Constructing
Democratic Governance
in Latin America

An Inter-American Dialogue Book

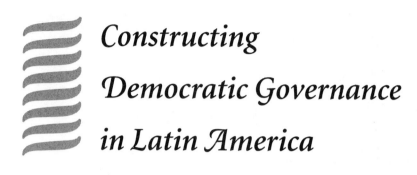

Constructing Democratic Governance in Latin America

THIRD EDITION

Edited by

Jorge I. Domínguez
Michael Shifter

THE JOHNS HOPKINS UNIVERSITY PRESS
Baltimore

© 1996, 2003, 2008 The Johns Hopkins University Press
All rights reserved. First edition 1996
Third edition 2008
Printed in the United States of America on acid-free paper
9 8 7 6 5 4 3 2 1

The Johns Hopkins University Press
2715 North Charles Street
Baltimore, Maryland 21218-4363
www.press.jhu.edu

Library of Congress Cataloging-in-Publication Data

Constructing democratic governance in Latin America / edited by Jorge I. Domínguez,
Michael Shifter.—3rd ed.
    p.   cm.
Includes bibliographical references and index.
ISBN-13: 978-0-8018-9004-8 (hardcover : alk. paper)
ISBN-13: 978-0-8018-9005-5 (pbk. : alk. paper)
ISBN-10: 0-8018-9004-7 (hardcover : alk. paper)
ISBN-10: 0-8018-9005-5 (pbk. : alk. paper)
    1. Latin America—Politics and government—1980–   2. Democracy—Latin
America.   I. Domínguez, Jorge I., 1945–   II. Shifter, Michael.
JL966.C677   2008
320.98—dc22   2008006610

A catalog record for this book is available from the British Library.

*Special discounts are available for bulk purchases of this book. For more information,
please contact Special Sales at 410-516-6936 or specialsales@press.jhu.edu.*

The Johns Hopkins University Press uses environmentally friendly book materials,
including recycled text paper that is composed of at least 30 percent post-consumer
waste, whenever possible. All of our book papers are acid-free, and our jackets and
covers are printed on paper with recycled content.

Contents

Preface

Since its inception in the early 1980s, the Inter-American Dialogue has been fundamentally and consistently committed to advancing democratic governance throughout the Americas. This core concern has shaped and informed the Dialogue's programming in a variety of areas, including social policy, trade, and remittances. It has also contributed to a considerable body of work in the study of democracy as well as to effective and realistic policy ideas at the local, national, and hemispheric levels.

In the early 1990s, coinciding with the end of the Cold War and the turn to civilian, democratic governments throughout Latin America, the Dialogue launched its most ambitious and systematic project on the central challenge of democratic governance. This effort sought to engage the best analyses produced by a diverse group of leading scholars in the Americas and Europe to help track the progress of democratic governance in the region. The idea was to test the myriad claims about advances and setbacks in the quality of democratic practice and institutions, over time and across countries. This endeavor pursued a middle ground between fashionable but somewhat oversimplified indexes of democracy and purely academic treatments with little practical value in the policy realm. The result was the first edition of *Constructing Democratic Governance in Latin America*.

This edition is the third of a series whose volumes seek to take measure of the quality of democracy at intervals of roughly five or six years. The first edition was published in 1996, the second in 2003. The baselines and reference points they record are enormously helpful in judging whether progress is being made in individual countries and in the region as a whole. Although we strive to achieve some continuity in the themes and countries covered—and in the authors commissioned to write about them—each edition contains a distinct mix of topics and writers, in part reflecting the evolving priorities in the study of democratic governance. This volume contains eight country studies and three chapters on relevant crosscutting themes. The result, we

hope, is an in-depth and wide-ranging interpretation of democratic governance throughout the region.

In each edition we have applied a particular template or terms of reference that seem most pertinent. Central to the original and continuing concept of the project are such critical dimensions of democratic governance as
the performance of political parties, civilian control over the armed forces,
the protection of human rights, emphasis on social inclusion, productive relations between the executive and the legislature, and harmony between
democratic practices and market reforms. In some cases these dimensions
have merited separate chapters, while in others they have been carefully examined by the authors of the country studies.

In all three editions we have been extremely fortunate to have benefited
from the intellectual direction and extraordinary knowledge about Latin
America provided by Jorge I. Domínguez, Antonio Madero Professor of
Mexican and Latin American Politics and Economics and vice provost for international affairs at Harvard University as well as a long-standing member
of the Inter-American Dialogue. Few, if any, scholars are as tireless and pro-
lific, and Domínguez's contribution to this exercise has been indispensable.
His experience in conceptualizing, organizing, and producing a volume of
this sort is without peer. It has been a tremendous pleasure to collaborate and
co-edit this edition and the previous one with him. He co-edited the first edition with Abraham Lowenthal, the Dialogue's founding director and professor of international relations at the University of Southern California. We
thank Harvard University's Weatherhead Center for International Affairs,
which provided support to Domínguez over the course of this project.

The chapters went through a number of drafts, benefiting enormously
from extensive feedback from the authors and members of Washington's
think tank and policy community. The discussions, both private and public,
at a two-day conference in Washington, D.C., in September 2006 substantially enriched the quality of the final product. The Dialogue particularly values the open and frank exchanges about the challenges to democratic governance in Latin America that took place at the public meeting between
decision makers and analysts. For their sharp insights and stimulating,
thoughtful commentary we thank Tom Carothers of the Carnegie Endowment for International Peace; Peter DeShazo of the Center for Strategic and
International Studies; Cynthia Arnson and Paulo Sotero of the Woodrow
Wilson International Center for Scholars; Mariclaire Acosta of the Organization of American States; George Vickers of the Open Society Institute;
Flavio Espinal, ambassador from the Dominican Republic to the United
States; and Riordan Roett of the Johns Hopkins School of Advanced International Studies. We were also extremely pleased that Assistant Secretary
of State for Western Hemisphere Affairs Thomas Shannon delivered the

keynote address at the conference, focusing his remarks on how the U.S. government is working to assist Latin American partners in improving the quality of democracy in the region.

None of the three editions of *Constructing Democratic Governance in Latin America* would have been possible without Henry Tom of the Johns Hopkins University Press. His constant encouragement, unfailing patience, and unmatched professionalism have been absolutely vital. We are also grateful to Alan Hynds and Patricio Mason for their fine translations of chapters in this volume.

The Inter-American Dialogue's research and publications are designed to improve the quality of public debate and decision making on key issues in Western Hemisphere affairs. The Dialogue is both a forum for sustained exchange among leaders and an independent, nonpartisan center for policy analysis on economic and political relations between the United States and Latin America. Its research agenda focuses on four broad themes: democratic governance, inter-American cooperation, economic integration, and social equity.

At the Dialogue we are particularly indebted to Dan Joyce, who was chiefly responsible for coordinating this effort and bringing it to fruition. His exceptional editing skills, superb judgment, and good cheer were invaluable. Vinay Jawahar deserves special thanks and recognition for his fine contribution during the initial stages of the project. We are also grateful to several interns who ably performed a variety of tasks essential to the production of this volume, including Fatima Asvat, Sarah Enright, Jessica Fleuti, and Sergio Gúzman.

The Inter-American Dialogue expresses its gratitude to the Open Society Institute and, in particular, its former regional director for Latin America, George Vickers. The Institute's generous support enabled the Dialogue to commission the chapters for this volume and organize the 2006 meeting in Washington.

Michael Shifter
Vice President for Policy
Inter-American Dialogue

Contributors

Fernando Cepeda Ulloa is the Colombian ambassador to France. He has served as ambassador to Canada and Great Britain as well as permanent representative to the Organization of American States and to the United Nations. He has also been the minister of government, minister of communications, and vice minister of economic development. At the Universidad de los Andes in Bogotá he held the positions of rector, director of the Political Science Department, and director of the Center for International Studies. He has published several books and reports on topics including party systems, economic reform, and intergovernmental relations.

Javier Corrales is associate professor and chair of the Political Science Department at Amherst College. He is the author of *Presidents without Parties: The Politics of Economic Reform in Argentina and Venezuela in the 1990s* (University Park: Pennsylvania State University Press, 2002) as well as a number of recent articles on the political situation in Venezuela. He has focused on presidential systems, energy politics, and international financial institutions in Latin America.

Carlos Iván Degregori is a political analyst and director of the Instituto de Estudios Peruanos in Lima. He served as a commissioner of Peru's Truth and Reconciliation Commission. He has a background in anthropology and has taught at the Universidad Nacional Mayor de San Marcos, Princeton University, the Free University of Berlin, Columbia University, and the University of Wisconsin–Madison. His recent work has focused on social movements, pluralism, and the relationship between political memory and violence.

Jorge I. Domínguez is the Antonio Madero Professor of Mexican and Latin American Politics and Economics in the Department of Government and vice provost for international affairs at Harvard University. He has been co-editor for all three editions of *Constructing Democratic Governance* and is a founding member of the Inter-American Dialogue. His recent work addresses U.S.–Latin American relations and the Cuban revolution, among other topics.

Denise Dresser is professor of political science at the Instituto Tecnológico Autónomo de México (ITAM) and a senior fellow at the Pacific Council on International Policy. An expert on Mexican political economy and U.S.-Mexico relations, she has taught at Georgetown University and the University of California–Berkeley. She was also a senior visiting fellow at the Inter-American Dialogue. She writes a political column for the Mexico City newspaper *Reforma* and is the author of *Neopopulist Solutions to Neoliberal Problems: Mexico's National Solidarity Program* (San Diego: University of California–San Diego, 1991).

Eduardo A. Gamarra is professor of political science at Florida International University, where he has also served as the director of the Latin American and Caribbean Center and the editor of *Hemisphere,* a magazine on Latin American and Caribbean affairs. He is the author of numerous books, reports, and articles on the politics of the Andean region countries, the political economy of drug trafficking, democratization, and civil-military relations.

Mala Htun is assistant professor of political science at the New School for Social Research in New York. She is the author of *Sex and the State: Abortion, Divorce, and the Family under Latin American Dictatorships and Democracies* (New York: Cambridge University Press, 2003). Her work on the political role of gender and ethnic minorities has appeared in many journals and edited volumes. She has held fellowships at the University of Tokyo, Harvard University, and the University of Notre Dame.

Steven Levitsky is associate professor of government and social studies at Harvard University. His areas of research include political parties, informal institutions, and regime change, with a particular interest in Argentina and Peru. He is the author of *Transforming Labor-Based Parties in Latin America: Argentine Peronism in Comparative Perspective* (New York: Cambridge University Press, 2003) and co-editor of *Informal Institutions and Democracy: Lessons from Latin America* (Baltimore: Johns Hopkins University Press, 2006).

David J. Myers is associate professor of political science at Pennsylvania State University. He has analyzed party systems, electoral institutions, and comparative politics in South America. He is co-editor of *The Unraveling of Representative Democracy in Venezuela* (Baltimore: Johns Hopkins University Press, 2004). He was a Fulbright scholar at the Universidad del Norte in Barranquilla, Colombia, and has taught at the Central University of Venezuela, the Instituto de Estudios Superiores de Administración, and the Raúl Leoni Foundation in Caracas, Venezuela.

David Samuels is associate professor of political science at the University of Minnesota–Twin Cities. His numerous books and journal articles have focused on Brazilian and Latin American politics, U.S.–Latin American relations, and comparative politics. He is the author of *Ambition, Federalism, and Legislative Politics in Brazil* (New York: Cambridge University Press, 2003) and co-editor of *Decentralization and Democracy in Latin America* (Notre Dame, Ind.: University of Notre Dame Press, 2004).

Michael Shifter is vice president for policy and director of the Andean program at the Inter-American Dialogue. He is the author of numerous articles and reports on U.S.–Latin American relations, democratic governance, and politics in the Andean region, and he was co-editor for the second edition of *Constructing Democratic Governance*. He is an adjunct professor at Georgetown University's School of Foreign Service, where he teaches Latin American politics.

Peter M. Siavelis is associate professor of political science at Wake Forest University. His research focuses on legislative institutions, electoral laws, party systems, and local governance in the Southern Cone. He is the author of *The President and Congress in Post-authoritarian Chile: Constraints to Democratic Consolidation* (University Park: Pennsylvania State University Press, 2000). He has written many articles and chapters on Chilean politics and taught at the Pontificia Universidad Católica de Chile.

Laurence Whitehead is official fellow in politics and director of the Centre for Mexican Studies at Nuffield College, Oxford University. He has focused on the impact of globalization, democracy, and economic liberalization on Latin America. He is the author of *Latin America: A New Interpretation* (London: Palgrave, 2005) and *Democratisation: Theory and Experience* (New York: Oxford University Press, 2002).

Acronyms and Abbreviations

General

FDI	foreign direct investment
FTAA (ALCA)	Free Trade Area of the Americas (Área de Libre Comercio de las Américas)
GDP	gross domestic product
IFI	international financial institution
ISI	import substitution industrialization
LAC	Latin America and the Caribbean
NAFTA	North American Free Trade Agreement
NGO	nongovernmental organization
TCO	transnational criminal organization

International Organizations

IDB	Inter-American Development Bank
IMF	International Monetary Fund
Mercosur	Mercado Común del Sur (Common Market of the South)
OAS	Organization of American States
SIP	Sociedad Interamericana de Prensa (Inter-American Press Society)

Argentina

ARI	Afirmación para una República Igualitaria (Affirmation for an Egalitarian Republic)
FREPASO	Frente País Solidario (Front for a Country in Solidarity)
MFR	Movimiento Federal Recrear (Federal Movement to Recreate)

MODIN	Movimiento por la Dignidad y la Independencia (Movement for Dignity and Independence)
NUD	Necessity and Urgency Decree
PJ	Partido Justicialista (Judicialist Party; Peronist)
PRO	Propuesta Republicana (Republican Proposal)
UCR	Unión Cívica Radical (Radical Civic Union)

Bolivia

ADN	Acción Democrática Nacionalista (Nationalist Democratic Action)
ASP	Alianza Social Patriótica (Social Patriotic Alliance)
INRA	Instituto Nacional de Reforma Agraria (National Institute for Agrarian Reform)
LPP	Ley de Participación Popular (Law of Popular Participation)
MAS	Movimiento al Socialismo (Movement toward Socialism)
MIP	Movimiento Indígena Pachakutik (Pachakutik Indigenous Movement)
MIR	Movimiento de Izquierda Revolucionaria (Revolutionary Left Movement)
MNR	Movimiento Nacionalista Revolucionario (Nationalist Revolutionary Movement)
PODEMOS	Poder Democrático y Social (Democratic and Social Power)
UN	Unidad Nacional (National Unity)

Brazil

PFL	Partido da Frente Liberal (Liberal Front Party)
PL	Partido Liberal (Liberal Party)
PMDB	Partido do Movimento Democrático Brasileiro (Brazilian Democratic Movement Party)
PSDB	Partido da Social Democracia Brasileira (Brazilian Social Democracy Party)
PT	Partido dos Trabalhadores (Workers' Party)
PTB	Partido Trabalhista Brasileiro (Brazilian Labor Party)

Chile

AFP	Administradoras de Fondos de Pensiones (Pension Fund Administrators)

AUGE	Acceso Universal con Garantías Explícitas (Universal Access with Explicit Guarantees)
FONASA	Fondo Nacional de Salud (National Health Fund)
ISAPRES	Instituciones de Salud Previsional (Private Health Insurance Companies)
PDC	Partido Demócrata Cristiano (Christian Democratic Party)
PPD	Partido por la Democracia (Party for Democracy)
PRSD	Partido Radical Socialdemócrata (Social-Democratic Radical Party)
PS	Partido Socialista (Socialist Party)
RN	Renovación Nacional (National Renovation)
UDI	Unión Democrática Independiente (Independent Democratic Union)

Colombia

AICO	Autoridades Indígenas de Colombia (Indigenous Authorities of Colombia)
ANAPO	Alianza Nacional Popular (National Popular Alliance)
ASI	Alianza Social Indígena (Indigenous Social Alliance)
AUC	Autodefensas Unidas de Colombia (United Self-Defense Forces of Colombia)
CRIC	Consejo Regional Indígena del Cauca (Regional Indigenous Commission of the Cauca)
ELN	Ejército de Liberación Nacional (National Liberation Army)
EPL	Ejército Popular de Liberación (Popular Liberation Army)
FARC	Fuerzas Armadas Revolucionarias de Colombia (Revolutionary Armed Forces of Colombia)
FEDESARROLLO	Fundación para la Educación Superior y el Desarrollo (Foundation for Higher Education and Development)
M-19	Movimiento 19 de Abril (April 19th Movement)
ONIC	Organización Nacional Indígena de Colombia (National Indigenous Organization of Colombia)
UNO	Unión Nacional de Oposición (National Opposition Union)

El Salvador

ARENA	Alianza Republicana Nacionalista (Nationalist Republican Alliance)

FMLN   Frente Farabundo Martí para la Liberación Nacional (Farabundo Martí National Liberation Front)

Mexico

IFE   Instituto Federal Electoral (Federal Electoral Institute)
PAN   Partido Acción Nacional (National Action Party)
PRD   Partido de la Revolución Democrática (Party of the Democratic Revolution)
PRI   Partido Revolucionario Institucional (Institutional Revolutionary Party)

Nicaragua

FSLN   Frente Sandinista de Liberación Nacional (Sandinista Front for National Liberation)

Peru

APRA   Alianza Popular Revolucionaria Americana (American Popular Revolutionary Alliance)
CODE   Convergencia Democrática (Democratic Convergence)
CONAPA   Comisión Nacional de Pueblos Andinos, Amazónicos, y Afroperuanos (National Commission on Andean, Amazonian, and Afro-Peruvian Peoples)
FIM   Frente Independiente Moralizador (Independent Moralizing Front)
PP   Perú Posible (Possible Peru)
SUTEP   Sindicato Unitario de Trabajadores de la Educación Peruana (Unified Workers' Union of Peruvian Education)
UN   Unidad Nacional (National Unity)

Venezuela

AD   Acción Democrática (Democratic Action)
Causa R   Radical Cause
CESAP   Centro al Servicio de la Acción Popular (Center at the Service of Popular Action)
CNE   Consejo Nacional Electoral (National Electoral Council)
COPEI   Comité de Organización Política Electoral Independiente or Partido Social Cristiano de Venezuela (Social Christian Party of Venezuela)

CTV   Confederación de Trabajadores de Venezuela
                (Venezuelan Confederation of Workers)
FEDECAMARAS   Federación de Cámaras y Asociaciones de Comercio y
                Producción (Federation of Chambers and
                Associations of Commerce and Production)
MAS   Movimiento al Socialismo (Movement toward
                Socialism)
MEP   Movimiento Electoral Popular (Popular Electoral
                Movement)
MVR   Movimiento Quinta República (Fifth Republic
                Movement)
PCV   Partido Comunista de Venezuela (Communist Party
                of Venezuela)
PDVSA   Petróleos de Venezuela (National Petroleum
                Corporation of Venezuela)
PPT   Patria Para Todos (Fatherland for All)
URD   Unión Republicana Democrática (Democratic
                Republican Union)

PART I

Introduction

1

Emerging Trends and Determining Factors in Democratic Governance

Michael Shifter

A Promising Round of Elections

As if any further proof were needed, the unprecedented concentration of national elections in Latin America in 2006 demonstrated that they perform multiple, essential functions in democracies. In conferring legitimacy, elections are a necessary—though far from sufficient—feature of a democratic form of government. In addition, they serve as safety valves and shock absorbers that allow views and preferences to be freely expressed, and frustrations to be accommodated, without derailing the constitutional order. Of course, they also serve as x-rays that reveal a great deal about the quality of democratic institutions and democratic practice.

It is no surprise, then, that political analysis reached a high point—if not of quality, then surely of quantity—during the intense cycle of elections in the region that roughly coincided with the production of this volume, the third edition of *Constructing Democratic Governance in Latin America*. Pundits and political scientists alike had a field day. The consensus was that the round of elections was, by any reasonable historical measure, a resounding success. Citizens went to the polls in overwhelming numbers, electoral institutions functioned according to acceptable norms, and (with the notable exception of Mexico) the losing side did not dispute the outcome. The elections subjected Latin America to an exceptional test of media and international scrutiny—and the results were largely favorable. In this critical sphere of democratic governance, the chapters in the current book document a steady and welcome progression from the situations described in the previous volumes. The advance may not be irreversible, but it is becoming increasingly ingrained, and voting, happily, is a tough habit to break.

Although all of the country chapters here—on Argentina, Bolivia, Brazil, Chile, Colombia, Mexico, Peru, and Venezuela—take appropriate note of the widespread practice of elections, they also explore and assess other critical dimensions of democratic governance in Latin America. Moreover, the three crosscutting, thematic chapters focus on the impact of globalization, market reforms, and social inclusion on the nature and quality of democratic governance in the region. Taken together, these nuanced appraisals suggest that the quality of democracy—measured in terms of political representation as well as institutional discipline and independence—may have suffered a modest decline overall since the previous volume was published in 2003, highlighting the huge challenges in the years ahead for governments and citizens alike.

Lingering Inequality

Perhaps the core challenge—long Latin America's Achilles' heel—is reducing the stubbornly high levels of social and economic inequality, which become particularly salient in political terms in the context of accelerated globalization. Previously excluded groups, with greater access than ever to information technology and often tied to transnational networks, are now taking a more active part in their countries' politics and are insisting on their rightful share of the national wealth. Social demands and expectations have been on the rise. The chapter on social inclusion points out that women, the indigenous population, and Afro-descendants in such countries as Brazil and Colombia are taking full advantage of democratic openings and a politically fluid landscape to play more prominent roles in fundamental functions of governance. As the respective country chapters make clear, the election of the first indigenous president in Bolivia and the first woman president in Chile are undeniable measures of significant and salutary social change in those countries and in Latin America as a whole.

Governmental responses to deal with such mounting pressures have been varied. The Brazil chapter highlights the importance and effectiveness of Luiz Inácio "Lula" da Silva's Bolsa Família social program in transferring income, reducing extreme poverty, and thus bolstering the country's governance. In Venezuela, Hugo Chávez has directed a considerable share of the windfall from the oil bonanza to underwrite a variety of different social programs, called *misiones,* ranging from literacy classes to public health centers and subsidized food outlets. Such programs have clearly helped build political support for Chávez among the country's very poor. The key question, however, is whether such programs are sustainable and whether they will help generate the employment that is essential to overcome long-standing inequalities and achieve broad-based development.

A Nagging Institutional Deficit

In general, Latin America's government institutions remain woefully ill equipped to handle such growing social pressures. This, of course, was the principal focus of concern for political scientist Samuel Huntington in his classic study of political development over four decades ago. With very few exceptions, the region's political parties and justice systems, for example, have little capacity or coherence, and there are few signs that their performance has improved in recent years. The demands for representation, for the delivery of basic services—including police protection, high-quality education, and reliable infrastructure—are largely unmet, which is a recipe for enormous social frustration and discontent. There are, in short, tremendous democratic deficits on a variety of fronts.

The Peru chapter, for example, shows that despite sustained and impressive macroeconomic results and even a slight reduction in poverty levels during the administration of Alejandro Toledo (2001–6), there were frequent street demonstrations and a high degree of social turbulence. As the most recent election revealed in Peru—and in other countries in the region, such as Bolivia, Ecuador, Mexico, and even Brazil—there are profound social, ethnic, and regional cleavages. If anything, these divisions are becoming more acute, which poses a formidable obstacle to building effective democratic governance. Positive economic growth and even falling poverty indicators can easily mask a transformation to a polarized and often ominous political geography.

High levels of citizen insecurity and transnational crime pose one of the gravest threats to democratic governance in Latin America. In country after country, the data on violence are alarming, while governmental responses and approaches have been inadequate. Indeed, it is hard to think of a more serious, intractable problem confronting political leaders in the countries covered in this volume—including Argentina, Brazil, Colombia, Mexico, Peru, and Venezuela. In addition, governance institutions in Central American countries—particularly in Guatemala—as well as in smaller, highly vulnerable nations of the Caribbean, run the risk of being overwhelmed by uncontrolled violence, much of it fueled by the pernicious and expanding drug trade. Police forces, often corrupt and poorly trained, are no match for the sophisticated, agile, and well-organized transnational criminal networks.

Not surprisingly, the relatively poor performance of basic governance institutions has further eroded public trust and confidence. This is a global phenomenon, of course, but it has peculiar manifestations in Latin America, where social mobilization appears to be substantially outpacing institutional responsiveness in a number of countries. Although survey after survey has shown that most Latin Americans continue to see democracy as the preferred political model or system, broad dissatisfaction with government performance has led to a looser definition of democracy and to more varieties of democracy than prevailed a decade ago.

The Venezuela chapter, for example, invokes the term "electoral autocracy," which emphasizes a Rousseauian rather than a Lockean conception of governance and does not exalt the virtues of checks and balances, separation of powers, or strict adherence to the rule of law. Whatever Chávez may mean by "twenty-first-century socialism," it does not appear to be steeped in Jeffersonian democratic principles. The Bolivia chapter similarly portrays a regime that barely corresponds to a representative or liberal democracy. It seems safe to assume that the debate about the nature of democracy in the region will continue to rage. To be sure, the Chile chapter suggests that the government there has admirably undertaken noteworthy reforms in a representative democratic framework, and the analysis of Brazil similarly points out promising trends. Nevertheless, aside from regular elections—the minimalist, Schumpeterian standard of democracy—a broad and firm political convergence on key questions related to democracy has all but disappeared from the region, as noted in the chapter on globalization.

Finding the Right Leadership Balance

The fundamental challenge for the region's political leaders is to forge a national consensus to pursue serious institutional reforms that address deep-seated inequities. Higher-quality education and judicial systems as well as effective legal protection from criminal violence belong at the top of the agenda. In a 1971 essay, "Underdevelopment, Obstacles to the Perception of Change, and Leadership," the distinguished political economist Albert O. Hirschman talked about the central importance of developing effective political leadership, combining charisma with a stronger emphasis on skills in perceiving and successfully acting on possibilities for real change. As many of the chapters in this volume make clear, political leadership, too often regarded as a mere residual variable, can make a critical difference in whether or not governments capitalize on opportunities for economic and social progress. In many instances, the resources and structural conditions for reform exist, but political will and ability are severely lacking.

The Peru and Mexico chapters respectively assess the political setbacks of Toledo and Vicente Fox, both of whom generated high, perhaps unrealistic, expectations. Both presided over periods of relative democratic stability but were unable to deliver on their promises. In the case of Toledo, the contrast with the Fujimori period was stark, and Fox certainly represented a change from the long era of domination by the Partido Revolucionario Institucional (Revolutionary Institutional Party). The chapter on Argentina offers a mixed appraisal of Néstor Kirchner, who, through a measure of political skill and perhaps some luck, managed to exceed expectations and bring the country back from the depths of the economic crisis of late 2001 and early 2002. However, the chapter points out some possible costs in terms of political independence and robust institutions—especially the Supreme Court and Congress—under Kirchner's administration. The Colombia chapter highlights the effective leadership displayed by Álvaro Uribe, particularly compared to his immediate predecessors, in carrying out the strategy of democratic security and undertaking important political reform. The question, though, is to what extent the positive economic and security accomplishments have been offset by weakened institutions and an excessive reliance on a single individual.

The circumstances of each particular situation necessarily dictate the effectiveness of presidential leadership and institutional development. Both are important and mutually reinforcing, and to argue in favor of strong leadership does not imply that a president can ride roughshod over institutions. On the contrary, it underscores the need to mobilize resources and forge alliances in pursuit of reforms that ultimately buttress institutions. Indeed, analysts note that governability can be undermined by presidents who are either too weak or too strong.

In this regard, there has been considerable debate in recent years about the wisdom of reelection in Latin America and its implications for the quality of democratic governance. This undoubtedly represents a trend in the region. Recently, constitutional reelection reforms have been enacted in Argentina, Brazil, Colombia, the Dominican Republic, Panama, and Peru, with similar signals emerging from Bolivia and Ecuador. These changes enabled three of the presidents treated in this volume—Chávez, Lula, and Uribe—to return to power. Chávez attempted to go a step further, pressing for indefinite reelection. Provided rules are clearly defined and followed, it is hard to object to the notion of reelection per se. However, there are valid and legitimate concerns about the wider institutional context. The lack of sufficient constraints and checks can increase the potential for arbitrary decision making and autocratic rule.

Moreover, it is worth noting that the empirical evidence regarding second terms in Latin America—both those that have occurred consecutively and those that have occurred after a period of time has elapsed—is not altogether reassuring; the case of Fujimori is perhaps the most egregious and cautionary. Reelected presidents tend to lose touch with the public, become attached to power, and develop indifference or disdain toward deeper institutional consolidation. The rationale for reelection may have some merit, but the record in the region to date suggests an understandable need for wariness about the idea.

An Unraveling Global Consensus

Although the *Constructing Democratic Governance* project has focused chiefly on analysis of particular countries and pertinent themes in Latin America, the authors and editors have been acutely aware of the importance of international factors in shaping internal developments. The chapter on globalization highlights the recent unraveling in the consensus around the core tenets of democratic governance, which no doubt hinders progress. For a variety of reasons, the international context is less hospitable to international democracy promotion than it was in the mid-1990s or even just a few years ago.

The "push back" to efforts to promote liberal democracy in many parts of the world has contributed, often indirectly, to the overall decline in the quality of democratic governance in Latin America. The Organization of American States (OAS) responded to several democratic ruptures in the 1990s (for example, in Haiti, Peru, Guatemala, and Paraguay), but the region's profound mistrust and notable disarray has hurt the OAS's will and capacity to respond to today's various challenges. The fading of a shared vision and willingness to respond is an important element of the overall political landscape.

The declining influence of the United States and the sharp increase in anti-American sentiment make up another important piece of the overall global environment. The U.S. military invasion of Iraq and the attendant violations of international human rights standards have substantially undercut any U.S.-led effort to encourage democracy in the world. U.S. support for autocratic governments like those of Egypt and Pakistan in the name of fighting terrorism has not gone unnoticed in the Western Hemisphere. The charges of hypocrisy and double standards have made it exceedingly difficult for Washington's exhortations to find any resonance in an understandably skeptical Latin America. This situation will take many years to repair even under the best of circumstances and sets the period covered in this volume apart from the periods covered in other studies over the past dozen years of democratic governance in the region.

Decentralization of Power and Perspectives

The set of dimensions germane to democratic governance is vast, so this volume is necessarily selective. Some important topics are addressed in the country chapters but do not receive the systematic treatment they warrant. The first is the question of decentralization and federalism, which has no doubt deepened in recent years, in contrast to the historical legacy of centralized governments in Latin America. For example, democratic accountability has been enhanced by the fact that mayors in the region are no longer appointed but are elected locally by their constituents, enjoy substantial authority, and have access to ample resources. Performance is also on the rise, as reflected by impressive improvements carried out by mayors in a number of cities, including Colombia's two largest, Bogotá and Medellín. At the same time, however, decentralization reforms have contributed to the overall tendency toward political fragmentation in Latin America. In some cases they have strengthened anti-democratic local authorities and exacerbated fiscal pressures.

Two additional elements of democratic governance that are evolving and bear close watching are the media and civil society. Press freedom, of course, is an essential element of democracy and one of its clearest measures. Progress on this score has been uneven. To be sure, the media have become more vibrant and diverse in a number of countries, and access-to-information laws have been adopted in such countries as the Dominican Republic, Honduras, Jamaica, Mexico, Panama, and Peru. Implementation of such laws, however, has been problematic at best. Further, criminal defamation or so-called insult laws are fortunately being revoked in some countries and invoked with less frequency in others. Of course, they are still being selectively applied in some situations, such as in Ecuador, where disparaging the media can yield valuable political rewards.

Of particular concern is the violence directed against journalists who investigate crime and corruption, often related to drugs. According to the Committee to Protect Journalists, in 2006 Mexico had the highest number of journalists killed anywhere but Iraq. Many parts of Colombia, too, remain extremely dangerous for journalists practicing their trade. Unfortunately, impunity for those responsible continues to be the norm. In situations dominated by fear, self-censorship is understandable and is reportedly on the rise. Fresh and critical topics on the region's press freedom agenda include media concentration, a serious concern in a number of countries, and protection from the arbitrary allocation of government advertising. In 2007, for example, in a landmark case Argentina's Supreme Court ruled that a provincial government had violated the free speech rights of a newspaper by withdrawing advertising in retaliation for critical coverage.

Civil society continues to play a vital role in strengthening democratic governance throughout the region. Yet, though they can often articulate interests, defend causes, and deliver services, such organizations cannot possibly supplant political parties. Instead, a proper balance between both sectors needs to be established. Indeed, bolstering single-issue, fragmented politics may enhance pluralism but risks weakening overall governance. Further, laws were proposed in Peru and Venezuela to regulate external funding for domestic and international nongovernmental groups. These efforts fit in with the general move toward a push back against democracy promotion activities and reflect an attempt to reassert sovereignty.

Final Thoughts

No doubt Latin America's political landscape is highly complex and displays contradictory currents and tendencies. As these chapters convincingly show, the region is in considerable flux and will probably remain unsettled for some time. Highly competitive elections and vibrant media coexist with pockets of instability, profound social distress, and anger. Based on the most recent round of elections, many have plausibly argued that there has been a shift to the left, away from market-friendly governments and toward greater independence or "elbow room" from the United States.

The left-right labels, however, have limited utility and tend to obscure the fundamental reality of democratic governance in a region struggling to find a place in an increasingly interconnected but competitive world. The challenge of globalization is tantamount to that of being hit by the flu, and it is easy to see from these chapters that some countries have better resources and resistance than others. Far more than ideological preferences, different leadership styles and institutional capacities account for the diverse paths taken by Latin American countries. The authors of this volume, thanks to their discerning and imaginative analyses, have contributed to a richer understanding of both the accomplishments and the pending challenges involved in constructing democratic governance in Latin America.

PART II
Themes

2

The Fading Regional Consensus on Democratic Convergence

Laurence Whitehead

Under favorable circumstances, the four international dimensions of democratization—control, conditionality, contagion, and consent—can be mutually reinforcing and can therefore produce a strong regionwide process with cumulative momentum and a well-defined time frame. The enlargement of the European Union provides the classic example, but the Summit of the Americas process launched in Miami in 1994 promised similar effects.[1] However, more than a decade later, the Mar del Plata, Argentina, summit of 2005 displayed considerable disarray, and the prospects for regionwide democratic convergence in the circumstances current at the time of this writing (early 2007) are quite discouraging. In this new setting, the aforementioned four dimensions are not so mutually supportive and do not generate such regionwide momentum or consensus. In the absence of a shared vision, rival and partial projects are liable to emerge and to clash. If so, control and conditionality become less workable, and progress in regionwide democratization must therefore depend more heavily on the remaining two international dimensions—contagion and consent.

The first Summit of the Americas, convened most appropriately in Miami in December 1994, held out to the peoples of Latin America and the Caribbean (LAC) the promise that thenceforth the entire Western Hemisphere would be united around a shared project. This project would include the liberalization of trade and investment and a private sector–led process of market integration (that would not, however, include the labor market) together with mutually reinforcing pro-democratic political reforms including free elections, accountable government, a more vigorous human rights regime, and the strengthening of the rule of law. It was recognized that not all these desiderata could be fully achieved in all countries at once. By building on the Enterprise for the Americas Initiative (launched by President George H. W. Bush in 1990) and on the contemporaneous launching of the North American Free Trade Agreement (NAFTA) (by President Bill Clinton in 1994), however, the Summit of the Americas process was envisioned as a coherent regional standard by which all actors and institutions could be evaluated. Cumulative reinforcements and incentives would bring every country (even Cuba) into the common fold within a decade. The basic assumption was that the United States already fulfilled all these requisites and that, by projecting its "soft power" through multiple channels of influence, it could extend its constitutional free market model of democracy throughout the Americas. This would reaffirm U.S. values, reinforce U.S. security and international leverage, and be good for business at the same time. A timetable was set, and the Free Trade Area of the Americas (FTAA)—open only to those states classified in Washington as democracies—was to be completed by 2005. When that deadline was missed and the FTAA process was indefinitely postponed, it opened the way for an acrimonious summit at Mar del Plata.

Looking back from the vantage point of early 2007, it seems timely to reevaluate the strengths and limitations of this project and to revisit the assumptions on which it rested. It is not possible to provide a comprehensive historical and analytical survey of the intervening 13 years in one short chapter. Because the central objective of this volume is to assess the conditions and prospects of democracy and democratization in *today's* Latin America, this chapter focuses on the current panorama. It outlines the international dimensions bearing on that assessment. This requires consideration of negative as well as positive components; it includes developments outside the Western Hemisphere as well as those within it; and it cannot omit the disagreements that have arisen since 1994 in understandings of what "democracy" and "democratization" are really about. Because the agenda is therefore very large, in this chapter I have to be highly selective.

In the mid-1990s I sketched an analytical framework for the study of the international dimensions of democratization deploying the four broad headings of control, conditionality, contagion, and consent.[2] In this chapter I return to these overlapping categories as they relate to the current state of the Western Hemisphere. Under each heading I sketch a summary interpretation of conditions in the LAC region in 2006–7. Although the focus is on the "new" democracies in Latin America, a discussion of international dimensions necessarily includes the United States as well. Both its democracy and its support for democratization are perceived quite differently in 2007 than they were in 1994. In this chapter I focus on the immediate present risks being overtaken by short-term events but also highlight the scale of the changes that have recently taken place. A snapshot at one point in time can also help us to cope with the cross-sectional diversity and complexity of the process under examination. The opening reference to the hopes and expectations trumpeted in December 1994 can serve as a brief reminder of the pace of change involved. It also points to the wide margins of possibility that remain open if we look forward from our present standpoint. The main sections of the chapter review the four international dimensions of democratization as they operate in the Western Hemisphere at the current time, leaving to the conclusion a discussion of the implications for the future of the region and for our theorizing about democratization processes in general.

Control: The Clash of Civilizations and the (Potential) Closure of Borders

When Francis Fukuyama interpreted the fall of the Berlin Wall as the "end of history" and the permanent enthronement of liberal democracy, Samuel P. Huntington responded by anticipating a "clash of civilizations" that might bring the "Third Wave" of democratizations to a halt or indeed throw it into reverse. The 1994 Miami Summit was convened during a peak of optimism over liberal internationalism that reflected Fukuyama's worldview. By 2007, at least from the vantage point of Washington, D.C., the more pessimistic extrapolations of the Huntingtonian alternative may be reaching a crescendo in the Middle East. The advocates of regime change and democratization through invasion and occupation ("control" in my parlance) are losing valor as it transpires that, at least in Afghanistan and Iraq, it is easier to precipitate a civil war than to build a liberal democracy. Why would a people liberated from autocracy by the noble deeds of the world's greatest democracy not simply rally to the cause of their benefactors and seize advantage of the new freedoms bestowed on them from without? One possibility is that they would like to if only the residual autocrats could be neutralized (i.e., more control is needed). A second is that they lack the civilizational foundations of the Western democratic system. Yet a third is that, failing these two interpretations, it may become necessary to consider whether the very theory of democracy by imposition is missing something. Could it be that Western self-understanding has failed to connect with local historical memories, that the coercive "mode of transition" can resemble an organ transplant in that it is liable to provoke systemic rejection, that the kind of democracy achievable in the Afghan or Iraqi context would have to be homemade according to a recipe very different from that known to the occupiers? The verdict on these issues may still be in dispute in Washington and London, but in most of the world, including the rest of the Western Hemisphere, firm conclusions have already been drawn.

In the LAC region there are few left who believe in the first alternative. Not even in post-Castro Cuba does it seem credible that the islanders would simply welcome an external liberator. It is true that this did happen in Grenada, and (with more effort) the invasion of Panama can also be viewed within this framework. The case of Haiti, however, warns us all (including the Argentines, Brazilians, and Chileans who have contributed peacekeepers) that it is not only in the Middle East that democratization through occupation can go astray.[3] Throughout the Caribbean, Mexico, and Central and South America it is generally regarded as an obvious and self-evident lesson of more than a century of regional history that coercive intervention brings more bitterness and conflict than it removes and that for democracy to flourish the region needs less external control, not more. (Plan Colombia may constitute a partial exception to this generalization, but the authorities in Bogotá would stress that they retain full sovereignty.)

Even fewer in Latin America can swallow Huntington's latest argument, that their region may lack the civilizational foundations of Protestant Anglo-Saxon democracies.[4] It could be moderately instructive to explore the relationship between the soft power projected by the British in the Caribbean before decolonization and the subsequent, generally successful, histories of democratic continuity. For this argument to achieve any mileage at all, however, it needs to be developed with great caution, not overlooking the slavery and racism of the Protestant rulers or the anti-democratic essence of colonialism.

That brings us to the third alternative, which very much represents the consensual take in LAC on what has gone wrong in Iraq and elsewhere. The protagonists of coercive democratization in the Middle East may still be unsure what lessons to draw from their disappointments, but not so the governments of Latin America, which—with some Central American exceptions—followed domestic public opinion rather than rallying to support the "coalition of the willing." Whatever solidarity with the United States was elicited by the terrorist attacks of September 11 and thereafter, Latin Americans have simply not felt the same existential threat and have been unable to share the discourse of the George W. Bush administration. To equate the United States with universal freedom and then to subordinate the concerns of bystanders to the logic of a one-dimensional conflict between good and evil has simply not proved marketable in most of the Western Hemisphere under conditions of open democracy. The White House position was understood as a policy stance that would permit the downgrading of other objectives closer to the interests of the LAC democracies and that would block dialogue and joint endeavors in the most promising areas that had been highlighted under the Summit of the Americas timetable. It seemed to require a rewriting of history and the suppression of any sense of co-responsibility for the global challenges that had come to the fore. With Washington's distinctive memories of the Cold War (during which a bipolar conflict had provided cover for an episodic disregard of human rights and democratic aspirations in much of the hemisphere), its new Manicheanism recalled the national security regimes of the 1970s. Torture, rendition, disregard for the Geneva Conventions, selective application of international laws, and so forth have provided almost daily reminders of this unlovely parallel.[5] Hence the growing evidence that coercive democratization is proving a failure in the Middle East elicits different responses in different parts of the Western Hemisphere. For some in the United States it may reinforce the sense of existential threat and the need to heighten security controls. For the many who were never persuaded that the U.S. response was justified in the first place, however, its ineffectiveness reinforces the argument of the principle that democracy needs to be promoted and protected by other means.

Admittedly, we should beware of oversimplifying the North-South divergence. Many in the United States would share part of the sentiments just attributed to the Latin Americans. The current governments of Colombia and El Salvador seem to share many of the assumptions of the Bush White House, and there are certainly powerful groups with similar alignments in most LAC democracies. Freedom of expression includes the right both to watch CNN and Fox News and indeed to join evangelical revivals that express a Manichean worldview. In addition, democratization via control contains a wider range of possibilities than those displayed in Iraq. It includes the Balkan pattern as well as that on display in the greater Middle East. Haiti may be more like Kosovo than Iraq, in which case the end of the story may not be so grim. Democratization through decolonization was once another important manifestation of control, and this pattern could still have a little further to go in some residual parts of the Caribbean. Therefore, the first argument of this section is not that all variants of regime change through international control can be ruled out for all of the Western Hemisphere for all time, but that in 2007 this category of possibilities is exceptionally out of favor.

The second argument of this section is that among the freedoms promised or implied by the Miami Summit process, the easing of controls on international migration was a prospect with great popular appeal throughout the poorer parts of the Western Hemisphere. This is not usually regarded as an integral component of democracy or democratization according to the standard academic literature (although it is a prominent theme in the rhetoric of U.S. democratic exceptionalism, e.g., in the "huddled masses" imagery). If we are to take seriously the international dimensions of democracy and democratization, however, we can hardly fail to consider this crucial issue. There are now signs that the democratization of Haiti is supposed to legitimize the closing of its borders. Once the people of Haiti have been helped to achieve their political rights at home, can they then be denied the chance of exit, or even be forcibly repatriated, with greater ease than when the international community classified it as an autocracy or as a failed state? If democratization were to pave the way to the ever tighter closure of national frontiers, it would carry very different implications for the welfare (and even the freedom) of the average citizen than if it were associated with an international project to liberalize human and commercial exchanges "from Alaska to Tierra del Fuego" (to quote the original language of the Enterprise for the Americas Initiative).

The war on terror, the massive U.S. Department of Homeland Security, and prospective changes in U.S. immigration law all convey a strong message about the kind of democracy currently in favor in North America (Canada may be a little different from the United States but seems to move in parallel with it). The protection of a certain kind of democracy through the reinforcement of control at the borders can have multiple and far-reaching consequences both for the balance of power and for the nature of rights in all the affected democracies ("receiving" democracies transmit powerful pressures in this area to their "sending" counterparts, and many states in between both send and receive). There are important contrasts here between the European Union (with its promise of a single market, a single passport, and a single currency uniting 27 or more democracies in a regional integration project) and the regionalism envisaged by the Miami process of 1994. From the perspective of 2007, the European Union has proceeded dramatically in one direction, producing many problems and tensions both internal and between these 27 democracies and the outside world.[6] At the same time, the much more tentative hopes associated with the plan for liberalizing exchanges across a democratic Western Hemisphere have not been so fully realized and could well face further disappointment as frontier controls are tightened.

This is a huge and complex topic, much entangled with different conceptions of democracy as a project or constitutional order. There is space here only to provide a single illustration of the kinds of dynamics we need to study if students of democratization are to keep up with real-world developments in their field. This example is a positive development from the standpoint of international initiatives to address the political consequences of global migration. In 2007, Spain held municipal elections in which it was agreed by all the main political parties that foreigners with residence permits in order should be allowed to participate. They pay taxes and consume local services and therefore should have the same democratic rights at the municipal level as people with Spanish citizenship. This proposal enfranchised about 867,000 non-Spaniards from other EU countries. There are also just under two million non-EU nationals with residence permits. They, too, will be allowed to vote in Spanish local elections whenever Spanish nationals are granted reciprocal rights. This applied this year to approximately

211,000 Colombians, 82,000 Argentines, 26,000 Venezuelans, and 24,000 Uruguayans.[7]

Conditionality: Balance of Payments Relief and the Relaxation of Intrusive Political Conditionality

Democracy promotion was not envisaged as the central purpose of either the European Union or the FTAA. They were designed with other economic, security, and political objectives in mind. However, as a condition of membership they both specified that a participatory state's regime should be classified as democratic. In the European Union the power of this democratic conditionality clause gradually became more apparent, and it was quickly recognized in the FTAA process as well. In fact, the Miami Summit played up the democratic aspect of the process to offset the ambivalence felt by key participants over the commercial implications. Thus, only regimes classified as democracies could attend the 1994 Miami Summit or benefit from the prospective FTAA. This is one particularly vivid example of the political conditionality that has long been in operation in Latin America. Only regimes classified as democracies could enjoy the unilateral benefits of the Caribbean Basin Initiative established by the U.S. Congress in 1984. Similarly, from 1996 onward, the Mercado Común del Sur (Mercosur; Common Market of the South) has added a democracy clause, used in particular to discourage *golpista* tendencies (a predisposition to carry out coups d'état) in Paraguay. Likewise, the Organization of American States (OAS) has acquired a "Democratic Charter" that is supposed to be binding on all its members. The Millennium Challenge Account also includes a weak form of democratic conditionality. The EU trade preference regime for African, Caribbean, and Pacific states has been modified to include a democratic conditionality component of the Cotonu Treaty, and this was sufficient to prevent the incorporation of Cuba. Outside the Americas, this form of democratic conditionality has also been very much in vogue, in particular as the European Union expanded first southward (to Greece, Spain, and Portugal) and then into postcommunist eastern Europe; Turkey is currently the key test case for this approach.

Other types of democratic conditionality also exist. Such conditionality may be functional or sectoral, for example, participation in the Inter-American Commission of Human Rights, the International Parliamentary Union, and even, arguably, the Sociedad Interamericana de Prensa (SIP; Inter-American Press Society).[8] Some international activities, such as election observation, justice system reform, the training of congresses, and so on, are normally included under the rubric of international democracy promotion. For a while in the late 1990s, even the U.S. Southern Command was in on the act, training military officials in the protection of human rights.[9]

Following the failure to complete the FTAA agreement by the 2005 deadline and in view of the imminent termination of the Bush administration's "fast track" negotiating authority in this area, these initiatives currently appear tired and have perhaps even been discredited. On the basis of a loose definition, every country in the Western Hemisphere (except Cuba) is currently classified as a democracy, has enjoyed that status for one or two decades almost without a break, and may well continue to receive such classification into the indefinite future. Therefore, the earlier preoccupation with "locking in" democratic procedures and creating disincentives to authoritarian regression has lost much of its urgency. However, this is not because anxieties over the stability of the LAC democracies have all evaporated but only because the system of classification used by the international community has proved so imprecise. Major strands of political opinion within key countries (including Mexico and Venezuela) openly challenge the belief that a minimally adequate level of democratic institutionality can be said to exist there. As long as periodic elections are held and contested, however, it is almost out of the question that any of the countries officially classified as democracies would be subjected to regional censure as openly undemocratic. If the Haiti of President René Préval qualifies despite the peculiar circumstances of the 2006 election there, on what grounds could Venezuela be disqualified? After all, even the domestic opposition in Venezuela has accepted that President Hugo Chávez won reelection in December 2006 (albeit in a lopsided contest). Influential voices in Washington have nevertheless argued that Chávez has abandoned democracy. Argentina and Brazil will not easily be persuaded to agree, however, and indeed Venezuela has just been admitted to Mercosur, untroubled by its democratic conditionality. If Colombia is a democracy despite its internally displaced population and its *secuestros* (kidnappings), who can object to the inclusion of Guatemala and Guyana? In short, international conditionality tied to regime type serves right now only to isolate Castro's Cuba, and it seems to have little further capacity to discriminate between good performance and bad. Admittedly, the European Union also faces analogous problems (concerning Bulgaria, Croatia, Cyprus, etc.), but its conditionality incorporates more precision, through the Copenhagen criteria defining the conditions for EU membership, and applies more leverage.

The current deflation of political conditionality extends beyond Europe and the Americas, however. The situation in the Middle East and elsewhere also has to be considered. We are asked to accept that Afghanistan and Iraq have qualified as democracies because the West "liberated" them, whereas Iran and Palestine do not because "terrorists" have been elected to high office there. Lebanon was considered a model democracy as long as it stood against Syria, but it became suspect as soon as it put up resistance to Israel. Russia and the Ukraine flip from one status to the other and back according to the geopolitical calculations of Western strategists. What of the democratic credentials of those doing the reclassifying? When the British prime minister scolds the Iranians for ignoring the will of the "international community," he assumes an authority he no longer possesses. If the European Union is to pass judgment on Turkey's fitness for inclusion in the world's club of leading democratic nations, it is fair to ask, "Who chose the European Commission, what was the role of the Parliament, and why is there no updated constitution? And if governments are to be upbraided or even sanctioned by the rest of the world for gross human rights violations, are the governments of the United States and Israel to be included—or not?" In synthesis, the moral authority and institutional neutrality required for an effective international structure of democratic conditionality is not currently available. The liberal internationalist zeitgeist of the 1990s has not survived into the new millennium. Unless and until it is reconstructed, Western attempts to apply democratic conditionality are likely to be regarded with cynicism in most parts of the world, including much of the Americas.

Latin Americans are well aware of this international context, as well as the selectivity and distortions that have periodically been in evidence when democratic conditionality has been applied in the Western Hemisphere. The recent record has been very patchy. There was some success in Peru at the end of Alberto Fujimori's term, but the OAS Democratic Charter played no part in the course of Argentine politics after the flight of Fernando de la Rúa, in Bolivia after Gonzalo Sánchez de Lozada's inelegant exit, or in Venezuela's coup in 2002 (or indeed subsequently). It is irrelevant to the current dispute in Mexico and is unlikely to help if Ecuador or Paraguay go off the rails in the next few months. Conditions might be different if compliance with the charter remained, as intended, very closely aligned with access to or denial of major economic benefits not available elsewhere.[10] However, this material foundation for international democratic political conditionality has in general been nullified (at least for the time being) by the disinterest of the U.S. Congress in the FTAA process, as well as by the upsurge in commodity prices and by the rise of Asian political and economic alternatives that leave Washington's traditional mechanisms of international financial institution (IFI) guidance stranded. As successive Latin American countries pre-pay their multilateral debt, not even traditional International Monetary Fund (IMF) conditionality remains in place.

In theory, the IMF, World Bank, and Inter-American Development Bank do not get directly involved in political conditionality. They are supposed to limit their advice and economic incentives to areas outside the strictly political realm (although "good governance" is an expanding area that can blur this distinction). In practice, their credit and advice have often been extended to the LAC countries on a basis that is locally perceived as highly intrusive and politicized. This is a story with a long history, and it did not end when the entire Western Hemisphere (other than Cuba, which is barred from all IFI financing) became uniformly democratic. The IFIs were deeply involved in promoting first the "Washington Consensus" and then the second- and third-generation pro-market reforms that followed. This was all congruent with the vision of a market-friendly liberalized democratic hemisphere as per the Miami Summit project. However, it became increasingly controversial and politically charged as that project faded and as many voters in the new democracies formed increasingly negative judgments of the results of the policies being foisted on them from without. The democratic accountability (and sometimes even the probity) of many of the officials most closely associated with the Washington policy network have also been brought into question in some countries. The consequence of all this is that in 2007 it has become a major political liability in most parts of the region for politicians or policy makers to be too closely associated with IFI conditionality. Latin America's large recent surge in export revenues (partly due to rising commodity prices as well as the benefits of earlier IFI-backed liberalizing reforms) has made it possible to secure project financing from other sources. In Latin American political circles, it can prove highly popular to be seen as casting off the shackles of the subcontinent's historical vassalage. Mounting foreign exchange reserves facilitate the pre-payment of conditional debt. The smaller and less competitive economies of Central America and the Caribbean are not exempt from this temptation because they tend to receive the largest proportional flows of remittances sent by nationals working in North America and Europe. In addition, the Venezuelan government has been vocal and active in offering subsidized oil and other inducements to those willing to pursue an anti-IFI agenda, for example, offering the administration of Daniel Ortega in Nicaragua benefits that match the previous level of U.S. aid (about which more is said in the next section). Therefore, economic conditionality has become more diversified. The Asian giants are also willing to step in with financing that hitherto could have been obtained only on "neoliberal" terms. For the purposes of this chapter, the crucial result is that neither the U.S. government, the IFIs, nor the European Union can exercise anything like the leverage they used to have. Not only economic policy but also political objectives can be pursued more easily by using home resources or by embracing alternative non-Western sources of financial support. This reinforces the relaxation of political conditionality as regards democratic performance.

Contagion: *Democradura* and Illiberal Democracy

Democracy by contagion is the third broad dimension of democratization that I see. Contagion can obviously overlap with both control and conditionality. The key distinction is that whereas the latter two are forms of external direction or influence that are intentional (and, in the best of circumstances, coordinated), contagion involves a set of international influences that operate by example or diffusion and therefore operate in a way somewhat independent of deliberate pro-democracy public policy. But these dimensions are on a continuum, of course, rather than being sharply divided. Some forms of contagion may be assisted or even directed by government policy (Radio Free Europe, TV Martí, or even the World Wide Web).[11] Single channels of diffusion may not be that powerful—contagion probably works best when it comes from multiple sources and penetrates diverse levels of society.

With these considerations in mind, let us review the current state of democratic contagion in Latin America and the Caribbean. As already noted, this is such a broad canvas that it is hard to know where to begin. Perhaps the following summary of one day's television news coverage in South America can provide a starting point. On August 22, 2006, the main news items on CNN and BBC World were as follows:

- Tehran will not curb its nuclear ambitions.
- Israel reserves the right to continue its self-defense in Lebanon if Lebanese or United Nations forces cannot.
- Terrorists trying to destroy civil airliners flying from the United Kingdom to the United States are named and accused by the British police (prior to any trial) with a great display of incriminating evidence.
- President Bush insists that allied troops must stay in Iraq until "the job is done."

The same day, the main news items on Telesur (a public news broadcasting system mostly funded by the Venezuelan government) included these:

- It is the 34th anniversary of the Trelew massacre, in which the Argentine armed forces (acting, according to the report, under the direct instructions of President Alejandro Agustín Lanusse and in concert with the Pentagon) slaughtered 16 unarmed Montonero prisoners.
- The left achieves victory in the Chiapas gubernatorial elections despite unprecedented collusion by the Partido Acción Nacional (National Action Party) and the Partido Revolucionario Institucional (Revolutionary Institutional Party) to block the popular will.

- Andrés Manuel López Obrador continues to resist the apparent electoral fraud orchestrated by the administration of Vicente Fox.
- Amnesty International urges President Morales not to allow U.S. nationals in Bolivia to be exempted from action by the International Criminal Court.
- On the eve of crucial elections in Nicaragua, the privatized Spanish electricity company (backed by the World Bank) imposes sweeping power cuts.

My summary of the coverage offered by these two types of news organizations is merely an illustration of the diversity of discourse that can be disseminated on a single day through pluralist media operating within a broadly democratic framework. Telesur's news may seem propagandistic, but if one judges by the normal standards of journalistic professionalism, it is not falsifying its reports any more than CNN does. It is merely selecting its coverage according to quite different assumptions about what is meaningful and newsworthy. Of course, the opinions of many more Latin Americans are influenced by CNN than by Telesur (the BBC is probably the least influential of the three). In any case, August 22, 2006, may not be representative, and the news items I have listed may reflect my personal interests.[12] Most television watchers have their political orientations shaped by milder outlets less prone to the kind of totalizing imagery that saturates CNN and Telesur alike. Other more fragmentary sources of political contagion will usually have a greater impact on public opinion than these highly structured news media.

Consider a further example of indirect political influence disseminated by the left. In Bolivia, for example, there are over 1,500 Cuban medical personnel providing free health care to over 275,000 persons, many of whom were not benefiting from adequate attention under the previous democratic regime.[13] The Cuban method of literacy training has also taken effect, with the declared aim of eradicating illiteracy by 2008 (including that among non-Spanish speakers). There are clear signs that this indirect form of political socialization can produce unintended effects (adverse reactions both from local doctors and from urban *maestros*), but this example shows that contagion can operate at many levels. In the context of Bolivian democracy, free health care can be as potent as any Fulbright program.

In contrast to these messages from the left, what are today the dominant assumptions governing the form and content of a good democracy, as disseminated by mainstream Anglo-Saxon media, culture, and example? My impression is that the underlying message serves to promote what O'Donnell and Schmitter termed "*democradura*"—an assemblage of democratic procedures and structures constrained by the fear of individuals or groups deemed "sufficiently dangerous" that their citizenship rights should be restricted.[14] This is not the variety of democracy that proved so contagious in Europe at the end of the Cold War. It is also not the Miami Summit picture of what a regionwide convergence on democratic values could produce. If *democradura* has become "the only game in town" (or at least in Washington, D.C.), it will be hard to disseminate across the Americas, because the "war on terror" simply fails to resonate in most of the LAC democracies. This is partly because *democradura* is not very inclusive (those who fail to display the necessary loyalty and discipline are liable to be marginalized). Moreover, it emphasizes security threats rather than economic opportunities, whereas most Latin American voters fear economic insecurity more than terror attacks. Those citizens who place tolerance, dialogue, and respect for divergent viewpoints at the heart of the democratic project tend to be alienated, because *democradura* requires unity and certainty and therefore does not welcome much dissent. Whether *democradura* of this kind is the appropriate response to the challenges we all confront is a topic for separate discussion elsewhere. As regards the topic of this section, in contrast to earlier and more inclusive variants of democracy discourse, *democradura* is simply not very contagious.

From the perspective of Latin America in 2007, this version of democracy is liable to be perceived not only as unattractive but also as unnecessary and unviable. When Chileans turn to their media for enlightenment about terrorism, they see programs alleging that Eduardo Frei was the victim of a government assassination plot. Uruguayans see the confessions of the self-described "ideological author" of Operation Condor. Bolivians see corpses of their lost leaders disinterred. In such a climate, Washington-encouraged visions of *democradura* may even be viewed as threatening to the fragile democratic consensus that had been in the process of emerging in this part of the Western Hemisphere. Because it fails to capture the public imagination and to win many new converts to its cause, it leaves a void that might, under certain circumstances, be filled by alternative discourses. These would be based on more locally intelligible and appealing conceptions of democracy. Some analysts refer to this as the return of "populism" or even of simple "charisma." However we label it, what seems capable of proving more contagious is the appeal of an inclusive and rhetorical discourse that tends to devalue formal democratic institutions and structures and instead to judge democratic quality by the tests of popular enthusiasm and redistributive intent.

Arguably, this tendency would find an outlet whether or not President Chávez was around to capitalize on it. It is as much about collective identities and aspirations for social justice as about economic populism. In most countries, such international clashes over the discourse of democracy reach few *televidentes* (television viewers). For the most part, traditional local channels prevail, and their cautious news coverage usually responds to advertiser preferences, with a fairly high degree of macroeconomic orthodoxy and business pragmatism. However, it seems that a contest of loyalties is evident in the background, as manifested in successive election campaigns. If so, what are its implications for the stability and integrity of democratic institutions? From a political perspective, what seems to be proving most contagious is the belief that formal rules of the democratic game do not deserve much respect. They are too easily captured and manipulated by a discredited political class at the service of unreformed elites. From this view, the non-contagiousness of Anglo-Saxon *democradura* leaves the way clear for a highly contagious version of illiberal distributive democracy. Telesur commenced round-the-clock broadcasting only in October 2005, and its message is certainly that of a very limited minority, but according to this analysis, its potential capacity to gain new adepts should not be underestimated.

Consent: International Pluralism and the "Bolivarian Alternative"

The fourth of the international dimensions of democratization I proposed was "consent." Few will doubt the central role of consent in any but the most mechanistic conceptions of democracy. Again, there is an overlap among these categories. It is possible to consent to control, to conditionality, and to contagion, just as it is possible to withhold consent. The more relevant questions have to do with why consent should be included as an *international* component of democratization and whether it can be placed on an equal footing with the first three categories considered. My contention is that in addition to the indispensable internal basis of consent, on which any national democratic regime must be founded, there is also a powerful extranational dimension of consent whereby democratic regimes can reinforce themselves and strengthen their international authority through mutual recognition, adjustment, and support.

An early example was provided by Franco's Spain. In the absence of a principled stand by the European Union, it is possible that some variant of "Franquismo sin Franco" (Francoism without Franco) might have been attempted, and might even have secured fairly widespread acquiescence from the Spanish population.[15] For Spanish regime change to have been acceptable to its European neighbors, however, there would have had to be some regional and external recognition and consent. In fact, it would have threatened the democratic integrity of the European integration project to leave the issue of regime change to be settled exclusively by the constrained choices of the Spanish polity. On that basis and on the assumption that democratization involves the affirmation of some values and principles that cannot be confined within a single closed political system, it can be argued that there is an important international dimension to the establishment of democratic consent. It can also be argued that the first three components of this analysis (control, conditionality, and contagion) would be insufficient to stabilize a democratic transition in the absence of consent understood as a process of legitimation with multiple strands, both internal and international. Thus, consent as a category is of a higher order than the others.

How does this line of reasoning apply to the process of democratization in Latin America and the Caribbean today? There is an evident analogy between Spain in 1975 (when Franco was about to die) and Cuba today. There may well be substantial domestic support on the island for a continuation of some variant of "*Castrismo* after Fidel." However, the international structure of incentives, guidance, and support that eased the transition to democracy in Spain is not present in the same way in Cuba. The president of Costa Rica and Nobel Prize winner Óscar Arias may have considerable moral authority here, but his political base is constrained. In addition, his attempt to be even-handed (arguing that the United States should lift its blockade *and* withdraw from Guantanamo in order to enable Latin American democracies to press Cuba for a peaceful transition to full democracy) risks alienating both sides and falling between the cracks. The American counterparts to the regional organizations that had exerted growing influence on Spain before the transition seem considerably weaker and less credible in relation to Castro's Cuba. Whereas all the European democracies trying to assist the Spanish transition were themselves quite robust and were able to work in tandem, their Latin American counterparts are more divided and often more internally troubled. Mexico, for example, may well prove too absorbed by its own problems to play a leading role with regard to Cuba. Venezuela (still an "electoral" democracy of sorts, albeit an illiberal one) will work hard for regime continuity on the island. Recent democratic elections in Ecuador and Nicaragua have brought about the victory of candidates sympathetic to the current Cuban regime. In summary, international consent for the democratization of Cuba is unlikely to operate as it did in southern and eastern Europe. Even the European Union may be quite divided over Cuba (e.g., between the more open position of Spain and the hardline approach of the Czech Republic).

The Cuban issue is significant, but it is only one case in a larger constellation. Consider the ongoing political division in Mexico as a result of the July 2006 elections. President Bush naturally rushed to congratulate Felipe Calderón on his apparent victory, no doubt thinking that in Mexico, as in the United States in 2000, the best response to a very narrow and disputable outcome is to build momentum behind the ostensible winner so that the opposition's challenge will fade away. The legacy of López Obrador's slender defeat, however, can be expected to cast a longer shadow over Mexican democracy than Al Gore's similarly close defeat in the U.S. presidential election of 2000. While few democrats in the rest of Latin America are likely to lend much support to the losing candidate in Mexico, many still have a general sense that some degree of electoral fraud is the norm there, rather than the exception, and that the Fox administration probably overreached in its attempts to keep the governing party in office. For some of these bystanders, a real democratization of Mexico requires a clear break with the past, and that is the key issue at stake rather than the precise details of the electoral arithmetic. Again, Mexico is just one case in a larger constellation. The general point is that here, too, as in the Cuban case, there is no strong regional consensus that might reinforce the construction of domestic consent and guide Mexican democracy in a more consensual direction.

In Bolivia, Evo Morales was the first president since the democratization of 1982 to win a clear majority of the popular vote on the first round. The resulting universally accepted constitutional legitimacy is reinforced by a discursive claim also accepted almost as widely. Morales's government projects itself as the first to represent what is said to be the indigenous majority of the population and the first to "decolonize" the nation, as exemplified by the establishment of a constituent assembly and the renationalization of base resources. Judging from current opinion surveys, this government is still highly popular and is still seen as basically democratic, although past experience suggests that this domestic consent may prove volatile. How about the reinforcing and steering effects of regional and international consent? The most effective support is coming from Venezuela, and the clear objective is that of guiding Bolivia in a "Bolivarian," or chavista, direction. Argentina, Brazil, and Chile might all in principle exercise some limited influence, but they cannot coordinate their actions, they all have bilateral problems with Bolivia that negate their potential, and they have difficulty treating the Bolivian polity with respect as an equal. As regards the other potential bearers of democratic consent (the European Union, the United States, and the OAS), it must suffice to offer the flat assertion that right now they have little to offer. In Bolivia, too, international guidance and support for a volatile democracy are conspicuously weak. Arguably, it might not have taken much for a well-designed, coherent, intelligent initiative from the international community to have produced major positive effects on Bolivia's democratization in the first half of 2006. That moment has passed, however, and instead huge efforts have been channeled toward less promising landlocked locations (such as Afghanistan and Kosovo).

One more case demands attention to complete this section. The international community's stance on the status of democracy in Venezuela provides a striking counterpoint to the initial case of Spain or to the comfortingly convergent template envisaged by the Miami Summit process. For some, the Chávez government is completely undemocratic; for others, it represents the best example of inclusive transformation, with popular support periodically reaffirmed at the polls. There is a recall mechanism (not available in most Latin American republics), and in 2004 President Chávez accepted the challenge and (probably) won the recall. He clearly secured reelection in December 2006, but Venezuelan society is deeply polarized on this issue. His Quinta República does not rest on a very stable foundation of domestic consent.

What role has been played by the surrounding regional community of democracies? It is impossible to deal adequately with this large and controversial question here. The events of April 2002 certainly provide us with insight. Whatever criticisms one could direct against Hugo Chávez, from a domestic perspective he was unquestionably the duly elected president, and he fell captive to an authoritarian coup. Any doubt about the democratic inclinations of the conspirators was dispelled by their actions during their brief occupation of the presidency. They not only arrested the president (falsely pretending he had resigned) but also closed the National Assembly and the Supreme Court.

Did the Bush administration oppose the coup? Here is what one respected analyst wrote immediately after the crucial events:

> For nearly 20 years successive American governments have worked hard to persuade Latin Americans that Washington cares about democracy in the region, and is prepared to use its power to support and defend democratic governments. However, those two decades of effort might well have been undercut in a single day (April 12) when the Bush administration's comments appeared to welcome the overthrow of Venezuela's elected president, Hugo Chávez, and to deny that what happened in Venezuela was a military coup.[16]

Anyone who watched coverage of this process on CNN at the time would have to acknowledge that the Western media were not precisely forthright in their coverage of this grave setback to democracy in the Americas. (In fact, the subsequent Venezuelan decision to fund Telesur was apparently spurred by dissatisfaction with CNN on this score.) In my own case, it was only by following coverage in the Portuguese media that I was alerted to more or less what was really going on and what was at stake.

How did the OAS respond? On the fateful day of September 11, 2001, the OAS had adopted the Inter-American Democratic Charter, which spelled out the full panoply of institutional requirements for a functioning representative democracy and committed the organization to monitor compliance and take action in the event of any interruptions to democratic normality. President Chávez had previously attempted to block the adoption of a democratic charter, but he finally went along with it. He was also the beneficiary of its provisions in that, on April 13, 2002, OAS Secretary General

César Gaviria for the first time invoked Article 20, which condemns an alteration of constitutional order. The Rio Group (of 19 Latin American republics) also condemned the coup while it was still in process.

These international moves may have contributed to the foundering of the conspiracy and thus to the reinstatement of the constitutional order. Overall, however, it seems clear that at the crucial moment of the coup the American democracies were divided on how to react to it and that the most powerful government in the community was at least somewhat inclined to grant its consent to the violent overthrow of a recognized democratic government in Venezuela. No doubt that would also have required Washington to make light of the repression that was intended to follow. Long after the fact, there would presumably have been a conscience-salving change of stance. In an hour of need, however, little or no solidarity with the elected authorities would have been forthcoming. At any rate, this is the lesson the chavistas drew from the reactions of other American nations when they returned to office, and they never hesitate to remind their friends in other Latin American countries of it: "If you want to use democratic means to challenge the established order, do not expect your conformity with standard electoral procedures to provide you with any real guarantees of support or protection from the so-called democratic community around you."

In the absence of a credible regional commitment to uniform standards of consistency in upholding liberal democracy, that message is capable of gaining traction with a significant segment of Latin Americans. It seems an easier message to transmit than the grim security obsessions of the *democradura* alternative. It is contagious because it seems hopeful and relevant to local understandings of politics and because it can claim the possession of certain truths (no doubt very partial ones) that pass forgotten or unrecognized elsewhere. It also appeals to Latin Americans because it challenges the authority of formal institutions that are often felt not to have served the common interest and not to have proved as neutral and transparent as the advocates of conventional democracy would have everyone believe. (The conventional wisdom is "Only the gullible would rely on the OAS to defend a democracy that Washington wished to overturn," just as "Only the gullible would trust President Fox to allow his rival an electoral victory when he has scope to fix the succession," etc.) Whether or not these arguments are well founded, they currently seem plausible to many Latin American voters. These are not just chavista deceptions; they reflect a good deal of the popular understanding in a large number (but not all) of the LAC democracies. Of course, their impact is enhanced by the well-funded actions of the Venezuelan government and by the evidence from other countries that Chávez's Bolivarian Alternative to the FTAA has some regional support. Their impact is further maximized to the extent that the FTAA fails, neoliberalism falters, Washington offers only *democradura*, and, in place of open debate, defenders of the status quo just dismiss this discourse as anti-democratic. Dissident currents of opinion have gained momentum since 2002, in considerable part because Washington and its allies have ceded the terrain of inclusive democracy to the critics.

In practice, outside the United States and a handful of Central American republics, it is not possible to silence the assertions of the Bolivarian Alternative by simply reclassifying Chávez as another Castro. Whatever the limitations of contemporary democracies in Latin America, they do allow a considerable degree of pluralism of opinions. There is an open space, a framework that is not seen as openly anti-democratic, for those who wish to criticize the state of democracy in the Western Hemisphere. There is a high degree of "democratic pluralism" in most of the LAC countries, and within that public space advocates of a Bolivarian Alternative can operate as freely as those who want to promote *democradura*. A key reason that the international dimension of democratic consent in the Americas is so weak is that neither of these conceptions is currently able to prevail over the other.

There are always objections to this placing of discourses of Washington and Caracas, or of CNN and Telesur, on an equal footing for comparison. After all, Venezuela's credentials as a democracy are far weaker than those of the United States (not to mention Canada). Chávez seems increasingly irresponsible and erratic. The Bolivarian Alternative rests on a small and fragile domestic base and may well prove to have limited staying power or international appeal. If the leading democracies of the hemisphere were once again to give genuine priority to their shared democratic values and aspirations, enshrined in the 2001 Democratic Charter, and were to act consistently and effectively to demonstrate the superiority of their version, they could, in principle, achieve a strong reversal of opinion. At least at present, however, the climate for this is not propitious. For the time being, the United States' lack of credibility on the democracy issue leaves its critics in the region with open terrain on which to advance alternative positions. The discussion in this chapter is limited to a transversal assessment of the structure of international support for democracy in the Americas in 2006 and 2007. From that limited perspective, the level of international consent is low and the dissidents are enjoying an almost entirely free run. For the time being, at least, many in the Western Hemisphere believe that these rival discourses operate on almost an equal footing in terms of trustworthiness, if not in terms of power.

For committed democrats, this is a troubling situation. The claim that different variants of democracy are appropriate for different historical and socioeconomic settings is notoriously vulnerable to misuse. It can be used to cloak or excuse all manner of retreat from basic democratic values, and even negation of those values. *Democradura* can, and historically has, easily paved the way for the outright repudiation of democracy (as in Uruguay during its campaign against Marxist "subversion" in the 1970s). Conservative politicians who rely on harsh "*super mano dura*" (extremely iron-fisted) policies against crime and insecurity to guarantee their electoral majorities risk creating such a siege mentality that all legal restraints and democratic checks and balances come to seem superfluous. Thus, *democradura* can prove contagious and, if pursued to excess, can also be fatal to core democratic values of tolerance and respect for human rights.

Similarly, whatever the current attractions of distributivist and participatory democracy, its disrespect for formal institutions and neutral procedures makes it vulnerable to authoritarian temptations. If an incumbent president immediately rewrites the rules to allow for an additional term of office, it is problematic but not necessarily fatal to democracy. However, if an incumbent rewrites the rules to allow indefinite or lifetime reelection to office (as was recently attempted in Venezuela), it is perilously close to anti-democratic, no matter what the circumstances. The reason is simple: if citizens subsequently regret their decision, they may no longer be able to rely on the ballot box to provide a constitutional way to correct it; if not, other, more conspiratorial, methods of restraining or ousting their ruler will become pivotal. Likewise, when a constituent assembly is elected to rewrite a constitution, it may be tempted, as in Bolivia, to claim unlimited democratic authority, displacing the existing Congress and the judiciary. Even if the assembly's recommendations require ratification by referendum, this degree of institutional discontinuity is perilous for a democracy. No matter how much the new constitution improves on the provisions of it predecessor, these advances come at a heavy price. If the old institutions can so easily be disregarded, that fragility will also weaken the new ones. This does not make the convening of foundational constituent assemblies inherently anti-democratic, but it does flash a warning. Again, if the citizens approve a new constitution but then subsequently regret their decision, the most obvious remedy may be simply to repudiate it rather than to work for its amendment from within. Likewise, it is not necessarily anti-democratic for defeated challengers to allege electoral fraud and even to mount civil disobedience campaigns, but it is perilous for them to publicly send "to the devil" such crucial institutions as the recently reformed election agency and its electoral court (as López Obrador has done in Mexico). Only a very compelling justification would be strong enough to offset the risk of precipitating a free-for-all between contenders after every close election. All these risks of authoritarian regression are currently live issues in the Western Hemisphere, and all could well prove contagious. They risk undermining the social consent, both internal and regional, that is needed to stabilize formal rules of the democratic game.

Control, Conditionality, Contagion, and Consent—A Southern Reprise in 2006

This chapter began with a brief reminder of the expectations concerning the advance of democratization throughout the Americas that were generated by the Miami Summit process, launched in 1994. The assumptions underlying that project were quite coherent and interlocking. They reflected a certain fairly agreed idea of what was to count as democracy and democratization. The aim was to reinforce recent liberalizing developments in most of the individual republics of the region, articulating a coordinated international strategy that was not directed mainly toward democracy promotion but did incorporate multiple proposals to lock in the type of democracy then in vogue. This international project could reasonably be analyzed according to the four overlapping categories—control, conditionality, contagion, and consent—that could, at that time, be extracted from the tendencies then observable in the Americas (as well as the EU counterpart practice).

Sixteen years later, we can reprise the international dimensions of democratization in the Western Hemisphere, revisiting the original concepts and assumptions in the light of subsequent experiences. However, subsequent experiences have been so varied and turbulent that it is not feasible to trace them all in a single chapter. Moreover, the current panorama of democratic advances and retreats remains quite unstable. This chapter contains a cross-sectional survey of the state of affairs as of early 2007 that leaves much room for doubt about the future direction of political change in the Western Hemisphere. This conclusion addresses some of the conceptual and analytical issues arising from the survey. It is not concerned either with prediction or with prescription.

In the mid-1990s there was a surprisingly wide consensus in the Americas about what kind of democracy was within reach and about how and why the many diverse nations of the Western Hemisphere should come together to support and reinforce it. This consensus was reinforced by a wider liberal internationalist zeitgeist reflecting the unexpectedly complete and easy Western victory in the Cold War, but looking back from the current vantage point it is hard to avoid the conclusion that this was in fact a somewhat strained consensus. Beneath the surface, a variety of partially overlapping but also significantly diverging ideas were in play. There were somewhat varying conceptions of what the ideal of political democracy should include. There were also substantial differences over how to cope with the inevitable gap between ideals (possibly shared) and "really existing" democratic practices (which were much more likely to be contested by those who felt they were losing out or not getting the share they were due).

In addition to these ambiguities over the "what" of democracy, there were already quite evident and keenly felt differences over its "how" (and, in particular, over the extent to which regional or international procedures and obligations might displace or even supersede purely internal or domestic dynamics). The "why" question was also bound to elicit somewhat different responses depending on the vantage point of each observer. Those just emerging from the insecurity and brutality of authoritarian rule (or perhaps even civil war) might offer rather more urgent and more directly political justifications. On the other hand, those already secure in their own democratic institutions might need more prodding to attach the same priority to international democracy promotion and might be inclined to take up the cause only if it could be linked to some other desired objectives (e.g., enhanced regional security or increased prosperity). The United States, as the lead democracy, needed reassurance that a stronger commitment to regional democracy and liberal internationalism would not threaten its other major foreign policy interests. Given these somewhat discordant regional responses to what/how/why questions, the agenda of the Summit of the Americas would progress only if it could develop a strong unifying discourse and powerful spokespersons. This the Miami process provided—a unified message backed by the full weight of both the U.S. administration and Congress. The message contained a fairly precise promise (that the FTAA would be in place by 2005) and rested on a fairly explicit basis of teleological argumentation.[17] In contrast to the policy stamina of the European Union, however, that of Washington is limited. Whatever the message of 1994, the policy makers of today are free to endorse a completely different script. The same volatility will apply to promises of future U.S. administrations.

Sixteen years after Miami, the cracks in this apparent consensus are all too apparent. The overly optimistic zeitgeist of the early post–Cold War years (1990–94) has been displaced by a grim new security obsession (2001–present). For clarity of analysis, we need to work out where the greatest problems have arisen and separate those from the passing and superficial setbacks. From a normative perspective, we also need to reflect on which aspects of the original consensus can be relinquished or modified and which elements are so fundamental to any principled conception of democracy that they must be defended against challenges from any source. The response to these analytical and normative puzzles will go far toward indicating what kind of Americas-wide consensus (if any) could prove more durable and convincing than before. More particularly (for this chapter), it will help show what weight can be attached to the first pair of regional and international dimensions discussed here (control and conditionality)—as opposed to the second pair (contagion and consent). A shift in emphasis toward the second pair would imply leaving each country as free as possible to build its own system of representative government from within with the minimum of external intervention.

A variety of practical problems have arisen from the crumbling of the somewhat artificial regional consensus of the mid-1990s, as illustrated by the following questions: Is it now permissible to build a democratic regime in the Americas on the foundation of public ownership and control of a nation's natural resources? Is regional convergence around norms of democratic integration compatible with much tighter immigration controls, the possible large-scale deportation of *indocumentados* (undocumented residents), and the denial of basic health care or driver's licenses to those who are not citizens? Can nonnationals be granted voting rights, perhaps based on transnational reciprocation? Are there circumstances in which it is justified to torture for freedom, to wiretap, or to detain those suspected of crimes without trial? How do projects of decolonization (and the restoration of allegedly long-suppressed indigenous rights) relate to democracy and democratization? What privileged status (if any) should American democrats accord to the extraterritorial decisions of the U.S. Congress or the U.S. Supreme Court? If the electorate of a particular Latin American republic decides, in a free and fair election, to rewrite the republic's constitution so as to abrogate existing laws and institutional commitments, is that an affirmation of democracy or a violation of the rule of law? Does Telesur operate within the freedom-of-speech protections that should be upheld in all American democracies, or is it a mouthpiece of anti-democratic subversion to be censored or shut down? If international observers qualify an election outcome as clean, can there ever be justification for disregarding their verdict and resorting to civil disobedience against what the losers regard as electoral fraud?

Whereas most—if not all—of these questions could have been answered unambiguously by a mainstream democratic consensus in the mid-1990s, today the responses are likely to be more qualified and divided. It is currently possible to group the options at two poles—I have labeled these the *democradura* and the illiberal distributive options, respectively—but neither of these is stable or all-encompassing. Other variants and combinations are easy to envisage and may well crystallize as competitive options in coming years. In any event, practical dilemmas of the kind represented by the questions raised earlier are more likely to proliferate than to disappear. If so, more than two competing discourses could well bid against each other for acceptance as really existing democracies adapt to current conditions in the Americas. A pluralism of proposals seems more likely than a return to *pensamiento único*.[18]

Therefore, from a comparative democratization perspective, the remaining issues to consider are (1) how much pluralism and diversity of practice can be accepted within the framework of an overarching commitment to democratic principle and (2) which variants of international collective effort are most compatible with this degree of discursive flux and contestation. On the first issue, there is little new that can be said about the various elements of political democracy at the national level that need to be defended on principle. The basic list is extremely familiar: free and fair elections; the possibility of periodic alternation in public office-holders; some constitutional separation of powers with accountability mechanisms; and some fundamental individual and collective rights, including protection for minorities, access to information, an inclusive or participatory ethos of some kind, and so on. Each of these general points has been refined and elaborated to the highest degree, and even those who consider the Inter-American Democratic Charter of 2001 out of date can use it as a solid basis for subsequent improvements. The principles are still reasonably clear. However, our survey of the current state of affairs has revealed considerable scope for tension between the various competing elements and for differences of interpretation about how they apply in specific contexts. Consider "fundamental rights" and Mexico or an "inclusive ethos" and Bolivia (or even "access to information" and CNN). Out of this mixture it is possible to distill more than one set of democratic priorities that can be defended on the grounds of highest principle. Moreover, beyond this long but restrictive list of components it would be possible to identify additional features that are regarded in certain contexts as integral to democracy for *some* societies (upholding free market principles, opposing totalitarian evil-doers, correcting historical injustices against excluded population groups, etc.) but not for others. In short, it is possible for more than one constellation of democratic principles to capture the collective imagination of a political community. In the specific case of the democracies of the Western Hemisphere, it is far from clear that a single, unified ensemble of democratic criteria can command consensual support across the entire region. In some countries, the sense that this is "our" version of democracy (homegrown, not imitating foreign models) may be vital for the legitimation of democracy.

Finally, if there is indeed a plurality of democratic conceptions or aspirations in play across the Americas, what dimensions of international support or reinforcement are likely to prove most relevant, and which might turn out to be divisive or counterproductive? In terms of the dimensions of democratization discussed earlier, what channels or procedures for mobilizing support are most appropriate? In this setting, control and most forms of conditionality seem inappropriate methods of reinforcing regional democratization patterns. Indeed, both could easily prove counterproductive. By contrast, because there is still a loose regional consensus in favor of a broadly democratic orientation in the Americas, this is a favorable setting for international democracy promotion by contagion, mutual accommodation, and locally driven consent. The key issue is the legitimacy (or lack of same) of each type of international influence.

Starting with control, it is not enough for an initiative to be proclaimed democracy-promoting; it is not enough for the proclamation to be seriously intended, properly researched, and adequately funded. The recipients of the initiative have to accept the truth of all of that and need to share an understanding of the what, how, and why of the initiative with its promoters. They also have to believe that this external input will add more to the chances of success of a democratizing process than it subtracts (by diluting the authority of the domestic actors involved or by tacking on additional unwanted considerations). Externally directed and controlled endeavors *can* be effective when all these conditions are fully and clearly met (as in Grenada in 1984). Even when they are largely but not entirely present (as in Panama in 1989), they may still succeed, although at higher risk in terms of subsequent conflict over legitimation. When most of these requirements are weak or absent, democratization via external imposition is inappropriate and, if attempted, likely to fail. The argument of this chapter is that, at least at the current juncture, very few if any of these conditions are present (even in Cuba).

With regard to conditionality, the conclusion could be a little less categorical, but not by much. Conditionality ranges from the nearly coercive to the nearly consensual. The first variety can sometimes be successful but only under the same restrictive conditions that work for control. At the more consensual end of the spectrum, there may still be tensions over authenticity. This point requires illustration. Citizens might ask, "Are we really adopting this reform because we want to and it is in our own interest, or are we deferring to foreign fashion rather than concentrating on building a domestic support base?" Some good examples of the seesaw nature of this dilemma can be seen in contemporary Turkey. Still, EU membership can constitute a relatively nonintrusive form of conditionality. At least as regards Spain in the 1970s, the dominant message was "You are, of course, free to choose your own regime and political system, but if you want to join our club there are certain membership conditions that you need to fulfill. Take your own time, take it or leave it, but don't expect us to vary our rules." (By the time the European Union's Copenhagen criteria were defined for the eastern enlargement, this nonintrusive posture had been superseded in Brussels.) Turning to the Americas, Mexico entered NAFTA on only the most indirect and nonintrusive of political conditions. (Some would say that there was no political conditionality at all, but that is not my reading. More likely, all signatories implicitly understood that previous extremes of fraud and repression would need to be curbed and that progress toward more competitive elections could not be entirely resisted.) Paraguay entered Mercosur with no explicit conditionality. Once inside, it tested the limits of membership; however, the underlying parameters became more sharply defined. During the Cold War, coercive conditionality was directed mainly against governments of the left, especially the Sandinistas and, prospectively, the Cubans. However, under the current conditions this formula is likely to prove counterproductive (easing the task of Caracas, stoking anti-imperialist imagery). Even the softest variants of conditionality carry some ambiguity and therefore risk misfiring.

By contrast, a loosely pluralist international environment may be particularly conducive to various forms of democratic contagion. One feature to notice here is that the contagion may flow in both directions. If Mexico's electoral institutions emerge reinforced after the current trial of their strength, an important message will be transmitted to officials in comparable institutions elsewhere in the hemisphere. At the same time, if Telesur's news coverage proves more relevant and persuasive than that of CNN or Televisa, under current conditions it can readily attract more viewers, subscribers, and imitators. The SIP's *pensamiento único* will have to be converted into a more persuasive and open dialogue if it is to embrace all the forms of free expression that are currently proliferating across the hemisphere. This "multivocal" type of contagion poses problems for *democraduras* as well as for chavistas.

Finally, therefore, the democratization of the Western Hemisphere remains an open project, equally capable of sharp regression and of swift recovery. Despite the current difficulties, there remains scope for advancement in a broad process of democratic dialogue and mutual accommodation based on the consent of all the parties involved, both domestic and international. Consent of this kind, however, will not arise from spontaneous agreement based on common values and assumptions. But if there is no single consensual model of democracy and democratization, openness to regional influences and discordant viewpoints tests the extent of pluralism and toleration in all the polities involved, not only those tilting toward illiberal distributivism but also those single-mindedly geared to security. So consent would have to be built up over time, requiring efforts of tolerance and imagination from all sides. In contrast to the assumptions of the Miami Summit process, it would uncover important areas of disagreement and even quite strong clashes of views between rival conceptions of democracy, alternative understandings of the region's history, and competing models of political participation and institutional design. While many of these debates would take place within the domestic politics of each American democracy, they would also find expression in rival projects of regional cooperation, integration, and democratic affirmation. Whether or not events will actually take this course is a separate issue. However, this is what regional consent to democratic pluralism in the Americas is likely to involve if it indeed materializes over the next few years.

3

The Backlash against Market Reforms in Latin America in the 2000s

Javier Corrales

The most salient political story in Latin America since the late 1990s has been the political defeat of market-oriented incumbents and candidates. With the exceptions of Chile, Colombia, Mexico, and several Central American nations, the electoral trend between 1998 and 2006 has been averse to pro-market political forces.

The new winners have tended to be figures whose electoral platforms are decidedly less enthusiastic about market economics than was the case in the 1990s. Presidents Hugo Chávez in Venezuela (1998), Alejandro Toledo in Peru (2001), Luiz Inácio "Lula" da Silva in Brazil (2002), Lucio Gutiérrez in Ecuador (2002), Néstor Kirchner in Argentina (2002–3), Tabaré Vázquez in Uruguay (2004), Evo Morales in Bolivia (2005), Rafael Correa in Ecuador (2006), Daniel Ortega in Nicaragua (2006), and Alan García in Peru (2006) all campaigned farther to the left than the incumbents they challenged. In Mexico and Peru, two explicitly anti-neoliberal candidates, Andrés Manuel López Obrador and Ollanta Humala, came close to winning in 2006. Although their levels of market aversion varied, all these new presidents and presidential candidates campaigned on more market-critical platforms than did other candidates. While it is true that in the 2000s economic issues during elections are concerned more with how to generate growth and improve distribution than with market reforms, there is no question that political forces advocating some form of statism are doing well electorally.[1]

Is there any chance for advancing market reforms in Latin America in this political context? On the surface, it seems that the answer is no. One way to read the political victories of these statist forces is to simply conclude, as suggested by Przeworski and more emphatically by Chua, that democracy and market reforms are incompatible: the reforms produce a majority of losers, and democracy empowers these losers to capture the state and block further market reforms.[2] This would be the most pessimistic reading of the trend of the 2000s—one that, I argue, may be incorrect. Although the rise of statist forces constitutes evidence of democratic opening, this trend is not exclusively fueled by losers or entirely incompatible with further market reforms.

In this chapter I argue that the rise of the left is fueled by a variety of complainants—blocs of voters from different sectors of society who have different views about the status quo and thus different agendas. I propose viewing the current wave of leftist movements not as a relatively homogenously "moderate" left or even a dichotomous left split between good and bad, but rather as the amalgamation of many disparate movements representing diverse constituencies, often with conflicting goals.[3] All these constituencies advocate change—and that is what unites them—but they differ on the institutions that they want to see changed (their policy targets), how far those changes must go (their degree of radicalism), and the appropriate means by which to attain those changes (their degree of respect for rules and political opponents). In short, the left is fueled by a variety of forms of discontent, not all of it radical or anti-market. Understanding this internal diversity within the rising left, both within countries and across countries, is also important for understanding the performance of these forces once their candidates assume office.

The Turn to the Left

Statist political forces are not new in Latin America.[4] By statist I mean displaying a programmatic orientation to use laws, decrees, and other state resources to restrict market activities (e.g., trade barriers; regulations; state ownership of productive assets; restrictions on competition; price, interest rate, and exchange rate controls; equity and content requirements). Between the 1930s and the late 1970s, statist political forces were dominant in most Latin American countries. Some were oriented more to the left (advocating stronger redistribution toward labor groups and closer collaboration with the Soviet bloc). Others were oriented more to the right (advocating more investments in infrastructure development, which tended to favor business groups). Others offered a combination of these strategies. Frequently, statist forces had a strong presence across states and also across society. Leftist forces (unlike populist forces) seldom captured the state, but they still had strong access to civil society through their penetration, and sometimes control, of labor groups (whose loyalties they disputed with other populist parties and, in some cases, with Christian Democrats). Most social and economic policy in Latin America's postwar period was negotiated among these various statist groups.[5] The difference between populism and the left is treated in more detail later in the chapter. For now, suffice it to say that on the whole, the leading political forces in Latin America from the 1930s onward were similarly reluctant to liberalize markets.

The minoritarian and weak status of pro-market political forces began to change in the 1970s with the rise of military regimes in Argentina, Brazil, Chile, Peru, and Uruguay that, rhetorically at least, called for less state intervention. But except for the Pinochet government in Chile, none of these military regimes achieved any real change in favor of economic freedoms; some did not even try. It was not until the mid-1980s that the region began to see the rise of political forces that decided to govern with the explicit intention of lessening statism, achieving real movement in this direction and achieving reelection.

The new salience of statist parties in the 2000s is thus remarkable only in comparison to the 1990s. During the 1990s, the trend was for statist and leftist parties to move to the right, both on the campaign trail and in office. This rightward move, so electorally rewarding in the 1990s, underwent a change in Latin America at the end of that decade. Both the former populist and the traditional leftist parties have begun to shift back to more statist electoral platforms, and new political movements expressing market discontent have emerged. Unlike in the 1990s, these newborn or reborn statist movements are doing well electorally.

Argentina is a good illustration of this back-to-the-left phenomenon. For the purposes of illustration, we will discuss the political spectrum in that country in terms of three political forces at the moment of each presidential election: those of the incumbent president (I) and the main leading candidates, the one who actually wins (C_W) and the loser (C_L) (Figure 3.1). In the early 1980s, both the winning candidate (Carlos Menem of the Partido Justicialista, or Judicialist Party) and the losing candidate placed themselves on the left, certainly more so than the incumbent (Raúl Alfonsín of the Unión Cívica Radical, or Radical Civic Union), who was trying to implement an increasingly market-oriented stabilization program. The more statist candidate, Menem, prevailed.

In 1995 (and to some extent in 1999), the candidates' positioning within the political spectrum was radically different from that seen in the late 1980s. Both the incumbent, who was running for reelection, and the leading opposition candidates placed themselves closer to the right than had candidates in the 1980s. No candidate advocated significant change of the economic reforms already set in motion, which at that point were deemed far-reaching by world standards.

Figure 3.1. Presidential Candidates' Positioning vis-à-vis Market Economics

Argentina, 1989

C_W C_L I

Statism   Free markets

Argentina, 1995

C_L C_L I_W

Statism   Free markets

Argentina, 1999

C_W C_L C_L

Statism   Free markets

Argentina, 2003

C_L C_W C_L C_L

Statism   Free markets

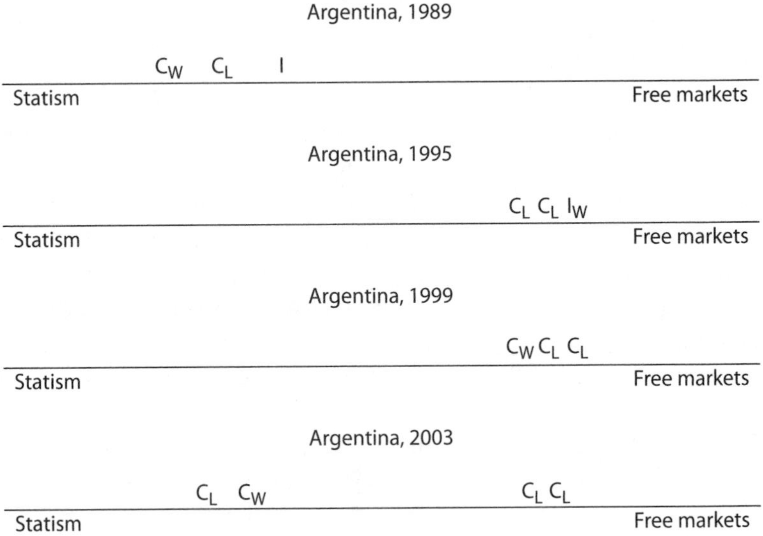

Notes: C_W, winning candidate; C_L, losing candidate; I_W, winning incumbent; I_L, losing incumbent.

But in the 2003 elections, the winning candidate (Néstor Kirchner) campaigned on a platform that was more statist than that of any major candidate since the 1990s, though it was more centrist than the platforms of the candidates in 1988. A second change in 2003 was that the electoral space occupied by pro-market forces remained strong. The two more pro-market candidates, Carlos Menem and Ricardo López Murphy, obtained 40.7 percent of the votes combined. If anything, the 2003 election offered far more diversity of choice for voters, at least in terms of candidates' positioning vis-à-vis market economics.

A similar "back-to-the-left" phenomenon was evident in Brazil's 2002 presidential race, to cite another example. Three major opposition candidates (Lula, Anthony Garotinho, and Ciro Gomes) came from parties that are typically classified as being on the left.[6] As in Argentina, the winner, Lula, was from this more statist camp. The more pro-market candidate obtained 23.2 percent of the vote in 2002 and 39.2 percent in 2006.

Argentina and Brazil thus offer three puzzles about electoral positioning vis-à-vis market reforms common to many countries of the region in the last three decades. First, why did statism become trendy again in the 2000s, albeit in a more modest manifestation than in the 1980s? Second, why has the electoral turn to the left not been more sweeping, with pro-market forces remaining electorally relevant? Finally, what explains the extent to which statist forces actually move away from market-oriented reforms once in office?

The answers to the first two questions have to do with economics. The mixed record of market reforms in the 1990s lends itself to a more divided electorate, and hence a more diversified electoral race. The answer to the third question, on policy movement, is harder to arrive at, but I contend that it has to do with the answer to the second question as well as with political party variables. Specifically, where party institutionalization is strong, it has served to moderate policy volatility in the 2000s.

Neoliberalism in the 1990s as an Explanation for the Return of Statism in the 2000s

The Blame Game

Perhaps the explanation most often heard for the return of the left is the "disappointing" performance of market reforms of the 1990s. A change of opinion has taken place. In the mid-1990s, there was a certain sense of "market triumphalism."[7] It was a time when everyone seemed to believe that market forces were winning, even if by ideological imposition.[8] Geddes even talked about the "ineffectiveness of popular opposition" to reforms.[9]

In the mid-2000s, in contrast, the climate could very well be described as one of "market defeatism": a feeling among analysts and politicians that the market reforms of the past two decades, at least in Latin America, involved too much pain for very little gain, maybe even retrocession. Meager growth in the 1990s, financial crises in the late 1990s and early 2000s, and unstable politics in many Latin American countries have led many perennial critics of the market to feel vindicated and many supporters of market reforms to feel dumbfounded. The "failure" of neoliberalism in addressing pressing social issues, the argument goes, explains the rise of the left.

But how terrible was the record of the 1990s? And, more important, how much can the economic record of the 1990s be blamed for the political rise of statist movements? Defenders of market reforms must contend with the fact that the record of the 1990s was less glittery than initially expected. Yet critics of market reforms cannot paint a picture of "overall devastation."

If anything, it is difficult to come to clear-cut judgments about the effects of market reforms. A variety of contradictory conclusions about the socio-economic impact of reforms can be drawn from the same type of evidence. Next I review some evidence with the goal of showing that all sides in this blame game make strong points, but none can claim conclusive victories. Whereas in the 1980s both analysts and Latin American citizens could easily agree that the experience of the previous decade had been negative and was thus worth revamping, in the 2000s no such consensus about ills and prescriptions seems possible.[10] And this disagreement about how to assess the performance of the 1990s is influencing politics on the ground.

Stabilization, Growth, and Poverty

One of the primary objectives of market reforms was to restore growth and eradicate inflation, which, at least since the 1960s, has been an endemic, poverty-multiplying economic malaise in many Latin American countries. Inflation abatement is perhaps the one area in which market reforms produced astounding success. Latin America moved from the position of world champion of inflation—a true global outlier—to one of the most price-stable regions in the world. Furthermore, this gain in price stability has proven to be sustainable, surviving even the most recent recession (1999–2002), an accomplishment that eluded the region in the past. Weyland suggests that, by saving the region from economic instability, neoliberalism actually safeguarded the new Latin American democracies from possible authoritarian reversals.[11]

Defenders of market reform can also argue, rightly, that the reforms produced a "sustainable recovery" (Figure 3.2). This was a huge change from the past, in which the region had either unsustainable growth rates (i.e., growth with inflation and debt in the 1970s) or economic collapse (with even more inflation and debt in the 1980s). Instead, Latin America had growth without inflation in the 1990s and has had growth with declining debt in the 2000s. Furthermore, there is some evidence that, overall, poverty has declined in the region. All in all, the 1990s and 2000s have not been bad decades.

However, the story of success is not as clear-cut. Figure 3.2 also shows that in the 1990s growth levels were modest in relation to both the region's development needs (i.e., they were insufficient to generate the levels of employment needed to combat poverty) and their record prior to the 1980s. Furthermore, from 1998 through 2002, Latin America experienced negative growth (suggesting excessive vulnerability), and during the recovery period after 2003, the region's growth underperformed compared to that of Asia and the Pacific regions. From this perspective, the performance of the period was modest, maybe even mediocre.[12]

Far-Reaching Reformers versus the Rest

One problem with the macro figures discussed thus far is that they do not differentiate among degrees of market reforms. I have argued that there were different levels of market reformers in Latin America, ranging from aggressive reformers (e.g., Argentina, Chile, Mexico, and Peru) to reform laggards (e.g., Ecuador, Paraguay, and Venezuela).[13] Some sectors of the economy were universally reformed (inflationary pressures, trade), but reform in other sectors was uneven across countries.[14] Did the more (or less) market-oriented countries or sectors perform noticeably differently than the rest?

Figure 3.2. GDP Growth per Capita by Region, 1970–2005

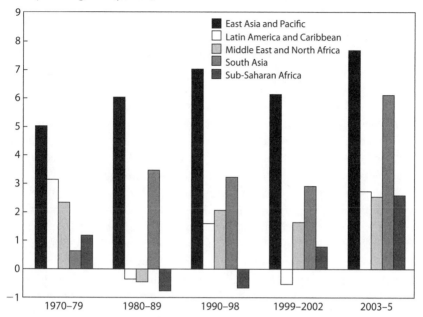

Per capita GDP growth (percent)

Source: World Development Indicators.

This question is not easy to answer because there are different ways of ranking degrees of market reform, and each produces different assessments. For instance, Huber and Solt classify countries according to whether they scored above or below the median on a widely accepted index of market-oriented reform from 1982 to 1995.[15] Their aim is to assess whether countries that changed policy (from statist to pro-market) most rapidly and extensively between 1982 and 1995 performed better or worse in terms of economic growth, volatility, inequality, poverty alleviation, and political rights between 1990 and 1998. They conclude that more aggressive and rapid reformers actually scored less well than the rest.

But Huber and Solt have faced direct criticisms. Walton, for instance, has explicitly challenged them by arguing that there are no statistically significant correlations across the variables that Huber and Solt study.[16] Furthermore, he contends that Huber and Solt's classification of countries is "unconvincing," in part because it gives too much emphasis to policy changes in the 1980s, when countries were mostly muddling through rather than actually achieving real market-oriented reforms.

The debate of Huber and Solt versus Walton highlights a broader methodological controversy. There are many ways to classify degrees of market orientation. Huber and Solt focus on one metric: changes in a given reform index. But one could instead propose a different index, such as the Heritage Foundation's *Index of Economic Freedom,* which is used to rank countries on a large array of pro-market policies. Alternatively, one could classify degree of market orientation by focusing on actual outcomes, such as degree of private sector investments. Yet another option is to rank countries on the extent to which private investments (as a percentage of gross domestic product, or GDP) have increased in the region. Yet another alternative is to focus on a particular measure of privatization (e.g., private investments in traditional state-owned sectors, such as utilities and transport) or liberalization (e.g., number of procedures needed to start a private business).

Table 3.1 shows how each of these metrics, including Huber and Solt's, yields different groupings of "far-reaching" market-oriented countries. For each metric, the countries that scored the highest values are shaded gray in the table. For all columns except column 4, the standard for a high score that I use is based on a comparison with Chile's ranking: the metrics of countries that matched or surpassed Chile's score are indicated in gray. The reason I use Chile's score as the dividing point is that almost all analysts agree that Chile has been Latin America's most market-oriented country since the early 1990s. Column 4 reflects Huber and Solt's classification.[17]

Table 3.1 shows that there is in fact variation across countries and across domains: being a far-reaching reformer in one domain does not mean that a country is a far-reaching reformer in another domain. Not one country scores high in all categories. Only Chile, mostly as a result of definitions, and Trinidad and Tobago appear as far-reaching reformers in four of the five rankings covering the late 1990s.

One problem with many of these metrics is incomplete data: coverage does not include recent years or all the countries. For this reason, it might make sense to focus on the *Index of Economic Freedom,* which contains data for the largest number of countries from 1995 to the present. Another benefit is theoretical: this index contains metrics that closely resemble the components of the Washington Consensus, and furthermore, most studies on the subject conclude that this index is positively correlated with economic growth.[18]

Table 3.2 lists all Latin American countries included in the Heritage Foundation's *Index of Economic Freedom* and indicates in light gray the scores of those countries that matched or did better than Chile's score in 1995 (2.6 points), the first year for which this index is available. The scores of countries that matched or did worse than Venezuela in 1995 (3.23 points), one of the region's most prominent reform laggards, are indicated in dark gray.

Table 3.1. Aggressive Reformers According to Different Metrics (circa late 1990s)

Country	A Private investments as a percentage of GDP (proxy for degree of reliance on market activities)	B Private investments in utilities and transport (proxy for privatization)	C Economic freedoms (level achieved by 2002)	D Distance traveled (largest change in market reform index between 1982 and 1995)	E Procedures necessary to start a new business
Argentina			HIGH		
Barbados	NA	NA		NA	NA
Belize	NA	NA		NA	
Bolivia	HIGH	HIGH			
Brazil		HIGH		Above	
Chile	HIGH	HIGH	HIGH		Few
Colombia		NA			
Costa Rica	HIGH	NA		Above	
Cuba	NA	NA		NA	
Dominican Republic	NA	HIGH		Above	
Ecuador		NA			
El Salvador			HIGH	Above	
Guatemala				Above	
Haiti		NA		NA	
Honduras	NA	NA			
Jamaica	NA	NA		Above	
Mexico	HIGH				Few
Nicaragua	HIGH	HIGH		NA	Few
Panama		HIGH	HIGH	NA	Few
Paraguay				Above	
Peru	HIGH			Above	
Trinidad and Tobago	HIGH	HIGH	HIGH	NA	Few
Uruguay		NA	HIGH		
Venezuela					

Sources: World Development Indicators; Heritage Foundation; Huber and Solt, "Successes and Failures of Neoliberalism."

Notes: Shading indicates countries whose scores match or surpass Chile's. NA, data not available.

Column A—HIGH indicates countries whose scores in 1998 matched or surpassed Chile's score in 1989 (18.2 percent of GDP), the earliest year for which there are data on Chile.

Column B—HIGH indicates countries whose level of private investment in telecoms, energy, water and sanitation, and transport in 1998 matched or surpassed Chile's levels in the early 2000s.

Column C—HIGH indicates countries whose scores in 1998 matched or surpassed Chile's score in 1995 (2.6 points).

Column D—Above indicates countries that experienced a degree of change that was above the median on the Morley, Machado, and Pettinato index of economic reforms; the classification appears in Huber and Solt, "Successes and Failures of Neoliberalism."

For Column E—Few indicates countries whose scores matched or surpassed Chile's score of 9 procedures (same as Iran).

Table 3.2. Economic Freedom Index for Latin America

Country	1995	1996	1997	1998	1999	2000	2001	2002	2003	2004	2005	2006	Change 1995–2002	Change 2002–6
Argentina	2.85	2.58	2.70	2.48	2.23	2.28	2.29	2.63	3.09	3.43	3.49	3.30	−0.22	0.67
Bahamas	2.36	2.09	2.05	2.16	2.16	2.23	2.23	2.06	2.15	2.25	2.25	2.26	−0.67	−0.23
Barbados	NA	3.15	2.98	2.63	2.86	2.74	2.59	2.48	2.24	2.41	2.35	2.25	−0.11	0.04
Belize	2.85	2.74	2.71	2.96	2.76	2.84	2.64	2.74	2.69	2.69	2.71	2.78	−0.50	0.30
Bolivia	3.16	2.56	2.51	2.61	2.61	2.56	2.31	2.66	2.54	2.64	2.75	2.96	−0.30	−0.03
Brazil	3.41	3.61	3.33	3.41	3.24	3.46	3.26	3.11	3.06	3.10	3.20	3.08	−0.72	0.00
Chile	2.60	2.56	2.26	2.10	2.13	2.04	2.03	1.88	2.06	1.91	1.86	1.88	−0.06	0.17
Colombia	3.05	3.10	3.23	3.19	3.09	3.14	3.05	2.99	3.10	3.13	3.21	3.16	−0.31	−0.04
Costa Rica	3.04	3.00	3.03	3.00	3.00	2.83	2.84	2.73	2.76	2.66	2.76	2.69	−0.12	−0.73
Cuba	4.95	4.95	4.85	4.90	4.85	4.83	4.83	4.83	4.48	4.13	4.24	4.10	−0.44	0.20
Dominican Republic	3.63	3.34	3.24	3.26	3.20	3.80	3.09	3.19	3.29	3.51	3.54	3.39	−0.47	0.13
Ecuador	3.39	3.33	3.26	3.15	3.14	3.19	3.56	3.60	3.58	3.60	3.49	3.30	0.21	−0.30
El Salvador	2.89	2.68	2.55	2.61	2.38	2.10	2.21	2.28	2.35	2.24	2.20	2.35	−0.61	0.07
Guatemala	3.36	3.10	2.94	2.96	2.94	2.91	2.88	3.00	3.01	3.16	3.18	3.01	−0.36	0.01
Guyana	3.70	3.38	3.40	3.55	3.30	3.35	3.35	3.23	3.15	3.08	3.08	3.11	−0.20	−0.10
Honduras	3.58	3.58	3.58	3.51	3.71	3.51	3.50	3.38	3.24	3.53	3.43	3.28	−0.15	−0.20
Jamaica	3.11	2.94	2.91	2.94	2.96	2.66	2.96	2.96	2.68	2.81	2.76	2.76	−0.09	−0.13
Mexico	3.05	3.31	3.35	3.41	3.30	3.09	3.05	2.96	2.81	2.90	2.84	2.83	−0.85	−0.18
Nicaragua	4.08	3.65	3.75	3.68	3.65	3.65	3.49	3.23	3.14	2.99	2.90	3.05	−0.02	0.02
Panama	2.70	2.55	2.49	2.50	2.48	2.61	2.58	2.68	2.64	2.83	2.74	2.70	0.34	−0.02
Paraguay	2.99	2.94	2.96	3.09	2.95	3.06	3.34	3.33	3.40	3.44	3.45	3.31	−0.71	−0.02
Peru	3.59	3.01	3.08	2.91	2.61	2.69	2.56	2.88	2.91	2.88	2.83	2.86	−0.20	0.01
Suriname	NA	4.10	4.00	4.10	4.08	3.98	3.98	3.98	4.01	3.96	3.93	3.60	0.70	0.23
Trinidad and Tobago	NA	2.69	2.63	2.60	2.49	2.43	2.59	2.49	2.54	2.40	2.54	2.50	−0.22	0.67
Uruguay	3.03	2.85	2.65	2.59	2.60	2.50	2.35	2.56	2.50	2.55	2.60	2.69	−0.67	−0.23
Venezuela	3.23	3.58	3.53	3.48	3.43	3.38	3.78	3.93	3.76	4.23	4.09	4.16	−0.11	0.04

Source: Heritage Foundation, *Index of Economic Freedom,* 1995–2006.
Notes: Light shading indicates the scores of those countries that matched or did better than Chile's score (2.6 points) in 1995, the first year for which this index is available. Dark shading indicates the scores of countries that matched or did worse than Venezuela (one of the region's most prominent reform laggards) in 1995 (3.23 points). NA, data not available.

The first point that emerges from this exercise is that, according to this classification, the number of deep reformers (light gray) in Latin America has never been very large. The peak year was 2001, when 10 of 26 countries matched or exceeded Chile's 1995 score. Second, the category of reform laggards (dark gray) is large: 9 of 26 in 2001. Third, by 2006 the number of far-reaching reformers had declined by half (down to 5), whereas the number of reform laggards had declined by only one (8 of 26). This is an important trend that is discussed later in the chapter. For now, suffice it to say that the overall economic performance of Latin America in 1996–2006 cannot be used to evaluate "neoliberalism" because, according to this metric, the region is neither entirely nor consistently neoliberal.

Public Opinion: The Dislike of Privatization

Is there evidence of discontent with market reforms regardless of the model's performance?[19] Latinobarómetro has conducted surveys of attitudes toward market economics. Its findings present a curious paradox. Although there is overwhelming support for "market reforms" in almost all countries (on average, 57 percent of the population supported market reforms in 2003), "privatization" was rejected (an average of 22 percent supported privatization in 2003, down from 46 percent in 1998).[20] This low level of support for privatization in a region where there is overall support for market reform and macroeconomic stability seems odd because privatization is a cornerstone of market reform.

Dislike of privatization prior to the sale of a firm has always been easy to understand: privatization is likely to generate concentrated losses (uncompetitive workers lose income and jobs), uncertain gains, and new hardships for winners (longer hours, job insecurity, and greater job pressures for retained workers). But intense dislike of privatization after the sale, as seen in parts of Argentina, Bolivia, Ecuador, Mexico, and Peru, is more mysterious because, as recent studies have shown, privatization has not been that nefarious: privatization (in infrastructure) may not have generated as much growth and investment or as low prices as expected, but it does not generate poverty or maldistribution of income, and in many cases it has significantly expanded access.[21] What might explain this discontent in Latin America?

The answer may have to do with the fact that discontent with privatization after the sale is indicative of discontent with politics more than with economics.[22] When privatizations are carried out in a transparent fashion, they still generate suspicion of collusion and state favoritism. When they are carried out in a less than transparent fashion, the suspicions explode, which is arguably what occurred in many Latin American countries.[23] Both Corrales and Schamis show that many of these irregularities, or what I call "rents as baits," were offered to entice initially reluctant buyers.[24] Murillo shows that, consequently, privatization laws related to telecommunication companies (more than to electricity) created legal monopolies in order to increase the value of assets, promote investment, and smooth the end of cross-subsidies, which led to reform unpopularity.[25] That is why Lora and Panizza find that discontent with privatization is correlated not so much with the degree of reforms in a given country as with the degree to which the people perceive their country to be corrupt or the degree to which monopolies were created.[26] Thus, the dislike of privatization after the sale seems to reflect a dislike of political institutions more than a dislike of markets in general.

Examining Urban Labor Markets

Critics of market reforms point out that the strongest evidence of "devastation" can be seen not by looking at macro numbers such as those for growth, inflation, or unemployment but by more microscopically examining labor markets, which, after all, are one of the factors that determine the type and quality of jobs, and thus poverty levels. A lot of research by sociologists and economists has been devoted to examining the response of labor markets to the economic reforms of the 1990s. There is agreement that the more far-reaching reformers have been able to generate winning sectors (competitive firms) and winning workers (high-skilled employees). But these researchers focus on the plight of the losers, which are found even in the best-performing economies. These researchers contend that the size of the losing sectors is large and that they are neglected.

These studies paint a clear picture of how market reform (more than labor market reform, which did not advance considerably) negatively affected labor markets. First, wages did not grow sufficiently, even during good times, perhaps because the race to stay competitive forced firms to keep wages down, or, more important, labor productivity increased at a snail's pace.[27] Second, private employment creation was insufficient, while public employment declined, leading to persistent or growing unemployment.[28] Third, wages and employment benefits for some workers in some privatized firms declined, while prices of some privatized services increased. Furthermore, the decline of trade unions' power in manufacturing sectors, the availability of cheap imports, and the rise of temporary contracts led to the expansion of informal or unstable jobs (to the detriment of more formal jobs), where working conditions were more precarious and unstable.[29] The result was a fragmentation of the labor market along these lines:

1. Skilled workers gravitated toward high-productivity sectors and liberalized sectors.[30] These workers are the real winners of market reform.

2. Women and less skilled workers gravitated toward the informal sector.[31] These workers are partial losers: they find incomes but also encounter precarious labor conditions.

3. Many young males and less skilled workers were unable to find (well-remunerated) jobs in either sector. They are the major losers of reforms.

4. Criminal activity (and drugs) became the magnet for these young males; urban gangs became their "employer/family/support-system" of last resort.[32]

5. Crime expanded in many urban areas, generating a demand for private security; older adult males found employment in the security labor market as private security guards, but most faced scarce job opportunities.[33]

Critics of market reform argue that these massive disruptions within labor markets—unemployment, underemployment, informality, criminalization, declining state support (e.g., unemployment insurance was rare and insufficient), and, more important, brutal shifts in workers' labor positions and expectations—had a powerful impact on politics. They led low-income groups to feel an intense discontent with the status quo.

Sometimes these arguments seem suspect because they tend to minimize the extent to which the pre-reform period (i.e., the 1930s through the 1980s) was plagued by inequality, marginality, plain hardship, and profound political protest.[34] In the 1960s, it was already clear that the formal economy was generating insufficient labor demand, which suggests that there must have been pervasive underemployment and unemployment and that workers in the formal economy, especially manufacturing, were earning good wages.[35] Together with the urban-biased social programs in place in the region, which excluded rural and informal workers from most welfare benefits, import substitution industrialization led to a dichotomous situation across urban sectors: formal, urban sector workers were doing well, the rest far worse, at least in some countries.[36] For that reason, Almeida and Johnston suggest that not just the austerity policies of the 1990s, but also the existence of a new "globally informed way of interpreting" hardship, together with new political opportunities, explain these presumably anti-austerity protests of the period.[37]

Nevertheless, it is hard to dispute that market reforms have led to disruptions in Latin America's labor market. The debate is about whether these effects are really the result of market reforms themselves or are instead unrelated factors (e.g., the aftershocks of the collapse of the 1980s, demographic forces, low levels of labor productivity, exogenous economic shocks, insufficient flexibility of formal labor markets, or failure to revamp public education systems and social services).

Furthermore, it is unclear whether this devastation, even if fully accurate, is the most important driver of anti-market movements in the region in the late 2000s. The argument by many market critics is predicated on the idea that the losers of market reforms are the main engines of these anti-market forces. However, there is a rival theory: that some of the most important drivers of anti-market backlash are not the losers themselves but rather the winners.

The Winners' Protest: Issue-Shifting, Frustrated Achievers, and Newcomers

Scholars have produced at least three theoretical statements about how political discontent might be stemming, at least in part, from economic and political winners of the 1990s rather than from losers. The first is Remmer's, resulting from work on determinants of the vote for incumbents.[38]

At the most basic level, Remmer's main point is that the Latin American electorate rewards incumbents who address key macroeconomic issues and punish incumbents who do not. But a more sophisticated version of her argument is what could be described as issue shifting. Latin American voters value macroeconomic variables when evaluating incumbents, but once those concerns are addressed, voters shift in issue preference; they begin to evaluate incumbents on other, newer issues. Some of these newer issues have to do with economic policy (e.g., addressing deficiencies in human capital), others with institutional reform (e.g., combating corruption or policy efficiency). In the late 1990s, this long list of poststabilization issues came to be known as "second-generation reforms."[39] The key point is that success with the first set of issues does not automatically mean success with the subsequent ones. Voters initially reward incumbents for delivering sustainable growth, but then they want other things. In Brazil, for instance, after stabilization voters began to prioritize inequality and transparency; in Argentina, they became concerned with corruption and inattention to unemployment; in Peru, they became less tolerant of autocratic-militaristic practice as the salience of key political issues requiring such an approach—the fight against the Sendero Luminoso (Shining Path) insurgency and an obstructionist Congress—declined.[40] The rise of the left in the 2000s could very well be seen as an anti-incumbent trend resulting from what Weyland, discussing the Fujimori case, calls "the paradox of success": after success was achieved in the first round of reforms, voters moved in issue preference, but the incumbent did not move in issue deliverance.[41]

The second argument about the possibility that winners fuel the anti-market backlash involves what Graham and Pettinato call "frustrated achievers."[42] In studying support for market reforms in the region, these authors find that "upwardly mobile" citizens are more critical in their self-assessments than less mobile people. The reason is that these "winners" compare themselves to the wealthy rather than to their cohorts. One could also posit that these winners are the ones who worry more about "postmaterialist" issues such as probity, institutional checks and balances, promoting a pro-women's agenda, and so on. Graham and Pettinato's research thus suggests that the rise of anti-incumbent, leftist movements in the late 1990s might have been fueled not entirely by the economically disadvantaged sectors but by economic winners dissatisfied with their gains or, as Shirley would add, those who believe that the bigger winners owe their gains to cheating, corruption, and foul play.[43] This explains why some of the strongest anti-incumbent, pro-left votes in Argentina (1999), in Brazil (2002), and in Peru (2000–2001) occurred in relatively wealthy, urban neighborhoods, exactly where these "frustrated achievers" are concentrated.

The third argument has to do with the decline in barriers to entry to new political organizations in the 1990s. Students of contentious politics have long argued that the rise of protest movements is contingent on two variables: gripe and opportunity. Gripe refers to the existence of complaints about the status quo; opportunity refers to the degree to which the political system becomes more amenable to collective action by protesters. A key trend in many Latin American countries was precisely the expansion of political opportunities for the traditional leftist parties, as Cleary says, *and* for new forces mobilizing unorganized groups, as Weyland says.[44] Four factors explain the rise in mobilizing opportunities in Latin America in the 1990s. The first is decentralization.[45] In numerous countries, new rules were created to give voters more direct opportunities to vote for, and monitor the performance of, local state officials.[46] A second factor was declining clientelistic mechanisms of control, which opened opportunities for citizens to reorganize from below and present new citizenship claims.[47] Third, there were greater mechanisms for the accountability of national-level politicians: electoral reforms that allowed for more direct election of legislators; the creation of *defensores del pueblo* (ombudsmen) and truth commissions; and the establishment of more independent courts. In Bolivia, these institutional changes made possible the act of "denouncing legal wrongdoing" and thus provided opportunities for "new social forces" to challenge the status quo.[48] The fourth trend, related to the first two, was the collapse of traditional parties and, in some cases, the complete party system. The causes of party collapse varied from case to case, but the effects seem similar everywhere: like decentralization, party collapse creates opportunities for new actors to mobilize old and existing voters and capture the political space. Van Cott invokes precisely these variables to explain the rise of indigenous movements in the 1990s; Corrales invokes them to explain the rise of "newcomers," that is, candidates who run for president without prior electoral or administrative experience.[49] Insofar as the rise of the left is the product of expanding mobilizing opportunities, it is a mistake to think that this trend is fueled strictly by reform losers.

In short, the 1990s produced new *economic winners* who turned anti–status quo, or at least anti-incumbent (due to issue shifting and rising reference points) and *political winners* who were able to challenge the status quo (due to new opportunities). The opening of these opportunities might explain why political protest in Latin America after market reforms has been less acrimonious than was the case prior to the reforms.[50] The left that rose to power in the late 1990s was composed not just of marginalized sectors, as much of the literature romantically or disparagingly suggests, but also of winners.

Varieties of Discontent

In the previous section I attempted to show that neoliberalism produced a variety of outcomes within countries, and consequently a diversity of assessments of market reforms. Rather than thinking that reforms produced a uniform sentiment, it is better to think of a variety of responses to or complaints about the reforms. In this section I discuss prominent manifestations of this discontent.[51]

The Radicals

The radicals are Latin America's old revolutionaries. They have not changed much since the 1960s. They still harbor the same passion (angry romanticism) and reasoning (dislike of markets and existing institutions). In the 1990s, scholars believed that their numbers and passion had subsided, but this might have been a premature assessment. What might have changed are their tactics. In the 1960s, radicals were infatuated with armed guerrillas and radical priests; more recently, they have developed a penchant for street protest and electing neophytes—politicians with little political experience who promise to kick out the bad guys. Their commitment to violence has diminished, but their commitment to contentious politics (roadblocks, paralyzing strikes, disrupting public events) has not. "*¡Qué se vayan todos!*"—Let's get rid of everyone!—is their slogan, and it became a refrain during the 1999 Constitutional Assembly in Venezuela, the 2001 financial crisis in Argentina, and the 2003 street protests in Bolivia. In some countries, the radicals' most important targets have been political parties, which they blame for most ills. On this topic, the radicals find support across different sectors of society, given that the distrust of political parties is widespread in Latin America.[52]

The Protectionists

Many business owners and union leaders throughout Latin America support tariffs and protection against cheap imports from Asia or even neighboring countries. Protectionists are found in a wide array of sectors: auto parts, light manufacturing, agriculture, toy and apparel production, financial services, and the media. This camp lost a lot of ground with the reforms of the 1990s, and it seeks to regain control of trade policy. Protectionists are particularly motivated to defeat efforts to open Latin American markets even further. Their slogan is "*No al ALCA* (Área de Libre Comercio de las Américas)," or No to the FTAA (Free Trade Area of the Americas), which the United States and various Latin American governments are advocating.

The Hyper-nationalists

Latin America's unexpected alignment with the United States on trade and drug policy during the 1990s alarmed this group. Inheritors of the "Yankee go home" mentality, the hypernationalists vent their anger against President George W. Bush, the International Monetary Fund (IMF), the Drug Enforcement Administration, and immigration officials at the Department of Homeland Security. Hypernationalists pervade Latin America's university sector and parts of the media, the military, and the middle class. Mahon has found, through multivariate analysis, that the best predictor of the rise of leftist governments in the region (stronger than indicators of "economic failure") is "negative attitudes" toward the United States: where discontent against the United States or Bush is stronger, the chances that the left will rise are greater.[53]

The Commodity Nationalists

The rise in the price of commodities, especially energy, since 2003 has generated a group that could be called the commodity nationalists. These are the heirs of the old economic nationalists.[54] They feel that the state is not capturing enough of the profits from the revenues generated by land-based exports. They are interested in greater taxation, even more state control of these sectors, and perhaps less leeway for foreign interests. As the mining minister in Bolivia stated, they are looking for "partners" to develop their mineral riches but do not want "bosses" in their mining and hydrocarbon sectors.[55]

The Crusaders

The crusaders are part of loosely organized citizen-based watchdog groups such as Alianza Cívica (Civic Alliance) in Mexico. In some cases, they are the heirs of the pro–human rights civic groups that mushroomed in the 1970s; in the 1990s, they began to advocate greater transparency in government, more public participation in policy making, less corruption, and better-functioning courts. The crusaders gravitated toward the left in the 1990s but more recently have displayed weaker ideological moorings than other groups. In Peru in the 1990s, for instance, it was impossible to find a single crusader group that was not affiliated with a leftist party; now they are less party-attached. In Brazil, the Partido dos Trabalhadores (Workers' Party) became the standard-bearer of the anti-corruption vote in the 2002 elections.

The Big Spenders

The big spenders want to invest more in old-fashioned progressive policies such as delivery of social services (education and health) and in statist projects such as infrastructure and energy development. They are tired of more than two decades of budget controls. They are not inherently anti-market, but they reject the pro-cyclical fiscal policies of the past two decades, which they blame on the IMF and bond traders. Lomnitz labels this sentiment the new form of Latin American "consumerism."[56] Like anti-party radicals, protectionists, and nationalists, big spenders include strange bedfellows, from business groups seeking state contracts to teachers' unions seeking higher wages. Infrastructure spending will be a big winner. The Inter-American Development Bank (IDB) predicts that infrastructure spending will reach 6 percent of GDP in the coming years, far higher than the 1.5 percent average of the early 2000s. In Peru, for example, President Alan García is actively raising funds from private financiers, foreign governments, and multilateral organizations to build new airports and roads.

The Egalitarians

A hybrid between the revolutionaries and the big spenders, the egalitarians advocate redistributive policies to help the poor. Andrés Manuel López Obrador's slogan in the 2006 Mexican presidential elections offers a good summary of this thinking: "For the good of all, the poor first." For egalitarians, the state should prioritize investment in the poor above all else.

The Equalizers

Not to be confused with the egalitarians, the equalizers want to help the poor by equalizing *access* to the market through low-priced privatized services, lower interest rates, expanded credit opportunities for low-income groups, more and better education, more consumer protection, and overall, greater opportunities for business to make profits. The collection of finance, education, and infrastructure ministers recruited by Chile's leftist governments since 1990 is a good example of this form of thinking. These ministers have famously cooperated with each other to fight the enormous barriers that continue to exist to market and education access and still preserve fiscal prudence. Their slogan has been "Free market social economy." Rather than pushing for one at the expense of the other, equalizers seek to promote strong states and strong markets simultaneously.

The Multiculturalists

The multiculturalists want to address the ethnic apartheid that is so prevalent in parts of Latin America, especially the Andes, where long-neglected indigenous groups lack political representation and economic assets. This sentiment helped elect Alejandro Toledo in Peru in 2001, Lucio Gutiérrez in Ecuador in 2003, and Evo Morales in Bolivia 2005, all of whom campaigned on an explicit pro-indigenous platform.

The Macho Bashers

"Macho bashing" is one of the newest trends in the Latin American left. Fighting to make these macho societies a bit less macho and, more recently, a bit less homophobic, there is no question that parts of the left today are a far cry from Fidel Castro's macho "*Patria o muerte*"—Fatherland or death—style of leftism.[57] In the 1980s, groups of this movement shifted their focus toward granting women more access to state office (not just more power in the family) or showing more respect for women's rights. The movement has succeeded in getting 11 countries since 1991 to enact laws requiring political parties to nominate a minimum percentage of female candidates for the legislature and encouraging presidents to nominate more female ministers.[58] In 2005, this sentiment encouraged Chileans to elect Michelle Bachelet, the first elected female president to campaign on an explicit platform of "gender parity."

To come to power, the left in Latin America has had to draw support from people with all these varieties of discontent. No government was able to rely exclusively on one issue or one constituency. Consequently, each of the leftist movements that has come to power since the late 1990s has included—in different proportions—people with all these different forms of discontent. Because of this variety of constituents, the vision of a united leftist coalition of Latin American nations is an illusion.

Leftist Factions and Their Impact
on Democracy and Market Reforms

What impact does each of these varieties of discontent have on democracy and market reforms? On the impact of democracy, I suggest that each of these forms of discontent offers the potential for enhancing democracy but also for hurting it. For instance, radicals can push parties and representative institutions to renew themselves, but they can also push for the demise of party life, which would undermine democratic competition. Protectionists and nationalists offer the promise of asserting the nation's interest vis-à-vis globalization, but they can also undermine accountability with their proclivity for blaming international actors (more than state officials or themselves) for domestic ills. Crusaders can enhance government accountability, but they can easily be co-opted by their funders, including the state. Egalitarians can address social needs, but they can also disregard institutional procedures and fiscal health in their obsession with redistribution. Equalizers are able to promote both the big and the little guys in the national economy, but they can also be too risk-averse with regard to social programs. Multiculturalists have the opportunity of ending racial apartheid, but they can also appear too threatening to others, especially to nonmembers of their groups. The macho bashers can lessen patriarchalism in institutions, but they can also ignore merit in the name of filling quotas. In short, the left has its democratic side, because its components seek to address many items on the second-generation reform agenda, but it also has an undemocratic side. The vision of the left as uniformly democratic (or not) is also an illusion.

On the question of the impact of people with the different varieties of discontent on market reforms, it is not entirely clear that these varieties of discontent are entirely or fully adverse to such reforms. The discontent of radicals, protectionists, and, to a lesser extent, nationalists makes them the most serious opponents of market reforms. But the other types of discontent represent demands that could easily be met while simultaneously pursuing economic reforms; they are more supplementary to market forces than incompatible with them.

A crucial question, therefore, is which of these factions end up prevailing within each leftist government? The answer might have to do with each country's recent experience with the implementation of market reforms: the bumpier the recent experience, the more likely it is that anti-market, radical, nationalist, anti-party factions will prevail within a government.

Table 3.3 depicts levels of bumpiness by looking at basic economic indicators (GDP growth per capita, unemployment and poverty levels, and trends in poverty alleviation) and political crisis indictors (executive-legislative gridlock, street protests, and political party dealignment) in the few years prior

Table 3.3. Problem Policy Area at the Time of Election of Leftist Governments

Case		Average GDP per Capita, Past Three Years	Annual Unemployment Rate[a]	Poverty Rate[b]	Poverty Trend	Political Crisis[c]	Recent Party Dealignment
Full (and Smooth) Implementation of Market Reforms							
Chile	2005	4.24	7.4	2.00	—	—	—
First-Generation Reforms Implemented, with Gaps							
Argentina	1999	1.68	14.1	2.00	—	—	—
Brazil	2002	1.07	9.2	8.20	—	—	—
Chile	1990	5.35	5.7	4.90	↑	—	—
Peru	2006	3.61	10.5	12.50	—	—	—
Uruguay	2005	6.22	16.8	2.00	—	—	—
Recent Economic and Political Crises							
Argentina	2003	−3.09	15.6	7.09	↑	PR, SP	—
Bolivia	2005	1.65	5.5	23.20	↑	EL, PR, SP	Yes[d]
Ecuador	2003	2.90	11.3	15.78	—	EL, PR, SP	—
Ecuador	2006	3.56	11.4	15.78	NA	EL, PR, SP	Yes[d]
Nicaragua	2006	1.80	7.8	45.00	↑	EL	—
Peru	2001	−0.29	7.9	18.10	↑	PR	—
Venezuela	1998	0.91	10.0	19.16	↑	—	Yes

Sources: Figures from *World Development Indicators;* political crisis indicators from country chapters.
Notes: Shading indicates crisis areas. NA, data not available.
[a]Data from the latest year available prior to election.
[b]Percentage of population living on less than $1 a day; data from latest year available prior to election.
[c]EL, executive-legislative gridlock; PR, presidential resignation; SP, street protests.
[d]Most dealignment occurred with indigenous populations; see Raul L. Madrid, "Indigenous Parties and Democracy in Latin America," *Latin American Politics and Society* 47, no. 4 (2005): 161–79.

to the rise of a given leftist administration. Shaded indicators reflect areas of deep crisis, that is, situations in which performance is particularly alarming.

The table shows three different contexts in which the left has come to power. The first context is successful and smooth implementation of market reforms. In this context, the left can come to power provided that it addresses the problem of issue shifting. In Chile toward the late 1990s, postmaterialist values, especially related to gender issues, became salient across the electorate, and the Concertación, led by the Socialists, responded by offering candidates and policies accordingly and was thus reelected.

The second context is that of countries that implement first-generation reforms but with a few salient "gaps," or trouble spots, in any policy area, such as growth rates, poverty, unemployment, transparency of institutions, and so on. In this context, the left has a chance of being elected, and the prevailing factions within the new government will likely consist of individuals interested in carrying out second-generation reforms. This was the experience of Chile in 1990, Argentina in 1999, Brazil in 2002, Ecuador in 2003, and Uruguay in 2005. In such cases of mild bumps on the path to the market, the left, if elected, is likely to form cabinets with a greater presence of equalizers than of radicals. The political problem that these administrations will potentially face is that the more moderate, pro-market groups will have to share the space of, and learn to tame, the less market-oriented factions within their ranks. A struggle between the equalizers and the egalitarians, to mention one example, is likely.

If, instead of mild gaps, a country suffered from recent large-scale crises both in economics (a huge economic recession, very high levels of unemployment, rampant poverty) *and* in politics (chronic street protests, executive-legislative gridlock, recent dealignment of voters), a leftist victory is likely to produce a cabinet with a predominance of less moderate, less pro-market factions. However, even these forces will still have to contend with more moderate factions. The only two surprise cases in this classification are Peru in 2001 and Ecuador in 2003. In the case of Peru, moderates ended up prevailing in the Toledo administration (in part because the more radical left gravitated toward the alternative candidate on the left, Alan García). In Ecuador, President Gutiérrez tried to implement more pro-market policies, but most of the groups allied with him were farther to the left, provoking a serious rift that brought the government down.

The key point is that the left has come to office in different contexts, and therefore with different prevailing factions, within each administration. In some cases, the more market-friendly factions have dominated (Brazil under Lula, Chile under Aylwin, and Peru under Toledo). Other times, the least pro-market factions have prevailed (Argentina under Kirchner and, more to the left, Venezuela under Chávez). Regardless, each of these leftist administrations has faced huge internal frictions between the different factions that compose it, at least at first. In some cases, the infighting has brought governments down (Argentina in 1999–2001, Ecuador in 2003–5). In yet other cases, the left has come to office after having suffered serious schisms (e.g., in Nicaragua in 2006, the more moderate groups left the Sandinistas; in Peru in 2001 and 2006, the more radical groups defected toward the alternative leftist candidates, Alan García in 2001 and Ollanta Humala in 2006). Either way, these administrations have all faced huge internal struggles between the different factions within their ranks and even outside their ranks.

If the story of the 1980s was how the authoritarian-statist formula of the postwar period unraveled, and if the story of the 1990s was how inflation and economic isolation ended, the story of the 2000s could very well be how different forms of market discontents fight among themselves once in office. A question yet to be answered is how far each of these winning factions is able to influence policy, if at all.

Has There Been a Leftward Trend in Economics?

Thus far, I have discussed the *political* leftward trend in Latin America, examining the electoral return of leftist-statist political forces. The next question is whether there has been a comparable leftward shift in *economic* policy. Have Latin American states relaxed their commitment to pursue market reforms?

Cleary and others argue that in the 2000s the left-leaning governments have exhibited "moderation" in economic policy, never quite repeating the excesses of the populist governments before the 1980s or in other parts of the world.[59] There is no question that, compared to this historical record, the return of the left in the 2000s is better described as a tropical storm than as a tsunami.[60] Yet this assessment belies the fact that there has been noticeable variation within this moderation. In the case of Kirchner, for instance, there is evidence, discussed later, that the state has rolled back some market-oriented institutions. Other leftist governments in the region (e.g., that of Chávez in Venezuela) moved even farther to the left, whereas yet other leftist administrations moved less (e.g., that of Tabaré Vásquez), and still others have moved hardly at all (e.g., that of Toledo in Peru).

One way to examine this question is to look at the economic freedom scores in Table 3.2, which track commitment to market reforms from year to year. Several observations are possible. First, on average, most of the countries did move in the direction of greater economic freedom from 1995 to 2001: the average score for the region moved from 3.24 to 2.97. All 23 countries except 3 (Ecuador, Paraguay, and Venezuela) moved in the direction of greater freedom during this period, albeit at different speeds.

Second, since 2002, the average score for the region has remained fairly stable: the regional average score for 2006 is virtually identical to that for 2002. This suggests that, on average, the progress toward market reform of the 1990s has halted, which is evidence of some leftist policy influence, but the reversal, on average, has not been drastic, which is evidence of moderation.

Third, there was far more variation in the direction of movement in 2002–6 than in 1995–2002. Between 2002 and 2006, more than half of the countries on the list experienced reversal of market reforms, which is in stark contrast with what happened in 1995–2002, when most countries were moving in the same direction, toward greater freedom.

Finally, some of these reversals have occurred in governments that are not led by the left (e.g., in Colombia and in Uruguay prior to 2005), suggesting that factors other than partisanship or ideology are influencing this leftward shift in economic policy.

Figure 3.3 offers one way to visualize this greater variation in direction during 2002–6. This figure plots each country's economic freedom score in 2002 (ranging from 5 to 0 on the horizontal axis) against the total change in scores experienced by each country from 2002 to 2006 (ranging from –0.8 to +0.08 along the vertical axis). The figure shows that there is widespread variation along both axes. The first few sections of this chapter addressed the issue of variation along the horizontal axis. I now turn to variation along the vertical axis: changes in commitment to market reforms since 2002.

It is too early to offer definitive conclusions about the sources of an economic leftward shift; after all, maybe not enough time has passed to allow us to assess the causes of a trend, or even whether a trend exists. However, we can offer some possible hypotheses, drawn from various works cited in this and other chapters of this volume. The first set of hypotheses has to do with economic factors, which explain the incentives that states face to deepen (or relax) market reforms. The second set of hypotheses has to do with political factors, which explain the capacity of partisan factions to carry out policy.

Economic Factors: External Shocks and Domestic Economic Institutions

Part of the explanation for the slowdown of market reforms in the 2000s (why so many countries are near zero or in the negative range along the vertical axis of Figure 3.3) may have to do with two external economic shocks that have hit the region since 1999. One was negative, the other positive. The negative shock was the regional recession of 1999–2002 (see Figure 3.1), which in some countries was profound. This economic contraction diminished enthusiasm on the part of the public and politicians for market reforms and increased the number of economic losers in countries where it hit hardest.[61]

A second factor was the boom in the world economy (2003, 2004, and 2005 were the best years in the world economy since the early 1970s) and in the prices of export commodities that matter to the region—oil, gas, iron, copper, zinc, wheat, and cement. These booms have had a mixed effect on the state's commitment to market reforms.[62] On the one hand, by boosting export revenues, capital flows, and economic activity in general, these external booms have allowed countries to maintain fiscal discipline. On the other hand, by reducing fiscal pressures and encouraging capital inflows, the

Figure 3.3. Economic Freedom Scores in 2002 and Change 2002–2006

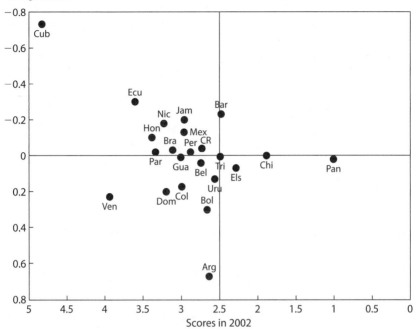

Change 2002–6

Source: Heritage Foundation, *Index of Economic Freedom,* 2002–6.
Notes: Arg, Argentina; Bar, Barbados; Bel, Belize; Bol, Bolivia; Bra, Brazil; Chi, Chile; Col, Colombia; CR, Costa Rica; Cub, Cuba; Dom, Dominican Republic; Ecu, Ecuador; Els, El Salvador; Gua, Guatemala; Hon, Honduras; Jam, Jamaica; Mex, Mexico; Nic, Nicaragua; Pan, Panama; Par, Paraguay; Per, Peru; Tri, Trinidad and Tobago; Uru, Uruguay; Ven, Venezuela.

booms have diminished the incentives—so strong in the 1990s, when external conditions were less favorable—to create more business-friendly domestic policies and thus to embrace the costs of pushing forward for greater market-oriented reforms. The result has been that, except for Venezuela, countries have been able to maintain healthy primary fiscal surpluses while still expanding spending and slowing the pace of market reform.[63] This change in the external environment is one reason that in the 1990s the Cardoso administration in Brazil, in the words of Hunter and Power, was a "government of *reforms* whereas Lula's has been a government of *programs,* a qualitative difference."[64] It is one more reason that Mahon finds a strong correlation between current-account balances and the incidence of leftist governments.[65]

However, as Figure 3.3 reveals, not all countries have responded to these two external influences similarly. Some countries have accelerated their commitment to market reforms, some have stood still, and others have reversed their economic freedom scores since 2002. Part of the explanation for this variation has more to do with domestic (than with external) economic conditions.

Figure 3.3 also shows that countries that advanced the furthest in consolidating economic reforms domestically in the 1990s (Barbados, Chile, El Salvador, Panama, and Trinidad and Tobago) have been less susceptible to deviation in the 2000s (i.e., they responded to the external shocks by either sustaining or deepening their commitment to economic freedom). This suggests that that there may be a certain threshold of economic freedom after which the reforms become deeply consolidated, maybe even widely supported by the political system, and thus resilient to external shock. On the other side of this threshold (apparently, the 2.5 score on the *Index of Economic Freedom*), the commitment is less secure. In these cases, market reforms are perhaps not yet consolidated; consequently, modest change in either direction is possible.

Political Factors: Party System Institutionalization

To explain policy variation among the cases that have not crossed this threshold, it may be necessary to invoke other variables. Schamis and the IDB, drawing from Mainwaring and Scully's seminal work, have emphasized a crucial point: party system institutionalization, defined as the creation of systems in which parties are stable and valued by citizens, have roots in society and ties with civil organizations, and enjoy organizational independence from strong leaders.[66] Where both the ruling party *and* the opposition parties are institutionalized, the chances of policy moderation and accommodation improve, as do the chances of policy implementation success. Where party politics are disjointed, on the other hand, the chance for parliamentary negotiation is weak and political disputes move to the streets. In this context, the executive branch either succumbs to policy chaos or, alternatively, concentrates too much power in an effort to survive in office, transforming regimes into "super presidencies." At this point, policy moderation declines along with respect for democratic institutions.

An institutionalized ruling party yields moderation because in such parties, mechanisms are in place for different internal factions to work out disagreements. An institutionalized opposition yields moderation because it has greater bargaining leverage vis-à-vis the government to effectively block efforts by the ruling party to deviate too radically from policies preferred by the opposition and can force the executive to try to work with the existing legislative channels.

Table 3.4 shows how prominent cases of the left in office fare in terms of this asymmetry in party institutionalization. The first category consists of countries in which both the ruling and the opposition parties are compara-

Table 3.4. Leftist Administrations, Party System Institutionalization, and Policy Outcomes

| Case | | Degree of Party Institutionalization/Cohesiveness | | Outcome |
		Ruling Party	Opposition	
Argentina	1999	Low	High	Government collapse
Argentina	2003	Medium	Low	Less moderation / concentration of power
Bolivia	2005	Increasing?	Declining?	Less moderation / attempt to change the constitution
Brazil	2002	High	Medium	Moderate changes / acceptance of existing institutional channels
Chile	1990 –present	High	High	Moderate changes / acceptance of existing institutional channels
Ecuador	2003	Low	Medium	Government collapse
Peru	2001	Low	Low	Moderate changes / stable politics and economics
Uruguay	2004	High	High	Moderate changes / acceptance of existing institutional channels
Venezuela	1999	Low	Medium	Serious defections from ruling party / political instability
Venezuela	2004	Medium	Low	Less moderation / concentration of power

bly institutionalized: Brazil in 2002, Chile since the 1990s, and Uruguay in 2004. The result in these cases, as predicted, is moderate policy deviation. The executive adheres to existing legislative mechanisms to achieve policy change.

The second category consists of countries in which the ruling party lacks institutionalization or cohesiveness relative to the opposition: Argentina in 1999, Ecuador in 2002, and Peru 2001. In both Argentina and Ecuador, the ruling coalitions succumbed to internal disarray. In Argentina, because the opposition was institutionalized, it was able to regain command of the country after the collapse; in Ecuador, where the opposition was less institutionalized and more fragmented, no powerful force was able to take control, and the country remained unstable. Again, Peru represents a somewhat anomalous case: despite a low level of institutionalization, the ruling party remained moderate and respectful of the rule of law and even survived until the end of its term, despite low approval ratings.

The third category consists of countries in which the party systems are in flux and asymmetrical: Argentina in 2003, Bolivia in 2005, and Venezuela in

1998. In these cases, if the ruling party manages to achieve greater institutionalization while the opposition continues to deinstitutionalize, the likely result will be greater concentration of power in the hands of the executive, and thus a greater possibility of radical policy deviation. In Argentina, Néstor Kirchner has been able to reorganize the ruling party, while the opposition's organizational and fund-raising capacity has continued to decline. Consequently, he has been able to engage in greater policy deviation. In Venezuela, this trend is even more advanced. In Bolivia, the same trend in party system institutionalization was visible in Morales's first year in office, but it is still too early to tell.

In short, asymmetries in party institutionalization matter. These are not the only factors that matter, but they are not insignificant, either. When both the ruling and the opposition parties are comparably institutionalized, policy change will be moderate and likely to be negotiated through normal legislative channels. When the ruling party is more institutionalized relative to the opposition, policy may shift more drastically in the direction of the particular partisan faction in office. When the opposition is more institutionalized than the ruling party, instability is likely.

The Left and Populism

The return of the left has also reopened an old conceptual debate in comparative politics about the difference between the left and populism. Scholars recognize that populism and left-wing ideologies share an affinity for using state resources to favor nonelite groups but also recognize that sections of the left, historically and currently, are repelled by populism.[67] How, then, should one think about the difference between the left and populism? The political variables discussed thus far—different ideological factions and asymmetries in party institutionalization—can help elucidate the differences (and overlap) between them. But first, a brief discussion of the concept of populism is necessary.

In the late 1980s, scholars tended to think of populism as a set of economic policies—mostly fiscal profligacy and protectionism—in the service of a particular political project, namely, the concentration of political power in the hands of the executive, the undermining of intermediate institutions of representation, and the construction of a multiclass, majoritarian coalition that mobilizes previously excluded groups.[68] But with the rise in the 1990s of presidents who pursued neoliberal economic policies in the service of similar political goals, scholars began to drop the economic aspect of the definition and think of populism strictly in political terms.[69] Thus, Weyland argues that populism ought to be defined as "a political strategy" in which a leader seeks concentrated power based on "direct, unmediated, uninstitutionalized" support from "unorganized" followers; others would stress lack of respect, or *ventajismo,* in relation to organized opposition groups.[70] In addition, Mudde emphasizes not just the notion that populism divides the world between organized and nonorganized groups that matter, but rather the notion that it sees the two sides as "antagonistic groups," with one camp seen as "the pure people" clashing with the other camp, seen as the "the corrupt elite."[71] Precisely because it views the other side as objectionable and adversarial, populism has a difficult time extending democratic rights to the other side. It is the mirror image of elitism and the antithesis of pluralism.

Defining populism based on its political features (state-society relations) rather than economic features has been a conceptual step forward because it has made it possible to accommodate populists who pursue both leftist and right-wing economic policies (e.g., Alan García in Peru in the 1980s versus Alberto Fujimori in the 1990s).

I propose that the difference between populism and the left has to do with the degree to which different factions of the left, in their efforts to achieve their own policy objectives, condone this form of state-society political relation (concentrating power in the executive and disfavoring organized opposition). In Latin America, leftist governments have exhibited different degrees of preference for this form of state-society relations: at one extreme, in the 1960s Fidel Castro in Cuba espoused complete power concentration and a disregard of organized opposition; at the other extreme, in the 1990s the Concertación in Chile exhibited a complete rejection of the model; meanwhile, in the 1980s Alan García in Peru embraced a less extreme version of it.

Drawing from the previous discussion of varieties of discontent and party institutionalization, I can now situate contemporary leftist administrations along this populist spectrum, defined in political terms. When the left comes to power by mobilizing mostly unorganized groups in which more radical varieties of discontent (those of radicals, protectionists, and nationalists) prevail and where the party system is asymmetrically institutionalized, conditions are favorable for a leftist-populist project to emerge. In contrast, when the left mobilizes predominantly more traditional voters led by factions that embrace less extreme views about the need to change institutions, and when both the ruling party and the opposition parties are similarly institutionalized, checks will be placed on any populist tendencies. In these cases of symmetrical party institutionalization, both the ruling party and the opposition prevent the president from concentrating power and mistreating organized groups.

In Figure 3.4 I have tried to capture these relationships. The upper rectangle presents the factors that determine variations in state-society relations (populism versus pluralism). Mobilized factions and party institutionalization play the key roles here. The lower rectangle adds the economic orientation of the leading faction within each government.

Figure 3.4. The Left and Populism

	Politics: Party institutionalization and mobilized groups		
	Asymmetrical party institutionalization (pro-incumbent), and unorganized groups:		Symmetrical party institutionalization plus postmaterialist groups
	Ruling party is young	Ruling party is traditional and large	
Political: Outcome in power concentration	Excessive	Significant	Respect for institutions of accountability

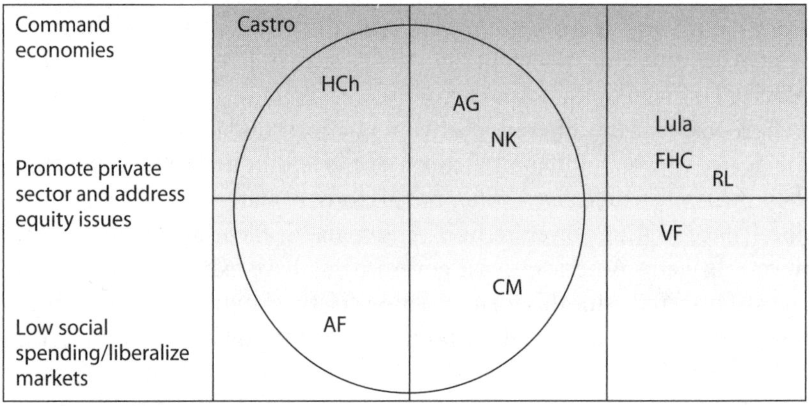

Notes: The shading indicates areas that the left can occupy. The oval indicates the area that populism can occupy. Cases: AF, Alberto Fujimori (Peru, 1992); AG, Alan García (Peru, 1988); Castro, Fidel Castro (Cuba, 1960s); CM, Carlos Menem (Argentina, 1992); FHC, Fernando Cardoso (Brazil, 2001); HCh, Hugo Chávez (Venezuela, 2006); Lula, Luiz Inácio Lula da Silva (Brazil, 2005); NK, Néstor Kirchner (Argentina, 2006); RL, Ricardo Lagos (Chile, 2005); VF, Vicente Fox (Mexico, 2005).

Economic orientation can range from extreme statism (command economies) to extreme neoliberalism (concern with liberalizing markets without regard for equity issues). Somewhere in the middle is an orientation that tries to promote both markets and human capital concerns (second-generation reforms, if you will). Leftist factions occupy different positions between this middle position and a command economy.

Combining both rectangles illustrates the areas of overlap and separation between populism (as a model of state-society relations) and the left (as both an economic and a political project). Essentially, the left can occupy any space in the shaded gray area: different degrees of statism in economic policies and different degrees of support for populist or pluralist political projects. Populism, on the other hand, can occupy only the area marked by the oval: all populist leaders are on the same side of the state-society relations model (i.e., strong leaders and disrespect for organized opposition groups and for institutions that hold the executive branch accountable), albeit in different degrees. However, they can exhibit any number of economic policies, ranging from high levels of statism to extreme neoliberalism.

Different cases of populist versus liberal and left-wing versus right-wing governments from the past 20 years can now be placed in the different areas of Figure 3.4. In the family of left-wing populists, the most extreme contemporary case is that of Hugo Chávez in Venezuela: economically and politically, Chávez has reversed economic and political freedoms the most, but never as much as Castro. The Chávez case meets the causal conditions depicted in Figure 3.4: Chávez came to power with the support of many unorganized groups, with radical varieties of discontent prevailing, and in the context of party deinstitutionalization. Néstor Kirchner is a less extreme version, although still within the family of left-wing populism. He was supported by unorganized groups with various forms of market discontent, although they were less radical leftists than the groups under Chávez. He also came to power under conditions of party institutionalization similar to those that elevated García in the 1980s, that is, with a ruling party that was more institutionalized than the opposition. Because the opposition was weak, Kirchner enjoyed enormous political leeway. But because his party was more institutionalized than the ruling party (less controlled by the leader), it prevented the president from concentrating as much power as is the case under Chávez, whose ruling party is mostly a self-serving machine of followers.

Likewise, within the family of right-wing populists (prevalent in the 1990s), there was variation in the degrees of party institutionalization: Fujimori had a more personalistic party, if one could even call it a party. Consequently, Fujimori was able to pursue a more extreme form of right-wing populist project.[72]

Figure 3.4 also shows the degree to which the democratic left and the democratic right have converged in contemporary Latin American politics. These groups reject the populist political project entirely (they respect institutions and organized groups) far more than do groups on the left side of the figure. They all emerge in contexts of more symmetrical party institutionalization. This type of context makes it difficult for populist political tendencies to emerge and prevail. In addition, these political forces also mobilize groups that embrace more moderate, more postmaterialist varieties of discontent. They are dominated by ideological factions that share a consensus on larger policy questions: agreement on the need to foster *both* human capital and private sector development.

The democratic left and the democratic right are therefore in agreement about the overall contours of economic policy (market liberalization, fiscal prudence, and social spending), but they differ on what some might call the minutiae of policy: the appropriate tax rate, the parameters of the tax base, the degree of labor market flexibility, the extent of labor and environmental regulations in free trade agreements, the degree to which competition and choice are introduced in the delivery of social services, the degree to which marital affairs and sexuality ought to be deregulated, and so on. The differences between the groups appear too small only to those observers who are situated close to the extreme ideological positions—extreme statists or neoliberals. For everyone else in the middle, these differences are the stuff of tough political competition.

Conclusion

In this chapter I have sought to address two main questions. First, what explains the electoral rise (or return) of leftist-statist parties in Latin America? I have argued that the economic experience of the 1990s offered a variety of outcomes and thus a variety of assessments, even a variety of forms of discontent, across the region. Leftist politicians were able to challenge incumbents by drawing from this wide variety of forms of discontent. The result was the rise of strong electoral coalitions, especially where barriers to entry for new political forces were lowered. However, these leftist forces had to compete with stronger pro-market forces on the one hand, and also had to cope with a set of constituents within their ranks who disagreed widely on which institutions to change, how much to change them, and which means are appropriate to bring about change. Internal disarray more than coherent policy implementation tended to characterize most leftist governments, at least in their first years in office.

The second question is what explains the degree of deviation from the path toward market reform that has been prevalent in the region since the late 1980s? This deviation has been moderate relative to previous episodes of statism in the region, but there has nonetheless been less policy continuity than some have argued: in most countries, progress toward market reforms has slowed considerably; in others, it has even reversed.

Two external conditions seem to have lessened the region's commitment to deeper reforms: the externally induced recession of 1999–2002 and the post-2003 boom in the world economy and export commodity prices. However, the decelerating impact of these shocks has been mitigated by domestic politics and institutions: countries that had achieved greater degrees of economic freedom have been less susceptible to policy volatility. In the rest of the cases, party system variables (asymmetries in the degrees of institutionalization between the ruling party and the opposition), together with the prevailing orientation of the dominant faction within each leftist coalition, explain the deviation from previous policy choices.

Contrary to what was initially believed in the mid-1990s, the region does not seem to be moving entirely toward greater convergence in the acceptance of the market and democracy. Some cases, mostly those in which party systems are institutionalized, exhibit convergence. In the rest, democracy and the market remain highly contested ideas. Where the radical anti-market forces have gone the furthest (Venezuela), they have also faced enormous political resistance. The Chávez government has produced the highest degree of market reversal and also the largest degree of political polarization in Latin American since the Sandinistas were in office in Nicaragua in the 1980s. One lesson that the left can draw from the Chávez administration is that attempting to reverse market institutions as far as Chávez has can end up destabilizing a country.

By the same token, where the more moderate left has taken control of policy, the story is not so rosy, either. In Peru, Toledo was able to preserve and pursue market reforms, but his popularity ratings were dismal. In Ecuador, the Gutiérrez government suffered a premature collapse because more leftist factions abandoned him. And Néstor Kirchner decided to pursue some market-friendly policies (e.g., competitive exchange rates and fiscal prudence), but he preferred to keep them a secret and instead flaunt his anti-market policies (an anti-IMF/Bush discourse, a hard line against privatized utilities, and overtures to Chávez).

These experiences reveal that the concepts of market economics and adherence to democratic norms remain enormously contentious issues, or at least are lower priorities in countries where the minimum features of modern state governance are lacking.

Countries like Chile, which have been able to find ways to make state and rule-of-law forces work in harmony with (rather than in opposition to) market and competitive forces seem to enter into a virtuous cycle of political stability and economic prosperity. In the other countries, this virtuous cycle seems more elusive.

4

Political Inclusion and
Social Inequality

Women, Afro-descendants,

and Indigenous Peoples

Mala Htun

Latin America is racially and ethnically diverse. Its population is divided equally between men and women. Looking at its leadership ranks, however, one would hardly be aware of these facts. Since the conquest, light-skinned Spanish- or Portuguese-speaking men have dominated political life. Even as suffrage broadened to include women and indigenous peoples, their numbers in elected office—as well as those of Afro-descendants—remained pitifully small. History books and the walls of government offices feature portraits that scarcely resemble average citizens.

By the last decade of the twentieth century and the first decade of the twenty-first, this situation had changed (somewhat). Chile had a female president, both houses of Congress in Argentina were more than 30 percent female, and women had served as mayors of the region's two most populous cities—São Paulo and Mexico City. Bolivia had an indigenous president, and an indigenous-led party held a majority in Congress; Ecuadorian Indians had occupied a plurality of cabinet posts; and indigenous-led parties had won national congressional races in Colombia, Peru, and Venezuela. Brazil had introduced quotas for blacks in university admissions and public sector hiring (the numbers of blacks elected to office are still very low), and Colombia had reserved legislative seats for rural black communities and indigenous peoples. Though their presence in power lags their proportion of the population, the political representation of historically excluded groups—namely women, blacks, and indigenous peoples—is increasing.

How did these various groups gain access to power? Will their greater in-clusion improve democracy, reduce inequality, and give the region a chance for social justice? Since the early 1990s, Latin American governments have made dramatic moves to guarantee access to power for historically excluded groups. Eleven states in the region adopted national laws establishing a min-imum percentage of participation for women as political party candidates in national elections, and a twelfth, Colombia, introduced quotas for positions in the executive branch (Table 4.1). (Venezuela has since revoked its law.) Two countries, Colombia and Venezuela, offered reserved seats in Congress to in-digenous peoples and rural black communities (Table 4.1). Latin American countries have thus taken a leading role in global trends. At the turn of the century, dozens of countries have made moves to incorporate diverse sectors of the citizenry into leadership. Altogether, over 50 countries have allocated access to political power along the lines of gender, ethnicity, or both.[1]

Compared to traditional ways of promoting equality, such as promoting access to education, land reform, infrastructure, protection of informal sec-tor workers, and so on, political inclusion is relatively cheap. It does not re-quire raising taxes, constructing roads and buildings, throwing people off their land, or angering teachers' unions. At the same time, bringing women, blacks, and/or Indians into power is highly visible. By doing so, governments can claim to voters and the outside world that they are actually doing some-thing to combat inequality. Members of oppressed groups seek greater access to power, and governments (as well as international organizations) believe they can demonstrate their commitment to equality and inclusiveness by providing such access.

The crucial questions are these: What, if anything, have guarantees of po-litical inclusion done for the problem of inequality? Are new interests and perspectives being included in decision making? Do beneficiaries of quotas and reserved seats act to improve the well-being of nonelite group members? Does their political inclusion lead to changes in policy and practice? If not, why should we care about diversity among elected officials at all?

When applied correctly, quotas and reserved seats diversify the ranks of elected officials by enabling the participation of women and/or subordinate ethnic and racial groups.[2] This inclusion is important: the presence in power of some members of a group confers status and dignity on all its members. Political presence changes the social meanings attached to certain ascriptive characteristics (gender, skin color, ethnic origin), particularly those that have been stigmatized or devalued in the past.[3] Descriptive representation, how-ever, is neither necessary nor sufficient for the promotion of interests. Policy advocacy and policy change on behalf of women and other excluded groups can occur without guarantees of representation and when few group mem-bers are in power. What is more, even when a group holds a majority, it may

Table 4.1. Policies regarding Group Representation in Latin America

Country	Date of Law	Minimum Percentage of Participation by Women as Party Candidates (top) and Number of Seats Reserved for Ethnic and Racial Minorities (bottom) in National Elections
By Gender[a]		
Argentina	1991	30% of candidates for Chamber, Senate, and 22 of 24 provincial legislative elections
Bolivia	1997	30% of candidates for Chamber and 25% for Senate elections
Brazil	1997	30% of candidates for Chamber, state legislature, and municipal council elections
Colombia	2000	30% of appointed executive posts
Costa Rica	1997	40% of candidates for unicameral Parliament and municipal councils
Dominican Republic	1997	33% of candidates for lower house
Ecuador	1997	35% of candidates for unicameral Parliament
Mexico	1996	30% of candidates for Chamber and Senate elections (numerous states also have quotas)
Panama	1997	30% of candidates in primary elections
Paraguay	1996	20% of candidates in primary elections for Chamber and Senate
Peru	1997	30% of candidates for unicameral Parliament and municipal councils
By Race or Ethnicity[b]		
Colombia	1991	2 Senate seats reserved for indigenous peoples, 2 House seats for "black communities," 1 house seat for indigenous peoples
Venezuela	1999	3 congressional seats reserved for indigenous peoples

[a]Honduras also has a gender quota law, but it is not enforceable.
[b]Peru has a candidate quota law governing regional elections in the Amazon (but not national elections): 15 percent of those competing in such elections must be indigenous.

be unable to produce all the changes it wants. Policy change comes about in various ways, not all of which are related to descriptive representation.

This chapter fleshes out these arguments by studying three recent cases of political inclusion: the adoption of quota laws regarding women candidates in 10 countries, Colombia's use of reserved seats for indigenous peoples and rural black communities, and the success of indigenous-led parties in Bolivia. The case studies show how various groups have struggled against odds to gain power: in the first two instances, by fighting for guarantees of representation, and in the third, by winning office without quotas or reservations. They also show that being in power does not guarantee policy change. Inclusion, however, is a worthy goal for its own sake.

Inclusion: Presence and Outcomes

Political inclusion is not political representation. To understand the difference between inclusion and representation, it is helpful to return to the different dimensions of representation described by Hannah Pitkin in her classic study *The Concept of Representation*.[4] On the one hand, we can think of representation as "standing for." Legislators represent their constituents descriptively when they resemble them physically, share their experiences, and serve as symbols evoking certain emotions or attitudes. This descriptive dimension of representation corresponds to what I mean by political inclusion. What counts is presence. Quotas and reservations are one way to bring it about.

On the other hand, we can think of representation as "acting for." Legislators represent by acting on behalf of the voters who put them in office. They promote interests. They introduce bills, make speeches, join coalitions, ask questions, demand funding, criticize, cajole, and cooperate. Through elections, voters authorize representatives to act on their behalf and then hold them accountable for good or bad behavior. This substantive activity of representing may be, but is not necessarily, linked to descriptive representation and therefore is possibly, but not necessarily, connected to quotas and reservations.

Many works on representation portray these potential or probabilistic relationships as causal certainties. Scholars of gender and politics, for example, argue that having more women in power leads to the introduction of more feminist bills and amendments and changes the tone of legislative deliberations.[5] Iris Marion Young claims that the inclusion of excluded groups ensures that all relevant perspectives are present in decision making and that policy outcomes will be more just.[6] Jane Mansbridge declares that the descriptive representation of women improves their substantive representation in every polity for which we have a measure.

These arguments may hold in certain cases. However, we need to *show* that they are true rather than simply *assuming* that they are. To facilitate such analysis, it will be helpful to distinguish the two dimensions of representation and to disaggregate each dimension:

1. *Descriptive representation of excluded groups,* also known as political inclusion or the presence of bodies. This can be achieved through (a) regular elections or (b) guarantees such as candidate quotas or legislative reservations.

2. *Substantive activity of representing,* ideally leading to policy outcomes on behalf of excluded groups. This activity can be performed by (a) group members, including those who gain power thanks to quotas or

reservations and those who gain power through regular elections, or (b) non–group members, such as politicians from a political party committed to gender and ethnic equality.

Figure 4.1 depicts the two dimensions of representation (1 and 2) and the component variables of each dimension (1a and 1b, 2a and 2b). The solid line connecting 1a and 2a represents the causal relationship claimed by advocates of quotas and reservations and by much of the literature on gender politics and minority politics: excluded groups, once in power thanks to quotas or reservations, will act on behalf of the interests of the rest of the group.

The relationship represented by the solid line is not the only potential relationship among the components of representation, however. At least two other relationships are theoretically possible, represented by the dashed lines: (1) members of a group gain power through regular elections and go on to promote the interests of the group, or (2) members of a group gain power through regular elections and go on to do little on behalf of the group, but the rest of the legislature begins to promote the interests of that group. It is also possible that there is no relationship between the variables. Descriptive representation could be completely unrelated to substantive activity of representing on behalf of excluded groups.

Finally, exogenous factors could affect the substantive activity of representing by group members as well as non–group members: (1) influenced by their party platform and ideology, legislators push through new policies to promote women and/or subordinate group interests; (2) to win more votes, legislators make promises to excluded groups during their campaigns and then follow through once in office; and (3) legislators are influenced to act

Figure 4.1. Dimensions of Representation for Excluded Groups

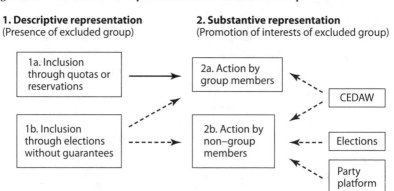

Notes: CEDAW, Convention on the Elimination of All Forms of Discrimination against Women. See text for meanings of solid and dashed lines.

by international norms and agreements such as the Convention on the Elimination of All Forms of Discrimination against Women.

There are different paths toward descriptive representation: members of excluded groups can gain power through quotas or reservations or by winning elections without guarantees. What is more, the relationship between descriptive and substantive representation is probabilistic rather than certain. Finally, the activity of representing—promoting the interests of the represented and otherwise acting on their behalf—can be performed by group members and non–group members. It may be stimulated by exogenous factors unrelated to political inclusion. Equipped with these conceptual tools, we are better prepared to study the politics of inclusion in Latin America.

Women and Gender Quotas

Gender quota laws are responsible for bringing record numbers of women into national legislatures across Latin America. Between the early 1990s (before the laws were adopted) and 2004, women's presence in legislative chambers with quotas increased by an average of 10 percentage points (from 9 percent of the total to 19 percent) (Table 4.2).[7] This is a remarkable achievement, and it is worth studying how and why quotas were adopted. Yet on their own, such laws are insufficient to advance women's substantive representation. Not all female politicians promote policies of gender equality.[8] Among those who do, not all came to power by means of a quota.

The idea of gender quotas emerged from coalitions of women politicians and activists. Angered by the gender discrimination excluding them from power and inspired by the use of quotas in European parties and international agreements such as the Beijing Platform for Action, they introduced quota bills, organized seminars, and began to educate their male colleagues and the general public about the relationship between democracy and women's participation.[9] These coalitions consisted of an elite vanguard; they did not originate from a grassroots movement and were only remotely connected to the demands of average women. The small and elite nature of these groups is one factor explaining their success. According to one Bolivian activist, "We are people with links to power. We are part of the elite that runs the country. . . . We spent one year living in Congress."[10] Another added: "Quotas were achieved by a group of middle class female intellectuals who had access to power and wanted to extend this right to others. It wasn't a massive demand surging from society but rather from a small group of women."[11]

Successful quota coalitions were also multipartisan. In Argentina, the quota movement began in the late 1980s when women from both the Unión Cívica Radical (Radical Civic Union) and the Partido Justicialista (Judicialist [Peronist] Party) began to meet at seminars sponsored by the Friedrich

Table 4.2. Results of Quotas in Latin America

Country	Legislative Body	Percentage of Women before Law	Percentage of Women after Law	Change (%)
Argentina	Chamber	6	34	+28
	Senate	3	33	+30
Bolivia	Chamber	11	19	+8
	Senate	4	15	+9
Brazil	Chamber	7	9	+2
Costa Rica	Unicameral Parliament	14	35	+21
Dominican Republic	Chamber	12	17	+5
Ecuador	Unicameral Parliament	4	16	+12
Mexico	Chamber	17	23	+6
	Senate	15	16	+1
Panama	Unicameral Parliament	8	17	+9
Paraguay	Chamber	3	10	+7
	Senate	11	9	−2
Peru	Unicameral Parliament	11	18	+7
Average		9	19	+10

Source: Mala Htun, "Women, Political Parties and Electoral Systems in Latin America," in *Women in Parliament: Beyond Numbers; A New Edition,* ed. Julie Ballington and Azza Karam (Stockholm: International IDEA, 2005).

Ebert and Karakachoff Foundations to formulate a strategy for writing a quota law. They were inspired by the successful use of quotas in the Spanish and German socialist parties and in the Economic and Social Council of the United Nations, which in 1990 had endorsed the objective that women should make up 30 percent of national decision makers by 1995. Though the first quota bill was sponsored by a female senator from the Unión Cívica Radical, her colleagues from the Partido Justicialista worked for passage of the law. They ended up playing critical roles in convincing then-president Carlos Menem (also a Peronist) and cabinet members to support the proposal.[12]

In Mexico as well, women from all parties (including initially skeptical politicians from the right) united behind quotas, to secure passage first of a weak law in 1996 and then of a stronger one in 2003. The Mexican quota coalition appealed not to principles but to self-interest. Specifically, they compelled male colleagues to support the quota to eliminate the advantage such support would give to other parties. As Lisa Baldez observes, Mexican men ended up supporting quotas not to claim credit but "to avoid being punished for failing to adopt it. Parties have adopted gender quotas in order to avoid being publicly portrayed as chauvinist." Right-wing men from the Partido Acción Nacional (National Action Party), for example, eventually supported quotas when they feared that their continued opposition would create an opportunity for other parties to claim to the electorate that the party was against women.[13] In this way, women politicians used their counterparts from other parties as leverage against the recalcitrant men in their own ranks.

Contrast these two cases to Chile, where multipartisan coalitions backing quotas have failed to form. Women from the Partido Socialista (Socialist Party), the Partido por la Democracia (Party for Democracy), and the Partido Demócrata Cristiano (Christian Democratic Party), all of whom are united in the governing Concertación coalition, support quotas. In fact, these three main Concertación parties use quotas for internal leadership positions and for candidate positions. However, women from the opposition parties of the right—Renovación Nacional (National Renovation) and the Unión Democrática Independiente (Independent Democratic Union)—have consistently been opposed to quotas. They believe that individuals should rise to power on their own merits and not through categorical guarantees. Without more widespread party support and advocacy from the executive, quotas have little hope.[14] Quota bills have been submitted twice since 2000 but have not made it even to a vote on the floor.

How did women from different parties come to agree on a radical measure such as quotas? They had tried other strategies to combat discrimination, such as leadership training, greater access to campaign finance, mentoring, networking, and gender preferences. Organizations such as the United Nations Development Fund for Women and the Ford Foundation had sponsored national efforts to convince women to run for office and to prepare them to conduct successful campaigns. Since the 1980s, many parties had included in their statutes rhetorical commitments to equality. For example, in response to a national gender equality law, Costa Rica's Partido de Liberación Nacional (National Liberation Party) reserved 10 percent of its budget for leadership training for women and required parity in nominations for internal executive posts. Yet the measure was inconsequential: the number of women in party leadership was virtually unchanged between 1985 and 1993.[15] In Mexico, parties began to introduce gender preferences in the early 1990s, and in 1996 the electoral law requested that parties nominate women to 30 percent of candidate slots. Yet, following the 1997 elections, the number of women in Congress actually decreased.[16]

The failure of these gradualist measures turned more female politicians toward quotas. They became convinced that without a radical requirement, parties would never change locked-in institutional rules and procedures to accommodate women. As Amalia García, a former president of Mexico's Partido de la Revolución Democrática (Party of the Democratic Revolution) and senator, put it, "Politics is a rude fight where what matters is beating the other. Women should not have to descend to this level. That's why we need a quota."[17] Even women from right-wing parties opposed to the idea of affirmative action began to endorse quotas once the intractability of male dominance became clear.[18]

What is more, quota coalitions had limited goals: achievement of quota laws. Quotas were not part of any larger package of proposals on policies related to issues such as abortion, sexual harassment, social expenditures, and other issues on which women from different parties were likely to disagree.

After the laws were passed, women politicians and activists played a crucial role in their application. In Argentina, they checked party lists to make sure women were included and challenged noncompliant lists in court to have them declared invalid.[19] In Ecuador, activists petitioned the courts to modify procedural laws that created a loophole in the quota law, effectively permitting parties to cluster the names of women at the bottom of the party lists instead of alternating them with those of men.[20] Bolivian activists, annoyed at the way party leaders tended to comply with the quota law by counting from the top of the list to the bottom (thereby minimizing women's chances to get elected), campaigned to make them count horizontally. If they counted across lists, from *titular* (officeholder) to *suplente* (substitute), the third slot of each list would correspond to the second *titular* position.[21]

Activists could therefore help ensure that women were placed on party lists in the ways specified by the law. However, they had no control over which women were actually included. In most cases, it was up to party leaders to decide—the same party leaders whose reluctance to include women had motivated the quota movement in the first place. These party elites were more interested in loyal candidates than in independent feminists. Often (but not always) they selected candidates with little connection to the feminist movement and little inclination to fight for change on sexual violence, reproductive rights, and the like. Feminist activists I have interviewed complain that strong women are not put on party lists and that the candidates chosen by parties are weak.

These realities have sparked heated debates among activists about the relationship between political representation and gender equality. Is the presence of bodies important for its own sake? Or does women's presence matter only if they are strong politicians committed to advancing gender interests? According to one observer:

> If women from one day to the next become deputies, they don't assume their role in public responsibly. They aren't participating in major national deci-

sions. I've done training courses for candidates and the women are totally ignorant. Quotas help women get there, but what we need is women who have worked all their lives and are ready to participate for real. . . . For quotas to have a symbolic effect, the women who are present have to be good. If women are supposed to open up opportunities for other women, they have to be good.[22]

Another activist concurred: "I'd rather have three good feminists than 60 women who sit there and do nothing."[23]

Other activists believe that the very presence of women marks progress toward equality, regardless of who they are and what they do: "Even by the mere fact of having women in power, parliament has democratized. . . . The fact of seeing these women there justifies all the work we have done."[24] As former Bolivian minister Gloria Ardaya puts it, "Quotas aren't a panacea but they produce a demonstration effect. They help change culture by setting a good example. It may take generations. It's a long process, and you can't judge it after only two mandates. Women too are carriers of a patriarchal culture."[25]

All else equal, women are more likely than men to actively promote feminist policies. In her study of legislators in Argentina, Colombia, and Costa Rica, Leslie Schwindt-Bayer found that women were more likely than their male counterparts to introduce bills to promote gender equality (1.5 percent of bills presented by men tackled the issue compared to 6 percent of bills introduced by women).[26] According to data gathered by Roseanna Heath, Schwindt-Bayer, and Michelle Taylor-Robinson, Honduran female legislators are significantly more likely than their male counterparts to sponsor bills and make speeches on behalf of women's rights.[27] Gender-related activism, however, represents only a small part of the legislative agendas of women (and men) politicians. When it comes to other policy issues, men's and women's views and behavior are substantially similar.[28]

Women tend to be marginalized within legislatures. They are overrepresented on the weaker committees dealing with women's and social issues and underrepresented on more powerful legislative committees such as those dealing with economics and foreign affairs. This asymmetry becomes more acute as women's legislative presence grows.[29]

In spite of women's numerical gains in Latin American legislatures, advocacy of gender equality policies is incomplete. Group rights have achieved women's legislative presence but are more weakly linked to women's substantive activity of representation. One reason, suggested earlier, is that not all female elected officials have the interest or motivation to pursue a women's rights agenda. Another reason is discrimination and marginalization of feminist politicians, a problem found not just in Latin America. Mary Hawkesworth, for example, has explored the "racing-gendering" of the U.S.

Congress and found that women representatives, especially ethnic minority ones, are silenced, interrupted, and more likely to have their proposals buried by committee chairs than are other legislators.[30]

Finally, most politicians are constrained by party discipline. When women enter power, they do so as members of political parties and not as members of a women's caucus. Their views and behavior reflect partisanship more than gender. In our study of Brazilian legislators, Tim Power and I found party affiliation a more consistent predictor of views on gender-related policies than the sex of the respondent.[31] Being from a leftist party, not being a man or a woman, explained a legislator's progressive position on gender issues. Similarly, Alatorre's study of Mexico found that gender policy advanced only when it corresponded to partisan interests.[32]

Party ideology and party interest are two of the factors that affect whether politicians will promote gender equality policies. Public opinion, religious pressure, civic mobilization, and personal beliefs, among numerous other factors, are also important. Some individuals have made great efforts on behalf of women's rights; others have done little. Quota laws have the potential to help more women get into power, but they are agnostic when it comes to these women's commitment to gender equality.

Reserved Seats for Indigenous Peoples and Black Communities in Colombia

In 1991, Colombia became the first country in the Americas to guarantee access to power on the grounds of ethnicity. Its Constitution offered two reserved seats to indigenous peoples in the Senate; implementing legislation later gave black communities two reserved seats in the lower house.[33] The text also granted indigenous peoples political and juridical autonomy, recognized their collective title to land, and endorsed the ethnic and cultural diversity of the nation.[34] In subsequent years, indigenous candidates were elected to the reserved Senate seats and won national seats against the general field. Afro-descendant candidates representing ethnic organizations took the seats in the lower house.

Have these legislative reservations led to the promotion of minority interests in Colombian politics? By bringing more indigenous and black politicians to power, they improved political inclusion. Recognition of Indians and blacks as subjects of collective rights has reversed decades of effort, at least rhetorically, to build a homogeneous national polity.[35] Yet politicians elected to represent indigenous and rural black communities have had a hard time promoting policy changes. Their numbers have been too small. In fact, it was the small size of these groups that made constitution makers willing to grant them rights in the first place. A larger group—the majority of black

Colombians—was denied similar collective rights. As this suggests, the state has endorsed multiculturalism in theory but has not consistently done so in practice.[36]

Three indigenous delegates participated in the Constituent Assembly convened by then-president César Gaviria in 1990.[37] Their mere presence was important: they wore traditional dress during the deliberations and spoke indigenous languages, thus making visible in the mainstream politics and media a way of life largely unseen by many Colombians. The indigenous delegates worked to see most of their proposals included in the final text of the Constitution. It also helped that white and mestizo delegates felt a sense of historical debt. The Constituent Assembly had coincided with hemisphere-wide preparations among indigenous activists to protest the commemoration of the 500th anniversary of Columbus's "discovery" of the Americas. (As one leader said to me in an interview, "We should be grateful to those people who wanted to beatify Columbus, since if they hadn't acted, we would not have reacted.")[38] Public sympathy for the indigenous cause saw many provisions adopted without extensive debate.

Perhaps the most important factor in the promotion of minority interests in Colombian politics, however, was the small size of the indigenous population.[39] This helps to explain the government's turnaround on the issue of reserved seats. The government had rejected indigenous proposals for reserved seats for elections to the Constituent Assembly. (As it turns out, Indians won seats anyway and used them to exercise tremendous influence.) However, the Constituent Assembly embraced ethnic reservations. Why? Because Indians make up only 1.5 percent of the citizenry and are a majority in two isolated provinces and a significant minority in just two more, the costs of accommodating their demands are small. The Constitution's crafters saw few risks to expanding indigenous rights and did not consider them a major challenge to the state. According to Supreme Court Justice Manuel José Cepeda (who drafted the government's text of the Constitution), "Mexico is one thing, Guatemala is another, and Colombia a third. [Indians] are not a threat. The guerrillas never took up the indigenous cause. Rather, the indigenous are against the guerrillas. They have been victims of everyone. *It was not dangerous to go so far.*"[40] Meeting indigenous demands has been somewhat costly for Colombia, but not as radical as, say, reserving half of Bolivia's congressional seats for Indians, teaching Quechua in Lima schools, or ceding law enforcement throughout the Guatemalan highlands to Indian tribunals.

Meanwhile, Colombia's Constitution granted rights to members of the *"communidades negras"* (black communities), who represent only about 7 percent of the total black population.[41] Transitory Article 55 (of 60 total) obliged Congress to pass a law recognizing the collective property rights of the *communidades negras* in the rural Pacific who had been occupying vacant or unused land "in accordance with their traditional productive practices."[42] Afro-descendant organizations failed to elect a representative to the Assembly, so their demands were forwarded by the indigenous delegates, who proposed that blacks be granted rights similar to those claimed by Indians. These rights, according to indigenous delegate Francisco Rojas Birry, were not for the "black race" but rather for black communities that had "been able to conserve a traditional cultural legacy . . . [and] able to conserve a territorial zone that comprises their habitat. The rights defended here are for those communities with a cultural identity, their own authorities and land used collectively [such as] the *palenques* [towns of free Afro-Colombians] and black rural communities of the Chocó and some regions of the Pacific."[43] Thus, blacks who were given rights in the Constitution were those whose lives most resembled those of indigenous peoples. Constitutional provisions, including two reserved seats in the lower house, were later implemented through Law 70 of 1993.[44]

Colombia's legislative reservations helped promote the maturation of indigenous parties.[45] After 1991, these parties contested elections not just in the special indigenous Senate district but also in the ordinary one. The Constitution had created a 100-seat Senate elected nationwide, furnishing incentives for indigenous groups and other groups formed by religious and political minorities (as well as former guerrillas, paramilitaries, and drug traffickers) to form parties and, eventually, to gain seats in Congress.[46] The Organización Nacional Indígena de Colombia (National Indigenous Organization of Colombia) and the Autoridades Indígenas de Colombia (Indigenous Authorities of Colombia) both contested the first elections held under the new regime and won the reserved seats.[47] In addition, in 1991 and 1998 at least one indigenous candidate gained a regular seat, and in 2002 two indigenous candidates won seats against the general field, bringing the total number of indigenous senators to three and four, respectively. In 2002, an Indian representative was elected to a reserved seat in the lower house. The most successful indigenous party, the Alianza Social Indígena (ASI; Indigenous Social Alliance), formed from the Consejo Regional Indígena del Cauca (Regional Indigenous Commission of the Cauca) movement and the demobilized Quintín Lame guerrillas, won the general Senate seats mentioned earlier (with its candidate, Jesús Piñacué, finishing 15th nationwide in 1998 and 12th nationwide in 2002), as well as two gubernatorial races and numerous municipal council and provincial deputy seats, including in Bogotá.[48] These elected officials have attempted to promote indigenous rights and denounced abuses committed against their communities.

Yet Colombia's indigenous parties have been frustrated in their attempts to secure legislative changes to implement those parts of the Constitution related to their rights. For example, though the 1991 text authorized the creation of *entidades teritoriales indígenas* (indigenous territorial entities) and separate jurisdiction for customary law, both provisions have been highly controversial, and legislation stalled in Congress. The situation of indigenous peoples continues to be grave. As indigenous Senator Gerardo Jumí explained:

> With a Constitution that recognizes our rights, with indigenous people present in the Congress, there are still murders, massacres, evictions, a lack of public investment, a lack of social policy and big public works projects. This is what is happening, in spite of everything. So why are there rights written in the Constitution? Why are there five indigenous legislators? Why should we participate? But if I don't participate, who will complain about this situation? We must be there.[49]

Unable to produce immediate changes, indigenous legislators believe that their political presence is still important. Senator Jesús Piñacué summed it up: "The reserved seats are not really to defend indigenous rights because this is very difficult. We are not in the majority. Rather, the idea is to help build a party that at some point can offer a broader understanding of what it means to defend indigenous rights." Piñacué's ASI party, in its attempt to promote this awareness, has incorporated many non-Indians into its ranks. Though this has helped the party grow, it has also generated conflict.[50]

How have the black representatives fared? In contrast to indigenous peoples, who were always excluded from power, a small number of blacks had risen to prominent positions in the government even before the 1991 Constitution was written.[51] In the early 2000s, a total of six seats in the lower house of Congress were occupied by blacks: the two reserved seats, two seats from the Pacific coastal province of Chocó, and two from the province of San Andrés (the Caribbean islands occupied by the Raizal ethnic group). One black woman held a Senate seat: Piedad Córdoba from Medellín, a member of the Liberal Party who has advocated for black rights, women's rights, and human rights. In practice, however, only the two reserved seat deputies are seen—and see themselves—with the mandate to represent the Afro-descendant population. Black deputies from Chocó and San Andrés belong to traditional parties, were not elected on platforms of ethnic rights, and, while not unsupportive of Afro-descendants, do not champion their issues in Congress.

As is the case with indigenous peoples, electoral institutions allow only representatives of black communities to run for the reserved seats, but the electorate as a whole may cast votes for them. Candidates for these seats must "be members of such a community and previously sponsored by an organization registered with the Directorate for Black Community Issues in the Interior Ministry." In practice, this is incredibly permissive: over 1,000 such organizations are registered, and there is little monitoring of their activities or the constituencies they claim to represent. Candidates in the regular elections, by contrast, must have the support of a party or movement that has succeeded in gathering 50,000 signatures. (Since the 2003 political reforms, a party must receive 2 percent of the national vote to register.) As a result, Cunin says, "black politicians in the special national district have not nearly the same legitimacy and transparency as other candidates."[52] Like the indigenous, they appear on every ballot throughout the country and have attracted more protest votes from people disenchanted with traditional parties than from their intended constituencies.

The first black deputies were elected to the reserved seats in 1994, but their record disappointed the black movements that had sponsored their candidacies. They fumbled from a lack of political experience and were contaminated by the scandal surrounding allegations that then-president Ernesto Samper had received campaign donations from drug traffickers. Much to the chagrin of supporters, both black deputies joined the coalition defending Samper.[53] Nonetheless, in 1996 the government passed a law granting Afro-descendant university students access to a public credit for scholarships (decree 1627 of 1996). Then, due to a technical error, the seats were ruled unconstitutional, and no elections to fill them were held in 1998. Their loss provoked little protest or concern, however. Neither the black movement nor the black communities of the Chocó mobilized on behalf of their two representatives.

This lack of connection between most black voters and deputies from the black community is evidenced by electoral data. Even though the Chocó was the main area to benefit from the Constitution, in the 1994 elections only 4,000 people there voted for black community candidates (of a total of around 131,000 votes cast nationwide for the reserved seats).[54] In a pattern resembling support for indigenous candidates, most of the votes for "ethnic" politicians came from urban areas, including 32,000 from Bogotá.[55] In 2002, out of 23 candidates contesting the seats reserved for the black community, the victors were two star athletes: a woman who had won a gold medal in weightlifting at the Sydney Olympics in 2000 (the only one ever earned by Colombia) and a champion soccer player of the 1970s. Much as in the 1994 elections, most of the votes for the victorious candidates did not come from those areas of the country benefiting from the new Constitution.[56]

In addition to reinforcing racist stereotypes associating blackness with athletic prowess (and not legislative competence), the election of the two deputies was criticized due to their lack of connection to Afro-Colombian social movements, demands for land rights, or the Law 70 process.[57] Yet, since they have been in power, the two deputies have attempted to champion black rights. They pushed the president to include within the National Development Plan a subplan on the development of black communities and presented a bill to Congress to create a quota for blacks in decision-making positions in the executive branch. The quota proposal encountered tremendous resistance in committee, however; other deputies made the familiar argument that the quota would lead to a cascade of demands from other groups.[58]

Like their indigenous counterparts, blacks suffer because of their small numbers. Like women elected through quotas, they are a diverse group, and not all members spend their time advancing black rights. For example, black deputies are divided between traditional parties and independent movements registered with the Interior Ministry. Reflecting on the difference between himself and Edgar Torres, another black deputy, Ortiz remarked that though Torres is sensitive to issues of race, he is "mostly concerned with his province. He works for the Chocó, but I have to work for blacks everywhere. It's at cross purposes."[59]

In summary, the Constitution, Law 70, and the allocation of two reserved seats in Congress marked an advance over the state's historic neglect of Afro-descendants. Yet these rights, directed at only a small portion of the black population, are inadequate to tackle mainstream racism. Brazil, by contrast, has tackled the problem through affirmative action in universities, government ministries, and the foreign service; a state secretariat and a national policy for racial equality; and a requirement that public schools teach Afro-Brazilian history and culture.[60] Thus far, Colombia has entertained few discussions of affirmative action for the entire black population.

Indigenous Peoples and Majority Power in Bolivia

Unlike their counterparts in Colombia, Bolivia's indigenous peoples have not sought reserved seats to guarantee their representation. Reserved seats may be desirable for a minority. Bolivian Indians, however, have not framed their demands in the language of minority rights. They want to "refound" the country according to the will of its original and authentic majority.[61] This implies the need for political power, and to achieve it, Indians have formed and joined parties and contested elections on a regular basis. In their view, reserved seats would impose a ceiling. They have been right: the largest of the indigenous-led parties, the Movimiento al Socialismo (MAS; Movement toward Socialism), swept the national elections in December of 2005, and its leader, former coca grower Evo Morales, became the first Indian president of the country.

Morales and the members of the MAS have symbolically and substantively represented their supporters. They wear ponchos and speak indigenous languages in Parliament. In addition, they have rejected neoliberal economics, taken steps to nationalize oil and gas, and convened a Constituent Assembly.

Unlike other scholars, however, I do not consider the MAS an ethnic party or an indigenous party.[62] These labels are too narrow. The MAS is a normal political party, which is defined by Downs as a team seeking to win elections.[63] It includes representatives of diverse currents, including indigenous authorities, leaders from the traditional left, and intellectuals. Vice President Álvaro García Linera, Morales's running mate, is a white intellectual who calls himself the "bridge" between the indigenous groups and the middle classes. For these reasons, I call the MAS an "indigenous-led party," not an indigenous party or an ethnic party.

To be sure, the MAS frequently appeals to pre-Columbian traditions. The party's strength, according to former senator Alicia Muñoz, is to "understand and accept the strong identity claims behind socioeconomic demands, . . . [but the MAS] is not an ethnic party. It is a new party."[64] As she explained, "We are a party of the Left, but we believe in nature, we respect mother earth, the water. . . . We are a party with cultural identity. This makes us different from a mere Leftist party based on class. We are a combination of class and culture."[65]

This statement alludes to the difficulty of disentangling the ethnic and the economic. The MAS represents the interests of the lower classes, including *cocaleros* (coca growers), slum dwellers, and peasants. Does the fact that these people are dark skinned make their demands ethnic and not economic? According to one Bolivian observer, "The MIP [Movimiento Indígena Pachakutik; Pachakutik Indigenous Movement] is the real ethnic party. In MAS [ethnicity is] a secondary issue. . . . Evo doesn't use the ethnic card that much, but he knows that the ethnic theme sells very well abroad. . . . [In Bolivia] the hydrocarbon issue generates much more mobilization than the issue of autonomy for the Aymara nation."[66]

The fact that leaders of the movement to nationalize hydrocarbons wear ponchos and speak indigenous languages, however, is symbolically significant. Morales's ethnic heritage earns him support among Indians. Consider the following observation by Jim Schultz, director of the Democracy Center in Cochabamba:

> I saw indigenous identification with Morales up close in October when I spent five days in a small Quechua Indian village three hours off into the mountains. On a sunny afternoon, I sat with the village leader, Lucio, a man I have known for almost a decade. I asked him if the coming elections were big on people's minds. "No, we are really more worried about whether it will rain soon." I asked him if people were excited about Evo Morales and the prospect of electing an Indian as president. "Well, he is really just a politician." Then I asked him whether the people of the village would vote. "Oh yes, we will vote. All 400

of us will walk together 45 minutes to the place where we vote and we will all vote for Evo."[67]

The MAS's victory is the culmination of decades of growth of indigenous-led parties. They boomed only in the mid-1990s but had emerged as early as the 1970s. Then they attracted only a small number of votes. One problem was the configuration of political institutions. For example, the scarcity of municipal organization in Bolivia minimized opportunities for local political action among indigenous groups. In much of the countryside, where Indians lived, there was little penetration by the state in terms of public investment or political party mobilization. What is more, national electoral laws required that parties whose candidates received fewer than 50,000 votes share the cost of printing ballots. Failure to pay the fines would result in loss of registration. The National Electoral Court disqualified many indigenous parties on these grounds in the 1980s and 1990s. None won more than 3 percent of the national vote.[68] Though white and mestizo parties recruited some indigenous leaders, these leaders were rarely promoted to senior positions.

What changed in the 1990s? In addition to the growing legitimacy of the indigenous category in global discourse, Bolivia reformed its political institutions. The 1994 Ley de Participatión Popular (LPP; Law of Popular Participation) established 314 municipal districts and procedures for the direct election of city councilors. It also allocated around 20 percent of the national budget to these municipalities for direct distribution according to the size of their populations. These political and fiscal opportunities stimulated Indian activism. According to former vice president Victor Hugo Cardenas, "None of the movements of 2002 and 2003 can be explained without the LPP. It gave the majority contact with local governments and gave excluded people a taste of decision-making power. With the LPP, resources went for the first time to excluded areas."[69] Meanwhile, a government-sponsored registration campaign added to the rolls more voters who would likely support parties with indigenous leaders.[70] Ironically, these changes were introduced under a government led by the neoliberal Gonzalo Sánchez de Lozada, who was despised by indigenous leaders and esteemed by Washington. A decade later, indigenous leaders who had gained power by virtue of the reforms this president introduced were instrumental in deposing him.

The reforms of Sánchez de Lozada bore fruit immediately: in the 1995 local elections, record numbers of Indians (around 470) were elected to municipal councils: they represented 29 percent of the total and 62 percent of councils in the highland regions.[71] The majority had been nominated by traditional political parties, though one indigenous-led party—the Alianza Social Patriótica (ASP; Social Patriotic Alliance), a group of coca growers led by Evo Morales, who would later form the MAS—elected around 49 coun-cilors and 10 mayors.[72]

Changes in national electoral rules furnished further incentives for indigenous-led parties. Previously, the country had elected deputies through closed-list proportional representation from a single national district with an effective 3 percent threshold. This system favored the larger traditional par-ties. However, a 1995 constitutional reform created a mixed system in which half of the lower house of Congress would be elected in single-member dis-tricts and half in national-list proportional representation. For the first time, voters were permitted to cast two votes: one for a deputy contesting one of the country's 65 single-member districts and the other for the president (and his chosen slate of legislators). In the 1997 national elections, nine deputies from indigenous-led parties gained power, including four from the ASP, the party of coca growers that had made gains in the 1995 local contests (a 10th was elected by means of the presidential vote).[73]

As the economy stagnated and coca eradication devastated rural areas, indigenous-led parties continued to grow. They assumed the traditional leftist cause of combating neoliberalism and were champions of social jus-tice. Leftist parties defeated at the ballot box decided to lend their names and legal registrations to Indian leaders (the MAS, a defunct leftist party, was reinvigorated when the bulk of Morales's movement of coca growers reassem-bled under its banner), and leftist voters supported them. Nationalism also helped; voters linked their opposition to coca eradication with a defense of sovereignty and traditional cultural identity. In 2000, indigenous leaders joined teachers and labor unions in organizing nationwide protests against poverty and exclusion, anti-coca policies, an increase in water prices, and multi-national corporations' participation in the water sector. These conflicts nearly brought down the government, further weakening traditional parties.[74]

A turning point came in the 2002 elections, when indigenous-led parties and candidates won record numbers of votes and Evo Morales came close to winning the presidency. The MAS gained 21 percent of the votes cast na-tionwide (placing second behind the ruling Movimiento Nacionalista Rev-olucionario, or Nationalist Revolutionary Movement, led by former presi-dent Gonzalo Sánchez de Lozada), and Felipe Quispe's MIP, the true ethnic party in Bolivian politics, took 6 percent. These two indigenous-led parties came to hold 33 of 130 seats in the lower house of Congress and 8 of 27 Sen-ate seats.[75] The MAS acquired control of the second vice presidency in the lower house as well as leadership of several important committees. For the first time in Bolivian history, legislators attired in traditional dress made speeches in indigenous languages.

In 2003, President Gonzalo Sánchez de Lozada fled to the United States amid massive popular protests. His plan to sell natural gas to multinational corporations at below-market prices proved a tipping point: tens of thousands of people took to the streets to protest a deal they perceived as compromising national sovereignty and organized a blockade around the capital city. The state responded with violence, leaving dozens dead. After deposing the president, radical social movements and opposition parties, including those led by Morales, Quispe, and the neighborhood associations of El Alto, used the threat of continued unrest to compel the president's successor, Vice President Carlos Mesa, to agree to various concessions, including the convocation of a Constituent Assembly and immediate reform of the Constitution to permit indigenous and other associations to contest elections independent of political parties.

Why has the Constituent Assembly been so important? Indian leaders see it as the embodiment of a new social pact, the refounding of the country on different terms. As Morales later put it: "The majority of people in this country—people from more than 30 indigenous groups—did not participate in the foundation of Bolivia in 1825. We have to re-found Bolivia in order to end the colonial state, to live united in diversity, to put all our resources under state control, and to make people participate and give them the right to make decisions."[76] As this quote suggests, indigenous-led parties (and others, too) have entertained high hopes about the outcome of the Constituent Assembly. Yet these expectations are dangerously high. As Electoral Court Justice Salvador Romero points out, "In Bolivia people expect that a new country will be made. . . . People want change, and they believe these two magic words ["asamblea constituente"] will bring it about. There will be a shock when people see that the only thing to emerge from the process will be a constitution."[77]

Debates about popular representation in the Assembly demonstrate how the policy of reserved seats was perceived to limit indigenous power. Indigenous reservations were part of the initial proposal submitted by Congress in the first few months of 2005. The bill would have reserved 26 seats for indigenous peoples (which would represent 14 or 22 percent of the total because the bill assumed an assembly of either 180 or 116 delegates). The same bill included a candidate quota of 50 percent for women, requiring that their names be alternated with those of men on party lists.

Though reserved seats were allegedly for the benefit of indigenous peoples, indigenous leaders and parties with strong indigenous support, such as the MAS, were critical of the proposal for reservations. In addition, Felipe Quispe claimed that the government wanted indigenous peoples merely to decorate the assembly as members of a minority and declared, in typical fashion, that if Indians were not the majority, the Aymara would separate from Bolivia and form their own constituent assembly.[78] Vice Minister for Women's Affairs Teresa Canaviri, herself indigenous, reflected that the indigenous quota worked at cross purposes to real inclusion: "I'm not in favor of quotas for indigenous peoples. It limits us. Why only 26? And it could be exclusionary. I don't believe they should give us these spaces to distract us and not include us in a fully intercultural society. It is very easy for the quota to become a ghetto. The same is true with spaces in government. The Indigenous Affairs Ministry is the only space we have, and it has led to conflicts between indigenous peoples."[79]

Reserved seats, moreover, could weaken indigenous-led parties. The seats would likely be filled not through secret votes for parties but through the local *usos y costumbres* of each group. Delegates filling the seats would represent their own home areas, not national political parties. The MAS could therefore stand to lose allies as indigenous leaders defected from the party to run from their home constituencies.[80] For these reasons, MAS Senator Alicia Muñoz was critical of the idea of reserved seats. She argued that the proposal came from members of traditional parties who intended to divide and weaken the MAS.[81]

Amid more protests and demands for the nationalization of oil and gas, Carlos Mesa resigned and was replaced by yet another caretaker president. National elections were scheduled for December. Evo Morales won 54 percent of the popular vote against 29 percent for his opponent, Tuto Quiroga. The MAS gained 72 of 130 seats in Congress; Poder Democrático y Social (Democratic and Social Power), the largest opposition party, won 43. This victory, touted as a political revolution, was also perceived to herald the rise of the indigenous majority. As Morales declared, speaking to Aymara and Quechua on the day of his victory, "For the first time we are president."[82]

When discussion was renewed about the Constituent Assembly, the ruling party opposed the proposals for reserved indigenous seats put forward by other parties and by indigenous social movements. As a matter of principle (and political calculus), the MAS opposed all forms of "corporatist" representation, including demands for guarantees by unions, peasants, and even the police.[83] Not surprisingly, it won a majority of the seats in the new Constituent Assembly (for which elections were held in July 2006) but later stirred considerable controversy by proposing that changes be approved only by a simple majority of delegates rather than the two-thirds vote originally agreed upon. In the political climate that prevailed at the end of 2006, it was not the indigenous majority but rather the white and mestizo minorities that seemed likely to need reserved seats and other minority protections.

Majority power has enabled the indigenous-led MAS to implement important elements of its agenda. Besides convoking the Constituent Assembly, Morales declared that the oil and gas industries would be nationalized, forcing foreign companies to renegotiate their contracts on terms more favorable to Bolivia. He ended up collecting over US$1 billion in taxes. Morales

announced plans to end the eradication of coca and decriminalize its production and brandished a coca leaf during a speech at the United Nations in
New York. He also appointed radicals to positions of power. Abel Mamani,
who as leader of the Federación de Juntas Vecinales de El Alto (Federation of
Neighborhood Boards of El Alto) had spearheaded massive protests against
previous governments, became minister of water. The education minister
called for an end to religious teaching and issued a decree requiring all schools
to offer classes in indigenous languages. The government made moves toward
land reform and announced that visitors from the United States would
need to obtain visas before arriving in Bolivia. With such moves, Morales
represents his constituency descriptively with his presence and substantively
through his policies.

Conclusion

Most Latin American polities have become more inclusive of women,
Afro-descendants, and indigenous peoples, groups historically excluded from
elected office. In some cases, this inclusion has come about thanks to the
state's adoption of representational guarantees such as gender quotas or reserved seats for ethnic groups. In other cases, subordinate groups have formed
parties and fought elections on their own. Once in power, many members of
these groups have struggled to change policy to benefit their constituents.
Not all have, and not all of those who have tried have succeeded. Change in
the descriptive dimension of representation is not always accompanied by
changes in the substantive activity of representing. The policy-making
process is complex and is influenced by many factors beside the gender and
race of officeholders.

In conclusion, it is worth examining how changes in political inclusion relate to the broader context of democratic politics explored in the rest of this
book. As Jorge Domínguez notes in his concluding chapter, the balance for
democratic governance is more negative than when the previous two editions
of this book were published. Though democracy is on a more solid footing
than it was a generation ago, several measures of progress—including citizen
satisfaction, the stability and effectiveness of parties, and "horizontal accountability," or the ability of different branches of government to check the
power of one another—are in trouble. Many polities have been unable to address crucial social problems, and several of the region's presidents have attempted to exert their authority in a sultanistic manner.

Though democratic prospects vary considerably by country, it is curious
that several of the countries where democracy seems most at risk—Bolivia,
Ecuador, and Venezuela—are also those that have made considerable progress
in including indigenous peoples. Colombia—a more stable but far from un-

problematic polity—has also improved in terms of political inclusion. Women's political presence has grown significantly in all four countries. This raises the question of why these Andean polities are becoming more inclusive of historically excluded groups at the same time that their democracies are faltering. Are the two phenomena causally related? That is, is the weakness of their democracy motivating these polities to be more inclusive? Or is their greater inclusiveness undermining their democratic stability?

In contrast to Aristophanes, whose *Lysistrata* depicted how angry women can destabilize a state, I see little correlation between the number of women present in government and the stability of democratic institutions. Why? In virtually every polity on the planet, gender crosscuts partisan divisions. All parties have male and female members. There are almost no electorally successful men's parties or women's parties (except in countries where women are denied the vote or the right to run for office). As a result, the inclusion or exclusion of women occurs through the existing party system; it is not a matter of adding new parties or subtracting old ones. Whether women are present or absent determines the composition of party personnel but not the relationship of parties to one another or to the polity as a whole. It is these relationships that matter most to the stability of democracy. Women's presence certainly improves the representativeness of democratic institutions and may even boost their responsiveness, but it does not have a significant effect on whether they succeed or fail.[84]

Ethnicity, however, is a different matter. In many polities, ethnicity coincides with party divisions. Ethnic membership determines how people vote and influences party membership. Often enough, minority (or majority) ethnic groups enter politics not through the existing party system but through the rise of a new party (such as La Confederación de Nacionalidades Indígenas del Ecuador, the Confederation of Indigenous Nationalities of Ecuador) or the transformation of an old one (such as the MAS in Bolivia). This presence of a new party and its rise (or fall) cause (or reflect) changes in the party system as a whole—dealignment, realignment, fractionalization, or breakdown. As the various editions of this book have pointed out, party system change is intimately related to democratic stability. Ethnically led and ethnically oriented parties, therefore, have implications for the fate of democracy that bringing women into existing parties does not. Ethnic political inclusion is more likely to be related to the performance and stability of democratic regimes than is gender. This still begs these questions: Are inclusion and democratic stability related? If so, how?

Let us consider the first hypothesis suggested by these questions, that inclusion and democratic stability are related.[85] Governments facing a democratic deficit in some sectors may seek to compensate in other sectors. Whereas failure to provide decent social services, stem rising crime rates, and reduce poverty erodes the legitimacy of a state, bringing in previously excluded social sectors enhances it. Governments unable to advance toward solving major problems such as poverty may feel motivated to produce visible progress on other social agendas. Introducing quotas for women or ethnic minorities is relatively costless compared to the expenditures required to fight poverty or guerrilla forces.

The Colombian Constitution, arguably Latin America's experiment in radical democracy, adheres to some of this logic. The late 1980s were characterized by escalating political violence, economic decline, flagrant activity of drug traffickers with impunity, and growing popular protests. Widely perceived as illegitimate, the state sought to rewrite the social contract by convening a Constituent Assembly. The new Constitution created a much more inclusive regime: electoral laws were redesigned to facilitate the representation of ethnic and political minorities, citizens could challenge the constitutionality of any governmental decree, many official decisions would require popular consultation, and Congress was called on to ensure the effective presence of women in public service.[86]

There is also evidence for the second hypothesis, that greater inclusion has contributed to the instability of democracy. In his classic study of political development, Sam Huntington argued that inclusion without institutionalization results in instability. If participation exceeds the ability of parties to channel and moderate it, a country runs the risk of degenerating into a praetorian society ruled not by law but by raw power. These arguments are relevant to recent events in Bolivia. As this chapter has shown, reforms in the mid-1990s, including the LPP and the introduction of a mixed-member electoral system, facilitated the unprecedented political inclusion of indigenous peoples and ethnic parties.

The problem is that the country's institutions have been too weak to accommodate the participation explosion. Bolivia's party system, already suffering from a legitimacy problem, now confronts movements, parties, and leaders that have expressed hostility to the procedures of liberal representative democracy.[87] Still, indigenous mobilization is but one factor (and likely not the determining one) behind the country's troubles. Light-skinned residents of the eastern Santa Cruz province also have organized protests and strikes and, to a much greater extent than their highland indigenous counterparts, expressed a desire for political autonomy and even an independent state. Andean polities are unstable for a variety or reasons, including corruption, economic mismanagement, inequality, drug trafficking, poor social services, and the like.

In summary, it is far more likely that the faltering of democracy is fueling moves toward inclusion than vice versa. Intractable political and social problems motivate voters to reject the old guard of politicians and turn to fresh candidates untainted by the crimes of the past. In this context, guarantees of inclusion such as quotas and reservations give democracy a facelift. Saving democracy, however, is about more than political presence. It requires action, not just by ethical and committed elites but also by citizens. Citizens need to educate themselves about public affairs, they need to help strengthen parties and other institutionalized channels of participation, and they need to work together in their neighborhoods, homes, and schools to build the civil societies that undergird successful democracies.

PART III

Country Studies

5

Argentina

Democracy and Institutional Weakness

Steven Levitsky

Argentine democracy defies easy evaluation. In many ways, it has been a success. Unlike most of its neighbors, Argentina has been fully democratic since 1983. The constitutional order has never been interrupted, elections have been free and fair, civil liberties have been broadly protected, and the military—author of five coups between 1930 and 1976—has disappeared from the political stage. The regime has also proven remarkably robust. It survived a Weimar-like hyperinflationary crisis in 1989, radical market-oriented reform during the 1990s, and a collapse into depression in 2001–2. At the same time, however, Argentine democracy has also been remarkably crisis-ridden. The 1989 and 2001 economic crises brought the country to the brink of political chaos, forcing presidents to leave office before the end of their mandates. Moreover, the regime remains more prone to executive abuse, such as court packing and extensive rule by decree, than many other middle-income democracies in the region.[1]

This chapter examines the strengths and weaknesses of contemporary Argentine democracy. It argues that democracy has benefited from a broad societal consensus against military rule, a robust civil society, and relatively strong political parties. A vibrant media and civil society increased the probability that state abuses would be exposed and denounced. Party strength—particularly that of the (Peronist) Partido Justicialista (PJ; Judicialist Party)—ensured relatively smooth executive-legislative relations, limited the space for anti-system outsider appeals, and facilitated the implementation—under democracy—of radical economic reforms. At the same time, however, democracy suffered from persistent and widespread institutional weakness. Although Argentina's core democratic institutions are robust, the rules and procedures governing numerous areas of political and economic life are widely contested, frequently circumvented or violated, and repeatedly changed. The result is high levels of uncertainty, narrow time horizons, and minimal trust and cooperation, all of which leaves both the economy and the polity vulnerable to crisis.[2]

Strengths and Weaknesses of Argentine Democracy

Argentina's post-1983 democracy has benefited from several important strengths. One is the emergence of an unprecedented democratic consensus. The brutality and failures of the 1976–83 military dictatorship broadly discredited the armed forces and led all major social and political actors to embrace democratic rules of the game. At the elite level, business, the right, labor, and Peronism—all of which had backed nondemocratic alternatives in the past—invested seriously in electoral politics after 1983.[3] At the societal level, the traumatic experience of the "Dirty War" had a powerful impact on political culture, giving rise to a new "rights-oriented politics" that helped entrench civil liberties to an unprecedented degree.[4]

A second source of democratic strength has been a robust civil society. The human rights movement of the 1970s and 1980s engendered a "second wave" of rights-oriented organizations aimed at monitoring and combating state abuses.[5] These groups formed a "permanent associative network for the supervision of state authorities."[6] Together with a vigorous and independent media, they served as agents of "societal accountability" that exposed and denounced (and thus raised the political costs of) state abuse.[7] For example, in 1990, when Catamarca's provincial government attempted to cover up the murder of teenager María Soledad Morales (in which members of the governing clan were implicated), civic and church groups organized a series of massive "marches of silence" that drew national media attention and forced a federal takeover of the case, paving the way for a conviction. In 1997, after the killing of news photographer José Luis Cabezas (arranged by a mafia boss with ties to the government), civic and media groups organized a massive and successful campaign—flooding Buenos Aires with "Who Killed Cabezas?" posters, fliers, and advertisements—to bring the perpetrators to justice.[8] In December 2001, when President Fernando de la Rúa declared a state of siege, public repudiation was so overwhelming that he was forced to resign.

A third source of democratic strength lies in the party system. Through the mid-1990s, Argentina maintained a predominantly two-party system, with the PJ representing the working and lower classes and the centrist Unión Cívica Radical (UCR; Radical Civic Union)—together with small left-of-center, conservative, and provincial parties—representing the middle and upper middle classes. The PJ was the key to governability. As Argentina's largest party, the Peronist party maintained a powerful grassroots organization, with strong ties to the labor movement and deep roots in working- and lower-class society.[9] Although the Peronists' labor-based populism had once threatened economic and military elites, repeatedly leading them to embrace nondemocratic rule,[10] union influence eroded during the 1980s, and the party transformed itself into a patronage-based machine.[11] As a result, the party system took on features of what Collier and Collier call an integrative party system, in which the PJ's working-class ties enhanced rather than undermined democratic stability.[12]

The PJ contributed to democratic governability in three ways. First, extensive ties to working- and lower-class society helped PJ governments gain popular sector cooperation or restraint during periods of crisis. This capacity was clearly seen with respect to organized labor. Despite the erosion of union influence during the 1980s, the vast majority of union leaders remained Peronist and active in the party.[13] These ties have given union leaders a stake in the success of Peronist governments—and an incentive to limit public opposition. Thus, whereas Radical President Raúl Alfonsín (1983–89) faced 13 general strikes during his presidency, Peronist President Carlos Menem (1989–99) gained a remarkable degree of labor acquiescence, despite far more conservative policies. The Confederación General del Trabajo (General Labor Confederation) did not lead a single general strike during Menem's first three and a half years in office and led only one general strike during his entire first term. The PJ's vast infrastructure of neighborhood branches and clientelist networks also helped dampen popular sector protest. For example, during the 1989–90 hyperinflationary crisis, Peronist activists employed a variety of means—from persuasion to the operation of hundreds of emergency soup kitchens to the physical expulsion of leftist activists—to prevent rioting and looting in their neighborhoods. Throughout the 1990s, Peronist "problem-solving networks" distributed food, medicine, disability pensions, and odd jobs to people who lacked alternative sources of social assistance.[14] Although the impact of these activities is difficult to measure, they almost certainly helped prevent the kind of riots that brought Raúl Alfonsín and Fernando de la Rúa's presidencies to an early end.

Second, the Peronists' electoral success provided the party with considerable legislative strength. Thus, whereas non-Peronist presidents have generally faced a divided government, Peronist presidents have always enjoyed legislative majorities (or near-majorities).[15] This legislative strength has helped Peronist administrations avoid the kind of executive-legislative deadlock that has undermined governability elsewhere in Latin America.[16] During the 1990s, for example, working legislative majorities facilitated the smooth passage of the Menem government's economic reform program and reduced the incentive for the president to bypass Congress or—as occurred in Guatemala, Peru, and Venezuela—attempt to shut it down.

Third, the PJ's continued strength among the working and lower classes limited space for the kind of anti-establishment—and often authoritarian— outsider appeals that threatened democratic stability in Ecuador, Guatemala, Peru, Venezuela, and elsewhere (Table 5.1). Notwithstanding severe political and economic crises in 1989–90 and 2001–2, the vast majority of low-income voters remained solidly Peronist, and, as a result, anti-establishment out- siders failed repeatedly to gain a foothold among the electorate. The closest approximation to a *chavismo*-like phenomenon in Argentina, the ultra- nationalist Movimiento por la Dignidad y la Independencia (MODIN; Move- ment for Dignity and Independence) of former military rebel Aldo Rico, never surpassed 9 percent of the vote.

In sum, Peronism has been an important source of governability since 1989. Although Peronist governability has little to do with standard (e.g., World Bank) conceptions of "good governance" (in fact, it has often involved means—patronage, clientelism, legislative vote buying, graft—that run *di- rectly counter* to those conceptions), it has clearly contributed to democratic stability. It is no coincidence that whereas both non-Peronist presidents elected since 1983 (Alfonsín and de la Rúa) were forced to leave office pre- maturely due to waves of mass rioting and looting, their Peronist successors (Menem and Eduardo Duhalde) successfully dampened social protest.[17]

Yet, if a broad democratic consensus, a vibrant civil society, and a strong Peronist party enhanced democratic governability in post-1983 Argentina, persistent institutional weakness posed a constant threat to that governabil- ity. Institutional strength may be defined along two dimensions: (1) *enforce- ment,* or the degree to which the rules that exist on paper are complied with in practice, and (2) *stability,* or the degree to which formal rules survive mi- nor fluctuations in the distribution of power and preferences).[18] Many Ar-

Table 5.1. Argentine Presidential Election Results, 1983–1999 (percentages of major parties and alliances only)

Party	1983	1989	1995	1999
Partido Justicialista (PJ; Justicialista Party; Peronist)	40.2	47.3	49.9	38.3
Unión Cívica Radical (UCR; Radical Civic Union)	51.9	32.4	17.0	
Frente País Solidario (FREPASO; Front for a Country in Solidarity)			29.2	
Alianza por el Trabajo, la Justicia, y la Educación (Alliance for Jobs, Justice, and Education) (UCR and FREPASO)				48.4
Unión del Centro Democrático (UCEDE; Union of the Democratic Center)		6.4		
Acción por la República (Action for the Republic)				10.2

gentine political and economic institutions are weak on one or both of these dimensions.[19] Between 1930 and 1983, Argentina suffered a period of regime instability—marked by five military coups—during which the Constitution, the electoral system, Congress, the Supreme Court, and other institutions were repeatedly suspended, circumvented, or modified. This period established a pattern of institutional fluidity that persisted for decades. To take one example, between 1928 and 2003, the presidential mandates prescribed by the Constitution were never once complied with in full. In 1930, 1962, 1966, 1976, 1989, and 2001, elected presidents were removed before the end of their mandates. Two presidents—Juan Perón and Menem—completed their terms, but both of them modified the Constitution to permit a second term. Similarly, although the Constitution guarantees Supreme Court justices lifetime tenure security, this constitutional guarantee has routinely been violated since the 1940s; incoming governments—civilian and military—have routinely removed unfriendly justices and replaced them with allies.[20]

Although core democratic institutions strengthened after 1983, other areas of political and economic life continue to be plagued by institutional weakness. The rules of the game governing executive-legislative relations, the judiciary, federalism, candidate selection, taxation, and central bank independence have been repeatedly challenged, violated, manipulated, or changed. Institutional manipulation was particularly widespread during the Menem years. For example, President Menem frequently circumvented the legislative process through Necessity and Urgency Decrees (NUDs), which were not explicitly granted by the Constitution prior to 1994.[21] Whereas all of Argentina's presidents had issued a *combined total* of fewer than 30 NUDs between 1853 and 1989, Menem issued 335 of them between 1989 and 1994.[22] In the judicial realm, Menem pushed through legislation—despite strong objection by the opposition—expanding the size of the Supreme Court from five to nine. He then packed the court with loyalists, creating an "automatic majority" that rarely ruled against the government on issues of importance.[23] Finally, Menem twice sought to modify or circumvent the Constitution in order to run for reelection. In 1993, he bullied UCR leaders into accepting a constitutional reform—via the Olivos Pact—by threatening a plebiscite on the issue. In 1998, he (unsuccessfully) sought to run for a third term via either a constitutional reform or a favorable Supreme Court ruling.

Institutional weakness has had a range of negative consequences. In the absence of stable rules of the game, polities and economies can resemble a Hobbesian world of great uncertainty, narrow time horizons, and low levels of trust and cooperation.[24] In the economic realm, the result has been unstable policy making and poor performance.[25] In the political realm, institutional weakness has brought greater vulnerability in two senses. First, compared to other middle-income democracies in the region (e.g., Brazil, Chile,

Mexico, Uruguay), Argentina experiences crises that are more likely to trigger institutional meltdowns in which extreme uncertainty over the rules of the game—whether or not they will be complied with, how long they will endure—dramatically narrows time horizons and undermines cooperation. Such crises occurred in 1989 and 2001. Second, Argentine democracy is more vulnerable to executive abuse than the democracies of other middle-income countries in the region. Whereas institutions of horizontal accountability have strengthened considerably in Brazil, Chile, Mexico, and Uruguay, they remain weak in Argentina, permitting a degree of executive domination unseen in these other democracies.[26]

In sum, the political foundations of Argentina's post-1983 democracy were somewhat contradictory. Although a broad democratic consensus and strong civic and political organizations permitted the emergence of robust core democratic institutions, many of the rules of the game *within* the regime remained unstable. The result has been both continuity and change relative to the past. As in the past, Argentina remains vulnerable to political and economic crisis. Unlike in the past, however, Argentine democracy has survived these crises. The following sections examine these patterns since 2000.

The Crisis of 2001–2002: Democratic Survival amid Economic Collapse

When Carlos Menem left the presidency in 1999, Argentine democracy was more stable than at any time in history. The Menem government had ended hyperinflation with the 1991 Convertibility Law (which pegged the Argentina peso to the U.S. dollar at a one-to-one rate) and carried out far-reaching market-oriented reforms. Military influence had eroded dramatically, and the specter of military intervention had disappeared. Although the PJ's electoral dominance and Menem's concentration of power triggered fears of a "Mexicanization" of Argentine politics, democratic institutions effectively blocked Menem's 1998 "re-reelection" bid, and Peronist candidate Eduardo Duhalde lost the 1999 presidential election to Fernando de la Rúa of the Alianza por el Trabajo, la Justicia, y la Educación (Alliance for Jobs, Justice, and Education), a coalition of the UCR and the center-left Frente País Solidario (FREPASO; Front for a Country in Solidarity).

The rise of the Alliance appeared to usher in a period of more institutionalized democratic politics. Almost immediately, however, Argentina plunged into another episode of crisis. This crisis had political and economic components. On the political side, widespread perceptions of unchecked corruption and abuse of power during the 1990s had eroded the credibility of representative institutions and widened the gap between citizens, particularly middle-class citizens, and the political elite.[27] Disaffected middle-class voters were poorly represented in the party system.[28] Argentina's traditional middle-class party, the UCR, had been weakened by the disastrous performance of the Alfonsín government and the 1994 Olivos Pact (which many middle-class progressives viewed as a "sellout" to Menem). During the 1990s, a large number of Radical voters migrated to FREPASO, a new, media-based party that adopted a progressive, anti-corruption platform. In 1999, most of these voters backed the Alliance, which campaigned on a platform of clean government.[29] However, the Alliance failed to deliver on its promise. In August 2000, allegations surfaced that government officials had bribed a handful of senators in an effort to pass labor reform legislation. Vice President (and FREPASO leader) Carlos "Chacho" Álvarez called for a serious investigation, and when de la Rúa balked, he resigned, triggering the collapse of the Alliance. The Senate scandal shattered the Alliance's claim to represent a "new way" of doing politics and left much of the middle-class electorate alienated from all the major parties.[30] Neither the UCR nor FREPASO ever recovered.

The crisis was even deeper on the economic front. Although the Menem government stabilized the economy and restored growth during the 1990s, the neoliberal decade left several problematic legacies. One of them was growing social exclusion and inequality. The unemployment rate soared to a record 18.6 percent in 1995, creating a marginal underclass not seen since the 1940s. Moreover, the Menem government did virtually nothing to create a social welfare net for the "losers" under neoliberalism, particularly the poor and unemployed.[31] Out of these sectors emerged new forms of social protest, such as *piquetes* (street blockades), that would gain prominence during the 2001–2 crisis.[32] A second problematic legacy was the Convertibility Law, which effectively turned the Central Bank into a currency board. Because it was widely credited with having ended hyperinflation (and because many Argentines had accumulated debts in dollars and could ill afford a devaluation), convertibility enjoyed broad public support. Indeed, it became politically untouchable—a "third rail" of Argentine politics. However, by taking monetary and exchange rate policy out of the hands of policy makers, convertibility left them without the tools to respond to economic downturns.

The constraints imposed by convertibility became tragically clear under the Alliance. The de la Rúa government inherited a recession rooted in a series of external shocks, including the Asian financial crisis, a strengthening U.S. dollar, and Brazil's January 1999 devaluation. Yet because it was wedded to convertibility, it could not use either exchange rate policy (devaluation) or monetary policy (expansion of the money supply) to reactivate the economy. To make matters worse, Argentina's debt burden effectively ruled out Keynesian anti-cyclical spending. Due to a combination of declining tax revenue and increasing debt payments, the government faced a deepening fiscal crisis that accentuated its dependence on bonds. The fiscal crisis, however, eroded investors' confidence in Argentina's capacity to make debt payments, causing the interest rates on its bonds to soar. Shoring up investor confidence required evidence of fiscal solvency, which meant low budget deficits. The International Monetary Fund (IMF) similarly demanded greater fiscal austerity. Thus, rather than fighting the recession through deficit spending, as most industrialized countries do, de la Rúa was pushed to implement procyclical austerity measures that were likely to deepen it. Argentina fell into a vicious recessionary circle: recession eroded the tax base and exacerbated the fiscal crisis, which rattled bond markets and generated new pressures for austerity, which in turn only prolonged the recession. Consequently, the Alliance, which during the 1999 campaign had promised to put a "human face" on neoliberalism, delivered only a series of austerity packages and unending recession. By 2001, the recession was well into its fourth consecutive year.

The depth of public frustration was made manifest in the October 2001 midterm legislative elections. Not only did the Alliance lose badly, with its vote share falling nearly 50 percent relative to 1999, but the percentage of voters who cast blank and spoiled ballots—in protest against the entire political elite—soared to an unprecedented 22 percent. The blank and spoiled vote exceeded that of the Alliance, and in two of the country's largest districts, the city of Buenos Aires and Santa Fe, it exceeded that of *all* parties.

De la Rúa never recovered. Within weeks, mounting fear of debt default or currency devaluation triggered a financial crisis. In November, in an effort to stave off financial collapse, the government imposed strict limits on currency movements and bank deposit withdrawals. The so-called *corralito* (playpen) deprived the middle classes of their savings, starved the cash-dependent informal economy that sustained many of the poor, and brought economic activity to a standstill. The political consequences were devastating. On December 18 and 19, the country exploded in a wave of rioting and protest. Widespread looting erupted in Greater Buenos Aires, and in various parts of the country unemployed *piqueteros* (protesters) blocked major roads and highways. In the capital, citizens took to the streets banging pots and pans in protests known as *cacerolazos*. The government declared a state of siege and ordered police repression that resulted in more than two dozen deaths. The killings eroded the last vestiges of de la Rúa's authority. The protests intensified, and a day later the president resigned. With the vice presidency vacant, Congress selected Peronist Governor Adolfo Rodríguez Saá to serve as interim president. Rodríguez Saá immediately declared a default on Argentina's $132 million debt—the largest default in history. He did little else. Another round of rioting and internal conflict among the Peronists forced his resignation on December 30.

On January 1, 2002, when Congress selected PJ Senator Eduardo Duhalde as Argentina's third president in less than two weeks, Argentina stood on the brink of anarchy. What had begun as anti–de la Rúa protests had grown into a massive rebellion against the entire political elite. Protesters surrounded each branch of government, banging pots and pans and demanding the resignation of all members of Congress and the Supreme Court. The public mood was crystallized in an extraordinary slogan: *"Que se vayan todos"* (Throw everyone out). Citizens' anger reached such heights that politicians were repeatedly attacked—in some cases, physically—when they ventured out into public: on downtown streets, in restaurants, and even in their own neighborhoods. At the same time, the international community abandoned Duhalde. The U.S. government and the IMF, which had acted swiftly to help Mexico recover from its 1994–95 financial crisis, made no effort to rescue Argentina. Indeed, the IMF conditioned further assistance on deep spending cuts,[33] a prescription that was questionable in economic terms and unthinkable in political terms.[34]

One of Duhalde's first moves was to end convertibility, which, though inevitable, plunged the economy further into chaos. Within weeks, the value of the peso had deteriorated by more than 70 percent, triggering fears of hyperinflation. With the banking system paralyzed and no immediate prospect of international assistance, economic activity ground to a halt. Supply chains broke down; contracts were broken. As the currency evaporated, people resorted to barter. The economy, in recession since 1998, collapsed into the worst depression in Argentine history. Its GDP contracted by 11 percent in 2002. The unemployment rate reached 21 percent, and more than five million people fell into poverty, pushing the poverty rate—just 22 percent in 1994—to more than 50 percent.

The economic collapse pushed the political system to the breaking point. Social protest reached levels unseen anywhere in Latin America for more than a decade. Throughout the country, poor and unemployed people— *piqueteros*—blockaded major roads and highways, demanding food and jobs. The number of roadblocks, which had increased from 252 in 1999 to 1,383 in 2001, reached a stunning 2,336—or 194 per month—in 2002.[35] By 2002, *piquetero* groups had crystallized into several national organizations and threatened to displace organized labor as the most important channel for popular sector protest. Middle-class protest also proliferated. *Cacerolazos* were ubiquitous in Buenos Aires and other urban centers: protesters gathered daily in front of Congress, the presidential palace, the Supreme Court building, and other government buildings, demanding that government officials resign. According to one count, there were 859 *cacerolazos* in the city and province of Buenos Aires between December 2001 and March 2002.[36]

Early 2002 also saw the spontaneous emergence in Buenos Aires of "neighborhood assemblies" that mobilized large numbers of people in marathon exercises in participatory democracy.[37] Highly radicalized, the assemblies demanded the immediate resignation of all public officials, followed by the election of a constituent assembly to write a new constitution.

Consequences and Causes of the 2001 Crisis

The 2001 crisis had a devastating impact on Argentine political and economic institutions. Rules and procedures governing everything from the exchange rate, property rights, and central bank autonomy to judicial independence, presidential mandates, and the electoral cycle were circumvented, violated, or eliminated. Core economic institutions (e.g., convertibility, central bank independence) were changed or dismantled in a matter of hours—and virtually without legislative debate. Elections were rescheduled four times. For months there was little certainty as to when elections would be held, which offices would be up for election, or how candidates would be selected.

The crisis also weakened the party system. FREPASO disintegrated, and, as the 110-year-old UCR fell to the brink of extinction, aspiring Radical politicians abandoned the party. Elisa Carrió, a legislator who had emerged as a prominent anti-corruption crusader, formed the left-of-center Afirmación para una República Igualitaria (ARI; Affirmation for an Egalitarian Republic), and Ricardo López Murphy, a de la Rúa cabinet minister, launched the conservative Movimiento Federal Recrear (MFR; Federal Movement to Recreate). Although the PJ fared better, the intensity of public hostility toward the political elite raised the specter of party system collapse like those in Peru and Venezuela.

Yet as remarkable as what occurred in 2001–2 was what *did not* occur: despite the worst depression in Argentine history, widespread social protest, and an atmosphere of virtual anarchy, the country did not suffer an interruption of democratic rule. The military refused to repress protesters, made no attempt to change the government, and did not seek to exert behind-the-scenes influence over political events. No serious thought was given to a presidential coup of the sort that had been carried out by Alberto Fujimori in Peru, and civil liberties remained largely intact. Indeed, state abuse met with vigorous civic mobilization that punished the politicians responsible for them. Thus, the December 2001 repression triggered a massive civic mobilization that forced de la Rúa's resignation. Similarly, the civic opposition that followed the June 2002 police killing of two *piqueteros* so badly weakened President Duhalde that he was forced to cut short his interim presidency. Given the depth of the crisis and Argentina's history of regime instability, the survival of its core democratic institutions was a remarkable achievement.

Many accounts of the 2001–2 crisis locate its causes in the political arena. According to these analyses, the roots of the crisis lay in pervasive corruption and clientelism, runaway spending, and a cartel-like party system, or *partidocracia* (partyarchy).[38] Yet, compared to what has been seen in other middle-income countries in Latin America and elsewhere, the levels of corruption, clientelism, and fiscal profligacy in Argentina were moderate.[39] Moreover, the party system was far from closed. Minimal legal requirements for party formation and a low-threshold proportional representation system allowed a variety of parties to gain representation in Congress. Indeed, a wide range of partisan alternatives—including the center-left Partido Intransigente (Intransigent Party) and FREPASO, the center-right Unión del Centro Democrático (UCEDE; Union of the Democratic Center) and Acción por la República (Action for the Republic), and the nationalist MODIN—were available to voters during the 1980s and 1990s.

Two factors distinguished Argentina from other middle-income democracies in 2001. One was the depth of its economic crisis. Shackled by convertibility, successive Argentine governments were unable to dig the country out of the recession for four years. The crisis was exacerbated by the international community's refusal to help stave off financial collapse. Had international actors intervened in late 2001 or early 2002, allowing the government to salvage the financial system, the country's history might have played out quite differently. The second distinguishing factor was institutional weakness. As in past Argentine crises, political and economic institutions quickly unraveled in 2001–2. In the absence of stable rules of the game, time horizons narrowed, and politicians, business leaders, *piqueteros,* and even Supreme Court justices turned to praetorian tactics. The contrast with the situation in Uruguay is striking. Although Uruguay also suffered a severe economic downturn in 2001–2, political and social actors responded to the crisis by working through institutional channels rather than circumventing or derailing them, and there was no descent into near-praetorian chaos.

The Restoration of Democratic Governability

The Duhalde government restored democratic governability. After four years of recession, the economy began to recover in late 2002, and under the pragmatic stewardship of Minister of the Economy Roberto Lavagna it grew briskly in 2003. At the same time, Duhalde implemented some effective emergency social policies, including an innovative program to distribute low-cost medicine and a massive Heads of Households social insurance program that distributed monthly $50 subsidies to more than two million families. Duhalde's capacity to defuse popular protest was enhanced by the PJ's strength in working- and lower-class society. Peronist activist networks distributed food and subsidies in poor neighborhoods, worked to dissuade local residents from looting supermarkets, and occasionally "cleared the streets" of left-wing activists. The government also began to co-opt factions of the *piquetero* movement, in part by allowing *piquetero* groups to distribute Heads of Households subsidies. Though the Duhalde administration hardly provided a model of World Bank–style good governance, it proved effective at restoring democratic governability. Social protest declined, and, as the 2003 election approached, political activity was channeled back into the electoral arena.

The 2003 campaign began in a context of great uncertainty. The party system was in disarray. With FREPASO dead and the UCR barely registering in opinion polls, personalistic candidates such as Carrió and López Murphy ascended. Leftist and nationalist parties called on voters to cast blank ballots in an effort to "throw everyone out." Although the PJ remained strong in electoral terms, it was ridden with internal conflict between Menem, who sought to regain the presidency, and Duhalde. Seeking a candidate to defeat Menem, Duhalde turned to Néstor Kirchner, the little-known governor of Santa Cruz. Former interim president Rodríguez Saá also sought the presidency. The Peronists failed to agree on rules of the game for selecting a candidate, and the nomination process descended into a naked power struggle. (PJ statutes called for a primary, but Duhalde, fearing a Menem victory, derailed a vote.) To avoid a rupture, PJ leaders decided not to officially nominate a candidate but instead to allow Menem, Kirchner, and Rodríguez Saá to run outside the party.

Five candidates emerged as serious contenders in the 2003 presidential race. Three were Peronist: Rodríguez Saá, who campaigned as a populist outsider; Menem, who ran as a law-and-order conservative; and Kirchner, who adopted a progressive center-left platform. Two others were former Radicals: Carrió, who adopted a left-of-center, anti-corruption platform, and López Murphy, who combined an appeal for clean government with a conservative, market-oriented platform.

The election went remarkably smoothly. The results showed a marked departure from the anti-establishment protest politics of 2001–2. Turnout was a healthy 78 percent, and establishment candidates carried the day (Table 5.2). The top two finishers were established Peronists: Menem, a former president, won 24.4 percent of the vote, and Kirchner, the incumbent government's candidate, won 22.0 percent. No anti-establishment outsider received even 2 percent of the vote, and the blank and spoiled vote fell from 22 percent (in 2001) to just 2.5 percent. Because no candidate secured 45 percent of the vote, Menem and Kirchner qualified for a runoff election. In the second

**Table 5.2. Argentine Presidential Election Results,
2003 (First Round)**

Candidate/Party	Percentage of Valid Vote
Carlos Menem (Peronist)	24.4
Néstor Kirchner (Peronist)[a]	22.0
Ricardo López Murphy (MFR)	16.3
Elisa Carrió (ARI)	14.1
Adolfo Rodríguez Saá (Peronist)	14.1
Leopoldo Moreau (UCR)	2.3
Others	6.8

[a]Declared the winner after Carlos Menem declined to participate in
a runoff election.

round, the anti-Menemist vote coalesced behind Kirchner. Facing the prospect
of overwhelming defeat, Menem abandoned the race, handing the presidency to Kirchner.

The 2003 elections thus had an uneven impact on the party system. On
the one hand, the established non-Peronist parties were virtually wiped out.
FREPASO disappeared, and UCR—whose candidate, Leopoldo Moreau,
won just 2.3 percent of the vote—suffered unprecedented decline. On the
other hand, Peronism proved remarkably resilient. Peronist presidential candidates won a combined 60.5 percent of the vote, and in legislative elections
later that year, the PJ captured a majority of both houses of Congress. The
PJ's persistent strength thus prevented a full-scale meltdown of the party system. In Peru and Venezuela, the success of outsider candidates was rooted in
the collapse of established populist parties, which left a large number of low-
income voters available for "neopopulist" appeals.[40] In Argentina, by contrast, the established populist party survived. Rather than collapsing in the
wake of the *que se vayan todos* protests, the PJ scored an impressive victory.
The anti-establishment vote was largely confined to the (predominantly
middle-class) non-Peronist electorate, which limited the space for neopopulist outsiders.

The Kirchner Presidency

Néstor Kirchner's first term was marked by two striking developments.
The first was a reconcentration of executive power. Kirchner took office in a
weak position: he had won only 22 percent of the vote in the 2003 election
and was indebted to former president Duhalde and his powerful Buenos
Aires machine for his victory. It was widely believed that Duhalde would

wield considerable power behind the scenes. Yet Kirchner turned out to be "the most centralizing president in Argentina's modern democratic history."[41] The new president moved quickly to establish control over the PJ, using federal levers of power—such as the allocation of discretionary funds to the provinces—to ensure the allegiance of Peronist governors. Kirchner aggressively challenged and defeated Peronists who resisted his leadership, including Duhalde, who, as boss of the PJ's Buenos Aires machine, remained Peronism's second most influential political figure.[42] In the 2005 midterm elections, Kirchner challenged the Duhalde machine by sponsoring an alternative slate of candidates—headed by his wife, Cristina, a senator—for Congress in Buenos Aires Province. Most local bosses defected to Kirchner, and the Kirchner list defeated the official PJ slate (headed by Duhalde's wife, Hilda) by a margin of more than two to one. The victory gave Kirchner a level of uncontested control over Peronism exceeded only by Perón himself.

Kirchner's concentration of power went beyond Peronism, however. Like Carlos Menem in the early 1990s, President Kirchner governed in a highly centralized fashion, often at the expense of institutions of horizontal accountability. During his first two years in office, he issued 140 NUDs, compared to 73 issued by de la Rúa and 128 by Menem.[43] Congress played a role in hollowing out its own powers, extending annually an Economic Emergency Law that delegated vast budgetary and regulatory powers to the executive and passing a law in 2006 that granted the president vast discretionary power to modify budgets after their approval. Thus, despite the economic recovery, Kirchner retained emergency powers that allowed him to revise spending priorities and undertake major policy initiatives without legislative approval. Kirchner also packed the Supreme Court. Soon after taking office, the new president pushed his allies in Congress to carry out impeachment proceedings against the Menemist court. Within weeks, eight justices—five Menem appointees plus three Alfonsín appointees—faced a minimum of 50 charges each.[44] Over the next two and a half years, two justices (Eduardo Moliné and Antonio Boggiano) were impeached, three others (Guillermo López, Julio Nazareno, and Adolfo Vásquez) resigned from the court in the face of pending impeachment, and a sixth (Augusto Belluscio, who also faced charges) resigned, invoking his proximity to the court's mandatory retirement age. The purge allowed Kirchner to remake the court. Unlike Menem, Kirchner instituted new procedures to enhance the transparency of the Supreme Court nomination process, and the four justices he nominated—Carmen Argibay, Elena Highton, Ricardo Lorenzetti, and Raúl Zaffaroni—were distinguished jurists with reputations for independence. However, the scope of Kirchner's intervention—a purge of two-thirds of the Supreme Court in less than two years—was striking even in Argentina.

The second major development under Kirchner was a significant shift to the left. Although the Kirchner government's fiscal and (to a lesser extent) monetary policies were fairly conservative (it ran large budget surpluses each year), in other areas it abandoned the market orthodoxy that had been dominant since 1989. State intervention increased markedly. For example, despite strong pressure from the IMF and foreign capital investors, Kirchner maintained the freeze on public utility rates imposed in January 2002. This brought him into conflict with power and water companies, and when Suez, the French company that provided water and sewage services in Buenos Aires, cut back its investment, the government rescinded its contract and formed a state-owned company to take over the water service.[45] Although Kirchner did not reverse the large-scale privatization of the 1990s, a few other privatized entities—including the post office and a major railroad line—were renationalized, and the state launched a new airline, an energy company, and even a satellite manufacturer. Although Kirchner maintained the export-oriented model established during the 1990s, he taxed—and at times restricted—exports to a degree not seen since the 1980s.[46] Kirchner also responded to rising inflation—which reached 12 percent in 2005—in a heterodox manner. Whereas mainstream economists attributed rising prices to wage gains and increased public spending, Kirchner blamed large companies, attacking them for price speculation. In 2005, he called for a boycott of Royal Dutch / Shell stations after that company raised gasoline prices (soon afterward, pro-Kirchner *piqueteros* seized 32 gas stations in Buenos Aires).[47] Kirchner also attacked major supermarket owners for raising food prices and then bullied them into negotiating a price freeze on several hundred food products.[48] The result was extensive price controls for the first time in nearly two decades.

Although the Kirchner government did not invest heavily in social policy, it was far more supportive of labor, pensioner, *piquetero*, and other redistributive demands than its predecessors had been.[49] Kirchner was the first Argentine president in more than a decade to actively push wages upward, both by promoting corporatist wage bargaining and by increasing the minimum wage.[50] Wages increased by about 20 percent in both 2005 and 2006, nearly doubling the rate of inflation.[51] In addition, Kirchner raised the minimum pension rate eight times during his first three years in office, more than doubling its 2003 rate.[52]

The Kirchner government also moved in a nationalist direction. For example, it adopted a hard-line position in debt renegotiations in the aftermath of the 2001 default. Argentina's offer of a debt swap worth about 30 percent of the defaulted debt—the largest debt "haircut" in history—was strongly opposed by the IMF, but the government held firm and eventually won out.[53] Kirchner maintained a hard line in negotiations with the IMF (refusing, for example, to meet IMF demands for a primary fiscal surplus of 4 percent of GDP, despite the fact that the Lula government in Brazil had committed to a similar surplus), and in December 2005 Argentina dipped into its foreign reserves to pay off its entire $9.8 billion debt to the IMF. On the diplomatic front, Kirchner abandoned the Menem government's policy of "carnal relations" with the United States, joining Brazil and Venezuela in their objections to the U.S.-inspired Free Trade Area of the Americas, rejecting U.S. demands of immunity for its military personnel, and angering U.S. officials by maintaining good relations with Hugo Chávez's Venezuela.

Finally, on the human rights front, Kirchner abandoned the civil-military accommodation in place since the Alfonsín presidency and reversed many of the concessions made to the military over the previous 16 years. He pushed Congress to declare null and void two Alfonsín-era laws, the Final Point and Due Obedience Laws, which had limited the scope of human rights trials.[54] In June 2005, the Supreme Court upheld Congress's declaration, and by early 2006 more than 500 former military and police officers had been brought up on charges.[55] Kirchner also pushed through legislation declaring March 24 (the day of the 1976 military coup) a national holiday, transformed the Naval Mechanics School (a notorious torture site during the Dirty War) into a human rights museum, and appointed a former leftist militant, Nilda Garré, defense minister.

Kirchner's shift to the left had a polarizing effect. Although business profits soared in the context of a rapidly growing economy, rural producers' organizations chafed under export taxes and restrictions on beef exports. In December 2006, for example, they carried out a massive nine-day farm strike to protest these measures. At the same time, Kirchner's public attacks on the military and his vigorous push to reopen human rights trials generated considerable animosity within the armed forces. For the first time in years, retired military officers and families of military personnel began to organize and protest in defense of the armed forces. More ominously, in late 2006 two witnesses in the new human rights trials, Luis Gerez and Jorge Julio López, were apparently abducted. (Gerez was soon released, but López remained missing as of January 2008.)

Kirchner's Political Success

Kirchner's first term was remarkably successful. In the economic realm, soaring world prices for soy, beef, and other commodity exports, together with a competitive exchange rate, triggered an export-led boom. Argentina experienced "Chinese" growth rates that averaged nearly 9 percent a year between 2003 and 2006 (Table 5.3). Fiscal revenue soared to record levels,

Table 5.3. Basic Argentine Social and Economic Indicators, 2000–2006 (percentages)

	GDP Growth	Average Inflation	Unemployment	Poverty
2000	−0.8	−0.9	14.7	33.4
2001	−4.4	4.0	18.3	35.9
2002	−10.9	26.0	17.8	53.0
2003	8.8	13.4	15.5	54.7
2004	9.0	6.1	14.8	44.3
2005	9.2	12.3	12.1	38.5
2006	8.5	13.4	10.4	29.2

Sources: Instituto Nacional de Estadística y Censos (National Statistics and Censuses Institute); World Bank.

which allowed the government to increase social spending while maintaining a steady fiscal surplus. Social indicators slowly but steadily improved. From a high of 21 percent in 2002, the unemployment rate fell to just over 10 percent in 2006, while the poverty rate fell from nearly 55 percent in 2003 to just over 31 percent in 2006.

Kirchner also consolidated the fragile governability achieved by Duhalde. *Cacerolazos* and other forms of middle-class protest diminished sharply, and although the *piquetero* movement remained active, the government took steps to co-opt and demobilize it. Building on the practice established under Duhalde, it allowed *piquetero* groups to distribute Heads of Household subsidies to as many as 200,000 people.[56] It also built political alliances with several *piquetero* groups. Leaders of four *piquetero* groups—the Federación de Tierra y Vivienda (Land and Housing Federation), the Frente Transversal, Nacional y Popular (Transversal National and Popular Front), Movimiento Barrio de Pie (Neighborhoods on their Feet), and the Movimiento de Trabajadores Desocupados–Evita (Movement of Unemployed Workers–Evita) —gained positions in government.[57] These groups moderated considerably. Although several *piquetero* groups remained in militant opposition, overall *piquetero* mobilization was considerably lower than it had been in 2002.

Kirchner enjoyed considerable political success. Due in large part to the booming economy, public support for Kirchner soared, hovering around 70 percent throughout his first term. Kirchner's popularity helped his allies win decisively in the 2005 legislative elections. Kirchner's Front for Victory—a coalition of Peronists and progressive non-Peronists—won the election with 39 percent of the vote, while other Peronist lists won an additional 10 percent. Although important local victories were scored by opposition parties—

the Socialist Party in Santa Fe, the center-right Propuesta Republicana (PRO; Republican Proposal) in the capital—the Peronists dominated at the national level. Indeed, no opposition party won even 10 percent of the national vote.[58] The governing party retained control of the Senate and won a working majority in the Chamber of Deputies. After the election, Kirchner's (mostly Peronist) allies held a plurality of between 110 and 118 (out of 257) of the seats, and non-Kirchnerist Peronists held an additional 30 seats. The opposition was left weakened and fragmented: the UCR retained 39 seats, ARI retained 14 seats, and PRO's representation grew to 23 seats.

Kirchner consolidated power after the 2005 election. He named a more leftist and pure Kirchnerist cabinet, sacking Minister of the Economy Roberto Lavagna, the only cabinet member with an independent base of support. He also further weakened the opposition through co-optation. Within months, several members of the dissident Federal Peronism legislative bloc had joined the pro-government camp. In addition, five of six UCR governors maintained a pro-Kirchner profile, backing many of the president's legislative initiatives and positioning themselves to support his reelection.

Although Kirchner would have been easily reelected in 2007, he ceded the PJ's presidential candidacy to his wife, Senator Cristina Fernández de Kirchner (thereby permitting himself to run again in 2011). Running as an incumbent and facing a weak and fragmented opposition, Fernández won easily, capturing 45 percent of the vote, compared to 23 percent for Elisa Carrió and 17 percent for former minister of the economy Lavagna, who was backed by the UCR. The PJ and allies captured large majorities in both legislative chambers and more than three quarters of Argentina's 23 governorships. Peronism thus emerged from the 2007 election in a dominant position. Opposition forces were split into at least three blocs (the UCR, the ARI-led Civic Coalition, and the center-right PRO), none of which posed a serious national-level challenge. Indeed, future challenges seemed more likely to come from within the PJ.

Kirchner and Democracy

The Kirchner presidency had both positive and negative effects on Argentina's democratic institutions. On the positive side, Kirchner reestablished governability and reinvigorated public institutions such as the Supreme Court, whose credibility had eroded to dangerously low levels. For example, Kirchner's impeachment of Menem's "automatic majority," creation of procedures to ensure greater public accountability in the judicial nomination process, and nomination of respected independent jurists enhanced the court's legitimacy.

More generally, Kirchner restored a measure of public trust in government. The 2001–2 crisis had triggered a "massive withdrawal of public trust" in the political elite.[59] According to the annual Latinobarómetro survey, the percentage of Argentines expressing confidence in the country's political parties fell from 29 percent in 1997 to a stunning 4 percent—the lowest in Latin America—in 2002.[60] Even more disturbing, the percentage of Argentines who agreed with the statement "Democracy is always the best form of government" declined from 76 percent in 1995 to 62 percent in 2002.[61] Although this public disaffection was partly a response to perceptions of unchecked corruption, it was also rooted in a generalized perception that governments were unresponsive to public demands.[62] For example, the halting (and later reversal) of legal action against military officials implicated in human rights violations was perceived to be rooted in military pressure, not societal demands. And policy making under Menem (whose economic minister declared that the economy was on "autopilot") and de la Rúa (who promised social justice but delivered only austerity) convinced many Argentines that the desires of international creditors and bond markets outweighed their votes in shaping social and economic policy. The perception of a disconnect between public opinion and public policy seriously eroded citizens' trust in government.

Kirchner reversed this pattern. Whereas de la Rúa had seemed constrained to the point of paralysis, Kirchner dedicated himself to expanding the government's (real or perceived) room for maneuver. Thus, he launched high-profile battles against the very entities that had been seen to constrain governments since the 1980s: the military, the IMF, bondholders, and foreign and domestic capitalists. Although the economic merits of some of Kirchner's policy initiatives (e.g., restricting beef exports, paying off the IMF debt) were open to question, the *political* merits were clear. The fact that most Argentines embraced these policies is not insignificant. Responsiveness to public opinion matters in a democracy. Although policy making that is overly oriented toward public opinion—what international observers are quick to deride as "populism"—may be destructive, the 2001–2 crisis showed that policy making that is overly divorced from public opinion may be at least as destructive. Thus, although the longer-term economic consequences of the Kirchner government's left turn remain uncertain in 2008, the medium-term political consequences were clear and important: Argentines perceived their government as having responded to public demands, and, consequently, their support for Kirchner, faith in the system, and optimism about the future all increased considerably.

The Kirchner presidency also had important negative effects on democratic institutions. Like Menem during the early 1990s, Kirchner concentrated power at the expense of institutions of horizontal accountability, and he frequently circumvented, manipulated, or changed the rules of the game in pursuit of this objective. In the area of executive-legislative relations, for example, Kirchner retained "emergency powers" delegated during the 2001 crisis to rewrite budgets and make key economic decisions without congressional approval. In 2006, Congress made these presidential "superpowers" permanent, passing legislation that granted the executive vast discretionary power to modify budgetary allocations. (As the Buenos Aires newspaper *Clarín* put it, the new law allowed the executive to "do practically anything."[63])

Similar patterns were seen in judicial politics. Although Kirchner's purge of the Supreme Court was both technically legal and widely popular, it reinforced the pattern, in existence since the 1940s, of incoming presidents' remaking the court to their liking.[64] Kirchner further assaulted judicial independence in 2006 when—despite strong opposition from leading legal, civic, and human rights organizations—the court he had remade pushed through Congress a reform that enhanced executive control over the Magistrates Council, a body created by the 1994 Constitution to oversee the appointment and removal of federal judges.[65] The reform reduced the size of the Council from 20 to 13 but left the executive with five seats, which would allow it to block a quorum.

Finally, Kirchner at times displayed intolerance for criticism and opposition. Although the government did not seriously violate civil liberties (and in some areas, such as the nonrepression of protest, it demonstrated a marked improvement over its predecessors), it was reprimanded by the Argentina Press Association and the Inter-American Press Association for its harsh verbal attacks on media critics, its use of government advertising to punish media outlets, and in one case, its use of pressure to cancel the radio program of journalist José Eliaschev.[66] Also troubling was the government's response to the anti-crime movement led by Juan Carlos Blumberg, whose son, Axel, was kidnapped and killed in 2004. When in August 2006 a Blumberg-led protest became a major focal point for right-wing opposition, the government organized a "countermarch"—headed by pro-Kirchner *piquetero* leader Luis D'Elia—that was criticized as undemocratic even by its allies.[67]

Kirchner's concentration of power aroused fear among the opposition that Argentina was moving in an autocratic direction. Opposition leaders described Kirchner's Argentina as ruled by "tyranny,"[68] and even "on the brink of fascism."[69] Some critics worried that Kirchner and his wife, Cristina, would alternate in office to allow for a three- or four-term Kirchner family presidency. These fears were reinforced by the PJ's growing electoral dominance, which led some observers to warn of a "Mexicanization" of Argentine politics.[70]

Such an outcome is unlikely. Argentina is not as vulnerable to democratic decay as Bolivia, Ecuador, Peru, or Venezuela. Not only are its core democratic institutions stronger, but the civic and societal "antibodies" that have checked executive abuse since 1983 remain in place. Indeed, new forms of civic opposition—such as the anti-crime movement—continue to emerge, and serious violations of democratic procedure continue to bring political costs. Two examples from 2006 are worth noting. First, surveys found that 96 percent of citizens were opposed to the government's "countermarch" against the August 2006 anti-crime rally, leading political analysts to characterize it as one of the most serious blunders of the Kirchner presidency.[71] Second, when Kirchner backed an initiative by Misiones Governor Carlos Rovira to reform the provincial constitution to permit unlimited reelection (a move that many in the opposition viewed as potentially having national-level implications), civic and opposition forces, led by the Catholic Church, organized a broad opposition campaign and defeated the PJ in the Constituent Assembly election. The defeat had an immediate and powerful impact at the national level: governors in Buenos Aires and Jujuy abandoned their reelection projects, and any sort of national initiative became unthinkable.

Yet, even if an autocratic turn is unlikely, Kirchner's concentration of power is problematic. In the absence of congressional oversight or credible challenges from within or outside Peronism, Kirchner and his inner circle answered to virtually no one during his first term. Whenever the level of executive accountability is low, the risk of abuse and serious mistakes will be high.[72] Moreover, even if the opposition's fears are exaggerated, their mere existence is troubling. Such fears are a legacy of widespread rule breaking in the past (which generates expectations of future rule breaking), but they also make manifest the increased polarization of Argentine politics.

Conclusion: Issues and Prospects for the Future

The performance of Argentine democracy is not easy to evaluate. Like those of Chile, Uruguay, and, to a lesser extent, Brazil and Mexico, Argentina's core democratic institutions are solid. Indeed, in 1989 and 2001–2 the regime survived crises of the sort that have historically destroyed all but the most established democracies of the world. Yet, due to the persistent weakness of its political and economic institutions, Argentina remains vulnerable to crises that have rarely been seen in the aforementioned democracies. This final section examines two areas that will be critical in the near future.

The Future of the Party System

In this chapter I have argued that relatively strong parties were critical to democratic governance in post-1983 Argentina. After 1999, however, the party system suffered a partial collapse. The collapse was partial because—

contrary to many expectations—the PJ remained intact. As in the past, vast ideological differences and severe internal conflict did not produce permanent rupture within Peronism. There are several reasons for this. First, the PJ's loose organizational structure permits it to serve as a broad tent. Peronism's fluid boundaries, lax membership rules, and lack of internal disciplinary mechanisms allow dissident factions to operate inside it with ease, and even to leave the party for an election or two and then return.[73] Second, because the PJ is a patronage-based party with a successful label, Peronists have powerful incentives to back winners. As patronage seekers, Peronists must remain on good terms with PJ officeholders. These incentives are reinforced by the electoral value of the PJ label. Because factions that have permanently abandoned the PJ have consistently failed to win votes, defectors have great difficulty convincing fellow Peronists to join them. Rather than defection, then, Peronists routinely choose conversion. Thus, just as Menem's shift to the right induced many nationalist and left-of-center Peronists to embrace neoliberalism, Kirchner's shift to the left led scores of erstwhile neoliberals to (re)embrace statist and nationalist positions.

Yet, though the PJ remained intact after 1999, the rest of the party system collapsed. The UCR, which had been the only national-level democratic alternative to Peronism since the 1940s, was virtually destroyed by the successive failures of the Alfonsín and de la Rúa governments. The Radicals finished sixth in the 2003 presidential race, with just 2.3 percent of the vote.[74] After 2005, five of the UCR's six governors and more than a third of its 476 mayors broke with the party leadership and effectively aligned with Kirchner, backing Cristina Kirchner's presidential bid in 2007. After the 2007 election, the Radicals' representation in Congress (30 of 257 seats) fell to a historic low. Although the UCR retains a national infrastructure of local leaders and activist networks, it has not seriously contended for the presidency since 1999, leaving the party's status as a national-level electoral force very much in doubt.

The prospects for the emergence of stable new parties appear dim. Since the rise of Juan Perón in the 1940s, only Peronism and the UCR have built national organizations, mobilized large memberships, and established stable identities in the electorate. Because the spread of mass media technologies has reduced politicians' incentives to invest in party organization, party building has proven extremely difficult in the contemporary period. Indeed, all of the nationally oriented parties that emerged during the post-1983 period —including the center-left Intransigent Party and FREPASO, the center-right UCEDE and Acción por la República, and the nationalist MODIN— were loosely organized, Buenos Aires–based parties that failed to penetrate the national territory. None survived for much more than a decade. The two major parties that emerged in 2003, ARI and the MFR, have fared little better, giving rise to new organizations, such as the center-right PRO, led by businessman Mauricio Macri. Consequently, the party system has become a fragmented universe of personalistic vehicles, provincial parties, and short-lived (media-based, Buenos Aires–centered) programmatic parties. An unprecedented 24 presidential tickets competed in the 2003 election. In 2004, 696 parties were legally registered (41 at the national level), and 40 different blocs existed in Congress.[75] Outside of the PJ and the UCR, none of these parties possessed a national structure or even minimal roots in society.

Such fragmentation may threaten democratic governance in several ways. First, it exacerbates Peronism's political dominance. In the 2003 presidential election, the top two finishers were *both* Peronist, and in 2005, no party other than the Peronists' won as much as 10 percent of the national vote. Cristina Kirchner was never seriously challenged in the 2007 presidential election. Because much of Argentina's large middle class leans anti-Peronist (which makes the PJ beatable whenever opposition forces unite or a single party or candidate emerges as a focal point), long-term Peronist hegemony is unlikely. The real problem is governing. As Calvo and Murillo have argued, opposition parties' lack of strength in the legislature, in the provinces, and in society make governing extremely difficult.[76] These weaknesses have been greatly accentuated since 2001, and there is little sign of reversal. Thus, non-Peronist candidates may capture the presidency, but they are increasingly unlikely to win control of the legislature or capture more than a handful of governorships. Without a real grassroots presence, they remain vulnerable to the kind of governability crises that destroyed the Alfonsín and de la Rúa presidencies.

Finally, party system failure may exacerbate crises of political representation, with important consequences for democracy. Much of the non-Peronist electorate was left without effective partisan representation in the wake of the Alliance's failure, which encouraged anti-systematic behavior. It was largely this sector that cast blank and spoiled ballots in October 2001 and joined the *que se vayan todos* protests in 2001 and 2002.[77] Without a party, these voters may turn to political outsiders. Even worse, the erosion of the party system could bring a return to the problems of sociopolitical representation that plagued Argentine democracy between 1930 and 1976.[78] If key social and economic actors lack effective representation in the party system, they will be more likely to pursue their goals outside the electoral arena.

The Question of Institutional Strength

A second issue has to do with institutional strength. This chapter has argued that although Argentina's core democratic institutions are strong, in numerous other areas rules and procedures are weakly enforced and/or repeatedly changed. Widespread institutional weakness helps explain why Argentina remains more prone to political and economic meltdown than other middle-income democracies, such as Brazil, Chile, Mexico, and Uruguay. It may also explain the growing gap between Argentina and these countries in the development of effective legislative and judicial branches. The Argentine Congress has few experienced leaders, virtually no professional staff, and little technical expertise, while its committee system and oversight bodies are badly underdeveloped.[79] Legislative ineffectiveness is rooted in several factors, including the repeated closure of Congress by the military between 1930 and 1976.[80] Yet whereas the Brazilian, Chilean, and Mexican legislatures steadily grew stronger during the 1990s and 2000s, Argentina's did not. Since 1989, core legislative functions have repeatedly been delegated away via "emergency laws" that granted budgetary and regulatory "superpowers" to the executive. Moreover, few politicians invested seriously in legislative careers: the average legislative career in Argentina is 2.9 years, compared to 5.5 years in Brazil, 8 years in Chile, and 9 years in Uruguay.[81] "Amateur" legislators are less likely to invest in specialization, serious committee work, or building effective institutions of legislative oversight.[82] Indeed, the Argentine Congress is deficient in all of these areas. On the Congressional Capability Index of Stein et al., which measures technical expertise, committee strength, and the professionalization of legislators, Argentina scores "low" (along with Guatemala, Honduras, and Peru), whereas Brazil, Chile, and Uruguay rank "high" and Mexico ranks "medium."[83]

A similar story can be told about the judiciary. On the World Economic Forum's 2004 index of judicial independence, Argentina ranked 13th out of 18 Latin American countries—below Ecuador, Guatemala, Honduras, and Peru.[84] A major source of executive dominance over the judiciary is the weakness of judicial tenure security.[85] Although lifetime tenure security for Supreme Court justices has been enshrined in the Constitution since 1853, this law has been violated repeatedly since the 1940s.[86] This did not change with democratization. Indeed, three of the four presidents elected since 1983 (Alfonsín, Menem, and Kirchner) successfully pressed for the removal of sitting justices, and two of them (Menem and Kirchner) reshuffled the court's membership in their favor. Due to repeated court packing, the average tenure of Argentine Supreme Court justices between 1960 and 1995 was barely four years, which is less than half the corresponding figure in Brazil and less than a third that in Chile.[87]

Crisis and institutional weakness tend to be mutually reinforcing. Institutional weakness increases the likelihood of political and economic crisis, which in turn triggers efforts to circumvent or change the rules. For example, the 2001–2 crisis gave rise to widespread demands that the institutional slate (again) be wiped clean: there were calls for immediate elections (existing mandates notwithstanding), a purge of the Supreme Court, a new constitution, and an overhaul of the electoral system. The crisis clearly facilitated Kirchner's encroachment on legislative and judicial authority. Although Kirchner's actions helped restore credibility to many public institutions, they nevertheless reinforced the dominant pattern since 1930: when crises hit Argentina, the players and the rules are changed. The Supreme Court provides a clear example of the type of dilemma that arises. During the 2001–2 crisis, many Argentines complained about the absence of judicial independence *and* demanded a purge of the court. Kirchner's purge produced a better court and one considered more legitimate by the public, but it came at the cost of another blow to the institution of judicial tenure security, which reinforced existing patterns of judicial weakness.

Building stable institutions is difficult. It often requires that institutions weather some major storms. It also requires that political and economic actors adhere to them even when they expect the rules to yield short-term inefficiencies or losses. Through 2007, many political and economic institutions in Argentina were not sufficiently robust to weather either crises or changes of government. As long as this pattern persists, shortsighted, noncooperative, and socially irresponsible behavior will be the rule.

In years to come, favorable structural conditions, such as high levels of wealth and education and a strong civil society, will likely contribute to the survival of Argentina's core democratic institutions. However, these conditions are insufficient to ensure high-quality democracy. For democracy to function well over the long haul, politicians must do more than get the institutions right. Rather, they must undertake the more difficult—and often less politically rewarding—task of sustaining and strengthening those institutions. President Kirchner's extraordinary popularity created a rare opportunity to invest in institution building. By doing so, Kirchner could have potentially avoided the fate that had befallen nearly all of his predecessors: seeing initial successes wiped away by subsequent crises and policy overhauls. For the most part, however, Kirchner took the easier road of building power at the expense of institutions. Argentina has been down this road before. Good times notwithstanding, the specter of (yet another) crisis remains.

6

Bolivia

Evo Morales and Democracy

Eduardo A. Gamarra

The January 2006 inauguration of President Evo Morales turned the attention of the world on Bolivia. No president in the history of Bolivia has received as much attention from other heads of state, the world press, nongovernmental organizations (NGOs), and others. Morales, a former migrant laborer in Argentina, band member, soccer player, and above all, leader of six coca growers' unions, entered the old Palacio Quemado bearing promises to end social exclusion in Bolivia.[1]

The coming to power of Evo Morales and his Movimiento al Socialismo (MAS; Movement toward Socialism) represented a major watershed in a quarter century of democratic rule. Some observers have equated Morales's assumption of power to the historic transition that ended apartheid in South Africa. Although the reality is much less dramatic, in electing Morales Bolivia did elect its first-ever indigenous president, who had run on a promise of carrying out a "democratic revolution." Indeed, since January 2006, Bolivian democracy has changed; a major realignment of political actors has occurred, to the point that an elite that had governed the country since the 1950s has been replaced by a new and more heterogeneous set of actors.[2] Whether these changes have deepened democracy in Bolivia remains an unanswered question.

This chapter evaluates the state of Bolivian democracy by focusing on the first 16 months of the Morales administration. It offers an analysis of the coming to power of Evo Morales, examining the historical and structural factors that contributed to his election. Then the chapter analyzes the MAS and the electoral promises that led to its dramatic victory in the December 18, 2005, national elections.

The December 2005 Elections

Evo Morales's complex and heterogeneous political organization, registered in the National Electoral Court as the Movimiento al Socialismo, is a vehicle through which a 15-year-long struggle to achieve political power was completed. The MAS is not a party based on a specific ideological doctrine. It includes Marxist militants among its ranks, but it is not a Marxist party. Marxist militants are newcomers to the party; the party's name is circumstantial, not doctrinal. The coca growers' unions that created the party defined it as and wanted to name it the Instrumento Político por la Soberanía del Pueblo (Political Instrument for the People's Sovereignty) but were unable to register it as such in the National Electoral Court. Coincidentally, in 1996 David Añez Pedraza, a former right-wing *"falangista,"* transferred the legal name of his own party, which he had called Movimiento al Socialismo, to Evo Morales. The MAS was a faction of the traditional Falange Socialista Boliviana (Bolivian Socialist Falange) and had not participated in any election. The party obtained legal recognition before the current, stricter electoral law was approved.

It is probably more accurate to compare the MAS with the Movimiento Nacionalista Revolucionario (MNR; Nationalist Revolutionary Movement) of the 1950s; the contemporary version of *movimientismo* represents a continuum of certain dynamics of Bolivian political culture. These include corporatist notions of political representation; the role of the state in correcting social, political, and economic inequality; and a state-centered development strategy.[3] Again, the similarities of these dynamics to those of the current moment are important, because each of these basic ideas has found a profound echo in the movement that brought Evo Morales to power. While there is much new in Bolivia in 2005, the basic conceptual frame that guides the MAS is firmly rooted in the country's political history.

One of the more significant aspects of Bolivian *movimientismo* is the push toward single-party rule. Throughout the revolutionary period, the MNR attempted to eliminate all other political contenders through both legal and de facto means. In contemporary Bolivia, the MAS experiences the same urge, encouraged less by developments in Venezuela under Hugo Chávez than by a homegrown and historic corporatist need to control the opposition and limit its size.

On December 18, 2005, the MAS won 53.7 percent of the vote, soundly defeating all traditional political actors. It was also the first time since the transition to democracy in 1982 that the president of Bolivia would not be elected by the National Congress.[4] Although Morales won by a landslide and the MAS won the Chamber of Deputies, the party did not win a majority in the Senate.[5]

The December 2005 election was also the first in which prefects (or governors) were popularly elected. Until then they had been appointed by the president and had served at the will and whim of the chief executive. Appointed prefects allowed presidents to impose central authority in Bolivia's nine departments, although, with some exceptions, their power was mainly ceremonial. The change that allowed the election of prefects was the result of a broad process of social mobilization organized mainly by regional civic committees and other local groups that had long demanded some sort of decentralization of political power. The most powerful of these were the myriad groups in Santa Cruz, including the Comité Cívico Pro Santa Cruz (Pro Santa Cruz Civic Committee), the Cámara de Industria y Comercio (Chamber of Industry and Commerce), and the Cámara Agropecuaria del Oriente (Eastern Chamber of Agriculture). These groups led a march in January 2005 that brought together half a million Santa Cruz residents demanding the convocation of a national referendum on regional autonomy. The referendum was finally held on July 2, 2006, alongside the election of a constituent assembly, which will be analyzed later.

The significance of the election of prefects was that although Morales and the MAS achieved a landslide victory for the presidency, their candidates for prefect won in only three of Bolivia's nine departments (Chuquisaca, Oruro, and Potosí). The MAS candidates failed to win in Cochabamba and La Paz, where the party's base is located. The message from the electorate was a bit less clear than most have assumed. They wanted to rid the system of traditional parties and, at the same time, to limit the power of the new president and his party. As we shall see, the prefects—especially in the opposition departments of Beni, Pando, Santa Cruz, and Tarija, together called the "half moon" because of their geographical shape—have become the principal source of opposition to the president.

To understand the logic of political competition in Bolivia since the MAS has come to power, it is important to understand the driving logic of the Morales administration. The MAS presented an electoral platform that encompassed a broad array of promises. On the ideological front, it framed an "anti-imperialist and anti-neoliberal" discourse that included several dimensions. It proposed first and foremost a nationalist and class-based identity that promised the inclusion of those who had historically been excluded from power. The appeal to "indigenism," which is now the central element of the party's rhetoric, was incorporated late in the development of the MAS and, paradoxically, as a result of the incorporation of mestizo ideologues of "indigenism."

The principal expositor of this thinking is Vice President Álvaro García Linera, a middle-class Mexico-educated mathematician and self-described Marxist sociologist. García Linera spent the late 1980s and the early 1990s as a member of the Ejército Guerrillero Túpac Katari (EGTK; Túpac Katari Guerrilla Army), which blew up electrical towers, stole the payroll of the Universidad Mayor de San Simón in Cochabamba, and committed other such acts. He was jailed in 1972 along with Felipe Quispe, the EGTK's leader, and was released in 1997.[6]

The second element of the MAS's party platform called for the elimination of the practices of the "traditional parties" that had governed the country for the two previous decades.[7] These parties—including the MNR, Acción Democrática Nacionalista (ADN; Nationalist Democratic Action), Movimiento de Izquierda Revolucionaria (MIR; Revolutionary Left Movement), Nueva Fuerza Republicana (New Republican Force), and others that belonged to the multiple ruling coalitions that had governed Bolivia between 1985 and 2005 under a "pacted democracy"(*democrácia pactada*)—had suffered an enormous erosion of their appeal. In 2005, the popular perception of these parties and their leaders was that they were, at a minimum, corrupt and that the neoliberal policies that they had imposed on the country after 1985 had not only impoverished the country but also deepened inequality in an already unequal society. The traditional parties were also perceived as having been responsible for selling off the country's natural resources to the lowest bidders through privatization programs dubbed capitalization.

One of the most important charges against the traditional political parties had to do with the very nature of pacted democracy. To ensure governability, every ruling coalition enacted legislation and provided key support to the executive branch. The pacts by which they did so were fundamental to the enactment of so-called neoliberal measures and at the same time allowed for the imposition of states of siege to control labor and social unrest. Although these governing pacts were not unlike those found in any multiparty presidential or parliamentary system, as the democratization experience progressed, the nature of the pacts dramatically changed toward pure and simple clientelism. These patrimonial dynamics were not new in Bolivia and are firmly rooted in the country's political culture.[8]

A survey of the political pacts that ruled Bolivia between 1985 and 2003 reveals two traits. At the beginning of that period, when the MNR and ADN formed the so-called Pact for Democracy, the aim of the coalition was in large measure to provide the political stability required to end hyperinflation and to set a new course of political economy. Thus, the original pact subordinated clientelism to the programmatic necessity of the moment. This is not to say that patrimonial dynamics were absent; they simply took a back seat to the immediacy of the crisis.

As the crisis of the mid-1980s subsided and the parties exerted control over the political system, patronage came to dominate the program and relegated even class-based interests. The epitome was the so-called megacoalition that provided the support that allowed General Hugo Banzer and Jorge "Tuto" Quiroga to govern between 1997 and 2002. Beginning in the year 2000 and even during the most extreme moments of the political and economic crisis that engulfed Bolivia, the petty patronage needs of the parties that made up the ruling coalitions were privileged over the urgent need to provide comprehensive policy reform to address both.

This situation dramatically showed up again during the short-lived second administration of Gonzalo Sánchez de Lozada (August 2002–October 17, 2003). During his 14-month tenure, the fate of Bolivia's multiparty system was sealed. In sharp contrast to his first government (1993–97)—when he forged significant reform measures, including the controversial capitalization strategy that privatized Bolivia's principal state enterprises and established the conditions for foreign direct investment (FDI) in areas such as hydrocarbons, telecommunications, railroads, electricity, and airlines—his second proved fatal to the pacted democracy.[9]

Accosted by politicians demanding patronage and a civil society that sensed the weakness of the government, Sánchez de Lozada was paralyzed by inaction, and the situation gradually deteriorated. Negotiations with social groups, especially with Evo Morales's coca growers, failed to reach any agreement, and in January 2003 conflict exploded between the Chapare-based unions and police forces attempting to eradicate coca leaves to fulfill agreements with the United States. At the same time, the government was continuously forced into a pattern of expanding the size of the ruling coalition to prevent traditional party politicians from subverting Sánchez de Lozada.

All of these attempts were for naught; the first explosion of violence came in February following the government's ill-conceived attempt at tax reform. A major police revolt resulted in a huge gun battle in the national palace and in the looting and burning of dozens of government buildings and the headquarters of the MNR and the MIR. When the gunfire subsided, 29 people had lost their lives in the crossfire, including police and military officers and numerous civilians.

Between February and October of 2003, the government could do little to contain the forces that wanted to see Sánchez de Lozada leave office. In this context of turmoil, the president unwisely pushed ahead with a plan to sell natural gas to the United States through Chile. This became the perfect excuse for social groups to initiate an intense campaign not only to prevent the plan from going forward but also finally to push Sánchez de Lozada out of office. In the end, social mobilization achieved its objective when the government had to use military troops to put down a revolt that left the city of La Paz without access to basic goods and fuel for several days.[10]

More than any other party, the MAS was able to capitalize on the tragic incidents of October 2003, when nearly 60 Bolivians died as a result of the civil unrest, and on the government's unfortunate response. The accusation of genocide against the former president and his ministers resonates well with the average Bolivian when any reference is made to the traditional parties and to Sánchez de Lozada.

The demonization of the traditional political parties has worked well in the new Bolivia under Evo Morales. Two months into the third year of his term, they are still as unpopular as they were in 2005, and this negative sentiment has also favored the government's overt plan to construct a single-party system on the ashes of the old regime. In public opinion polls, the combined ratings of Jorge "Tuto" Quiroga of Poder Democrático y Social (PODEMOS; Democratic and Social Power) and Samuel Doria Medina of Unidad Nacional (UN; National Unity), the two most important leaders of the opposition and the principal candidates in the 2005 elections, is barely 16 percent. The government's anti–traditional party message is likely to prevail in the midterm election because no one in the opposition can muster enough strength to challenge Morales and the MAS.[11]

Another dimension of the MAS's electoral platform was the call to make the Bolivian state a dignified sovereign entity. While this was in some measure redundant with regard to the anti-imperialist and nationalist message, this notion largely encompassed two pragmatic offers: (1) to nationalize natural resources to recover income for the state and (2) to convoke a constituent assembly to "refound" the country and to enable the coming together of diverse sectors of the Bolivian people.

The first offer was the most important given Bolivia's political-economic realities. The nationalization of hydrocarbons was one of the key demands made of the Sánchez de Lozada administration, especially in view of that government's attempts to export natural gas through Chile. Even in the hydrocarbon-producing departments of Santa Cruz and Tarija, nationalization was a very popular notion.

In early February 2004, Carlos Mesa—Sánchez de Lozada's vice president, who had assumed office as president following the resignation of Sánchez de Lozada on October 17, 2003—announced a new hydrocarbons law that levied taxes on the multinational investors who had capitalized the industry and discovered Bolivia's amazing natural gas wealth. At the same time, Mesa called for a referendum in July 2004, principally to settle the question of exporting natural gas. Both the law and the outcome of the referendum strengthened Morales and the MAS, who claimed that the referendum's results had confirmed the average Bolivian's support for the nationalization of the hydrocarbons industry.

Mesa's short-lived government (October 2003–June 2005) set in motion the convocation of a constituent assembly, the second pillar of the MAS's pragmatic stance. However one analyzes the civil unrest that led to Sánchez de Lozada's resignation, the MAS and the sectors of the civil society that led the October revolt argued that in addition to the export of natural gas through Chile, the refusal to convoke a constituent assembly was the principal reason for the extremity of the social explosion. Mesa attempted to resolve these immediate political issues. He vainly attempted to achieve a nation-saving social pact among disparate movements, political parties, and regional groups, each with its own laundry list of impossible demands. In 2003, the country's principal analysts and political leaders convinced Bolivians that the creation of a constituent assembly was a fundamental step toward saving the country. As we shall see, a simple reading of the experience of Andean countries with constituent assemblies reveals that, far from solving problems, they tend to exacerbate them. Given Bolivia's extreme ethnic, racial, and regional problems, the creation of a constituent assembly is unlikely to result in a new institutional architecture. More important, it will not resolve the profound regional and political differences in the country.

In summary, the MAS won in 2005 because it encompassed the overwhelming demand for change and the promise that it would open the political system to the indigenous masses. Now that Evo Morales and the MAS have governed Bolivia for over two years, it is arguable that the political system and its practices have changed. In the remaining sections of this chapter, I attempt to evaluate how the Morales administration has performed.

The Legacy of Neoliberalism

The Morales administration has dedicated much of its time to legitimizing itself by attacking the "legacy of neoliberalism." Neoliberalism is blamed for everything that is wrong with contemporary Bolivia. This message has been repeated time and again, to the extent that the conventional wisdom in Bolivia blames slow growth, increases in poverty, and the deepening of inequality on the neoliberal strategies of the 1980s and 1990s.

Depending on where one sits on the ideological spectrum, Bolivia either reduced poverty rates during this 20-year period or experienced a significant increase in poverty and a parallel process of deepening inequality. The latter view, however, is the one that has prevailed in Bolivia and has been the basis of the dominant charge against the traditional political parties that governed the country and the "neoliberal model" they imposed.

Left-of-center groups, especially those linked to Evo Morales, have capitalized on this predominant view. While social exclusion was and continues to be Bolivia's most serious problem, today, in contrast to the early 1950s, socioeconomic indicators have improved considerably. A more correct approach to explain the current situation might be to argue that democracy unleashed expectations that went unmet during 25 years of democratic rule, thus causing a huge long-run and recurring problem for weak democratic governments with a very small social and political base.

The Morales government has proposed a development strategy in which the principal actors are the country's main economic agents and social movements within a framework of interculturalism. The objective is the internal accumulation of wealth, the redistribution of income, and the eradication of poverty. The government's plan aims to create a new era for the state through the recovery and industrialization of renewable and nonrenewable resources.

The new strategy proposed seeks to "create a communitarian, complementary and solidarious economy to break with the neocolonial and neoliberal past." The aim is to "live well by achieving development with sovereignty, overcoming the ethnocentric content of traditional development, postulating a Cosmocentric vision based on communitarian elements rooted not only in agrarian communities and nomadic peoples but also in urban communities and organizations."[12]

President Morales's proposal contains a strong dose of nationalism and economic developmentalism that promotes the return of the state through public enterprises and development banks. As noted earlier, this strategy strongly resembles the 1952 National Revolution agenda, which called for the nationalization of natural resources, agrarian reform, and ethnic-social integration.[13]

I will analyze the specific components of the implementation of this strategy later in this chapter. The point here is that the Morales government came into office with a plan that benefited from a very favorable economic context. This context was much more favorable than those that had preceded the 1952 Revolution and certainly much better than that of 1984–85, when neoliberalism was put in place by the traditional political parties. In sharp contrast to those periods, the economic timing of the Morales administration's coming to power could not have been better.

In 2006, the Bolivian economy found itself in an extremely favorable international context, perhaps the best since the 1800s. The prices for Bolivian exports (minerals, natural gas, agricultural products, and nontraditional exports) rose, international interest rates dropped, remittances increased, dollars from the illicit economy flooded the country, and the Latin American region registered sustained rates of economic growth. To make matters even better, a large part of Bolivia's bilateral and multilateral foreign debt was written off. Since the return to democracy in 1982, no government had had the good fortune of inheriting such an economic situation. In short, the legacy of neoliberalism was much better than the Morales government has claimed.

Propelled by these internal and external factors, in 2006 the rate of real GDP growth reached 4.5 percent. This figure signaled that the low level of growth seen during 1999–2004 appeared to be over.[14] The most dynamic sectors were mining and metallurgy. Bolivia's unemployment rate sank from 9.4 in 2005 to 7.6 percent in 2006. After Morales's first year in office, the economic indicators contradicted the dire warnings of foreign and domestic analysts who had predicted that the country would face a serious economic crisis soon after he and the MAS rose to power.

The important point about the set of conditions that existed just before Morales's election—which included the discovery of large reserves of natural gas, the economic crisis of 1998–2004, high rates of unemployment, and the collapse of the traditional party system—is that the MAS was able to bring these factors together under a platform that grasped the broad-based demand of citizens for a redistribution of the pieces of the economic pie, which, at least in their view, had increased in size.

Several factors are of considerable concern in the postneoliberal era. First, as a result of the policies pursued by the government and the uncertainty they have generated, FDI has fallen dramatically. The collapse of FDI in Bolivia is likely to have a considerable impact on growth rates in the medium to long term, and this could affect the stability of the country's economy.

A second factor has to do with how international firms are looking at Bolivia. Standard and Poor's, for example, downgraded Bolivia to a B– investment rating in December 2006, mainly because of the political instability resulting from growing political fragmentation in the regional, social, and political arenas. The Morales government pays little attention to these types of reports, claiming that foreign capital can be attracted to Bolivia regardless of the degree of conflict prevalent in the country.

A third consideration has to do with the management of the economy, even assuming that neoliberalism can be replaced by an alternative policy. Owing to a rise in job specialization, the level of technical skills of public sector employees has deteriorated considerably. The political criteria used to select employees do little to ensure that good managers are hired.[15]

How Indigenous Is Bolivia?

In analyzing Bolivia today, it is common to start from the premise that it was the country's South Africa–like conditions that allowed Evo Morales to rise to power. This analogy must not be taken too far. The 1952 Revolution and the democratization process that has been under way since 1982 have represented significant efforts at sociopolitical inclusion. No one can seriously argue that the democratization experience of the last two decades has not provided the space for the political participation and growth of alternative parties and groups. That Evo Morales is president today is evidence of the open nature of the system.[16]

Under Morales, social exclusion has taken on serious racial overtones, to the point that even the period of democratization is described by the government and its supporters as a racist period in which Bolivia's indigenous masses were kept out of politics. While there is some truth to this observation, the reality is more complicated. Most important is the fact that Bolivia is racially complex; thus, it is not accurate to describe the country as divided between white oligarchs and the indigenous masses. To get to the heart of the ethnic composition of Bolivia and how politicized it has become, it is important to consider the results of the 2001 National Census and subsequent surveys.

The 2001 National Census asked Bolivians over the age of 15 if they considered themselves to belong to any of the following groups of original peoples: Quecha, Aymara, Guaraní, Mojeño, or other. The census did not provide any other response options, such as mestizo, thus skewing the outcome. The results revealed that 62 percent of respondents self-identified with those indigenous groups. This is the figure often cited to support the argument that nearly two-thirds of all Bolivians are indigenous.

Surveys such as those done as part of Vanderbilt University's Latin American Public Opinion Project (LAPOP), however, show a more complex situation. In 1998, the LAPOP survey measured ethnic self-perception, producing the following results: indigenous or *originarios,* 9.8 percent; mestizos, 62.8 percent; and whites, 23.3 percent. In 2004, the LAPOP survey showed these results: indigenous or *originarios,* 15.6 percent; mestizos, 60.6 percent; and whites, 19.4 percent. In the 2006 LAPOP survey, 19.3 percent considered themselves indigenous or *originarios,* 64 percent mestizos, and 11 percent whites. Two-thirds of the population still identified itself as mestizo. As Carlos Toranzo argues: "Perhaps owing to the boom of the indigenous discourse and the coming to power of Evo Morales in January 2005, indigenous self identification grew to almost 20 percent. That the MAS government promoted enthusiasm for indigenism—which led many middle class intellectuals and other professionals to dress in indigenous garb or to espouse the ideology of the MAS—might explain this growth."[17]

Racial and social exclusion are inextricably linked to the emergence of the MAS. Race is a fundamental ingredient of the MAS platform. The reality is that in Bolivia social exclusion transcends race and ethnicity, as it does elsewhere in the Americas. In this sense, social exclusion is a very serious challenge to the Morales government. It continues to be a fundamental reality that was exacerbated by the inability of governments (democratic and authoritarian) to deal with poverty. At the same time, inequality was deepened by the clientelistic nature of Bolivian democracy and by the perquisites and spoils that the traditional political class enjoyed.

Is the Political System More Open and Democratic Now?

On the surface, the Morales government has contributed to the opening of the political system. The incorporation of political actors who previously lacked direct access to decision-making channels and were able to present only street-based demands is indeed a dramatic change in Bolivia's political system. Indigenous, social, and political movements today are the beneficiaries of the distribution of cabinet posts and have direct access to the president. As Ximena Costa argues, they demand public service positions, power spaces, and attention to their problems not just as demands but as orders to the government.[18]

The political system has renewed itself and has opened up; society is more empowered than ever in what appears to be an irreversible process. For the foreseeable future, this process of inclusion will continue, at least in terms of expanding the levels of participation by those sectors previously excluded from decision-making circles. At the same time, it appears that the expectations unleashed by the election of Morales and the way in which he has governed have led to an explosion of contradictory demands that the government has had a difficult time meeting.[19]

Simultaneously, a new pattern of exclusion has also become evident. The exclusion of those who were previously in charge is obvious; the Bolivian political system at the level of the national government has little room for anyone even remotely associated with the neoliberal period. In the contemporary setting, governability is ensured by the *movimientista* vision, which is imbued with a particularistic, corporatist, regional, and ethnic logic of the country's future. This view fits well with the authoritarian traits that remain deeply ingrained in Bolivian political culture.

Another way of examining the pattern of inclusion and exclusion during the first year and a half of the MAS government is to describe it as reproducing the basic elements of job faction politics. While Bolivia was under pacted democracy, jobs and posts were distributed among the political class; today the MAS requires membership in the party, recommendations from party leaders, and other such credentials of those seeking state employment. The laying off of thousands of state employees and their replacement with MAS supporters has been amply documented by the press.[20]

In other words, the system as such has not changed. The patrimonial dynamic of the past has simply been reproduced. Today public posts are not only handed out to members of the MAS; they are doled out to members of allied parties and movements. The headlines about power have changed, but traditional behaviors remain the same. Change refers to the opening of the system but not to overcoming the practices of the past that are still prevalent, expanding, and unlikely to disappear.

Any discussion of whether the Bolivian political system is more democratic under Morales must consider the biases on both sides of the spectrum. Opposition sectors—and independent analysts—often criticize the concentration of power that appears to be occurring and the increasing conflict between the branches of government as demonstrating that the system is increasingly authoritarian and that Evo Morales is simply attempting to impose a chavista model of governance. His public tirades against the press and against the Constitutional Tribunal and the Supreme Court are pointed out as examples of this trend.[21]

At the same time, his supporters point to the inclusion of social movements and the way in which the government discusses public policy matters with different social sectors as a more democratic way of doing politics in Bolivia. Public opinion data reveal that the average Bolivian agrees with this view.[22]

Trust in the Political System

One of the more interesting paradoxes of the advent of Evo Morales and the MAS is the restoration of trust in the political system. Several polls reveal that people again believe in democracy, the government, Congress, the judiciary, and even the often-questioned National Police. In other words, the level of social trust in the political system has changed.

The level of trust in traditional political parties, however, remains low. As noted earlier, they are seen as guilty of all that has gone wrong in Bolivia. Given the high level of rejection of the leadership of these parties, it is unlikely that they will be able to compete in an electoral setting with the MAS and Evo Morales.

Interestingly, the MAS is not yet perceived as a political party and thus retains high levels of favorability in contrast to that accorded the traditional political parties. This is significant because of recurring allegations of acts of corruption—such as influence peddling, nepotism, self-enrichment, and illegal use of public resources, among others—committed by members of the MAS.[23]

Nationalization

Anti-imperialism and anti-neoliberalism did not translate into the "nationalization" of the hydrocarbons industry. As we shall see, the government simply extended the deadline for the renegotiation of contracts with the companies in a not-so-transparent process that was reminiscent of the much-criticized corruption of the past.

On May 1, 2006, the government announced the nationalization of hydrocarbons in a media-orchestrated event that included the presence of military troops in plants belonging to Petrobras, the Brazilian state company that owned the largest share of Bolivia's natural gas industry. The nationalization of hydrocarbons, which was implemented only after a six-month period of negotiation with the private petroleum companies, ended up as simply a change of contracts. This change allowed the Bolivian state to recover property and control over the hydrocarbons industry without expelling foreign companies. It also allowed for the relaunching of the Yacimientos Petrolíferos Fiscales de Bolivia (National Oil Fields of Bolivia) as the state enterprise charged with directing the "nationalization" process.[24]

The most important dimension of this contract renegotiation was the change in the tax structure for the natural gas and petroleum sector. The change did produce a significant increase in revenue for the Bolivian state at the levels of the central and local governments. At the end of the process, nationalization simply established a new set of rules for state involvement and for private company investors. This agreement is very distant from what the public was led to expect by the rhetoric of nationalization that has consistently led to the administration's high polling figures. In contrast to the nationalization of the mining sector in 1952 and even the nationalization of Gulf Oil in 1969, the nationalization of hydrocarbons in 2006 is still quite neoliberal in content.

Just as the dust was settling on the nationalization of the hydrocarbons industry, the government nationalized the smelting company at Vinto and gave signals that it would not respect investment treaties or the laws that were used to sell off these enterprises.[25] This violation of *seguridad jurídica,* or legal certainty, gradually made companies less than willing to smelt their minerals there.

The government's nationalization drive has not yet ended. In April 2007, the government announced the nationalization of the Empresa Nacional de Telecomunicaciones (ENTEL; National Telecommunications Company). Although the terms are still vague and the negotiations with the Italian firm that capitalized ENTEL are at a standstill, concern has increased that the government's control may mean the end of competition in this sector and the decline of the quality of service offered to the public.

The nationalization of hydrocarbons, the Vinto Smelter, and ENTEL are reminiscent of the state-led development strategies unleashed by the 1952 Revolution. Critics of this pattern note the "rent-seeking" behavior that it sparked in the 1950s. In Laserna's view, "Rent seeking behavior seeks to maximize particular benefits, income, or benefits for individuals or groups through the exercise of direct political power or through influence on the decision making process. Rent seekers use power and influence to obtain control or gain from existing wealth such as revenue or utility generated from the exploitation of natural resources."[26]

This patrimonial dynamic has prevailed since the country achieved independence in 1825.[27] In contemporary Bolivia, rent-seeking behavior has not changed. The MAS and Evo Morales, like the MNR in the 1950s, put forth an economic development strategy that is more likely to exacerbate the problems of rent seeking.[28] The discovery and exploitation of Bolivia's natural gas reserves and the forthcoming revenues will likely exacerbate rent-seeking behavior and patrimonialism. The political consequences of this "state-led development" strategy merit closer scrutiny.

President Morales's nationalizing thrust is well protected by polling figures. Most Bolivians believe his speeches and the government's media messages about nationalization. Despite all the evidence, which points less to nationalization than to confiscation as in the past, most Bolivians believe that the government has indeed nationalized hydrocarbons. Until this perception changes, the Morales administration is likely to remain popular.

Agrarian Reform

Another important objective of the Morales administration has been land reform. Land tenure is a very significant indicator of inequality—and also of Bolivia's serious regional divide, which will be discussed later. The 1952 Revolution had agrarian reform as one of its key measures. In the five decades that followed, land tenure patterns in Bolivia returned to pre-Revolution extremes, mainly because of a pattern of land reconcentration in the western part of the country and a massive doling out of landholdings to political supporters, relatives, and others by military authoritarian rulers and democratically elected presidents alike. As a result, it should not be surprising that Evo Morales's promises to resolve the land concentration issue played well in rural areas and contributed enormously to his victory.

The issue of land tenure is one that has caused division not simply between large landholders and poor landless peasants. In the mid-1990s, the Sánchez de Lozada government attempted through legislation to establish an orderly process through which land disputes could be resolved. The so-called Instituto Nacional de Reforma Agraria (INRA; National Institute for Agrarian Reform) Law established mechanisms for land distribution and titling even in the department of Santa Cruz, where land concentration was the greatest. A decade later, the INRA process had failed dramatically, not necessarily as a result of the resistance of large landowners. Although large landholdings do in fact exist, many are the sites of productive farms that have been the key to the development of a large export sector, especially for soybeans.

Under Morales, agrarian reform became a controversial policy area. Based on a study whose results showed that 87 percent of all land—48 million hectares—is in the hands of 7 percent of owners and that indigenous people have access to only 13 percent of the total arable land in Bolivia, the government introduced the Ley de Reconducción Comunitaria de la Reforma Agraria y la Revolución Agraria Mecanizada (Law for the Communitarian Redirection of Agrarian Reform and Mechanized Agrarian Reform). The central objective of this law is to give land a social function. Those lands that perform no social or productive function are to be redistributed among the indigenous population and communities. This reform, which above all tackles the large landholdings (*latifundios*) of the Bolivian eastern lowlands, has stirred the resistance of large commercial agricultural interests.

As in the case of the nationalization of hydrocarbons, the inflammatory discourse surrounding this so-called second agrarian reform has translated into legal and institutional processes that may indeed facilitate a negotiated process of land distribution rather than a violent confrontation between landholders and *campesino* invaders. At the same time, the rhetoric of agrarian reform, which has been largely aimed at the landholders of the Santa Cruz department, could generate conflictive situations in the future.

More important than the imagined conflict with large landholders is the real threat of conflict as a result of land invasions by groups of landless *campesinos* all over Bolivia, not just in the Santa Cruz department. *Campesino* invasions have stirred sometimes violent reactions, as in the case of the indigenous groups in the Madidi National Reserve.[29] The government now finds itself in the unenviable position of having to resolve problems of its own making. In other words, its early rhetoric about agrarian reform has encouraged land invasions. Bringing them under control will be a difficult task.

The Constituent Assembly and Departmental Autonomy

For several years, the sense prevailed that a constituent assembly was the only way that the conflict that had characterized Bolivia since 2000 would cease. The driving notion was that only a constituent assembly would bring together the different political, regional, cultural, and ethnic forces into a new and dramatic refounding of the country. A wide range of cultural and ethnic groups argued that a constituent assembly should resolve discrimination and prejudice and finally lead to the establishment of a state that would more accurately reflect the country's racial composition. Regional forces, especially in the half-moon departments, hoped that a constituent assembly would end the debate about centralization and its alleged limit on to the development of the country's key regions.[30] In sum, a constituent assembly became all things to all people; as such, from the beginning it was condemned to fail one group or another.

Interviews and focus groups I have conducted in Bolivia over the past three years have revealed a variety of the views on this topic and how high expectations have risen regarding the capacity of a constituent assembly to transform the country.[31] These high expectations are unlikely to be met by the Constituent Assembly now that it has been constituted, because politics as usual appears to have governed its behavior while it has been in session.

This is not the first time that Bolivia has experienced a constituent assembly and that constitutional change has been a regular exercise. The most recent constitutional amendment process occurred in 1994. Changing the architecture of politics, however, has done little to change the fundamental dynamics of political behavior. This is not to say that in the past political rules did not condition some behavior, such as the recurring need to form coalitions to ensure governability at the local and national levels. At the same time, unless the concrete behavior of political actors changes dramatically, the results of the Constituent Assembly will simply be cosmetic.

Several basic notions have become realities during the course of the functioning of the Assembly, which was elected on July 2, 2006. Warnings related to the composition of the Assembly have become realities, because the MAS has imposed a corporatist logic that has made the sessions unruly and has resulted in little concrete action. Achieving consensus has been extremely difficult, especially in a polarized setting in which the MAS majority and the PODEMOS and UN minority find little room for consensus building. Rather than becoming the cathartic setting from which a new Bolivia would emerge, the Constituent Assembly has become a most conflictive body in which consensus is difficult to achieve.

The area of greatest concern is the profound tension that exists between notions of national unity and notions of what divides Bolivians. My focus groups have revealed the magnitude of these divisions. While regional variations occur, most respondents have perceived conflicting and irreconcilable notions of autonomy. The most commonly cited dichotomies are those between east and west, autonomy and centralism, political sectors and citizens, continuity and change, the country and regions, indigenous people and whites, "my family" and politicians. In other words, the general sense among respondents has been that, rather than resolving these tensions, the Constituent Assembly has indeed exacerbated them.

The prevalent view among focus group respondents regarding the members of the Assembly is also indicative of the problems that body has faced. Some see the members as the same politicians as always, especially those in the opposition sector. Others see the MAS bench as a collection of union members handpicked by the party and its leadership and completely manipulated by Evo Morales. As a result, by mid-2007 the Constituent Assembly was perceived as a "collective farce," and few respondents—even those who identify with the MAS—believed that a new Bolivia would emerge from it in August 2007, when the making of the new Constitution was set to be concluded. They were indeed proven correct, as the deadline has been extended repeatedly.

The more problematic issue related to the Constituent Assembly concerns the view that all Bolivians wanted it and have fought for it. The reality may be a bit more complex. The Assembly was largely pushed by a very active but small portion of the electorate, especially those sectors tied to the MAS and other groups. At the same time, political parties vying to retain some presence in the new context that existed after Morales assumed office in January 2005 helped develop the national sense of urgency that surrounded the convocation of such an assembly. Similarly, prominent academics ranging from conservatives to the more radical also legitimized the idea that a constituent assembly was absolutely necessary. These views were also reflected by the media, and soon the perception emerged that the formation of such an assembly was indeed a universal nation-saving aspiration

As can be seen from the focus group results, however, it is not as clear how much the average Bolivian wanted a constituent assembly. Most knew little about such an assembly or what it might actually do for the country. While it was generally viewed positively, few had a real notion of its role. Still others believed that nothing would change in Bolivia after the creation of a constituent assembly. Lack of knowledge about the reach of the Constituent Assembly and the disparity of interests and views has led to a general sense of disbelief regarding the transformative capacity of citizens in organizations such as this one.

Although nearly everything became contentious in the Constituent Assembly, nothing has been more controversial than the autonomy question. The July 2006 Autonomy Referendum was also inconclusive and ratified the idea that unless the questions are clear and leave no room for varying interpretations, the results may exacerbate the initial problem. In this particular instance, the results have contributed to the regional polarization of the country and in some instances have even led to violent episodes.[32]

Fearing that the government would prevail, in December 2006 Santa Cruz civic and business organizations and Ruben Costas, the popular prefect, staged an impressive million-person march with the objective of "defending democracy, the two-thirds vote in the Constituent Assembly and the Yes vote on departmental autonomy." While it may be arguable whether a million people congregated in the streets of Santa Cruz, the impact was huge and gave credence to the notion that departmental autonomy is not just an elite aspiration. On the same day, Manfred Reyes Villa, the prefect of the department of Cochabamba, staged his own less impressive rally. Similar events were convoked by the respective prefects and civic organizations in the departments of Beni, Pando, and Tarija.[33]

The government's response to these events was less than democratic. In a failed attempt to prevent people from reaching the Santa Cruz march, MAS supporters staged violent road blockades near the town of San Julian.[34] The government's response to the Cochabamba rally did not come until early January 2007. The Morales government did little to contain a massive and violent demonstration of coca growers, labor leaders, and MAS elected officials and supporters demanding Prefect Reyes Villa's resignation. The violent and racially motivated deaths of a coca grower and a middle-class "white" teenager during this clash suggest that the traditional regional cleavages have deepened as a result of a racial-ethnic divide promoted in part by the government. The violent confrontations ended largely as a result of the expression of concern over the direction of Bolivian democracy by European ambassadors.[35] While Vice President García Linera refused to recognize a parallel departmental government elected by the marchers, the Cochabamba incidents demonstrated the Morales administration's reliance on social organizations to control dissent of any kind.

These events and others since then demonstrate the increasing significance of prefects in Bolivia. With autonomy as their driving message and goal, they have occupied the position historically held by political parties. The role of the half-moon prefects has managed in some measure to temper attempts to impose a mandate the government believes it was granted by the December 2005 elections. By mid-2007, even the prefects in the departments of Cochabamba and La Paz had joined the half moon in demanding that the results of the autonomy referendum be respected by the MAS majority in the Constituent Assembly.

As of this writing, the Constituent Assembly has spent 9 of the 12 months it has been in session without passing a single article of the new Constitution. Nothing has been refounded. On the contrary, instead of becoming a mechanism for the coming together of diverse groups, the Assembly has contributed to the polarization and fragmentation of the country. The perceived intrusion of the government in the affairs of the Constituent Assembly has contributed to making this institution nothing more than a sideshow. Whether the government and the opposition will be able to come together to resolve insurmountable differences is anyone's guess; however, it seems unlikely that they will overcome their impasse in just a few days.

Coca and Cocaine under the Morales Administration

Evo Morales's entry into politics did not end his role as Bolivia's foremost coca union leader. While he was a deputy in Congress pushing legislation forward, he was also engaged in directing road blockades and other union strategies to protest anti-drug policies, often paralyzing the country. He has opted to follow this dual role even as president. On February 14, 2006, Morales was reelected head of the coca growers' federation and promptly announced that unless the opposition in Congress voted in favor of his law to convoke a Constituent Assembly, he would order the coca growers to march on La Paz. Although Morales is a national leader with a broad base of support, he will always rely on the coca growers (*cocaleros*) to achieve specific government goals.

Morales's union role was always questioned by the traditional political parties, which sought ways to force him out of the Chamber of Deputies. In 2000, they found a reason to expel him from Congress following a still unsolved incident that involved the kidnapping, torture, and execution of four police officers by coca growers allegedly under Morales's orders.[36] He was finally expelled in February 2002 in the middle of another electoral process. Rather than hurting his public image, his expulsion served to launch his electoral campaign for the presidency.[37] In the June 2002 election, he placed second only to Gonzalo Sánchez de Lozada, demonstrating that he had become a national political force and the head of the opposition.

This analysis of Evo Morales's first year in office would not be complete without a discussion of the consolidation of a vast and complicated coca-cocaine complex that includes coca farmers, displaced mineworkers, security forces, and drug traffickers. Both the growth of the complex (with its concomitant web of corruption) and joint Bolivian-U.S. efforts to combat its proliferation taxed Bolivia's weak political system. The coca-cocaine complex has profound ramifications that extend well beyond those seen from a simple perspective of law enforcement or national security. It is this particular sector that was responsible for the rise to power of Evo Morales, who (as was noted earlier) also heads the coca growers' federation in the Chapare Valley in Bolivia's central department of Cochabamba.

The coca-cocaine complex has held a central position in the Bolivian economy and politics for the past three decades. Since the transition to democracy in the early 1980s, coca growers' unions have resorted to a combination of strategies that have included taking advantage of the political space and opening provided by democracy and relying on a long tradition of union activism and tactics. In the former case, coca growers opted to run candidates for office whenever they were able to, thus gaining spaces in the National Congress. Although Evo Morales was the first coca grower to win a single member-district seat in the lower house, these unions had had representatives in the legislature under different party tickets as early as 1982.[38] At the same time, however, coca growers' unions successfully employed road blockades, marches, and strikes to resist not only the imposition of U.S.-funded eradication efforts but also to combat the so-called neoliberal policies. The fact that Bolivia's major roadway connecting the east and the west runs through the Chapare gave the coca growers a strategic advantage, because they could periodically block the country's exports and flows of goods from one side of the country to the other.

The importance of the *cocaleros* to the emergence of Evo Morales cannot be overemphasized. They were the key to his rise to national prominence in the 1980s and 1990s and were fundamental to his ascension to the presidency in 2005. It is also important to reiterate the significance of the so-called *instrumento político* (political instrument) that led to the establishment of the MAS. As noted earlier, well before 1997 coca growers achieved political representation in Congress by being included in the lists of political parties such as Izquierda Unida (United Left). In the mid-1990s, the coca growers essentially rented a party (which became the MAS of today) from David Añez Pedraza, a right-wing politician who had a legally registered party. This instrument enabled Morales to enter Congress and then build a national platform that he used to very slowly and carefully construct an urban and rural party structure. In this sense, while the traditional parties focused on distributing state patronage between and among themselves, Morales and the MAS constructed an unsophisticated but effective national electoral machine.

Although the MAS is now the most important political tool of President Morales, it is also the case that the *cocalero* unions play an ever-more-significant role. They are the president's praetorian guard, ready to be mobilized in defense of their leader whenever he is threatened or needs them. For this reason, the fact that the president called on them on February 14, 2006, to mobilize against the opposition in Congress and then again in January 2007 to oppose the elected prefect of Cochabamba should not have been surprising.[39]

This background is necessary to understand what has occurred since Morales assumed office in January 2006. The enthusiasm for Evo Morales and the coming to power of the MAS in Bolivia appear to have camouflaged a worrisome trend in the South American drug industry. In this section, the main argument is not that the Morales government is responsible for the current explosion of drug production, trafficking, consumption, and related crimes in Bolivia but that its policies have contributed to the consolidation and acceleration of these activities. Turning the tide will be an impossible task without greater international involvement, which has largely waned as a result of both the lack of interest of the Bolivian government in interdiction policies and the decline in European and U.S. funding.

The Bolivian Approach

In 2004, President Carlos Mesa attempted to minimize sociopolitical conflicts by giving in to nearly every demand placed before him. He also gave in to nearly every group, such as the ones that had mobilized extensively to bring down the Sánchez de Lozada government in 2003. This strategy, dubbed "rope-a-dope" by a creative U.S. diplomat at the time, proved futile in the long run, because Mesa was also forced to resign in favor of Eduardo Rodríguez, the president of the Supreme Court, whose main task was simply to hold elections in December 2005. Although Mesa's other economic and social policies had poor results, it appears that the decisions he made on the drug front are having serious repercussions after only a few years. Carlos Mesa allowed each coca-growing family in the Chapare Valley to legally grow up to one *cato* of coca.[40] The logic was that the restrictions imposed on the production of coca by agreements with the United States and the international community had resulted in a critical scarcity in the amount available for legal consumption.[41] Mesa's agreement was based on the promise by Evo Morales's coca growers that an independent study would be commissioned to determine once and for all how much coca was legitimately used for traditional purposes, not cocaine production. Morales and his followers argued that an independent study could not be funded by the United States and that even U.S. universities could not participate in such a study.[42] For over three years, the debate over who would fund the study continued; at one point, it was agreed that the European Union would fund it. By mid-2007, no agreement had been reached over when or even whether the study would be conducted.

In the meantime, Chapare growers meticulously worked their *catos*. As the production of coca increased dramatically in the Yungas Valley in the department of La Paz, growers there also demanded and obtained the right to grow their own *catos*. Dissatisfied by the *cato* approach, in late 2006 the Morales government announced that it was authorizing an increase in coca production, from 12,000 to 20,000 hectares.[43] The government argued that the industrialization of coca, the central pillar of its strategy, required the 8,000 additional hectares to meet internal and external demand for old and new products made from coca.[44] With great fanfare and with the Cuban and Venezuelan ambassadors in attendance, President Morales launched his coca industrialization plan in June 17, 2006. The Venezuelan government pledged to fund the construction of a coca plant in the Chapare. Nearly one year later, the plant had yet to begin production.

As noted earlier, the Bolivian government has deep roots in the coca growers' unions; therefore, no one expected a continuation of the eradication strategies of the past two decades. The great irony was that the very security forces that had targeted—and even tortured—Morales in the past were now under his direct command. Be that as it may, Morales appointed Felipe Cáceres, a former MAS mayor of a Chapare town with long and close ties to the president, as Bolivia's new "drug czar."

Nearly two years later, Cáceres has had a very interesting tenure. He has not done away with Law 1008, the 1988 U.S.-crafted law that calls for an end to the production of coca in Bolivia. At the same time, he has allowed the anti-narcotics units to carry out significant operations. The interdiction record of these units has improved over the past year, netting a larger number of cocaine seizures and arrests. In certain areas of the Chapare, clashes between coca growers and the anti-drug units have resulted in the wounding or death of soldiers and coca growers, a pattern not unlike that of the past two decades.

Cáceres has been the person most responsible for implementing the government's official position of "no to zero coca and yes to zero cocaine." In practice, this position has translated into a three-step approach. As noted, the first pillar is the industrialization of the coca leaf, which requires an expansion of coca production from 12,000 to 20,000 hectares per year. The second step involves the interdiction of cocaine production wherever it occurs in Bolivian territory. The third step involves voluntary, community-based eradication of coca production beyond one *cato* per family. This is an approach proposed for several years, not only by coca growers but also by many in the NGO and academic communities, who argued that this was the only way both to obtain the support of the coca growers and to reduce the violence that had characterized successive governments' attempts to forcefully eradicate coca production. Although it is still too early to properly evaluate this policy, it is probably safe to assume that it has not been effective in controlling the expansion of coca production beyond the self-imposed limits. It is true, however, that for the most part the violence of the forceful eradication campaigns has diminished considerably.

The Consequences of This Approach

Several evaluations of the Morales approach ("no to zero coca and yes to zero cocaine") are available.[45] Based on these reports, it appears that Bolivia is regaining prominence in the coca-cocaine circuit for a variety of reasons. Space constraints limit discussion of the depth required to explain each, but they include the following: a dramatic increase in the production of coca leaf, a concomitant increase in the production of cocaine, the significant presence of transnational criminal organizations, a consolidation of Bolivian family clans engaged in drug trafficking activities, the still recent wave of immigration to Europe, the increasing role of Argentina and Brazil as consumer nations, and a significant decline in U.S. and European funding of alternative development and interdiction programs.

The dramatic increase of coca production in Bolivia since 2004 can be attributed to the decline in coca eradication activity since the Mesa government put in place the policy of one *cato* per family. Moreover, the expansion of the number of hectares under cultivation by the Morales administration appears to have further expanded this trend. Reports of coca cultivation in even Bolivia's ecological reserves have become common as *campesinos,* pressed by drug traffickers, have invaded land in the Madidi and other parks.[46]

U.S. Ambassador Philip Goldberg has made the case that more coca inevitably results in more cocaine production. While the case could be made for simple correlation rather than a causal relationship, the figures do reflect a significant growth in cocaine production in Bolivia. By some measures, Bolivia may be producing more cocaine today than at any time in its history, despite nearly three decades of U.S.-driven policy. By mid-2007, cocaine production was not limited to the Chapare and Yungas Valleys. Reports of cocaine labs are now widespread. These include family-based labs that dot the entire Altiplano region, including the cities of La Paz, El Alto, Cochabamba, Sucre, and even Potosí. Although these labs are family-based, the highland family clans are responsible for moving both Yungas and Chapare coca paste and refined cocaine to Argentina, Brazil, and Peru. They also appear to be significantly involved in the movement of precursor chemicals into Bolivia from these three countries. The movement of drugs and precursor chemicals takes many forms and employs many methods.[47]

Of greater concern is the apparently large presence of transnational criminal organizations (TCOs), especially in the departments of Beni, Pando, and Santa Cruz, though they have a national presence. These TCOs include Colombian groups such as the Fuerzas Armadas Revolucionarias de Colombia (FARC; Revolutionary Armed Forces of Colombia) and Autodefensas Unidas de Colombia (United Self-Defense Forces of Colombia); Peruvian organizations; Brazilian organizations such as Partido Comando Capital (Capital Commando Party), which led the prison-based revolts in São Paolo in 2006; and organizations from northern Argentina based in the state of Salta (Table 6.1).[48] Working closely with local growers and family-based clans, these organizations are moving cocaine out of Bolivia to all neighboring countries and increasingly to Europe.[49]

This movement of cocaine to Bolivia's neighbors is a result of the huge demand from mainly Argentine and Brazilian consumers. This explosion has led to repeated complaints by the Brazilian government that Bolivia's approach of "no to zero coca and yes to zero cocaine" is responsible for the flood of drugs that is pouring into São Paolo, Rio de Janeiro, and other large cities. At the same time, trafficking networks are transporting Bolivian cocaine across Brazil and into Europe, especially through Spain. The increase in the migration of Bolivians to Spain has also resulted in the arrests of dozens of small-time traffickers.[50]

Table 6.1. FELCN Comparative Drug Interdiction Activities, January–March 2006 and 2007

Activity	Quantity	2006	2007	Change (%)
No. operations carried out		1,806	2,533	40.25
Drug Interdiction				
Cocaine hydrochloride	Grams	158,978.00	700,399.00	340.57
Cocaine base	Grams	2,353,036.37	2,900,958.82	23.29
Total cocaine	Grams	2,512,012.37	3,601,357.82	43.37
Marijuana	Grams	24,472,919.73	151,130,937.54	517.54
Total drugs seized	Grams	26,984,932.10	154,732,295.36	473.40
Precursor Seizures				
Liquid chemicals	Liters	147,497.22	566,714.48	284.22
Solid chemicals	Kilograms	59,186.86	106,208.61	79.45
Coca leaf	Pounds	563,329.53	850,427.77	50.96
Related Activities				
Arrests		994	1,203	21.03
Maceration pits destroyed		1,164	1,332	14.43
Labs destroyed		746	838	12.33

Source: Adapted from "Organizaciones internacionales absorben narcos bolivianos," *La Razón,* March 28, 2007, www.la-razon.com/Versiones/20070328_005859/nota_256_407691.htm.
Note: FELCN, Fuerza Especial de Lucha contra el Narcotráfico.

Despite these trends, U.S. and European anti-drug assistance to Bolivia has declined considerably. The United States argues that, given the change in focus of the Morales administration, funding for alternative development and interdiction programs is no longer relevant. Moreover, the United States appears somewhat unconcerned because less than 2 percent of all Bolivian cocaine produced is making its way to U.S. shores. Europeans are facing an important increase in Bolivian cocaine, but they are hesitant to show concern given their increasingly complicated relationship with the Morales administration. In contrast, Brazil has expressed concern, although it has also done little to tackle the situation due its similarly delicate relationship with Bolivia.

A final aspect of the problem is the increase in drug-related violence throughout Bolivia's largest urban centers. A major problem in the country is microtrafficking to meet the growing consumer demand for both cocaine and marijuana. Like other countries in South America, Bolivia will soon face a serious problem of internal violence if it does not begin to address these trends.

Conclusion

This brief and limited survey of the first year and a half of the Morales administration allows for a quick look at what the future may bring to Bolivia. The outcome of the Constituent Assembly will be decisive in terms of whether a new architecture will be established for the political system, and it is also likely to set the terms of the political debate for years to come. At this writing, all signs suggest that Bolivians will be subjected to several more months of uncertainty.

On the other hand, if a new constitution does emerge from the Constituent Assembly, Bolivia will probably enter into another electoral year, one in which citizens will be given the opportunity to ratify or reject its text. There is also a strong possibility that Bolivians may face another presidential election if the MAS prevails and President Morales is allowed to run for reelection. Given the MAS's electoral strength and the president's favorable rating, it is unlikely that the rather disorganized opposition that prevails in Bolivia will be able to block the MAS's constitutional project.

Nonetheless, if the MAS prevails and imposes a constitution of its own making, Bolivia could again enter into a very serious moment of sociopolitical conflict. Departmental autonomy will be the main issue to observe, especially if the government and the MAS impose their version of autonomy. If this situation develops, prefects from the half moon are likely to become an even more formidable political force. This is the case because under the MAS's version prefects would again become subordinate to the central government, making indigenous communities and municipalities the key agencies of autonomy and decentralization.

Several voices claim that the trend toward authoritarianism is clear. They point to the government's communication strategy—under which, with Venezuelan assistance, the state-owned channel has been modernized and an extensive national radio network has been developed—as evidence of President Morales's mimicking of Hugo Chávez. They also claim that the government harasses those in the media who do not sell out.

At the same time, the government's battle with the opposition in Congress and with the judiciary has led to widespread accusations that President Morales is attempting both to rein in the opposition and to pack the courts with pro-MAS judges. Concern over the independence of the National Electoral Court has also been voiced owing to the government's charges that it, too, is a holdover from the traditional political parties and pacted democracy.

One of the most important dimensions of the MAS's vision for Bolivia has been their quest for sovereignty and national dignity. Public opinion polls reveal that Bolivians are proud of the way in which President Morales has stood up to the United States and has put Bolivia on the map with his frequent trips abroad and his close relations with Fidel Castro and Hugo Chávez. At the same time, however, a growing sector is incensed by the perceived (and real) intrusion of the Cuban and Venezuelan governments. The ambassadors of both countries have become fixtures at political rallies and government-sponsored events. Not only have members of these legations threatened the opposition and the media for criticizing the government, but some even claim that the Cubans and Venezuelans push the Bolivian military around.

Moreover, the growing role of the Venezuelan government in controversial areas such as funding the armed forces, providing helicopters for President Morales and his cabinet, and selling natural gas to Bolivia to meet a winter shortage has sparked sharp criticism from the media and from the public at large. The perception that emerged in mid-2007 is that the government may have recovered the dignity it lost to the United States, but it has turned it over to the Cubans and Venezuelans for much less and at a greater cost to Bolivia in the long run. Relations with the United States remain strained and are unlikely to improve significantly. Nonetheless, Bolivia will probably benefit from its position in the Andean region and become a beneficiary of the extension of the Andean Trade Preference Act. This may help an important textile industry in Bolivia and save a few thousand jobs. It is highly improbable, however, that a larger aid package will be in the works for Bolivia. In fact, since Morales's arrival U.S. assistance has declined considerably, even in the drug-control area.

The more complex dimension of relations with the United States will once again be in the coca and cocaine circuit. This chapter has noted the possibility of broader participation by Bolivia in the international drug circuit as more Brazilian, Colombian, and Peruvian organizations select this country as the place to produce cocaine and transport it to the markets of South America and Europe. How this trend develops will influence the way in which the United States responds in the medium term.

In the final analysis, the dramatic change that the Morales government promised has indeed occurred. Yet, no matter how much appears to have changed, much also remains the same. The old political elite may have been soundly defeated and is now seeking a legitimate way to return to power. At the same time, the new—albeit poorer—ruling elite is revealing patterns of behavior that show once again that patrimonial dynamics prevail irrespective of who takes power in Bolivia.

Postscript

Since this chapter was written, the situation in Bolivia has become increasingly complex, to the point that the very future of the country is now seriously at stake. As expected, the deadlines for achieving consensus on a new constitution expired, and political maneuvers by the government extended the process until December 2007. The inability to reach consensus on key issues—such as whether Bolivia should be considered a pluriethnic nation with 36 official languages, or the nature of land reform, or just how broad the definition of autonomy should be, or just where the national capital should be located—resulted in a sad outcome, with all political actors violating what little was left of the law. At the same time, all actors justified their illegal and unconstitutional acts by appealing to perverse interpretations of the laws under which the Constituent Assembly was convoked in the first place.

Events had come to a violent climax in November, when the government, unable to obtain a quorum, orchestrated a meeting of the Constituent Assembly within the halls of a military academy in the city of Sucre. Surrounded by the dozens of police and hundreds of members of social movements bused in by the government from around the country to prevent the entry of opposition members, the majority bench, comprised of members of the MAS and its allies, approved a constitution that, by most accounts, few Assembly members had read. Meanwhile, in the streets of Sucre protesters clashed with the police, rejecting not only the way in which the government was forcing through its constitution but the fact that the document did not include Sucre's demand to become the full-fledged capital of Bolivia. In the end, three university students were gunned down by the police, although the government subsequently and ludicrously claimed that the bullets were fired from within the student movement. In addition, hundreds of people were injured in the battle.

The government claimed that the illegal meeting of the Constituent Assembly was necessary because the opposition had manipulated students and others in Sucre to prevent a quorum from being achieved. While there is some truth to this claim, it is also true that the police and the social movement members the government had bused in prevented opposition Assembly members from entering the military school.

Less than a week later, the government again bused in hundreds of social movement members—which have become the equivalent of the Bolivarian groups in Venezuela—to circle the National Congress in La Paz and prevent opposition members from entering the building so that they could not vote against a modification of the original law that had established the rules for the Constituent Assembly. The tactic worked; opposition members who attempted to enter the building were beaten by the government-convoked mob.

With the law changed, the government moved the venue of the Constituent Assembly to Oruro, where, again surrounded by police and social movement members, opposition delegates were not allowed to enter the theater where the new constitution was to be approved. As expected, the government-controlled Assembly passed the Constitution, setting off yet another fierce round of confrontations with the opposition.

In response, the half-moon departments, especially Santa Cruz and Tarija, approved their own Autonomic Statutes, which reject the government Constitution's version of autonomy. Instead, they introduced several additional layers of autonomy, including an extreme form of autonomy from departmental governors for the indigenous community. On December 16, 2007, Bolivia was essentially split along two irreconcilable poles. In the west stood Evo Morales and his vision of an indigenous and socialist Bolivia, while in the east the half-moon departments staked their claim to departmental autonomy and clearly rejected a state-centered view of the world.

The end-of-the-year festivities and the Carnival holidays of early 2008 temporarily delayed a full-blown confrontation. For a short while, it looked as if the regional opposition and the government would achieve some kind of Solomonic solution during a very brief two-week hiatus in the hostilities when both sides sat down to engage in a dialogue. By late February 2008, however, the irreconcilable polarization between the MAS's new Constitution and the regional opposition's Autonomic Statutes widened.

At this writing, in late March 2008, the half-moon departments are moving swiftly toward referenda intended to ratify the Autonomic Statutes that each approved between December 2007 and February 2008. The government has declared all departmental referenda illegal and has even threatened to use force if necessary to "preserve national unity." Meanwhile, the government inexplicably postponed the referenda on its new Constitution.

Bolivia appears headed toward confrontation, and the possibility of a peaceful outcome does not appear likely given the distance between Morales and the regional opposition groups. In the past, Bolivian political conflicts always appeared to subside as leaders resourcefully found alternatives to violent conflict. Since 2005, violence has escalated considerably, and all actors are now more prone to resort to violence to settle differences. This pattern does not bode well for the future, and, as Humberto Vacaflor has already noted, Evo Morales may become the last president of a country once known as Bolivia, or he could rise to the occasion and become the leader of all Bolivians, united less by a constitution than by geographic and historical commonalities.[51]

7

Brazil

Democracy under Lula and the PT

David Samuels

On January 1, 2003, for the first time in over 40 years, one popularly elected Brazilian president passed the sash of office to another. The election of Luiz Inácio "Lula" da Silva was historically significant for Brazilian democracy in several ways. At the most general level, his inauguration symbolically closed the book on Brazil's transition to democracy. The full incorporation of the country's middle and lower classes into politics had begun in the late 1970s, and Lula's victory completed the process. Lula had emphasized this facet of his trajectory and that of his party in his campaign, promising even greater participation for civil society in the government process.

Lula himself differs from all previous Brazilian presidents, and his party, the Partido dos Trabalhadores (PT; Workers' Party) differs substantially from Brazil's other parties. Lula and his party are "outsiders" in that they do not have much in common with the traditional Brazilian economic, political, or social elites. To this day, Lula carries with him the marks of his humble origins—the finger shortened by half in an industrial accident, his unrefined Portuguese. The ascension to power of a poor, uneducated migrant worker who had worked as a metal lathe operator, become a nationally prominent union leader, and helped found the PT is symbolically significant: it suggests that not only can average Brazilians legitimately participate in *selecting* the nation's rulers; they can *become* those rulers. This idea embodies everything the PT claims to stand for: the promise that ordinary Brazilians can take the reins of their own political destiny.

As for the PT, even though it has heavily relied on state-supported unions for its growth, it is the first important Brazilian party to be formed largely autonomous of state influence or of political or economic elites themselves.[1] The party grew out of a confluence of union, Catholic Church, and social movement activism in the 1970s and early 1980s and matured into an organization that catalyzed, mobilized, and channeled an extraordinarily broad network of individuals who sought political change both locally and nationally. The PT sought to develop a deeper sort of participatory democracy, beyond elections and voting, and to reorient government policy toward the interests of poor and working-class Brazilians. As it grew, its organizational strength, programmatic coherence, and administrative innovation transformed it into the anchor of the opposition within Brazil's fragmented party system and helped it, in contrast with every other Brazilian party, amass a large and loyal following of partisan identifiers (*petistas*).[2]

Assessing Democracy in Lula's Brazil

Since its inception, the PT has advertised itself as "different." An evaluation of democratic governance in contemporary Brazil must therefore ask, "What is different about the Lula/PT administration, and what difference, if any, has the Lula/PT government made for Brazilian democracy?" In this regard, the most important point is not that Lula and the PT are outsiders, but that for the first time Brazil's leader not only boasts of considerable personal popularity but also leads a highly institutionalized political party with deep roots in society. At the time of Lula's inauguration, nearly one in four Brazilians identified themselves as *petistas*, not just *lulistas*, an astonishingly high proportion when one considers the weakness of Brazil's other parties in terms of mass partisan identification. Other presidents could boast of convincing electoral victories, but their histories and fates were never so intimately linked to those of a political party—and vice versa. José Sarney (1985–89) was hardly a paladin of the fight of the Partido do Movimento Democrático Brasileiro (PMDB; Brazilian Democratic Movement Party) against the military regime; Fernando Collor's (1990–92) Partido da Reconstrução Nacional (National Reconstruction Party) was a legal fiction; and even Fernando Henrique Cardoso's (1995–2002) Partido da Social Democracia Brasileira (PSDB; Brazilian Social Democracy Party), after eight years spent controlling the national government, had put down only weak roots in society.

Given these differences, the Lula administration provides a new lens through which to assess the long-standing debate—ongoing both in comparative politics and in the analysis of Brazilian governance specifically— about the allegedly "difficult combination" of presidentialism and multipartism.[3] Analysts of Brazilian politics contentiously debate the nature of the country's executive-legislative relations, which are unproblematic to some, chaotic and paralyzing to others, and neither here nor there to still others. Prior to Lula's ascension to power, never before had the Brazilian political system—also the subject of intense academic debates about the alleged weakness of its parties and party system—been tested by the ascension to power of a popular leader backed by a highly institutionalized political party.

Lula's electoral victory forced the PT to face up to several challenges, including those that any party confronts when it assumes control of the apparatus of the state for the first time and those that confront historically leftist parties in particular when they assume such control. Moreover, in the PT's case such challenges differ from those faced by other leftist parties because the PT's trajectory emerged from the *non-communist* left. The PT and its supporters have historically exhibited a philosophically ambiguous stance regarding the exercise of state power given their exaltation of the power of civil society organizations to radically transform state-society relations. Finally, even though its presidential candidate had earned a smashing personal electoral majority, the PT had to address all these challenges as a minority government. As a cohesive leftist party with far greater ideological motivation as well as organizational density and cohesion than Brazil's other parties, the PT has demonstrated governance dynamics that necessarily differ from those of a government led by any of Brazil's other parties. All of these issues add layers of complexity to the questions regarding the dilemmas of multiparty presidentialism, Brazil's default situation.

The PT remains a novelty in Brazilian politics despite its moderation over the 1990s and the experience of the Lula government since 2003. Any evaluation of Brazilian democracy under Lula must therefore focus not only on policies enacted as opposed to those that were left on the table and the stability of executive-legislative relations but, more important, on the tension between government policies and performance and how well the administration measured up to the aspirations and hopes of the PT and its supporters. Consideration of this latter question, which emphasizes the relationship between the president and his party, has not been unknown in analyses of previous administrations, but it merits far more scrutiny in the case of Lula's government. This chapter explores this tension, focusing particularly on the consequences of the administration's coalition-building strategy in terms of the PT's ability to implement its vision for Brazilian society.

Evaluating the *Modo Lula de Governar*

How can we compare Lula's presidency to previous administrations? Although the definitive evaluation of the administration of Fernando Henrique Cardoso remains to be written, many observers agree with Bolívar Lamounier's assessment in the previous edition of this book, that the Cardoso administration "may well turn out to be seen as one of the most effective in Brazilian history."[4] Yet despite Cardoso's many accomplishments, especially in terms of institutionalizing economic stability and improving education and health, his reform agenda remained incomplete. His policies substituted hyperinflation for crushingly high interest rates and a massive increase in the national debt; economic growth was mediocre; unemployment remained stubbornly high; the crime rate increased inexorably; the country's energy, communications, and transportation infrastructure begged for investment; the social security system's deficit mounted; and the tax system remained hopelessly complicated and burdensome.[5]

Lula's 2002 Campaign: Contradictory Signals

During his campaign Lula heaped blame on Cardoso and vowed to aggressively confront these problems, calling them a *"herança maldita"* (accursed legacy). Lula had repeatedly condemned the Cardoso government's reforms and economic policies as insufficient and inappropriate. His campaign motto, *"Um Brasil para todos"* (A Brazil for everyone), and his campaign platform expressed a desire not just to build on the Cardoso administration's achievements but to do so in a way that put PT ideals into practice.[6] The PT had long expressed its key principles as the so-called *"modo petista de governar"* (PT way of governing), a critical element in the PT's self-image and public presentation as "different." The *modo petista de governar* has three pillars: greater popular participation in setting government policies, an "inversion" of government policy and investment priorities toward the poor, and greater government transparency and honesty.[7] Lula's campaign and election victory thus raised the hopes of those who expected his government to redirect government priorities and change the relationship between citizens and the state.

Yet, despite these expectations, the presidential campaign sent conflicting messages. Although Lula and the PT had adopted more pragmatic policy stances since the mid-1990s, growing economic instability in the runup to the 2002 election indicated that the market had yet to fully appreciate the extent of the PT's moderation.[8] Thus, while Lula promised to provide what Cardoso could not, he also sought to placate international financial markets. To bolster his credibility, Lula chose as his running mate a prominent representative of Brazil's business class and a member of the conservative Partido Liberal (PL; Liberal Party). He also released a statement of principles—purportedly addressed to the Brazilian people but in reality aimed at domestic and international financiers—that emphasized his acceptance of the rules of the economic and political game.[9] Prior to his inauguration Lula also publicly supported an International Monetary Fund (IMF) stabilization plan negotiated and signed during the last months of the Cardoso administration. Lula's policy proposals were clearly constrained by international market considerations, and his 2003 campaign sent contradictory signals: he sought votes based on traditional *petista* ideals, but he also sought to portray himself as someone who would not undo the hard-won economic stability the Cardoso administration had achieved.[10]

The Modo Petista de Governar *under Lula*

Lula's campaign successfully bolstered his image as a political moderate, but it also suggested to Lula's core supporters that he was willing to sacrifice ideology in the name of expediency. Once Lula reached the corridors of power, to what extent did his government live up to the expectations the PT's long trajectory had encouraged? It is certainly the case that the administration (and thus the PT) can trumpet a series of positive economic and social statistics. For example, in its first three years Brazil's GDP growth was positive, and although it was not as spectacular as that of China, for example, it was slightly higher on average than the rate of growth during Cardoso's two terms. The rate of inflation remained fairly low and stable, interest rates declined slightly (although they remained high by global standards, stifling investment), formal employment levels increased, the export volume nearly doubled, Brazil eliminated its debt with the IMF, and the country's national debt level declined as a proportion of GDP.[11]

Given these positive economic signals, Brazil's "country risk" (a measure of the premium that international markets demand before investing in a country) declined, indicating that the international finance community regarded Brazil as stable and thus as a good investment opportunity. Nevertheless, despite all this apparent good news, before the administration had even reached its midpoint many observers concluded that Lula's ascension to national power meant the abandonment of the *modo petista de governar.* To what extent was this conclusion justified? Had Lula achieved success in the economic sphere (which helped him win reelection in October 2006 by a huge margin) at the cost of abandoning his own party's long-standing principles, the three pillars of *modo petista de governar*?

The First Pillar: Popular Participation

It is safe to say that Lula's administration has not yet met the PT's longstanding goal of greater popular participation in setting government policy and investment priorities. Observers have suggested that the Lula administration has never even given "participatory governance" an opportunity. For example, the administration's much-vaunted Conselho de Desenvolvimento Econômico e Social (Social and Economic Development Council), which in theory would have brought dozens of representatives of civil society organizations onto a policy advisory board, has been absolutely irrelevant. Likewise, no effort was made to apply the PT's much-vaunted "participatory budgeting" process, which the party touted as a major success in many of its municipal administrations, at the national level.[12] These failures to put ideals into practice sorely disappointed many PT supporters, for whom mobilization and participation define what it means to be a *petista*.[13]

The Second Pillar: An Inversion of Priorities

In the eyes of many PT supporters, the administration failed to enact the PT's goal of inverting government policy toward the poor. Some even suggested that Lula's presidency could be mistaken for a third Cardoso term given the large dose of policy continuity and the emphasis on economic stability rather than transformation of the country's economic model. Lula filled key economic management positions with moderates who focused on maintaining Brazil's international credibility rather than with party ideologues, and he largely maintained the Cardoso administration's policy of high interest rates, which had been designed to keep inflation in check. He also sought to enhance his government's market credibility by *exceeding* the Cardoso administration's austerity measures: Lula's first finance minister set a primary budget surplus target of 4.75 percent of GDP rather than 3.75 percent. Setting aside a larger proportion of GDP to pay off debts meant, of course, that the government could do less to meet the PT's own long-standing demands for greater social spending, but it also meant that Lula was not tagged an "economic populist" of the Hugo Chávez style.

In terms of policy proposals, the Lula government also emphasized continuity with Cardoso's policies. For example, the government proposed granting autonomy to the Central Bank, a move the PT had long opposed. (Such autonomy means that the political party in power exerts less influence over monetary policy; instead the central bank is free to concentrate exclusively on market considerations.) Lula also initially sought to hold the line on minimum wage rate increases, even though he had promised to double the minimum wage by the end of his administration (he did propose minimum wage increases eventually). And although much of his leftist support base erupted in protest, Lula proposed public sector pension reforms to reduce a deficit in the social security system. The proposal sought to lower benefit payments, increase social security taxes, and restrict eligibility for benefits. Under Cardoso the PT had opposed any such reform—because public sector unions comprise an important element of the PT's base—but Lula fought for and obtained its passage in an effort to continue to put Brazil's fiscal accounts in order.[14]

The government claimed its policies were necessary to ensure macroeconomic stability. This may well be true, but its critics complained that the government failed to counterbalance the emphasis on economic stability with sufficient attention to social policy. Academic observers reported that such critiques quickly became widespread among civil society organizations.[15] For example, the government's much-publicized "Zero Hunger" program was criticized as inefficient and designed for publicity rather than to end hunger; some observers suggested that most of the administration's social programs merely continued policies enacted under Cardoso. The government's allies also decried Lula's perceived failure to keep a campaign promise to expand Cardoso's land reform program, calling Lula's efforts in this area "absolutely residual and peripheral."[16]

The government's focus on continuity and stability rather than on change and confrontation of the established economic interests came at a high political cost. The PT's left wing, along with other parties in the president's electoral coalition, harshly criticized Lula's pragmatism. The administration's leftist critics perceived a disjuncture between its economic policies and its political and social support bases, and they reacted violently to their perceived abandonment or betrayal. Some disillusioned *petistas* even concluded that Lula had actually converted to neoliberalism. Whatever the case, Lula's choice to adhere to conservative economic policies precluded radical change in the realm of social policy. This served to alienate his closest political allies and weaken the government's legislative support.

However, the government's leftist critics have missed an important point. Those who claim that the government has failed to enact an inversion of government priorities ignore substantial evidence that Brazil's poor have enjoyed improved living standards under the Lula government, including a sizable real increase (if not a doubling, as of late 2006) in the minimum wage, which has improved the purchasing power of Brazil's poorest citizens.[17] The proportion of Brazilians living below the "absolute poverty level" (those who earn less than R$115, or about US$50, per month) declined by only 2.2 percent between 1995 and 2003, but declined by 19.2 percent just between 2003 and 2005 (Figure 7.1).[18] Brazil has long been one of the world's most unequal societies, but under Lula income inequality has declined: between 1995 and 2003, Brazil's Gini coefficient improved by 2.75 percent, yet in just the first three years of Lula's administration it improved by another 2.55 percent, reaching its lowest point since 1981 (Table 7.1).[19] Among other indicators, infant mortality declined and the proportion of residences with access to sanitation increased.[20]

The Lula government attributes these gains in social welfare to its increases in the minimum wage and in targeted social spending. In particular, Lula has highlighted his Bolsa Família (roughly translated, Family Scholarship) program, which provides R$50 a month (plus R$15 per child, up to R$45 additionally) to families earning less than R$100 per month. This program expanded rapidly under Lula, and by the end of 2006 it covered nearly everyone eligible—almost 11 million families.

Figure 7.1. Percentage of the Brazilian Population Living below the Absolute Poverty Level, 1992–2005

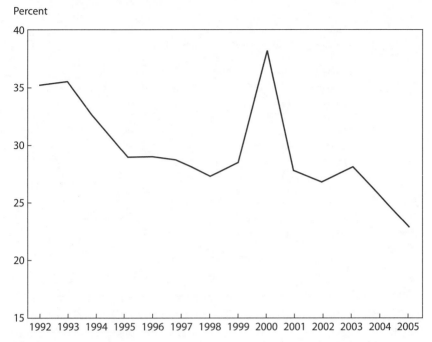

Source: Fundação Getúlio Vargas, "O segundo real," PowerPoint slide presentation, Centro de Pesquisas Sociais, Fundação Getúlio Vargas, Rio de Janeiro, 2006, www.fgv.br/cps/pesquisas/site_ret_port/RET_Apresentacao_port.pdf.

It is true that some of Brazil's social indicators have been improving for years, and it remains unclear what is distinctly leftist or even *petista* about Bolsa Família and the other programs that Lula highlights as the key social welfare policies marking his presidency. Nevertheless, the results of the 2006 elections indicate that redistributive programs helped Lula defeat his rivals and win reelection.[21] Without looking at the political impact of government economic policies and distributivist programs, it is extremely difficult to understand the strength of Lula's political support among Brazil's lower classes.

Lula has always relied on his personal charisma and has always claimed to represent the interests of Brazil's less fortunate, but he failed to win his 1989, 1994, and 1998 presidential campaigns because he could not overcome the resistance by members of Brazil's poorer classes to his candidacy. "Poor folks don't vote for poor folks" is commonly heard in Brazil. Yet after his 2002 election Lula engineered a political realignment and quickly established his popularity with Brazil's poor majority, largely through the consolidation of social welfare spending and its expansion to Brazil's poorest classes. In so doing, Lula reassured his own reelection.

Table 7.1. Gini Coefficients for Brazil, 1992–2005

Date	Gini Coefficient
January 1, 1992	0.583
January 1, 1993	0.607
January 1, 1995	0.599
January 1, 1996	0.602
January 1, 1997	0.600
January 1, 1998	0.600
January 1, 1999	0.594
January 1, 2001	0.596
January 1, 2002	0.589
January 1, 2003	0.583
January 1, 2004	0.572
January 1, 2005	0.568

Source: Fundação Getúlio Vargas, "O segundo real," Power-Point slide presentation, Centro de Pesquisas Sociais, Fundação Getúlio Vargas, Rio de Janeiro, 2006, www.fgv.br/cps/pesquisas/site_ret_port/RET_Apresentacao_port.pdf.

Given this dynamic, there is a disjuncture between the perceptions of many leftist critics and the perception of millions of Brazilian voters as to whether there has been an inversion of government priorities. The truth is surely a matter for debate, because many policies of the Lula government indeed simply represent the expansion and/or consolidation of policies begun under President Cardoso and are not *petista* policies per se. It is also remains unclear to what extent these distributivist programs are actually redistributivist (i.e., fundamentally attack Brazil's vast inequalities) and to what extent they represent a true inversion of priorities of the Brazilian government. (And of course any government can do *more* for the poor.)

The Third Pillar: Ethical and Transparent Governance

Prior to the explosion of scandals during Lula's first term, most observers of Brazilian politics—and most *petistas* themselves—believed that corruption pervaded every party *except* the PT. Lula and the PT built their reputation not only by calling for broader participation and advocating change in government priorities but also by railing against corruption and political impunity. Elected PT officials sought to cultivate a reputation for putting into practice what they demanded of others. However, this third element of the party's self-portrait contrasts with the practices of the PT as the governing party, and the PT's image has suffered as a result.

The fundamental problem Lula confronted when he took office was how to transform his large electoral coalition into a stable governing coalition.

This is a common dilemma under multiparty presidentialism. As Abranches presciently argued before Brazil had even elected its first president following military rule, coalition presidentialism is the greatest Brazilian institutional dilemma, bar none.[22] Presidents' coalitions illustrate how they propose to resolve the tension between the majoritarian institution of the presidency and the power-sharing requirements of Brazil's other political institutions.

Brazil's institutions do not foretell presidential success or failure. Presidents make choices, and the experiences of Fernando Collor, Itamar Franco, Cardoso, and Lula reveal (in very different ways) that those choices matter a great deal. Presidents can try to govern more or less alone, as Collor did initially, by relying on laws in the form of decrees and on other unilateral measures such as the use of their appointment and budgetary impoundment powers. Collor sought to exploit the majoritarian and plebiscitary aspects of the presidency. In contrast, Cardoso sought to negotiate a wholesale distribution of power and resources in order to construct a broad majority coalition.

How did Lula seek to meet the challenge of coalition presidentialism? At first glance, his coalition and policy choices might suggest that the PT fully capitulated to rather than changed the Brazilian political system. However, this is an inaccurate inference. Hunter suggests that Lula's administration highlights the incompleteness of the PT's transformation into "just another party."[23] Lula made strenuous efforts to protect his party—and, more specifically, to protect his allies within the party—from the power-sharing incentives that drive coalition presidentialism in Brazil. He refused to wholeheartedly adopt pork-barrel politics, and he refused to share control of bureaucratic appointments with allied party leaders. Thus, to maintain support in the legislature, his administration sought allies on the cheap and relied on corruption, at least in part. This is a key point, for it suggests that Lula sought to chart a political path different from what either Ames or Figueiredo and Limongi say is "politics as usual" in Brazil. Ames suggests that ad hoc "retail" clientelism is the norm and results in unstable governance, while Figueiredo and Limongi argue that "wholesale" distribution of the spoils is the norm and tends to generate stable party coalitions.[24]

Brazilian presidents possess substantial leeway to choose between the extremes of a purely unilateral strategy (an extreme version of the strategy used by Collor) or a purely cooperative approach (an extreme version of that chosen by Cardoso). Lula's approach to governing was not as unilateral as Collor's, nor was it as cooperative as Cardoso's. The critical way in which governance differs under Lula is that he clearly has sought to favor his own political party. As suggested earlier, Lula's presidency is not different simply because he is sociologically or ideologically "different" but because his presidency is the first since Brazil's redemocratization (perhaps the first in the country's history) in which the president, imbued with substantial popular legitimacy and charismatic authority by virtue of his direct election, has sought to govern in tandem with a highly bureaucratized political party that possesses a powerful sense of mission and an activist membership numbering in the hundreds of thousands but holds nothing close to a majority of the seats in the legislature. Lula and the PT have confronted dilemmas of multiparty presidentialism unlike those faced by any previous Brazilian president.

Upon taking office, Lula confronted the need to perform a complicated balancing act, to obtain a majority without alienating his base. The results of the 2002 legislative elections shaped his options. The PT became the largest party in the Chamber of Deputies (equivalent to the U.S. House of Representatives), winning 17.7 percent of the seats, but the parties in Lula's electoral coalition controlled only a total of 25.3 percent of the seats in the Chamber, along with 29.7 percent in the Senate. To get anything done, much less to reach the 60 percent threshold required to pass constitutional amendments, Lula would have to reach out to parties outside his electoral coalition, even to parties that had supported the Cardoso administration.

Lula constructed a governing majority by bringing eight parties into his first administration (January 2003–January 2004). This was not only the most fragmented government since redemocratization but also the "most fragmented ministry ever formed in the history of Latin American presidentialism."[25] The coalition was also ideologically diffuse, incorporating parties from across the political spectrum. Yet even a coalition as broad and this initially failed to provide a legislative majority. The government achieved this majority by capitalizing on many politicians' weak attachments to their parties and on the tradition of *governismo* (a pragmatic desire to obtain the clientelistic benefits of being in the government rather than remaining in the opposition), enticing several deputies to abandon the party that had helped them win election and switch into one of the cabinet's two center-right parties, the Partido Trabalhista Brasileiro (PTB; Brazilian Labor Party) or the PL (it should be noted that in Brazil, approximately a third of all sitting members of Congress, on average, switch parties during a term).

Lula could have constructed a broader coalition, but he opted to seek a bare majority. He personally vetoed the participation of the centrist and relatively large PMDB, which held 14.4 percent of the seats in the Chamber at the start of the legislature compared to the PTB's and PL's 5.1 percent and 4.3 percent, respectively. Couto and Baia suggest that Lula adopted this tactic because he believed he did not need wider congressional support given his convincing electoral victory, his personal legitimacy, and his high level of public support at the start of his administration.[26] Or perhaps Lula's opinion of Congress remained as it had been in 1993, when he famously stated, "There is a minority in Congress that works for the good of the country, but there is a majority of three hundred jerks (*picaretas*) who only defend their own interests." The insult suggests a deep aversion to depending on a group of "jerks" for support. The PT reinforced that disposition, because Lula confronted resistance from within his party to ceding power to the party's ostensible enemies. Thus Lula sought to distribute as few ministries as possible to members of nonleftist parties as a way to forestall protest from his own support base against policies he was soon to propose, such as that regarding pension reform.

For a brief period, Lula managed to balance the concerns of his leftist supporters with an ability to provide just enough of what members of the PTB and PL wanted to keep them in his cabinet. And so, during the first half of his first term, Lula's government passed several important pieces of legislation, including contentious reforms of the financial system (granting greater autonomy to the Central Bank), the government employees' pension system (noted earlier), the tax system (gaining continued collection of "temporary" levies initially imposed under Cardoso), the bankruptcy law (making it easier for companies to declare bankruptcy, with the aim of easing the cost of doing business in Brazil), and the judicial system (seeking to limit nepotism and corruption and to speed the judicial process).[27]

Despite these successes, Lula's governing strategy proved fragile. Lula's problems began when his supporters on the left opposed his social security reform. This reform passed only because Lula ignored his leftist base and reached out to the opposition PSDB and the Partido da Frente Liberal (PFL; Liberal Front Party), as well as to the PMDB, which at that time was neither formally in the government nor in the opposition. It was at this point that criticism of Lula's abandonment of the *modo petista de governar* intensified. After social security reform passed, one of the leftist parties in Lula's cabinet withdrew from the government. Worse, the PT expelled several members who had persistently opposed the reform, exposing irresolvable internal fractures in what observers had long regarded as Brazil's most cohesive party.[28]

The Second Cabinet: An Attempt to Strengthen the Governing Coalition

Lula's policy choices forced him to lean more heavily on parties to the PT's right, and in January 2004 he reversed his earlier decision and brought the PMDB into his government. His nominal legislative majority thus surpassed even the 60 percent threshold necessary to amend the Constitution. Nevertheless, the government's control of the legislative agenda subsequently weakened.[29] What explains this paradox? The degree of fragmentation and heterogeneity of Lula's cabinets do not provide the key, but the proportionality of the distribution of portfolios does. After the PMDB was invited into the cabinet, the distribution of portfolios became less proportional: the PT controlled only 29 percent of the coalition's seats but took 60 percent of the ministries. In contrast, the PMDB, PL, and PTB held almost 50 percent of the seats in the coalition but were awarded a total of only 12 percent of the portfolios.[30]

Thus, even though Lula appeared to broaden his legislative base after a year in office, his choices served to weaken the political pillars that support any legislative coalition, the distribution of the spoils of office and the influence over policy formulation that coalition members expect as fair trade in exchange for their support in the legislature. This situation increasingly generated dissatisfaction among the center-right parties. Lula was caught between a rock and a hard place: his policies (as well as the inclusion of the PL, PTB, and PMDB in the cabinet) angered his leftist base, but the disproportional distribution of cabinet portfolios angered his partners to the right.

Lula's distribution of cabinet portfolios indicated an unwillingness to concede substantial access to government resources and control over policies to parties other than the PT.[31] The PT sought to maintain control of policy as well as the power to hire and fire down through the second and third echelons of the federal bureaucracy.[32] Thus, although Lula's coalition was nominally broad, his coalition partners had relatively little power to enact policy and grew frustrated at their inability to appoint friends and allies to plum government posts.[33] Instead of giving his coalition partners what they most wanted by purchasing their support "wholesale" and conceding substantial control over the levers of power, Lula relied on a "retail" coalition-building strategy. In principle, this strategy could resemble a simplified version of the picture of Brazilian politics Ames provides, wherein the president negotiates support on a vote-by-vote, deputy-by-deputy basis in exchange for the distribution of clientelistic resources. Although there is nothing illegal about this strategy, observers regard it as politically and economically inefficient.[34]

The weakness of the government's legislative coalition—and Lula's inability to control both moderates and radicals within the party—soon became transparent. In early 2005, the government failed to elect its chosen candidate as president of the Chamber of Deputies. Traditionally the largest party in the Chamber elects the president of that body. However, sectors of the PT as well as a substantial proportion of opposition deputies rejected the government's nominee. The PT split so badly that a second PT deputy put forth his name, undermining the government's candidate. In the end, the government nominee lost, the PT's independent candidate lost, and a backbencher with little stature obtained the Chamber presidency. This result illustrated that Lula could even not control the moderates within his party, much less organize a coherent majority coalition.[35]

The Descent into Scandal

The government's problems worsened. In May 2005 a minor postal service bureaucrat was caught on film demanding a bribe on behalf of PTB leader Roberto Jefferson. As accusations against him mounted, Jefferson accused the government of constructing its coalition through payola, by exchanging monthly cash "allowances" (the so-called *mensalão*) for support on particular legislative votes and by using cash to "encourage" deputies to switch into parties in the government coalition. These accusations implied that Lula had constructed his first cabinet not through perfectly legal if inefficient "retail" pork-barrel politics but through corruption. The PT's treasurer admitted that the illegal payments had been made but claimed that the government was not bribing its way to a majority but was instead providing under-the-table campaign finance (known as *caixa dois,* or the "second cash box") to its allies to retire debts from 2002 and to cover expenses from the 2004 municipal campaigns. The scandals spread, affecting members of both branches of government, and Lula's approval ratings plummeted.[36]

The scandals badly damaged the reputation the PT had built over the previous two decades, but the *mensalão* was just the proverbial tip of the iceberg.[37] Media and congressional investigators obsessed over the question of where the cash for the payola had come from, and soon they discovered that the PT had constructed a massive, organized *caixa dois* scheme, disguising its illegal fund-raising just as other parties had done in the past. The scandals forced Lula's chief of staff to resign from the cabinet (he returned to his seat in Congress, which expelled him) and also forced out several other administration and party officials, including the finance minister and the president of the PT. These powerful figures had played key roles, helping to articulate Lula's policy proposals, maintain connections with the PT's organization, and establish links with the business community.

Roberto Jefferson blew the lid off the PT's scheme to save his own skin, but he, too, was eventually expelled from Congress. Once he realized he would not enjoy impunity, he decided to go down with guns blazing. His self-serving justifications for his corruption possessed a certain perverse coherence: on the one hand, he readily admitted to having no objection, in principle, to *caixa dois.* Yet, on the other hand, he protested that the *mensalão* crossed some sort of ethical line because it violated a cardinal rule of Brazilian politics, well expressed by the famous expression of St. Francis of Assisi: "*É dando que se recebe*" (It is in giving that you receive).[38] In Jefferson's world, "business as usual" meant that parties used their control of government agencies to generate kickbacks. (Private sector businesses often depend on government agencies for contracts, generating a give-and-take relationship.)

Jefferson alleged that the PT sought to monopolize control of these kickbacks and distribute the money as it saw fit, but he claimed that he had refused to play by the PT's rules. Up until that point, he had had no problem taking what the PT had given him, including several million *reais* to distribute to his copartisans, and his legal defense did not depend on revealing the political dynamics of the PT's corruption schemes.

The Political Roots of the Scandals

We may never know whether Jefferson's allegations were wholly true, but the general contours of his accusations have been supported by subsequent investigations. Corruption has always existed in Brazil, and Brazil is certainly not the "most corrupt" country; in 2006 it ranked 70th out of 163 countries in the Transparency International Rankings, slightly more corrupt than in 2005.[39] Yet given the PT's trajectory and public image, what explains the corruption in the Lula government? The scandals cannot be blamed on "PT incompetence," an allegation some Brazilian conservatives have long made, because that lets Lula and the PT off the hook by eliding their political agency. Other conservatives have alleged that the PT is a wolf in sheep's clothing—that it is an anti-republican organization that seeks to steamroll democratic institutions, conquer the state by any means necessary, and put it in the service of the party.[40] After Lula's victory, those who hold this view pointed to Lula's disproportional cabinets and efforts to give the PT a greater say over appointments to the government bureaucracy, his government's efforts to undermine the already fragmented party system through the use of payola, and the PT's illegal campaign finance scheme as evidence in support of their views.[41]

One cannot simply dismiss the accusations against the PT as politically motivated because the party's leaders have admitted that a substantial part of what has been said is true. The PT and its supporters dismissed attempts to paint the party as anti-democratic, yet its leaders' responses to the scandals left many of its supporters ashamed. PT leaders initially suggested that administrative incompetence within the party resulted in misguided and admittedly illegal efforts to raise campaign funds.[42] They used this excuse in an attempt to isolate the few "bad apples" from the rest of the party—and, more important, from Lula's government. Yet, as suggested earlier, this explanation is unsatisfying. Lula's own attorney general affirmed that immediately following the 2002 elections a criminal organization within the PT had taken root in Lula's administration to work toward the PT's long-term political project.[43]

If one of Lula's own appointees is willing make such an affirmation in public, we can be sure that when PSDB and PFL leaders level accusations at the administration they do not merely seek to score political points with voters. The attorney general's statements left Lula in the uncomfortable position of having to explain how such an organization could take shape at the PT's highest level and install itself inside the Palacio do Planalto without his knowledge, and how and why his closest confidants could so profoundly betray him. He had no option but to play the fool (in which case he could also play the victim) or admit he was a liar. Not surprisingly, he chose the former. Yet, when pressed to acknowledge and explain their party's use of *caixa dois,* both Lula and PT leaders have downplayed the scandals' significance and have even resisted admitting that they did anything wrong. At the height of the scandal, Lula could only bring himself to say, "The PT only did what other Brazilian parties have done all along."[44]

It is clear that the scandals are the fruit of the PT's long-standing yet increasingly problematic relationship to campaign finance.[45] PT candidates have always trailed candidates from other (nonleftist) parties in their ability to raise funds, largely because the party historically possessed few links to wealthy private sector patrons.[46] The PT compensated for its poverty by relying on the coattail effects of Lula's popularity and, more important, on the strength of its organization, its message, and its party label.[47] Campaigns are expensive in Brazil, not simply because money affects election outcomes but also because most politicians lack tools besides money—most notably, affiliation with a strong party label—to attract voter support.[48] The key to the PT's growth, in other words, was not Lula's personality but the resonance of the party's image among broad swaths of the Brazilian electorate and the extensive network of partisans it could mobilize. Yet, in the 1990s, as Lula and the PT moderated and adopted a more pragmatic approach to campaigns, elections, and electoral alliances, the party's leaders came to rely less on the party's traditional mobilizational techniques and increasingly on campaign tactics similar to those used by other parties. However, as the party sought to expand its appeal, it consistently failed to obtain the funds it needed to compete successfully.[49]

According to Hunter, the temptation to resort to *caixa dois* is the flip side of the party's moderation over the course of the 1990s.[50] There is much truth to this. Given the party's persistent lack of access to legitimate sources of campaign finance, Lula's ascension to power opened innumerable doors to temptation. After all, Lula would need money to win reelection, and the party needed money to continue to grow. Yet Lula's statement that the PT did what other parties have done is an excuse, not an explanation, and in important respects it is also wrong. Desperation to increase the flow of money does not explain why elements within the PT engineered a centrally organized, illegal *caixa dois* scheme. After all, governing provides access to various forms of political power that can be leveraged at the next election, and it also opens the spigots of legal campaign finance.

Lula is correct when he acknowledges that the PT stooped to the level of the tawdriest Brazilian politics when it sought to raise campaign funds illegally. *Caixa dois* is widely practiced in Brazil; the official campaign finance reports, it is said, account for only 10–30 percent of real expenditures. Yet, as typically practiced, *caixa dois* is highly decentralized, just as is the rest of the Brazilian campaign finance market.[51] All party organizations receive yearly subventions from the government, but parties receive no funds to support their candidates' campaigns, and national party organizations have never controlled the raising of campaign funds and their distribution to candidates for any office (except the presidency), as they do in most countries. The Lula administration's scandals are novel—even unprecedented—in Brazilian politics, and Lula's statement is incorrect in an important way, because for the first time in Brazilian history a highly organized political party sought to leverage its control of the national government to raise funds on its own behalf, to influence or even control the flow of campaign funds to its candidates (and even to its allies), and to discriminate against its rivals.[52]

PT leaders did not engage in illegal activities simply to enrich themselves personally (although many of them certainly did so), as is often the case in Brazil and elsewhere. They did so as part of a quest for power, on behalf of a party and its candidates. We can be even more specific about the partisan nature of the campaign finance scandals under Lula, and thus how they differ from previous scandals, by noting the particular intraparty dynamic of the scandal. Efforts to accumulate funds through *caixa dois* reflect a long-standing effort on the part of elements within the PT's dominant faction to tighten their grip on the party machine—to help the party grow but particularly to help their allies within the party. Ideology and geography both played a role in this story of intraparty competition; Lula's allies sought to retain control of the party in the face of competition from factions to their left and also from politicians from outside the state of São Paulo, home to most of Lula's closest associates. Seeking legal campaign donations would have forced members of this group to report their activities both to the party and to the general public, and probably would have forced them to distribute all contributions according to party-determined proportional criteria, but they sought to avoid such controls.

Apparently such illegal campaign finance activities had been ongoing within the PT since the 1990s but on a smaller scale.[53] Lula's ascension to power transferred the personnel involved in illegal activities to the center of national power. Their behavior continued, on a much larger scale, but the scheme proved untenable. Previously such activities could be hidden behind the closed doors of party meetings, but secrets are harder to keep when more people know about them and when the scale of the operation grows. As in the case of Fernando Collor's move from the tiny state of Alagoas into the national spotlight, the PT's shift in scale caught the attention of far more people and generated far more political friction.

Party Politics and the Distinctiveness of the Lula Administration's Scandals

The campaign finance scandals under Lula are thus distinctive relative to previous scandals because at root they concern control of a national political party, not winning this or that particular election, "buying" votes in Congress to pass this or that bill, or (for the most part) personal enrichment. The connection between the *caixa dois* and the *mensalão* reveals differences between these scandals and previous ones as well, because the *caixa dois* aspect of the scandals does not explain why Lula (or rather his minions, if we are to believe Lula's claims) adopted a coalition-building strategy that included the *mensalão. Caixa dois* and *mensalão* are linked, but not simply because the money either came from or was to be used for off-the-books campaign finance. They are linked because they reflect the Lula administration's and the PT's inability to resolve the dilemma posed by coalition presidentialism. Fernando Henrique Cardoso had demonstrated that the obstacles of Brazil's consociational institutional matrix are not insurmountable, so the questions are whether Lula was unable or unwilling to adopt a similar approach, given somewhat different constraints, and why he chose to adopt a different tactic to generate legislative support.

As noted earlier, Lula initially chose to construct as narrow a coalition as possible, but just one year into his term he appeared to broaden his coalition to include the PMDB. Yet appearances can be deceiving, for this coalition was built on a weak foundation. Lula's critical problem was not his inability to construct a coalition (due to the refusal of other parties to enter the government) but rather his and the PT's unwillingness to share power. The numerous academic observations to this effect echo (and serve to confirm) what Lula's conservative opponents (including Roberto Jefferson) have alleged from the start.[54] In the end we must conclude that the PT committed the same political error (albeit for different reasons) as Fernando Collor: it refused to share.

Taken as a whole, the exposure of the *mensalão* and the *caixa dois* scandals illuminates the shadowy corners of a larger picture that includes the administration's cabinet coalition-building strategy and the PT's *aparelhismo*, its effort to employ the apparatus of the government bureaucracy to serve the party's long-term political interests. These are all elements of a strategy privileging one faction within the PT over the others and privileging the PT over other parties, the flip side of which involved a refusal to cede control of important ministries and secondary echelons of the government bureaucracy to supposed coalition allies.

This was the strategy Lula chose to use in his effort to address the challenge of coalition presidentialism, and it is useful to put this choice in perspective. Lula and the PT chose to purchase legislative support "on the retail market," but they chose not to do so the way that Ames suggests such coalitions are cemented: by judicious distribution of pork-barrel disbursements and by sharing control of bureaucratic appointments.[55] This distinction is important: a "retail clientelism" strategy may be politically "inefficient," but there is nothing illegal or unethical about it. Yet the Lula administration did not wholeheartedly adopt such a strategy, because it favored the PT's efforts at *aparelhismo* and disbursed relatively little pork.[56] Instead of relying on the political currency of pork and bureaucratic appointments, the government used actual currency, at least in part. Because there is no honor among thieves, this is a dangerous tactic for constructing a governing coalition.

Lula could have chosen different tactics, but he was unable to thread the needle between the demands of the PT and the demands of coalition presidentialism.[57] Although the PT had moderated over the years, it retained aspects of its unique organizational and ideational character. A broad perspective of the Lula administration thus highlights the fact that for the first time in Brazilian history a highly organized political party has had to confront the dilemmas of governing. In particular, the experience of Lula's first term tells a story of how leaders of a political party sought to use their party's control (or perceived control) of the apparatus of the state to enhance their long-term hold on political power in terms of both intraparty and interparty politics. This sort of thing happens all over the world, but even without any illegal activity it is new to Brazil. And in this case we cannot dismiss the corruption; instead we must connect the novelty of the party-state nexus and all its dilemmas to the fact that leaders of the PT engaged in illegal activities to work toward their goals. The Lula administration also differed from previous presidencies because its scandals were the fruit of a struggle for power within an enormous party organization and of the conflict between that party and its rivals rather than a function of the foibles of this or that politician or even of a clique of individuals within the government. In short, the dilemmas faced by the president and his government were inextricably related to his party's dilemmas, and vice versa, a dynamic relatively absent in previous administrations.

Conclusion

Since the 1980s Brazil has undergone two parallel and profound structural transformations: economic liberalization and democratization. These changes have substantially weakened the developmentalist and authoritarian aspects of the Brazilian state that have been dominant since the 1930s. Transformations in the political, social, and economic spheres turned the country toward a moderately liberal economic model by the end of Fernando Henrique Cardoso's administration, while the process of democratization ended only with the election of Lula. Sallum suggests that both of these processes are irreversible, because no political movement with sufficient weight advocates a return to the developmentalist state and because anti-democratic political forces lack support.[58]

Yet within the structural confines of this moderately liberal and largely capitalist democracy, there is substantial debate about how well Brazil's institutions function. What can the Lula government teach us about this debate, and what can we therefore learn about Brazilian democracy through an evaluation of Lula's presidency? For many scholars, Brazil's combination of the majoritarian institution of the presidency with a set of institutions that disperse political power hinders democratic governance.[59] "Power-fragmenting" institutions in Brazil include a high degree of party-system fragmentation; the effective number of legislative parties in Brazil was 8.5 in 2003, among the highest in the world. As one can see from Table 7.2, political parties rarely win more than 20 percent of the seats in Brazil's Chamber of Deputies. The PSDB, which was created only in 1988, peaked at 19.3 percent of the seats in 1998, and the PT, which had only 7 percent of the seats in 1990, peaked at 17.7 percent of the seats in 2002. Legislative fragmentation, as noted, requires the construction of broad and heterogeneous coalitions.

Other "power-fragmenting" institutions include federalism, strong bicameralism with a high level of malapportionment in both legislative chambers, an electoral system that promotes individualistic campaign behavior, a cumbersome judiciary, and an extremely detailed Constitution. Lamounier had difficulty reconciling Cardoso's many successes with his view of the political consequences of these institutions. Indeed, in the previous edition of this book he stated that Cardoso's success is paradoxical given the "manifest dysfunctionality" of Brazil's political system.[60]

This assessment seems exaggerated even in light of Lula's more modest achievements, especially given the problems that plague some of Brazil's neighbors. Under Lula GDP growth has been positive, if not the "spectacle" that Lula promised on the campaign trail. Inflation has remained low and stable, and the risk premium paid on Brazilian government bonds has declined substantially, indicating that international financial markets have accepted Lula's moderation and believe Brazil's economy is stable. As noted, several of Brazil's social indicators have continued to improve during Lula's presidency. Of course, several problems continue to bedevil Brazil's economy and polity. Interest rates remain among the highest in the world, making banking a highly profitable industry but crippling investment in productive activities. The ratio of public debt to GDP ratio remains high despite the gov-

Table 7.2. Seat Distribution in the Brazilian Chamber of Deputies, 1990–2006

Party	1990 No. seats	1990 Percentage	1994 No. seats	1994 Percentage	1998 No. seats	1998 Percentage	2002 No. seats	2002 Percentage	2006 No. seats	2006 Percentage
PT (leftist)	35	7.0	49	9.6	58	11.3	91	17.7	83	16.2
PSDB (centrist)	38	7.6	63	12.3	99	19.3	71	13.8	65	12.7
PP (rightist)	42	8.3	51	9.9	60	11.7	49	9.6	42	8.2
PMDB (centrist)	108	21.5	107	20.9	83	16.2	74	14.4	89	17.3
PDT (leftist)	46	9.1	34	6.6	25	4.9	21	4.1	24	4.7
PTB (centrist)	38	7.6	31	6.0	31	6.0	26	5.1	22	4.3
PFL (rightist)	83	16.5	89	17.3	105	20.5	84	16.4	65	12.7
Other left	19	3.8	29	5.6	30	5.9	54	10.5	77	15.0
Other center and right	94	18.8	60	11.7	22	4.3	43	8.5	46	9.0

Source: http://jaironicolau.iuperj.br/banco2004.html.
Notes: PT, Partido dos Trabalhadores (Workers' Party); PSDB, Partido da Social Democracia Brasileira (Brazilian Social Democracy Party); PP, Partido Progressista (Progressive Party); PMDB, Partido do Movimento Democrático Brasileiro (Brazilian Democratic Movement Party); PDT, Partido Democrático Trabalhista (Democratic Labor Party); PTB, Partido Trabalhista Brasileiro (Brazilian Labor Party); PFL, Partido da Frente Liberal (Liberal Front Party).

ernment's extraordinary efforts to extract budgetary surpluses. Unemployment remains high despite job growth. And despite some improvement, socioeconomic inequalities remain vast, perhaps contributing to Brazil's crime rate, which has been on the rise since the 1980s.

Prompted by Figueiredo and Limongi's analysis of presidential control of legislative agendas, many scholars have argued that there is no evidence that Brazil's institutions are "manifestly dysfunctional."[61] For example, Couto and Arantes note that despite party system fragmentation and multiparty cabinets, presidents have managed to pass dozens of constitutional amendments since 1988 (52 as of mid-2006), suggesting that even difficult policy reforms are within reach.[62] An exhaustive comparative study of the relationship between institutions and policy performance in Latin America prepared under the auspices of the Inter-American Development Bank (IDB) revealed that Brazil compares well with its neighbors in terms of policy performance.[63] Lula's survival through a rough presidency might just suggest that Brazil's institutions function well.

Yet institutional functionality is a narrow basis on which to assess Brazil's democracy. The discussion of the relationship between politics and performance in Brazil must consider a broader conception of democratic governance. The same IDB scholars who concluded that Brazil's policy performance is at least average also concluded that Brazil's political parties still poorly serve the country's citizens as agents of political representation and accountability.[64] Interested observers might concur that governability and deadlock no longer threaten Brazilian democracy, yet Brazilian democracy still faces several critical challenges.

Although Brazil certainly qualifies as fully democratic according to accepted minimal criteria and its policy process appears to function fairly well, debates about Brazil's political institutions overlook the fact that vast political inequalities persist (as they do in all countries to greater or lesser extents), in particular with regard to access to the government process and equality before the law.[65] Unequal political influence gives the lie to the "quality" of the formal institutions and highlights weaknesses in the rule of law. Money provides the wealthy with unequal access to government, undermining the notion that the "well-functioning" policy process reflects voters' expressed demands, even indirectly. While candidates spend billions of *reais* on election campaigns and Brazil's tax burden brings the government record tax revenue, elected officials bemoan a lack of resources to address pressing social needs, including greater access to health care and education and the development of a response to Brazil's growing crime and drug trafficking problems. Responsiveness to the needs of the general population remains problematic; it is no wonder that the vast majority of Brazilians express so little confidence in their elected leaders.

Moreover, although Brazil's electoral system, fragmented party system, and other institutions may not damage governability, they continue to impede voters' ability to identify clear policy alternatives in legislative elections and to hold elected officials accountable.[66] Both responsiveness and accountability presuppose political parties of a certain kind. For years the PT viewed debates about institutional reform proposals as "bourgeois concerns" with regard to governability and as irrelevant to the more important issues of expanding citizen participation in policy making and improving government transparency and accountability. That is, the PT presented itself as the agent of change that would bring greater responsiveness and accountability to Brazilian politics. However, Lula's political choices and the PT's descent into scandal may have sacrificed the PT's claim to carry the banner of "deepening" Brazil's clearly functional democracy. Indeed, the persistence of corruption under Lula suggests that political elites across all parties continue to believe in their own impunity, and it even suggests that Brazil has taken steps backward in terms of political equality, even as income inequality is declining.

In the end we have returned to square one in this debate, to the question of the quality of Brazil's political parties. Clearly the *qualities* of the PT affected the nature of the Lula administration, whether or not they determined it. Party-systems theory has long held a normative bias in favor of a Weberian "institutionalization" of the system and its component parts. In the Brazilian case this also implicitly suggests that the rise of parties like the PT positively reflects deep national cultural change, from the dominance of charismatic authority and informal patron-client relationships to a bureaucratic-rational mode of authority. Yet Brazil's first experience in which the bureaucracy of the state has been controlled by a highly bureaucratized political party whose vote base comes from the most developed sectors of society has not been an unmitigated success. What can this teach us about Brazilian democracy?

The Lula administration offers new perspectives on the debate about the "difficult combination" of presidentialism and multipartism. The experience of the Lula administration has revealed that different political dynamics emerge when a cohesive, organizationally complex party with deep roots in civil society governs from the position of legislative minority, in concert with parties that lack similar organizational characteristics, societal penetration, or ideological motivation. Lula's experience reveals that governing from such a position can seriously strain intraparty relations, in addition to having the usual problems of interparty coalition management.

As noted, the question of the relationship between the Brazilian president and his party has attracted relatively little attention, but the Lula government casts new light on this relationship. A president and his party face diverging incentives when they assume control of a government. First, a president wins election and must seek reelection and his place in history by appealing to a broad swath of the electorate. In contrast, members of his party can thrive on a much narrower electoral appeal. Second, a president knows that although he has won a majority of votes, if his party has not, his mandate is empty if he does not reach out to other parties in the legislature. Yet his party does not wish to share power and tries to hold the president to a narrower mandate.

Third, a president can survive in office and even successfully seek reelection without the support of his own party. Although Lula helped found the PT and spent years leading it and building up its organization, as the PT became mired in scandal Lula increasingly sought to distance himself from the party. Toward the end of his first term he increasingly sought to rely on his personal charisma rather than on the party organization for support. As his administration progressed, Lula's and the PT's goals increasingly diverged, and his coalition and policy choices served to fracture what observers had unanimously considered Brazil's most cohesive political party. Clearly the experience of governing has proved difficult for the PT.

Lula was unable to thread the needle between maintaining the solid support of his own party and the incentives and constraints of coalition presidentialism. By the midpoint of his first administration, his advocacy of centrist policies had cost him the support of his leftist base, yet he was unable to purchase consistent support from his center-right coalition partners. One cannot blame the administration's problems on weak support from his leftist allies, nor does the fault for the administration's problems lie with parties in opposition to the Lula/PT government. To blame leftist critics ignores the fact that most of the administration's problems originated from within the majority moderate faction within the PT, long controlled by Lula and his closest political allies.

The question is whether governability problems are the result of the oft-cited structural and institutional factors that fragment political power in Brazil or whether Lula and the PT made strategic and tactical errors. Presidential legacies are determined partly by structural conditions and partly by political choices; it is those choices that we must consider critical. A comparison across the Collor, Cardoso, and Lula administrations reveals the extent to which both intraparty and interparty negotiations are necessary for smooth governance in Brazil and the extent to which presidential strategy matters for governance in the context of a highly consociational political system. It is not the institutions per se that cause policy outcomes but rather the choices that political leaders make within those institutions. Legislative majorities are not automatic; institutional factors can make the construction of majorities problematic but not impossible.[67] The fate of each of Brazil's presidents since its redemocratization can be assessed in light of the dilemmas of coalition presidentialism.

Lula's administration is likely to be remembered for successfully building on the economic stabilization and political reforms that President Cardoso had achieved. However, it is also likely to be recalled for succumbing to and relying on traditional forms of clientelism and even for rationalizing patently illegal practices as the normal way of conducting political business. The adoption of illegal campaign finance techniques and their coordination from within the nerve center of Brazil's strongest national party spells trouble for the prospect that Brazil can successfully resolve the problem of the relationship between money and democracy. Calls for reform come from all parts of the spectrum, but political will appears to be lacking, largely because corrupt politicians are not consistently punished at the polls or in the halls of justice.[68]

The behavior of several key PT leaders, along with Lula's relatively nonchalant reaction to the scandals, may thus have sacrificed the party's authority to carry the mantle of political reform in the eyes of Brazilian voters, in particular in terms of questions of government transparency, accountability, and corruption. On the heels of the *mensalão* and the *caixa dois* scandals, many *petistas* called on the party to return to its principles. Yet internal elections in 2006 revealed that the party did not (and perhaps could not) undertake a full housecleaning. Some of the principal party leaders who were involved in the scandals are gone only in name, not in spirit, and it remains to be seen what kind of party the PT will become.

Even if the party has lost some of its luster, it is unlikely that the party's death will result from a perception that the PT is "just like" other parties in that some of its leaders are corrupt. The PT elected 83 deputies in the October 2006 elections, down from 91 in 2002 but still the second-largest delegation in the Chamber of Deputies. The party also elected five governors, achieving notable victories in the north and northeast regions of the country, where it has traditionally been weakest. More important, perhaps, it remains unclear whether Brazilians care much about corruption, and it is even unclear whether self-identified *petistas* among Brazilian voters care much about corruption.[69]

Even if some *petistas* have abandoned the party because of the corruption scandals, perceptions of corruption in one party do not necessarily lead people to vote for a different party; instead, they might withdraw from politics.[70] Still, a perception that the PT is no better or worse than any other Brazilian party could seriously damage the PT's long-term prospects because participation in politics literally defines what it means to be a *petista* for many party activists. Given the combination of corruption-induced apathy and a perceived failure on the part of the Lula administration to decisively implement the other two pillars of the *modo petista de governar* (participation and an inversion of government priorities), civil society organizations have become "profoundly disillusioned with electoral democracy and a party-based strategy for social change."[71] Many social movements now feel that *no* party represents their goals and interests. Their previous enthusiasm for Lula and the PT may have waned, implying a growing distance between the party and civil society organizations, a critical element of its base. The PT's trajectory remains uncertain: if it loses its strong links to civil society, it will indeed become more like most of Brazil's other parties. In some senses this would represent a step backward for Brazilian democracy, because it suggests that key aspects of citizen representation and accountability, especially in terms of broad societal interests, remain out of reach.

Although Lula is a "different" president, his administration may well be best remembered not for the ways in which it symbolically completed Brazil's transition to democracy but for its inability to clearly expand the contours of the reform agenda Cardoso had consolidated into "PT turf"—the much-vaunted *modo petista de governar* of greater popular participation, an inversion of government policy and investment priorities, and improved government accountability and transparency. Discussion of the legacy of Lula's administration for Brazilian democracy will no doubt focus on the degree to which the administration abandoned or implemented those principles.

8

Chile

The End of the Unfinished Transition

Peter M. Siavelis

Michelle Bachelet's historic election as the first woman president of Chile (and the first Latin American woman president who did not follow a politically prominent husband to office) captured international headlines as a watershed in Latin American politics. The focus on Bachelet's gender obscured a political reality that was perhaps more noteworthy. Bachelet's Concertación coalition has continuously ruled Chile for 16 years and, when she steps down, will have ruled Chile for two decades. The coalition has been the lengthiest among third wave democracies and is noted for having presided over a period of economic prosperity and political stability with few precedents in Latin America. In addition, while populism and nationalism of various forms reassert themselves across the region, Bachelet and her Concertación predecessors have led non-populist, non-nationalistic, center-left governments characterized by high levels of popularity and effectiveness. So while the election of a woman president in a country like Chile is remarkable, even more remarkable are the peace, stability, and coalitional continuity that have characterized the country during an era when economic and political distress have prevailed in much of the rest of the region. In addition, on a continent rife with deep and resurgent political and ideological struggles, Chile is known for its relative consensus and agreement. What explains Chilean exceptionalism?

This chapter argues that continuity in the pattern of postauthoritarian politics as well as much of the success of the so-called Chilean model of transition are due in large part to the establishment of a new informal social pact that has set down mutually and tacitly understood rules of the game. Although this type of agreement was elusive during the years when

Chile was controlled by General Augusto Pinochet and in the first years of the transition, it gradually developed from the mid-1990s on. Furthermore, the chapter argues that this type of agreement is not without precedent in Chile. The *estado de compromiso,* or compromise state, that characterized Chilean politics from the mid-1930s until the mid-1960s marked a similar period of agreement. In essence, the *estado de compromiso* emerged as a consensus on the basic outlines of Chile's socioeconomic structure, which included the protection of private property and business interests combined with state-led industrialization and a limited welfare state. Rather than being a purposefully negotiated settlement, it emerged primarily out of the recognition that no one social class had the ability to impose its will on the others, and a de facto agreement of accommodation gradually developed.[1]

The *estado de compromiso* dramatically broke down in the years leading up to the 1973 coup as the military, the ideological right, and the business class allied to attempt to impose their transformational project on the rest of the country. However, the aftermath of the Pinochet dictatorship demonstrated the failure of the military and actors on the right to definitively and completely impose their project on other social groups in Chile. Across the political spectrum, actors have again come to a new tacit agreement, albeit one distinct from that which characterized the *estado de compromiso*.[2] This chapter does not argue that Chileans agree on everything and that no divisions persist. Indeed, the transition has left in its wake winners and losers, and many remain dissatisfied and disenfranchised. Rather, the chapter argues that, once again, political actors have realized that a particular vision cannot be imposed on those who disagree, and a new tacit pact has emerged regarding the fundamental rules of the game.

The chapter proceeds as follows. First, it outlines the basic elements of this new agreement, underscoring consensus on the rules of the game regarding economic and social policy, political moderation, constitutional reform, and the role of the armed forces. In each of these sections it underscores the dynamic and gradual evolution toward a politics of agreement. However, just as the *estado de compromiso* was ultimately undermined and came to a violent end, this chapter does not suggest that the new political compromise is indestructible. Indeed, the second section of the chapter underscores the fault lines that can lead to the undoing of this compromise, arguing that nagging inequality and the lack of reform of the Pinochet-imposed legislative election system have the potential to undermine the tacit social and political pact at the root of Chile's success. Finally, the chapter concludes that, assuming the electoral system is reformed, Chile's widely cited "unfinished" transition can finally be considered finished.[3]

The New Compromise

Market Economics and Social Reform

In the mid-2000s, left-leaning nationalists and populists of various stripes across Latin America triumphed (in Argentina, Bolivia, Brazil, Nicaragua, and Venezuela) or nearly triumphed (in Mexico and Peru). Michelle Bachelet's victory was routinely cast as part of this generalized leftward trend.[4] Those critical of this characterization routinely underscored that Bachelet was no leftist given the Concertación's (and Bachelet's) wholesale adoption of Pinochet's market model and advocacy of U.S.-backed free trade policies. Both of these depictions are caricatures; the reality is that Bachelet's economic policies emerged from a negotiated consensus that is neither leftist in a traditional sense nor unapologetically pro-market with respect to the state's role in the economy and the provision of social goods.

The spectacular success of Chile's economy is well documented and need not be extensively reviewed here. The growth rates of Chile, commonly referred to as "Latin America's Asian Tiger," are unrivaled in Latin America in terms of their size and consistency (Table 8.1). Between the return of democracy in 1990 and 2005, GDP growth rates averaged over 5.6 percent per year, reaching as high as 10.8 percent in 1995.[5] Between 1995 and 2005, growth remained impressive, and despite a downturn in 1999, it averaged 4.7 percent during this period. Democratic governments have successfully contained inflation, with rates below 9 percent between 1995 and 1998 and below 4 percent between 1999 and 2005.[6] Furthermore, between 1995 and 2005 the overall size of the economy increased by almost 50 percent and unemployment rates were held under 10 percent, peaking at 9.8 percent in 1999 but gradually dropping to 8 percent in 2005. In addition to these impressive macroeconomic indicators, in 2005 Chile had the highest GDP per capita in South America and its international debt as a proportion of GDP was 43.2 percent, having fallen from a high of 90.7 percent in 1983.[7]

Despite its many successes, the Chilean economy continues to be plagued by some enduring difficulties. As the economy has grown, income distribution has become skewed, making Chile one of the least equitable countries, along with Brazil and Colombia. Despite remarkable success in fighting poverty, there is an important sector of the population that remains in chronic and extreme poverty and that, despite the best efforts of the government, has been difficult to reach. In addition, despite increases in social spending, Chile is far from a social policy paradise.[8] The privatized health care, educational, and pension systems have benefited the upper and middle classes but have provided little security for popular and working classes, creating a dual society in terms of the provision of social goods.[9]

Table 8.1. Major Chilean Economic Indicators, 1995–2005

Indicator	1995	1996	1997	1998	1999	2000	2001	2002	2003	2004	2005
Economic growth (annual percentage change in GDP)	10.8	7.4	6.6	3.2	−0.8	4.5	3.4	2.2	3.3	4.9	6.0
Size of the economy (GDP, billions of US$)	71.3	75.8	82.8	79.4	73.0	75.2	68.6	67.3	73.4	94.1	100.7
Inflation (percent per year)	8.2	7.4	6.1	5.1	3.3	3.8	3.6	2.5	2.8	1.1	3.0
Unemployment (percent)	7.3	6.4	6.1	6.3	9.8	9.2	9.1	8.9	8.5	9.1	8.0
Product per capita (GDP divided by population, in US$)	5,071	5,255	5,664	5,355	4,851	4,944	4,440	4,318	4,573	5,570	6,224

Source: Inter-American Development Bank and Instituto Nacional de Estadísticas de Chile, www.iadb.org .countries/indicators/cfm?language=English&id_country=CH&pLanguage=English&pCountry=CH&parid=8, www.ine.cl/canales/chile_estadistico/mercado_del_trabajo/empleo/series_estadisticas/desocupacion/php.

Nonetheless, despite these problems and indications of tension and potential conflict and in line with the central arguments of this chapter, contemporary Chile is characterized by a consensus regarding its fundamental economic organization that is unprecedented in Chilean history and rare in Latin America. Indeed, during the 1960s and 1970s there was deep disagreement concerning the basic economic organization of the country in the wake of the breakdown of the *estado de compromiso*. In addition, despite the end of the Cold War, across Latin America consensus on the essential nature of the role of the state in the economy has broken down with the crisis of neoliberalism, the unraveling of the "Washington Consensus," and the emergence of prominent politicians and presidential candidates who have questioned the basic tenets of market economics. No such politician has emerged in Chile. What is the nature and content of this consensus in Chile? Is it an elite consensus or a popular consensus? How can it be measured?

It is important to emphasize at the outset that the new consensus on economics is a negotiated one, not one arising from the simple forced acceptance of Pinochet's neoliberal model. Chile's capitalist model was never as uniformly free market as some contend. The ultra–free market "Chicago

Boys" are routinely cited as the intellectual authors of the current economic policy.[10] However, beginning with the economic crisis of 1982–83, the military government increasingly adopted a wider role for the state, and civilian governments continued this trend. Kurtz has shown that contrary to the usual association of Chile's export boom with free market policies, state intervention has been central to Chile's export-led model, especially in the fruit, fish, and forestry sectors.[11] The state has actively engaged in research and development, export promotion, and the identification of infant industries. Initially orthodox trade policy also became more pragmatic after the crisis of the early 1980s, with a range of state policies aimed at encouraging exports, including temporary and targeted tariff increases; the foundation of a semi-public trade promotion authority; and an active exchange rate policy.[12] In addition, on the fiscal side, the Chilean government offered tax breaks and tariff drawbacks to exporters in infant industries and, on the credit side, provided long-term loan guarantees to help exporters.[13] The production of Chile's major export, copper, is still in the hands of the gargantuan state-owned Corporación Nacional del Cobre (National Copper Corporation). Finally, unlike in other countries in the region, corporate taxes have actually increased since the end of the Pinochet government, and Chile has instituted controls and restrictions on foreign investment, particularly in areas targeted for export development.

With respect to social policy, contrary to some commonplace depictions of Chile as a free market jungle, where Concertación governments are simple clones of the military government, democratic governments have been active and successful in fighting poverty. The country's poverty eradication record stands out in the region, with the percentage of the population living in poverty decreasing from 45.1 percent in 1987 to 18.8 percent in 2003. The percentage in extreme poverty fell from 17.4 percent to 5.7 percent during this period. A combination of spectacular economic growth and intelligently designed social policies explains this success. Concertación presidents oversaw important changes in Pinochet's labor code, providing more benefits for workers in a system that had egregiously stacked the deck in favor of employers. Regular increases in the minimum wage, which have consistently been higher than inflation, have helped to improve salaries and acquisitive power. In 2004, the minimum wage in Chile, adjusted for inflation, was 93 percent higher than in 1990, and the number of minimum salaries required to purchase the basic basket of family necessities—a measure often used to quantify poverty in Chile—dropped from just under 4.5 to 2.1.[14] Along with a negotiated moderate increase in value-added taxes, government revenues from copper and higher taxes on corporate and individual earnings provided democratic governments additional resources to spend on health, education, and social welfare. Between 1990 and 2005, there was a tenfold increase in government spending on health and just under a tenfold increase in spending on education.[15] These policies, combined with efficient macroeconomic management, laid the groundwork for faster growth, job creation, and the dramatic decrease in poverty.

In terms of elite consensus, the reform process is just as instructive as the content of reforms. Very early in the democratic transition, economic management was recognized as the Achilles' heel of the new government. Concertación leaders had to consistently reassure the business community and the right that they were capable of successfully managing the economy. Early in his term, President Patricio Aylwin Azócar publicly acknowledged that the private sector was the primary "motor" of economic growth in the country.[16] This need to assuage powerful economic actors continued through all of the Concertación administrations. Indeed, despite finishing his term in 2005 as one of the most effective and popular presidents in Chilean history, as a candidate Socialist Ricardo Lagos was initially regarded with trepidation by the business community and the right, with public assertions that electing Lagos would represent a return to a chaotic and divisive government like that of Salvador Allende.

In addition, the Concertación was a new and inexperienced coalition operating in a system in which the right maintained significant veto power.[17] Building a new coalition for economic progress would entail convincing the right and the left to commit to the Concertación's stated goal of achieving *crecimiento con equidad* (growth with equity). If economic policy had strayed too far from the general outlines of the Pinochet model, there would certainly have been a backlash. At the same time, ignoring problems with the Pinochet model would undermine the legitimacy of the new government if a perception took hold that economic policy under democracy was no different than that during dictatorship. Thus, considerable political skill and purposeful action were devoted to building this new elite consensus; it did not simply emerge. How was it built?

The policy-making model developed and pursued by postauthoritarian Chilean presidents, particularly in the economic realm, was central to constructing this consensus. This model, generally know as the *democracia de los acuerdos* (democracy by agreement), refers to the extrainstitutional negotiations and discussions that preceded major policy initiatives by presidents, which were aimed at assuaging the fears of a potentially reactionary right while also considering the interests and demands of stakeholders.[18] These negotiations and discussions have consistently been carried out with the congressional opposition and with powerful social groups outside of Congress. The tax reform of 1990 is perhaps the most cited instance of what was a regularized and normalized pattern of informal pact making. Members of the executive branch consulted directly with the business community and producer groups to neutralize any potential opposition to the tax reform. The tax reform bill passed with very limited congressional input. Boylen argues that the very design of the bill was aimed at assuaging "powerful business interests in an environment of uncertainty." She shows that the "reform was characterized by a series of extra-parliamentary negotiations in which the government clinched the support of the chief opposition party, thus defusing any potential opposition to the reform and ensuring its rapid passage."[19] Executive branch officials have regularly met and negotiated with members of the opposition in relation to legislation on tax reform, labor standards, the minimum wage, and the far-reaching 2005 constitutional reforms.

Budgetary politics also consistently demonstrated this pattern of *democracia de los acuerdos*. The Chilean budgetary process as set out in the 1980 Constitution was designed with the idea that "President" Pinochet would be in charge. Accordingly, Chilean presidents were granted almost complete control. The president presents the national budget every year, and if Congress fails to approve it, the president's budget enters into force.[20] This arrangement presented a very tempting possibility for unilateralism in budget-making. However, rather than simply imposing their budgets, Concertación presidents have engaged in negotiations aimed at securing the votes of the opposition, even though presidents do not necessarily need these votes. During negotiations on most budgets, the Concertación's various ministers of finance have met and negotiated with opposition leaders. Despite their impressive formal budgetary powers, presidents have consistently chosen informal avenues of negotiation and consultation to come to budget agreements that have been acceptable to members of both the presidents' coalition and the opposition. These consultations have consistently reassured the opposition and the right that fiscal austerity would be maintained and that Concertación leaders could be trusted to responsibly make economic policy.

Chile's presidents have regularly and informally consulted with the business community, producer groups, and members of the conservative media. Silva notes the privileged access of business elites to the executive branch, which was granted to stem their fears that the neoliberal model would be abandoned. He goes as far as to characterize this influence as "institutional veto power."[21] He notes that business elites have directly lobbied the executive branch in relation to key legislation that has affected business and that Chile's main business lobby, the Confederación de la Producción y del Comercio (Production and Commerce Confederation), has been particularly influential in derailing initiatives perceived to be anti-business. While Silva characterizes this relationship as one that has sacrificed potentially progressive economic reform in exchange for political democratization, these relationships have also granted presidents the power to persuade conservative forces in Congress that business interests have been taken into account in elaborating budgets and controversial economic legislation. Concertación leaders have also often negotiated directly with influential actors on the left, primarily trade unions, when drafting and advocating the passage of controversial legislation, pointing to a consistent pattern of purposive consensus building even among the coalition's natural constituencies.

There are indications that there has also been popular consensus on the country's economic structure, though it is more difficult to measure. Survey data suggest that Chileans generally agree on the role that the state should play. When asked whether "private enterprise is the best way to solve economic problems in Chile," only 24.4 percent of Chileans disagreed or strongly disagreed.[22] In addition, when asked to choose the three most important determinants of personal success from a list of 14 categories, Chileans chose "educational level" (43.1%), the "economic situation of parents" (23.7%), and "*pitutos*," or personal contacts (20.4%). Economic help from the state was named by only 5.9 percent of the population, barely beating "luck" (5.5%) and significantly trailing "faith in God" (10.3%).

Did the Pinochet years, then, disabuse Chileans of their attachment to their traditionally interventionist state? Not entirely. Responses to other questions suggest that Chileans still want their state to be involved in the economy. For example, over 70 percent of Chileans polled in 2000 either agreed or very much agreed with the statement "It is the responsibility of government to reduce the differences in income between high income and low income people."[23] In addition, despite the widespread privatization of the health and educational sectors, when asked in 2006 which should be the three most important initiatives to which government resources should be devoted, 92 percent of those surveyed named health care and 80 percent named education. Therefore, while the case for a tacit popular consensus on the economy is of course thinner than that related to elites, there are few indications that there is widespread popular disagreement concerning the basic structure of the economy.

In sum, this new consensus (elite and popular) is not a simple consensus on Pinochet's neoliberal model. Chile remains a very open market economy based on export-led growth. However, within this broad framework set down by the military regime, successive Concertación governments have put greater emphasis on social policy, introduced more government regulation and oversight, and more closely regulated capital flows than did the authoritarian government. The consensus, then, is for a market economy characterized by a significant role for the state. However, the breadth and the depth of that role is subject to the consensus-making and consultative model that has characterized Chile since the democratic transition. What is more, the right and the left both agree on the essential model, in a pattern departing from the norm in much of the rest of the region. This economic consensus has provided fertile ground for what has also developed into a flourishing political consensus.

Moderate Politics

Throughout the 1960s and 1970s, Chilean party politics were character-ized by extreme polarization, precipitating the immobilism and crises that eventually led to military intervention.[24] Political parties were at the center of Chilean political life and were recognized to have very strong roots in so-ciety.[25] What is more, despite the best efforts of the military regime to trans-form the party system through a combination of severe repression and elec-toral engineering, the same basic pattern of preauthoritarian competition at the party level remains.[26] Does this continuity in what was formerly a frag-mented party system undermine the argument for growing political con-sensus in Chile? I argue that it does not for a number of reasons.

From the most basic perspective, few coalitions in the world have enjoyed as stable and lengthy support as the Concertación, which has continuously ruled Chile since 1990. Table 8.2 summarizes support for the two major coali-tions across Chamber of Deputies elections since the return of democracy. With the partial exception of the 2001 election, overall identification with the

Table 8.2. Percentages of Valid Votes and Seats Received by the Concertación and the Alianza in Chamber of Deputies Elections, 1989–2005

Party	1989		1993		1997		2001		2005	
	Percentage of Valid Votes	Percentage of Seats	Percentage of Valid Votes	Percentage of Seats	Percentage of Valid Votes	Percentage of Seats	Percentage of Valid Votes	Percentage of Seats	Percentage of Valid Votes	Percentage of Seats
Concertación	51.5	57.5	55.3	58.3	50.5	57.5	47.9	51.7	51.8	54.2
Alianza	34.2	40.0	36.7	41.7	36.3	38.4	44.3	47.5	38.7	45.0
Others	14.3	2.5	7.9	0.0	13.3	4.2	7.8	0.8	9.5	0.8
Difference between Concertación and Alianza	17.3	17.5	18.6	16.6	14.2	19.1	3.6	4.2	13.1	9.2

Source: Author calculations of votes based on data at www.elecciones.gov.cl; calculation of seats based on data at Congreso Nacional de Chile, www.camara.cl/.

two major alliances has remained relatively stable. However, there have been more dramatic shifts in support among parties within the major coalitions. Figures 8.1 and 8.2 summarize support for each of the constituent parties within the two major coalitions. They show that the major movement of voters in Chile has been away from the PDC and toward the PPD within the Concertación, and away from RN (with minor growth in support for the PRSD) and toward the UDI in the Alianza. Indeed, because the PS and the PPD have generally competed under a unified subpact on the left, Figure 8.3, which maps support for major parties and combines the total vote received by the left, is a more accurate representation of the evolution of support for major ideological tendencies. In this figure we see even more clearly that the movement has been away from moderate, more centrist parties (RN and the PDC) and toward the more extreme right (the UDI) and left (the PPD-PS). This conclusion may seem to contradict the argument presented here and may trouble those familiar with Chile's previous pattern of party centrifugation and its link to the breakdown of democracy.[27]

Figure 8.1. Evolution of Support for Parties of the Concertación in Chamber of Deputies Elections, 1989–2005

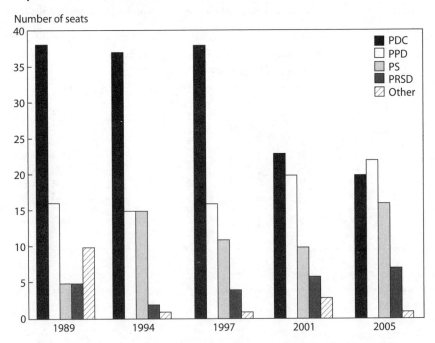

Notes: PDC, Partido Demócrata Cristiano (Christian Democratic Party); PPD, Partido por la Democracia (Party for Democracy); PS, Partido Socialista (Socialist Party); PRSD, Partido Radical Socialdemócrata (Social-Democratic Radical Party).

Figure 8.2. Evolution of Support for Parties of the Alianza in Chamber of Deputies Elections, 1989–2005

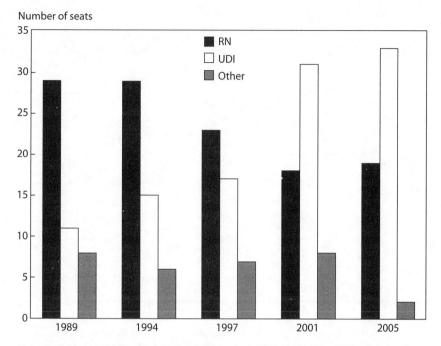

Number of seats

Notes: RN, Renovación Nacional (National Renovation); UDI, Unión Democrática Independiente (Independent Democratic Union).

However, this movement away from the center must be qualified in some important ways. Both the left and the right in Chile have significantly moderated their discourse since the advent of the democratic transition, with the UDI attempting to distance itself from the Pinochet government and the PPD-PS bloc presenting very moderate platforms. Most important, rather than representing any ideological movement, the growth in support for parties on each ideological wing can be traced to other variables more particular to the characteristics of the parties. On the right, the UDI is notorious for its excellent organization and infrastructure. Indeed, it is a remarkable how the UDI changed from a very loosely organized party that had trouble recruiting candidates in 1989 to one with a local-level party organizational network that rivals that of RN. In addition, among poorer Chileans the UDI has a much better reputation, because RN is perceived as the representative of the traditional, aristocratic, classist right. Similarly, part of the reason for the growing support of the PPD-PS bloc in the Concertación is certainly the re-

Figure 8.3. Evolution of Support for Major Chilean Parties, 1989–2005

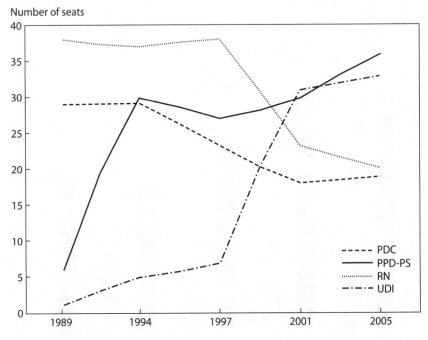

Number of seats

Notes: PDC, Partido Demócrata Cristiano (Christian Democratic Party); PPD, Partido por la Democracia (Party for Democracy); PS, Partido Socialista (Socialist Party); RN, Renovación Nacional (National Renovation); UDI, Unión Demócrata Independiente (Independent Democratic Union). PPD and PS seats have been combined as representing a single leftist bloc.

cent disorganization within and conflict with the PDC, along with the fact that the PPD-PS bloc is acknowledged to have done a better job of choosing attractive candidates.[28]

The 2005–6 presidential campaign also demonstrates the extent of the political consensus on the basics in Chile. While the presidential campaigns for these years in Bolivia, Mexico, Peru, and Venezuela were contested by candidates with broadly differing visions for the fundamentals of politics in economics (often reflecting very deep fault lines in their societies), Chile's major candidates campaigned toward the center.

Michelle Bachelet, a political neophyte who had never served in elective office, emerged as an early leader. Her personal story made her a compelling candidate. Bachelet's father, Air Force General Alberto Bachelet, had died in government custody after being tortured for noncompliance with dictates of the Pinochet government, and she and her mother had also been tortured at the notorious Villa Grimaldi military detention center. Later, as a practicing pediatrician working in the public sector, she had been appointed minister of health by Ricardo Lagos. Her success led Lagos to appoint her Latin America's first woman defense minister, an appointment that was all the more remarkable given her past. Further, as an avowed agnostic and divorced single mother (in a country that had legalized divorce only in 2004), Bachelet was not a traditional Chilean presidential candidate. This, of course, was part of her appeal; the Concertación sought to put a new face on an old coalition. Bachelet's main challenger for the nomination within her own coalition was former foreign minister and Christian Democrat Soledad Alvear, who dropped out of the race before the primary due to her lack of support in opinion polls following debates heralded as historic for pitting two women against each other.

In the general election, Bachelet was initially to face off only against the UDI's Joaquín Lavín, who was the standard-bearer for the Alianza. Lavín, formerly a successful mayor of one of Chile's wealthiest municipalities, Las Condes, and later of Central Santiago, had often been assumed to be waiting in the wings to become the first popularly elected conservative president of Chile since 1958. Lagos had defeated Lavín by a razor-thin 0.4 percent of the vote in 2000. Despite high hopes on the right for Lavín to parlay this momentum into a 2006 victory, Lagos's popularity, the success of the Concertación, and infighting on the right caused Lavín's popularity to flag. In addition, according to Chile's two-round presidential system, if no candidate garners a majority of the vote in the first round, a second-round election is held to decide between the top two finishers. The incentive structure of a two-round system encourages a larger number of candidacies because the system lowers the hurdle for success in the first round.[29] This institutional and electoral environment, coupled with the perception that the right was headed for a loss, led RN's Sebastián Piñera, a wealthy businessman, to throw his hat into the ring. An alliance to the left of the Concertación, Juntos Podemos Más (Together We Can Do More)—made up of the Humanist, Communist, and other far left parties—chose Tomás Hirsch as its candidate. However, because it received support from only about 5 percent of those polled in national surveys, Piñera's entry essentially made for a three-way presidential race.

All three candidates campaigned toward the center, albeit for different reasons. Bachelet sought to project her capitalist credentials, assuring the business community that her government would not depart significantly from the economic policies of the Lagos government. She had also been dogged during the presidential campaign by evidence of a brief romantic relationship with Alex Vojkovic, a spokesman for the Frente Patriótico Manuel Rodríguez (Manuel Rodríguez Patriotic Front), an armed group that had made an assassination attempt on Pinochet in 1986. Her goal was to avoid any tinge of radicalism, campaign to the center, and project a moderate image.

Lavín and Piñera found themselves in a difficult campaign position that also pushed their messages toward the center. Ricardo Lagos was an enormously popular president who would leave office with a 70 percent approval rating. Attacking Lagos and his policies was a losing strategy. Lavín also sought to distance himself from the policies of both Pinochet and his own UDI, the party most closely associated with the policies and personalities of the military government. The battle for the center transformed the campaign into one about personalities rather than ideology or issues. The party platforms of all of the Chilean candidates were replete with expressions of continuity. Rather than words like "transform," "revolutionize," or "change," the expressions more commonly found in all of the candidates' policy platforms included "improve," "continue," "strengthen," "widen," "deepen," "assure," and "advance." Indeed, Bachelet's renowned 36-point program for her first 100 days in office entailed primarily proposals to improve and build upon Lagos's policies. Similarly, because issues were rarely in play, references to the personal attributes of the candidates took center stage. Lavín repeatedly pointed to Bachelet's lack of experience and underscored that she lacked "traditional Chilean values" (presumably as an agnostic and divorced single mother). Lavín also repeatedly underscored that the Concertación was spent ("*agotado*") as a government and had been in power too long.

Piñera, on the other hand, employed a different strategy, though he used similar methods. His goal was to cultivate the support of traditional voters on the right who had a distaste for the UDI's association with the military government, as well as that of habitually more centrist Concertación voters who might be unwilling to vote for a woman, a divorcee, another socialist, or a professed agnostic. He underscored his status as a "Christian Humanist" and pointed to family roots in the PDC (his father had been a PDC activist). He also played to the center by speaking of the need for a more "compassionate state."[30]

In the months leading up to the December 2005 first-round vote, most polls showed Bachelet far ahead, leading with about 40 percent support, and Lavín and Piñera trailing in a virtual dead heat with about 20 percent each. Results from the first round gave Bachelet 45.9 percent, Piñera 25.4 percent, and Lavín 23.2 percent.[31] These results were not entirely encouraging for Bachelet. The 45.9 percent of the vote received by Bachelet was below the 47.9 percent received by Lagos in 2000 (when his candidacy had been seen as much more precarious). It was also less than the 51.8 percent received by the Concertación in the concurrent Chamber of Deputies elections, suggesting that some Concertación voters personally objected to her candidacy. Finally, and most worrying for Bachelet as she faced off against Piñera, the 45.9 percent of the vote she had received was lower than the 48.6 percent received by the two candidates on the right.

Despite these worrisome results, Bachelet managed to outpoll Piñera by 53.5 percent to 46.5 percent in the January 15, 2006, runoff vote. How did Bachelet win? New Bachelet voters were likely those who had initially voted for leftist Tomás Hirsch in the first round. However, Piñera actually received 140,000 fewer votes in the second round than the combined number of votes he and Lavín had received in the first round, suggesting that Bachelet did pick up some votes from the right. Piñera lacked appeal among two crucial sets of Lavín voters: women and the poor. Lavín had received more women's votes than Piñera in the first round, and the poor preferred Lavín's brand of right-wing populism to Piñera's traditionally classist conservativism.[32]

In the end, Bachelet and the Concertación managed to pull off a masterful bit of politics. By choosing a nontraditional politician, an outsider and a woman, the alliance managed to put a new face on what, at 16 years of age, was a geriatric coalition. However, more important for the arguments of this chapter, and in sharp contrast with the situations in most of the rest of the region, Chile's presidential election was free of deep conflict and was characterized by a rhetoric of moderation and compromise. It was reflective of a wider dynamic of consensus politics characterized by moderate, negotiated reform and agreement on the fundamental rules of the game. This pattern of consensus politics has also been reflected in the process of constitutional reform since the return of democracy.

Constitutional Reform

As the basic legal frameworks for representative democracy, constitutions must strike a balance between malleability and solidity. They must be malleable enough to respond to social and political change but solid enough to resist capricious and politically motivated change that undermines their legitimacy. Excessive malleability and unresponsive solidity can equally undermine constitutional legitimacy. Domínguez underscores the problematic tendency toward reform mongering in Latin America, where constitutions are too often unilaterally changed for politically motivated and short-term reasons.[33] He contends that constructing successful constitutional democracy is more likely where incremental constitutional reforms are the norm. Chile fits this pattern, which also reflects the country's new tacit social pact.

The 1980 Constitution, imposed by the Pinochet government and approved in a plebiscite of questionable propriety, limited the authority of civilian authorities and provided numerous benefits for the right.[34] It created an exaggerated presidential system, a weak legislature, a majoritarian electoral system that favored conservative parties, and a requirement of large majorities for constitutional reform. In addition, the Constitution created several institutions whose membership was determined by the military or institutions with a de facto pro-military majority. These included a Senate with nine members effectively appointed by the outgoing government (a number of whom would continue to be chosen every eight years by nonelected authorities influenced by the military), a National Security Council with extraordinary powers, and a Constitutional Tribunal with sweeping powers to judge the constitutionality of legislation at any stage of the legislative process.[35] In addition, presidents lacked power over the hiring, firing, and promotion of high-level military officials.

The 1980 Constitution had been criticized as a straitjacket because of its limits on civilian authorities and its establishment of multiple veto points and veto players that made it impervious to reform. However, successive civilian governments succeeded in reforming the Constitution in 1989, 1991, 1997, 1999, 2000, 2003, and 2005. Despite their frequency, these reforms do not represent the type of unilateral, politically motivated reform mongering to which Domínguez refers.[36] Rather, they were negotiated and incremental reforms characterized by wide-ranging consensus. More important, they were undertaken within the institutional and legal framework of the Pinochet constitution (despite its questionable legitimacy), pointing to an agreement to play by the rules of the game.

Departing from the usual pattern whereby elites adopt institutional frameworks that suit their interests and political goals, Chile's Constitution was imposed, which presented twin dangers. First, it would have been quite easy for democratic authorities to forge ahead with reforms and claim that the Constitution was simply illegitimate (presumably justifying change outside of the established rules of the game). Second, constitutions that are imposed rather than negotiated may ill fit the political context of a country, creating problems of governability. While the imposition of a constitution provided twin rationales for quick reform, elites resisted such temptations, with much happier consequences for Chile's democratic transition.

In the immediate post-authoritarian period, there was a significant distance between political forces on what Chile's legal framework should look like, but this distance has substantially narrowed through gradual negotiated reforms.[37] The 1989 and 2005 reform processes best demonstrate this dynamic. The 1989 reforms were hammered out in a context of intense negotiations between the Concertación and the more moderate party of the right, RN. Although the changes introduced by the 1989 reforms never challenged the core features of the 1980 Constitution substantively, they represented a first important step toward incipient negotiations and gradual confidence building that would lead to other negotiated reforms and culminate in the far-reaching reforms of 2005.

Given Pinochet's grip on power, one might ask how there could be any constitutional reforms at all before the 1989 elections. The political context was one of uncertainty and risk for both the military government and the opposition. Pinochet had lost the 1988 plebiscite, providing the opposition with a strong rationale to push for reform of the military constitution. In addition, having lost the plebiscite, the military and its allies were concerned that if they did not negotiate and appeared inflexible, the opposition might succeed in building a popular movement to do away with Pinochet's entire institutional framework. However, given the continuing strength of the military and the support of 43 percent of the population that Pinochet had garnered in the plebiscite, it would have been unrealistic and potentially destabilizing for the opposition to demand the general's resignation and the formation of a provisional government to write a new constitution. In addition, the opposition had achieved a victory within the rules established by the Constitution, and it would have been awkward to then question its legitimacy. Finally, though the opposition did not relish operating under the Constitution bequeathed to the nation by the general, it wanted to avoid giving Pinochet any excuse to renege on the constitutional deal that had been struck.

The agreement eventually reached for the 1989 reforms reduced the majorities necessary for constitutional reform and eliminated the requirement that all amendments to the Constitution be approved by two successive congresses. It changed the composition of the National Security Council to balance the representation of civilians and military authorities and substituted the words "*hacer presente*" (to make known) for language that had given the Council the power "*representar*" (to present) its concerns. The number of elected senators was increased from 24 to 38, effectively diluting the power of the 9 appointed senators.

The 2005 reforms were much more significant and represent the culmination of this pattern of gradual consensus reform, as well as the confluence of interests of the Concertación and the Alianza. The Concertación had a long-standing commitment to constitutional reform, while for the Alianza it was becoming clear that the Concertación was increasingly inheriting all of the authoritarian benefits provided by the Pinochet constitution and that the longer the Concertación retained power, the greater the benefits it would reap.[38] Indeed, one official noted that the Concertación had moved into the "house of authoritarianism" and found it "quite comfortable."[39] Most important, whoever controls the appointed and lifetime senators also controls the Senate. Left unreformed, the Constitution would have provided lifetime seats for former presidents Eduardo Frei and Ricardo Lagos. Appointed sen-

ators were also increasingly Concertación members because of the ability of
the president to directly appoint two senators, but also because of the influence of the Concertación in the appointment of officials to the other institutions involved in naming appointed senators, including the Supreme
Court, the Constitutional Tribunal, the Contraloría (comptroller), and the
high-level military command, all of which had previously been in the hands
of military and rightist sympathizers. The opposition knew that all of these
institutions would increasingly become dominated by Concertación appointees. Finally, while the rationale for shortening the presidential term was
to provide for concurrent legislative and presidential elections, the shorter
term also provided the Alianza with an incentive to support reforms, because
a shorter term could bring an Alianza presidency one year closer.

According to the 2005 reforms, all nonelective Senate seats were eliminated and the presidential term was shorted to four years. Presidential
control over the legislative process was reduced through the transfer of
agenda-setting power to the Chamber of Deputies. The quorum for reform
of the Constitution was reduced from three-fifths of both chambers to four-
sevenths. The composition of the National Security Council was transformed and its role made purely advisory, and the president's prerogative to
name, fire, and promote high-level military officers was restored. Lagos, who
succeeded in shepherding the reforms through Congress where his predecessors had failed, contended that the reforms created a new constitution and
signaled the end of the democratic transition. Though the Constitution is
not technically a new one, the changes are dramatic and bring Chile more in
line with other nations in its constitutional framework.

Chile's judiciary was also substantially, albeit very gradually, reformed
during the democratic transition. Before the Pinochet government came to
power, judicial independence had been the norm and the judiciary had been
a highly respected institution that, according to Valenzuela, "constituted the
bulwark for the protection and interpretation of a highly detailed legal code."[40]
In the 1970s, the Supreme Court asserted its independence with open challenges to the Allende administration. However, during the military government Pinochet packed high-level courts with supporters and the courts were
generally perceived as subservient. Further, as the transition approached
Pinochet offered incentives for elderly members to retire, then replaced them
with younger members, whose life tenure would be expected to last much
longer, in order insulate the courts from the influence of the new civilian governments. Upon taking office, President Aylwin rationalized that a Franklin
Roosevelt–style court-packing strategy would not be out of line for the new
democratic government given that Pinochet had so obviously attempted to
pack the court with conservative justices. Nonetheless, Aylwin's plan to expand the Supreme Court met with resistance early in his term, and he with-

drew the proposal amid charges that he was attempting to "decapitate" and "politicize" the courts. However, ultimately the negative performance and alleged corruption of several justices led to new calls for reform. In 1993, three judges were impeached for dereliction of duties; one was ultimately convicted and removed by the Senate. Further scandals on the court between 1994 and 1997 eventually convinced even the right that reform of the court was necessary, and the government of Eduardo Frei Ruiz-Tagle succeeded in expanding the size of the court from 17 to 21 members in 1998, effectively watering down the influence of Pinochet appointees. This process was hastened by the simple passage of time. Between 1990 and 1994, 7 of the 17 justices appointed by Pinochet either died or retired for health reasons.[41]

Reform of the criminal justice system has been equally important. The Chilean judicial and penal systems were once recognized as sluggish, secretive, inefficient, and often glaringly unfair. In most criminal cases, a single judge was responsible for investigation, prosecution, and sentencing. In 1998, the Chilean Congress approved the creation of a new Ministerio Público (State Prosecutor's Office) that was charged with the public investigation of criminal cases. Creation of the Ministerio was accompanied by a paradigm shift in the day-to-day handling of cases, moving from a legal, secretive, written form of testimony toward a more public, oral one. In 2000, a new penal code was adopted, followed by the creation of a Defensoría Penal Pública (National Public Defender's Office). Most analyses of judicial and penal reform find that these changes have substantially improved the criminal court system.[42]

Left unreformed, Pinochet's constitutional and legal framework would have undermined the legitimacy of the democratic government and created myriad problems of governability.[43] However, an attempt by the Concertación to simply impose its constitutional vision on the opposition would have been equally damaging to Chile's democratic prospects. The arguably unilateral process of constitution making in Venezuela, and that currently under way in Bolivia, show that imposed, forced, or "reform-mongered" constitutions fail to establish the foundations necessary for long-term governability. The Chilean case demonstrates that a constitution crafted through a longer-term process of gradual and negotiated reform better establishes this foundation. It is also more likely to result in congruity between a country's constitutional design and its political reality, better permitting political actors to achieve their goals within the rules of the game. While this is an important lesson for other countries, it is quite difficult to reproduce. Chile's reform process unfolded with a concomitant process of depolarization and the increasing congruence of all actors' preferences behind a reform agenda.[44]

All in all (and pending the electoral reform discussed later), from an institutional perspective the Chilean transition is finally complete. There is much to criticize about the reform process. It was profoundly elitist, involving negotiations at the highest levels of political parties. In addition, the 2005 reforms clearly did not represent the birth of a new constitution, as President Lagos contended when he signed the reforms into law. It is undeniable that the genesis of the 1980 Constitution was profoundly authoritarian. Indeed, some have argued that Pinochet is still fundamentally the father of Chilean democracy[45] and that Chileans should have done away with the 1980 Constitution altogether. This view is off the mark for a number of reasons. First, the Chilean Constitution parallels those of the world's established democracies in meeting the basic standards of democracy. Second, it was negotiated by the democratic actors governing Chile. Third, whatever the virtues of adopting a completely new constitution, doing so was practically impossible and would likely have derailed the Chilean transition. In the immediate post-transition period, the right and the military insisted on maintaining the Pinochet constitution, and attempts by the Concertación to impose a new constitution would likely have been met with a severe backlash. What is more, had such a new constitution been imposed unilaterally by the center left, the right would have regarded it as illegitimate, with profoundly negative consequences for the conduct of democratic politics. The reform process itself, interestingly, also built widespread support for the Constitution across the political spectrum.

Subordination of the Armed Forces to Civilians

In the immediate post-transition period, of all militaries in the Southern Cone, that of Chile was on many accounts the most entrenched and perceived to be the greatest threat to democracy.[46] More important, perhaps, the military was not isolated or without support as in Argentina and some other third wave democracies. There was deep division in society concerning the Pinochet government and the role of the military within it. Agüero notes that at the outset of the transition in the early 1990s the military-authoritarian project was still backed by General Pinochet's base: business elites, producer organizations, the military, and the parties of the right (the UDI and RN). The interests of these groups were protected by Chile's tutelary democracy and by constitutional provisions that provided the right with an advantage and veto power. They also accepted giving the military veto power, which was deemed an essential protection from the excesses of partisan politics. On the other side were groups who opposed the military regime, including the parties of the center and left, trade unions, and some professional organizations not tied to the military regime. These groups pointed to the institutionalized political role of the armed forces as evidence of the deficiencies of Chilean democracy. However, by the end of the Lagos government, a new consensus was shared by the right and the left on the need to eliminate the tutelary role and constitutional protections of the armed forces and to reestablish civilian control of the military.

How did Chile go from point A to point B? This consensus, like the others described in this chapter, did not just emerge but was formed by a combination of propitious conditions and purposive actions. Indeed, with the hindsight of success one forgets the military's significant challenges to civilian authority, including two military mobilizations—the *"ejercicio de enlace"* (coordinating exercise) of 1990 and the *"boinazo"* (rebellion, from *boina,* which means "beret") of 1993—and the tense moments following Pinochet's 1998 arrest in London. Indeed, it was a series of successful short-term responses to immediate conflicts that allowed the government to gradually institute more permanent transformations in civil-military relations. In each of these cases, democratic authorities faced down threats yet resisted antagonizing the military. Eventually, the public lost patience with the political machinations of the military and even those who had previously backed Pinochet increasingly moved to support the subordination of the armed forces to elected civilians. Gradually, Chile's economic success and status as a model in Latin America inspired pride in the country as a modern capitalist democracy. In this new vision of modernity (now shared by civilians of all political stripes and, increasingly, by the military), there is no place for an old-fashioned *golpista* (coup-prone) military.

The most significant transformations in the role of the armed forces in Chile have included the building of an independent Ministry of Defense, the gradual marginalization of General Pinochet from an influential role in politics even before his death, the real subordination of military authorities to the president, and the elimination of the institutional guarantees for the armed forces set out in the Constitution.[47]

During the Pinochet dictatorship, the Ministry of Defense was a career graveyard for former military officers, with most real defense-related activities centered within the armed forces. President Aylwin thus inherited a virtually powerless ministry. He appointed a veteran politician, Patricio Rojas, as minister, alienating high-level military officers. During the initial crises of the Aylwin administration, the military established a pattern of bypassing the ministry to negotiate directly with the president. However, Aylwin stressed that the Ministry of Defense should assert itself more aggressively, making pronouncements that helped to lead to the *boinazo.* Each successive administration sought to institutionalize an enhanced role for the ministry. For example, in 1995, during Eduardo Frei's government (1994–2000), the Supreme Court tried and convicted retired General Manuel Contreras as the intellectual author of the assassination of former Chilean diplomat Orlando Letelier in Washington, D.C. Frei insisted that negotiations over the status of Contreras, and ultimately his handing over to civilian authorities, be handled by the Ministry of Defense. Although there was some conflict between the ministry and the high levels of the Army at the time of Pinochet's arrest in London, the Frei government set down the bases for the continuing establishment of a strong Ministry of Defense.

The Lagos government (2000–2006) maintained this trend. When Lagos appointed Bachelet as minister, some feared that her experiences under the dictatorship would make her an enemy of the armed forces. Nonetheless, her training, combined with her success in the ministry, won her first grudging acceptance and later outright praise from military authorities. She updated and coordinated defense policies with the various armed services and made important changes in Chile's ineffective policy of compulsory military service, all without alienating the military. She also helped modernize the armed forces with respect to equipment, its budgetary system, and the internal functioning of the Ministry of Defense.

Augusto Pinochet's death in December 2006 roused bitter animosities concerning his role in transforming Chile, which would seem to contradict the argument presented here that a consensus had been formed on the role of the military. Nonetheless, though 60,000 mourners turned out for his wake and there were protests, skirmishes with police, and isolated acts of violence, Pinochet had largely ceased to be relevant to Chilean politics long before his funeral, as can be demonstrated by several trends.

First, despite initial unqualified support, the military had gradually and actively distanced itself from Pinochet. Although it had come to his defense in the early 1990s, by 2000, when the Supreme Court stripped Pinochet of his senatorial immunity, there was little reaction from the ranks of the armed forces. Military officials increasingly disassociated themselves from Pinochet, coming to regard his repeated political pronouncements as the bluster of an old man. Indeed, Lagos' commander-in-chief of the Army, Juan Emilio Cheyre, publicly differentiated his "new" army from that of the Pinochet government. Further, Cheyre offered the first public acknowledgment that civilian courts had jurisdiction over human rights cases.

Second, and perhaps more important, the parties of the right (especially the UDI) also gradually distanced themselves from Pinochet, even many of those that had previously supported or, indeed, served in his government. In the immediate aftermath of the transition, the parties of the right, particularly the UDI, tenaciously defended both Pinochet and his legacy. Increasingly, however, the UDI has attempted to style itself a party of the modern, globally oriented, technocratic right, and this image is at odds with that of the tinhorn, sunglasses-wearing Latin American dictator that Pinochet had

begun to project for many. Following his second electoral defeat, and perhaps because of it, Lavín issued a public mea culpa for blindly following the
Pinochet government. Furthermore, both Alianza candidates competing in
the 2005 presidential election were notably and symbolically absent from
Pinochet's funeral.

However, the most remarkable advance in civil-military relations has been
the armed forces' reassumption of a professionalized role, subordinate to
civilian authorities. During the Frei administration, Commander-in-Chief
of the Army General Ricardo Izurieta cooperated in investigations of human
rights abuses, stating categorically that he wished to leave this negative legacy
behind and concentrate on plans for the modernization of the armed forces.
Most concretely, he accepted an invitation by Defense Minister Edmundo
Pérez Yoma to participate in the so-called *mesa de diálogo* (roundtable) on
human rights. This body, which included politicians, human rights activists,
and victims of abuse, was charged with producing information on pending
cases of the "disappeared."

During the Lagos administration, the armed forces acknowledged that
human rights investigations should be left to civilian rather than military
courts, and they accepted (albeit with some reservations) the decision of the
Supreme Court to strip Pinochet of his parliamentary immunity. In a much-
publicized speech that represented a dramatic departure from Pinochet's
rhetoric, Cheyre declared that there had been no justification for human
rights violations in the past, nor were they ever justified, committing the military to "never again" repeat human rights violations. The most striking departure from the past, however, was that Cheyre met with President Lagos
before the speech to seek his approval of what he would say. Finally, the constitutional reforms of 2005 brought the de jure role of the military effectively
in line with its already de facto stance of subordination to civilians, and with
these changes, Chile is again within the norm of democratic nations in terms
of the role of its armed forces.

In sum, Chile's civil-military relations, though characterized by occasional threats and moments of tension, have been handled pragmatically by
both sides. The management of civil-military relations has, of course, involved trade-offs and left key actors dissatisfied. Families of the victims of
human rights abuses are outraged by the effective impunity granted to the
guilty in the armed forces. Proponents of the government contend that immediate and decisive action against human rights abusers would have elicited
a military backlash, effectively destroying democracy and potentially resulting in more human rights abuses. They argue that the gradual negotiated approach adopted in investigating human rights abuses and the limited and
targeted judicial actions taken against guilty parties was better for the coun-

try over the long term. On the military side, despite initially threatening behavior, the armed forces have increasingly accepted civilian authority as in the best interest of the military and the country for the long term. In the civil-military arena, dramatic divisions regarding the role of the military in society have been displaced by a new consensus for a military subservient to civilian authority.

Underwriting the New Consensus: The Challenges Ahead

Thus far, this chapter presents a perhaps excessively optimistic view of a conflict-free society at peace. However, the consensus argued for here is not without its fault lines. And, just as the *estado de compromiso* came to a violent end when the social pacts on which it had been based broke down, the current consensus can also break down if some deeper problems are not addressed.

Inequality

The first potential fault line revolves around issues of equality. In recent years Chile's Gini coefficient has hovered around 57, putting it in the same league as Brazil, Bolivia, and Colombia, the countries with the worst distribution of income in the Americas. Chile has the ignominious honor of ranking ninth worldwide in income inequality.[48] The long-term sustainability of democracy, as well as the consensus analyzed here, is endangered by such glaring inequality. However, increasing inequality of income is only the tip of the iceberg; different social classes in Chile lead dramatically different lives. Despite Chile's much-vaunted moves toward the privatization of social services, the by-product has been an asymmetrical duality in its health, education, and retirement systems. For example, the privatization of the health care system is often noted as one of the accomplishments of the military government. The reality that Chile actually has one health care system for the rich and another for the poor is often overlooked. The Fondo Nacional de Salud (FONASA; National Health Fund) provides state-funded health care, while the Instituciones de Salud Previsional (ISAPRES; Private Health Insurance Companies) provide privatized health care. Even after being in place a quarter century, the privatized system covers only about 18 percent of the population, the rest of which relies on the underfunded and lower-quality FONASA system or other government-funded health schemes. Indeed, while membership in the ISAPRES grew steadily until 1997, since then the percentage of the population covered by the ISAPRES has declined.[49] Of course, it is the wealthiest Chileans who are covered by the ISAPRES and have speedy access to the most modern and well-equipped hospitals, while the state system is characterized by long lines and long waits for services at older, less well-equipped hospitals.

In 2002, President Lagos introduced a reform package entitled Acceso Universal con Garantías Explícitas (AUGE; Universal Access with Explicit Guarantees), which sought to remedy some of this inequality. The plan targets 56 of the most serious illnesses, for which Chileans are guaranteed timely treatment at little or no out-of-pocket cost. If FONASA patients cannot access these treatments in a reasonable time within the public system, they can receive services at private clinics, which are later reimbursed by the government. However, while the plan has eliminated some of the most egregious inequalities in the system, questions remain about its cost and sustainability. What is more, for nonchronic diseases the two-tier system stands, and those relying on FONASA for noncritical care may experience actual declines in quality of care as more resources are dedicated to illnesses identified by AUGE and compensatory subsidies are paid to private hospitals.

This duality in social policy also extends to Chile's retirement system. While the statistics on coverage for the retirement system are better than those for the health care system, the much-heralded privatized pension system has also aggravated inequality. The Administradoras de Fondos de Pensiones (AFP; Pension Fund Administrators) system adopted by the Pinochet government is a defined contribution system that requires workers to contribute 10 percent of their income, up to US$22,000, to an individual retirement account managed by one of a series of private pension administrators. Currently over 95 percent of the formally employed population has at one point contributed to an AFP account.[50] However, the pension system is plagued with problems, including extreme volatility of returns, high expenses and fees, and evasion and underreporting. The most severe problem with respect to inequality is the recognized inadequacy of the system to provide a pension for the least advantaged. Though the formally employed have taken advantage of the AFP system, for the 28 percent of the Chilean workforce that is self-employed, participation is voluntary. Only 10 percent of those who are self-employed have voluntarily enrolled.[51] More serious, a study by the state regulator of the pension system (the Superintendencia de Administradoras de Fondos de Pensiones) found that about half of the system's affiliates will not save enough to provide even a minimum pension (which is set at about US$100 per month).[52]

Nagging inequality in the educational system turned into Bachelet's first major crisis, abruptly ending her administration's honeymoon. Bachelet had campaigned extensively on a platform of addressing inequality. In May of 2006, only weeks into her term, small-scale protests began among high school students in response to an increase in the price for college aptitude tests and rumored limitations on the *pase escolar*, the free student transport pass. The protests quickly escalated to focus on inequality and the poor state of public education more generally. The arrest of 600 students and accusations of heavy-handedness by the police and Education Minister Martín Zilic added fuel to an already explosive situation as citizen reaction took the government by complete surprise. On May 30, an estimated half-million students participated in a new protest, and in protests held in early June the numbers swelled to over 700,000 as high school students were joined by parents, university students, and union members, all demanding comprehensive reform of the Pinochet-era educational system.

A particular target became the unpopular educational law promulgated at the end of the military government, which had transferred the authority for public education from the central government to the municipalities, creating huge gaps between rich and poor areas. In addition, inequality had been further aggravated by the partial privatization of schools and the introduction of a voucher system that subsidized a vastly superior private education at the expense of public education. Inequality in funding had led to vast differences in quality and performance. For example, overall 50 percent of high school graduates fail the college entrance exam, while in privatized schools 91 percent of the students pass and can go on to college.[53]

Bachelet initially offered the students an additional US$60 million in emergency spending, which they rejected as inadequate. Ultimately, Bachelet agreed to US$200 million additional spending in the annual education budget, which represented a 2.78 percent increase. She also agreed to continue the policy of issuing free bus passes for students and to offer a free university entrance exam to all but the richest 20 percent of students. Bachelet announced the formation of a commission to study the educational system and recommend reforms. Students insisted on 50 percent representation on the commission, a demand Bachelet turned down, naming 6 high school and 6 college students to the 73-member body.[54]

The Bachelet government's handling of the situation was roundly criticized. Polls showed that over 87 percent of the population supported the students, and the president's favorable rating dropped from 54.5 percent at the beginning of May 2006 to 43.4 percent by July.[55] Bachelet announced a cabinet shake-up, replacing her ministers of the interior, economy, and education. Still, the replacement of these ministers did little to change most critics' perception of government ineptitude and indecision. Though they ended their strike, the student organizers vowed to continue pressing the government for deeper reforms of the educational system, which is largely unchanged from that bequeathed to the country by Pinochet.

The unwillingness or inability of future governments to address severe inequality imperils Chile's new consensus. Inequality is not new in Chile. Indeed, deep conflict over inequality and the polarization it produced ultimately led to the crumbling of the *estado de compromiso* and to the violent end of democracy. The recent student protests and labor unrest are the first indications of public disgust with inequality, and pragmatic policies to address it now, during Chile's boom period, can help to avoid the breakdown of the new consensus and the emergence of a more troubling form of conflict that is increasingly common across much of the region.

Reform of the Binominal System: The Last Authoritarian Enclave

The last remaining "authoritarian enclave" standing in the way of the completion of Chile's unfinished transition is the parliamentary election system imposed by Pinochet. The election system is not simply a curious institutional artifact of the regime; it has profound consequences for the quality of democracy and the maintenance of the tacit social pact in Chile.

The legislative election system, known as the binominal system, establishes two-seat districts for elections to Congress.[56] Each party can present two candidates in each of the 60 electoral districts for the Chamber of Deputies. The two-candidate list system is also used in the country's 19 Senate districts. In practice, both coalitions have negotiated to divide candidate slates among their constituent parties, providing for bipolar competition between the two coalitions. The lists are "open," meaning that voters indicate a preference for one of two candidates on their preferred list. The total votes for both candidates on each list are first pooled for the purposes of distributing seats to lists, and then seats are awarded to the individual candidate who receives the most individual votes on the list. Because seats are allocated by the D'Hondt Method, the first-place list in a district can win both seats only if it more than doubles the vote total of the second-place list; otherwise, each list wins one seat. In Chile's postauthoritarian pattern of two-coalition competition, this has created two effective thresholds: coalitions must win about 66 percent of the vote to win both seats in a district and about 33 percent to win one. It is this aspect of the system that led Pinochet to adopt it. The system allows the right to win 50 percent of the seats when it only effectively polls a little over one-third of the votes across districts. The flip side, of course, is that the effective thresholds also make it quite difficult for a coalition or party to muster the supermajority necessary to win two seats in a district (or to "double"). For the last five democratic elections for the Chamber (1989, 1993, 1997, 2001, and 2005) the center-left Concertación coalition succeeded in doubling in 11, 11, 9, 4, and 6 districts, respectively. The center-right Alianza por Chile has doubled only three times during this time, in 1 district in 1993, 2001, and 2005.

The arguments against this election system are familiar and do not need to be recounted in depth here.[57] Briefly, the system effectively provides a lock on power for the two major coalitions in the country. The outcome of an election is usually a foregone conclusion: except in a few cases, one member of the Concertación and one member of the Alianza is likely to win in each district, because each of the major coalition lists almost invariably polls between 33 percent and 66 percent, meaning each wins one seat.

In addition, the election system requires each coalition to negotiate two seat lists drawn from their constituent parties (with the understanding that one candidate is likely to lose). This creates a good deal of interparty squabbling about list partners, because every candidate and party wants a list partner whom he or she can beat. The complexity of this exercise shifts the power of candidate nomination into the hands of party elites who must make strategic calculations and engage in extensive negotiations on candidate placement, which translates into very little citizen input into the selection of candidates. Furthermore, following these negotiations, it is usually a foregone conclusion which candidate on a list will win. Therefore, in many cases party elites effectively choose legislators.

The system also makes it difficult for voters to hold legislators accountable once elected. Reelection rates are quite high, and it is very difficult to unseat an incumbent given the dynamics of the two-list system. To begin with, incumbents across parties are understood (with few exceptions) to be entitled to automatic renomination. In addition, because list votes are pooled, even a voter who chooses to sanction an incumbent by voting for the incumbent's list partner may actually contribute to the reelection of the incumbent! These problems provide disincentives to participation, with a growing perception in the Chilean electorate that voting does not matter because electoral outcomes are predetermined by elite negotiations.

For its proponents, the binominal system provided strong incentives for the creation of a two-coalition pattern that has been at the root of postauthoritarian stability.[58] These arguments tend to ignore the fact that the balance between the binominal system's benefits and trade-offs is time-dependent. It certainly did buy democracy a measure of security by providing strong incentives for coalition formation and maintenance that were functional and useful in the immediate postauthoritarian period. However, these benefits came with the understanding that the binominal system exacted a cost in terms of representation, competition, party turnover, internal democracy, and the impact of voters on outcomes. This cost-benefit balance has now changed. In a transformed environment in which Chile's democracy is now secure, the costs of the security and predictability created by the binominal system outweigh the benefits it provides. Democracy depends on accountability, legitimacy, and representation. By stacking the deck for winners, transferring the power of candidate choice to elites, and limiting the ability of citizens to sanction elected representatives, the binominal system limits all three. Voter disgust, disconnection, and perceived irrelevance could undermine what seems a perfect transition and shatter the tacit consensus outlined here.

There are compelling reasons to make reform of the binominal system the final in a series of reforms to the Pinochet constitution, signaling the end of Chile's democratic transition and its arrival as a full-fledged modern democracy. Every president has proposed a reform of the electoral system and the adoption of some form of proportional representation. In each instance, the proposal has failed. Michelle Bachelet pledged reform of the binominal system as part of her electoral platform, and shortly after taking office she formed a commission of experts to study electoral reform, headed by former minister and senator Edgardo Boeninger. The Boeninger Commission issued its report and recommended the adoption of a moderate proportional representation system for both the Chamber of Deputies and the Senate. Total Chamber membership would be increased from 120 to 150, and the Senate would expand from 38 to 50 members. For both houses, the reform envisions an election system with district magnitudes (seats per district) ranging between two and eight and employing the D'Hondt counting system.[59] In June 2006, President Bachelet sent the Senate a proposal to reform the Constitution in various ways to allow for the later introduction of a concrete reform such as that proposed by the Boeninger Commission. However, by the end of 2006, the legislation had not made it out of committee, and the Boeninger Commission's recommendation of a proportional system had been specifically and vocally rejected by both major parties on the right. By the middle of Bachelet's term in 2008, electoral reform was dead in the water.

During the 2005 presidential campaign, the right made a commitment to discuss electoral reform. However, beyond its reaction to the Boeninger Commission's report, the right's general stance on electoral reform has been mixed. The UDI has categorically discounted the possibility of electoral reform, while RN has been more willing to discuss reform with the government, mostly due to the party's own instinct for self-preservation. The UDI is currently the largest party in Chile in terms of electoral support and legislative representation. If the Alianza falls apart and each of its parties presents separate lists, the UDI is likely to maintain a large legislative contingent, while the possibilities for RN's exclusion are very real. Of course, with a proportional representation system, should such a division come to pass, RN could still maintain legislative representation, which in large part explains its willingness to consider electoral reform. Past efforts at electoral reform have been defeated because of the combination of the supermajority required for constitutional changes and the veto power of the appointed senators, both of which were eliminated by the 2005 constitutional reforms. If the government succeeds in striking a bargain with RN, the UDI's legislative contingent alone will be unable to block electoral reform. However, if the right remains unified, RN and the UDI together have the numbers they need to continue to block electoral reform.

Conclusion

In addition to the longer-term challenges of inequality and institutional reform outlined here, there are shorter-term challenges for Chile's major political actors that will test the durability of Chile's new social pact.

For Bachelet the most central challenge is to regain control of what was already being termed a lame duck administration by its midterm in early 2008 and to find policies that are genuinely hers. Bachelet did commit to promoting a new brand of citizen politics through her 36-point platform, which outlined proposed legislation aimed at helping and empowering everyday Chileans. However, there has been concrete success on only a few of these initiatives, and these successes were achieved during the first months of her government. Since then, her administration has seriously faltered, with allegations that the government is, at best, adrift and, at worst, incompetent. In addition to student protests, the government has been plagued by labor unrest, cabinet instability, and internal governmental divisions. However, the allegations of ineptitude related to a major reorganization of Santiago's transport system (known as the Transantiago Plan) have been far and away the most damaging to Bachelet. Though the plan had been designed by the outgoing Lagos government, Bachelet was responsible for its implementation. The Transantiago Plan's launch on February 10, 2007, was a complete disaster, and the system continues to be plagued with problems. In its first days, commuters were left stranded by a shortage of buses, and the GPS system designed to track the intervals between buses proved inoperable. The choice of routes was criticized, with riders complaining that the new routes were more complicated to understand than the old ones and actually took longer to complete. National newspapers printed dramatic photos of masses of stranded commuters and packed Metro cars as commuters abandoned buses in favor of the more dependable Metro. Given the centrality of public transport to the lives of everyday Chileans, the issue contradicted Bachelet's contention that she was the people's president.

Bachelet's responses to this series of crises have been widely criticized, and her government has suffered in public opinion polls. For her handling of the crisis of student protests the president was criticized for lack of decisiveness and firmness, two characteristics she must work hard to cultivate given perceptions about gender in the country. On a deeper level, the Transantiago debacle raised questions about the basic competency of Concertación governments. This is a serious threat to a coalition that has prided itself on its administrative and political acumen in managing both the economy and the political transition. If Bachelet's government is to go down in history for reasons other than the novelty of her gender, she must do more to put her own imprint on Concertación policies and more resolutely make decisions. Unfortunately for Bachelet, little time remains to do so, and early crises and failures have created an environment of government temerity, exacerbated by the reality that many of her supporters have jumped ship, their sights set on the next election.

From a longer-term perspective, the Concertación must face up to the problems of any aging coalition. Approaching two decades in power, it is one of the longest-lived continuously governing coalitions in the world. The Concertación came close to losing the presidential elections in 1999 and 2005. In the most recent elections it could rely on the personality of Bachelet as a novel candidate who made the coalition seem fresh and new. There are no fresh faces waiting in the wings, and it is quite difficult for any governing coalition to sustain itself for more than two decades.

More significantly, the Concertación must devise a new model of post-transition politics in order to continue to remain electorally attractive and to ensure the long-term vitality of Chilean democracy. The prevalent pattern of policy making through interelite settlement, including the *democracia de los acuerdos* and elite negotiations over legislative candidate selection, has been very effective in averting conflict, maintaining coalition unity, and underwriting Chile's vaunted "model transition." However, it has also marginalized Congress and voters while privileging the executive branch, ministries, and political party elites. Bachelet pledged to adopt a new way of doing politics in Chile, a promise she fulfilled largely through the appointment of a cabinet characterized by political outsiders and women. Bachelet's surprise at the scope and intensity of the student protests shows that even a politician who purports to be in touch with the people can be betrayed by the politics of interelite settlement. Up until now, there has been shared elite and popular consensus, but unless this model of politics changes, the Chilean political class risks widening the rift between it and voters, with potentially very negative consequences for democracy. The recent student and labor protests also suggest a bubbling discontent beneath what appears to be a successful transition. Electoral participation has been steadily declining in Chile since the return of democracy, which is perhaps a reflection of growing disillusionment with the transitional model of politics. The great irony is that the Concertación's very model of transition, which made Chile stand out as a success, may not be the model necessary for the long-term success of representative democracy.

The right also faces challenges. Democracy is fundamentally about alternation in power and choices. However, since the return of democracy to Chile, while the right has been successful in burying the ghost of Pinochet, it has been less successful in elaborating a vision for Chile's future that is sufficiently attractive for it to win elections. One of the reasons is that the Concertación has pulled off the seemingly impossible: it has adopted and adjusted the discourse of the right to establish a government with necessary elements of continuity while simultaneously casting itself as a force for change. The Bachelet race is emblematic. Even though Bachelet led a 16-year-old coalition, she was perceived as the "new" candidate, while Lavín was seen as the old one. Given the new consensus in Chile analyzed here, the programmatic space available in which to elaborate a new vision is of course constrained. While the elaboration of an overall vision for the country that differs from that of the Concertación may be elusive, the right must at the very least show an effective governing face. To do so, it must overcome its internal divisions. A good first step would be the institution of presidential primaries. The right could arguably have won the last election if it had avoided an internecine and damaging fight between its two sectors and presented a unity candidate.

Chile's return to democracy was slow, gradual, negotiated, and plodding, and it often left actors unsatisfied and demands unmet. However, ultimately its success is instructive for other countries. It shows that democratic success is more likely when the trappings of democratic government are underwritten by and attached to some deeper social consensus. Still, this is a difficult model to copy, because Chile was able to rely on two elements that are often lacking across the region. First, in Chile consensus could be rebuilt rather than built from the bottom up. Despite their violent breakdown in the 1970s, Chile had previously established strong patterns of social accommodation. Second, the new consensus came gradually, was negotiated, and was underwritten by a context of strong institutions and political parties within which agreements could be structured and enforced. The question is whether such a consensus can be built and maintained in other countries where similar social and institutional building blocks are lacking.

Chile is also instructive in the sense that even with these elements, democracy and consensus there are not immune to crisis. The violent end of the *estado de compromiso* and the continuing challenges to the current social pact underscore how consensus can break down, and this chapter has suggested some potential fault lines, the most important of which are nagging inequality and a less than optimal electoral system. In previous editions of this volume and elsewhere, analysts have consistently pointed to the "unfinished" and "incomplete" nature of Chile's democratic transition. Given Chile's new social consensus, and pending a reform of its electoral system, the country's unfinished transition may finally have come to an end. The challenge now is to transform Latin America's "model" democratic transition into the region's model democracy.

9

Colombia

Democratic Security and Political Reform

Fernando Cepeda Ulloa

Democratic governance has been seriously threatened at various moments throughout Colombia's history. Interparty conflict for over a century and a half led to multiple violent outbursts in the nineteenth and twentieth centuries. In 1970 this confrontation was overcome, apparently forever. Since then, however, new and serious threats to democratic governance have emerged, including illegal armed groups, drug cartels, organized crime and its inevitable consequences, corruption, a presidential election whose legitimacy was questioned by a group—the Movimiento 19 de Abril (M-19; April 19th Movement)—that went on to carry out high-profile terrorist acts, and human rights violations that went unpunished because of the ineffective justice system.

In 1991, after several unsuccessful attempts, a constituent assembly sought to restore institutional legitimacy, open political spaces, and create special mechanisms to make the justice system more effective. However, two governments that faced deep political, economic, and social crises (those of Ernesto Samper, Liberal, 1994–98, and Andrés Pastrana, Conservative, 1998–2002) undermined the objectives of the new Constitution. This resulted in a very serious crisis of governance and, for the first time in more than a century, the reelection of an incumbent president, Álvaro Uribe, a Liberal who presented himself as an outsider. His primary pledge has been to restore democratic governance in Colombia. This chapter is intended to shed light on the scope of his policies and their implications for strengthening democratic governance.

In an essay that has been reprinted several times, the historian Malcolm Deas wrote, "Colombia has at times been a violent country. It is not easy to state precisely how violent."[1] More recently, Sebastián L. Mazzuca and James

A. Robinson began a suggestive essay on Colombia's political conflict and the attempts to overcome it at different moments of the country's history with an assertion that also refers to the country's history of violence: "Colombia has not always been a violent country. In fact, for the entire first half of the twentieth century Colombia was one of the most peaceful countries in Latin America, standing out in the region as an exotic exemplar of a highly stable and competitive bipartisan democracy."[2]

What caused the periods of peace and also such painful periods of war, violence, and conflict? Mazzuca and Robinson went on to describe the violent side of Colombia:

> Colombia was not born peaceful. That half century of peaceful political existence [during the twentieth century] was itself a major novelty in Colombian history. Colombia's nineteenth century was politically chaotic even by Hispanic American standards: the record includes nine national civil wars, dozens of local revolts, mutinies and *pronunciamientos* [military coup declarations], material destruction equivalent to several years of economic output, and at least 250,000 deaths due to political violence.[3]

Why have violent periods been followed by decades of peace and then by new outbreaks of violence? According to Mazzuca and Robinson, "The emergence of order in Colombia is temporally correlated with a transformation in the political institutions shaping inter-party relations: internal pacification was concomitant with the introduction of special mechanisms for power-sharing between Liberals and Conservatives, Colombia's two dominant political forces."[4]

In Colombia, different forms of national unity governments have been attempted time and again.[5] In 1957, the country once again resorted to a power-sharing formula, the most comprehensive and longest-lasting in its history, and this time it was enshrined in the Constitution. The political agreement created the Frente Nacional (National Front) and ratified a referendum that was supported by a large percentage of the electorate.[6] Several fundamental points were agreed on, such as the even distribution of judicial and administrative posts between Liberals and Conservatives, the creation of a civil service to professionalize public administration, the introduction of a consensus-based system to ensure the independence of the judicial branch, and the neutrality of the armed forces. Hence, for a period of 12 years (later extended to 16), known as "parity in time," the two parties alternated in the presidency every four years. The Liberal Party began this era in power, and the Conservative Party finished it.

Thus, in the name of interparty peace, the Liberal Party, which had enjoyed a majority since the early 1930s, brought to an end one of the most violent periods in Colombian history. A military government had come to power, led by General Gustavo Rojas Pinilla with the backing of the Liberal Party and a majority of the Conservative Party, as well as most of the general population. Indeed, one of the patriarchs of the Liberal Party, Darío Echandía, said that the new arrangement was not a military coup but "an opinion coup," which is almost unheard of in Colombian politics.[7]

What went wrong? Why did the mechanisms for power-sharing described by Mazzuca and Robinson cease to bear the fruits of peace? The absence of a clear understanding of the limits of power has undermined political peace in Colombia. Majority parties have historically abused power, and minority parties have felt excluded or mistreated, while power-sharing schemes and electoral reform have repeatedly been tried as a way to overcome these obstacles. Mario Latorre Rueda described this situation very accurately in a legal text he wrote as a member of the Council of State:

> In different eras, the Conservative and Liberal parties have been, by turns, government and opposition: when in government, they have said they were seeking an understanding with the opposition and that they came up against an ardent and intransigent opposition; in the opposition, they have called for essential guarantees and have proclaimed that they were answered with arbitrariness and abuse. In government, they have justified their actions based on the legitimate attributions of power; out of government, on the legitimate prerogative to dissent and on tolerance.[8]

In sum, the abuse of power by the government or by the opposition triggered crises of democratic governance. The National Front was, undoubtedly, a successful way to end the recurrent interparty violence. By the time the National Front ended, however, the global and Latin American contexts had changed. The victorious revolution in Cuba, guerrilla movements in Central America, urban warfare in the Southern Cone, and liberation theology had helped change the nature of the use of violence in Colombia. The remnants of the Liberal guerrillas became the Fuerzas Armadas Revolucionarias de Colombia (FARC; Revolutionary Armed Forces of Colombia), Fidel Castro contributed to the founding of the Ejército de Liberación Nacional (ELN; National Liberation Army) in the 1960s, and a movement with a nationalistic ideology and conservative roots emerged after the administration of Carlos Lleras Restrepo (1966–70) purportedly committed fraud against the Alianza Nacional Popular (ANAPO; National Popular Alliance) during the elections on April 19, 1970. Other fringe groups emerged as well, including the Ejército Popular de Liberación (EPL; Popular Liberation Army), the Partido Revolucionario de los Trabajadores (Revolutionary Workers' Party), and the indigenous rights group Movimiento Armado Quintín Lame (Quintín Lame Armed Movement).

In 1968, a constitutional amendment was introduced that sought to gradually dismantle the National Front. Nevertheless, it preserved the spirit of the National Front by establishing that the party with the second-largest number of votes should receive a "proper and equitable" share of representation in government.[9] In this manner, the issues of parity and alternation were resolved and a power-sharing arrangement was indefinitely established "to permanently preserve . . . the spirit of the nation in the executive branch and in public administration."[10]

Another attempt was made in 1968 to use the power-sharing system described earlier to pave the way for peace in Colombia. However, this time the attempt was not fully successful because the illegal armed groups rejected the new formulas and electoral mechanisms for allocating power. In this new phase of the use of violence as a tool of political struggle, no longer was just the predominance of one traditional party or their share in the allocation of power at stake. President Alfonso López Michelsen (1974–78), a critic of the mandatory presidential alternation who won the presidency on the Liberal Party ticket when the National Front ended,[11] noted:

> Today we have a class struggle more than a party struggle. That is why [the parties] are divided between those who want to end the system and those who want to preserve it. Hence, the issue of how to make peace between Liberals and Conservatives no longer has currency. The issue is, rather, how to conduct the debate between friends of the status quo and those who aspire to a different order.[12]

In addition to the new nature of the illegal armed groups, three factors elevated the threat they posed and contributed to the crisis of democratic governance: involvement in the lucrative global drug trade, the subsequent military buildup (particularly by the FARC), and the profitable businesses of kidnapping and extortion. The power of these groups reached such a high level during the Samper administration that they were able to score highly publicized military victories.[13] A consequence of the weak Colombian state was the emergence and expansion of the Autodefensas Unidas de Colombia (AUC; United Self-Defense Forces of Colombia), incorrectly described as "paramilitary groups," which played the role of a counterguerrilla force.[14] Never before had the Colombian state faced the convergence of such threats, particularly ones with such substantial military capacity.

In 1991, a tripartite Constituent Assembly was convened, composed of Liberals, Conservatives, and former guerrillas, primarily from the M-19 but also including representatives of other illegal armed groups that had returned to civilian life.[15] The Assembly drew up new electoral rules and even went beyond this mandate by introducing the notion of a social state based

on the rule of law and mechanisms for grassroots participation, such as referendums, plebiscites, consultations, and town meetings. It reaffirmed the
election of mayors by popular vote, which had been introduced into the Constitution as Legislative Act 1 of 1986 and enacted through Law 78 of 1986 as
part of the unsuccessful peace negotiations between the administration of
Belisario Betancur Cuartas (1982–86) and the FARC.[16] The Assembly also
introduced the election of departmental governors by popular vote and
adopted a Charter of Political, Social, and Economic Rights. These rights
were to be—and in fact have been—guaranteed by the Constitutional Court
and by highly effective legal instruments, such as the *tutela* (appeal for constitutional relief) and *acción popular* (a collective appeal for human rights
enforcement). In strictly electoral terms, the Assembly established the vice
presidency of the republic (opening the door for minority factions to weaken
the majority party, in this case the Liberal Party) and drew up national districts for the election of senators (a mechanism to strengthen minority parties by allowing them to aggregate votes obtained in different departments),[17]
as well as special districts for indigenous groups, fro-descendants, and
Colombians living abroad.[18] It also designed a two-round system for presidential elections (encouraging the splintering of majority forces, principally
the Liberal Party, and facilitating coalitions with minority groups in the second round). From different angles, all these mechanisms helped encourage
power-sharing.

These new electoral institutions, mechanisms, and rules consolidated the
peace accords reached with the M-19, the EPL, the Corriente de Renovación
Socialista (Socialist Renovation Movement, a faction of the ELN), and others.
As was recognized at the 15th anniversary of the Constitution on June 4, 2006,
these mechanisms have helped channel numerous social, economic, and
political conflicts into institutional forums. Nevertheless, they have not succeeded in bringing the two leading armed groups, the FARC and the ELN,
into mainstream politics.

Democratic governance was further weakened during the administration
of Ernesto Samper as a result of a scandal over illegal campaign financing
from drug cartels, which tainted nearly his entire term.[19] Samper attempted
political reform, which failed despite being supported by a consensus of all
political forces and others representing civil society.[20]

The centerpiece of Andrés Pastrana's government was an effort to negotiate a peace agreement with the FARC. This endeavor went through three
phases. The first, known as Plan Colombia I, was based on a document prepared with the support of the Inter-American Development Bank and
sought to create a US$7 billion investment fund for peace to be administrated
jointly with the FARC.[21] The most salient feature was the absence of a military component. The second phase, Plan Colombia II, was drafted following

a visit by Thomas Pickering and other senior U.S. government officials on August 10, 1999, as well as a proposal by then–secretary of state Madeleine Albright, published in the *New York Times* on the same day. Secretary Albright pointed to the link between achieving peace and addressing the drug problem, highlighting the military component without ruling out a more comprehensive approach. "Efforts to stop the drug trade are linked to the quest for peace because of rebel and paramilitary involvement in drug trafficking," she wrote.[22] Although she ruled out a definitive military victory, Albright called for introducing a military element: "The question is whether [Pastrana] can muster a combination of pressure and incentives that will cause the guerrillas to respond."[23] The FARC called the new proposal "a counter-guerrilla strategy disguised as an anti-drug plan." During a trip to Cartagena on August 30, 2000, President Bill Clinton responded by saying that the plan was "pro-peace and anti-drugs."[24]

Various accounts, including those of both Clinton and Pastrana after they left office, reveal that the FARC was not altogether wrong. As ambassador to Washington, Pastrana stated that President Álavaro Uribe's strategy was a continuation of the one Pastrana had begun.[25] Clinton, referring to his visit to Cartagena accompanied by several congresspersons and cabinet members, later wrote, "We all wanted to reinforce America's commitment to President Andrés Pastrana's Plan Colombia, which was intended to free his country of the narco-traffickers and terrorists who control about one third of his territory. . . . When he failed, he had asked the United States to help him defeat them with Plan Colombia."[26]

The third phase of Plan Colombia—entered into after the 9/11 terrorist attacks, once the peace process had failed as of February 20, 2002, and in the midst of a presidential race—explicitly targeted the armed groups in the name of fighting terrorism. Both Ambassador Luis Alberto Moreno and Andrés Pastrana wrote columns—Moreno in the *New York Times* and Pastrana in the *Washington Post*[27]—inviting the United States to focus on Colombian terrorists rather than those in Afghanistan and other far-flung places.[28]

The Uribe Administration: Strengthening Democratic Governance

Once elected president, Álvaro Uribe embarked on a comprehensive strategy to strengthen democratic governance. For domestic and international political reasons, he called this strategy the "Democratic Security Policy." He emphasized the military element in the struggle against illegal armed groups that have since come to be known, both in the United States and in Colombia, as "narco-terrorist" groups. A law (Public Law 108-375) passed by the U.S. Congress on August 2, 2002, five days before Uribe's inauguration, had already expanded the State Department's powers to use funds assigned to

Colombia to battle not only the drug cartels but also guerrilla groups designated as terrorists or narco-terrorists in what was called a "unified campaign." The United States thus became directly involved in an internal conflict in another country for the first time since the end of the Vietnam War.[29] The convergence of the post-9/11 political climate, the resounding failure of the Pastrana government's peace process, and the wave of terrorism unleashed in Colombia between January 20 and February 20, 2002, created the conditions necessary for Clinton's vision of Plan Colombia to be fully realized during Uribe's term.

This analysis does not overlook the fact that Plan Colombia II brought about reform in the armed forces and secured military resources that allowed Uribe to quickly increase the military budget, in keeping with the requirements of the U.S. law enacted on August 2, 2002. This was achieved by creating an estate tax and declaring a state of emergency, which President Pastrana had refused to do because he felt that such a measure would be futile.[30] That tax made it possible to collect some 2.6 trillion pesos (US$1 billion).[31] In the opinion of Thomas Marks, "Unlike the predecessor *Plan Colombia* of the Pastrana/Clinton years (written with U.S. input), which had been a virtual catalogue of national ills with proposed solutions beyond Bogotá's ability to operationalize or fund, the new *Democratic Security and Defense Policy* (officially released in June 2003) was intended as a course of action."[32] This policy was developed in response to the emergence of an explosive combination of threats: "terrorism; the illegal drugs trade; illicit finance; traffic of arms, ammunition, and explosives; kidnapping and extortion; and homicide."[33]

The Uribe government's Democratic Security and Defense Policy lays out a comprehensive strategy involving all of the state agencies. This strategy is not for an isolated peace negotiation process or for a simple military buildup. Rather, it is a multidimensional strategy to strengthen democratic governance. It remains to be seen, of course, whether there will be sufficient financial resources to carry out the policy. The multifaceted strategy includes the following components:[34]

- Strengthening the state, specifically institutions that are beyond the vicissitudes of electoral politics, such as law enforcement, the independent judiciary, the board of directors of the Central Bank (which has autonomy to manage macroeconomic policy), and the regulatory commissions responsible for foreign investment, the provision of public services, television broadcasting, and elections.
- Strengthening the government at the national, departmental, municipal, and regional management levels. The Uribe administration carried out an ambitious reform to restructure 145 state companies. For example, Telecom went from 480 billion pesos (approximately US$170 mil-

lion) in losses before the reform to 950 billion pesos (approximately US$340 million) in profits in 2004. The elimination of the Industrial Development Institute has saved the government 300 billion pesos (approximately US$140 million) a year, and similar actions were taken with regard to other state institutions.[35]

The government succeeded in reducing foreign debt from 54 percent of GDP to 46 percent following the revaluation of the peso and a swap of dollar-denominated debt for peso-denominated debt.[36] It has restored authority in 168 municipal seats and in many other large urban areas that formerly had no police service and were at the mercy of guerrilla or paramilitary forces.[37]

One of the most effective tools in restoring democratic governance and a state presence in Colombia has been regional councils. They meet nearly every Saturday (except during a presidential race), and their meetings are broadcast on government television. There is strong participation of authorities and members of civil society at these meetings, which can last up to 12 hours. They are intended to commit authorities to carrying out government programs as well as to involve citizens in government spending allocation either individually or through the organizations to which they belong, which helps ensure transparency and accountability.

Nevertheless, since the very outset of their use, the regional councils have been criticized as

- mechanisms of deinstitutionalization that erode the authority of territorial officials;
- populist tools that create a direct relationship between the president and the citizenry, bypassing the institutional mechanism of mayors, governors, and other local authorities;
- outlets for distributing favors that ignore institutional procedures for developing budgets; and
- publicity ploys.

However, the regional council meetings have been an educational exercise allowing citizens to see for themselves budget constraints and the difficulties of prudently managing funds. It is true that they have unquestionably been one of the administration's most successful publicity instruments and one of the reasons for the high approval ratings the president has enjoyed since taking power. Indeed, the Law of Electoral Guarantees, which was passed to level the political playing field during Uribe's reelection bid, prohibited council meetings for the six months prior to the election. Criticisms of the regional councils, then, have more to do with their effectiveness in boosting the president's popularity than with other considerations.

The same applies to the president's interest in citizen security and the offices responsible for managing decentralized government agencies. Uribe closely monitors performance and each year holds public meetings in which ministers must justify their performance before the entire nation. Some observers, however, view these transparency mechanisms as another form of deinstitutionalization, adding that the councils of ministers have lost much of their value because their meetings are attended by numerous officials who are not ministers.

Although other actions and decisions have also served to strengthen democratic governance, those already mentioned provide a clear indication of the overall success of the strategy outlined in the Democratic Security Policy.[38] Colombian foreign policy is also an integral part of this strategy, as may be inferred from the title of a document released early in Uribe's first term, "Colombian Foreign Policy, 2002–2006: Democratic Governance, Shared Responsibility, and Solidarity." The introduction, written by Uribe, makes the divergence from previous policy abundantly clear: "The main task of the Colombian government on the domestic and foreign fronts is to strengthen democratic governance." Immediately following that, the report reads:

> This document, which maps out Colombian foreign policy, is based on the following assumptions: that our international policy is firmly interwoven with our entire domestic policy, that the efforts and sacrifices made by the Colombian government and people require the firm and resolute commitment of the international community, and that Colombia asks for the unwavering support of the world to defeat terrorism, just as Colombia has shown itself supportive of the worldwide struggle against terrorism in all its forms and manifestations wherever it may arise.[39]

The document reflects the administration's recognition of the highly complex nature of Colombia's situation and its intricate international dimensions: "In light of the principle of shared responsibility, Colombia supports and promotes all international efforts to combat activities that threaten democratic governance and foster terrorism and violence anywhere."[40]

Reelection as a Tool to Strengthen Democratic Governance

During the debate on eliminating the constitutional ban on reelection, the familiar arguments on this matter were voiced—principally that it was not advisable to amend the Constitution to benefit a sitting president. And there are valid reasons for this and other objections, such as those related to the possible abuse of power or the disadvantages in competing with a sitting president.

The October 2003 referendum had made clear that a well-organized opposition could defeat the president on one of his principal government programs, even when the level of his popularity was at its highest. Hence, the concerns about abuse of power, inequality, and so on were diminished. Besides, the arguments against allowing Uribe to run for immediate reelection ignored the postulates put forth in 1788 in *Federalist 72*.[41] This classic text presents five arguments in favor of reelection, that is, against the principle of temporary or perpetual exclusion:

1. A ban on reelection results in "a diminution of the inducements to good behavior" by the president. The hope of earning and obtaining continuity in power encourages good government and good presidential behavior.

2. Such a ban introduces a temptation for the president to abuse power and to unscrupulously take advantage of this unique opportunity. Even though, as *Federalist 72* says, "his avarice might be a guard upon his avarice," there is a fear that avarice might prove victorious over prudence.

3. Such a ban would be "depriving the community of the advantage of the experience gained" by the president.

4. A rule against reelection encourages instability because a change of officials inevitably brings a change in policies, and it is unlikely that there will be a change of persons without a change in policies.

5. The most relevant point for the Colombian situation is this: "There is no nation which has not, at one period or another, experienced an absolute necessity of the services of particular men in particular situations; perhaps it would not be too strong to say, to the preservation of its political existence."

Alexander Hamilton, the author of *Federalist 72*, offers two possible arguments to refute the objections to reelection outlined earlier, based on greater presidential independence and national security. The constitutional amendment allowing the reelection of the president of the republic, upheld by the Constitutional Court, is consistent with strengthening democratic governance because it would (1) give citizens the right to hold a president accountable for the exercise of his or her mandate and, consequently, give them the tools with which to renew a president's term or to vote the incumbent out and bring in someone else and (2) ensure the continuity of policies deemed successful—with some adjustments, based on criticism and the facts on the ground—and maintain the possibility for key officials to continue in office.

Uribe has broken with the tradition of "ministerial crises" that, three or four times each four-year term, have led presidents to reshuffle their cabinets in response to poor performance or pressure from Congress. Several ministers have now been in office for more than four years, and during Uribe's first term, there was not a single ministerial crisis. There were only individual resignations, including those of the minister of the treasury and public credit and the minister of the interior and justice, as well as two ministers of defense, and the replacement of the minister of environment, housing, and territorial development. Seven ministers from Uribe's first term have continued into his second. This unprecedented stability in the cabinet has been a significant institutionalizing factor.

Some observers have claimed that ministers do not perform a traditional role and act instead as vice ministers. It is argued, moreover, that the president micromanages, for instance by making direct calls to subordinate officials or giving instructions without clearance from the respective minister. Some ministers have voiced their displeasure and resigned, such as the first prime minister of the treasury and public credit.

Uribe has responded to criticism on various occasions by saying that a Harvard professor taught him that one must both macromanage and micromanage to be effective. In Colombia, it is difficult to achieve meaningful public administration objectives if one neglects the operational level.

Another objection repeatedly raised regarding presidential reelection has to do with checks and balances. The possibility of concentration of power in the executive has been raised because of the president's ability to influence appointments and select candidates for the principal oversight agencies and other autonomous entities. The Liberal Party recently proposed a constitutional amendment to ensure that the comptroller, Office of the Attorney General, Office of the Ombudsman, Office of the Prosecutor, board of directors of the Bank of the Republic, Constitutional Court, National Electoral Board, National Television Commission, and other agencies not be subordinate to the directives of the executive. This was one of many arguments made in the petition asking the Constitutional Court to rule on the elimination of the ban on reelection. However, the court determined that reelection would not cause the imbalances that some had alleged.[42] During the legislative session that began on July 20, 2006, Congress rejected a constitutional amendment on reelection proposed by the Liberal Party; in fact, the proposal failed to receive enough support to pass to a first-round vote.

Critics allege that the president has excessive power over the board of directors of the Central Bank, whose members are directly appointed by the president when the term of a member expires. It has been noted that a reelected president would be able to appoint a majority of the five members of the board—who serve for four years, subject to reappointment—because the president could replace two in each four-year term.[43] These officials, however, normally serve for eight years, except in the rare cases of resignation. This frees them from the direct control of the executive, as the history of the bank demonstrates.

The appointment of the current comptroller during Uribe's second term is a case in point. He was nominated by the state councilor for inclusion in the slate of candidates (the other candidates had been chosen by the Supreme Court and the Constitutional Court) and elected by both chambers of Congress. He received votes from all political parties, including the Liberal Party and the Democratic Pole from the opposition, while very few in Congress abstained or voted against the appointment.

The Impact of Presidential Reelection

For the first time in many years, Álvaro Uribe's reelection for the 2006–10 term has allowed for real continuity in the execution of public policies and the strategy for strengthening democratic governance. Expectations are very high, and the president has a great responsibility. Only time will tell if the arguments in favor of reelection prove more substantive than the risks highlighted by its opponents.

Congress amended the Constitution to allow reelection, not to reelect Uribe. The latter option was left in the hands of the electorate and the opposition, as is appropriate in a pluralistic democracy. Uribe won the first reelection of a sitting president in Colombian history, with two million votes more than he had obtained in 2002. He also took 31 of the 33 departments. The exceptions were Guajira, which borders Venezuela, and Nariño, which is adjacent to Ecuador. The president faced three experienced opponents of considerable standing: Carlos Gaviria, a former justice of the Constitutional Court; Antanas Mockus, twice mayor of Bogotá; and Horacio Serpa, in his third bid for the presidency. Figures 9.1 and 9.2 show the evolution of Uribe's public image between 2001 and 2006 and how he was perceived in comparison with his opponents before the 2006 election.

How did the forces on the left, which in Colombia have traditionally garnered far less than 10 percent of the vote, fare? They received 25 percent of all votes, an extremely high rate in historical terms. Indeed, opening the door to presidential reelection allowed the democratic opposition to flourish. The Democratic Pole, a coalition of forces on the left, and the Official Liberal Party are both vigorously playing roles as opposition forces, in Congress and in other political forums. The strengthening of the democratic left—to the detriment of illegal armed groups such as the FARC and the ELN—and the strengthening of the opposition are two significant contributions to democratic governance in Colombia.

Figure 9.1. The Evolution of President Uribe's Public Image over the Course of His Campaigns, September 2001–May 2006

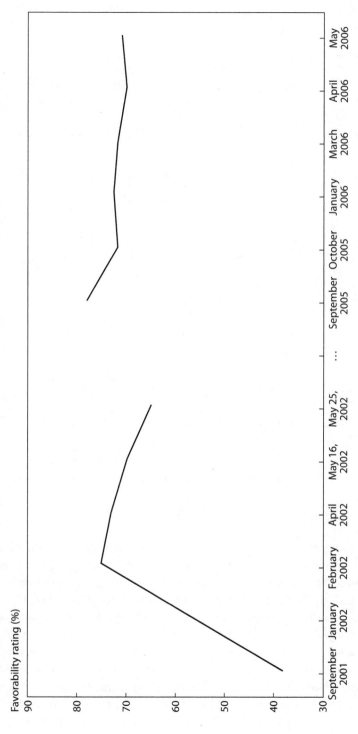

Favorability rating (%)

Source: Ipsos-Napoleón Franco, "El gran cubrimiento, 7 y Última Gran Encuesta," study no. 7456, prepared for RCN Radio and RCN Televisión, Semana y La FM, May 18, 2006.

Figure 9.2. Favorable Perceptions of Some Colombian Presidential Candidates, September 2005–May 2006

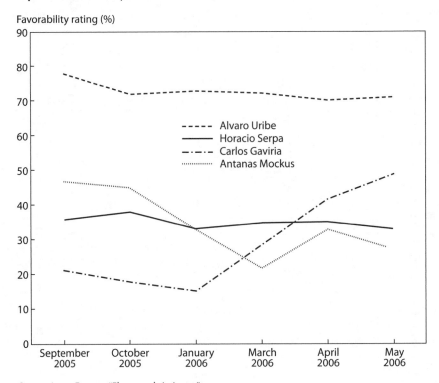

Favorability rating (%)

Source: Ipsos-Franco, "El gran cubrimiento."

Were there outbreaks of extreme violence, as some critics of reelection had predicted? Compared with past elections, this was the most peaceful on record.

The Parapolitics Scandal in Perspective

Paradoxically, the governance crises experienced by the Uribe government in the first months of its second term have helped strengthen governance in Colombia. Such crises are essential and result from the government's confrontation of the factors that threaten governance in Colombia. The proceedings that the Supreme Court initiated in November 2006 against senators, representatives, and other politicians with links to the AUC forces underscored the strength of the justice system, the presidency, and Congress, whose activities were seriously affected by these court decisions. As noted, attempts to overcome the threats to democratic governance cause temporary, acute crises of governance, and therein lies the institutional fortification described in this chapter. It is an illusion to expect threats to governance to be overcome without considerable costs and risks. In spite of the enormous threats, the tradition of democratic and civil law in Colombia has played a crucial role in maintaining democratic procedures and the rule of law.

The Colombian self-defense forces were ostensibly formed to protect citizens from guerrilla groups and the inability of the state to fulfill its basic security functions. Birds of a feather flock together, however, and the paramilitary groups ultimately morphed into criminal gangs, funding themselves from the same sources as the guerrillas: illegal drugs, extortion, kidnapping, and theft of state resources. A number of government officials and members of Congress became involved, prospering politically and financially from their connections.

This deplorable phenomenon has been called the "parapolitics scandal," that is, the involvement of the paramilitaries in political life. In the eyes of some, this scandal has tainted President Uribe because nearly all of the representatives in jail or on trial belong to his bloc of supporters in Congress. The arrest of Jorge Noguera, the former director of the intelligence service, as well as those of the father and brother of the former foreign minister, María Consuelo Araújo (who resigned as a result of the scandal), have only raised more concerns.

How has President Uribe responded? He argues that he has no formal connections to the accused legislators because he did not run on the ticket of a political party in either of his elections, opting instead to register through the process of citizen petition. Furthermore, this scandal has been uncovered only because of the president's policy of negotiation with and prosecution of the paramilitaries. The negotiation process has been overseen by the Organization of American States, whose Permanent Council periodically reviews the progress reports. A special Justice and Peace Law was passed by Congress —despite tremendous national and international controversy—to regulate this process and serve as the legal precedent for negotiations with other illegal groups. Colombia's judges have been granted all the support and independence they need to move forward with their mission. These actions opened the door for the provision of testimony against public officials and for public debate on the role of the self-defense forces in public life. Corrupt officials and paramilitary bosses can no longer count on the complicity and fear that, much like the Omerta code of silence, once protected these mafia-style criminal organizations.

In fact, the government has helped lead the movement against the AUC influence in politics, resulting in over 45,000 paramilitary demobilizations. These have included the demobilization of nearly 4,000 individual soldiers and 32,000 collective demobilizations, even though at the beginning of the process there were thought to be fewer than 15,000. In addition, the commanders are in maximum-security prisons, eligible for the reduced penalties promised under the Justice and Peace Law only if they fully cooperate with the judicial system and offer reparations to their victims.

Various officials have resigned, and more than 10 members of Congress have been imprisoned or are under investigation in the wake of the parapolitics scandal. As is common in these situations, the opposition has tried to implicate the government. The parapolitics scandal itself, however, is evidence of the government's successful campaign to eliminate the paramilitaries.

A New Power-Sharing Model

In his second presidential term, Uribe has the immense responsibility of strengthening democratic governance and pushing for two outcomes. First, he wants to minimize the capacity of illegal armed groups to undermine democratic governance. Naturally this entails eliminating or minimizing profits from drug trafficking, kidnapping, and extortion. Second, Uribe is striving to carry out political negotiations with the FARC and the ELN, the scope of which would be directly proportional to the extent to which the government is able to weaken the military power of these groups.[44] Given this state of affairs and provided that other threats to democratic governance can be addressed with some success, efforts to strengthen democratic governance in Colombia depend on designing a new power-sharing model.

Any political framework designed in the current circumstances is unlikely to resemble those employed at other moments of Colombia's history. Drafting new electoral rules and systems to ensure distribution of power to the satisfaction of illegal armed groups will not suffice, because this confrontation differs from those that repeatedly flared up between Liberals and Conservatives or from the one that allowed M-19 and other insurgent groups to return to civilian life in 1991–92. The new power-sharing arrangement will have to include other elements that would reform rural, urban, and financial property holdings without undermining the new economic model.

The scope and content of this new power-sharing formula will, as noted, depend on the extent of the military success against the insurgents. However, this does not preclude a certain political generosity, which, with some luck, could end the insurgents' use of violence as a tool for achieving political, economic, and social ends.

Undoubtedly, these four years are going to be decisive for strengthening democratic governance in Colombia. It can be said that the government is doing well, but this is not enough. The decisive cooperation of the international community and civil society is required, and continuing to encourage citizenship participation is a sine qua non.

The postconflict period is here, and Colombia cannot wait for the signing of peace accords before it implements public policies that are essential for victims and perpetrators to find their place in a society at peace. This is a huge undertaking requiring an immense commitment and effort not only from Colombia but also from the international community. All of this makes the task of the state, government, civil society, citizenry, and international actors particularly complex. After all, peace often requires more resources than war.

Political Reform

During his campaign for the presidency, Uribe harshly criticized the way Congress operated and the corrupt practices common to political activities. He announced that he would call a referendum to create a unicameral Congress and introduce other political reforms.[45] He kept this promise the very day of his inauguration, August 7, 2002. A thorny political process ensued, making it necessary to deal with two reforms simultaneously. First, the October 25, 2003, referendum failed to obtain the 25 percent turnout required for it to be valid, although those who voted overwhelmingly approved of the proposed measures (Table 9.1). Only the first of the 14 questions in the referendum received enough votes to pass. Second, a constitutional amendment that Congress had approved (through Legislative Act 1 of 2003) ultimately served as the legal framework for the territorial elections held later that year as well as for the 2006 elections for Congress and the presidency.

Why was political reform necessary after the passage of the 1991 Constitution? In truth, some institutions—for example, the board in charge of national electoral districting—were transformed into something significantly different from what had been envisioned. Others failed because of the weakness of the National Electoral Board, which did not completely fulfill its role as a regulatory and governing body. The effectiveness of other institutions was undermined by excessively strict regulations—for example, Law 134 of 1994, the Statutory Law on Citizen Participation. Making matters even worse, Congress did not meet fundamental political requirements mandated in the 1991 Constitution.

Traditionally, such reforms require several attempts before they finally succeed, and the new reform was no exception. The following antecedents should be taken into account.

The Commission to Study Political Party Reform (1995)

The first serious attempt at political reform, the creation of the Commission to Study Political Party Reform, was promoted by the Samper administration.[46] A consensus developed within the commission on a set of important recommendations.[47] For the most part, the reform would not have modified constitutional rules; the authors sought to preserve the 1991 Constitution as much as possible and preferred to update the 1991 reform through legal measures.

Table 9.1. Vote Totals for the Questions on the October 2003 Colombian Referendum

Question Number	"Yes" Votes	"No" Votes	Blank Votes	Total Votes	Percentage "Yes"	Percentage Participation	Unmarked Questions
1	5,874,193	294,348	125,266	6,293,807	93.33	25.11	379,243
2	5,871,354	232,121	119,213	6,222,688	94.35	24.82	450,362
3	5,839,612	295,616	125,850	6,261,078	93.27	24.97	411,972
4	5,319,557	703,634	124,915	6,148,106	86.52	24.52	524,944
5	5,668,819	283,030	104,406	6,056,255	93.60	24.16	616,795
6	5,328,733	295,908	105,040	5,729,681	93.00	22.85	943,369
7	5,403,139	208,100	93,982	5,705,221	94.71	22.76	967,829
8	5,602,823	493,563	124,926	6,221,312	90.06	24.82	451,738
9	5,557,950	460,941	117,946	6,136,837	90.57	24.48	536,213
11	5,714,738	283,440	109,104	6,107,282	93.57	24.36	565,768
12	5,668,878	270,039	100,384	6,039,301	93.87	24.09	633,749
13	5,778,469	285,842	123,228	6,187,539	93.39	24.68	485,511
14	4,907,283	1,063,877	141,545	6,112,705	80.28	24.38	560,345
15	5,457,866	420,859	115,300	5,994,025	91.06	23.91	679,025
18	5,475,951	270,249	97,197	5,843,397	93.71	23.31	829,653

Sources: Registraduría Nacional del Estado Civil, March 1, 2004, and *Diario Oficial* 45.070, January 21, 2003.
Note: Numbers at left are the numbers from the *Diario Oficial,* the source of the information.

The Pact between Andrés Pastrana and Ingrid Betancourt

During the 1998 presidential race, candidate Andrés Pastrana reached an agreement with fellow candidate Ingrid Betancourt to call for a referendum on political reform in order to gain her support in the second round. Although a draft referendum was drawn up, a concrete proposal for reform never materialized because a broader political agreement was reached, as I explain next.

The Casa Medina Political Pact

Representatives of the Liberal Party, the Conservative Party, the Opción Vida (Life Option) movement, independent organizations, and the Movimiento Liberalismo Renovador (Renew Liberalism) bloc signed the National Agreement for Political Reform on October 5, 1998. This agreement served as the basis for the Legislative Proposal to Reform Colombian Politics and Consolidate Democracy, which was submitted to Congress by Minister of the Interior Néstor Humberto Martínez as a first step toward peace and the modernization of political customs. A draft constitutional reform, submitted while this agreement was being prepared, would have substantially modified the 1991 Constitution. This stands in contrast with the cautious approach of the 1995 Commission, which limited itself to legislative mechanisms and proposed only moderate constitutional amendments. This proposed legal reform was submitted as Legislative Proposal 088 of 1998 in the lower house and as Legislative Proposal 018 of 1998 in the Senate.[48] This attempted political reform collapsed at the last moment because of a disagreement over the excessive executive powers proposed in Article 1.[49]

President Pastrana's Proposed Referendum

In a March 30, 2000, address, President Pastrana announced a constitutional referendum on sweeping new reforms to the Colombian political system. This was the first proposal making use of the participatory mechanism set forth in the 1991 Constitution to allow the Colombian people to express their opinion on important political matters. The administration's assessment of a corruption scandal triggered by the leadership of the lower house was blunt and categorically critical.[50]

The proposal called for a referendum on July 16, 2000. To this end, it also requested passage of Bill 261 of 2000 by the Chamber by Representatives. The proposed law contained 17 specific questions followed by 17 constitutional amendments, which were to be the text of the referendum to be submitted for approval by the electorate.

The administration's proposal set off a formidable political crisis that soon blocked the proposed referendum and led to two simultaneous reactions: the collection of signatures to support a grassroots referendum and the submission of a draft political reform in Congress by a group of senators that included Juan Martín Caicedo and Rodrigo Rivera. The administration's proposal and that of Congress failed, as did the grassroots initiative, at different times and for different reasons.[51]

The Proposal Initiated by Congress

A political reform put forth by several members of Congress began to make its way through the Senate. It was approved by the First Commission of the Senate on October 11, 2000, and a definitive text (Legislative Proposal 118 in the Chamber of Representatives, 06 in the Senate) was achieved in the first round, after review by a Temporary Mediation Commission on December 15, 2000. In late 2001, despite the efforts of many members of Congress as well as Ministers of the Interior Humberto de la Calle and, later, Armando Estrada, this proposed political reform also foundered. The issues debated were quite similar to those that had come into play in the preceding cases, although there were changes to the text as it made its way through the legislature.

Toward an Inevitable Political Reform

After the March 10, 2002, congressional elections, the issue of political reform once again came to the fore. The proliferation of candidate lists (321 for the Senate, with 2,979 candidates, and 906 for the Chamber of Representatives) once again underscored the chaotic state of the Colombian party system. The presidential candidates announced their unwavering intention to obtain passage of a reform, and some, along with individual members of Congress, proposed grassroots initiatives for holding a referendum. Meanwhile, candidate Uribe reiterated that on August 7 he would submit a proposal for a referendum on political reform.

The efforts of the Fundación para la Educación Superior y el Desarrollo (FEDESARROLLO; Foundation for Higher Education and Development) should be noted. FEDESARROLLO, a research organization supported by the Inter-American Development Bank and Colombian government agencies and foundations, embarked on an ambitious project to produce a document titled "Institutional Reforms in Colombia." At least three chapters specifically address political reform: decentralization, the division of powers, and Colombia's party and electoral system. The purpose of these proposals was to limit clientelism and political fragmentation by buttressing the party structure.

To everyone's surprise, the administration announced that it would submit a proposal for political reform to Congress before the end of its session, on July 20. Inevitably, this proposal met with resistance, though it did serve as a belated political statement.

The Uribe Administration's Political Reform

It is not surprising, then, that during the 2002 presidential race all candidates promised to carry out political reform. Uribe, who won the election in the first round by an overwhelming majority, pledged to propose a referendum to prohibit corruption and politicking at the very moment of his inauguration, August 7, 2002, at 5:00 p.m. The proposed law became Senate Bill 47 of 2002 and Chamber of Representatives Bill 57 of 2002. Of the 16 points that it initially contained, the most controversial called for replacing the bicameral system with a unicameral one (which would naturally require drastically reducing the number of members) in addition to a complex proposal to give the president discretion over the timeline for holding a referendum on revoking the mandate of Congress. If the president and Congress failed to reach an agreement on a date for holding elections for the unicameral assembly, the president would be empowered to call a referendum directly, without having to obtain Congress's authorization. Thus, the electorate would merely vote on whether to call early elections for a term that would end on July 19, 2006.

In the subsequent political give and take, the executive agreed to eliminate these highly controversial points. The referendum ended up including some political points and a substantial number of fiscal issues. New topics were incorporated into a referendum that already had 15 articles, not all of which would easily be understood by voters. The new points included the reversal of a Constitutional Court ruling dating back several years that allowed possession of a certain amount of illegal drugs for personal use. In its decision to allow the use of narcotics, the Constitutional Court had cited the constitutional principle of the "free development of personality." The reform also called for extending the term of incumbent mayors and governors from three to four years, reducing the salaries of deputies of departmental assemblies, and cutting funding for municipal councils.

In light of the country's extremely precarious fiscal situation, the referendum became a tool to address the fiscal problem (reducing pensions, making transfers to the rural sector, eliminating departmental representation offices and comptroller offices, and so on). The technocrats were delighted to have a way to make these changes without the need for the characteristic horse trading of congressional debate.

Many observers believed that the president was taking a great risk by including fiscal issues, which could lead to the formation of a "No" movement to defeat the referendum, which is what in fact occurred. Other observers argued that the referendum was going to turn into a referendum on the president's performance.

Passage of a referendum requires a turnout of at least 25 percent of eligible voters—that is, about six million people—and the casting of 50 percent plus one of the votes in favor of the referendum. In the end, the minimum threshold of voters was not reached, and the referendum failed. It is clear now that the introduction of the controversial fiscal component cost the referendum the votes it needed for approval.

By contrast, the political reform that Congress had drafted and approved (Legislative Law 1 of 2003) was still in effect. In the territorial elections of October 26, 2003, turnout fell by 82 percent compared to the previous elections. Since then, the country has been governed within a very different electoral framework. The changes of Law 1 were reinforced with the constitutional amendment allowing the immediate reelection of the president (Legislative Law 2 of 2004). They were also mandated by the constitutional amendment itself, the Law of Electoral Guarantees (Statutory Law 996 of 2005), the main objective of which was to protect the opposition.[52] The Law on Party Blocs, which governs the behavior of parties, was a necessary complement to the Law of Electoral Guarantees (Law 974 of 2005).[53]

Thus, the March 12, 2006, congressional elections and those for president on May 28, 2006, were held within a completely new legal framework. The central aim of this framework was to strengthen democratic governance. It did so in several ways. First, it allowed presidential reelection to ensure both accountability and policy continuity at a crucial moment in Colombian history. Second, it made the party system more rational by reducing the number of parties. Third, it placed limits on the behavior of political parties in Congress as well as in municipal councils and assemblies. Fourth, it guaranteed the opposition both funding and broadcast media airtime to publicize their political programs or criticisms, and it established other mechanisms to ensure electoral fairness. On campaign finance policy, the framework introduced at least two innovations: it mandated a preponderance (80 percent) of state financing and devised a system of advance payments worth more than US$2 million.

The political reform (Legislative Law 1 of 2003) was highly praised by Matthew Shugart, who had been following the issue.[54] In an in-depth study, Shugart made the following assertion:

The new system is thus a radical departure from the old one; in fact, it is one of the most fundamental reforms of an electoral system carried out anywhere in the world in the last decade or so. Whereas the old system undermined the cohesiveness of political parties and provided no guarantee that parties' shares of legislative authority would reflect their collective voting strength, the new one redresses both of these shortcomings.[55]

Later, in his conclusion, Shugart ventured to predict the effect of the reform:

The new electoral system, by mandating a single list for each party and by pooling votes at the party level nationally in the senate, and in each district in the house, greatly enhances the ability of parties to act collectively. It does so by doing two important things that the former system did not: (1) Ensuring that seat allocations will reflect the distribution of votes by party; and (2) Ensuring that a vote for any candidate of a party (in the case of parties presenting open lists) will aid the seat-winning potential of the party as a whole.[56]

The party system began to whither away before the 1991 Constitution entered into effect. In recent decades, particularly since the late 1970s, the nature of Colombia's party system has led presidents to deal with individual members of Congress rather than with party leaders. Hence, the institutional fabric that held the party system together has gradually weakened. It is true that Uribe has attempted neither to found a political party nor to run on the ticket of any party in the two presidential elections that he has won. His government, however, has sought to institutionalize parties and streamline congressional procedures. For example, it reformed the law on party blocs, which now requires that parties elect spokespersons and follow democratic decision-making procedures. The law did not take full force until October 19, 2006, and political parties had until that date to amend their bylaws to adjust to the new rules.

In the period from 1978 to 1998, the average share of the vote received by the different political parties was 54.6 percent for the Liberal Party, 37.0 percent for the Conservative Party, 3.3 percent for left-leaning parties, and 1.3 percent for the others.[57] Thereafter, the parties became highly splintered. For the March 12, 2002, congressional elections, 59 parties were legally registered (Table 9.2), partly due to the incentives of state financing and free access to television and radio airtime. As a result of the reform and in keeping with professor Shugart's expectations, the number decreased to 11 (Table 9.3), and the current number is 5.[58] In fact, seen through the prism of recent Colombian history, there are really only 3: (1) Liberals, those donning the masks of the Partido Social de Unidad Nacional or Partido de la U (National Union Social Party or U Party), Partido Cambio Radical Colombiano (Colombian Radical Change Party), Partido Liberal Oficial (Official Liberal Party), and Partido Colombia Democrática (Democratic Colombia Party), in addition to the Liberals present in some Conservative coalitions; (2) Conservatives, members of the Conservative Party and some predominantly conservative coalitions, such as the Movimiento Alas–Equipo Colombia (Wings–Team Colombia Movement) and the Partido Convergencia Ciudadana (Citizen Convergence Party); and (3) the Partido Polo Democrático Alternativo (Democratic Alternative Pole Party), a coalition of left-leaning groups. In addition, some minority political forces vie for the seats set aside for blacks and indigenous persons and for Colombians residing abroad.

For a political analysis of this type, it is instructive to note that forces that were once expected to be permanent features of the political landscape have disappeared since the last congressional elections (March 2006), including General Gustavo Rojas Pinilla's Alianza Nacional Popular (ANAPO; National Popular Alliance), Andrés Pastrana's Movimiento Nueva Fuerza Democrática (New Democratic Force Movement), Álvaro Gómez Hurtado's Movimiento de Renovación Nacional (National Renovation Movement), Noemí Sanín's Movimiento Sí Colombia (Yes Colombia Movement). All of these movements, except ANAPO, were clearly masking their true natures to obtain votes—principally Conservative votes, though Liberal independent votes as well—by taking advantage of short-term political trends. They were never destined to be permanent. People know who is a Conservative, who is a Liberal, and who is a leftist. It is useful to consider this when evaluating the groups currently masquerading as Liberals or Conservative to support Uribe.

Table 9.2. Colombian Political Parties or Movements Registered for the Elections of March 2002

1	Partido Liberal Colombiano (Colombian Liberal Party)
2	Partido Conservador Colombiano (Colombian Conservative Party)
3	Alianza Nacional Popular (National Popular Alliance)
4	Movimiento Nacional de Reconciliación (National Reconciliation Movement)
5	Movimiento Nacional Progresista (National Progressive Movement)
6	Partido Nacional Cristiano (National Christian Party)
7	Movimiento Unión Cristiana (Christian Union Movement)
8	Partido Opción Centro (Center Option Party)
9	Movimiento de Salvación Nacional (National Salvation Movement)
10	Movimiento Fuerza Progresista (Progressive Force Movement)
11	Movimiento Autoridades Indígenas de Colombia (Indigenous Authorities of Colombia)
12	Movimiento Conservatismo Independiente (Independent Conservative Movement)
13	Movimiento Alianza Social Indígena (Social Indigenous Alliance Movement)
14	Movimiento Compromiso Cívico Cristiano con la Comunidad (Civic Christian Commitment with the Community Movement)
15	Movimiento Cívico Independiente (Civic Independent Movement)
16	Movimiento de Integración Regional (Regional Integration Movement)
17	Partido Socialdemócrata Colombiano (Colombian Social Democratic Party)
18	Partido del Socialismo Democrático (Democratic Socialism Party)
19	Movimiento Independiente Frente de Esperanza (Independent Front of Hope Movement)
20	Movimiento Obrero Independiente Revolucionario (Independent Revolutionary Labor Movement)
21	Movimiento Convergencia Popular Cívica (Popular Civic Convergence Movement)
22	Movimiento Ciudadano (Citizen's Movement)
23	Movimiento Nueva Fuerza Democrática (New Democratic Force Movement)
24	Partido Popular Colombiano (Colombian Popular Party)
25	Movimiento de Participación Popular (Popular Participation Movement)
26	Movimiento Seriedad por Colombia (Seriousness for Colombia Movement)
27	Movimiento Apertura Liberal (Liberal Opening Movement)
28	Partido Convergencia Ciudadana (Citizen Convergence Party)
29	Partido Vanguardia Moral y Social de Colombia (Colombian Moral and Social Vanguard Party)
30	Movimiento Comunal y Comunitario de Colombia (Colombian Communal and Communitarian Movement)
31	Partido Cambio Radical Colombiano (Colombian Radical Change Party)
32	Movimiento Reconstrucción Democrática Nacional (Democratic National Reconstruction Movement)
33	Movimiento Sí Colombia (Yes Colombia Movement)
34	Movimiento Vía Alterna (Alternative Way Movement)
35	Movimiento Somos Colombia (We Are Colombia Movement)
36	Movimiento Unionista (Unionist Movement)
37	Movimiento Huella Ciudadana (Citizen Fingerprint Movement)
38	Movimiento Progresismo Democrático (Democratic Progressivism Movement)
39	Movimiento Voluntad Popular (Popular Will Movement)

Table 9.2. Continued

40	Movimiento Renovador de Acción Social (Renewal of Social Action Movement)
41	Movimiento Nuevo Liberalismo (New Liberalism Movement)
42	Movimiento de Participación Comunitaria (Communitarian Participation Movement)
43	Movimiento "Dejen Jugar al Moreno" ("Let Moreno Play" Movement)
44	Movimiento Únete Colombia (Join Colombia Movement)
45	Movimiento Político Ciudadanos por Boyacá (Citizen Political Movement for Boyacá)
46	Movimiento Integración Popular (Popular Integration Movement)
47	Movimiento Popular Unido (Popular Unity Movement)
48	Movimiento "MIRA" ("MIRA" Movement)
49	Partido Acción Social (Social Action Party)
50	Partido Colombia Siempre (Always Colombia Party)
51	Movimiento Político Grupo Organizo de Liderazgo Popular (Organized Group of Popular Leadership Political Movement)
52	Movimiento Republicano (Republican Movement)
53	Partido Unidad Democrática (Democratic Union Party)
54	Movimiento Frente Social y Político (Social and Political Front Movement)
55	Partido Social de Unidad Nacional or Partido de la U (National Union Social Party or U Party)
56	Partido Polo Democrático Alternativo (Democratic Alternative Pole Party)
57	Partido Colombia Democrática (Democratic Colombia Party)
58	Movimiento Colombia Viva (Colombia Life Movement)
59	Movimiento Alas–Equipo Colombia (Wings–Team Colombia Movement)

Source: Consejo Nacional Electoral, *Boletín de Prensa* 10, July 14, 2006, www.cne.gov.co.
Note: The numbers at left represent the order in which the parties or movements were created or registered.

Table 9.3. Colombian Parties That Survived the Political Reform

1	Partido Social de Unidad Nacional or Partido de la U
2	Partido Conservador Colombiano
3	Partido Liberal Colombiano
4	Partido Cambio Radical
5	Partido Polo Democrático Alternativo
6	Partido Convergencia Ciudadana
7	Movimiento Alas–Equipo Colombia
8	Partido Colombia Democrática
9	Movimiento "MIRA"
10	Movimiento Colombia Viva
11	Movimiento Apertura Liberal

Source: Consejo Nacional Electoral, *Boletín de Prensa* 10, July 14, 2006, 1.
Note: The numbers at left represent the order of the parties and movements according to the results of the congressional elections held on March 12, 2006.

Hence, the assertion that the two-party system is dead has been made for more than 30 years without any real connection to reality. It remains to be seen if this claim, which is being put forth once again, will prove accurate. For example, a private conversation in the halls of power might again give the Partido Liberal Oficial a majority in Congress and the presidency. The Conservative Party would keep its present status, and we would have a leftist party with high expectations. Whether that conversation will take place is another matter, one that could determine whether the masquerade ball will continue or whether Colombia will evolve toward a new party system. The truth is that the new legal framework is encouraging a new party system whose nature is still unclear.

The principal instruments that facilitated the reduction of the number of political parties were four: the single list of candidates, thresholds for elections both of senators (2 percent of the turnout) and representatives (50 percent of the electoral quotient), the introduction of the D'Hondt Method of allocating seats, and preferential voting (which is optional for the parties and voters).[59]

The Role of Constitutional Jurisdiction

Since the late nineteenth century, Colombia has had a system for the judicial protection of the Constitution that has remained one of the most comprehensive and advanced in the world. Under the 1886 Constitution, the Supreme Court had authority to override the president's objections to proposed laws that he or she considered unconstitutional. This power was consolidated in a 1910 constitutional amendment establishing what is known as a public unconstitutionality action.[60] The important role that constitutional justice played in the search for peaceful coexistence and democracy in the country has been explained by Manuel José Cepeda Espinosa, who writes that the 1904 inclusion of a public unconstitutionality action against presidential decrees issued during states of siege was intended to be "a useful instrument for reconciliation" of the government, Congress, and opposition forces.[61]

The 1991 constitutional amendment further strengthened this system by creating effective, easily accessible safeguards to ensure citizens' fundamental rights and by establishing the Constitutional Court as the body specifically designed to oversee matters related to those rights. A writ for constitutional relief (acción de tutela) allows anyone to obtain redress in 10 days for any fundamental rights violated or threatened by a public authority or, in certain cases, by private parties.[62] Through December 31, 2005, judges with jurisdiction over constitutional relief matters (jueces de tutela) had ruled on 1,262,346 writs, of which 23,497 were reviewed by the Constitutional Court.[63] Moreover, class action suits for constitutional relief, objections on grounds of unconstitutionality, and other mechanisms to ensure that the Constitution is followed have earned the judicial branch, particularly the Constitutional Court, special esteem among the population, who finally feel that effective justice is available to them.

In the 15 years since the Constitutional Court was created, it has ruled on a number of highly significant national issues, and its rulings are viewed with respect in international legal forums. Cases related to fiscal and budget policy, home financing, and displaced populations have come under the purview of the Constitutional Court.[64] Moreover, its rulings on presidential reelection and the peace process have been awaited with enormous anticipation.[65]

Nevertheless, the court has come under harsh criticism, especially from the bureaucracy, which accuses it of siphoning off government funds, impeding macroeconomic policy management, and generating legal insecurity, thereby deterring foreign investment. The nature of the court's duties and the scope of its jurisdiction have led some critics of this constitutional protection system to view it as a "government of the judges."[66] Moreover, the admissibility of writs for constitutional relief against court orders, even those handed down by the Supreme Court and the Council of State, has led to a phenomenon known as a "train crash" among the high courts.[67] Consequently, the Uribe government has sent several judicial reform bills to Congress in a bid to reduce conflicts among the top-level courts, clearly delineate jurisdiction on constitutional relief, and improve the constitutional protection system.

It should be stressed that the Constitutional Court has become the true final arbiter in Colombia's power structure. This same phenomenon can be seen elsewhere in the world, particularly in Europe, where the independent Constitutional Court now appears to be the cornerstone of an authentic separation of powers. Consolidating an independent, effective, and widely accessible constitutional protection system is essential for democratic governance, and strengthening that system has made it possible to instill confidence in institutions and the law.

Conclusion

Uribe's first term coincided with a significant strengthening of democratic governance in Colombia, and his second term should build on this progress. There are signs of this fortification in the executive, legislative, and judicial branches; in the decentralization process; and in the relations between the government and the opposition. Macroeconomic and budget management indicators also point to an undeniable improvement. Public perceptions of the direction of the country before the 2006 election are shown in Figure 9.3, and Figure 9.4 shows the change from 2002 to 2006. The president's favorability ratings before the election are shown in Table 9.4.

Figure 9.3. Opinions as to Whether Things in Colombia Were Moving in the Right or the Wrong Direction, September 2005–May 2006

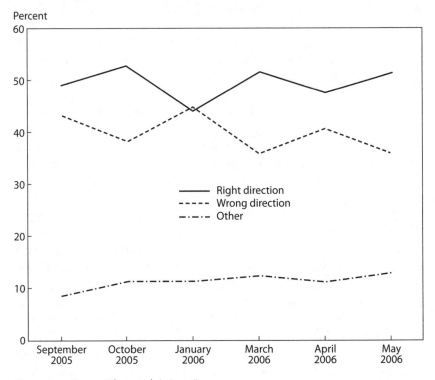

Source: Ipsos-Franco, "El gran cubrimiento."

The threats to democratic governance appear to be losing their virulence and power (Figure 9.5 and Table 9.5). The peace process has succeeded in demobilizing more than 40,000 armed fighters, including all the illegal armed groups that belonged to the AUC and many individuals from illegal organizations such as the FARC and the ELN. Nevertheless, this chapter does not underestimate the impact that dismantling criminal organizations or illegal armed groups has had on governance and the perception of Colombian institutions. From 1994 to 1998, the dismantling of the Cali drug trafficking cartel revealed the group's links with other sectors of society, particularly political leaders. Hence, an action of great significance for ensuring democratic governance temporarily triggered an acute governance crisis. The dismantling of nearly all of the AUC forces, starting in 2006, led to a similar phenomenon. The Supreme Court indicted several senators and representatives, triggering a crisis seen as worse than the one caused by the dismantling of the Cali cartel. The same will be the case when an attempt is made to demo-

Figure 9.4. Colombians' Perceptions of the Future, 2002 versus 2006

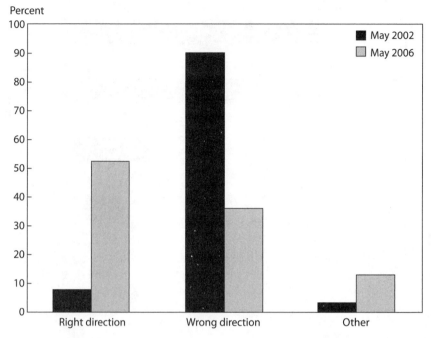

Source: Ipsos-Franco, "El gran cubrimiento."

Table 9.4. The Public Image of President Uribe, September 2005–May 2006 (percentage "yes" responses)

	September 2005	October 2005	January 2006	March 2006	April 2006	May 2006
Favorable opinion of Uribe	78	72	73	72	70	71
Uribe possesses management skills	67	62	68	64	66	67
Support Uribe	67	62	60	63	62	63
Uribe is fulfilling his promises	61	58	57	64	56	59
Intend to vote for Uribe	56	56	57	56	56	57

Source: Ipsos-Franco, "El gran cubrimiento."

Figure 9.5. Democratic Security: Number of Homicides and Demobilizations in Colombia, 2002–2006

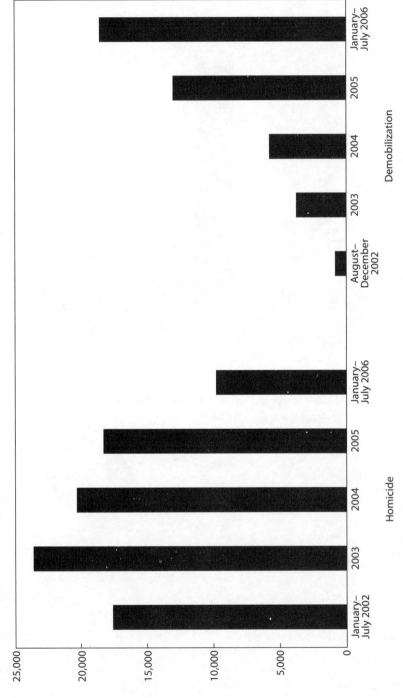

Source: Vice Presidency of the Republic, Office of Communications, "Derechos humanos y DIH en Colombia: Balance," February 1, 2008.

Table 9.5. Democratic Security in Colombia: Kidnappings, Massacres, and Terrorism 2002–2007

Crime	Time Frame	Total
Kidnappings	2002	2,882
	2003	2,121
	2004	1,440
	2005	800
	2006	687
	2007	521
Massacres	2002	680
	2003	504
	2004	263
	2005	252
	2006	193
	2007	128
Acts of Terrorism	2002	1,645
	2003	1,257
	2004	724
	2005	611
	2006	646
	January–July 2007	213

Sources: Presidency of the Republic of Colombia, www.presidencia
.gov.co/resultados/2008/victimas_13.pdf; Vice Presidency of the Republic, Office of Communications, "Derechos humanos y DIH en
Colombia: Balance," February 1, 2008.

bilize and dismantle other causes of ungovernability, such as the FARC and
the ELN. These crises are temporary, however, and if they are handled in an
appropriate manner—that is, rigorously, transparently, and credibly—they
will ensure better and more sustainable governance in the future.

The drug problem is being forcefully combated on several fronts. Under
Uribe, more than 400 Colombians with ties to drug trafficking have been ex-
tradited, while the eradication of drug crops—both manually and through
fumigation—is the most extensive in the history of Colombia's fight against
drugs.

The introduction of oral proceedings for criminal trials and of an accu-
satory system has greatly enhanced the expediency of criminal proceedings.
As this system continues to be introduced throughout the country, the rampant impunity and torpor that characterize the justice system should give
way to efficacy and timeliness. Thus, the threat posed by organized crime,
corruption, and other criminal activities will be substantially weakened. Surveys point to growing confidence in institutions (Figure 9.6 and 9.7), including those susceptible to widespread disdain, such as Congress.

Figure 9.6. The Public Perception of Various Colombian Institutions, May 2006

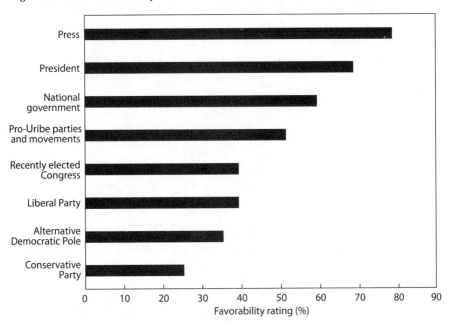

Source: Ipsos-Franco, "El gran cubrimiento."

As a result of all of these efforts to strengthen democratic governance, there is a much clearer political playing field in Colombia, with a government coalition and an opposition coalition. The opposition has increasingly gained legitimacy, and the party representing the democratic left is noticeably growing.

It appears that the weaknesses of the 1991 Constitution, particularly regarding political organizing, are being overcome with the new electoral legal framework, and the benefits of this are obvious. Indigenous and black minorities continue to receive special consideration, but there is still much work to be done.

In the previous edition of this book, in his chapter assessing democratic governance in Latin America in the 1990s, Jorge Domínguez spoke, justifiably, of the "deterioration of the constitutional government in Colombia."[68] He warned that Liberals and Conservatives "risked encountering a fate similar to their neighbors in Venezuela and Peru."[69] He added, "In the early twenty-first century, the democratic deficit of parties continues to be serious, and it is arguably worst in Colombia."[70] Today, Domínguez could say without hesitation that Colombia's constitutional government is significantly stronger. Moreover, the party system he then saw as so risky is now undergoing a realignment that will likely end up closer to what existed before the 1991 Constitution than to the party disarray that has emerged since.

Figure 9.7. The Public Image of the Colombian Armed Forces and Illegal Armed Groups

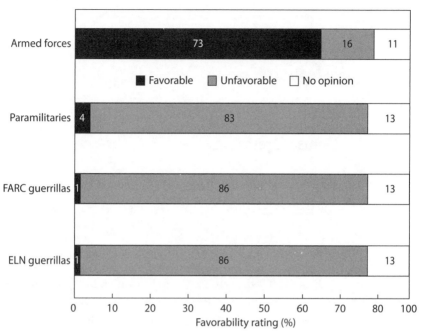

Source: Ipsos-Franco, "El gran cubrimiento."

It is abundantly clear that the consolidation of democratic governance in Colombia—particularly regaining the monopoly on the use of force and full control of the nation's territory—will depend on something more than the traditional power-sharing system that made it possible to achieve peace at other moments in the country's history. The changes to the electoral system will not be sufficient and must be complemented by instruments such as the National Front's power-sharing arrangement, which was designed to end the confrontation between Liberals and Conservatives. It will be up to political leaders to muster the ingenuity and creativity required to devise institutional formulas for ensuring democratic governance.

Once confidence in institutions and optimism about Colombia's future have been restored, we will be able to say that the country is on the right path, returning to democratic governance and securing its place in a competitive and globalized world.

10

Mexico

Dysfunctional Democracy

Denise Dresser

Six years after the historic election of Vicente Fox, a contentious and contested presidential race revealed that all is not well with Mexican democracy. The conflict that ensued after the July 2006 contest evidenced the shortcomings and flaws of Mexico's process of transition and consolidation. While it is certainly true that many of the authoritarian practices of the past have been left behind, many of the institutional vices associated with anti-democratic rule survive, precluding effective representation and governance.[1] Mexico's political system is not experiencing a linear evolution in the direction of democratic consolidation; instead, the political system seems to be caught in a permanent, uneasy tug-of-war between the past and the future, between change and the actors who seek to place obstacles in its path.

Mexican democracy was built with votes. In contrast with other democratic transitions, Mexico's was characterized by neither a rupture with the previous regime nor a foundational pact to inaugurate a new one. Instead the transition has come about largely as a result of reforms to electoral laws and institutions, as well as the competitive politics they produced.[2] But Mexico's "voted transition" has proved to be a double-edged sword. Mexican political elites have focused on electoral processes without paying sufficient attention to broader reforms to the political and institutional framework as a whole. Growing pluralism coexists uncomfortably within the confines of a presidentialist regime, and a competitive party system has yet to deal with heightened demands for better democratic governance.

The country's political system has become a peculiar hybrid combination of authoritarian remnants and newly established mechanisms for transparency. Under Fox, Mexico's electoral democracy made some strides toward greater openness and accountability, but several necessary reforms were sabotaged by the old authoritarian, corporatist structures. Unions, political parties, vested interests, and public and private monopolies have not learned to adapt to more democratic circumstances; they are exploiting them to their advantage by becoming "veto centers" opposed to further political and economic reforms.[3] Some of these authoritarian bastions, such as political parties, have experienced some degree of reform but have also sought to entrench their control over political life instead of contributing to its democratization. Mexico's new democracy is haunted by the old demons of corruption, patrimonialism, rent seeking, and the arbitrary exercise of power.

In contrast with the past, when Mexico's "imperial presidency" constituted one of the obstacles to democratic evolution, excessive concentration of power has been replaced by its dispersion. The problem is no longer too much power in the hands of the president, but too much power seized by those who want to sabotage and constrain him. Political and economic actors intent on preserving the status quo have been successful in their efforts to block further democratic change, and as a result, inertia has prevailed. Political battles among key actors during the Fox term were not about how to build a more effective representative political system but about how to maintain control of what political power they have or distribute it among their allies. The legislative branch, in particular, has become one of the most important mechanisms for the preservation of politics as usual. The Mexican Congress has used its newly acquired power not to push forward modernizing reforms but rather to control and thwart the president at every turn.

In contrast with the old authoritarian system, checks and balances to the power of the president do indeed exist. But few controls have been put into place to control and curb the power of those actors that have gained clout as the old imperial presidency has lost it. So what the presidency has given up or been forced to concede, Congress has gained. What the executive has relinquished, vested interests have been quick to pick up. Drug traffickers and organized crime have taken advantage of what the Mexican state is no longer able to ensure—such as a monopoly on violence.

Mexico's political system presents institutional problems, associated with other presidentialist democracies, that condemn it to low-grade representation and democratic governance. Mexico's democratization has stalled as a result of both dysfunctional institutional design and bad institutional performance. Political parties appear far removed from citizen demands, prone to making questionable decisions, beset by internal divisions, incapable of attending to deep-rooted problems of inequality and lawlessness, and prone to populist or authoritarian leadership—on both sides of the political spectrum —that presents itself as a redemptive force capable of saving the country from itself.[4] These problems are the product of a system of political representation with little accountability accompanied by a legislative process that frequently engenders gridlock due to the lack of incentives for collaboration.

Yet collaboration will be essential if Mexico is to combine democracy and citizen empowerment with market reform and social justice. As Jorge Zepeda Patterson argues in the book *El presidente electo,* "Mexico's problem is social, the solution is economic, and the route is political."[5] Mexico will need to tread further down the road of reform in order to surmount obstacles related to the country's institutional design and the legislative paralysis it has produced. Political elites will have to change an electoral system that was unable to guarantee a fair election or avoid a turbulent election outcome. And they will need to modify a party system that depends on large amounts of public financing and taxpayer money, which are avowedly used to shore up the credibility of Mexico's electoral process while distorting it. Mexico exhibits a low-grade democracy characterized by parties that are well financed but not particularly representative and by rules that allow elite rotation but do not ensure accountability because reelection is not allowed. Democratic governance faces the challenge of an increasingly expensive system for power-sharing—and for distribution of the spoils—that benefits Mexico's political class much more than its citizens.

Dysfunctional Institutions, Low-Grade Democracy

Citizen perceptions of democracy in Mexico reflect pessimism toward a political system borne from a much-applauded transitional election in 2000.[6] In 2003, 51 percent of the population stated that political parties were "not necessary" for the good of the country. Between 2002 and 2005, disapproval of Congress grew and citizens' satisfaction with the health of representative democracy decreased.[7] By the end of 2006, following the turmoil produced by a divisive election, 66 percent stated that the country was regressing instead of evolving. Public opinion seems disenchanted with a democracy incapable of offering tangible solutions to evident problems.

Although Mexican elections have become increasingly competitive, the party system and the political class have become further and further removed from societal interests. Over the past six years, Mexico has experienced numerous competitive elections, but they have not been accompanied by mechanisms for effective citizen representation. As in the past, an insulated political class continues to monopolize decision making while remaining unaccountable for its actions given the absence of legislative or governmental reelection. Mexico's democracy is indeed competitive, but it is also frequently unaccountable, routinely paralyzed, increasingly expensive, and far removed from the concerns of its citizens.

Electoral *alternancia* (alternation of power) has not been a sufficient condition for Mexico's democracy to be fully representative or accountable.[8] By themselves, elections have been too weak to guarantee decent democratic governance. In Mexico, they have been unable to keep predatory practices among those in the political class under control, to make public officials follow established rules, to keep them responsive to citizen preferences, or to deter them from channeling public funds into private hands. Indeed, the absence of institutional restraints on state actors has led to a "low quality democracy."[9]

Signs of low-grade democratic governance were abundant throughout the Fox term; almost weekly, the Mexican press reported stories of excesses, frequently committed with taxpayer money. Abuses continued to be widespread across the political system and encompassed most of the country's political institutions, including Congress, the judiciary, and political parties.[10] Cases in point were those of the governor of the state of Oaxaca who staged an assassination attempt to bolster his party's political fortunes in a local race, a senator from the Green Party who was videotaped negotiating a bribe from a businessman who wanted to build a hotel on an ecological reserve, a city government official also caught on tape as he received a bribe from a powerful contractor, the man in charge of Mexico City's finances gambling with them at a Las Vegas casino, and former governor and presidential candidate Arturo Montiel of the Partido Revolucionario Institucional (PRI; Revolutionary Institutional Party), who has accumulated at least seven expensive houses and apartments in Mexico and abroad by siphoning money from the public budget of his state.

Democratic Mexico has not eliminated corruption; it has just made it more evident. Democracy has inaugurated a political system that is freer but not necessarily cleaner than previous systems. Mexico continues to be a country of crimes without punishment, of people who are identified as guilty on the television screen but cannot be proved so in court, of politicians who enrich themselves because they still can due to the absence of "credible restraints" on the overarching power of the political class. Serious failures to ensure public accountability have contributed to the shallow, vulnerable state of Mexican democratic governance.

Accountability through elections is an essential component of democratic representation. Mexico's democracy, however, has been unable to ensure that the vote can function as a mechanism for rewarding or sanctioning behavior in office. Initiatives to reform the Constitution to allow reelection of legislators and municipal presidents have been consistently blocked by party leaders intent on maintaining control of their legislative factions. This has had the adverse effect of not only precluding accountability but also institutionalizing what many analysts call a *partidocracia* (partyocracy) that benefits from the status quo and the financial rewards it provides.

Mexico's electoral democracy has become extraordinarily expensive as a result of an electoral system based on large, publicly provided cash disbursements. As Alejandro Poiré has argued, this system was essential for a successful transition from electoral authoritarianism a decade ago, when significant reforms were introduced to level the playing field among political parties.[11] Political actors involved in the 1996 electoral reforms that instituted public financing believed that credibility and competitiveness had to be established even at a steep price. The logic at the time was that the provision of large amounts of public funding would lead to fairer competition and also deter the seeping of private, illicit funds into electoral campaigns.

That foundational decision, however, may have turned into an important obstacle to the consolidation of a deeper, more functional democracy.[12] The party finance system that once promoted Mexico's electoral democracy may be undermining its credibility. Evidence over the past decade shows that irregularities did occur and financing scandals were not avoided, even though fines were imposed by the Instituto Federal Electoral (IFE; Federal Electoral Institute). Despite the massive influx of public funds, Vicente Fox's campaign resorted to illegal fundraising though "Amigos de Fox" (Friends of Fox), and his contender in the PRI benefited from money channeled through the oil workers' union in a shady operation that came to be known as Pemexgate.[13]

At the same time that credibility was compromised, the costs of elections spiraled; in 2006 alone, the IFE disbursed US$572 million for political campaigns. In addition, 70 percent of that money was used by political parties to buy ad time in the electronic media, guaranteeing a financial bonanza during electoral periods for the television duopoly of Televisa and TV Azteca.[14] This system has created a vicious cycle that functions in the following way. People join political parties that depend on public financing whose origin is taxpayer money. Those political parties then nominate for Congress and the Senate candidates who subsequently get elected. Congress is then put in charge of designing and implementing the laws that regulate electoral competition, and it also participates in the selection of the members of the IFE as well as approving its budget. The IFE is then assigned the task of making increasingly large disbursements to the parties. The parties compete largely through the media and use two-thirds of their budgets to position themselves there. Powerful media conglomerates then pressure legislators to block any sort of reform to a system that provides them with large financial gains.[15]

Thus, the political class has very few incentives to change the rules of a game characterized by "extraction without representation."[16] Political debates related to the need for institutional transformation tend to focus on how to maximize the advantages and the power that political parties and their congressional representatives have managed to accrue. Few political actors are focused on how to imbue the political system with greater accountability, how to institutionalize checks and balances, and how to consolidate Mexico's democracy.

That task has been made more difficult by the existing political regime and the legislative paralysis on key pending reforms it has produced. According to Juan Linz, in a presidentialist regime in which the executive lacks a majority in Congress, there are very few institutional incentives for executive-legislative collaboration, especially if the president's opponents have the short-term expectation of winning the next presidential election.[17] This lack of collaboration is precisely what happened in Mexico after Vicente Fox's victory in 2000 when, time after time, initiatives submitted by the executive were blocked by the PRI and the Partido de la Revolución Democrática (PRD; Party of the Democratic Revolution).[18] Throughout Fox's six-year term, opposition parties made the rational calculation that the best way to bolster their own political fortunes was to sabotage the president at every turn. As a result, significant legislation either languished or was tossed out. Evidence from the Fox period underscores that Mexico does not have mechanisms to limit congressional paralysis on public policy issues, thus condemning it to minimalist change and perpetual political mediocrity.

In addition, Mexico's presidentialist institutional design accounts for much of the drama that accompanied the 2006 presidential election. The front-runners, Felipe Calderón and Andrés Manuel López Obrador, embodied the hopes and fears of millions of Mexicans. But when the race ended in a tie in which neither was able to garner more than 35 percent of the vote, and then the ultimate winner (Calderón) obtained a razor-thin victory, political warfare ensued. Almost 15 million voters viewed the outcome either as a total victory or as a total loss. In a first-past-the-post, winner-take-all electoral system, the loser leaves the race empty-handed. Even though the Mexican left tripled the vote it had received in the previous election, the loss of the presidency obscured other gains and fueled deep resentments.

Opportunities Squandered, Reforms Postponed

The combination of executive-legislative paralysis and little public accountability led to unfulfilled expectations regarding Vicente Fox's government (2000–2006) and to a widespread perception that little had changed under democratic rule. Toward the end of Fox's administration, many Mexicans began to talk not about what had been accomplished but about what could have been done. The country seemed to be speaking the vocabulary of disenchantment. The words *disappointment, disillusionment,* and *lack of leadership* came to be heard daily as part of the national conversation and as an integral part of the political analysis of the period. Although personally popular, Fox ended his term amid charges that he had been an ineffectual leader who had squandered a historic opportunity. He was seen as a decent but limited man—a president with good intentions but bad political instincts.[19]

Among political analysts, Fox was viewed largely as someone who knew how to be a good cheerleader but not how to make tough decisions, who knew how to sell ideas but not how to put them into practice, who knew how to charm the media but not how to horse-trade with Congress. Behind what was undoubtedly a stellar presidential candidate lay an inexperienced state governor who wanted to become president of Mexico but did not have enough experience for the task. Fox knew how to market his persona as a product during the 2000 presidential race but did not know how to govern. He entered into politics, but halfway through his term he confessed that it "wasn't really his thing." He wanted to reach Los Pinos, the presidential residence, but did not have the temperament or the vocation to be successful there. As he confided to his closest aides, he did not like confrontation or negotiation, the dark side of politics, and what it entailed.

Fox seemed to enjoy the public, ceremonial part of the presidency but not the difficult decisions that accompanied his role. This reticence explains the paradox underscored by Adolfo Sánchez Rebolledo: the conservatism of *el gobierno de cambio* (the government of change).[20] Fox arrived in office promising substantive change and a radical break with the past, but over time he became an energetic defender of the established order, as if his initial reformist efforts had already borne fruit. He proclaimed that he was happy all the time. He argued that the country was marching forward, despite what his critics said. He continually presented numbers and data that confirmed his rosy, optimistic views, however politically irrelevant they had become. He obsessed about his approval in the polls, even though they revealed that he was well liked but viewed as ineffectual. He ended his *sexenio* (six-year term) arguing that Mexico was "a democracy like any other," one in which democratic governance is ensured and a successful economic path has been definitively and consensually mapped out.

In several specific areas, democratic governance did indeed show signs of improvement. The Federal Institute for Access to Information was established, a law to prevent and eliminate discrimination was approved, electoral competition prevailed at the federal and state levels, freedom of the press and the media grew, the Seguro Popular health insurance program was established, macroeconomic stability was maintained, the Oportunidades poverty alleviation program was expanded, and the government made huge strides in public housing and consumer credit. Nonetheless, these undeniable accomplishments were also accompanied by substantive mistakes, errors of judgment, and questionable decisions that marked Fox's presidency.

The reasons behind Fox's failures are complex and varied: the appointment of a cabinet of people he did not know based on the advice of "headhunters," the misuse of his political capital during his first year in office when he placed the achievement of peace in the southern state of Chiapas above all else, the lack of clear policy priorities and concrete strategies to achieve them, the decision to negotiate with the PRI instead of dividing it after the 2000 election, the use of the bully pulpit in a country with no congressional or presidential reelection, the reliance on institutions created for dominant party rule, the uncontrollable activism and presidential ambitions of his wife, and the intermittent sabotage of Fox by members of his own party, among others. Fox painted himself into a corner but also allowed others to help him do so.

Given the constraints posed by a presidentialist system with a divided government in which Fox's party did not have a majority, the president attempted to bypass Congress by "going public" and appealing directly to public opinion.[21] But this strategy did not produce the desired results given that the absence of legislative reelection in Mexico has produced disciplined political parties whose loyalty lies more with the head of their congressional faction than with the president and his popularity. Although parties were able to agree on numerous legislative proposals throughout the Fox term, the perception of confrontation and paralysis prevailed, to a large extent due to congressional opposition to further structural reforms. Specifically, opposition parties rejected Fox's proposals for fiscal, energy, and labor reform, as well as other political initiatives related to the so-called reform of the state and the necessary reform of the judiciary and the police.[22]

On several other key fronts, the Fox strategy of hands-off, reactive governance displayed a "clear predominance of conjectural decisions based on a reaction to social pressures."[23] As Ernesto López Portillo, an expert in public security, argues, Fox left office as he had arrived in it: without a model of interpretation and actions that could deal with mounting problems of crime, drug trafficking, and violence. The president's political inexperience in dealing with the Atenco matter provided legitimacy to the argument that judicial mechanisms are ineffective in confronting abuses of state power and that therefore resorting to violence is a legitimate course of action for popular movements from below.[24] Finally, his efforts to promote the prosecution of political rival Andrés Manuel López Obrador—through a process known as the *desafuero,* in which a government official's immunity from prosecution is removed—proved that under the guise of legality, political interests prevailed in order to guarantee a discretionary application of the "rule of law" during the Fox administration.[25]

The Fox government's attempt to overcome the country's inertia on the one hand, and its blatant attempts to undermine a political rival on the other, had important consequences for the quality and credibility of democratic rule. López Obrador and the anti-institutional, confrontational political movement he led were the result of what Fox's government should have done but was reluctant to undertake. When Fox denied the need for the state to act as an agent of deeper institutional change, he set the stage for the emergence of a proto-populist, plebiscitary leader who called for more than the piecemeal change Mexico had experienced.

Fox spent more time applauding the country's institutional framework than trying to reform it. The president avoided initiatives that would have injected more competition into key sectors of the economy and promoted others that favored monopoly control. Fox refused to confront vested corporatist interests in the labor unions and ended up engaging in the kind of back-room deals that had characterized PRI rule. And when he did decide to use what remained of his presidential authority, he intervened in a crude, counterproductive effort to remove López Obrador from the presidential race, fueling the misgivings of López Obrador and his supporters regarding the fairness of the country's political institutions. Fox later campaigned against him, thus violating the electoral ordinance of presidential neutrality and providing grist for the conflict that ensued.[26] As a consequence, the first *sexenio* that followed Mexico's transition from dominant-party rule ended in crisis.

The 2006 Election: A House Divided?

The 2006 presidential election and its disputed aftermath seemed to turn Mexico into a house divided against itself. It was a polarized place where, months after the race, a political battle continued to be fought between those who supported PRD candidate López Obrador and those who endorsed Felipe Calderón, the candidate of the Partido Acción Nacional (PAN; National Action Party). Even after Calderón was declared the official winner—by less than half a percentage point—confrontation persisted among Mexicans who believed the election had been clean and Mexicans who insisted there had been a monumental fraud, among people who claimed that the country's institutions are perfect and those who argued that they must be completely overhauled. The two main contenders each commanded 35 percent of the vote, which also reflected a social divide between a relatively prosperous north that sided with the PAN and an impoverished south that largely voted for the PRD.[27] The PRI slouched to a distant third place and failed to carry any state.

The election evidenced the divide between left and right on economic policy and the lack of a national consensus about Mexico's political model, because the two main contenders presented radically different options. In the ranks of a split electorate, many continued to endorse market-led reforms instituted since the 1980s, while others called for a return to state intervention. Many supported the economic model of the past 20 years, championed by Calderón, while those who voted for López Obrador rejected it. Many continued to believe in the nationalist and protectionist principles linked to the ideology of the Mexican Revolution, and others sided with the PAN candidate who suggested throughout the campaign that Mexico needed to deal with the imperatives of a globalized world. Thirty-five percent of voters chose the change promised by López Obrador's "Alternative Project for the Nation," while 35 percent chose the continuity embodied by the PRI. The PAN appealed to constituencies that had benefited under the Fox government, and the PRD appealed to those who felt disappointed by its performance.

But neither candidate or his party received overwhelming support. Each camp held onto its piece of the country and its portion of the voters but was unable to expand its base beyond a third of the electorate. During the campaign, both Calderón and López Obrador addressed their hardcore supporters in the hope of getting them out to the polls. Both gambled on polarization and, as a result, were unable to garner the votes of centrist voters. Consequently, there was no overwhelming winner on July 2. Calderón and López Obrador reached Election Day constrained by the limits of the political model with which they had chosen to run.

Calderón was undoubtedly the "dark horse" of the race. In March 2005, after he had won the PAN primary in a startling upset of Fox's protégé and former minister of the interior Santiago Creel, most analysts suggested that Calderón's chances of winning were slim. Both his poll numbers and his name recognition were in the single digits, in contrast to those of López Obrador, the front-runner for over three years. As the popular mayor of Mexico City, López Obrador had managed to build a vast network of support based on clientelistic ties with groups linked to the informal economy, street vendors, small businesses, and transportation unions.[28] He had also appealed to members of the urban middle class through a strategy of public investment in public works and formation of a strategic alliance with businessmen such as magnate Carlos Slim to promote the rescue of Mexico City's historic center. And Fox's efforts to catapult him out of the presidential race in 2005 had undoubtedly contributed to his allure as an anti-establishment figure.[29]

Calderón, however, displayed an extraordinary degree of tenacity. He set up a "war room" staffed by young and savvy professionals, hired foreign campaign consultants, ran focus groups, and devised a highly negative yet effective campaign. Throughout the race, he behaved as the more professional politician: disciplined, prepared, hard-hitting. He was advised to conduct a campaign of contrasts, and he set himself to the task by heightening the "perception of risk" his adversary posed to the country's economic stability.

Calderón focused on how he was different from López Obrador, whom he portrayed as an irresponsible, anti-institutional populist. He promised to brandish a "firm hand" in order to establish the rule of law, and he offered continuity to those who would benefit from it. Calderón positioned himself as the candidate of stability, common sense, and comfortable, gradual change.[30]

Calderón's campaign slogan—"López Obrador: a danger for Mexico"—undoubtedly turned the election in his favor, because the fear he created transcended class divisions. It became a kind of universal corrosive that cut across social groups and economic regions. Many voters, including the poor, remembered the years of instability produced by macroeconomic mismanagement in the 1970s and 1980s and did not want to relive them. Many remembered the times of crisis and did not want to resurrect them. Fair or not, Calderón's message had the resonance and impact he sought; as he stated in an interview during the campaign, "We had no other choice."[31] Calderón won by sowing fear of his adversary; as a result of that fear, he was able to garner the support of a broad spectrum of voters by activating economic reasoning among those who had favorable views of the economy and mobilizing them in favor of the PAN.[32] The Calderón campaign also capitalized on key mistakes made by López Obrador, such as his recurrent confrontation with Fox and his decision not to attend the first presidential debate. However, the Calderón strategy was not enough to clearly overcome his adversary; he won the election by no more than 238,000 votes, according to the official results presented by the Federal Electoral Tribunal after a partial recount.

Paradoxically, something similar happened to López Obrador. The political positions he espoused during his campaign frequently seemed exclusionary and monochromatic. López Obrador presented himself as a polarizing figure intent on governing a country that had room only for the poor. He never stated what he would offer the middle class or how he would foster its growth. He constantly offered to relieve poverty but did not put forth public policy proposals on how to create wealth. He behaved as a charismatic, providential leader but not as a professional politician in a tight race whose outcome would be defined by independent voters. López Obrador never understood the need to move toward the center of the political spectrum and lead a modern, progressive, tolerant left from there. He never grasped that the moderation of recalcitrant leftist stances had brought to power politicians such as Tony Blair in the United Kingdom, Ricardo Lagos in Chile, and Felipe González in Spain.

López Obrador could not or did not want to temper his message or the confrontational "us-against-them" tenor of his campaign. He insisted on making history when he should have been engaging in electoral politics. He insisted on talking about his Alternative Project for the Nation, but did not articulate credible and viable proposals about how to achieve it. He insisted on addressing only those at the bottom, alienating those at the top and ignoring those in the middle of the class spectrum. López Obrador thought it would be enough to win the presidency merely by offering what he did: to fight corruption, penalize the privileged, eliminate influence peddling, and help the dispossessed, who had been left behind by economic liberalization. He believed he could win given the just nature of his cause, and therefore he never focused on the imperatives of electoral competition. He never thought that he needed to convince the electorate; he assumed that it was enough to be in the race.

The Left and Its Labyrinth

The left's electoral front, the "Coalition for the Good of All," undoubtedly faced multiple irregularities in the 2006 election that eroded the credibility of the country's electoral institutions.[33] Among these were an interventionist president and the playing field he distorted through a media campaign against López Obrador, Calderón's promotion of the fear vote and the hardball campaigns to which his team resorted, aggressive business elites and the electoral rules they bent by disseminating campaign ads that warned against a populist takeover of the country, and incompetent electoral institutions and the doubts they planted in the first couple of days after the election.[34] The IFE committed several specific errors that became politically relevant and opened the door for the left's claims of widespread fraud.[35] As Pedro Salazar has argued, "The negligent inexperience of one group and the disloyalty towards democracy of another jeopardized the country's electoral institutions."[36]

But this chronicle of legitimate grievances does not take into account the mistakes that López Obrador made and the opportunities he squandered by, for example, not attending the first presidential debate. López Obrador's own failings contributed to the outcome he then proceeded to shun. His promises resonated among some segments of the disaffected electorate but alienated others, mainly stakeholders in the system, who felt they had something to lose. The *campaña del miedo,* or fear campaign, provoked a national epidemic because López Obrador had not vaccinated himself against it. On the contrary, he fed animosity toward his cause by engaging in the incessant rhetoric of class division: the rich against the poor, the elites against the masses, rapacious businessmen against marginalized Mexicans.[37]

After the July 2 election, López Obrador adopted increasingly radical, anti-institutional stances in en effort to get the election results annulled. He set up encampments along Mexico City's main avenue; delivered fiery speeches in which he yelled, "To hell with your institutions"; and decided to create a "legitimate" parallel government and name himself the president of it. He also drew constant comparisons between the country's postelectoral conflict and the tension that had preceded the Revolution of 1910. When the Federal Electoral Tribunal ruled against the Coalition for the Good of All, López Obrador called for peaceful civil resistance while making veiled threats of ensuing violence and also proclaimed the establishment of a National Democratic Convention that would draw up a new constitution. At the time, these tactics suggested that López Obrador had decided to abandon the electoral route in order to become the combative, critical, radical conscience of the country. Unmoored by the constraints of conventional politics, he could then do what he knew how to do best: fight, denounce, mobilize, and become a permanent thorn in the political system's side. He could go down in history not as just another president, but as a revolutionary icon like Emiliano Zapata, whom he admires.[38]

López Obrador's decision to contest the election and mobilize mass protests were, however, completely rational.[39] He gambled on confrontation and claims of fraud as a way of strengthening his movement's position on Mexico's ideological spectrum and differentiating himself from the PAN. But that long-term goal was based on short-term decisions that backfired on him and the left as a whole.[40] The radicalization of López Obrador and his party and their reluctance to play the role of a constructive, loyal opposition hurt their political and electoral standing. Both López Obrador and PRD leaders assumed positions that were perhaps morally unimpeachable but electorally damaging. They adopted testimonial stances that "the people" applaud but voters reject. They promoted the tactic of seizing the congressional dais—to block Calderón's arrival in office, for example—instead of representing citizens, and they applauded the strategy of blocking streets instead of thinking how to win elections. As a result, the left's support declined dramatically after the election; a party that doubled its vote in 2006 now faces the prospect of its support declining by half in 2009.[41]

López Obrador and the PRD paid the price for presenting themselves as a political force that focused less on how to legislate but more on how to block: a left that seems incapable of surmounting the intransigence that strengthens the right instead of reining it in, a left that acts not as a protagonist of Mexico's politics but as its predictable victim, a left that has not decided whether it wants to be a loyal opposition because it has not decided what to do with López Obrador.

The quandary for the left as an electoral alternative is that López Obrador called for the destruction of a political system in which the PRD had just achieved its largest gains ever. He shunned the very institutions that his party helped build and of which it is an integral part. López Obrador's maximalist, scorched-earth stance ran counter to the kind of modern, tolerant, institutionalized left that Mexican democracy needs and voters want. This is a reality revealed in poll after poll, survey after survey. Electoral support for the PAN has grown as electoral support for the PRD has declined. What López Obrador lost, Calderón has picked up. What a radicalized and belligerent left sowed, an empowered right reaped. The postelectoral behavior of López Obrador did not foreclose spaces for the PAN; quite the contrary.[42]

Every time López Obrador launched a frontal attack on the country's institutions, he fueled more Mexicans willing to defend them—despite their obvious flaws—because most voters prefer that they be reformed rather than destroyed. Every time the PRD's moral leader referred to "the spurious presidency" or called Calderón *el pelele* (the puppet), he led more citizens to defend the presidential chair, even if they had not voted for the PAN's candidate. The left's maximalism produced a diaspora in favor of the PAN and more moderate, centrist options, including the PRI. As Kathleen Bruhn and Kenneth Greene have documented, the ideological polarization among elites that characterized the 2006 election does not extend to voters.[43] Voters—especially a growing number of independents—tend to be more moderate than party leaders or candidates. Even voters who identify with the PRD and the PAN coincide with their candidates on certain issues, but in general they congregate around the average voter, who tends to be centrist.[44] So López Obrador's attempts to act as a "polarizing fiduciary" of a combative, confrontational left pushed him further away from voters instead of mobilizing them.[45]

Paradoxically, despite the Mexican left's self-sabotage, all the reasons for its existence are still there and have yet to be addressed by the political system: poverty, inequality, corruption, discretionary justice, the concentration of wealth, and the postponement of solutions to redistribute it better. But PRD elites (with the exception of Marcelo Ebrard's government in Mexico City) and López Obrador seem too occupied with denouncing the system to focus instead on how to remodel it. If the left continues to act in this fashion, it will end up making Mexico not more equal but more predisposed to vote for the PAN. It will not empower the dispossessed but rather help the party that appeals to a "firm hand" to deal with them. If the left remains incapable of translating social demands into reasonable public policy options, it will further undermine Mexico's dysfunctional democracy instead of helping to fix it. If the PRD is not capable of attending to the concrete demands of its natural constituencies, it will end up sacrificing them.

Mexican democracy requires a functional, institutional left that can act as an effective counterweight to the conservative tendencies of PAN leaders: a left that can temper the PAN instead of providing justifications for Calderón to govern alone or exclusively in tandem with the PRI. It also requires a moderate political force that can act as a catalyst for progressive change and not just provide a pretext for conservative gradualism. In order to move in that direction, both López Obrador and the PRD would have to discard their efforts to block, sabotage, and thwart the government and instead work to make it increasingly accountable.[46] The PRD would have to renounce the easy immediacy of confrontation for the difficult long-term commitment of changing Mexico law by law, institution by institution. And the left—both as a political party and as representative of a social movement—would have to fight for a better cause than Felipe Calderón's political destruction, because the kind of deep transformations that will benefit the poor and strengthen Mexican democracy will not be accomplished by merely fueling legitimate grievances instead of addressing them. Mexico will not end up in a better place if López Obrador's hatred of a flawed political system precludes the possibility of reforming it.

Felipe Calderón: The Mexican Gulliver

"Prudent," "programmatic," "measured," "with political acumen," architect of a "good beginning"—these were the words frequently used to describe Felipe Calderón during his first months in office after the political turmoil he had faced. These assessments were accurate insofar as they accounted for the unequivocal achievement of actually assuming the presidency on December 1, 2006, when—given the country's postelectoral conflict—many had thought he would not be able to do so. In the first six months of his term, Calderón was able to build a modicum of presidential authority, but he faced significant challenges: maintaining political stability in the face of López Obrador's recalcitrance, legitimizing Mexico's institutions in the aftermath of questions regarding their fairness and impartiality, implementing needed institutional and economic reforms that would enable better democratic governance through legislative alliances with opposition parties in Congress, and promoting sustained economic growth in order to address the inequalities and injustices López Obrador's movement had brought to the fore.[47]

Through skillful political decision making—such as resorting to the military to combat public insecurity—Calderón was initially able to project an image of personal force. That image and the approval it garnered, however, obscured the problems of Vicente Fox's legacy: a constrained presidency at the helm of a weakened state, a presidency tied to the ground by a hundred ropes that limit its room to maneuver and govern effectively. Like Gulliver ensnared by the Lilliputians, Calderón was metaphorically tossed on the beach after a shipwreck and awoke to discover that the Mexican presidency had become a prisoner of numerous vested interests in the political and economic system. A survivor of the tempests, cyclones, and mutinies produced by the 2006 election, Calderón assumed the helm of a rudderless ship, because the power that the Mexican presidency had lost, other actors—

including drug traffickers, state governors, opposition parties, union leaders, monopolists, and sundry veto centers—had been quick to accumulate.[48]

Given that the conditions that enabled presidentialism to flourish no longer exist, the Mexican presidency can no longer resort to traditional mechanisms to process, negotiate, co-opt, convince, assimilate, or repress as it did for so long.[49] Just like his predecessor, Calderón faces a divided Congress that has few incentives to collaborate with the president and many reasons to sabotage him. Confronted with a growing north-south economic divide and social demands that continue to grow in scope and intensity, Calderón encountered a fiscally weak state incapable of addressing these issues. But in contrast to Fox, Calderón understood that he did not have the luxury of "muddling through" for six years due to the conflict-ridden way he arrived in office. The election underscored that continuity alone is not enough to ensure political stability, that a more equitable country must be built on Mexico's hard-won gains.

Among the things Calderón first needed to do was to recognize that drug trafficking, organized crime, and public insecurity had eroded the state's monopoly over violence. Restoring order, particularly in northern states plagued by unrest, became the new administration's method for reestablishing the authority of the state in order to promote its transformation. The Calderón government had no choice: a *sexenio* of half-hearted and ineffectual government action had left behind a slew of infiltrated institutions, decapitated policemen, corrupt judges, and widespread lawlessness. In a country where thousands of people a year are killed in drug-related violence, insecurity has become a primordial concern for many Mexicans. During the Fox administration, Mexico turned into a more violent country than Colombia; in just the first three months of 2007, Mexico witnessed over 600 executions, or approximately 6 per day.[50]

The security imperative explained Calderón's metamorphosis from mild-mannered party bureaucrat to commander-in-chief, courting and promoting the Mexican military at every turn while putting it in charge of security operatives in select states. Over the long term, Calderón hoped to overcome the corrupting influence of the drug trade by creating a new national police force, as well as a special anti-drug division similar to the U.S. Drug Enforcement Agency. His administration argued that, endowed with greater resources and more autonomy, those in charge of combating crime would not end up succumbing to it. But creating a new agency and extending its reach may not be enough. In order for the Mexican government to gain the upper hand in a war perhaps without end, political elites will need to deal with Mexico's pervasive culture of illegality and widespread impunity. In addition, the corrupting influence of the drug trade could seep into the military, as it has in the past. So resorting to the army as a roving cleanup force may solve some short-term image problems but create other, intractable, ones.

Nonetheless, the emphasis on security allowed Calderón to act quickly and forcefully, breaking the perception of paralysis that had plagued Vicente Fox. After announcing military operations to combat insecurity, he presented a series of social programs, including day care for preschoolers; he cut government salaries by 10 percent; and he negotiated a reform of the pension system with the PRI, obtaining its approval by Congress. Little by little, he cut several of the ropes that had constrained the Mexican presidency and had limited its room to maneuver. The pending question, however, is whether the Mexican Gulliver will be able to liberate himself sufficiently to address unsolved dilemmas revealed by the 2006 election or if he will even want to do so considering that part of what he has promoted is more rhetoric than reality, more smoke and mirrors than substance, particularly where drug trafficking is concerned. Some measures he proposed seemed designed to generate applause and not necessarily to solve problems. Some decisions, such as that to return highway concessions to private hands, suggested bad responses to old issues. Several of the measures adopted, such as brokering a deal with labor union leader Elba Esther Gordillo, suggested that the Mexican president might prefer to live with some of the ties that bind instead of cutting them. His governing style seemed better suited to pragmatic minimalism than to transformative reform.

Calderón's approach, however, may not be appropriate for the magnitude of what the government must do if it wants Mexico to become, as Finance Minister Agustín Carstens suggested in an interview with the *Financial Times,* a developed country like Ireland or Spain in twenty years.[51] The achievement of this goal would require an opening of the energy sector to private investment, fiscal reform to widen the tax base and enhance the meager state revenues, the introduction of greater flexibility in the labor market, and institutional reforms that could enhance democratic governance and address pending problems with the electoral system. Hard decisions will need to be made by the political class if Mexico is to become a more modern economy, a more representative democracy, a more equal place. But these changes will not occur if Calderón ignores the strongest ropes that encircle his presidency. The election revealed a country that is not changing quickly or deeply enough for a third of its people, a country where democratic institutions frequently do not fulfill their roles. And although Calderón won by inciting fear of his main adversary—López Obrador—the challenge will be to recognize the reasons for the existence of a populist, anti-institutional actor who garnered over 14 million votes.

López Obrador is a product of Mexico's failed efforts over the past 20 years to modernize using half-hearted neoliberal reforms. Mexico followed the path mapped out by the "Washington Consensus" but did it badly, with botched privatizations that transferred public monopolies into private hands, with economic reforms that benefited a handful of businessmen but few consumers, and with poor results: an economy that does not grow enough, a business elite that does not compete enough, and an economic model that concentrates wealth and does not redistribute it well enough.

Along with dysfunctional democratic institutions, Mexico is held back by what economist Joseph Stiglitz and others have called "crony capitalism," an intricate web of privileges, kick-backs, union vetoes, and "dominant positions" in the market that inhibit the creation of a more level playing field for economic transactions. It is a dense network that operates on the basis of favors, concessions, regulatory protection, and collusion that the government offers and the private sector—or union leaders—demand in return for political acquiescence.

Mexico's economy is riddled with rent seekers and entrenched vested interests in key sectors such as telecommunications, financial services, transportation, energy, and education. Those bottlenecks preclude Mexico's development in a globalized, competitive world and are one of the key reasons for the persistence of social inequality. Those veto centers concentrate economic and political power at the tip of the socioeconomic and political pyramid while blocking competition and milking consumers. They perpetuate an economic system that is based not on market reforms but rather on their avoidance.

The privileges that López Obrador alluded to throughout the presidential campaign are real. They exist. They are embodied in every bottleneck that impedes effective democratic representation and capitalism that operates on a level playing field. They are evidenced by the US$572 million in public financing political parties received last year, by the new media law that benefits the dominant duopoly in the sector, by the tax evasion in which Mexico's top companies routinely engage, by the privatizations carried out in the 1980s and 1990s that simply transferred public monopolies into private hands without ensuring effective regulation that would dismantle them. These are irrefutable signs of an oligopolistic economic structure that neoliberal reform did not transform sufficiently to ensure effective competition.

Therefore, it is not surprising that López Obrador received the support of 35 percent of the population in the 2006 presidential race. He is a providential politician created by a dysfunctional economic system. He exists because of everything that Mexico's business and political classes should have done a long time ago: they should have created real opportunities for ordinary people by reforming Mexico's electoral democracy and political economy. They did not do so, and the privileges granted the few at the expense of the many explain why López Obrador's message resonated as it did. It was as if he held up a mirror and forced the country to look at the reflection of the inequalities many refuse to acknowledge. There are too many Mexicans for whom the status quo simply does not work. There are too many people who seek a profound transformation of a country that has historically excluded them or forced them to migrate to the United States in search of the social mobility to which they can not aspire in Mexico. The election was a wake-up call, and those of the political elite who ignore it do so at their own peril.

Unfortunately, many members of the country's political and economic elite do not know exactly how to deal with López Obrador. They think that it is enough to simply despise him. They think that by presenting the election as a "mission accomplished" they have weakened the position of López Obrador sufficiently that he will self-destruct. But what many members of the political class and the business elite fail to comprehend is that López Obrador is a symptom of the deep problems that Mexico needs to address. Inciting hatred for a man who is perceived as being close to the dispossessed will not eliminate their legitimate grievances. And that is the real danger for Mexico in the aftermath of the election: that in their efforts to disavow López Obrador, Mexico's ruling class will disregard the conditions that produced him.

If Calderón wants to govern more effectively than his predecessor did, he will have to acknowledge these conditions and confront them eventually. He will have to recuperate the state's monopoly on violence and inaugurate its capacity to regulate and reform in the public interest. At some point in his administration, he will need to distance himself from the powers that be and domesticate them. He will need to send unequivocal signals of how he will deal with the veto centers that are blocking Mexico's democratic consolidation and economic growth: rapacious monopolists, protected union leaders, inefficient quasi-state entities, privileged corporate executives, blackmailing television networks, and party leaders who resist accountability.

These people and practices—as well as the institutions they have put at their disposal—are at the root of the problems that the 2006 election brought to the surface. They explain why over 14 million people voted for an "alternative" economic strategy, however unviable it might have been. For all of those who have breathed a sigh of relief in face of the self-destruction of López Obrador and the Mexican left, it is important not to shy away from the sound of the wake-up call he and his movement embodied and of which they were symptomatic. And it is crucial that they recall as well that Calderón's offer of economic continuity won by less than 1 percent of the vote. So although the new president has offered and shown a firm hand, in the future he will have to do much more than that if he truly wants to create the "country of winners" he promised. Calderón's tied-down administration will free itself only when the president understands that he will have to strengthen the state and level the market, promote competition with one hand and equity with the other, establish conditions for wealth creation and redistribution, consolidate electoral democracy and enhance its representativeness. In other words, he will have to liberate his government sufficiently to regulate the existence of Lilliputians with more power than the government, more weight than the electorate, more interests than the public interest.

This challenge is not Calderón's alone, and the political opposition has a great responsibility, because it will run against Calderón's interests to take on the powers that helped him get into office. He will do so only if pressured, cajoled, and convinced that he has no other choice. But the PRI is not going to push him to that point. Transformed by the postelectoral dynamics of the "loyal" opposition, the PRI has become an uncomfortable ally that the PAN needs to invite, seduce, and negotiate with in order to push forward a reformist agenda in Congress. Calderón may be able to obtain what he wants by creating a pact with the PRI through its corporatist leaders—as he did with the reform of pensions for the Instituto de Securidad y Servicios Sociales de los Trabajadores del Estado (Institute of Social Security and Services for State Workers)—but this collaboration will come at a cost both for Calderón and for Mexican democracy: the maintenance of political privileges and political immunity for some of Mexico's anti-reformist political groups.

Making Democracy Work

An analysis of the Fox administration and its aftermath—the divisive 2006 election—suggests that flawed institutions were the cause of Mexico's low-grade democratic governance and that institutional transformation will be needed to improve it. This will entail working on multiple fronts, not only in the electoral arena as had been the case with reformist efforts of the past. On one hand, the political class must eliminate the political incentives for executive-legislative gridlock while promoting greater governmental accountability and more effective citizen representation. On the other, state leaders must design and develop public policies that dismantle Mexico's system of crony capitalism while promoting both equality and social mobility. Mexico continues to face many of the same challenges it did when Fox won the presidency, but those related to institutional design and government performance are among the most important.

In order to address the problem of gridlock, political leaders need to consider whether Mexico will require a regime change in order to overcome legislative paralysis. Some have argued that Mexico will achieve effective democratic governance only if it implements a transition from presidentialism to semiparliamentarism, "parliamentarizing" its politics through institutional reforms that strengthen the legislative branch and further weaken the presidency.[52] Others have argued for the reverse: for the expansion of democratic presidentialism through measures that shore up its power, such as instituting a presidential runoff or reducing proportional representation. As Mexico proceeds to a third round of institutional and electoral reforms, one of these models will have to be chosen and acted upon, because currently the institutional framework is caught in the worst of both worlds: a presidentialist system that operates with a parliamentary logic and precludes the formation of stable legislative alliances for reform.

Necessary changes should also include constitutional reform to allow for reelection of legislators, governors, and municipal presidents, because accountability cannot be achieved without it. The current model of extraction without representation has only widened the gap between the political class and the citizens it is supposed to represent. Reelection would allow for the creation of a basic system of accountability capable of producing more responsive, responsible, and committed public authorities. It would also affect the collective behavior of Congress by eliminating the perverse incentives that result in more loyalty to party leaders than to the electorate.[53]

In addition, those considering further electoral reforms should contemplate a fundamental overhaul of the relationship between politics and the media, which explains why the cost of Mexican democracy has soared in recent years.[54] The current legislation has created a perverse cycle in which political parties receive large amounts of public financing that, come election time, they hand over to the country's radio and television oligopolies. Although public financing of parties was conceived of as a way of leveling the playing field among contenders, the amount and destinations of the funds collected must be revised. In the name of competition, key ingredients of democracy such as accountability, representation, and trust are being sacrificed. One way in which this problem has been addressed is through the reduction of publicly provided cash disbursements to political parties. A broad electoral reform passed in November 2007 prohibits parties' purchase of media time in order to run campaign ads. Campaigns were also reduced in length, to six months; thus, Mexican democracy should cost less by delivering more.

The government should recognize that anti-competitive, monopolistic, and rent-seeking interests have become more evident and, as a result, more damaging to democratic legitimacy. In the context of a weakened presidency, private interests have been able to impose their choices, their vetoes, and even their own laws. They have all too frequently been able to capture regulatory agencies and representative institutions such as Congress and the Senate, as was revealed by the approval of the new media law in April 2006.[55] The Mexican government has allowed the perpetuation of privileges instead of working to dismantle them, and it has also provided regulatory protection to rent seekers instead of changing the rules that have allowed them to prosper. If more effective democratic governance is to be promoted rather than postponed, the political class will have to target the monopolies it intends to dismantle and the anti-competitive practices it will sanction in order to promote a market system with a more level playing field. Political leaders will need to convince Mexico's power centers that the longevity of the democratic regime and its rulers is in their best interest.[56] But in the face of an ever-present populist challenge, that desired longevity can be ensured only by reforms that make domination less obvious and more legitimate.

If the political class cannot agree on how to strengthen democratic governance and promote greater economic equality, Mexico will continue to have a crisis-prone political system saddled by political institutions it has been unable to remodel, legislators it has been unable to make more accountable, public and private monopolies it has been unable to dismantle, and corporatist structures it has been unable to democratize. It will be what Calderón calls "a country of winners" where the same privileged groups always win. It will be a country where 23 million Mexicans barely survive on US$2 a day and too many people are forced to dilute their hopes, live with their hands outstretched, march angrily down the streets, yell because they think no one in the government is listening, cross the border in search of opportunities they are unable to find at home, or vote for a populist, anti-institutional figure because Mexico does not change as deeply as it should or as its citizens deserve. And Mexico will remain a dysfunctional democracy governed by presidents who continue to witness its inertia instead of modernizing it.

11

Peru

A Missed Opportunity

Carlos Iván Degregori

Alejandro Toledo's inauguration in 2001 lasted two days. It began in Lima on July 28, Independence Day, with a solemn *Te Deum* blessing at the Lima cathedral, followed by an address to the nation from Congress, with a grand finale of clarions and trumpets thrown in for good measure. The following day, Toledo flew to Machu Picchu. Decked out in the traditional poncho and *chullo* dress of Cusco, the ancient Inca capital, and flanked by his wife and foreign dignitaries, Toledo and Quechua leaders led a ritual offering to the Pachamama while *pututus* blared in the background.[1]

It could hardly have been otherwise, as Toledo was Peru's first indigenous president. He had come to power at the helm of a party whose emblem was the sacred *chakana* and offered the downtrodden masses a new Pachacuti who would lead them back to power after five centuries of oppression.[2] During the first round of voting, in April 2001, Toledo had made a clean sweep among the rural, poor, mostly native population that had borne the brunt of armed conflict.[3] In the 1980s, they had voted for the left, then for Alberto Fujimori.[4] Now they had finally had a chance to vote for one of their own.[5] Two months later, Toledo beat incumbent President Alan García, the most skillful politician in Peru, by a thin margin of 53 percent to 47 percent.[6] The poignant story of the shoeshine boy who had gone to Stanford and taught at Harvard turned into a legend. Combined with Toledo's market-friendliness in a region where the Washington Consensus was starting to unravel, his life story earned him support among the Peruvian elite, international lenders, and even George W. Bush. Toledo was one of Bush's only friends among Latin American presidents.

Toledo was elected amid widespread optimism following the collapse of Alberto Fujimori's authoritarian regime in November 2000 and Valentín Paniagua's successful interim government. In stark contrast to Fujimori's fraudulent vote of the year before, in eight months Paniagua had organized a clean election. He had sacked senior military officers corrupted by Fujimori's disgraced intelligence adviser Vladimiro Montesinos, launched a sweeping investigation into corruption under Fujimori, and set up a Truth and Reconciliation Commission to reconstruct the events that had transpired during the armed conflict of 1980–99.[7] Paniagua's caretaker government had crowned its achievements with an important victory against corruption: the capture of Montesinos in Venezuela and the repatriation of millions of dollars embezzled by prominent members of the previous regime.

Yet, a few weeks into his administration, Toledo rapidly started to lose support (Table 11.1). The unprecedented extent of his slide would stun friend and

Table 11.1. President Toledo's Approval Ratings, February 2002–July 2006 (percent)

Year and Month	Approval	Disapproval
2002 February	27	65
August	16	75
December	24	66
2003 April	17	75
August	12	84
December	11	84
2004 April	8	89
August	10	85
December	9	87
2005 April	8	87
August	13	83
October	11	86
November	10	86
December	11	86
2006 January I	13	82
January II	15	78
February	17	75
March	18	75
April	28	63
May	31	60
July	33	59

Source: Apoyo Opinión y Mercado S.A.
Note: The first Apoyo survey dates back to August 2001 and measured national support. In August 2001, Toledo had 59 percent support and 16 percent disapproval ratings. By November his approval rating had dropped to 32 percent, and by February 2002 it had fallen to 28 percent.

foe alike. In subsequent years, impeaching the president became a recurring theme for politicians and the press.[8] Just how did Toledo squander his initial approval, the success of Paniagua's caretaker government, and the good will shown by all quarters? How did he manage to regain some of his lost popularity in his final, lame duck days, when Peru had a new president-elect? And what is the legacy of his five-year term? A few possibilities are outlined in this chapter.

An Inheritance of Violence and "Anti-Politics"

Toledo's rise in 2000 and his victory in 2001 took place as Peru's political system was emerging from over a decade of degradation. The new president found himself leading a country with institutions in shambles after the economic crisis of the 1980s, the collapse of the political party system, a devastating armed conflict, and, above all, the "anti-politics" of the Fujimori regime. After his coup in 1992, Fujimori had dissolved what was left of democratic institutions, gutting them and turning them into mere formalities at the service of his rule. The results were politically feeble institutions beset by cronyism and clientelism with pockets of technocratic excellence.[9]

A Question of Character

When institutions are weak, a leader's personality tends to play a central role. Of little consequence in other circumstances, in Toledo's case the issue of character was very relevant. In order to understand his impact on Peruvian politics, it is first essential to examine the nuances of Toledo's character.

Toledo's tide began to turn barely a month into his administration, when the new president boasted to foreign correspondents, "Governing is easier than I thought."[10] This statement exposed him as a political outsider and novice while also casting light on aspects of his character that his opponents had noted on the campaign trail: his frivolity and his irresponsibility in his private life.[11] The comment was not an isolated blunder. During his first days in office, Toledo doubled his salary to $18,000 a month (the highest in the region), ordered costly renovations to the Presidential Palace, and began making frequent retreats at Punta Sal, an exclusive resort more than 1,000 km north of Lima.[12] These were not minor details to a populace that expected him to be frugal and hardworking.[13] Rumors about a president who was never on time, had developed a taste for Blue Label scotch, and took ostentatious holidays were devastating in a profoundly racist country that might have forgiven the same transgressions in an aristocrat but could not ignore them in a leader of indigenous descent.

More Label than Party

As a political outsider, Alejandro Toledo did not emerge from a consolidated or well-known party. He was the natural leader of País Posible (Possible Country), a group he had founded in 1994. The following year, without benefit of a solid organization, he had hastily run for the presidency as a technocrat with a touch of Bolivian-style *indigenismo*.[14] His central campaign promise was *"Fujimorismo* without Fujimori"—a more democratic way of carrying out the reforms Fujimori had left unfinished. País Posible, in conjunction with the small Convergencia Democrática (CODE; Democratic Convergence) alliance, garnered just 3.2 percent of the vote and five of the 120 seats in Congress.[15] After this failure, Toledo promptly returned to academia and vanished from the political scene. His parliamentary quintet disintegrated: the two from CODE went over to Acción Popular (Popular Action), a traditional party that had faded; two entered the Fujimori camp; and one sat as an independent. País Posible went into hibernation until, a year ahead of the 2000 presidential campaign, Toledo dusted it off and remade it into Perú Posible (PP; Possible Peru), the platform from which he would again try his luck as a presidential candidate. A few months before the elections, PP barely registered in the polls (Table 11.2).

In the first months of 2000, however, the Fujimori-Montesinos media machine methodically shredded every other presidential hopeful with a chance of winning.[16] Toledo rose to second in the polls as the last hope of the 50 percent of voters who wanted Fujimori out, and on April 9, Toledo successfully prevented him from winning a first-round victory.[17] Table 11.2 illustrates how the Fujimori demolition machine created a window of opportunity for the anti-Fujimori groups to declare Toledo their leader, a new alternative that Montesinos did not have time to attack. In some sense, the rise of Toledo came about as an unintended side effect of Montesinos's smear campaign against more prominent adversaries.

Toledo took advantage of his opportunity, situating himself at the head of the fight against authoritarianism, charging Fujimori with electoral fraud, and refusing to participate in the runoff election. He found support for his decision in Eduardo Stein, the Guatemalan head of the Organization of American States (OAS) observer mission, who had the courage to call a spade a spade and warn that Fujimori indeed intended to commit fraud.[18] Though latecomers to the struggle against Fujimori, Toledo and PP were suddenly swept to the head of a democratic resistance movement that culminated in the "March of the Four Corners of the Incan Empire."[19] The massive protest march, on July 28, 2000, convulsed Lima and forced Fujimori to take his third oath of office in the safety of Armed Forces Headquarters rather than in Congress.

Table 11.2. Voter Preference Ratings for the Four
Leading Candidates in the 2000 Election, January
1998–April 2000 (percent)

Year and Month	Fujimori	Andrade	Castañeda	Toledo
1998 January	35	23	8	2
February	34	28	8	3
March	30	27	8	3
April	26	28	10	
May	31	23	5	2
June	27	29	10	
July	24	31	13	
August	30	24	12	
September	23	25	14	
October	23	35	14	
November	21	35	17	
December	21	36	18	
1999 January	21	33	18	
February	24	30	19	3
March	28	31	17	3
April	25	32	15	4
May	25	25	19	3
June	29	25	24	4
July	31	22	25	4
August	35	21	22	3
September	34	18	26	5
October	33	16	24	7
2000 January	41	16	14	7
February	39	14	12	10
March	37	6	6	27
April	46	5	3	39

Sources: January 1998–October 1999: *Apoyo S.A.*; January–April
2000: Martín Tanaka, *Democracia sin partidos: Perú, 2000–2005;
Los problemas de representación y las propuestas de reforma
política* (Lima: Instituto de Estudios Peruanos, 2005).

During this period, Toledo wisely built bridges—indeed, he *was* the bridge
—between those who had had enough of Fujimori and the mostly rural and
indigenous underclass, which had not benefited from a centralist economic
model that neither redistributed income nor created enough jobs.[20] While
Toledo played a prominent role in the democratic resistance, Vladimiro
Montesinos drew into his web of corruption a number of opposition legislators who came to be known as "the turncoats," including some elected on
the slates of political parties that existed only in name.[21] Within just three

months, he had bought off 8 out of the 29 PP legislators—fully 27.5 percent of the caucus.[22]

While Toledo wanted reforms within PP, he had not had the time to realize them, so when he took office, his party had not changed substantially. As a result, rather than serving as a pillar of governance, PP became a headache for the president and for the country at large.[23] By the end of Toledo's tenure, the number of PP legislators had dwindled from 45 to 32. The defections were almost never based on political or ideological motivations. Instead, they were primarily driven by personal ambition, squabbles over sinecures, and small-time corruption.

Toledo loyalists demanded a presence in the cabinet and the bureaucracy. Time and again, honest and capable cabinet ministers were shunted aside in favor of PP party loyalists who often lacked the basic requirements for the job.[24] An emblematic case is that of fishing magnate Javier Reátegui, who, based on his experience in the fishing industry, was minister of fisheries in the first year of Toledo's term and then, based on his friendship with Toledo, became minister of transport and communications in the second, minister of production for the following seven months, and minister of the interior for two months in 2004 and 2005. After practically running out of cabinet posts, in September of 2005 Reátegui was elected secretary general of PP. According to a former minister under Toledo, the reason for the back-and-forth—in addition to party pressure—was that Toledo was most comfortable in the company of close friends and party associates.[25]

The contours of the party were blurry and porous, often including nonpolitical actors such as members of the president's extended family, hometown friends, and members of his graduating class at the Escuela de Administración de Negocios (School of Business Administration). These people enjoyed preferential access to the president, which gave rise to a string of complaints about nepotism and corruption. Relative to the systematic large-scale corruption of the Fujimori years, the small-time corruption of the Toledo administration was minor. Precisely because it was not as centralized and veiled as before, however, it seemed more overt. The media covered with relish Toledo's "Court of Miracles" comprised of inept, corrupt advisers and relatives, who provided perfect fodder for editorial cartoons and comedy shows.

As befits a court, the Toledo administration had its courtiers. As never before in the history of contemporary Peru, the president surrounded himself with legions of advisers who were often in competition rather than cooperation, did jobs that would have more properly been done by ministries, and spent work time socializing with friends and relatives. Rather than providing expert advice, his courtiers trapped Toledo in a bubble that prevented him from dispassionately evaluating his achievements and mistakes—had he ever cared to.[26] Under Toledo, Peru transitioned from Fujimori's anti-politics to a "partyless democracy," with the political parties replaced by a confusing fluctuation of professionals and cronies.

A Restrictive Policy on Alliances

Toledo's aversion to being a "big-league" politician was evident in his alliance policy, which he designed at the beginning of his term. In July 2001, he was flush with the political capital amassed over the previous year and a half and had a range of options for securing a majority in Congress. As Fujimori's power grab had become evident in the last days of his second term, the battered opposition parties had begun to cooperate. With OAS support, they had joined with a broad range of civil society groups in setting up a forum that played a key role in bringing about the collapse of the Fujimori regime.

Thus, to set up a broad-based government the new president had only to draw on the legitimacy and consensus he had built in previous months. In August 2001, he seemed to be doing just that when his prime minister called on civil society and congressional parties to convene a national policy forum that would transcend individual administrations. Talks were held in late 2001 and early 2002, and on March 5, 2002, participants signed a "National Accord" that was intended to "provide a basis for a transition to and consolidation of democracy, an affirmation of national identity, and the formulation of national policies enshrining a shared vision for the country."[27] But although the accord was endorsed by leading civic organizations and political parties, it failed to translate into concrete action and soon faded into irrelevance.

One of the reasons for this disappointing outcome was that Toledo had actually hedged his bets by forming an alliance with the Frente Independiente Moralizador (FIM; Independent Moralizing Front), a single-issue group founded in the 1990s as traditional parties collapsed and led by Congressman Fernando Olivera. Why did Toledo accept Oliviera's entreaties to join with the FIM? This question still puzzles observers. If Toledo wanted stability, he could have called on any one of the National Accord signatories. True, times had changed and the allies of 2000 had been the electoral adversaries of 2001, but the Alianza Popular Revolucionaria Americana (APRA; American Popular Revolutionary Alliance), first runner-up in 2001, had made friendly overtures, and he had ignored them. Although the National Accord was a far cry from Chile's Concertación, if the government and main parties had kept it active, it could well have helped reverse a decade of anti-politics in which political parties had been undermined and demonized.[28] Another option was an alliance with Unidad Nacional (UN; National Unity) and Lourdes Flores—the most market-friendly candidate—but UN distanced itself from

Toledo, possibly due to concern with the swiftness of his drop in popularity and effectiveness.

Why did Toledo side with the FIM? Was it because of his political inexperience, fear of the APRA, or strong neoliberal convictions? If so, why did he not build stronger links to UN? There were several reasons and two prevailing factors. One was a lack of political experience on the part of the president and his associates and their attendant fear of traditional parties, especially the APRA. These fears, systematically encouraged by the FIM, were shared by Toledo's economic team and the business elite, in whose minds the rampant populism and disastrous end of the first García administration were still fresh.[29] Any hopes of closer ties to the APRA were dashed after the regional elections of October 2002, when the APRA won in 12 of the 25 regions, the ruling PP in just 1.[30] Yet, Toledo's key reason for choosing the FIM seems to have been the limited range of his goals.

Comprehensive reform of state institutions, so fundamental in a society emerging from eight years of authoritarian rule and almost two decades of armed conflict, required wisdom and political will. In addition to economic growth, the country needed to reach out to the vast masses of poor, dispossessed Peruvians. But the will to undertake major political reform, which had appeared in Toledo and PP during the protests against Fujimori and Montesinos, was weak and eventually faded as the administration ran its course.

Toledo's alliance with the FIM proved fatal to his popularity. The FIM, whose only political capital was proximity to the president, did all it could to block other parties and popular independent figures such as Beatriz Merino, who was president of the Council of Ministers for five months in 2003. As Toledo's administration drew to an end, Olivera had become the politician everyone loved to hate. His discredit exacerbated Toledo's unpopularity and undermined his ability to govern.

Could anyone have governed differently in a partyless democracy? Saying that the situation was "difficult but not impossible" is almost a cliché, but the key was to have pushed through the aforementioned political reforms, which would have consolidated the transition. Thus, the fate of the Toledo presidency would be decided on three fronts: institutional reform, macroeconomic stability, and the international economic and political context.

An End to the Will to Reform

Two decades of institutional decay and violence, as well as profound changes in the economy and the international situation, had made wide-ranging state reform an immediate priority. The proper conditions existed: after Fujimori had fled to Japan and his regime had collapsed, there was no need for a negotiated transition. Local power groups had been seriously weakened, particularly the armed forces, which were in disarray, with most senior officers implicated in Vladimiro Montesinos's web of corruption. Interim president Valentín Paniagua had fired two consecutive sets of joint chiefs of staff on corruption charges, the first such development in the history of the republic. Dozens of generals and other high-ranking officers were in prison, on trial, or on the run. The armed forces had publicly apologized to the country, expressed regret for their involvement in organized corruption, and accepted the Truth and Reconciliation Commission, which had been established to investigate human rights violations over the previous two decades.

In this context, Toledo included in his first cabinet prominent PP members as well as prestigious and capable independents from the right and the left. A few months later, some PP ministers were replaced by more independents due to ineptitude and poor performance. After that, it was clear sailing. The anticorruption drive was going well, and the Truth and Reconciliation Commission was working without interference. But the second year of Toledo's administration was a different story altogether. Besieged by party pressures and palace intrigues, stunned by the growth of social discontent, and demoralized by his party's meager performance in the October 2002 elections, Toledo began to ignore everything other than the economy and the preservation of democracy. Toledo neglected to undertake a number of reforms that the Truth Commission described in its Final Report a year later as crucial to preventing a recurrence of political violence: reforms of the armed forces and the police, the judiciary, the education system, and the political party system.[31] These reforms were necessary as part of a wider process of state reforms, including the development of an urgently needed decentralization plan.

When the new president had first announced the appointment of a civilian as minister of defense, it seemed that the time had come to put the armed forces under civilian control, align them with the democratic system, and retool them for the twenty-first century. Toledo also appointed an independent as minister of the interior, with powers of oversight over the National Police, an institution so corrupt that it had plundered its own pension fund. From the moment of his swearing-in ceremony, the new interior minister launched a process of aggressive reforms. He was joined in January 2002 by a new defense minister with more expertise and a stronger reformist bent.[32] However, both soon found themselves up against powerful vested interests, long-neglected grievances, and large pockets of corruption, especially in the Interior Ministry, which had not been effectively cleaned up by the interim government. Their attempts at reform could not prevail over the reverential fear the president and the political establishment held for the armed forces as protectors of the state and guarantors of internal security.

The first of Toledo's appointees to go was Interior Minister Fernando Rospigliosi, fired in June 2002 in the wake of a general strike in Arequipa, Peru's second-largest city, and a wave of unrest in the city of Puno. A bewildered, alarmed government had ordered the armed forces to restore order in the latter, an order that had resulted in the killing of a student. In an attempt to signal that police reform would continue, Toledo replaced Rospigliosi with his deputy, Gino Costa. This was a way to snatch an easy victory from the APRA, which had campaigned for Rospigliosi's removal. But police reform was doomed. Powerful groups within the National Police had regrouped just as the government was growing concerned about mounting social unrest. In this context, Toledo's approval ratings plummeted and the ruling PP lost the regional elections of October 2002. In January 2003, Costa resigned.[33] In late 2003, Defense Minister Aurelio Loret de Mola also resigned after watching his reforms languish. He was replaced with retired General Roberto Chiabra, a former chairman of the joint chiefs of staff, who was in turn replaced with PP member Marciano Rengifo in September 2005. By this time, the will to reform was as good as dead.

The outlook in other strategic areas requiring reform was no better. The justice system was in the hands of the FIM throughout the Toledo administration, and the FIM was more interested in advancing its agenda than in reforming the judiciary. In addition, the justice system once again proved unable to reform itself. In the previous decade, a corrupt government had controlled a corrupt judiciary. Now the judiciary was still corrupt, but the government could not bring it under democratic control.

The education system was a singular case. Decades before, educational institutions had played a central role in sparking armed conflict, and Toledo himself had proclaimed that his government would be that of education. He liked to emphasize that the world had entered the age of knowledge, and he cited himself as an example of how education could lift Peruvians from poverty. Yet, his "education reform" consisted of no more than providing wage increases for teachers and developing disjointed programs that lacked a global approach, such as distributing computers to rural schools that often had no way of using them.[34] Although reputable civil society groups such as the Foro Educativo (Educative Forum) had advanced sophisticated education proposals, Toledo failed to make any significant progress in reforming the sector. By the time the Education Ministry's National Education Council had completed a long-term reform plan, it was too late in Toledo's term to put it into practice. Meanwhile, reliable foreign and domestic evaluations of the quality of education showed that Peruvian students were behind practically everyone else in Latin America in reading comprehension and in mathematics.[35]

Little wonder, then, that the teachers' union—the Sindicato Unitario de Trabajadores de la Educación Peruana (SUTEP; Unified Workers' Union of Peruvian Education)—was controlled by a radical Marxist-Leninist party or that a 2004 teachers' strike was hijacked by groups with even more radical leanings. These groups led strikers to torch buildings and destroy public property in Ayacucho, where Peru's bloody armed conflict had started in 1980.[36] Some 24 years later, little had changed in Ayacucho's education system.

Social Movements

The SUTEP was not the only union to rally against the government. In 2005, the Confederación General de Trabajadores del Perú (General Confederation of Workers of Peru), a survivor from the golden era of the union movement (1956–90), called a nationwide strike. The institutional collapse did not affect just the political parties; it also involved all the traditional national organizations. Toledo was soon facing a growing barrage of isolated but intense conflicts. Table 11.3 shows the number of conflicts identified by the Interior Ministry's Intelligence Directorate.

The fragmentary nature of these conflicts is evident in reports prepared by the Ombudsman's Office starting in 2004. But because the Interior Ministry counted every protest and the Ombudsman's Office tallied only conflicts that grew into major mass movements, the latter tally provides a better picture of the conflicts that plagued the Toledo administration. From 2004 to 2006, the Ombudsman identified a total of 251 protests (Table 11.4). Of these, 137 (54.6%) targeted local, district, or provincial authorities. Prominent among the rest were 34 conflicts confronting rural communities and

Table 11.3. Social Protest in Peru, 2001–2005

Year	Number of Conflicts
2001	1,826
2002	6,240
2003	8,532
2004	8,494
2005	5,240

Source: Carlos Basombrío and Fernando Rospigliosi, *La seguridad y sus instituciones en el Perú a inicios del siglo XXI: Reformas democráticas o neomilitarismo* (Lima: Instituto de Estudios Peruanos, 2006).

Table 11.4. Conflicts and Scenarios, 2004–July 2006

					Total	
Scenario	Description	2004	2005	2006[a]	No.	Percentage
Municipal	Disputes with local authorities	64	35	38	137	54.6
Environmental	Clashes between communities and natural resource companies	6	14	14	34	13.5
Communities	Disputes among communities over demarcation, ownership, or access to resources		12	16	28	11.2
Unions	Labor grievances	18	7	7	32	12.7
Regional	Disputes among regions over territorial boundaries or access to resources	5	2	5	12	4.8
Coca farming	Opposition to crop eradication policies		2	2	4	1.6
Universities	Disputes with university employees or authorities	3	1	—	4	1.6
Total		96	73	82	251	100.0

Source: Defensoría del Pueblo.
[a]As of July 2006.

mining or logging companies, 28 disputes within communities over boundaries or resources, and 32 conflicts over labor grievances. Other types of events, though less numerous, had a much greater impact. Although regional conflicts accounted for only 12 protests, they included the serious Arequipa clashes noted earlier. There were only 4 protests staged by coca farmers, but they can also be considered serious because they included clashes with regional governments over the legalization of coca crops, growing violence by organized gangs and members of the Sendero Luminoso (Shining Path) insurgency, an increase in the amount of land used to grow coca, and a shift away from production and shipment of coca base in favor of pure cocaine.

The number of municipal conflicts dropped from 64 in 2004 to 35 and 38 the following two years, while those confronting communities and mining companies jumped from 6 in 2004 to 14 in the same time frame. These trends illustrate the types of conflicts Alan García would inherit when he was re-elected to the presidency in 2006.[37]

The kind of strife Toledo faced was local and would frequently target corrupt or unrepresentative officials, often elected with less than 20 percent of the vote. The fragmentation and parochial character of the movements made it difficult for the government and agencies such as the Decentralization Council to find valid partners with which to negotiate.

Poor handling of conflicts brought on three emblematic events: the April 2004 killing of the mayor of Ilave, an Aymara provincial capital in Puno, on the border with Bolivia; the January 2005 revolt in the mostly Quechua province of Andahuaylas led by Ollanta Humala's more radical brother Antauro, an *etnocacerista* chieftain; and the failure of the October 2005 referendum to create "macroregions."[38]

The Ilave Case

While extreme, the appalling lynching of the mayor of Ilave—broadcast live to most of the country—was by no means an isolated case.[39] Rather, it symbolized the widespread crisis facing local governments, the decentralization process, and the democratic transition in general. Ilave was simply the place where trends that had been brewing since the 1990s collided head-on. Most of these trends had arisen in the rural areas that bore the brunt of armed strife. These included:

1. The breakdown of the political party system, the rise of short-lived movements, a proliferation of party slates, a fragmented electorate, and the election of local officials by very low pluralities.

2. The vacuum left by political parties, which was filled by local power brokers whose extreme pragmatism harked back to the authoritarian, pork-barrel legacy of the Fujimori era and the radical left of old.

3. A radical stance, the manipulation of collective decision making, confrontational politics, and an uncompromising agenda embodied in slogans such as "Radicalize the struggle" and "Fight to the bitter end."

4. A mix of pragmatism and radicalism placed at the service of personal or local interests.

5. The replacement of respect for procedural norms by the pursuit of quick results and complete victories imposed by force. This often happens when institutions are fragile, party politics is discredited, and an informal economy and rural poverty prevail.[40]

If democracy is a mechanism for institutionalizing conflicts, the murder of Ilave's mayor and other cases show that it was far from working well. This failure, along with weak institutions, made for a dangerous scenario because there was no outlet for grievances, which reinforced the demands and promoted radicalization. Conflicts were fought out without benefit of the limits imposed by institutions and were pursued to the bitter end, as in Ilave.

In the absence of broader institutional and political frameworks, these struggles became fierce, focusing on narrow local or special interests, also as in Ilave. Over time, this state of affairs paved the way for violent anti-system stances. A notorious example was Antauro Humala's Andahuaylas revolt on New Year's Day 2005, in which several peasants and police officers were killed.

A Difficult Decentralization

Regionalization ran into trouble from the outset. The regional elections of October 2002 took place *before* the decentralization act was passed. The Decentralization Council was a highly bureaucratic entity with an unclear mission and trouble communicating with its constituency. The difficulties had as much to do with the institution itself as with the inherent intricacies of negotiating with widely scattered interests that most regional, provincial, and district governments often would not or could not channel. Special-interest movements proliferated in spite of participatory mechanisms first imposed on Fujimori by international lenders such as the World Bank and later enhanced by Paniagua and Toledo. Under Toledo's administration, however, participation in itself proved to be no silver bullet.[41]

A glaring weakness of the 2002 Decentralization Act was that it merely re-designated the 24 existing departments and one "constitutional province" as regions. Most observers agreed that 25 regions were not viable and that existing departments should be merged into no more than 5 to 10 socially and economically viable regions. The government tried to start the process from the bottom, asking departments or regions willing to merge to submit a request and call a referendum.

In October 2005, 16 departments and regions held merger referendums. As sensible as it was that the many regions should merge into fewer but more viable entities, and in spite of technical arguments supporting the merger, discontent with the government and with the conduct of the process was so great that the proposal met with a resounding refusal. Spearheaded by the APRA, those voting "no" garnered 69.1 percent of the vote, while "yes" proponents obtained a mere 22.9 percent.[42]

An Indigenous President, an Anthropologist First Lady, a Failed Diversity Policy

Given Toledo's indigenous heritage and his anthropologist wife (who used to heap scorn on the racist views of the Lima elite), special mention should be made of his cultural diversity and indigenous policy, especially in light of related events unfolding in Bolivia and Ecuador at the time.

Toledo set up a Comisión Nacional de Pueblos Andinos, Amazónicos, y Afroperuanos (CONAPA; National Commission on Andean, Amazonian, and Afro-Peruvian Peoples) and put his wife at the helm. But the commission failed to produce any substantial initiatives benefiting the indigenous and Afro-Peruvian population, focusing instead on Peru's indigenous past and present as a travel promotion tool. This peculiar approach reached its apex in 2005 when Alejandro Toledo hosted *Royal Tour* on the Discovery Channel.[43] *Royal Tour* is a travel-oriented show on which presidents, prime ministers, and kings host a grand tour of their countries.[44] The production was an initiative of the Peruvian government through the PromPerú promotion agency.[45]

Toledo did well in parading Peru's natural, historical, and cultural heritage for the world to see. Unfortunately, CONAPA failed to address a range of pressing issues, including the following three (in addition to poverty):

1. Amazonian peoples are under relentless, often illegal, pressures from Andean settlers, coca farmers, and logging companies with ties to unscrupulous native leaders. But little headway was made on Amazonia land titling and management issues under Toledo.

2. Although the 1993 Constitution states that Peru has many cultures and languages, over five million Peruvians have no access to justice in their native tongues. This basic individual right remained utterly neglected under Toledo.

3. There has also been a failure to adopt intercultural bilingual education as government policy. Native speakers who use Spanish often do so because they are fully cognizant that their mother tongues are not used in the public sphere.[46]

These unaddressed issues reflect a much deeper problem: ingrained racism. Long thought to be on the wane in Peru, racism resurfaced with a vengeance during the armed conflict. It became more subtle and elusive afterward, only to permeate public discourse once again after Ollanta Humala came onto the scene during the 2006 presidential campaign. In early, 2006 Peru was discussing ratification of a free trade agreement (FTA) with the United States, and Humala had come out against it. Speaking at an international conference in Lima, Prime Minister Pedro Pablo Kuczynski said: "Changing the rules, revising contracts, and nationalizing assets is ruinous, disastrous. Those are ideas that prevail only up there in the Andes, where the air is thin and not enough oxygen reaches your brain." House Speaker Ántero Flores Araoz was asked by the press if he thought an FTA ratification referendum should be held. He replied: "Of course not. Who are you going to ask, the llamas and the vicuñas?"[47]

The reference to the "oxygen-deprived" Andean population and the likening of indigenous peoples to llamas and vicuñas became a recurring theme throughout a campaign also marked by Ollanta Humala's more understated but no less evident "reverse racism."

The Threat of Impeachment

Even before his first year in office was out, both in Congress and on the Peruvian streets people were busy talking about impeaching Toledo on moral grounds over his refusal to acknowledge having fathered a daughter born out of wedlock. The campaign was whipped up by a still strong pro-Fujimori press, which used the issue to discredit the democratic regime with a view to paving the way for a coup. Toledo, who eventually decided to acknowledge his daughter, was severely weakened.

Impeachment returned to the agenda in April 2004, when Toledo's approval ratings hit rock bottom at 8 percent. His numbers plummeted following the discovery of a "signature factory" that had been fabricating the signatures of thousands of people presumably registered in his party and submitting them to the National Electoral Board. In light of this scandal, in July Congress moved to increase the number of votes required to impeach a president from half to two-thirds of sitting legislators. The issue was debated through May 2005, then receded as the 2006 election campaign went into gear. Although Toledo's character was the grounds for impeachment both times it was brought up, the mounting discontent and widespread public disapproval were the factors that really motivated the charges.

Calls for impeachment eventually faded away. It never became a real option, because the opposition preferred to remain in Congress than be forced to operate in the larger society (very much as had been the case in Bolivia's political establishment in 1984–2003), large sectors of society became more moderate as the economy began to improve, and political parties and significant segments of public opinion refused to see themselves in the mirror of instability held up by neighbors Bolivia and Ecuador; all of these factors ensured that impeachment never became a real option.[48]

Democracy and Growth: A Solid Lifeboat

Toledo failed to consolidate democracy or improve the lot of the long-suffering rural and indigenous underclass. However, he not only survived but managed to end his term with a remarkably high approval rating, 33 percent, after spending more than a year in single digits (see Table 11.1). The reason was that he had two key accomplishments to his credit: (1) economic growth and macroeconomic stability and (2) the preservation of democracy in the face of massive discontent and political ineffectiveness.

Democracy and Human Rights

"I leave democracy intact," a grim Fernando Belaúnde had said in 1985 as he finished a presidency marred by political violence, intractable inflation, and low approval ratings.[49] Toledo could have said something similar, although— luckily for him and the country—the context was completely different.

As a man without a political past, Toledo benefited from having no connection to the massive human rights violations perpetrated under Belaúnde (1980–85) and García (1985–90).[50] He was also safely distanced from Fujimori's crimes against humanity. Therefore, Toledo felt much freer than traditional parties not to, for example, interfere with the Truth and Reconciliation Commission, which was watched with suspicion and even ill will by political parties. His relations with the Inter-American Court of Human Rights were good, and he acquiesced to several adverse rulings relating to the Fujimori era. Rebel leaders who had been sentenced in summary judgments were given new trials, and as his term drew to a close, Toledo drafted a National Human Rights Plan that was fairly advanced for the region. However, Toledo began to let up in the fight against corruption, especially as his own scandals came to light.

As part of the general sapping of the reformist spirit, the Toledo administration left the attorney general's office weakened in its ability to fight corruption, especially when cases against his administration began to arise. Still, Peruvians knew that Toledo was no friend of Fujimori's and had no connection with the megacorruption he had fostered.[51]

Economic Growth

Partly because of Toledo's liberal convictions—he said he would never resort to populist measures to regain credence—and partly because of his own survival instinct, he never lost his bearings regarding the economy. This, along with a highly favorable international context, allowed the Peruvian economy to grow for an unprecedented 57 consecutive months (Figure 11.1).

Throughout Toledo's term, the Ministry of Economy remained largely immune to the ambitions of PP and the constant changes in cabinet composition they prompted. Pedro Pablo Kuczynski, an economist with close ties to the business community and international financial institutions, held the portfolio for almost half of Toledo's term. When he left the ministry to become prime minister, the post passed to Fernando Zavala, his heir apparent.[52]

Figure 11.1. GDP Growth, 1990–2006

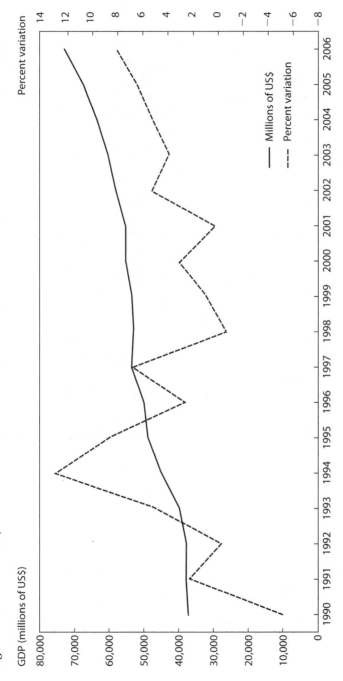

Source: Apoyo Opinión y Mercado S.A.
Note: The first *Apoyo* survey dates back to February 2002 and measured support in Lima. In August 2001, Toledo had 59 percent support and 16 percent disapproval ratings. By November, his approval rate had dropped to 32 percent, and by February 2002 it had fallen to 28 percent.

Like medieval monks at the service of the market and feeling besieged by what they saw as economically illiterate barbarians adept only at demanding a piece of the pie, the ministry practitioners, CEOs, and even leading economic writers set out to shield the economy from politicking during Toledo's five-year term. To them, politics had become "noise" outside the walls of their economic fortress built on tax incentives and other mechanisms, most inherited from Fujimori. This was not a wholly unreasonable view, given the mediocrity of the cast of political actors. Overall, public opinion agreed that the best aspects of the Toledo administration were infrastructure development, the signing of the FTA with the United States, and economic stability. The worst had been Toledo's ethical and character flaws, especially where his family was concerned. Table 11.5 shows the results of a survey conducted at the end of his mandate. Interestingly, adherence to democracy is far down on the list of achievements cited, while serious economic issues, such as unemployment, are also low on the list of shortcomings.

A Mixed Assessment, A Disjointed Administration

The final result was a disjointed administration that left behind a GDP growth of 22 percent and set the stage for the next government to continue benefiting from economic stability. However, Toledo failed to reduce poverty or economic and regional inequality to a significant degree (Table 11.6), formulate effective social policies, or implement urgent institutional reform. Worst of all, his inability to act as a serious politician prevented him from

Table 11.5. Ratings of the Best and Worst of Alejandro Toledo's Administration

Best	Percentage	Worst	Percentage
Housing programs	37	Scandals of relatives	62
Completion of Cusco–Lima gas pipeline	35	Wife's attitude and statements	53
Beginning of the southern inter-oceanic highway	33	Corruption	44
Free trade agreement with the United States	30	Too many promises	44
Economic stability	30	Unemployment	42
Development of the tourist industry	25	Delay in recognizing his daughter	37
Export growth	22	Lack of leadership skills	31
Adherence to democracy	17	Frivolity and lack of austerity	24

Source: Apoyo Opinión y Mercado.

Table 11.6. Poverty and Extreme Poverty under Toledo, 2001 and 2005 (percent)

	2001		2005	
	Poverty	Extreme Poverty	Poverty	Extreme Poverty
Total	54.3	24.1	48.0	18.1
Rural	77.1	49.8	72.5	40.3[a]
Andes	70.6	43.2	67.7	36.5[a]

Source: Council of Ministers / National Statistics Institute.
[a]Data for rural and Andean regions are from 2004.

restoring politics to its rightful place and from making progress in building a democratic nation of empowered citizens.

As a result, although the sustained growth of the economy and a limited reduction in poverty played a role in Toledo's final approval rating, he left a number of ticking time bombs in his wake. The first to explode was that represented by Ollanta Humala. A radical nationalist outsider, not to mention a follower of Hugo Chávez, Humala surprised everyone by taking first place during the first round of voting in April 2006. His candidacy served as a conduit for long-simmering grievances between rich and poor, between urban and rural Peru, between Lima and the provinces, and between the northern coast and the central region on one side and the Andean south and Amazonia on the other.[53] Humala became the standard-bearer for half of a country divided from the rest in part by the policies of a government that was itself fractious.

The electoral map after the first round reflected this division almost exactly and signaled the total collapse of government parties. The FIM disappeared, while PP obtained just 4 percent of the vote (the same as in 1995), picking up a paltry two seats in Congress.[54] Yet, as Table 11.1 shows, Toledo himself escaped almost unscathed; his 33 percent approval rating was the highest for an outgoing Peruvian president since the 1980s.

Toledo was most popular before his inauguration and after he became a lame duck president. Oddly enough, his support in 2006 came from regions and segments of society that had little to do with those that had propelled him to the presidency in 2001. His later support came from regions that had voted for conservative candidate Lourdes Flores in the first round of 2001 voting and for Alan García in the runoff. As he left, Toledo had a 67 percent approval rating among the wealthy and 22 percent among the poor—not insignificant levels, given his past performance.[55] It was as if voters from the integrated parts of the country wished to thank him for the modest yet sustained growth he had overseen. They were also relieved that Peru, unlike its Andean neighbors, had not succumbed to what Marcelo Cavarozzi called "dizzying political consumption," the search for a political savior. These voters now looked with some condescension on this blundering but well-meaning president, who may be looking to return to the Peruvian political scene in 2011.

12

Venezuela

Delegative Democracy or Electoral Autocracy?

David J. Myers

Today ends a cycle, what is best called a 3,000-day period of transition. . . .
Until now what we have done is to lay down a base upon which we shall
construct the building.
    —Hugo Chávez, third presidential inaugural address, January 10, 2007

Eight years of rule by Hugo Chávez Frías have deepened the divide sepa-
rating supporters and opponents of his Bolivarian Revolution. Supporters
argue that his post-1999 "Bolivarian Republic" replaced an oligarchy that had
masqueraded as a democracy for over 40 years. They portray the current
project as a transitional regime that opened the way for "twenty-first-century
socialism," true democracy that will empower citizens and reduce glaring inequalities in wealth, status, and power among Venezuelans. The Bolivarian
Republic already has improved linkages between *el soberano* ("the people")
and their leader, according to supporters. They applauded on January 9,
2007, when President Chávez announced that he would revise the 1999 Constitution and restructure the economy to create the Socialist Republic of
Venezuela by year's end.

Many elements of President Chávez's socialist republic were already in
place prior to his announcement on January 9. During the Bolivarian Republic, his government had increased the role of the national executive,
reduced the autonomy of regional and local governments, and limited the
influence of private business. Individuals were encouraged to involve themselves in communal projects ranging from neighborhood garden plots to
self-help housing. President Chávez also expropriated property that he considered badly used, reallocating it for projects described as beneficial to

society as a whole. Most Venezuelans trusted President Chávez to do the right thing and supported his efforts to create a "different democracy." Until the referendum of December 2, 2007, he dominated electoral politics. However, concerns over proposed changes to the Constitution that diluted the right to own private property and allowed for the indefinite reelection of the president gave even government supporters cause for pause. In addition, in 2007 the vaunted socialist distribution system faltered and concerns over government corruption and a lack of personal security raised doubts about the character of the revolutionary regime. Many of President Chávez's supporters abstained from voting in the 2007 referendum, and by the narrowest of margins, it failed to pass. Thus, while there was continuing support for dismantling "savage capitalism," a system that President Chávez condemned for marginalizing and exploiting the poor, there was growing unease over how the government was using its already considerable powers.

Opposition to capitalism also orients President Chávez's regional foreign policy. He positions himself as a vocal opponent of the United States, especially the Free Trade Area of the Americas (FTAA) initiative promoted by President George W. Bush. Chávez's antagonism toward the FTAA dates to the Quebec Summit of April 2001, where he felt excluded and ignored when he argued for a section supportive of social justice and economic democracy to be included in the initiative. President Chávez's hostility toward the U.S. government intensified after a failed coup on April 11, 2002. On that day, demonstrators opposed to the government veered from the approved route and shots rang out as they surged toward the presidential palace (Miraflores). Opponents claimed that police fired into the mass of protesters, while the government countered that the demonstrators first attacked the police. Soon afterward, the military arrested President Chávez and took him to La Orchila, an island off the Venezuelan coast.

While factions in the provisional government fell to fighting among themselves, a swell of popular support for President Chávez surged from the slums of Caracas, and on the morning of April 14 the armed forces returned him to power. Despite denials from the U.S. government, President Chávez concluded that his removal from office had been orchestrated from Washington. Subsequently, the Venezuelan president tarred his domestic opponents as agents of the United States (which he referred to as the "Evil Empire"[1]), and he embarked on a crusade against the United States throughout Latin America. Thus, when President George W. Bush visited South and Central America in March 2007, President Chávez journeyed to Buenos Aires. At a sports stadium in the Argentine capital, before a rally of 40,000 anti-American leftists, the Venezuelan president railed against the hypocrisy, greed, and immorality of the United States.[2]

Venezuelan opponents of the Bolivarian Revolution, even those with reservations about the George W. Bush presidency, have a view of Hugo Chávez that differs dramatically from that of his supporters. They argue that Chávez's government destroyed the indigenous liberal democratic institutions that reformers had heroically crafted following the overthrow of the dictatorship of General Marcos Pérez Jiménez in 1958. These defenders of post-1958 democracy (also known as the Punto Fijo regime[3]) argue that governments between 1958 and 1998 made impressive gains in protecting human rights and increasing the quality of life for Venezuela's rapidly increasing population. They acknowledge that the economy performed erratically after 1983, but claim that the declining economic momentum was the consequence of falling international petroleum prices, a turn of events beyond the government's control. Defenders of post-1958 democracy also point out that political reforms in 1989 and economic reforms in the early 1990s were valiant attempts by true democrats to revitalize the Punto Fijo system. Defenders argue that these changes were never implemented as intended, but they still produced many positive results, most of which President Chávez has undone. Finally, opponents of the Bolivarian Revolution chide President Chávez for exacerbating tensions between socioeconomic groups and vilifying the productive middle class.

These contrasting views of Venezuela under the leadership of Hugo Chávez have little in common. Opponents argue that the way in which the president has defined *el soberano* all but excludes the opposition. Consequently, Bolivarian revolutionaries feel little obligation to provide political space from which opponents can compete for power or make effective demands. One reason that President Chávez has all but excluded the opposition from *el soberano* is that the opposition is dominated by groups and individuals who prospered and gained influence during the Punto Fijo period: the middle class, unionized labor, business interests and the politicians that dominated the ruling parties. It is these groups that Bolivarian revolutionaries portray as oligarchs exploiting *el soberano.*

In the presidential election of December 3, 2006, the opposition challenger to President Chávez, Governor Manuel Rosales of Zulia state, received 37 percent of the total vote. His defeat, the opposition's fourth at the hands of Hugo Chávez in eight years, was both expected and demoralizing. Most Rosales supporters agreed with him when he pointed out that President Chávez had used state resources in ways that made it all but impossible for the opposition to win. Their assessment is reflected in the 2006 Latinobarómetro poll taken several months before the presidential balloting, which found that 44 percent of all Venezuelans believed that elections in their country were neither clean nor free of fraud.[4] This picture is complicated by a survey performed in the same year by the University of Chicago's National Opinion Research Center, which found that a larger proportion of Venezuelans than citizens of any other country except the United States were brimming with national pride.[5]

Proponents and opponents of the Bolivarian Revolution want a different kind of democracy. Proponents favor direct democracy in the Rousseauian mode, whereby an elected leader embodying the general will acts under few constraints. Increasingly, President Hugo Chávez has argued that socialism is the only form of government that safeguards the people's interests. Opponents, in contrast, favor checks and balances to guard against what they view as the tyranny of the majority. The prospects for crafting a variant of liberal democracy acceptable to Bolivarian revolutionaries are all but nonexistent. Political regimes with checks and balances lost much of their legitimacy when those who crafted Venezuela's post-1958 democracy became isolated, arrogant, and corrupt. After decades in power, they refused to make way for a new generation of leaders. Finally, as noted earlier, they were unable to reverse the economic downturn that began in the 1980s and worsened during the 1990s.

The magnitude of Venezuela's economic decline during the final decades of the Punto Fijo period is breathtaking. No measure better captures the drama of this decline than the change in real per capita income between 1958 and 1998. Figure 12.1 shows per capita income rising steadily until about 1978, when it began its progressive decline. As of 1999, Venezuelans had slipped back to commanding a per capita gross domestic product (GDP) that was about the same as it had been in 1962, and the purchasing power of their average salary was only 33 percent of what it had been in 1978.

The plunge in per capita income after 1978 reversed the upward mobility on which the architects of Punto Fijo democracy based their right to rule. In 1978, roughly half of all Venezuelans had incomes that placed them somewhere in the middle class; ten years later, 31 percent were living in poverty. By 1998, the year in which Hugo Chávez was first elected president, two-thirds of all Venezuelans were living below the poverty line. In addition, after 1987, inflation (which had risen at an annual rate of 15 percent or less between 1958 and 1986) increased dramatically. Punto Fijo governments had squandered resources in good times, so there were few financial reserves to lessen the pain when the country began experiencing lean years. Inflation rates skyrocketed because the government could no longer provide public utilities such as telephone and electricity services at subsidized prices. Nor could the government bail out state enterprises accustomed to losing money while producing subsidized steel, cement, and fertilizers. During the 1990s, when subsidized products were replaced by goods and services priced at market value, the annual increase in the rate of inflation approached 100 percent in some years.

Figure 12.1. GDP per Capita and Average Real Salary, 1957–2001

Thousand 1984 bolivars

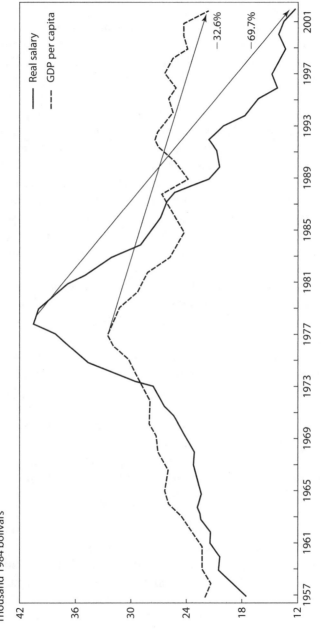

Sources: Central Bank of Venezuela, Central Office of Statistics and Information, and MetroEconómica.

The poor and those living on fixed incomes suffered the most as living standards declined sharply.

Venezuela's economic decline in the 1990s resulted from the convergence of several developments. Most important, as suggested earlier, was the plunge in oil prices that occurred following the first Gulf War. Social scientists classify Venezuela as a "rentier state," meaning that its economy is driven by the "rent" (income) that it receives from the sale of a single natural resource—in this case, petroleum. During the late 1950s, just before oil production from the Middle East came online, Venezuela was the world's largest exporter of petroleum. Although Saudi Arabia subsequently claimed this distinction, Venezuela has remained among the top five petroleum-exporting countries. In the negotiations leading to the Constitution of 1961, Venezuelan elites (party leaders, businesspeople, clergy, and organized labor) agreed to share power, most importantly the power to distribute income derived from the sale of petroleum.[6] Their capability to distribute resources to political clients increased dramatically after 1973, when the price of petroleum skyrocketed from under $15 a barrel (in constant 2006 U.S. dollars), first to $40 a barrel and, subsequently, to just under $70 a barrel in 1982. This decade-long "petrobonanza" came to an end in 1983, and by 1998 petroleum was selling for around $11 a barrel. Correspondingly, the two dominant political parties, Acción Democrática (AD; Democratic Action) and the Comité de Organización Política Electoral Independiente, usually referred to as the Partido Social Cristiano de Venezuela (COPEI; Social Christian Party of Venezuela), were unable to meet the expectations of their supporters—subsidized goods and services in return for electoral support. Once AD and COPEI could not keep up their end of the bargain, their supporters looked for alternatives. Hugo Chávez offered something quite different from the traditional political parties, first as a leader of the unsuccessful military coup of February 4, 1992, and subsequently as the presidential candidate of the anti-establishment Movimiento Quinta República (Fifth Republic Movement).

During the first eight years of Hugo Chávez's presidency (1999–2007), the opposition behaved in ways that called into question its willingness to accept the legitimacy of any government that redistributed their wealth, reduced their political influence, or restricted private economic activity, even if that government's mandate derived from victory at the polls. Opponents resorted to extraordinary measures (including coups, general strikes, and electoral abstention) in an effort to force President Chávez from office, but each failure left the opposition weaker and more disorganized. Following an unsuccessful revocatory referendum of August 2004, President Chávez pressed his advantage. Demoralized and reeling, the opposition made only perfunctory challenges in the regional elections of October 2004 and the municipal council elections of August 2005. They abstained altogether from the National Assembly elections of December 2005. In August 2006, however, the opposition united around a single candidate, Governor Manuel Rosales of Zulia, and mounted a vigorous challenge in the presidential election of December 3, 2006. President Chávez, while falling far short of his goal of 10 million votes, won reelection by a slightly greater margin than he had achieved in the 2004 referendum. Nevertheless, opponents hoped that Governor Rosales's respectable showing in defeat (37 percent of the total vote) would convince President Chávez to reserve political space from which the opposition could exercise influence and compete for power during the 2007–13 presidential term.

President Chávez's announcement on January 9, 2007, and his inaugural address the following day gave little hope that Bolivarian revolutionaries would take the opinions of their opponents into account when making policy. The president's inauguration speech began with rhetorical flourish: "Fatherland, socialism, or death—I swear it." He continued by repeating his promise to accelerate the march toward socialism by nationalizing three sectors controlled by foreigners: telecommunications, electricity, and the "heavy oil" petroleum facilities found in Venezuela's Orinoco Tar Belt.

President Chávez also announced his intention to take advantage of the 1999 Constitution's provision allowing him to request unrestricted legislative powers (Ley Habilante) from the National Assembly. If such a request is granted, the National Assembly does not meet during the period in which the powers are in force. On January 11, 2007, President Chávez requested a Ley Habilitante from the National Assembly, stating that he intended to use the special powers to rewrite the Constitution and eliminate institutions and checks that restricted his ability to build twenty-first-century socialism. Singled out for special attention were the municipal and regional governments and the Central Bank. Decentralization legislation passed during the second government of Carlos Andrés Pérez (1989–93) had given these institutions considerable autonomy, which President Chávez intended to scale back. The president's plans were placed on hold following voters' rejection of the constitutional reforms proposed in the December 2007 referendum.

President Chávez's presentation of his new cabinet on television (January 9, 2007) and his inaugural address the following day confirmed his resolve to create a militantly socialist regime dedicated to improving and equalizing living conditions among Venezuelans. Dialogue with his opponents and affirmation of their right to organize were not part of the socialist project he described, although on December 4, 2006, following Manuel Rosales's congratulatory message, President Chávez did opine that he would listen to ideas from the loyal opposition. Nevertheless, the president's behavior between his election and his inauguration on January 10, 2007, suggested that the political regime he intended to create during his next government would be either some form of "delegative democracy" or "electoral autocracy," or perhaps a sui generis mixture of both. These two models have been developed by social scientists to describe political regimes that fall into a "gray zone" between full democracy and autocracy. Before continuing with our discussion of Venezuelan politics, we shall briefly digress to examine the basic characteristics of delegative democracy and electoral autocracy.

Political Regimes and Democracy's Gray Zone

Most of the literature on democratic transitions views political regimes as falling along a continuum between full democracy and closed autocracy.[7] This work, following O'Donnell, Schmitter, Whitehead, and Schedler, embraces the definition of *political regime* that focuses on the rules governing access to political power (who may compete, what resources and strategies may be used, and the basic rules for gaining power).[8] A great deal of effort has been expended in distinguishing subtypes of democratic and autocratic, or even hybrid, regimes. This emphasis on the competitiveness and freedoms of the electoral process does not imply that the *exercise* of power (as opposed to *access* to power) is unimportant. Indeed, the exercise of power and the curtailment or expansion of basic freedoms shapes the electoral process and the quality of freedom.[9] Hybrid political regimes display a mixture of the characteristics that mark access to power and the exercise of power in full democracies and closed autocracies. They dwell in the continuum's gray zone, between the poles.[10] Partisans of full democracy sometimes refer to gray zone political regimes as "defective democracies."

For the purposes of examining recent political developments in Venezuela, we differentiate among four types of political regimes: full liberal democracy, delegative democracy, electoral autocracy, and full autocracy. Observers have suggested additional subtypes and debated their utility for understanding how political change occurs and why the breakdown of many autocracies in the 1980s did not lead to the establishment of full democracies. Because we are interested in examining the type of political regime that is emerging in Venezuela, the finer points of the debate over subtypes of full democracy, delegative democracy, electoral autocracy, and full autocracy are beyond the scope of this work.. Characteristics of the four basic types of regime are as follows:

- *Full liberal democracy*—regimes with highly responsive polities that allow for elections based on universal suffrage, full contestation, and the rule of law.[11] They protect individual freedoms, shield citizens from abuse of state power, and deny any group reserved domains of power.[12]
- *Delegative democracy*—regimes with positive traits such as minimally acceptable elections and responsiveness to the majority.[13] They also in-

corporate important defects, at least from the perspective of partisans of full liberal democracy. Something is amiss; most often, the basic freedom of organization is curtailed and horizontal accountability is sacrificed to the exigencies of governance.[14] Corrales, Roberts, McCoy, and Panizza argue that large disparities in wealth and power favor the neopopulist variant of delegative democracy.[15]

- *Electoral autocracy*—regimes that allow some competition, but do not meet minimum acceptable standards for meaningful elections.[16] The defects of delegative democracy are magnified to the point at which opponents who play by the sanctioned rules of the game have little chance of exercising power or modifying policies.[17]
- *Closed autocracy*—regimes with no elections or in which simply ritualistic, uncompetitive plebiscites are held. A range exists within this category as well.

This discussion of regime types assists us in placing Bolivarian Venezuela within its political and historical tapestry. The first thread of this tapestry that we examine is the unraveling of post-1958 democracy that opened the way to the Bolivarian Revolution. Our primary concern, however, is how Venezuela has changed since President Chávez came to power. The first groups whose political activities we scrutinize are organized interests and civil society, with special attention given to the armed forces. Next, we focus on how other important groups create coalitions in their quest to influence policy making. The emphasis is on political parties and movements, although we discuss the aggregative activities of national bureaucracies such as the Ministry of the Interior and Justice and the Ministry of Infrastructure. Elections —national, regional, and local—provide a critical prism for assessing the role of opposition political forces and the extent to which Venezuela under Chávez remains democratic. The political practices of the national executive also yield information essential for assessing the quality of democracy during what is now labeled the "transitional phase" to twenty-first-century socialism. Additional data for making this assessment come from examining the other branches of the central government: the National Assembly, the judiciary, the Electoral Power, and the Citizen Power. Movement away from liberal democracy in the regional and municipal polities between 1999 and 2007 is the final development from which we draw conclusions about the nature of Venezuela's political regime.

The Unraveling of Liberal Democracy in Venezuela

The second inauguration of President Carlos Andrés Pérez, on February 2, 1989, began on a high note, with lavish celebrations attended by a glittering constellation of international dignitaries. It also quickened the unraveling of Venezuelan liberal democracy.[18] Pérez, the candidate of AD in the presidential election of December 4, 1988, had served as president earlier, between 1974 and 1979, a time of prosperity and economic growth. Most Venezuelans anticipated that Pérez's second government would bring the nation similar success. This illusion was shattered three weeks into the new administration, when President Pérez announced that the country's foreign reserves were severely depleted: the country had run a fiscal deficit exceeding 9 percent of GDP in 1998, the current account balance had its largest deficit in history, and all prices in the economy were artificially low and impossible to maintain. The new government turned to the International Monetary Fund, but the price of its assistance was implementation of a bitter austerity program. Popular outrage over the frustration of expectations raised in the presidential election campaign set off two days of rioting in 10 cities (the infamous *Caracazo* of February 28 and 29, 1989). Neither the police nor the National Guard could contain the violence. The army finally restored order, but at the cost of least 200 deaths. The economy continued to contract throughout 1989 but improved in 1990 and boomed in 1991. Nevertheless, the *Caracazo* had greatly damaged the legitimacy of the political regime, which was never repaired.

The economic recovery in 1990 and 1991, which President Pérez engineered using the neoliberal model, proved a mixed blessing. It created wealth, but the ruling classes appropriated most of the new revenue. The glaring disparity between the new wealth captured by the elites and the plight of the poor intensified societal alienation. By the middle of the 1990s, most Venezuelans wanted something different from the established party-dominated democracy,[19] which they eventually found in Lieutenant Colonel Hugo Chávez's Bolivarian Republic. Such a turn of events had been inconceivable when President Pérez set out on his neoliberal adventure.[20]

After the *Caracazo,* Venezuela settled into a deceptive calm. People appeared resigned to painful adjustments even though conditions screamed that petroleum-fueled distribution networks could no longer sustain the existing institutions. It was in this period of calm that President Pérez imposed his neoliberal economic package, El Gran Viraje (The Great Turnaround).[21] This radical departure from the past relied on four sets of policies: macroeconomic stabilization, trade liberalization, privatization, and deregulation. Macroeconomic stabilization included measures such as the establishment of a single freely floating rate for foreign exchange, the elimination of price controls on all private goods and services (except those on a list of 18 specific staple items), market-determined interest rates, reductions in real public spending, and significant increases in the prices of public utilities as well as goods produced by the public sector.

Trade liberalization and privatization changed Venezuela. Government planners removed nontariff barriers covering 94 percent of local manufactures and eliminated special permits for exports, simultaneously restructuring the tariff system. This lowered the country's average tariff level from 35 percent in 1988 to around 10 percent in 1990. Entry into the General Agreement on Tariffs and Trade consolidated the freest trade regime since the Constitution of 1961 had entered into force. Foreign commercial banks responded by restructuring US$20 billion of Venezuela's public debt. Finally, new foreign investment regulations eliminated most restrictions on foreign investors and minimized bureaucratic interference in their financial, commercial, and technological transactions.

The Pérez government took steps to privatize deficit-prone state enterprises. By the end of 1992, four commercial banks, the national airline, the telephone company, the cellular telephone system, a shipyard, the ports, sugar mills, and several hotels had all been sold. Other enterprises slated for privatization included horseracing tracks, a second airline, additional hotels, the Caracas water supply system, regional electricity distribution facilities, and the public television network.[22] These changes were a dramatic reversal for a president who had nationalized petroleum and led the Latin American Social Democratic Movement, and they confirmed that the state had experienced a serious loss of distributive capability.

Deregulation, as suggested earlier, accompanied macroeconomic stabilization, trade liberalization, and privatization. It also forced changes to be made in the government's social programs. Subsidies in which payments and other allocations were transferred to specific private firms producing basic staples (e.g., corn, flour, milk, sugar, poultry, sardines, and so forth) to keep their prices low were no longer feasible. The government's intent was to replace them with a nutritional grant program that would establish a direct cash transfer to the mothers of children enrolled in schools located in poor areas. The government also announced a maternal health care program and a worker protection plan based on unemployment compensation payments for six months. AD and COPEI opposed and undercut these measures because President Pérez's approach ended their control over the distributive mechanism that party leaders used to service their clienteles. Implementation of this new approach to social problems was also hindered by the magnitude of the changes involved, the rigidities of established bureaucracies, and the scarcity of funds.[23]

The repercussions of President Pérez's neoliberal restructuring were felt throughout the 1990s. Early in the decade, Venezuela's economy set world records for macroeconomic growth, but these records masked the deterioration of state institutions, which became less capable of acting on the basis of technical and professional criteria. Poor performance by the state undermined the living standards of those who depended on public sector resource distribution. Their purchasing power declined, and many supplemented their income through activity in the informal sector. Decay seemed pervasive, and the government's legitimacy continued to erode.

The social tensions and economic downturn that undermined support for President Pérez also intensified the contempt for liberal democracy within the armed forces. During the late 1970s, the professional military promotion system established following the overthrow of General Pérez Jiménez had been relaxed and politicized. Intrigues inside the officer corps became commonplace as aspiring factions blocked or even sabotaged the career development and possibilities for promotion of their rivals. Those who lost in these Byzantine intrigues were appointed to mid-level executive positions within the myriad state enterprises. This practice became less commonplace as budgets tightened and the public sector contracted during the fiscal crisis of the 1980s.[24]

Another consequence of the fiscal crisis for the armed forces was that the daily needs of enlisted soldiers and junior officers became grossly underfunded. This fed resentment toward the senior ranks, which were viewed as increasingly remote and preoccupied with contracts to procure sophisticated military hardware. During the country's petro-bonanza, junior officers had been given opportunities to complement their military training with professional education at home and abroad, thus differentiating their experience in the profession from that of senior officers and exacerbating tensions. The younger officers were appalled by the rampant corruption that was undermining national development, and they became disillusioned with liberal democracy. The senior officers, in contrast, supported centrist liberal democracy and belonged to a generation that had come of age in the 1960s and cut their teeth on the struggle against leftist insurgents. Thus, reduced economic circumstances and distinct generational experiences in the armed forces conspired to create distrust, erode discipline, and undermine cohesion. The military ceased to be a bulwark of support for the Punto Fijo regime after the urban riots of February 28 and 29, 1989.

The crisis broke on February 4, 1992, when a group of junior military officers known as the Bolivarian Military Movement attempted a coup that came perilously close to succeeding. Although much in the movement's program was confused, its call for the affluent and dishonest to be tried for crimes against the nation struck a responsive chord among the majority, who were experiencing economic hardship. Although the coup failed, it emboldened the opponents of President Pérez's austerity plan and even longforgotten enemies of the Punto Fijo regime.

The 15 months that separated the February 1992 coup attempt from President Perez's suspension from office in May 1993 proved remarkable for its political turbulence and intensifying opposition to the government's neoliberal economic policies. Former president Rafael Caldera (1969–74) stopped just short of proclaiming that the Bolivarian Military Movement's cause was just. Former president Isaías Medina's (1941–45) last minister of the interior, the intellectual Arturo Uslar Pietri, suggested that forcing Pérez from office before the end of his term would make amends for the Revolution of 1945, which had brought AD to power in the first place. In late November 1992, the military (this time the navy, air force, and marines) mounted a second unsuccessful coup, and Venezuela's once-robust macroeconomic indicators faded.

Even though the reforms of the second Pérez government had strengthened regional and local governments, a move popular with the middle classes, economic decline and political discontent doomed that government.[25] In March 1993, the attorney general, Ramón Escovar Salom, went public with evidence that the president had "misused" government funds from the *partida secreta* (secret executive budget).[26] On May 20, the Supreme Court found "merit" in these charges, and the national Congress suspended Carlos Andrés Pérez from the presidency the following day.

The eight months that followed raised more questions than they answered. After AD and COPEI came to an agreement, the Senate selected one of its own, Ramón J. Velásquez, to serve as interim president. Velásquez, a political intellectual, oversaw free and open elections for the presidency, Congress, and the state legislatures in December 1993. During his brief stewardship, however, the economy failed to recover, privatization stalled, and bitterness over declining living standards intensified. No candidate captured the public imagination in the 1993 presidential election, which former president Rafael Caldera won with just over 30 percent of the total vote.

Caldera's expulsion from COPEI in early 1993, as he was organizing his run for the presidency as an independent, allowed him to capitalize on hostility toward the two dominant political parties and their neoliberal agenda.[27] During his first two years in office, Caldera attempted to turn back the clock to an earlier time when the state had funded import substitution industrialization (ISI) and services for the less affluent. One initiative he undertook to demonstrate outrage over his predecessor's neoliberal policies involved squeezing the financial institutions that had benefited from privatization under El Gran Viraje. To this day, many in the Venezuelan financial community believe that Caldera's actions were a vendetta against institutions that had bankrolled his rivals in the 1993 presidential election. They point out that none of the banks that supported his presidential candidacy perished, while others defend Caldera's actions as well intentioned but poorly managed. Regardless, the initiative had the unintended consequence of collapsing the banking system, which liquidated almost 60 percent of all deposits in Venezuelan banks.[28]

During his first two years in office, President Caldera attempted to expand the safety net for the less affluent and to stimulate production at existing ISI enterprises, most of which ran chronic deficits. These policies could not be sustained, because the banking crisis and falling petroleum prices weakened the central government's financial position. In 1996, the rate of inflation approached 103 percent and foreign public debt rose to $26.5 billion. To extricate Venezuela from this financial quagmire, Caldera negotiated a structural adjustment agreement with the International Monetary Fund that reinstated many of the neoliberal reforms (under a program now labeled Agenda Venezuela) that he had criticized during the 1993 presidential election campaign.

Agenda Venezuela also reversed many of the decentralization reforms that middle-class reformers admired. President Caldera negotiated an arrangement with Luis Alfaro Ucero, the secretary general of AD, who had opposed the decentralization reforms. The agreement gave the government control of Congress, which quickly passed neoliberal legislation and refrained from investigating President Caldera's failure to abide by procedures stipulated in existing decentralization legislation. The cooperation between President Caldera and AD convinced most Venezuelans that the supposedly reformist Caldera administration was no different from the party-dominated governments that had ruled since 1958. It also unmasked AD, the dominant political party of the Punto Fijo era, as the president's silent partner. Caldera and Alfaro Ucero appeared untrustworthy and self-serving, and neither enjoyed much political credibility.

The opportunity to make dramatic changes in what most citizens viewed as an unresponsive political regime came with the national elections of 1998. Voters went to the polls to choose the president and members of Congress. COPEI and AD nominated presidential candidates with fatal flaws, which underscored their isolation. Just prior to the presidential voting, the two traditionally dominant political parties abandoned their nominees to support the promising but ultimately unsuccessful candidacy of Enrique Salas Römer, the semi-independent governor of Carabobo. The real story of the presidential election campaign, however, was the meteoric rise of Hugo Chávez. His promise to construct a "different democracy" resonated with voters disillusioned by the incompetence and arrogance of AD and COPEI while calming fears that he would not govern as a democrat. On December 6, 1998, almost three out of five voters cast their ballots for the former lieutenant colonel.

President Chávez moved quickly to change the status quo. At his February 2, 1999, inauguration, he vowed to replace the existing "moribund" and "unjust" Constitution of 1961 with one that empowered the people. He organized a referendum in which 85 percent of the voters authorized elections that would select delegates to a Constituent Assembly charged with drafting the new constitution. One important reason that the new president moved so quickly to change the existing Constitution was that the political opposition, based on their showing in the legislative elections of November 1998, controlled Congress. A Constituent Assembly dominated by Chávez supporters would neutralize the most important institutional check on the president's ability to create a different democracy.

The decision to call for a Constituent Assembly yielded rich dividends for President Chávez. On July 25, his supporters won 122 of the 131 seats in the Constituent Assembly even though opposition candidates received almost 40 percent of the total vote. Once the Assembly began drafting the new constitution, it was clear that the Bolivarian delegates would approve a constitution with few checks on President Chávez's power to act on behalf of *el soberano*.[29] The Bolivarians also crafted provisions that would reduce the influence of the traditional political parties, private corporations, and the regional governments. Somewhat unexpectedly, the Constituent Assembly asserted that it, rather than the Congress, had the power to legislate. The opposition-dominated Congress challenged this usurpation of its authority, which led President Chávez to mobilize his supporters and blockade the Congress building. The Supreme Court then issued a ruling that supported the position of the Constituent Assembly, and soon afterward Congress dissolved itself. The Constituent Assembly then intervened in the judiciary and removed judges that it deemed corrupt, weeding out many jurists with ties to AD and COPEI.

Once President Chávez had eliminated the most important institutional checks on his power and it became clear that a populist constitution would emerge, economic elites began transferring capital abroad. Capital flight exceeded $4 billion in 1999, and the economy contracted by 5.5 percent. President Chávez, however, remained focused on restructuring political institutions. Venezuelans rewarded his persistence in a national referendum on December 15, 1999, when 72 percent of voters approved the new Constitution.

The Constitution of 1999 was not necessarily fatal for the continuance of Venezuelan liberal democracy; everything depended on how the government would implement it.[30] The 1999 Constitution created two new branches of government—the Citizen Power and the Electoral Power. Each had the potential to hold the executive accountable over a significant range of issues. From the start, however, President Chávez undermined the 1999 Constitution's liberal democratic potential in the political sphere. On the other hand, his economic policies were not significantly different from those of his predecessor, at least until 2002. This reflected his reciprocity for the support he had received from important sectors of the business community during his 1998 presidential election campaign and prior to the failed military coup of April 2002.

The first elections under the Constitution of 1999 were held on July 30, 2000. At stake was the presidency, all seats in the National Assembly and state legislatures, and all regional governorships and mayoralties.[31] Voting was not compulsory, unlike in elections conducted under the 1961 Constitution. However, penalties for not voting during the Punto Fijo regime were light and seldom assessed. During the 1960s and 1970s, the legitimacy of the regime was considered high and abstention rates in presidential elections were low, below 10 percent, rising to 12 percent in 1988 and 18 percent in 1988.[32] Forty percent of eligible voters abstained in the 1993 presidential election, following the *Caracazo* and two unsuccessful coups in 1992, and 36 percent abstained in the presidential election of 1998. The most widely accepted explanation for the sharp increase in rates of abstention during the 1990s is alienation from the political regime. Forty-four percent of eligible voters abstained in the July 2000 "megaelections," which suggests that voter alienation (or apathy?) remained an important feature of the Venezuelan polity. On the other hand, 6 of every 10 voters who did participate in the megaelections opted for President Chávez and candidates offered by the government and its allies. The victory of the chavistas in the megaelections of 2000 and their success in gaining control of key national government institutions all but ended the possibility of embedding horizontal accountability in the new political regime.

Seven months after the 1999 Constitution entered into force, the "Fifth Republic" of Hugo Chávez approximated the delegative democracy regime type. The Bolivarian variant of delegative democracy, as suggested earlier, was populist from the beginning and has become more so. The course of events between the unsuccessful recall election on August 15, 2004, and the first months of President Chávez's second administration under the 1999 Constitution suggests a trend toward electoral autocracy.

Our attention now turns to the political structures and processes that have taken shape in Venezuela since the megaelections of July 30, 2000. To repeat, we focus on the following: interest groups and civil society, political parties and elections, the powers of the central government, and relations among national, regional, and state political systems. We are interested in the operational characteristics of institutions and whether their transformation since the unraveling of liberal Punto Fijo democracy suggests a metamorphosis into electoral democracy or into electoral autocracy. As part of this concern, we will discuss the forces within these institutions that support each of these political regime types.

Interest Groups and Civil Society in the Fifth Republic

Bolivarian Venezuela is less supportive of demand making by organized interests than was post-1958 liberal democracy. Hugo Chávez, as discussed earlier, views democracy from the perspective of Jean Jacques Rousseau, not that of John Locke. Nevertheless, in the early years of the Bolivarian Republic many institutional and associational interest groups enjoyed meaningful autonomy and exercised significant influence. The armed forces and the church, both historically elitist, were the most influential of the institutional interests.[33] The similarly elitist business community and professionals operated in the associational mode, as did such mass-based groups as labor and the peasantry.[34] These groups' influence declined after the coup of April 2002 and the unsuccessful demonstrations and strikes of December 2002–January 2003. On the other hand, the urban poor gained in influence. They provided the greater share of the votes that allowed President Chávez to survive the recall election in 2004 and win the presidency in December 2006. When many in the shantytowns abstained from voting, the president's December 2007 proposal to reform the 1999 Constitution was defeated.

The military, along with the church and the landed elite, had dominated Venezuela from the time of its independence until General Pérez Jiménez fled the country on January 23, 1958. The provisional junta that took power faced nationwide strikes supported by business, labor, and other groups demanding civilian political rule. Confused and dispirited, the army acquiesced to the election of its nemesis, Rómulo Betancourt (1959–64), as president. The Betancourt government also fought an insurgency mounted by leftist guerrillas who intended to establish a Castroite regime in Venezuela. The counterinsurgency effort that defeated the guerrillas forged a bond between the armed forces and civilian leaders. Until the leaders of Punto Fijo democracy called on the army to put down the urban riots on February 28 and 29, 1989, this bond remained a formidable obstacle to direct military intervention in politics.

After 1989, the armed forces could not be depended on to make demands through constitutional channels. Instead, they became institutions that, under conditions judged favorable by the officer corps, might intervene directly in politics. There are several reasons for this transformation. First, simmering frustration with party-based governments' management of the economy made violent protests increasingly common, and on several occasions the last two Punto Fijo governments turned to the armed forces to assist the police in preserving order. The officer corps faulted liberal democratic governments for not maintaining police capabilities and raised questions about how budgets had been administered.

Corruption and institutional decay underlay other military concerns with post-1958 democracy. The experience of using force against protesting civilians led many in the military to question their support of an unpopular, party-centered regime dominated by autocratic gerontocracies that appeared unscrupulous and isolated. Finally, the opulent lifestyles of young politicians and businessmen during the 1990s contrasted with the economic difficulties experienced by junior officers, creating resentments in the armed forces against the political and economic establishment. President Pérez sought to address these grievances after the unsuccessful coups of February and November 1992, and in early 1994, President Caldera made his own special overtures to the officer corps. Neither was able to return the armed forces to the regime-supportive stance that they had maintained between 1960 and 1989.

When Hugo Chávez first assumed the presidency, Venezuela's military was divided into three factions. One supported the Bolivarian Revolution, another was vehemently opposed, and a third argued that the armed forces should remain apolitical and focus on professional enhancement. President Chávez was determined to transform the armed forces into a pillar of support for his regime because he viewed the military as special, an institution more honorable than any other, and he saw the bureaucracy as corrupt and incompetent. Thus, he launched Plan Bolívar 2000, an improvised departure that funneled funds for infrastructure maintenance and development through regional military garrison commanders. Some officers opposed this policy, while others used the opportunities that accompany the contracting of public works for personal enrichment. In general, Venezuela's physical infrastructure deteriorated under this military stewardship.

In early 2002, factions in the military opposed to President Chávez became concerned over his use of discretionary powers to undercut the autonomy of a broad range of institutions and interests. They were especially uneasy over his campaign to replace the professional managers of the state oil company Petróleos de Venezuela (PDVSA; National Petroleum Corporation of Venezuela) with revolutionary loyalists. On April 11, 2002, a march in Caracas by hundreds of thousands of government opponents ended in shootings that killed and wounded more than 15 individuals. The opposition and the government blamed each other, and the incident became an excuse for military officers opposed to President Chávez to remove him from office. They replaced him with Pedro Carmona Estanga, president of the umbrella business confederation FEDECAMARAS (the Federación de Cámaras y Asociaciones de Comercio y Producción or Federation of Chambers and Associations of Commerce and Production).

Carmona based his short-lived government on support from a narrow segment of the opposition, especially entrepreneurs and the Roman Catholic hierarchy. He ignored organized labor, most political party leaders, and the civil society organizations that had blossomed in the 1990s.[35] Rather than promising an investigation of the April 11 violence, Carmona abolished the National Assembly and the courts and indicated that he would replace elected regional governors with his own appointees. These decisions raised fears that Carmona's backers intended to establish a right-wing dictatorship, a regime that few Venezuelans favored. President Chávez's supporters regrouped, played on divisions within the opposition, and took the offensive. In less than 48 hours, they returned the ousted president to power.

Chávez never fully trusted the armed forces after the coup of April 11. He not only purged officers known to have sympathized with the coup but also marginalized those with only a tepid commitment to the Bolivarian Revolution. In addition, because President Chávez saw the hand of the United States government as behind the coup, he began to search for alternative weapons systems that would reduce the military's dependence on U.S. armaments. Following his victories in the October 2004 regional and municipal elections, the president organized militias among unemployed slum dwellers.

President Chávez also changed official military doctrine, giving priority to preparing the armed forces for asymmetric warfare (*guerra asimétrica*). This doctrine recognized that Venezuela could not resist a conventional invasion by the United States (now seen as the country's most likely military opponent). Instead, the armed forces would refine their capability to wage insurgency. Once troops of the "empire" (the new designation for the United States) had landed on Venezuelan soil, the militias (asymmetric forces) would conduct guerrilla warfare and wear down the will of the American people to support the invasion. This doctrine also gave the Chávez government a national security rationale for arming forces dominated by the urban poor, the social strata most supportive of the Bolivarian Revolution. As of early 2008, President Chávez was well into reorganizing the military for use against his international and domestic foes. He appeared justified in counting on this force to support whatever policies he chooses during his second presidential term and to protect the Bolivarian Revolution against all enemies, domestic or foreign.

The ecclesiastical hierarchy, in spite of being uncomfortable with AD's anti-clerical tradition, supported post-1958 liberal democracy.[36] Church leaders viewed the Punto Fijo regime as preferable to any other viable alternative in spite of shortcomings that included corruption, politicization of resource distribution, and favoritism toward the two dominant political parties. In the 1970s and 1980s, the Jesuit think tank Centro Guimilla leveled especially biting criticism at AD and COPEI. After the urban riots of February 1989 and the two unsuccessful coup attempts in 1992, the Episcopal Conference issued statements intended to put distance between the church and the neoliberal policies of President Pérez. The second Caldera government, even after it restored neoliberal policies with Agenda Venezuela, received strong backing from the Catholic bishops. In 1997, Pope John Paul II dispatched an emissary to Caracas in an unsuccessful attempt to heal the breach between Rafael Caldera and COPEI. This division dramatically weakened Venezuela's Christian Democratic movement and facilitated the rise of Hugo Chávez.

Venezuela's Roman Catholic bishops viewed the rise of Hugo Chávez with alarm. His preference for militant Marxists, whose antagonism toward parochial education predated the revolution of October 1945, resurrected almost forgotten enemies from past church-state confrontations. Although the president's one-time second in command, Francisco Arias Cárdenas, had studied for the priesthood, the bishops had few contacts inside Chávez's inner circle. In hope of reaching a modus vivendi with the popular president, church leaders took no official position in the referendum in which the 1999 Constitution was approved, although some clergy argued that ratification would be a first step toward depriving the church of cultural influence.

Church-state relations were cool but polite in 2000 and 2001 as the government veered to the left and laid the groundwork for tighter control. On April 12, 2002, several well-known individuals associated with the Roman Catholic hierarchy appeared at the proclamation of Pedro Carmona's short-lived provisional government. President Chávez was outraged and accused the Church of being anti-revolutionary. For a time he contrasted the Church's behavior with the more supportive stance of Venezuela's evangelical Protestant movement, which was making significant inroads among slum dwellers in the large cities. However, President Chávez's enthusiasm for the evangelicals evaporated when the Reverend Pat Robertson, a well-known fundamentalist pastor in the United States, suggested on his *700 Club* television program that President Bush should use the Central Intelligence Agency to "assassinate" the Venezuelan president.

To summarize, relations between the Roman Catholic Church and the Venezuelan government deteriorated sharply between 2000 and 2007. On January 10, 2007, during President Chávez's second inaugural address, the president turned to the bishop of Coro—a critic of the government's decision to terminate the broadcasting license of an opposition television station —and opined that he would see the bishop in hell. The potential alliance between evangelicals and the Bolivarian Revolution stalled before gaining any political significance. Finally, in an unanticipated shift of strategy, President Chávez attempted to undermine the Roman Catholic Church and evangelical Protestant movements by importing and subsidizing *babalaos,* or shamans of the Santería religion, from Cuba.

Private sector interests in Venezuela are diverse, ranging from local agribusinesses to multinational manufacturers. During the *trienio;* the three years from 1945 to 1948, businesspeople were united in their opposition to the emphasis on regulation and statist economic intervention of AD's reformist Marxism. Like the military and the church, however, the business community accommodated to party-dominated democracy and prospered between 1958 and 1998. Its two hundred individual groups are organized under an umbrella organization, FEDECAMARAS, which is dominated by four pivotal sectors: industry, trade, cattle, and agriculture. Each possesses its own chamber: CONINDUSTRIA (the Consejo Venezolano de la Industria or Venezuelan Industry Council) for industry, CONSECOMERCIO (the Consejo Nacional del Comercio y los Servicios or National Commerce and Services Council) for commerce, FENAGAN (the Federación Nacional de Ganaderos or National Federation of Cattle Ranchers) for cattle, and FEDEAGRO (the Confederación de Asociaciones de Productores Agropecuarios or Confederation of Associations of Agricultural Producers) for agriculture. Because these key interests have different and sometimes conflicting priorities, the single-interest or intermediate chambers are as important as FEDECAMARAS as centers of political demands.

Private business leaders, as suggested earlier, initially believed that they could embed themselves within the Chávez administration, as they had with Punto Fijo–era governments. Thus, many supported Chávez's presidential candidacy in 1998. When forming his first cabinet, however, President Chávez rejected private sector candidates for the important posts of minister of the Treasury and president of the Central Bank, and only one businessperson served in that cabinet. After the 2000 presidential elections, the government seldom consulted the private sector and assumed ever more control over the economy. Relations between President Chávez and the business community turned frigid after Pedro Carmona agreed to serve as provisional president following the coup of April 11, 2002. Following his reinstatement, President Chávez ignored FEDECAMARAS and undermined its influence. For a time he even favored multinational corporations over local businesses interests.

Multinational corporations have long been important players in domestic Venezuelan politics. After President Pérez implemented his Gran Viraje in 1989, a torrent of foreign capital flowed into the country. It fled following the unsuccessful coups in 1992 and returned in force during 1996, when the state petroleum company signaled a willingness to accept overseas assistance to implement plans that would double Venezuela's oil production capability. Capital flight began anew in 1998 and accelerated in 1999, when President Chávez rejected consultation with business leaders. Nevertheless, the multinational oil companies continued upgrading their already large investments in facilities to process Venezuela's massive reserves of viscous oil, even after the government tripled the rate at which they were taxed.

President Chávez remains uncomfortable with his country's dependence on multinational oil companies based in the United States and Western Europe. The Orinoco Tar Belt of Venezuela holds vast reserves of viscous oil that must be processed and upgraded before it can be used. The high price of petroleum makes such processing economically feasible. Multinational corporations such as Exxon Mobil, Royal Dutch / Shell, and ConocoPhillips have invested billions of dollars in facilities to process heavy oil for commercial use. In his inaugural address of January 10, 2007, President Chávez announced that his government would be taking control of the operations of the multinational oil companies in the Orinoco Tar Belt. Even before this announcement, President Chávez stepped up his efforts to tap alternative sources of investment and technical expertise in Brazil, Iran, and Russia. He demanded that the subsidiaries of the multinational oil corporations operating in the Orinoco Tar Belt cede majority ownership to the Venezuelan state oil company PDVSA. Two of the largest multinationals, ConocoPhillips and Exxon Mobil, refused and asked for compensation.[37] The Chinese moved into the picture in September 2007, when they promised to invest US$10 billion to extract petroleum from the Orinoco Tar Belt and refine it for use in China.

Organized labor and peasants, two important associational interest groups, began participating in Venezuelan politics in the late 1930s. A third associational interest group, professionals, traces its origins to the nineteenth century. AD and COPEI organized workers and peasants as part of their mobilization strategy in the 1940s to wrest political power from the entrenched Andean cabal. During the Punto Fijo era, the two dominant political parties incorporated their labor and peasant federations into the policy-making process. Unionized workers and peasants, as well as allied professionals, were subject to party discipline. Failure to comply with instructions from one's political party risked sanctions and possibly expulsion. Expulsion from the party entailed loss of leadership positions within the relevant federation and possibly one's ability to earn a living.

Following approval of the 1999 Constitution, the leading labor organization, the Confederación de Trabajadores de Venezuela (CTV; Venezuelan Confederation of Workers), opened negotiations with President Chávez. CTV leaders sought a deal whereby they would eliminate the influence of AD and COPEI in their member unions. In return, the CTV would be certified as the official voice of organized labor. President Chávez rejected the idea of an autonomous labor movement and began to organize his own Bolivarian trade unions. The CTV then joined with FEDECAMARAS and other opponents of the government in a series of strikes that convulsed the country in December 2002 and January 2003. In March of 2003, after breaking the final and most virulent wave of strikes, President Chávez discharged 17,000 workers belonging to FEDEPETROL (the Federación de Trabajadores Petroleros or Federation of Petroleum Workers), the most influential union of the CTV. The president of the CTV, Carlos Ortega, went into exile. He returned to Venezuela less than a year later. Ortega was captured in Caracas and sentenced in December 2005 to 15 years in prison for treason. Eight months later, he escaped from jail under mysterious circumstances. The CTV carries on, and it backed the candidacy of Governor Manual Rosales in the 2006 presidential election, while the Bolivarian trade unions supported the reelection of President Chávez. The CTV is a shadow of its former self, and the Bolivarian trade unions are creatures of the government with no autonomy.

Until the mid-1980s, the urban poor were only weakly integrated into Punto Fijo democracy. Political parties with the greatest appeal to slum dwellers early in the Punto Fijo era lost out to AD and COPEI, neither of which crafted institutions capable of attending to the interests of slum dwellers. The political demand-making structures that crystallized among slum dwellers were different from the party-dominated associations of workers, peasants, and professionals. Slum dwellers organized out of frustrations caused by the failure of AD and COPEI to use the state's ample revenues during the petroleum bonanza to improve their living conditions. Initially, the most important organization to represent the urban poor was the Centro al Servicio de la Acción Popular (CESAP; Center at the Service of Popular Action). During the 1980s, CESAP settled on the strategy of working within the existing political regime. This choice undermined its legitimacy when the second Pérez government and the Caldera government adopted neoliberal policies. This convinced the urban poor that when resources contracted, Punto Fijo elites would take back the meager benefits they had given.[38]

The perception that AD and COPEI cared little for poor people underpinned the massive support that slum dwellers gave to Hugo Chávez in the presidential elections of 1998, 2000, and 2006 and in the recall referendum of 2004. Soon after taking office in 1999, the president began organizing supporters in the slums into diverse Círculos Bolivarianos (Bolivarian Circles). On one hand, they taught young women to sew and manage small businesses, and they provided needed child care. On the other, they assisted the government in identifying its supporters and opponents. There was much concern among opposition leaders that the Círculos Bolivarianos were precursors of institutions that would exercise dictatorial control over the urban poor, but the diverse character of the circles precludes their use for this purpose.

Círculos Bolivarianos remain active in many locales, but other revolutionary organizations such as the electoral Comando Maisanta, the irregular asymmetric warfare battalions, and the communal councils have become the cutting edge of the political regime in the slums. Finally, the resource-distributing *misiones* (missions) controlled directly out of the president's office have established regional centers in most poor neighborhoods. Operating under the powers given to him by the Ley Habilitante of January 2007, President Chávez appointed a commission that in July 2007 proposed constitutional reforms that were intended to streamline this potpourri of overlapping bureaucracies and harness them for the task of building twenty-first-century socialism.

Political Parties and Elections: What Kind of Interest Aggregation?

Events between 1998 and 2007 radically transformed the Venezuelan political party system. AD and COPEI, as we have seen, dominated national politics between 1958 and 1998. Both had strong indigenous roots, although the former developed an ideological affinity with European Social Democrats and the latter identified with the Christian Democrats. For many years, AD and COPEI efficiently performed the functions most often associated with modern political parties: mobilizing supporters, recruiting individuals to fill government positions, mediating the demands of competing interests, and creating symbols that strengthened support for the political regime. However, in 2006, during the presidential election campaign, identification with the AD party hovered around 5 percent, and COPEI commanded even less support. Both were shells of the organizations that had established and dominated Venezuela's competitive centrist party system.

Other political parties played important roles during the Punto Fijo era, but until the elections of 1993 only the nominees of AD and COPEI were able to win the presidency. The Unión Republicana Democrática (URD; Democratic Republican Union) was a personalistic movement that drew support from urban professionals and slum dwellers during the 1960s before internal conflicts led to its demise. In 1967, Luis Beltrán Prieto Figueroa, a founding member of AD, split from the party following divisive primary elections. Prieto founded the Movimiento Electoral Popular (MEP; Popular Electoral Movement), which had fleeting success among the urban poor, but five years later most MEP voters returned to AD. The third political party of the Punto Fijo era, the Movimento al Socialismo (MAS; Movement to Socialism) began as a faction inside of the Partido Comunista de Venezuela (PCV; Venezuelan Communist Party). It was dominated by younger militants who had split from the PCV when the founding generation supported the Soviet invasion of Czechoslovakia in 1968. The defection caused the demise of the PCV as a competitive electoral force. Finally, yet another group broke away from the PCV and formed Causa Radical (Causa R; Radical Cause). Over two decades, Causa R built support within organized labor in the state of Bolívar and among the urban poor of Caracas. The party enjoyed little success until the presidential elections of 1993, when it mounted a strong but unsuccessful challenge to established political forces. In the aftermath of this defeat, Causa R's leaders fell to quarreling among themselves, and their supporters drifted into the Bolivarian camp.

The loss of support by Venezuela's traditional political parties allowed Hugo Chávez to collapse the traditional political party system. In 1997, he organized the Movimiento Quinta República (MVR; Fifth Republic Movement) as an electoral vehicle to support his presidential candidacy. At that time, Chávez was running a distant second in the public opinion polls to Irene Sáez, the former beauty queen who had been elected mayor of Chacao, an upscale municipality in eastern Caracas. Sáez's popularity began to decline in early 1998, with a dramatic plunge occurring in June, when she accepted the presidential nomination of COPEI. Support for Hugo Chávez rose in tandem with Sáez's decline. Chávez assembled an anti-establishment coalition of 13 political parties known as the Polo Patriótico (Patriotic Pole). The "Pole" included political parties that were little more than hollow shells —the PCV, URD, and MEP—and remnants of other challengers that AD and COPEI had defeated and marginalized. Two political parties that joined the Polo Patriótico retained important electoral followings: the MAS and Patria para Todos (PPT; Fatherland for All). PPT was the majority faction of the former Causa R. In May 1998, public opinion polls showed Hugo Chávez pulling ahead of all other presidential contenders.

Party leaders, labor bosses, and sectors of the middle class mobilized to defeat Hugo Chávez once they realized the magnitude of his appeal. In the closing days of the 1998 presidential election campaign, Chávez's opponents coalesced behind the presidential candidacy of independent Enrique Salas Römer, the progressive governor of Venezuela's richest and most highly industrialized state, Carabobo. Earlier in the electoral campaign, the once-dominant AD had committed the greatest blunder in its history. Party elders nominated septuagenarian Luis Alfaro Ucero, the AD secretary general, as its presidential candidate. These same elders jettisoned Alfaro for Salas when Alfaro's support never passed 10 percent in the public opinion polls. Hugo Chávez won the December 6, 1998, presidential election with just under 57 percent of the popular vote.

Twenty months later, on July 31, 2000, Venezuela held elections for the first time under the 1999 Constitution. In what came to be known as the mega-elections, voters chose the president, all governors and mayors, and all members of the new unicameral National Assembly. AD and COPEI declined to contest the presidency. Chávez's only significant challenger was Lieutenant Colonel Francisco Arias Cárdenas, his second in command during the unsuccessful military coup of February 4, 1992. Arias had split with Chávez over the president's leftward drift and anti-clericalism. He received one-third of the total presidential vote, and Chávez captured 60 percent, slightly more than in 1998. The MVR secured 46 percent of the seats in the National Assembly, while AD and COPEI together held only 21 percent. The remaining third of the seats in the National Assembly were controlled either by allies of the MVR or by regional political parties that had backed Arias Cárdenas. Hugo Chávez's supporters controlled the National Assembly, but significantly, they lacked the two-thirds majority necessary to change the Constitution.

Institutions supportive of the government increased their domination over the party system between the megaelections of July 2000 and presidential elections of December 3, 2006. AD and COPEI, as discussed earlier, were shadows of the national political parties that had dominated Venezuela for more than four decades. The MAS declined, suffering from the perception that its leaders were opportunistic and corrupt. One new opposition party, Primero Justicia (Justice First), did develop a loyal following. Support for Primero Justicia remains concentrated in the upper-middle-class neighborhoods of Eastern Caracas and a few other cities of the center region. Un Nuevo Tiempo (New Time), the political party of presidential candidate Governor Manual Rosales, served as a mechanism for voters who opposed President Chávez to express their opposition. Un Nuevo Tiempo began the 2006 presidential election campaign with an organization that was confined largely to Governor Rosales's home state of Zulia. Efforts to transform Un Nuevo Tiempo into an opposition party capable of challenging the chavistas on a national scale have been largely successful.

In the early years of the Bolivarian Republic, when the defeated opposition parties enjoyed more support, they coalesced as a loose umbrella organization, the Coordinadora Democratica (Democratic Coordination). The Coordinadora Democratica spearheaded the previously discussed failed efforts to force President Chávez's resignation in 2002 and 2003 as well as the unsuccessful revocatory referendum of August 15, 2004.[39] The fallout from these failures paved the way for resounding electoral victories by President Chávez and his allies in the regional and local elections of October 2004 and August 2005. Public opinion polls in advance of the December 4, 2005, elections for the National Assembly indicated that opposition voters were disheartened. Many of them planned to abstain, and it appeared that the MVR and its allies would win up to 80 percent of the National Assembly seats. Opposition leaders decided to boycott the election in the hope that their failure to participate would discredit the results. However, the most important consequence of the decision to boycott the elections was that pro-Chávez candidates captured every one of the 167 seats in the National Assembly. The opposition was left without any voice to challenge the government in the national legislature.

The 2006 presidential election was free, if not entirely fair. The government used its patronage and domination of political communication in ways that severely disadvantaged the opposition. Nevertheless, international observers declared that voters were not coerced by the government and that the

National Electoral Council tabulated the ballots accurately. The result was not encouraging for the opposition; President Chávez's percentage of the total vote increased by 4 percent over what he had received in 2000, and the rate of abstention declined from 44 percent to 25 percent. Table 12.1 shows the results of Venezuelan elections from the presidential election of December 1988 through the presidential election of December 2006.

President Chávez and leaders of the political opposition maneuvered to consolidate their forces in anticipation of the decrees that would implement twenty-first-century socialism. On several occasions following his January 10 inauguration, President Chávez repeated that he expected the minor politi-

Table 12.1. National, Congressional, Regional, and Local Election Results in Venezuela, 1988–2005

Month/ Year	Type	Winner, Party	Percentage of Vote	Percentage of Punto Fijo Regime Ruling Parties	Percentage of Anti–Punto Fijo Regime Parties	Percentage Abstention
12/1988	Presidential	Pérez, AD	53	94	6	18
12/1988	Legislative	AD	43	74	27	18
12/1989	Regional/Local	AD	40	71	39	55
12/1992	Regional/Local	COPEI	42	78	32	60
12/1993	Congressional	AD	24	46	54	40
12/1993	Presidential	Caldera, CNE/MAS	31	46	54	40
12/1995	Regional/Local	AD	35	56	44	55
11/1998	Congressional	AD	25	37	63	46
12/1998	Presidential	Chávez, MVR	56	11	91	36
7/2000	Presidential	Chávez, MVR	59	0	100	44
	National Assembly	MVR	46[a]	21[a]	79[a]	44
12/2000	Municipal Council	MVR	39[a]	28[a]	72[a]	76
10/2004	Gubernatorial	MVR/allies	21/23	9[a]	91[a]	
	Mayoral	MVR/allies	238/335	29[a]	71[a]	55
8/2005	Municipal Council[b]	MVR/allies	1911/2389	17[c]	80[a]	68
	National Assembly	MVR/allies		Abstained	100[a]	

Source: Author's calculations based on official statistics of the Consejo Supremo Electoral (1958–98) and the Consejo Nacional Electoral (2000, 2005).
[a]Percentage of seats. Party alliances varied from electoral district to electoral district, so it is not possible to calculate the national percentage of the National Assembly vote received by each political party.
[b]Does not include election results for neighborhood councils.
[c]Three percent of the seats were won by local candidates whose ties to the government and the opposition are unknown.

cal parties (the PCV, the PPT, and PODEMOS—Poder Democrático y Social or Democratic and Social Power) that had supported him in the 2006 presidential election to dissolve themselves and merge into the new Partido Unido de la Revolución Socialista (United Party of the Socialist Revolution).[40] When PODEMOS, the PCV, and the PPT dragged their heels, President Chávez made it clear that he would not wait indefinitely and that there would be no place for independent parties in the new socialist government. Governor Rosales was almost as dogmatic as the president in attempting to merge the opposition into his party, Un Tiempo Nuevo. Some opposition leaders indicated their interest in joining, but others spoke openly of crafting a nonconfessional alternative similar to the Partido Popular in Spain. Resistance to Governor Rosales's call for unity is yet another indication that President Chávez's opponents will have great difficulty in presenting a coherent alternative to the government.

The Bolivarian State

Venezuelan state organization has been in flux since 2000, when the shift to institutions envisioned by the Constitution of 1999 began. This Constitution mandates a presidential system with five separate branches of government: the executive, the legislative, the judicial, the Electoral Power, and the Citizen Power. Twenty-three states and a capital district comprise the polity, whose leaders have yet to agree on the balance of power among the central, regional, and local governments. Under the previous 1961 Constitution, especially after the reforms of 1989, the balance of power had grown more decentralized. The 1999 Constitution retains this decentralization by providing for a Federal Council of Government to oversee relations among the central government, regions, and municipalities. Nevertheless, for reasons peculiar to the unitary, centralistic tensions in Hispanic and Roman Catholic constitutional development, Venezuela's subnational politics have always exhibited a preference for centralization and national elites. Following his inauguration on January 10, 2007, President Chávez, as discussed earlier, appointed a commission for constitutional reform, giving it the charge to restructure the state to better implement socialism for the twenty-first century, but the centralizing recommendations of this commission were put on hold after voters rejected modifications to the 1999 Constitution on December 2, 2007.

The National Executive

The national executive of the 1999 Constitution is more powerful than its predecessor, which was itself viewed as strong. A popularly elected president presides over the central government and is eligible for election to a second consecutive six-year term. The president is commander-in-chief of the armed forces and appoints a cabinet composed of 25 ministers, who can be removed by the president.[41] The constellation of cabinet ministries, ranging from the powerful Ministry of Interior Relations and Justice to the recently created Ministry of Food, reflects the Bolivarian preference for state control. The president is also empowered to name and remove at will a vice president, who assumes the presidency if that office falls vacant.

A unique feature of the Chávez presidency has been its reliance on the ad hoc *misiones* to allocate resources. From the beginning, President Chávez was clear that he considered the Punto Fijo bureaucracy corrupt and incompetent, and he looked for ways to bypass entrenched public administrators. His solution was to mobilize regional military commanders to allocate resources. After the unsuccessful military coup of April 2002, however, President Chávez was less sanguine about entrusting the armed forces with administering the state. Instead, he gave this responsibility to the newly created *misiones,* controlled directly out of his office or through the Ministry of the Interior and Justice. For example, President Chávez ignored the Ministry of Education when he created special programs to increase literacy (Misión Robinson), expand high school diploma programs (Misión Ribas), and establish revolutionary universities (Misión Sucre). Other high-profile *misiones* have developed programs to provide services to the slums (Misión Barrio Adentro), distribute food to the poor at subsidized prices in popular markets (Misión Mercal), and plan socialist cities (Misión Villanueva). The official Web site of the Venezuelan government listed 21 such *misiones* (as of March 2008). Most funding for the *misiones* comes to the president directly from the state petroleum company PDVSA rather than passing through the Central Bank, as stipulated by the banking laws passed during the neoliberal reforms of the 1990s. The budgets of the *misiones* are closely guarded, and President Chávez can draw freely on the more than US$40 billion in reserves that the government is estimated to hold abroad. During the election campaigns leading up to the revocatory referendum of 2004 and the presidential election of 2006, resources were allocated by these *misiones* to groups whose votes President Chávez sought.

Legislative and Judicial Power

The 1999 Constitution substituted a unicameral National Assembly for the bicameral Congress mandated by the 1961 Constitution. The most important reason for eliminating the Senate was the populist ideology of the Bolivarian Revolution, which viewed any institution that represented territorial interests as an unacceptable limitation on the power of *el soberano*. Indeed, all institutional modifications by President Chávez have included the elimination of veto points as a principal objective. Consequently, the 1999 Constitution gives the national legislature less autonomy and power than its predecessor. It allows legislation to be introduced into the National Assembly from seven sources: the national executive, the Delegative Commission of the National Assembly, the Supreme Tribunal, the Electoral Power, the Citizen Power, any three members of the National Assembly, or a petition bearing the signatures of 0.1 percent of registered voters. Should the National Assembly prove recalcitrant, the president can dissolve it and call for new elections. As well as confirming the Bolivarian preference for executive control, the weakening of the legislative branch in the 1999 Constitution reflects the disrepute into which the national congress had fallen at the end of the Punto Fijo era.

The unicameral National Assembly is made up of 167 deputies who are elected by universal, direct, personal secret vote. Each of the 23 states and the Capital District elect 3 deputies, as does the Amerindian community. The remaining 92 deputies are apportioned among the states on the basis of population. Sixty percent of each state's total deputies are elected in single-member, winner-take-all districts, and the other 40 percent are chosen by party list based on proportional representation. All deputies serve five-year terms and must appoint a replacement *(suplente)* to stand in for them in during periods of incapacity or absence (Article 186). Deputies can be reelected on up to two occasions (Article 192). Forces supportive of President Chávez have controlled the National Assembly since the megaelections of July 31, 2000. As discussed earlier, the MVR and its allies gained roughly 55 percent of the seats at that time. The current National Assembly has no opposition deputies.

The 1999 Constitution creates the position of National Assembly president and provides for two vice presidents. It also sets the number of permanent commissions at a maximum of 15. This limitation reflects President Chávez's belief that the numerous permanent commissions in the previous bicameral Congress had evolved into privileged sinecures from which corrupt party leaders peddled their influence for personal gain.

The 1999 Constitution places the Supreme Judicial Tribunal at the apex of the judiciary. The tribunal meets in several kinds of sessions: plenary, political-administrative, electoral, and those that deal with civil, penal, and social matters. Justices of the Supreme Judicial Tribunal are elected for terms of 12 years without the possibility of reelection and are forbidden to engage in partisan political activity during their time in office. Indeed, the 1999 Constitution goes to great lengths to shield the entire judiciary from the influence of political parties. For example, competitive examinations are required for entry to or promotion in the judicial system. Finally, the Constitution of 1999, like its predecessor, establishes separate courts for the military. Going back to the Castilian tradition of the military *fuero* (privilege), this system protects members of the armed forces from being tried by civilian courts.

The Constitution of 1999 was implemented in ways that limited the independence and power of the judiciary. Even so, from 1999 to 2004 the Supreme Court was equally divided between supporters and opponents of the Bolivarian Revolution. In December 2004, the National Assembly expanded the Supreme Court from 20 to 32 members, ostensibly to reduce the workload of individual justices. The Assembly gave itself greater authority to shape the Supreme Court (including adding more justices) by rewriting the applicable Organic Law.[42] This change tipped the partisan balance of the court to one with a pro-government majority in 2005. Since then, the Supreme Court has rubber-stamped the positions of the national executive.

Institutional Innovations: The Electoral Power and the Citizen Power

The 1999 Constitution establishes the Electoral Power as a separate branch of government in reaction to the Punto Fijo practice of allowing political parties to dominate the Supreme Electoral Council and oversee the tabulation of voting results. Party control of the Supreme Electoral Council played an important role in maintaining the electoral domination of AD and COPEI. These two were the only political parties with organizations in every municipality, and there is evidence that they sometimes divided among themselves the votes of third political parties at polling places where smaller parties had no observers. The worst excesses of this abuse occurred in the 1993 national elections, but five years later, the reorganized Electoral Council eliminated these problems when they mobilized a random sample of citizens as poll watchers. The megaelections of 2000 employed this system, as did the presidential recall referendum held on August 15, 2004, and the presidential election of December 3, 2006.

The independent Electoral Power envisioned in the 1999 Constitution fell under the control of President Chávez and his supporters at the beginning of the Fifth Republic. The government named talented and capable individuals to the Consejo Nacional Electoral (CNE; National Electoral Council) prior to the megaelections of 2000, but with some justification, the opposition viewed the Council as biased in favor of the government. In 2003 and 2004, when the opposition was gathering signatures for the revocatory referendum to remove President Chávez, the impartiality of the CNE became a critical political issue. The issue of CNE impartiality reached the boiling point when exit polling by the opposition suggested that the referendum had succeeded. The CNE, in contrast, certified results showing that roughly 60 percent of voters favored the retention of President Chávez. The Carter Center and other international observers found the official results valid, a judgment that many in the opposition never accepted.

The Citizen Power, a second new branch of government and a kind of ombudsman or watchdog, was established in reaction to the widely held belief that Punto Fijo governments had become abusive and corrupt. The main authority of this branch of government is the Moral Republican Council, an institution composed of three individuals: the public prosecutor (*fiscal*), the general comptroller (*comptrolador general de la república*), and an official known as the ombudsman (*defensor del pueblo*). The ombudsman "promotes, defends and watches out for abuses of constitutional rights and guarantees." By a two-thirds vote, the National Assembly designates the ombudsman, who serves for a single period of seven years. The authority and influence of the Citizen Power remained murky during the first seven years that the Constitution of 1999 was in force. Following his inauguration in January 2007, President Chávez stated that strengthening the Citizen Power would be given high priority when revising the 1999 Constitution.

Regional and Local Government

Venezuela's polity has been highly centralized since its independence. The lone important effort to empower subnational governments came during the final decade of the Punto Fijo period. Two conditions set the stage for this development. First, the leaders of AD and COPEI had promised to strengthen municipal governments as part of the process of implementing the 1961 Constitution. When the political regime came under attack from leftist insurgents during the first three liberal democratic administrations, however, the central government postponed any state reforms that might have interfered with its ability to maintain order in regions and the municipalities. Insurgency ceased to be a problem after 1974, and demands for decentralization surfaced almost immediately. Second, the Constitution of 1961 provided few points for citizen access within the centrally controlled regional and local governments. Until the late 1980s, Caracas controlled resource distribution, which was fueled by income from petroleum sales and dampened demands for subnational participation. Once petroleum income declined, those demands gathered force. However, the administration of President Jaime Lusinchi (1984–89) dealt with reductions in state income by tightening centralized control.[43] Regional and local leaders reacted to Lusinchi's policy and poor economic performance by intensifying their demands for decentralization.

President Carlos Andrés Pérez used dissatisfaction with government following the *Caracazo* to pass unprecedented decentralization reforms in 1989. Additional reforms followed in 1993 under the interim government of Ramón Velásquez. The centerpiece of these reforms was the popular election and empowerment of regional governors, who had previously been appointed by the president. In addition, the reforms created the elected posts of mayor and neighborhood (*parroquia*) councils. They also included an important economic component. The Constitution of 1961 stipulated that at least 15 percent of the national government's regular earnings was to be transferred to the states, with 30 percent of these of these transfers divided equally among the state governments, and the remainder was to be allocated based on population. The Organic Decentralization Law mandated that allocations to the states from the central government be increased 1 percent per year between 1991 and 1994 until they reached 20 percent. The municipalities also received in their transfer accounts a percentage of the state's regular income, starting at 10 percent in 1990, with a requirement that they reach 20 percent by 2000. The fiscal structure under which these changes occurred remained consistent with the Constitution of 1961, which directed that budgetary compensation to the regions be provided on a per capita basis.[44]

Advocates of a powerful central state immediately began looking for ways to weaken the decentralization reform. President Rafael Caldera's supporters had little strength in the regions and municipalities during his second administration (1994–99). The Caldera government compensated for this weakness by refusing many requests for the resource transfers and decision-making powers that states and municipalities had anticipated that they would receive under the decentralization reforms. Mayors and governors were forced into an uneasy coexistence with a hostile national government. During the 1998 presidential election campaign, Hugo Chávez veiled his position on decentralization. Soon after taking office, however, he decreed several measures that reduced financing to the regions and municipalities. The 1999 Constitution retained the traditional definition of Venezuela as a federalist state, but it contained provisions that weakened the state and municipal powers that the decentralization reforms had augmented.

The 1999 Constitution intended that the Federal Council of Government, composed of representatives of the three levels of government, would provide channels through which subnational governments could influence policy making in Caracas. The legislation that would have established the Federal Council of Government was not passed, and the Inter-regional Compensation Fund, foreseen by drafters of the 1999 Constitution as a replacement for the Fondo Intergubernamental para la Descentralización (Intergovernmental Fund for Decentralization), was never established. Most resource allocation to the states and municipalities between 2002 and 2007 was accomplished through the previously discussed *misiones,* shielded by constitutional provisions that effectively barred the public from finding out how they occurred. In July 2007, President Chávez presented constitutional reforms that restructured the process of resource allocation to the regions and localities envisioned in the 1999 Constitution. Following the rejection of these reforms by voters in December 2007, the most militant of Chávez's supporters urged him to make these changes through other means.

Conclusion

The struggle for democracy in Venezuela is multifaceted and, in some senses, exceptional. Lessons learned in the 1940s and 1950s primed leaders of the dominant and militantly socialist AD party to open political space for all but the most intransigent of their domestic rivals in the 1960s. Presidents Rómulo Betancourt (1959–64) and Raúl Leoni (1964–69) agreed to a constitution (1961) that mandated representative institutions and to veto points that restricted the ability of their political party to implement its militantly leftist agenda. This political regime respected diverse political interests and attempted to reconcile them in a representative democratic manner. Venezuela's reconciliation regime survived when other democracies of the period gave way to bureaucratic authoritarianism. In the late 1980s, however, when the aging leaders of AD and COPEI failed to open new channels for political participation or relinquish power, new generations began to look for alternatives to the established political parties. In addition, economic decline accelerated in the 1990s, which increased alienation because the downwardly mobile middle sectors and the poor concluded that no one was looking out for them. Most blamed their plight on the two dominant political parties, their allies in business and organized labor, and the reconciliation approach to governing that prioritized interclass cooperation. Alienation surfaced in the mid-1990s in public opinion polls, which found that 80 percent of Venezuelans wanted a different kind of democracy.[45] On the other hand, the overwhelming majority have long expressed a preference for democracy over any other form of government.[46]

President Hugo Chávez described himself as a different type of democrat in his 1998 presidential election campaign and in his inaugural address of February 2, 1999. He proclaimed that his power and authority came from *el soberano,* which included supportive sectors of the middle class and "enlightened" forces in the private sector. After the failed coup of April 2002 and the demonstrations of December 2002–January 2003, however, President Chávez equated *el soberano* with the underprivileged, especially the urban poor. In the political turmoil leading up to the revocatory referendum of August 2004, relations with the opposition (largely from the middle and upper middle classes) became so tense and conflictive that civil discourse all but disappeared. When critics accused the government of perpetrating fraud in the revocatory referendum, President Chávez explicitly excluded them from his interpretation of *el soberano,* labeling opposition leaders oligarchs and exploiters. Governor Manuel Rosales's public recognition of his defeat at the hands of President Chávez in the December 2006 presidential elections did little to change this situation.

Between 1999 and 2007, the Chávez government co-opted many institutions whose autonomy is the hallmark of liberal democracy. The president's 2007 inaugural address described these actions as creating a base on which to build socialism. The day after this second inauguration, President Chávez requested a Ley Habilitante that would send Congress into recess for 18 months and give him authority to legislate by decree in 13 critical policy areas: transformation of state institutions; popular participation; public functions and the economic and social environment; public and private finances (including insurance and taxes); citizen and juridical security; science and technology; national health; security and national defense; transportation and service infrastructure; telecommunications and information technology; the penitentiary system; regionalization; and territorial organization and food security. The National Assembly passed the Ley Habilitante at a special outdoor gathering in Plaza Bolívar on January 31, 2007.

After taking office on January 10, 2007, President Chávez opined that during the previous Constituent Assembly "oligarchic forces" had "infiltrated" their ideas into sections of the 1999 Constitution. He promised to change these sections, using the Ley Habilitante to rewrite the Constitution. The president named Celia Flores, president of the National Assembly, as chairperson of the Presidential Commission for Constitutional Reform. The document that emerged in July 2007 from The Flores Commission, and was rejected by voters in the December 2007 referendum, closely resembled its Cuban counterpart. There were few, if any, checks on the national executive—the power President Chávez views as embodying the will of el soberano—and regional and local political institutions would have been weakened in the short run. In the long run, they would have been likely to be replaced by communal councils engineered to encourage citizen participation and facilitate control from the center. These communal councils would have interacted directly with representatives of the national government, some of whom would be embedded in presidential misiones and others in reconstructed central bureaucracies.

Hugo Chávez has never modified his view that the institutions of Punto Fijo democracy, including those that reformers created through the decentralization reforms of 1989 and 1993, were impediments to the expression of the popular will. He has excoriated social democracy as a pale version of savage capitalism. From the Chávez perspective, decentralization reforms were designed to prop up a degenerate political regime, and they ended up creating new groups of corrupt politicians in the regions and municipios. Even after his supporters captured 21 of the 23 governorships and 80 percent of the mayors' offices in the regional and local elections of October 2004, President

Chávez has had little use for elected local officials. He views them as road-blocks to overcoming behavior that ingrained misery and poverty in the country over 40 years of liberal democracy.

With some exceptions, President Chávez has respected basic human rights and freedom of speech, even those of his opponents. Nevertheless, government power has been used to discredit opposition groups and undermine their capabilities to organize. This approach is unlikely to be reversed during the 2007–13 constitutional period. On the day before his inauguration, President Chávez called for a constitutional amendment that would allow for unlimited reelection. This change was recommended by the Flores Commission for constitutional reform. On more than one occasion, President Chávez has stated that he is in campaign mode for the 2012 presidential election, with an announced goal of winning more than 80 percent of the votes.

To summarize, liberal democracy is all but dead in Venezuela. The delegative democracy of the Bolivarian period (1999–2006) is giving way to a populist electoral autocracy that only grudgingly concedes political space to its opponents. The future of processes that sustain meaningful democracy is uncertain. Perhaps the best thing that those who are uneasy with the course of the Bolivarian Revolution can do to ensure the survival of real democracy in Venezuela is to defend the right of all groups to act in their own interest and to insist that the freedom to organize and speak one's mind be respected. These actions will help to sustain conditions that, if nurtured, will provide the opportunity for opponents of the government to make their case in free and open competition. For their case to resonate with the electorate, however, opposition leaders must convince voters that they can govern more fairly and reduce poverty more effectively than the Chávez administration. Given the number of previously marginalized citizens who have benefited from the Bolivarian Revolution and the substantial resources available to President Hugo Chávez Frías, this will be no easy task.

PART IV

Conclusion

13

Three Decades since the Start of the Democratic Transitions

Jorge I. Domínguez

As this book is published, Latin America—long the land of the coup and the home of dictators—celebrates the 30th anniversary of the start of its democratic transitions. In 1978, the Dominican Republic led the way when international intervention prevented an election fraud that had sought to extend President Joaquín Balaguer's 12-year term in office, making way for the first opposition victory in a free presidential election under universal suffrage in that country's history—and the start of Latin America's transitions to democracy.

The next year, constitutional democratic rule began to take hold again in South America. Ecuador and Peru held free and fair elections won by the candidates most opposed to military rule. During the 1980s, democratically elected civilian presidents would replace one after another of South America's military rulers, culminating in Chile in the 1988 defeat of General Augusto Pinochet in a plebiscite that he had called, unsuccessfully seeking voter approval to lengthen his 17-year dictatorship. In the 1990s, as Central America's complex domestic and international wars ended, peace made possible the spread of constitutional government. Mexico's transition from authoritarian rule began in the late 1980s and culminated in 2000 with the first opposition victory in a presidential election since the Mexican Revolution in the second decade of the twentieth century. As the twenty-first century began, the only Spanish-American country without free multiparty national elections was Cuba.

As those transitions started, few imagined that they would take hold. All of Latin America was plunged into a catastrophic economic crisis in 1982–83. The performance of Latin America's economies during the 1980s was the worst since the worldwide economic depression of the 1930s. The 1990s brought a financial panic in 1994–95 that severely hurt the region, especially Argentina, Mexico, and Uruguay. Brazil suffered its own financial panic in 1999, and the Argentine economy imploded in 2001–2. For many years, the prevailing wisdom among scholars, politicians, journalists, and political activists was that the newly installed civilian presidents would fall prey to military coups or insurgencies provoked by economic or other calamities. Moreover, many of Latin America's elected civilian presidents turned out to be as corrupt and ineffective as many of their military predecessors had been, further fueling the expectation that military coups would again mark Latin America's public life.

And yet, since 1976 (the year of the successful military coup in Argentina), no military ruler has come to the presidency by coup in any Latin American country since the start of a country's democratic elections. In that same time frame, only one elected civilian president has been toppled by a military coup (Jamil Mahuad in Ecuador in 2000), but even he was replaced by his civilian vice president. Only one elected civilian president, Peru's Alberto Fujimori, sponsored a military coup (1992) to topple Congress and the Supreme Court, and he went on to govern autocratically until he was forced out in 2000, following blatantly fraudulent elections and a massive corruption scandal. Constitutional democratic rule was restored in Peru thereafter, as Carlos Iván Degregori notes in his chapter.

Nevertheless, few citizens or analysts feel celebratory about the quality and record of Latin America's democratic performance. Nor do I. Especially worrisome has been the interruption of constitutional presidencies short of a successful military coup or insurrection in 7 of the 10 Spanish-speaking South American countries and Brazil as well as in the Dominican Republic and Guatemala.[1] Presidential resignations under threat of constitutional impeachment and conviction or of comparable congressional actions or threat of action occurred in Brazil in 1992, Venezuela in 1993, Ecuador in 1997, Paraguay in 1999, and Peru in 2000. Presidential resignations in the face of massive public protests took place in Bolivia in 1985 and 2003, the Dominican Republic in 1994, Ecuador in 2000 and 2005, and Argentina in 2001. In Argentina, the crisis that led to the president's resignation in December 2001 also led to an outbreak of mass lootings for food, an instance of collective violence that momentarily shook the foundations of Argentine democracy.[2] Presidential resignations also took place in Argentina in 1989 to shorten the time to the installation of the newly elected president because of a major economic crisis and in Guatemala in 1993 upon the failure of a president-led coup against Congress and the courts. Serious attempts to impeach a president were also undertaken in the 1990s in Colombia and Nicaragua, though neither succeeded.

Since the late 1990s, moreover, disappointed and at times rightly angry voters have defeated governing political parties or coalitions, often in a decisive rejection of preceding policies and practices, at least once in Brazil and each of the Spanish-speaking South American countries except Chile and Paraguay, in Spanish-speaking Central America except El Salvador, and in the Dominican Republic. Such widespread electoral punishment had not occurred since the economic desperation that prevailed at the end of the 1980s.

As Javier Corrales notes in his chapter, several of these elections were also associated with a rejection of the market-oriented economic policies that had come to prevail in the region in the 1990s. Running on a platform markedly less market-oriented than the incumbent administrations were successful presidential candidates in 7 of the 10 Spanish-speaking South American countries plus Brazil: Hugo Chávez in Venezuela in 1998, Alejandro Toledo in Peru in 2001, Luiz Inácio "Lula" da Silva in Brazil in 2002, Néstor Kirchner in Argentina in 2003, Tabaré Vázquez in Uruguay in 2004, Evo Morales in Bolivia in 2005, Alan García in Peru again in 2006, and every successful presidential candidate in Ecuador since the mid-1980s. All but Kirchner ran from the opposition, thereby underlining the credibility of Latin America's democratic practices in these elections. The same process was in evidence for the election of Daniel Ortega in Nicaragua in 2006.

How, then, should we assess the record and the prospects for constructing stable and effective democratic governance in Latin America?

Civil-Military Relations

Military governments had performed poorly and were no longer desired. A key factor in the growth of democratic governance has been the rejection of such poorly performing governments. This section explores the waning of the military as the driving force of government rule as well as the persisting problems in civil-military relations as an entry point for a later discussion of political parties and democratic governance.

Not only have successful military coups in Latin America become a nearly extinct species, but military coup attempts have been decreasingly frequent. In 2000, there were military coup attempts in Ecuador, Paraguay, and Peru. Since that time, the only coup attempt occurred in Venezuela in 2002—a failed attempt to overthrow President Hugo Chávez. The first decade of the twenty-first century has been the longest stretch since the transitions to democracy began three decades ago that has been free even from military mutinies.

Military influence in politics raises different issues, but the story in the current decade also underlines the strengthening of democratic institutions. In Venezuela, President Chávez politicized the military, especially after the failed coup attempt against him in 2002, and has made military involvement in society and economy one hallmark of his rule during the decade, as David Myers notes in his chapter. Venezuela is the only Latin American country where such trends have been under way in recent years.

Military influence in politics has remained great and relatively unchanged in Ecuador and Paraguay, thanks in part to the sustained electoral weakness of civilian presidents in Ecuador and the historically strong ties between the military and the Colorado Party in Paraguay. Military influence in politics declined markedly in Central American countries upon the end of the domestic and international wars, but high crime rates and old habits persist to sustain high levels of military influence in politics in the northern Central American countries.

There are contrary trends, however, that augur better for constitutional rule. As Fernando Cepeda shows in his chapter, Colombia has suffered from extremely high levels of political and criminal violence for a very long time. Its military and police forces, therefore, necessarily inhabit an important place in the country's affairs. Nevertheless, Colombia's President Álvaro Uribe clearly exercises civilian command over the armed forces that are engaged in domestic combat; military subordination to the civilian president has increased in Colombia in the 2000s.

Peru's military had played a decisive role in national and local politics nearly uninterruptedly since the end of the military government in 1979. From the early 1980s to the early 1990s, the military fought the Sendero Luminoso (Shining Path) insurgency. In 1992, the military supported President Fujimori's coup against the other constitutional powers and remained influential for the balance of his presidency until Fujimori's resignation in 2000. Interim President Valentín Paniagua decisively dismissed Peru's highest-ranking military officers, paving the way for the reassertion of greater, albeit still imperfect, civilian control over the military in the century's first decade, as Degregori shows in his chapter.

The most noteworthy story of the resurgence of civilian control over the military in recent years occurred in Chile. In most respects, Chile has had an extraordinarily successful transition from military to constitutional civilian rule alongside economic prosperity, declining rates of extreme poverty, and more effective social policies. As Peter Siavelis demonstrates in his chapter, civilian control over the Chilean military improved gradually but slowly during the 1990s and then took a giant leap forward following former dictator Augusto Pinochet's arrest in London in 1998. The actions of the Chilean Supreme Court and other Chilean courts revealed the abuses and corruption during the Pinochet dictatorship, impelling the armed forces and the political parties that once had supported Pinochet to distance themselves from the discredited dictator. As Siavelis notes, the highly professional Chilean armed forces became fully subordinate to civilian authorities and cooperated in the investigations of human rights abuses and political killings. Chile's constitutional reforms in 2005 abolished most elements of the privileged position of the military and terminated all hitherto constitutionally mandated authoritarian enclaves (such as a set of appointed senators)—except for the still privileged access of the military to the earnings from international copper exports.

In sum, successful military coups have been extremely rare, and since 1990 there has been no military president who has reached power by means of a coup. Unsuccessful military coups have also become rare, and there has been just one since 2000. Military politicization has increased in Venezuela but declined in Chile, Colombia, and Peru in the first decade of the twenty-first century, while it remains high but unchanged in Ecuador, Paraguay, and the northern countries of Central America. The problem of democratic civilian supremacy has not been solved, but important steps have been taken in that direction.

What explains such trends in civil-military relations? In the first edition of this book, Jeanne Kinney Giraldo and I identified two factors to account for the decline in the frequency of coups.[3] The "supply" of coup efforts dried up. The military governments, for the most part, did not end in glory. Beyond engaging in human rights abuses and the repression of public liberties, most also mismanaged the economy and fell prey to corruption, damaging the military institutions and personnel in the process. Military officers adversely evaluated those experiences.

The "demand" for coups also fell. Except for General Pinochet's government in Chile and, thanks to the oil boom, the Ecuadorian military government in the 1970s, no military governments managed the economy well. Instead, they presided over declining living standards. Some committed acts of cruelty. Neither political parties nor business elites came to think of military rule as an effective solution to the problems of governance. Moreover, since the transition to civilian rule, moderate center or center-right parties have performed well in elections in Brazil and the northern Central American countries, characteristically so in Colombia, demonstrating that such parties may win free elections. As Steven Levitsky shows in his chapter, not even in the midst of Argentina's economic collapse at the start of the century's first decade was there a significant demand for a military coup, and no such attempt was made.

A third factor (first mentioned in this book's second edition) became more evident by the end of the 1990s. There was a worldwide regularity in the decline in frequency of coup attempts, which suggests that an international explanation is also in order, and Laurence Whitehead discusses various aspects of such an explanation in his chapter. The end of the Cold War deprived would-be coup makers of anti-communist "national security" rationales and U.S. support for possible coups. Latin American governments also undertook to help prevent military coups, as Argentina and Brazil have done repeatedly in Paraguay. The Organization of American States became more effective in gathering support to prevent military coups from succeeding.

The variation in the level of military influence over politics short of coups cannot be explained, however, either by international factors or by the reduction in the demand for coups, because both of those explanations have converging and uniform effects across countries. Nor do such supply factors as the relative degree of military professionalization explain the variation in the likelihood of military influence. In the 1990s, for example, a highly professional military had much political influence in Chile but little in Argentina; a less professional military had much political influence in Peru but little in Mexico. More broadly, none of the factors used to explain the presence or absence of coups helps to explain the level of military influence in politics in these Latin American countries. For example, international and regional intervention has no effect on military influence within a country short of a coup.

The variation in civilian demand for military influence in politics does help to explain the variation in the level and changes in such influence; that is, agents exogenous to military institutions—civilian demand for a political role for the military—changed first, leading to a subsequent change in the level and trend in military influence in politics.[4] As noted in the earlier narrative, from the 1990s to the 2000s civilian demand for a high level of military influence in politics dropped in Chile (all political parties sought this outcome, especially after Pinochet's public disgrace), Colombia (under President Uribe's leadership and independent congressional action), and Peru (especially under the late president Paniagua's leadership), and military influence in politics declined in all three countries, though it remains substantial in each. Civilian demand for military influence in politics remained high and unchanged in Ecuador, Paraguay, and the northern Central American countries from the 1990s to the 2000s; military influence in politics remained equally high and unchanged. President Chávez politicized the Venezuelan military, at times over the opposition of many military officers; thus, military influence in politics increased.

In sum, constitutional democratic control over the military continued to advance in Latin American countries in the new century. As Rut Diamint has made clear, there is a low level of effective civilian governance of many aspects of military affairs according to the standards prevalent in fully democratic countries.[5] Nevertheless, the frequency of military coups, successful or unsuccessful, has continued to decline, as has military influence in politics, especially in the Southern Cone countries and Brazil. Civilian control of the military remains weak and must be strengthened much more, but it may be at the highest level in the region's history.

Responsible and Reliable Parties

Parties are the most effective instruments to articulate and aggregate social, economic, and political demands; set priorities; and respond to those
demands. Parties are key means to organize parliamentary politics to support or oppose the executive. Bargaining between parties reduces the intensity of acute conflicts and creates the political room for the rise and consolidation of "arbiter" institutions such as the courts.

A half-century ago, Anthony Downs identified two important traits of
parties in democratic politics: reliability and responsibility. "A party is reliable," he wrote, "if its policy statements at the beginning of an election period
—including those in its preelection campaign—can be used to make accurate predictions of its behavior." He also argued that a "party is responsible
if its policies in one period are consistent with its actions (or statements) in
the preceding period, i.e., if it does not repudiate its former views in formu-
lating its new program."[6] Partisan reliability and responsibility are at the very
core of democratic politics. Democracy must rest on the promise that politicians and their parties do not intend to deceive the voters and that their candidates would, at a minimum, govern within the broad parameters of their
preelection promises if elected. Voters should want more than just this from
politicians and parties, but they must want at least this much from them.

By those standards, many Latin American politicians and parties were unreliable and irresponsible in the late 1980s and early 1990s. As Susan Stokes
has shown, at that time there was a very wide gap between a presidential candidate's campaign promises and his policy choices as president, well beyond
what might be considered normal in politics.[7] Parties were not reliable. The
election campaigns of Carlos Andrés Pérez in Venezuela and Carlos Menem
in Argentina, both in 1989, or of Alberto Fujimori in Peru in 1990, gave no
hint of the strong market orientation of their economic policies once elected
to the presidency.

There was also a profound discrepancy between administrations of the
same political party. Venezuela's successive Acción Democrática (AD; Democratic Action) administrations of Jaime Lusinchi and Carlos Andrés Pérez
followed dramatically different economic policies before and after the 1988
presidential election. Mexico's long-ruling Partido Revolucionario Institucional (PRI; Institutional Revolutionary Party) followed policies that differed just as markedly before and after the 1982 presidential election, when
Miguel de la Madrid replaced José López Portillo. These parties were not responsible in Downsian terms.

Much has changed since then. Consider Stokes's evidence. Of the 15 presidential elections held between 1988 and 1991 in 15 Latin American countries,
7 featured a switch between what parties promised during the campaign and

what their candidates did once in office. Between 1992 and 1995, however, only 3 out of 14 presidential elections featured such a dramatic switch.[8]

Employing the same criteria for the same 15 countries for 1996–2000, we find that none of the 15 presidential elections was followed by such a drastic change from campaign promises to implementation. In the mid- and late 1990s, in contrast, Presidents Menem in Argentina, Fujimori in Peru, and Fernando Henrique Cardoso in Brazil ran for reelection on their records and sustained similar policies in their second terms. In Mexico, the economic policies of Ernesto Zedillo were consistent with those of his predecessor, Carlos Salinas; both men were from the same political party, the PRI. Thus, both partisan reliability and responsibility have improved markedly.

President Hugo Chávez, too, is an exemplar of reliability defined in these terms. In 1998, he ran against the Venezuelan establishment. His goals have been public, and he has successfully run for reelection on his record. He demonstrates that politicians averse to the predominance of market-oriented economic policies can mean what they say and persevere in their views and policies. Reliable and responsible, too, was Bolivia's Gonzalo Sánchez de Lozada, who, after one term out of office, won the presidency for a second time in the 2002 election after promising a continuation of the policies of his previous term. Also reliable and responsible has been his sharp opponent and eventual successor, Evo Morales, elected Bolivian president in late 2005; over time, both during the campaign and in the presidential office, Morales has acted as he has spoken. He has worked hard to fulfill his campaign promises. In the Dominican Republic, Leonel Fernández also won the presidency for a second term in 2004, having spent one term out of office, with the promise of replicating his record of government.

Partisan responsibility, understood in Downsian terms, has been especially noteworthy from the 1990s into the 2000s in El Salvador and Chile between the successive administrations of four consecutive presidents, respectively, from El Salvador's Alianza Republicana Nacionalista (ARENA; Nationalist Republican Alliance) and Chile's Concertación coalition between Christian Democrats and social democrats.

During the 2000s, as Denise Dresser considers in her chapter, in Mexico there has been comparable partisan responsibility in economic policy between the successive Partido Acción Nacional (National Action Party) presidencies of Vicente Fox and Felipe Calderón. Equally responsible in Downsian terms has been Mexico's leading opposition party on the left, the Partido de la Revolución Democrática (Party of the Democratic Revolution). Every Mexican president since the first seriously contested presidential election in 1988 has been "reliable"; his campaign foreshadowed the new administration's program.

In Central America, the levels of partisan reliability and responsibility have been high in El Salvador. Both the long-governing conservative ARENA party and the lead opposition, the Frente Farabundo Martí para la Liberación Nacional (Farabundo Martí National Liberation Front), have held to their programmatic orientations. The same has occurred in Nicaragua with the Frente Sandinista de Liberación Nacional (FSLN; Sandinista Front for National Liberation) and, to a lesser extent, the Liberals.[9] The FSLN share of the electorate has remained nearly constant over time; the party's Daniel Ortega won the presidency in 2006 principally because opponents divided.

In the 2000s, however, partisan unreliability has increased somewhat. In 2002, Lucio Gutiérrez was elected president of Ecuador promising a definite turn away from the pro-market economic policies that had characterized Ecuadorian macroeconomic policies in preceding years. Nevertheless, Gutiérrez's own policies diverged back toward market-conforming economic policies soon after his election. Such lack of reliability had, in fact, been typical of Ecuadorian elections and governments: only President Jamil Mahuad governed in a manner consistent with his campaign promises. Since the mid-1990s, none of the three elected presidents of Ecuador—Abdalá Bucaram, Mahuad, or Gutiérrez—has finished his term, with Bucaram and Gutiérrez deposed by Congress and Mahuad deposed in 2000 by a military coup led by Gutiérrez, then a colonel.

As Corrales notes in his chapter, in 2001 the campaign of Peru's Alejandro Toledo was pitched to the left of center, but his government sustained and deepened the market orientation of macroeconomic policies. President Toledo's administration was highly successful in promoting economic growth, but, in Downsian terms, he was unreliable.

David Samuels and Corrales note in their chapters that some of the supporters of Luiz Inácio "Lula" da Silva in Brazil were surely disappointed at the market-conforming thrust of Lula's economic policies that followed his election to the presidency in the 2002 elections. Once in office, in the name of party discipline the Lula loyalist majority within the Partido dos Trabalhadores (PT; Workers' Party) in Congress expelled some deputies from the PT caucus who opposed the Lula administration's economic policies. Some PT leaders broke with the PT and supported alternative presidential and legislative candidates on the left in the 2006 election.

In the 2000s, Lula and the PT pose problems principally for an assessment of partisan responsibility. As Samuels notes, during the 2002 election Lula's presidential campaign sought to placate domestic and international financial markets. His vice presidential running mate came from the world of business and a conservative party. Lula's platform emphasized his acceptance of market-oriented policies and differed plainly from the more left-oriented

PT party platform. During the campaign, Lula publicly supported an agreement with the International Monetary Fund (IMF) that the Cardoso administration had negotiated and pledged that, if elected president, he would comply with and implement the agreement with the IMF. He did. Lula and the PT government were thus reliable in Downsian terms. And yet, this Lula and this PT were surely different from those of the past, which is what partisan responsibility means in Downs's schema. To their credit, as Samuels points out, the Lula and PT government doubled the minimum wage and pursued other policies that significantly brought down poverty levels and infant mortality during Lula's first term.

Argentina's Partido Justicialista (Judicialist or Peronista Party) also changed course in the 2000s, although the economic policy shift should be called moderate. As Levitsky argues in his chapter, Peronista President Néstor Kirchner retained fairly conservative fiscal and (to a lesser extent) monetary policies, running large budget surpluses year after year. His government sustained the export-oriented macroeconomic model set in the 1990s and did not reverse the large-scale privatizations of the 1990s. Argentina's economic recovery and subsequent growth in the 2000s are explained, to a significant extent, by the persistence of such market-oriented policies. Kirchner and the Peronistas departed from economic orthodoxy in various ways, however. The Kirchner administration froze public utility rates, imposed price controls on energy and food, pushed up wages, rescinded the contract for the privatization of water and sewage services in Buenos Aires, renationalized the post office and a major railroad line, and launched a new state airline, energy company, and satellite manufacturer.

In the 2000s, Uruguay's Frente Amplio (Broad Front) continued its gradual march toward the political center. Founded in 1971 but unable to operate during the years of military dictatorship that ended in 1985, the Frente Amplio's first major success was the election of Tabaré Vázquez as the mayor of Montevideo in 1989. As mayor, Vázquez sought to reposition the Frente Amplio to gain the votes of the long-dominant parties, the Colorados and the Blancos. Ideological battles within the Frente Amplio between Vázquez, on the left, and Danilo Astori, a more moderate technocrat, were resolved in advance of the 2004 presidential election: Vázquez ran and won the presidency, the Frente Amplio's first such victory, with Astori as his pre-designated finance minister.[10] During the campaign, the Frente Amplio signaled that it would pursue market-conforming economic policies. The Frente Amplio government did, and the economy grew rapidly. Moreover, in January 2007 it signed a trade and investment framework agreement with the United States, which was a potential first step toward a free trade treaty; majorities of Uruguayans, including a majority within the Frente Amplio, support a free trade accord with the United States. At the same time, the Vázquez government pursued a vigorous effort to investigate human rights violations during the dictatorship.[11]

What explains the lack of partisan reliability and responsibility in the late 1980s and early 1990s, their rise thereafter, and their slight decline in the 2000s? As Corrales argued in the previous edition of this book, those who were elected president in the late 1980s and early 1990s believed that they had no other choice but to betray their campaign promises and the records of their political parties in order to enact policies that they deemed essential but for which there was little popular support. Otherwise, they discovered, their countries would plunge into an economic abyss.[12] Opportunistically, they ran on the left in order to get elected, yet they had to move to the political center in order to govern effectively. Theirs was a swing between opportunity and necessity.

Incumbent parties were compelled to run on their records in office, however. In the 1990s, incumbent political parties that ran the incumbent for re-election or ran different candidates for president had to reshape their base of support to succeed. In the 1990s, many incumbent parties were successful at turning the economy around and making other improvements. Success enabled politicians to become more reliable and responsible. As a result, incumbent parties succeeded in winning at least two consecutive elections in Argentina, Brazil, Chile, Colombia, El Salvador, Mexico, Paraguay and, less clearly, Nicaragua (where there was some coalitional discontinuity) and Peru (where Fujimori was reelected in 1995 in a personalist victory; he had destroyed existing parties and built none of his own, as Degregori has shown). Rational voters rewarded effective government.

Some of those same incumbent parties or coalitions continued to win in the 2000s (in Chile, El Salvador, and Paraguay), but even the once incumbent parties that lost elections in the 2000s remained important contenders— Brazil's Partido da Social Democracia Brasileira (PSDB; Brazilian Social Democracy Party), the Liberal Party in Colombia, the PRI in Mexico, and the Liberals in Nicaragua. In short, in the 1990s partisan reliability and responsibility increased because economic growth made them electorally valuable.

In the 2000s, there were two cases of decline in partisan reliability (Ecuador and Peru) and three other cases that pose questions regarding partisan responsibility (Argentina, Brazil, and Uruguay). For democratic accountability, the cases of Ecuador and Peru are serious. For opportunistic reasons, Lucio Gutiérrez returned to the pattern that had hitherto prevailed in Ecuador: run left, govern right. Betrayed, angry supporters forced him out of office. In Peru, Alejandro Toledo also positioned himself somewhat to the left for opportunistic reasons and, though he was not compelled to resign, became a stunningly unpopular president and remained so for nearly all of his term, as Degregori makes clear. Citizens held Gutiérrez and Toledo accountable for being unreliable; Toledo lost support as well because he was perceived to be both frivolous and inept, notwithstanding the Peruvian economy's boom during his years as president.

In Argentina, Brazil, and Uruguay, democratic accountability was better served. Lula and the PT publicly repositioned themselves during the 2002 presidential campaign. It is difficult to imagine a clearer, louder public signal of such repositioning for a Brazilian leftist party than endorsing an IMF agreement during the middle of a presidential campaign. In 2004, Tabaré Vázquez and the Frente Amplio also repositioned their campaign, principally through the choice of Danilo Astori at the outset of the campaign to signal a future market-oriented policy. In Argentina in 2003, Kirchner ran for president to the left of the Peronistas and in opposition to Menem's bid for one more reelection. He did so because he believed that Argentina's economic collapse in 2001–2 should have been blamed on some of the policies that his predecessors had enacted and sustained; that Kirchner governed from the center-left should have surprised no one.

Public partisan repositioning during a presidential campaign absolves the PT, the Peronistas, and the Frente Amplio of the ethical charge of partisan irresponsibility, though many citizens no doubt would remain bewildered that the verities of the past had changed for the PT and the Frente Amplio or that the economic anchoring of the Peronistas had changed so dramatically within the span of a decade. Therefore, such switches may have been appropriate. The practical problem of partisan irresponsibility—given the limitations of the information available to voters and the demands on their time to pursue the subtleties of political repositioning—remains, however; it should remain a serious concern in the assessment of democratic governability in Latin America.

In short, after the early 1990s, many Latin American politicians and political parties became more responsible and reliable in the sense defined by Downs. The trend for democratic accountability was positive. In the 2000s, retrogression in reliability occurred in Ecuador and Peru. In Argentina, Brazil, and Uruguay, in contrast, the winning presidential candidates and their respective parties signaled a policy repositioning during their campaigns —the only democratically acceptable way for parties to depart dramatically from the policies that they had hitherto advanced. Democratic accountability has maintained gains in most of these countries over the past two decades.

Equally noteworthy has been Latin America's greater diversity in partisan ideological outcomes. In the many national elections held in 2005 and 2006, presidential candidates on the left won in Bolivia, Ecuador, Nicaragua, and Venezuela. Presidential candidates on the right won in Colombia and Mexico. Center-left presidential candidates won in Brazil (confirming a move toward the political center) and in Chile, Costa Rica, and Peru. Parties of the right have continued to win elections uninterruptedly in El Salvador and

Guatemala. In Uruguay, the 2004 presidential election simultaneously implied a shift to a center-left victory but also a moderation of a left partisan coalition. In Argentina, the Peronistas have governed from the center-left during the current decade, in contrast to their governing on the center-right in the 1990s, but substantive policy discontinuity (except in the international debt arena) has been modest.

There is also considerable political pluralism within countries. For example, the right-wing ARENA has won the Salvadoran presidency consistently for two decades, yet El Salvador's left (the FMLN) is strong and well represented in parliament and local governments. The center-left Chilean Concertación coalition has won four consecutive presidential elections, yet the Chilean right-wing parties are also strong and well represented in parliament and local governments. Today Latin America is an ideologically plural continent on which parties and politicians characteristically mean what they say and contest each other vigorously.

Increased partisan and politician reliability—good for democratic accountability—may contribute to political polarization, however. Candidates feel responsible to honor the promises made to their voters and, as a result, may be less willing to compromise with other parties. Evo Morales, Hugo Chávez, and Álvaro Uribe have been exemplary presidential candidates in terms of Downsian reliability and responsibility, but, as a consequence, they are also highly polarizing presidents. El Salvador's persistently sharp ideological divide owes much to the pristine Downsian reliability and responsibility of the ARENA and FMLN parties. There is a tension between these important ingredients of democratic accountability, on the one hand, and political moderation, on the other.

We should not kneel before the Downsian altar of partisan reliability and responsibility, therefore, without also understanding their potential adverse side effects. Certain forms of political reliability and responsibility may construct a polity that is deeply and seemingly irreparably split and peopled by uncompromising politicians wedded to policies that may be failing or undermining democratic institutions and practices. This analysis, therefore, is not a paean to political rigidity. Rather, it is a call on behalf of public accountability: parties and politicians should be reliable and responsible but also open to changing the policies that they have hitherto advocated when these are wrong and misguided—but those changes in prior commitments must be made transparently for all citizens to witness and assess.

The Collapse of Parties and Party Systems

The story of political parties in Latin America is more troubling than the preceding section implies. In the 1990s, three long-established and once powerful political parties virtually disappeared. These were AD and the Comité de Organización Política Electoral Independiente, usually referred to as the Partido Social Cristiano (COPEI; Social Christian Party) in Venezuela, which had supplied the winner in every Venezuelan presidential election between 1958 and 1988 and between them had typically won more than four-fifths of the seats in Congress, and Peru's Alianza Popular Revolucionaria Americana (APRA; American Popular Revolutionary Alliance), which had been Peru's largest political party from its foundation in the 1920s to the end of the 1980s. Venezuela's traditional parties had already weakened substantially prior to Hugo Chávez's first presidential election in 1998, when they collapsed.[13] Peru's parties had also been decomposing prior to Alberto Fujimori's first presidential election in 1990; Peru became a no-party political system in the 1990s.

In the 2000s, Venezuela's AD weakened further. It had won about a sixth of the seats of the National Assembly filled in late 1999. As Myers notes in his chapter, AD and the COPEI declined to contest the presidency in the 2000 election. Then, in a suicidal decision, they boycotted the December 2005 legislative election in the hope of discrediting the result; the most important consequence, as Myers notes, was to enable pro-Chávez candidates to win every seat in the National Assembly.

In the 2000s, the same fate may have befallen Argentina's Unión Cívica Radical (UCR; Radical Civic Union), which elected its first president in 1916 and its most recent, Fernando de la Rúa, in 1999. In the 2003 presidential election, the vote for the UCR was negligible, even though the party retains a significant presence in public opinion and continues to elect some provincial governors. Similarly, in Costa Rica, the Christian Democratic coalition, which under various names had elected five presidents of Costa Rica from the 1960s to the early 2000s, in 2006 received just about a tenth of the legislative election votes—a repudiation too severe to be attributable merely to voter volatility.

As Eduardo Gamarra shows in his chapter, in the 2000s Bolivia has undergone a partisan dealignment and realignment. In December 2005, Evo Morales was elected president of Bolivia with an absolute majority of the votes for his mass-based party, the Movimiento al Socialismo (MAS; Movement toward Socialism), in an election with the first such margin of victory since the end of unelected governments in 1982 and the highest electoral turnout (nearly 85 percent) during that entire period. The MAS also won a majority of the seats in the Chamber of Deputies and by far the strongest plurality in the Senate. The parties that had governed Bolivia from the early 1980s to the early 2000s virtually disappeared: the Movimiento Nacionalista Revolucionario (MNR; Nationalist Revolutionary Movement), which had three times won the presidency in that time frame, and Acción Democrática Nacionalista (ADN; Nationalist Democratic Action) and the Movimiento de

Izquierda Revolucionaria (MIR; Leftist Revolutionary Movement), each of which had won the presidency once. The MAS has strong grassroots support and has been built from the ground up. The collapse of the older parties, however, leaves Bolivia with no comparable opposition counterpoint. Thus, Bolivia has undergone both a massive realignment that has brought perhaps half of the electorate to the MAS and a massive dealignment of voters with regard to the older political parties.

In Colombia, as Cepeda explains in his chapter, the Liberal and Conservative parties elected every president of Colombia from the nineteenth century until the close of the twentieth century. However, Colombia's party system fragmented and weakened over recent decades. Cepeda notes that by the end of the 1970s, presidents began to find it insufficient to negotiate with party leaders and instead bargained with individual members of Congress. The electoral law that followed the adoption of a new constitution in 1991 facilitated the proliferation of factional lists within the Liberal and Conservative parties. By the end of the 1990s, the labels "Liberal" and "Conservative" had lost much meaning, because hundreds of subparty lists appeared on ballots across the country. Nonparty candidates were elected to the mayoralty of Bogotá, and in 2002 a nonparty candidate, Álvaro Uribe (a former Liberal legislator and governor), won the presidency.

The collapse of party systems should be kept in perspective. In the 2000s, there has been one partisan resurrection. In Peru, the APRA staged a comeback in the 2001 legislative election; Alan García came in a close second in the 2001 presidential election and won the presidency in 2006 in a very close election. Moreover, as Cepeda shows, the Colombian situation is subtler than first impressions may imply. From one angle, the 2006 presidential elections suggest the death of the Conservative Party and the reduction of the votes for the Liberal Party—Colombia's largest party for much of the past half century—to fewer than 12 percent. President Uribe won reelection at the head of his own coalition of new parties and personalist supporters; a partisan coalition on the left impressively won 22 percent of the votes. From another angle, as Cepeda also demonstrates, it is not difficult to recognize the old Liberal and Conservative parties in Congress among the 11 parties with various names that won parliamentary seats in the 2006 legislative elections. The parties could be grouped into Liberal, Conservative, and Left clusters. From this second angle, the distribution of seats in Congress better represents Colombia's political diversity, which is an important democratic value for an electoral law to achieve. Moreover, the number of parties within each cluster is dramatically smaller than the number of subparty faction lists within the pre-reform Liberal and Conservative Parties. In Colombia, the death and resurrection of the Liberal and Conservative Parties may be said, from the perspective of time, to have occurred simultaneously.

What explains the collapse of parties and party systems and the variation over time and countries?[14] In the first edition of this book, Giraldo and I offered explanations for the breakdown of AD, the COPEI, and the APRA in the 1990s that also help to explain the subsequent breakdown of the Colombian party system, the collapse of the once powerful Bolivian traditional parties, and the decreased support for Costa Rica's once dominant parties in the 2000s.[15]

We argued, first, that AD and the APRA suffered from retrospective voting punishment; that is, voters assessed their performance in government and pronounced it dismal. Similarly, the implosion of Argentina's UCR in the early 2000s is best understood as retrospective voting punishment of UCR President de la Rúa's economic stewardship, which led to economic catastrophe in 2001–2. The same thing happened to the Liberals and Conservatives in Colombia from the mid-1990s to the early 2000s—specifically, during the Liberal presidency of Ernesto Samper (1994–98) and the Conservative presidency of Andrés Pastrana (1998–2002)—when the economy plunged in the Latin American country with the most sustained long-term economic performance during the second half of the twentieth century. In Colombia, levels of violence also escalated significantly during the late 1990s and early 2000s. In Bolivia, escalating social and political protest in the early 2000s ignited highly visible, albeit numerically modest, instances of political violence, leading to the resignation of President Gonzalo Sánchez de Lozada in October 2003. In the 1980s and 1990s, accusations of corruption had also plagued AD, the APRA, and the Liberal Samper administration, just as in the early 2000s they haunted Costa Rica's Christian Democrats and were an important factor in explaining Bolivia's partisan collapse.

Giraldo and I pointed to a second factor in the breakdown of parties, drawing from Michael Coppedge's work.[16] Long-established political parties that have seemingly colluded to create an oligopoly of power and employ the electoral laws to sustain their grip on public office, defying shifts in popular preferences, are vulnerable to voter revolt. Coppedge developed the concept of partyarchy to explain what ailed AD and the COPEI. Colombia has long been a principal example of coalescent behavior between the two allegedly rival political parties—the most enduring formal duopoly. Costa Rican parties increasingly cooperated on economic policies in the late 1990s. In the 2002 election, Costa Rica's two largest parties won only 63 percent of the legislative seats compared to 88 percent in 1998, and in 2006, as noted, Costa Rica's Christian Democrats collapsed. In Bolivia, the MNR, ADN, and MIR had been both adversaries and allies according to the circumstances—a classic example of oligopoly collusion. Gamarra notes that Bolivia's "pacted democracy" was also a key reason for the repudiation of the old parties in the election of late 2005.

Partisan collusion alone had not unraveled the Bolivian, Colombian, Costa Rican, or Venezuelan party systems in the past, however. Similarly, hard times before partisan collusion—the circumstances of Costa Rica and Venezuela in the 1980s, for example—had not sufficed to destroy parties or party systems. The combination of partisan collusion with hard times in terms of economics, corruption, or violence (retrospective voting punishment), however, explains the difference between the defeat of a party in one election and the collapse of a party altogether. In the 1990s and 2000s, such a lethal combination skewered Bolivia's MNR, ADN, and MIR; Colombia's Liberals and Conservatives; Costa Rica's Christian Democrats (Liberación Nacional was weakened but less so); and Venezuela's AD and COPEI.

Uruguay has also exhibited elements of partisan collusion over time under the cover of its complex electoral laws. Since the end of military dictatorship in 1985, however, Uruguayan political parties have been responsive to the voters. Uruguay has not suffered from much political violence in these years. Its economic crises in the mid-1990s and early 2000s were explained and understood as the effects of exogenous shocks from crises elsewhere. The presidential election victory of Tabaré Vázquez and the Frente Amplio in 2004, moreover, did not vanquish the Colorado and Blanco parties but instead reflected a gradual partisan realignment that better reflects voter preferences.

In the 2000s, a third factor in explaining the collapse of parties became clearer: a president's deliberate attempt to weaken political parties, at times including his own party. In the 1990s, Peru's President Alberto Fujimori had tried systematically to undermine and disorganize the already feeble opposition political parties. More striking is the fact that Fujimori had seemingly been allergic to the electoral vehicles that he himself had created, undermining his own political party and its allies.

This behavior had seemed idiosyncratic until it reappeared in President Hugo Chávez's Venezuela. Chávez has tried to pulverize the already weak opposition and, with an assist from inept opposition leaders who decline at times to contest elections, has had much success. More striking is the fact that Chávez's own Movimiento Quinta República (MVR; Fifth Republic Movement) was, yes, highly powerful and electorally effective but also a rather personalist political machine. As Myers makes clear in his chapter, the MVR lost key leaders and gained fair-weather supporters. Moreover, much of the significant civil society organizing that has been under way depends on identification with Chávez rather than on a political connection to national-level partisan organizations; the better organization of civil society has yet to strengthen the instruments for national-level democratic accountability, which only parties can provide.[17] In addition, upon winning reelection in December 2006, Chávez announced his wish to gather his disparate supporters in various parties into a single United Socialist Party of Venezuela, which required the disbandment not only of various allied parties but also of his own MVR. Some of those other pro-Chávez parties were reluctant to disband, yet they fall victim to Chávez's disdain even for parties that support him. Such disarray in the Chávez coalition may help to explain the defeat, in a plebiscite held in December 2007, of Chávez's attempt to eliminate the prohibition in the Venezuelan Constitution of a president's indefinite reelection; this was the first election he ever lost.[18]

A third example of a president's anti-party behavior may be found in Ecuador. In November 2006, Rafael Correa won the presidency of Ecuador. His party had nominated no congressional candidates and thus elected none. Correa, not surprisingly, soon called a Constituent Assembly to strengthen his position relative to the legislature and the parties. When Congress refused to consent to the call for a referendum, in March 2007 the Correa-aligned electoral court removed 57 of the 100 members of Congress—a civilian president's coup against a freely and fairly elected Congress, informed by the strategy that Venezuela's President Chávez had pioneered in 1999 and that Bolivia's President Morales had attempted without success in 2006–7. Correa's approach was as confrontational as that of Fujimori, who in his 1992 presidential coup had dissolved the entire Congress as well as the Supreme Court. Correa has employed the institutional powers of the presidency rather than constructing a democratic partisan base of support.

In the late 2000s, therefore, party and party system breakdown has advanced in Ecuador and Venezuela. It remains problematic, though less so, in Peru and, in still complex ways, in Colombia, and has become newly problematic in Argentina, Bolivia, and Costa Rica. On the other hand, despite many continuing problems, parties have remained capable, and some have become stronger, in Brazil, El Salvador, and Mexico. Parties have remained strong in Chile, the Dominican Republic, and Uruguay.

This balance is more negative for democratic governance than when the second edition of this book was published in 2003. Argentina, Bolivia, and Costa Rica have faced new instances of party breakdown in the 2000s, while this long-standing problem has worsened in Ecuador and Venezuela; in each of these two cases, deliberate presidential actions have emerged as a key explanation. Partisan life remains disorganized and feeble in Guatemala, and Nicaragua's Liberals are weaker and more fragmented. Only Peru has taken some steps toward partisan reconstruction. The optimistic hunch about Colombia's new parties remains to be tested. At the time this book's previous edition was written, the breakdown of parties and party systems seemed a special disease of the Andean countries. During the twenty-first century's first decade, these anti-democratic maladies have spread.

The Representational Deficit

Latin American countries have long been plagued by representational deficits, that is, the perception of a significant number of citizens that their views are represented not well or not at all in the national institutions, the political parties, and other public spaces. Some of the partisan realignment, dealignment, and plain partisan collapse just noted may be explained as stemming from these perceptions.

In his chapter, Corrales explores one dimension of this deficit, namely, discontent with the market reforms enacted in the 1990s. His 10 groups of the discontented may be regrouped into three clusters. Some of those he finds to be unhappy with market reforms, the radicals and the hypernationalists, never supported those reforms in the first place and have rarely exercised political power. The protectionists and the big spenders had political power in times past in nearly every Latin American country and were understandably unhappy to have lost it in the 1990s, not to regain it outside of Venezuela. In many ways, these groups express long-standing partisan disputes. Their lack of effective power in the 2000s has resulted from defeat in democratic politics, not from a representational deficit.

In the 2000s, Corrales's commodity nationalists gained power in Bolivia, Ecuador, and Venezuela, where they have been changing the political landscape. The multiculturalists have gained power in Bolivia and made important representational gains in Ecuador. Yet, they have made few such gains in Peru, notwithstanding its demographic similarities to neighboring Bolivia and Ecuador. Corrales's macho bashers made gains in a majority of countries through the enactment of gender-quota electoral rules, among other policy changes, and thus suffer from a representational deficit less than in the past.

Three of Corrales's categories, however, raise significant issues of political representation. Those he calls the crusaders advocate in favor of greater transparency, less corruption, better-functioning courts, and other means of improving democratic governance. Corrales's egalitarians advocate redistributive policies to help the poor; independent of the wisdom of specific policy proposals, they focus on central issues of social and economic inequality. So, too, do the quite different persons Corrales calls equalizers, who wish to help the poor by equalizing access to the market; the latter's policy preferences are quite consistent with a market economy approach but may also be opposed by anti-tax market supporters.

The latter three groups have had some clout over the past 20 years but not much. The equalizers—market-conforming market-access reformers—have had influence in the design and implementation of successful social policies in Brazil under the Cardoso and Lula presidencies, in Chile since 1990, and in Mexico with regard to certain welfare and health care policies under the presidencies of Ernesto Zedillo and Vicente Fox.[19] And the proponents of more open government have helped to open up archives on the most heinous crimes of dictatorships in Argentina and Chile and provided better access to information that ought to be public in Mexico. These remain exceptions, however; their greater success would augur improvements in governance.

Corrales's analysis, therefore, effectively distinguishes between those who are not well represented in politics because the electorate has not chosen them, those who had been underrepresented before 1990 but have been less so since that time, and those whose clout in politics remains weak, often to the detriment of more effective democratic governance.

In her chapter Mala Htun addresses other dimensions of the representational deficit pertaining to gender and ethnicity or race. She shows that the relationship between the method of election of a public official, on the one hand, and specific policy outcomes that serve substantive representational purposes, on the other, may be complex and, at best, indirect. The election of women members of parliament through electoral quota laws, and the election of ethnic minority deputies through reserved seats in the national legislature as guaranteed by constitutional amendment, seem to have had meager impact on the enactment of substantive gains for women or ethnic minorities. Htun perceptively notes that there have been descriptive representational gains; for instance, having a "person like me" in parliament is a value in itself that may have subtle important long-term effects on public discourse, private meanings, and childhood and adult political socialization. But these gains fall short of what their proponents have claimed in favor of their enactment.

Instead, Htun argues that cross-partisan advocacy coalitions have often effectively advanced reforms of gender policies. Such coalitions often involve women and men deputies as well as indigenous and nonindigenous deputies. A second path to policy change has been the election of a party committed to enacting such reforms, as an example of which the MAS in Bolivia is Htun's case study. In each instance, Htun identifies problems in need of remedy—severe gender or ethnic and racial discrepancies in exercising the rights of citizens. She examines potential remedies that turn out to be problematic, such as quota laws or reserved seats, as well as political remedies that have more effectively addressed representational deficits, such as cross-party coalitions or the development of a large party capable of enacting policy change.

The National Institutions for Democratic Governance

Since the late 1970s, the transition to democracy in Latin American countries has led many citizens and their representatives to consider the political and democratic adequacy of their constitutions and national institutions. Each of the countries studied in this book has reformed its constitution in this time span or is currently engaged in such a process. Institutional reform mongering often reflects broad dissatisfaction with governance.

Key amendments to the constitutions of Chile and Mexico enacted in the late 1980s and 1990s, and to Brazil's in the 1990s, sought to strengthen property rights and the constitutional context for market-friendly policies, along with laws enacted to the same effect. Constitutional reforms in Argentina, Colombia, Peru, and Venezuela were not principally focused on economic themes, but Argentina, Peru, and to some extent Colombia enacted far-reaching institutional changes with the same result. These pro–property rights reforms were part of a broad international movement in that direction that, as Laurence Whitehead suggests, had strong backing from the U.S. government and international financial institutions.

In Brazil, Chile, and Mexico, several constitutional reforms with explicit economic objectives were also an integral part of the process of democratic transition. In the late 1980s in Chile, the constitutional reform that secured the independence of the Central Bank was part of the bargain to permit the transition to democracy. In Brazil, the Constituent Assembly of 1988 sought to prescribe much of the country's social and economic life to match its prescriptions in politics; in the decade that followed, democratically elected Brazilian governments succeeded in amending the Constitution in piecemeal fashion to enact market-opening constitutional and other institutional changes. In the late 1980s and the 1990s, the multiple bargains that were part of the closing act of Mexico's authoritarian regime included political and economic changes, the latter providing for the elimination of statist economic regulations.

Only in Venezuela in the late 1990s did constitutional reform represent a setback for market-conforming policies. In addition, in 2006 and 2007, respectively, Bolivia's President Morales and Ecuador's President Correa both called constitutional assemblies for various purposes, one of which was to reinforce the role of the state in the economy and move away from market-reliant policies in various important respects, especially the ownership and operation of natural resource companies such as those dealing in petroleum and natural gas. In these three energy-resource-rich countries, since the late 1990s the increase in the international price of energy has been associated with an increase in the role of the state with regard to the energy sector and, more broadly, the domestic economy; this is reminiscent of worldwide practices among energy exporters in the early 1970s.

Apart from these three energy-producing countries, constitutional property rights protections have not weakened in Latin America in recent years, though, as Corrales shows generally and Levitsky for the Kirchner presidency in Argentina, a broader political process, short of constitutional amendments, has strengthened presidents who prefer that the state regulate markets.

In the 1990s, the motor for constitutional amendments in Argentina, Brazil, Peru, and Venezuela was not economics but the incumbent president's wish to remove the formal prohibition against immediate presidential re-election. That was a factor, too, in Bolivia and Ecuador in 2006–7. In Peru and Venezuela in the 1990s, as Myers and Degregori indicate in their chapters, many other changes disproportionately strengthened the powers of Presidents Alberto Fujimori and Hugo Chávez, weakening constitutional democratic practice in both countries. In no country have recent constitutional reforms strengthened the capacity of legislative institutions to more effectively represent the consent of the governed, although the electoral law that governed Colombia's legislative elections in 2006 did have that intention and may have such a result.[20] Yet, only in Peru and Venezuela in the 1990s, and in Ecuador and Venezuela in 2007, has there been an evident authoritarian design in the motivations and processes for revising the constitution. The attempt failed in Venezuela when voters defeated the Chávez proposals in the December 2007 plebiscite.

In Ecuador in 2007, for example, President Correa relied on the electoral court but disregarded the constitutional court in his battle to dismiss from office the majority of the members of Parliament—an example of arbitrary, authoritarian presidential behavior in both procedure and outcome. Correa's success in defenestrating the majority of parliamentarians was an explicit assault on constitutional governance.

From the perspective of democratic governance, the comprehensive constitutional revisions carried out in Colombia in the early 1990s and in Venezuela in the late 1990s, and attempted in Bolivia, Ecuador, and Venezuela in 2006–7, illustrate the perils of such exercises: they weakened constitutional democracy or governability.

In his chapter Myers documents the concentration of political power in the hands of President Hugo Chávez, mainly through lawful means, although they disempowered the other constitutional organs and undercut those civil society organizations not under the president's influence, such as the Roman Catholic Church and many labor unions. The comprehensive revision to Colombia's Constitution in 1991, as Cepeda notes in his chapter, weakened governability. The parties lost control of the use of the party label, a process that changed only a decade later via legislation. Colombia's 1991 Constitution also mandated fiscal transfers to subnational governments equal to nearly half of the ordinary revenues in the national budget, without providing for institutional support to use those resources effectively. Decentralization with weak means for accountability to constituents and national institutions impaired governability.

In 2006–7, as Gamarra notes in his chapter, Bolivia's constitutional assembly became embroiled in bitter disputes that endangered the territorial unity of the state, disputes focused on the distribution of powers between the center and regional authorities and between the presidency and other constitutional organs. The very process of comprehensive Constitution revision polarized and destabilized Bolivian politics. And, in Ecuador in 2007, the way the constitutional assembly was convened—by sacking the majority of Parliament—impaired democratic governance.

On balance, therefore, Latin America's experiences with systematic constitutional reform mongering have not been good. At their best, those reform efforts have opened up avenues for participation to nontraditional groups. Yet, overall the trends have been adverse for effective democratic governance, which is distressing because the region did not begin at a high level. Since the late 1980s, the most far-reaching constitutional revision attempts in Bolivia, Brazil, Colombia, Ecuador, Peru, and Venezuela have produced constitutions that have weakened either liberal democracy (in Peru, Venezuela, and possibly Ecuador) or governability (in Bolivia, Brazil, and Colombia). The construction and deepening of constitutional democracy was more likely through incremental reforms.

More effective, well-pondered constitutional reforms have occurred piecemeal or in limited fashion, as in Argentina, Brazil, and Mexico during the 1990s or, as Siavelis notes, in Chile in the 2000s. Experienced parliamentarians, conscious of ongoing political habits and limitations, knowledgeable about practical issues of government, and operating under party discipline, were likely to produce constitutional reforms that strengthened the capacity of the state and the value of democratic institutions.

Legislatures and Courts

Since the early 1990s, the cross-national variation in the performance of Latin America's national legislatures and supreme or constitutional courts has increased. At the start of this period, these were weak institutions everywhere, often badly staffed, poorly funded, and incapable of independent policy making. In the 1990s, the power of legislatures and supreme courts weakened markedly only in Peru and Venezuela, threatening democratic practices. The power of legislatures and courts stabilized or, in some cases, strengthened, though mainly for political reasons—the effects of party competition—rather than due to constitutional reforms.

In general, party competition makes it more difficult for the executive to impose its will on the other constitutional organs. Competition between parties and party discipline within parties creates the political space that parliaments require to exercise their constitutional autonomy. Weak party discipline, on the other hand, lets individual parliamentarians retain autonomy from party leaders, at the risk that they will use this independence for personal gain, thwarting the ability of parliamentary leaders to mobilize party leverage against the executive.

Competition between parties is also the key explanation for supreme or constitutional court independence. Such courts are political institutions that are likely to defer to the executive when only one party is likely to win elections. These courts—not unlike the U.S. Supreme Court—follow public opinion polls and election returns, tipping against long-dominant presidents and parties only when they anticipate their replacement in office. Where the level of party competition is high, the high court may expect to find support in powerful quarters when it rules against the executive. Competitive parties have an incentive to preserve the independence of such courts as neutral arbiters.

Until 1997 in Mexico, the president's PRI commanded a majority of both chambers of Congress. Not surprisingly, Congress characteristically approved nearly all executive bills, and the Supreme Court rarely ruled against the executive on important matters; no party competition, no legislative or judicial autonomy.

Presidents Hugo Chávez and Alberto Fujimori weakened national legislatures, supreme courts, and political parties in Venezuela and Peru, although, as Myers shows in his chapter, Chávez was unable to seize control of the Supreme Court until 2005—seven years after his first presidential election in what had been a highly competitive political system. In both countries, parties had crumbled before the respective elections of Fujimori and Chávez; each was elected in what had become a no-party political system. In both countries, as party competition declined, so did the independence of parliaments and courts. Chávez won control of the National Assembly through elections, and through the Assembly he would later pack the Supreme Court. Fujimori's 1992 coup was aimed in part at the Supreme Court, which he subsequently packed as well. Both Chávez and Fujimori favored plebiscites to augment their presidential powers in order to prevent the legislature from holding them accountable. In the mid-2000s, Morales in Bolivia and Correa in Ecuador also relied on plebiscites to weaken their parliamentary oppositions.

With greater party competition, there is more autonomy. In the 1980s and 1990s, about a third of presidential bills were defeated in parliament in Argentina, Brazil, and Chile, which was the same proportion as in once-competitive Venezuela (1959–88). In Colombia, half of the president's bills were defeated in Parliament in the late 1990s.[21] These countries—Argentina excepted—showed also the best evidence for Supreme or Constitutional Court autonomy.[22] All arrived at this outcome, however, following slightly different paths, two of which should be highlighted: (1) the executive is supported, or checked, by disciplined parliamentary parties or (2) the executive is supported, or hamstrung, through the efficacy or inefficacy of obtaining parliamentary votes deputy by deputy.

High levels of party discipline and competition and appreciably less political autonomy of parliamentary deputies are most likely to permit the representation of public interests and purposes. Chile since 1990 and Mexico in the 2000s have had among Latin America's most programmatic and disciplined legislative parties. They are also fiercely competitive. Patronage, once the mother's milk of Mexican politics, declined in importance along with the decline of the PRI in opposition after the 2000 election. In the 2000s, both countries have parliaments capable of defeating many presidential initiatives. Both countries have independent supreme courts. In Mexico, increased political competition is a key explanation for the Supreme Court's increased political autonomy.

Indeed, as Denise Dresser makes clear in her chapter about Mexico in the 2000s, a key problem in Mexico is no longer how to check the imperial presidency of the PRI years but rather how to enable a democratic executive to govern with parliamentary support and to enact an array of economic and social reforms that will contribute to Mexico's growth and welfare. The old authoritarian regime had buttressed presidential power by extraconstitutional means, principally the effective role of the PRI in making presidential rule possible. Such arrangements masked the constitutional weakness of the president's formal institutional authority. With the passing of the authoritarian regime, the president's relative weakness vis-à-vis Congress became evident and worrisome, making the governance of Mexico more difficult and deferring important reforms.[23]

In Chile, in contrast, the executive retained considerable powers in the transition from dictatorship to democracy. The Chilean Congress, for example, cannot appropriate more funds for the budget than the executive has proposed; it may reallocate funds only beneath the presidentially stipulated budget ceiling. In that context, the close division of highly disciplined parties led the executive to negotiate over the enactment of major changes— above all, as Siavelis shows, the 2005 constitutional reform, the institutional climax of Chile's constitutional democratization since the end of Pinochet's dictatorship in 1990. Similarly, the changes in the Pinochet-appointed Supreme Court occurred gradually over the 1990s as the parties of the government and the opposition worked to create an impartial arbiter that would serve the interests of a competitive political establishment and, in so doing, enhance democratic order itself.

The supreme courts of Brazil and Colombia and, as Cepeda notes forcefully, Colombia's Constitutional Court, play significant public roles in these countries. Brazil's Supreme Federal Court and Colombia's Constitutional Court have ruled unconstitutional some major economic proposals in each country. The Colombian courts have also ruled against the executive on issues such as the extradition of drug traffickers, budgets, taxes, amnesty for combatants in Colombia's many domestic wars, and so forth. These are outcomes of vigorous party competition on election day.

The Brazilian and Colombian congresses enjoy relatively high levels of political autonomy—certainly compared to those of Mexico under the PRI, Peru under Fujimori, or Venezuela under Chávez. In Brazil and Colombia, much more than in Chile or contemporary Mexico, however, the executive often relies on patronage or clientelist practices to elicit the support of parliamentarians. Samuels, in his chapter on Brazil, shows some of the adverse repercussions in terms of the spectacular levels of corruption associated with relying on methods that require the purchase, at times literally, of legislative support deputy by deputy. Nevertheless, the Brazilian executive can and often does prevail by constructing a support coalition that way.[24] Clientelist practices nurture a perverse form of congressional deputy autonomy, fostering corruption and weakening the means for democratic accountability. The pork-barrel behavior of politically autonomous, clientelism-motivated individual legislators is more pernicious where parties are less disciplined, because there such behavior is less restrained.

However, Brazil and Ecuador have long suffered from weak party discipline, which imparts special qualities to their executive-legislative relations. In both countries, in the 1980s and 1990s approximately a third of the members of Congress elected for any given term switched political parties by the end of the term. In Brazil, during the congressional term that concluded with the 2006 election, more than a fifth of the members of the outgoing Congress had switched parties.[25] Such switches may be justified at times, but routine recurrent defections weaken democratic accountability: voters think that they are supporting X and get Y instead. This behavior also makes the task of governing much more difficult. Nevertheless, the extent of partisan cohesion in Brazil has risen over time because two of the more disciplined parties, the PSDB and the PT, elected a larger proportion of Congress. Moreover, Brazilian party switching occurs principally within "ideological families," which implies more substantial ideological bloc cohesion.[26] Both Cardoso and Lula sought to foster sustained loyalties among their congressional supporters.

Finally, Argentina, as Levitsky shows in his chapter, illustrates the impact of the rise and fall of political competition on the autonomy of other constitutional organs. The high level of partisan competition in the 1990s made Congress an important arena for partisan contestation and greatly enhanced the Supreme Court's independence. In the 2000s, the collapse of the Radical Party and the failure to develop a significant counterweight to the Peronistas, along with the rise in President Kirchner's popularity, severely curtailed the capacity of Congress to countervail the president's power as well as the

Supreme Court's independence; Kirchner sacked the justices he did not like and packed the court with others of his choosing. Argentina is the only one of the large countries studied in this book to have transitioned between such different outcomes in such a short time.[27]

In the early twenty-first century, competitive and disciplined parties, significant legislatures, and independent courts were the triad on which Latin American constitutional democracy was built. Chile and Mexico best exemplified this outcome.[28] At the opposite end, Chávez's Venezuela was the principal counterexample, with worrisome trends also seen in Correa's Ecuador. Brazilian and Colombian legislators enjoyed considerable individual autonomy but provided fewer checks on executive power, relying on vigorously independent high courts to play such a role; judicial independence, however, made market-oriented economic reform more difficult, certainly slower in both countries.

These, in short, are the three trade-offs that Latin America's constitutional democrats have faced. In practice, the autonomy of individual parliament members was at odds with effective, corruption-light democratic governance. A very high level of parliamentary autonomy relative to the executive may impede social or economic reforms. And supreme court institutional independence may serve to safeguard liberty, but it may do so in part by preventing needed economic reforms.

Conclusion

Latin America made many significant democratic gains from the 1980s to the 2000s, and some of these gains deepened in the 2000s. Constitutional democratic government survived the economic crises of the 1990s and 2000s; this has been quite unlike the Latin American experience in the 1960s and 1970s, when constitutional governments tumbled in the face of economic turbulence. Since 1990, civilian authority over the military has remained the norm and has gradually taken steps forward, except in Venezuela. These outcomes have derived from the effective practice of democratic politics.

Political parties and politicians had been dramatically unreliable and irresponsible in the late 1980s and early 1990s. Since that time, partisan reliability and responsibility have risen across the ideological spectrum. Such reliability and responsibility, in Downsian terms, characterize President Hugo Chávez in Venezuela just as well as they do the repeatedly electorally successful right-wing ARENA party in El Salvador. Parties and politicians may—and at times should—change their policy preferences provided that they do so openly, transparently, and in advance of election day to enable the public to make an informed choice. Such democratic standards marked the election victory of Lula and the PT in Brazil in 2002, Néstor Kirchner's election in Argentina in 2003, and the Frente Amplio's electoral victory in Uruguay in 2004. During the 2000s, Alejandro Toledo's election in Peru and Lucio Gutiérrez's in Ecuador did not meet those standards; no wonder Toledo was deeply unpopular and Congress evicted Gutiérrez from office. Such heightened partisan reliability and responsibility have a problematic effect, however: deeper and more sustained partisan polarization. Polarization, too, has characterized politics at the start of this century.

The efficacy of parties, long a problem, took a turn for the worse in the 1990s and 2000s, however. Party system breakdown began in Peru and Venezuela in the early 1990s and spread to Argentina, Bolivia, and Colombia in the 2000s. The reasons for such collapse remained the same—retrospective voting to punish malperformance in office and to break up interparty collusion along with intensified presidential action to disorganize parties, especially in Ecuador and Venezuela in the 2000s. Only the APRA in Peru revived in the 2000s.

The representational deficit lingers, too. The region remains the worldwide champion of economic inequality, plagued as well by gender, ethnic, and racial inequalities. Nevertheless, in the 1990s and the 2000s important steps forward were taken in poverty reduction and social services provision in Brazil, Chile, and Mexico—countries where the majority of Latin Americans live.

Reforms to change the contours of democratic governance retained their fundamental features from the 1980s to the 2000s. Piecemeal, targeted constitutional reforms proved more effective in improving the quality and competence of democratic governance. Comprehensive constitutional revision via constitutional assemblies was more likely to weaken democracy or governability, or both. In the 2000s, piecemeal, targeted reforms deepened Chilean democracy, while comprehensive constitutional reforms threatened it in Bolivia and Ecuador.

Competition by disciplined parties served democratic constitutional government best because it held the promise of strengthening parliaments and courts. That competition developed in Chile in the 1990s and in Mexico in the 2000s. Unfortunately, the institutional weaknesses of the Mexican constitutional design also made it difficult to enact most reforms during the first half of the 2000s. The high courts of Brazil and Colombia continued to become more independent, though in part by blocking important economic or social reforms. Parliamentary autonomy weakened dramatically in Argentina and Venezuela in the 2000s, when both national legislatures authorized enabling acts that delegated vast discretion to Presidents Kirchner and Chávez. Ecuador's President Correa abused power to dismiss the parliamentary majority that opposed his designs. Kirchner reinstituted the previous pernicious practice of purging the Supreme Court of justices whom the president opposed.[29]

This is the third edition of this book. The trends toward democratic governance were hopeful in the mid-1990s, when we wrote the first edition. Military rule and its record of ineptitude and abuse were over. Chile had made its transition to democracy, and Mexico had begun its own. Central America's domestic and international wars had come to an end. Economic growth had resumed.

The trends in democratic governance remained positive at the start of the 2000s, when we worked on the second edition. Mexico had elected a president from the opposition. Democracy had survived a financial panic in Brazil in 1999 and a calamitous economic collapse in Argentina in 2001–2. Alberto Fujimori's autocratic rule had ended in his resignation and political disgrace. Thus, we concluded the second edition asserting, "On balance, most Latin Americans lived in more open societies and were freer to exercise their political rights, including the right to protest against the government. Their governments worked more effectively."[30]

The trends have been less positive toward the end of the 2000s than they were prior to the book's two previous editions. Democratic consolidation advanced in Mexico, but democratic effectiveness gained little. Constitutional government weakened in Argentina as Kirchner overshadowed Congress and the Supreme Court. Venezuela no longer meets appropriate standards of constitutional democracy, nor has its government become more effective in serving its citizens, although in 2007 the voters stopped the Chávez-sponsored constitutional reforms to further weaken legislative and judicial counterweights to the executive branch, recentralize the state away from the units of the federation, and authorize the president's indefinite reelection at the same time that the state expropriated more of the means of production and the executive united the parties in its ruling coalition into a single party. Bolivia and Ecuador are in the midst of tumultuous changes, with worrisome authoritarian practices being deployed by Ecuador's President Correa. In Brazil, massive corruption during the PT's 2002 election campaign and in the conduct of subsequent presidential and congressional relations was a severe setback for democrats everywhere. Colombia's parties have decomposed during the 2000s and remain in flux, making it difficult to envisage a counterweight to a powerful executive in a country still rocked by violence and scandals related to the processes of making peace. Costa Rica's party system has been weakened. In South America, only Chile, Peru, and Uruguay have taken important steps toward democratic deepening in the 2000s. Therefore, angry, disappointed citizens have defeated incumbent parties throughout the majority of South and Central American countries in the 2000s.

And yet, in the long view, Latin Americans live today in freer, more democratic countries than they did in the 1970s or 1980s. Latin American citizens are better educated and possess longer life expectancies; poverty rates have dropped in the countries where most Latin Americans live. Nearly all Latin American economies have resumed a growth path in the 2000s, even if much of this growth responds mainly to benign exogenous international price increases for the commodities that they export. In general, therefore, in the 2000s most Latin American governments have governed more effectively than their predecessors did a full generation ago.

The key to democracy remains the decisions of citizens. In their hands, and on their wisdom, rest the region's democratic prospects. As the region approaches the two hundredth anniversary of the start of its independence, Latin America's democratic star shines less brightly than it did a decade ago, but it still shines more brightly than it did for the preceding generation.

Notes

Chapter 2. The Fading Regional Consensus on Democratic Convergence

1. Jon Pevehouse, in particular, has recently elaborated the argument that regional communities of democratic states are constructed "top down" as much as "bottom up." See Jon C. Pevehouse, *Democracy from Above: Regional Organizations and Democratization* (New York: Cambridge University Press, 2005).

2. Laurence Whitehead, ed., *International Dimensions of Democratization: Europe and the Americas,* 2nd ed. (New York: Oxford University Press, 2001).

3. Guantanamo is not the only legal "black hole" in the Caribbean. Popular folk singer So Anne was held for 826 days in a Haitian jail as a supporter of ousted President Aristide. In 2004, the U.S. Marines seized her on suspicion of "possessing information that could pose a threat to the U.S. military force." The U.S. military subsequently accepted that it had no weapons or evidence to support the allegations against her. Nevertheless, the interim Haitian government (dependent on United Nations troops) held her on suspicion of incitement to violence without ever bringing formal charges against her. Former prime minister Yvonne Neptune was similarly detained for over two years until freed on appeal in mid-2006. Less prominent individuals remain incarcerated without charge. Of course, such abuses have a long history in Haiti, but this was a case of coercive democratization, so here, too, the international participants failed to fulfill their own standards for the promotion of the rule of law.

4. Samuel P. Huntington, *Who Are We? The Challenges to America's National Identity* (New York: Simon and Schuster, 2004).

5. The shifting normative foundations of regionalism in the Americas is reviewed in Louise Fawcett and Monica Serrano, eds., *Regionalism and Governance in the Americas: Continental Drift* (New York: Palgrave Macmillan, 2005).

6. Whereas the enlargement of the EU is gradually reducing free movement of labor within the Union, its effects on illegal migration from the rest of the world are much harsher and may also undermine its credibility as an agency of democracy promotion in the world at large, although Spanish policy indicates a way that this could be mitigated (discussed later).

7. Most data have been taken from "El Gobierno promueve que los inmigrantes 'con papeles' puedan votar en las municipales," *El País,* August 16, 2006, www.elpais.com/articulo/espana/Gobierno/promueve/extranjeros/papeles/puedan/votar/municipales/elpporesp/20060816elpepinac_10/Tes/. However, the majority of the one million Latin Americans legally residing in Spain will have to wait for the establishment of reciprocating agreements. This applies to 340,000 Ecuadorans, 86,000 Peruvians, 54,000 Dominicans, and

48,000 Bolivians, among others. There is a significant exception in the case of Cuba, where the Spanish view is that it remains impossible to establish a reciprocity agreement based on democratic criteria.

8. The SIP has tried to promote its conception of press freedom throughout the hemisphere ever since the first Peronist period. It currently represents over 1,300 enterprises engaged in the print media in almost all Latin American republics. For example, it has 16 affiliates in Bolivia covering all the main commercial dailies.

9. By contrast, on March 14, 2006, Southcom Commander General Bantz Craddock spoke at a hearing of the Senate Armed Services Committee of the need for South America's military to address unconventional new threats such as "ungoverned spaces, porous borders, corruption, organized crime and narco-terrorism." Southcom has also warned against threats of "radical populism" and "*indigenismo*" in Andean countries. The Pentagon is pursuing bilateral policies with each national military counterpart, thereby fragmenting regional cooperation. It is urging local militaries to become more like Central American "constabularies." A law before the U.S. Congress calls for an OAS multinational political task force primarily targeting the Argentine-Brazilian-Paraguayan frontier area. Argentina explicitly rejected this "new threats" argument in May 2006, and Brazil protested against the OAS proposal. Instead, Brazilian forces are being deployed in the tri-border area.

10. The Helms-Burton Act presumes that this will prove the case for a postcommunist Cuba, but even there, there is room for doubt.

11. The sense that the Internet can be appropriated by the user for his or her own purposes probably adds to its impact and assists its diffusion, though it also increases the uncontrollability and even the unpredictability of the effects.

12. The Americas executive editor for the BBC World Service, James Painter, is currently on a career break at the Reuters Institute of Oxford University researching new international news networks such as Telesur. His preliminary comparison of CNN and Telesur concluded that the two networks cover similar themes but have very different news priorities and different senses of what is newsworthy. In his opinion, neither network is falsifying news. Telesur is not a vehicle for state propaganda (as was Mexico's Televisa before 1990 or Radio Havana). It is a network "with an agenda." Of course, so is Fox News. Telesur broadcasts little or no criticism of its sponsor governments (Argentina, Cuba, and Venezuela). It may be missing an opportunity to deepen democratic debate in Latin America and to strengthen public sector broadcasting there. James Painter, "The Boom in Counter-Hegemonic News Channels: A Case Study of Telesur," conference paper, Reuters Institute for the Study of Journalism, Oxford University, December 2006.

13. According to Cuban Ambassador Rafael Daussá, quoted in "Cuba se disculpa y se compromete con la salud de Bolivia," *La Razón* (Bolivia), August 19, 2006, www.la-razon .com/versiones/20060819_005638/nota_250_322147.htm. According to the Associated Press, 562 non-Cubans graduated from medical school in Havana in 2006, adding to the 3,000 already qualified. They came from poor families in 26 countries of Latin America and received free education in return for a commitment to provide health care for poor communities in their countries of origin (notably Guatemala and Honduras).

14. Guillermo O'Donnell and Philippe C. Schmitter, in *Transitions from Authoritarian Rule: Tentative Conclusions about Uncertain Democracies* (Baltimore: Johns Hopkins University Press, 1986), propose the term "*democradura,*" or "limited democracy," as a counterpart to "*dictablanda,*" or "liberalized authoritarianism." Their explanation is that "once democratization has begun and its prudent advocates fear the excessive expansion of such

a process or wish to keep contentious issues off the agenda of collective deliberation, they may well continue old, or even create new, restrictions on the freedoms of particular individuals or groups who are deemed insufficiently prepared or sufficiently dangerous to enjoy full citizenship status." While this was a useful contribution to the democratization literature, it was arguably too narrow. Just as *dictablanda* had an earlier history as a term describing a fully fledged but not very repressive authoritarian regime (the dictatorship of Primo de Rivera in Span), so *democradura* first emerged in reference to the guerrilla-inspired withdrawal of democratic freedoms in a venerable but declining democracy (Uruguay after 1971). Current regime taxonomies recognize various "illiberal," "delegative," or "low-quality" possibilities between strong liberal democracy and outright authoritarian rule. In the new climate created by the "war on terror," even the best-established of old democracies may display features of *democradura* in the sense that full citizenship rights are conditioned by a severe security override.

15. In a recent survey of Spaniards over the age of 45, 76.4 percent said they had done "nothing" to bring the Franco regime to an end, and 16.6 percent said they had done "little." This held for voters of Partido Socialista Obrero Español (the Spanish Socialist Workers' Party) and for supporters of regional parties as well. Only the Izquierda Unida's electorate reported otherwise, and their pro-communist affiliations suggest that they were not necessarily seeking the current type of liberal market democracy. "El Franquismo a debate 30 años después," *El Mundo* (Spain), August 17, 2006, www.elmundo.es/papel/2006/08/17/espana/2012608.html.

16. Peter Hakim, "Democracy and U.S. Credibility," *New York Times,* April 21, 2002, http://query.nytimes.com/gst/fullpage.html?res=9E0CE4DA133FF932A15757C0A9649C8B63. White House bulletins of April 16 and 18 contain denials of the main press accusations, but these were discounted by many in Latin America as backtracking once Chávez was reinstated. On April 12, the Associated Press correspondent in Washington reported on the White House's desire to see democracy restored but also noted that the Bush administration blamed Chávez for the events that (supposedly) had led to his resignation, adding that "officials suggested that the interruption of the democratic process in Venezuela was justified." "U.S. Closely Watching Political Developments in Venezuela Following Ouster of President," Associated Press, April 12, 2002, www.lubbockonline.com/stories/041202/upd_075-8830.shtml.

17. In my view, it need not be seen as a criticism to note the teleological elements in a democratization project. The same applies to EU enlargement, an imagined better future that has been (at least partially) realized.

18. A single way of thinking.

Chapter 3. The Backlash against Market Reforms in Latin America in the 2000s

I am most grateful to the other authors of this project, as well as the editors, for their terrific comments on earlier drafts. I thank Tom Carothers, Robert Kaufman, Marcus J. Kurtz, Eduardo Lora, James Mahon, M. Victoria Murillo, Moisés Naím, Carmen Pagés-Serra, Liliana Rojas-Suárez, Ben Ross Schneider, and Kurt Weyland, who offered comments on parts or all of this essay. I am also grateful to the students in my advanced seminar Markets and Democracy in Latin America (Fall 2006), whose ideas, questions, and research helped me polish my own.

1. Diana Tussie and Pablo Heidrich, "América Latina: ¿Vuelta al pasado estatistapro-

teccionista o en la senda de políticas de consenso democrático?" *Foreign Affairs en Español* 6, no. 2 (2006): 43–52.

2. Adam Przeworski, *Democracy and the Market: Political and Economic Reforms in Eastern Europe and Latin America* (New York: Cambridge University Press, 2001); Amy Chua, *World on Fire: How Exporting Free Market Democracy Breeds Ethnic Hatred and Global Instability* (New York: Doubleday, 2003).

3. Matthew R. Cleary, "Explaining the Left's Resurgence," *Journal of Democracy* 17, no. 4 (2006): 35–49; Teodoro Petkoff, *Las dos izquierdas* (Caracas: Alfadil, 2005); Jorge Castañeda, "Latin America's Left Turn," *Foreign Affairs* 85, no. 3 (2006): 28–43. See also Franklin Ramírez Gallegos, "Mucho más que dos izquierdas," *Nueva Sociedad* 197 (2006): 30–44.

4. This section draws from Javier Corrales, *Presidents without Parties: The Politics of Economic Reform in Argentina and Venezuela in the 1990's* (University Park: Pennsylvania State University Press, 2002), and Javier Corrales, "Market Reforms," in *Constructing Democratic Governance in Latin America,* 2nd ed., ed. Jorge I. Domínguez and Michael Shifter (Baltimore: Johns Hopkins University Press, 2003), where I provide more detailed bibliographic references for many of the points here.

5. Ruth Collier and David Collier, *Shaping the Political Arena: Critical Junctures, the Labor Movement, and Regime Dynamics in Latin America* (Princeton, N.J.: Princeton University Press, 1991); Stephan Haggard and Robert R. Kaufman, *Recrafting Social Contracts: Welfare Reform in Latin America, East Asia, and Central Europe* (forthcoming).

6. Nathan M. Jensen and Scott Schmith, "Market Responses to Politics: The Rise of Lula and the Decline of the Brazilian Stock Market," *Comparative Political Studies* 38, no. 10 (2005): 1245–70.

7. Thomas J. Biersteker, "The 'Triumph' of Liberal Economic Ideas in the Developing World," in *Global Change, Regional Response: The New International Context of Development,* ed. Barbara Stallings (New York: Cambridge University Press, 1995).

8. Francis Fukuyama, *The End of History and the Last Man* (New York: Free Press, 1992); John S. Dryzek, *Democracy in Capitalist Times: Ideals, Limits, and Struggles* (New York: Cambridge University Press, 1996), 17.

9. Barbara Geddes, "Challenging the Conventional Wisdom," *Journal of Democracy* 5, no. 4 (1994): 104–18.

10. Nancy Birdsall, Augusto de la Torre, and Rachel Menezes, *Washington Contentious: Economic Policies for Social Equity in Latin America* (Washington, D.C.: Carnegie Endowment for International Peace and the Inter-American Dialogue, 2001).

11. Kurt Weyland, "Neoliberalism and Democracy in Latin America: A Mixed Record," *Latin American Perspectives* 46, no. 1 (2004): 135–57.

12. Underperformance has also been detected in terms of labor productivity (measured as the ratio of a country's GDP per capita to its labor force) and in the generation of high-skill, technology-intensive, nontraditional exports. See José Antonio Ocampo, "Latin America's Growth and Equity Frustrations during Structural Reforms," *Journal of Economic Perspectives* 18, no. 2 (2004): 67–88, and Eva Paus, "Productivity Growth in Latin America: The Limits of Neoliberal Reforms," *World Development* 32, no. 3 (2004): 427–45.

13. Corrales, *Presidents without Parties;* Corrales, "Market Reforms."

14. Corrales, "Market Reforms."

15. Evelyne Huber and Fred Solt, "Successes and Failures of Neoliberalism," *Latin American Research Review* 39, no. 3 (2004): 150–64; Samuel A. Morley, Machado Roberto, and Stefano Pettinato, "Indexes of Structural Reform in Latin America," *Serie de Reformas Económicas* 12 (Santiago: CEPAL, 1999).

16. Michael Walton, "Neoliberalism in Latin America: Good, Bad or Incomplete?" *Latin American Research Review* 39, no. 3 (2004): 165–83.

17. Huber and Solt, "Successes and Failures of Neoliberalism."

18. Jakob de Haan, Susanna Lundstrom, and Jan-Egbert Sturm, "Market-Oriented Institutions and Policies and Economic Growth: A Critical Survey," *Journal of Economic Surveys* 20, no. 2 (2006): 157–91.

19. For an argument on the idea that perceptions among Latin Americans are not entirely related to actual economic performance, see Frances Hagopian, "Conclusions: Government Performance, Political Representation, and Public Perceptions of Contemporary Democracy in Latin America," in *The Third Wave of Democratization in Latin America: Advances and Setbacks*, ed. Frances Hagopian and Scott P. Mainwaring (New York: Cambridge University Press, 2005).

20. See Leslie Elliott Armijo and Philippe Faucher, "We Have a Consensus: Explaining Political Support for Market Reforms in Latin America," *Latin American Politics and Society* 44, no. 2 (2002): 1–40; Weyland, "Neoliberalism and Democracy in Latin America."

21. Alberto Chong and Florencio López-de-Silanes, "The Truth about Privatization in Latin America," Working Paper R-486 (Washington, D.C.: Inter-American Development Bank, 2003); Nancy Birdsall and John Nellis, "Privatization Reality Check: Distributional Effects in Developing Countries," in *Reality Check: The Distributional Impact of Privatization in Developing Countries*, ed. John Nellis and Nancy Birdsall (Washington, D.C.: Center for Global Development, 2005); Inter-American Development Bank, *Good Jobs Wanted: Access to Labor Markets in Latin America* (Washington, D.C.: Inter-American Development Bank, 2004).

22. This is not to deny that many privatizations entailed direct economic costs to consumers and workers. First, there were clear microeconomic costs. In some sectors, for example, prices for privatized services were too high relative to the income of consumers; in other sectors, consumers who had previously obtained services for free (due to "illegal" connections) suddenly had to start paying for services. See Chong and López-de-Silanes, "The Truth about Privatization in Latin America." Privatized firms reduce employment by 20–30 percent, and laid-off workers suffer income losses (ibid.). Furthermore, the decline of support for privatization is also strongly correlated with declines in economic growth: discontent increased during the recession years. See Ugo Panizza and Mónica Yáñez, "Why Are Latin Americans So Unhappy about Reforms?" Working Paper 567 (Washington, D.C.: Inter-American Development Bank, 2006).

23. Raúl Zibechi, "Privatizations: The End of a Cycle of Plundering," special report, Americas Program, International Relations Center, Silver City, N.M., November 2004; Mary M. Shirley, "Why Is Sector Reform So Unpopular in Latin America?" *Independent Review* 10, no. 2 (2005): 195–207.

24. Javier Corrales, "Coalitions and Corporate Choices in Argentina, 1976–1994: The Recent Private Sector Support for Privatization," *Studies in Comparative International Development* 32, no. 4 (1998): 24–51; Hector E. Schamis, "Distributional Coalitions and the Politics of Economic Reform in Latin America," *World Politics* 51, no. 2 (January 1999): 236–69.

25. María Victoria Murillo, "Voice and Light: Political Competition, Partisanship, and Policymaking," unpublished manuscript, Columbia University, New York, 2006.

26. Eduardo Lora and Ugo Panizza, "The Future of Structural Reform," *Journal of Democracy* 14, no. 2 (2003): 123–33.

27. Inter-American Development Bank, *Good Jobs Wanted*.

28. Barbara Stallings and Wilson Peres, *Growth, Employment, and Equity: The Impact of the Economic Reforms in Latin America and the Caribbean* (Washington, D.C.: Brookings Institution Press, 2000); Juan Pablo Pérez Sainz, "Exclusion and Employability: The New Labor Dynamics in Latin America," in *Rethinking Development in Latin America*, ed. Charles H. Wood and Bryan R. Roberts (University Park: Pennsylvania State University

Press, 2005); Alejandro Portes and Kelly Hoffman, "Latin American Clan Structures: Their Composition and Change during the Neoliberal Era," *Latin American Research Review* 38, no. 1 (2003): 41–82.

29. Jaime Saavedra, "Labor Markets during the 1990s," in *After the Washington Consensus,* ed. Pedro-Pablo Kuczynski and John Williamson (Washington, D.C.: Institute for International Economics, 2003).

30. Stallings and Peres, *Growth, Employment, and Equity,* 150; David De Ferranti, Guillermo Perry, Francisco H. G. Ferreira, and Michael Walton, *Inequality in Latin America and the Caribbean* (Washington, D.C.: World Bank, 2003).

31. Inter-American Development Bank, *Facing Up to Inequality in Latin America: Economic and Social Progress Report, 1998–1999* (Washington, D.C.: Inter-American Development Bank, 1998).

32. Magaly Sánchez R., "Insecurity and Violence as a New Power Relation in Latin America," *Annals of the American Academy of Political and Social Science* 606 (July 2006): 196–215; Joseph S. Tulchin, Hugo Fruhling, et al., eds., *Crime and Violence in Latin America: Citizen, Security, Democracy, and the State* (Washington, D.C.: Woodrow Wilson Center Press, 2003).

33. Saavedra, "Labor Markets during the 1990s."

34. John Coatsworth, "Structures, Endowments, and Institutions in the Economic History of Latin America," *Latin American Research Review* 40, no. 3 (2005): 130–31, 143; Joseph L. Love, "The Rise and Decline of Economic Structuralism in Latin America: New Dimensions," *Latin American Research Review* 40, no. 3 (2005): 108–10; John Walton and David Seddon, "Food Riots Past and Present," in *Free Markets and Food Riots: The Politics of Global Adjustment* (Oxford, England: Blackwell, 1994); Marcus J. Kurtz, "The Dilemmas of Democracy in the Open Economy: Lessons from Latin America," *World Politics* 56 (2004): 262–302.

35. Werner Baer, "Import Substitution and Industrialization in Latin America: Experiences and Interpretations," *Latin American Research Review* 7, no. 1 (1972): 95–111; Mahon, "Was Latin America Too Rich to Prosper?"

36. Haggard and Kaufman, *Recrafting Social Contracts;* John Sheahan, "Development Dichotomies and Economic Strategy," in *Towards a New Development Strategy for Latin America: Pathways from Hirschman's Thought,* ed. Simon Teitel (Washington, D.C.: Inter-American Development Bank, 1992).

37. Paul Almeida and Hank Johnston, "Neoliberal Globalization and Popular Movements in Latin America," in *Latin American Social Movements: Globalization, Democratization, and Transnational Networks* (Lanham, Md.: Rowman and Littlefield, 2006).

38. Karen L. Remmer, "Elections and Economics in Contemporary Latin America," in *Post-Stabilization Politics in Latin America: Competition, Transition, Collapse,* ed. Carol Wise and Riordan Roett (Washington, D.C.: Brookings Institution Press, 2003).

39. Birdsall, de la Torre, and Menezes, *Washington Contentious;* Patricio Navia and Andrés Velasco, "The Politics of Second-Generation Reforms," in *After the Washington Consensus: Restarting Growth and Reform in Latin America,* ed. Pedro-Pablo Kuczynski and John Williamson (Washington, D.C.: Institute for International Economics, 2003); Carol Wise, "Introduction: Latin American Politics in the Era of Market Reform," in *Post-Stabilization Politics in Latin America,* ed. Carol Wise and Riordan Roett (Washington, D.C.: Brookings Institution Press, 2003), 1–31.

40. Jana Morgan Kelly, "Counting on the Past or Investing in the Future? Economic and Political Accountability in Fujimori's Peru," *Journal of Politics* 65, no. 3 (2003): 864–80.

41. Kurt Weyland, "A Paradox of Success? Determinants of Political Support for President Fujimori," *International Studies Quarterly* 44 (2000): 481–502.

42. Carol Graham and Stefano Pettinato, "Frustrated Achievers: Winners, Losers and Subjective Well Being in New Market Economies," *Journal of Development Studies* 38, no. 4 (2002): 100–140.

43. For Shirley, this explains the unpopularity of privatizations in Latin America. She argues that when two economic actors (say A and B) gain from a transaction but gains are asymmetrical (B gains far more than A), A will emerge dissatisfied if A perceives B's gains to be the product of corruption, cheating, or unfavorable rules. With privatizations, Shirley suggests that consumers were A and governments and private owners were B. See Shirley, "Why Is Sector Reform So Unpopular in Latin America?"

44. Cleary, "Explaining the Left's Resurgence"; Weyland, "Neoliberalism and Democracy in Latin America."

45. Christopher Sabatini, "Decentralization and Political Parties," *Journal of Democracy* 14, no. 2 (2003): 138–50.

46. An index of degrees of decentralization in the region from 1996 to 2004 places Argentina, Brazil, and Colombia further along in the decentralization process. Ecuador, Chile, Peru, and Honduras follow them. See Robert Daughters and Leslie Harper, "Fiscal and Political Decentralization Reforms," in *The State of State Reform in Latin America,* ed. Eduardo Lora (Washington, D.C.: Inter-American Development Bank, 2005).

47. Jonathan Fox, "The Difficult Transition from Clientelism to Citizenship: Lessons from Mexico," in *The New Politics of Inequality in Latin America: Rethinking Participation and Representation,* ed. D. A. Chalmers et al. (New York: Oxford University Press, 1997).

48. Pilar Domingo, "Democracy and New Social Forces in Bolivia," *Social Forces* 83, no. 4 (2005): 1727–44.

49. Donna Lee Van Cott, *From Movements to Parties in Latin America: The Evolution of Ethnic Politics* (New York: Cambridge University Press, 2005); Javier Corrales, "The Devil We Know . . . and the Devil We Don't: Expresidents and Newcomers Running for President, and Winning," *Latin American Politics and Society* (forthcoming). See also Scott P. Mainwaring, "The Crisis of Democratic Representation in the Andes," *Journal of Democracy* 17 (2006): 13–27.

50. See Kurtz, "Dilemmas of Democracy."

51. A shorter version of this section appears in Javier Corrales, "The Many Lefts of Latin America," *Foreign Policy* 157 (2006): 10–11.

52. Latinobarómetro, *Informe Latinobarómetro 2006* (Santiago, Chile: Corporación Latinobarómetro, 2006).

53. James E. Mahon Jr., "Origins of Latin America's Leftward Shift: Growing Inequality, George Bush, and Record Surpluses," unpublished manuscript, Williams College, Williamstown, Mass., 2006.

54. Jorge I. Domínguez, "Business Nationalism: Latin American National Business Attitudes and Behavior toward Multinational Enterprises," in *Economic Issues and Political Conflict: U.S.–Latin American Relations,* ed. Jorge I. Domínguez (Woburn, Mass.: Butterworths, 1982).

55. "Eco Minería," *Cambios* (Bolivia), October 9, 2006.

56. Claudio Lomnitz, "Latin America's Rebellion: Will the New Left Set a New Agenda?" *Boston Review* (September–October 2006), http://bostonreview.net/BR31.5/lomnitz.php.

57. Ibid.

58. Mala Htun, "Women, Political Parties and Electoral Systems in Latin America," in *Women in Parliament: Beyond Numbers; A Revised Edition,* ed. Julia Ballington and Azza Karam (Stockholm: International IDEA, 2005).

59. Cleary, "Explaining the Left's Resurgence."

60. Ken Frankel, "Forget about Right, Left—It's Latin America," *Globe and Mail* (Toronto), December 12, 2006, A23.

61. Panizza and Yáñez , "Why Are Latin Americans So Unhappy about Reforms?"

62. For a brief discussion of reforms and the international economic cycle, see Navia and Valesco, "The Politics of Second-Generation Reforms."

63. International Monetary Fund, *Western Hemisphere Regional Economic Outlook: 2006 Midyear Update* (Washington, D.C.: International Monetary Fund, 2006).

64. Wendy Hunter and Timothy J. Power, "Rewarding Lula: Executive Power, Social Policy, and the Brazilian Elections of 2006," *Latin American Politics and Society* 49, no. 1 (2007): 1–30, 17 (emphasis in original).

65. McMahon, "Origins of Latin America's Leftward Shift."

66. Hector E. Schamis, "Populism, Socialism, and Democratic Institutions," *Journal of Democracy* 17, no. 4 (2006): 20–34; Inter-American Development Bank, *The Politics of Policies: Economic and Social Progress in Latin America, 2006 Report* (Washington, D.C., and Cambridge, Mass.: Inter-American Development Bank and the David Rockefeller Center for Latin American Studies, 2005), 14.

67. Ludolfo Paramio, "Giro a la izquierda y regreso del populismo," *Nueva Sociedad* 205 (2006): 62–74.

68. Robert R. Kaufman and Barbara Stallings, "The Political Economy of Latin American Populism," in *The Macroeconomics of Populism in Latin America*, ed. Rudiger Dornbusch and Sebastian Edwards (Chicago: University of Chicago Press, 1991).

69. Kenneth Roberts, "Neoliberalism and the Transformation of Populism in Latin America: The Peruvian Case," *World Politics* 48, no. 1 (1995): 82–116; Alan Knight, "Populism and Neo-Populism in Latin America, Especially Mexico," *Journal of Latin American Studies* 30, no. 2 (1998): 223–48; Philip Oxhorn, "The Social Foundations of Latin America's Recurrent Populism," *Journal of Historical Sociology* 11, no. 2 (1998): 212–46; Kurt Weyland, "Clarifying a Contested Concept," *Comparative Politics* 34, no. 1 (2001): 1–22; Michael Coppedge, "Venezuela: Popular Sovereignty versus Liberal Democracy," in *Constructing Democratic Governance in Latin America*, 2nd ed., ed. Jorge Domínguez and Michael Shifter (Baltimore: Johns Hopkins University Press, 2003); Weyland, "Neopopulism and Neoliberalism in Latin America."

70. Weyland, "Neopopulism and Neoliberalism in Latin America." On military populism, see See Karen Remmer, *Military Rule in Latin America* (Boulder, Colo.: Westview, 1991). See also Michael Conniff, "Introduction," in *Populism in Latin America*, ed. Michael Conniff (Tuscaloosa: University of Alabama Press, 1999).

71. Cas Mudde, "The Populist Zeitgeist," *Government and Opposition* 39, no. 3 (2004): 541–63.

72. Steven Levitsky and Maxwell A. Cameron, "Democracy without Parties? Political Parties and Regime Change in Fujimori's Peru," *Latin American Politics and Society* 45, no. 3 (2003): 1–33.

Chapter 4. Political Inclusion and Social Inequality

1. Mala Htun, "Is Gender Like Ethnicity? The Political Representation of Identity Groups," *Perspectives on Politics* 2, no. 3 (September 2004): 439–58.

2. I use the term *subordinate ethnic or racial groups* instead of the more popular *ethnic or racial minorities* because the groups in question are often not minorities but majorities (indigenous people in Bolivia, Afro-descendants in Brazil, and so forth).

3. Manager A, for example, sees an indigenous finance minister on television announcing important and desirable changes to economic policy. This experience causes her to question some of her racist beliefs about the financial acuity of indigenous peoples. A week later, interviewing applications for an accountant position, she is less likely to exclude indigenous candidates on the grounds of their ethnicity alone. Eventually, Manager A may come to regard ethnic diversity as helpful for her business because it attracts indigenous customers.

4. Hannah Pitkin, *The Concept of Representation* (Berkeley: University of California Press, 1967).

5. Sue Thomas, *The Difference Women Make* (Chicago: University of Chicago Press, 2002), and Michele Swers, *The Difference Women Make: The Policy Impact of Women in Congress* (Chicago: University of Chicago Press, 2002).

6. Iris Marion Young, *Justice and the Politics of Difference* (Princeton, N.J.: Princeton University Press, 1999).

7. The effectiveness of the laws in getting women elected varies across countries depending on the structure of the electoral system and the details of the legislation: women's presence exceeds 30 percent in Argentina and Costa Rica but is as low as 9 percent in Brazil. At the local level, the effects of quotas have been even greater. In Bolivia, Ecuador, and Peru, women made up only 8 percent of municipal councilors before quota laws, but after they came to occupy a quarter to a third of seats. See Mala Htun, "Democracy and Political Inclusion: The Andes in Comparative Perspective," in *Nadando contra la corriente: Mujeres y cuotas políticas en los países andinos,* ed. Magdalena León (Quito and Lima: UNIFEM, 2005); Mala Htun and Mark Jones, "Engendering the Right to Participate in Decisionmaking: Electoral Quotas and Women's Leadership in Latin America," in *Gender and the Politics of Rights and Democracy in Latin America,* ed. Nikki Craske and Maxine Molyneux (London: Palgrave, 2002).

8. I refer to gender equality policies rather than the advancement of women's interests. The latter notion is controversial because it may imply that women are a homogeneous group with shared concerns rather than individuals capable of making diverse life choices. In this chapter, I define "women's interests" in the loosest possible sense: it encompasses all claims made on behalf of women to improve their quality of life and promote their equality. These include demands made by feminist movements as well as by grassroots women's groups.

9. For a fuller discussion of the factors behind the adoption of quotas, see Htun and Jones, "Engendering the Right to Participate in Decisionmaking"; Lisa Baldez, "Elected Bodies: The Gender Quota Law for Legislative Candidates in Mexico," *Legislative Studies Quarterly* 29, no. 2 (May 2004): 231–58; Mona Krook, "Reforming Representation: The Diffusion of Candidate Gender Quotas Worldwide," *Politics & Gender* 2, no. 3 (2006): 303–27. These works emphasize the role of international factors, diffusion effects, and strategic interests.

10. Bolivian feminist activists first forged an agreement among themselves, then got support from the government women's agency, and finally brought in women politicians, creating the Women's Political Forum. The forum carried out a national survey on women in politics and distributed the results; it held debates, meetings, and workshops; it sought allies; and it even distributed "*palomitas*" (popcorn) at a soccer match. The strategy was "very scientific and very planned." Diana Urioste, Women's Coordination, interview by the author, La Paz, May 12, 2005.

11. Jimena Costa, interview by the author, La Paz, May 13, 2005.

12. Marcela Durrieu, *Se dice de nosotras* (Buenos Aires: Catalogos, 1999).

13. Baldez, "Elected Bodies," 249.

14. Marcela Rios, personal communication with the author, FLACSO–Chile, September 11, 2006.

15. Mala Htun, *Moving into Power: Strategies to Expand Women's Opportunities for Leadership in Latin America and the Caribbean,* Policy Brief (Washington, D.C.: Inter-American Development Bank, 1997)

16. Mala Htun, *Women's Rights and Opportunities in Latin America: Problems and Prospects,* Women's Leadership Conference of the Americas Issue Brief (Washington, D.C.: Inter-American Dialogue / International Center for Research on Women, 1998).

17. Amalia García, interview by the author, Mexico City, 1997.

18. Cecilia Romero, PAN senator, interview by the author, Mexico City, July 2000.

19. Marcela Durrieu, *Se dice de nosotras.*

20. Vega Ugalde, "La cuota electoral en Ecuador," in *Nadando contra la corriente.*

21. Lisa Baldez and Patricia Brañez, "¿Cuánto hemos avanzado las mujeres con las couotas? El caso beliviano," in *Nadando contra la corriente.*

22. Jimena Costa interview, 2005.

23. Diana Urioste interview, 2005.

24. Rosario Paz, interview by the author, La Paz, May 12, 2005.

25. Gloria Ardaya, interview by the author, La Paz, May 11, 2005.

26. Leslie Schwindt-Bayer, "Legislative Representation in Latin America: A Comparative Study of the Descriptive, Substantive, and Symbolic Representation of Women," Ph.D. diss., University of Arizona, Tucson, 2003, 117.

27. Roseanna Michelle Heath, Leslie A. Schwindt-Bayer, and Michelle M. Taylor-Robinson, "Women on the Sidelines: Women's Representation on Committees in Latin American Legislatures," *American Journal of Political Science* 49, no. 2 (April 2005): 420–36.

28. Schwindt-Bayer, "Legislative Representation in Latin America," and Htun and Jones, "Engendering the Right to Participate in Decisionmaking."

29. Heath, Schwindt-Bayer, and Taylor-Robinson, "Women on the Sidelines."

30. Mary Hawkesworth, "Congressional Enactments of Race-Gender: Toward a Theory of Raced-Gendered Institutions," *American Political Science Review* 97, no. 4 (November 2003): 529–50.

31. Mala Htun and Timothy J. Power, "Gender, Parties, and Support for Equal Rights in the Brazilian Congress," *Latin American Politics and Society* (Winter 2006): 83–104.

32. Anna-Lizbeth Flores-Alatorre, "Government, Parties, Gender and Democratization: The Causes and Consequences of Women's Participation in the Mexican Congress," B.A. thesis, Harvard University, Cambridge, Mass., 1998.

33. In this chapter, I use the terms *reserved seats* and *legislative reservations* (or just *reservations*) interchangeably.

34. The Colombian Constitution called for the creation of new indigenous territories (called ETIs for "*entidades territoriales indígenas*"), which would have the same legal status as states and municipalities, sharing in fiscal transfers and with the authority to administer public health and education (Articles 286, 288, and 329). It also gave indigenous rulers political autonomy and legal jurisdiction, allowing them to govern (administer justice, design development programs, distribute resources, administer natural resources, and collaborate in the maintenance of public security) in accordance with their own customs (*usos y costumbres*) as long as they did not contradict the Constitution and other national laws (Articles 246 and 330).

35. Peter Wade, *Blackness and Race Mixture: The Dynamics of Racial Identity in Colombia* (Baltimore: Johns Hopkins University Press, 1993).

36. Kirsten Matoy Carlson, "Premature Predictions of Multiculturalism?" *Michigan Law Review* 100 (May 2002): 1470–87.

37. When elections for the assembly were held in 1990, the indigenous groups Organización Nacional Indígena de Colombia (ONIC; National Indigenous Organization of Colombia) and Autoridades Indígenas de Colombia (AICO; Indigenous Authorities of Colombia) fielded candidates and ended up winning two of the 70 seats in dispute. Following a peace agreement with the government, a third indigenous former guerrilla leader was able to participate in the assembly but without voting rights. Donna Lee Van Cott, *The Friendly Liquidation of the Past: The Politics of Diversity in Latin America* (Pittsburgh: University of Pittsburgh Press, 2000).

38. Antonio Jacanamijoy, ONIC leader, interview by the author, Bogotá, June 11, 2004.

39. For an alternative view, see an article by Juliet Hooker, who claims that size of population is unrelated to governmental willingness to grant greater rights to indigenous peoples than to Afro-descendants. She argues that Latin American states are inclined to accept claims based on cultural distinctiveness (which indigenous peoples have) but not racism. Juliet Hooker, "Indigenous Inclusion / Black Exclusion: Race, Ethnicity and Multicultural Citizenship in Latin America," *Journal of Latin American Studies* 37 (2005): 285–310.

40. Manuel José Cepeda, interview by the author, Bogotá, June 16, 2004 (emphasis added).

41. *Black* usually means "of African descent" or "having phenotypical features that suggest African descent." Estimates are that around 20 percent of Colombians fall into this category. Olivier Barbary and Mireille Rabenoro, "Measurement and Practices of Social and Racial Segmentation in Cali: A Survey of African Colombian Households," *Population* 57, no. 4/5 (July 2002): 763–92. They can be further subdivided into at least three different groups. The first is a heterogeneous population living in urban areas, as do the vast majority of Colombians, and participating in the majority culture. Peter Wade, "Introduction: The Colombian Pacific in Perspective," *Journal of Latin American Anthropology* 7, no. 2 (2002): 6–7. Second are the *"raizales,"* or residents of the Caribbean islands of San Andrés and Providencia. The third group is that of the black communities who are the main beneficiaries of the Constitution. They are rural blacks living primarily in the Pacific and number approximately 540,000 people, or 7 percent of the total black population. Odile Hoffmann, "Políticas agrarias, reformas del Estado y adscripciones identitarias: Colombia y México," *Análisis Político* 34 (May 1998): 16. Rather than addressing the advancement of the majority of Colombia's blacks, the Constitution directed its attention only to this small group. Wade, "Introduction," 2–33, and Hoffmann, "Políticas agrarias, reformas del estado y adscripciones identitarias," 3–24.

42. Applicable to other areas of the country "with similar conditions," the law also called for mechanisms to protect the rights and cultural identity of these communities and for the promotion of their social and economic development. Later, legislation to implement this provision allocated two seats in the lower house of Congress to black communities.

43. Francisco Rojas Birry, "Ponencia: Los derechos de los grupos etnicos," *Gaceta Constituyente* (Bogotá), April 30, 1991, 19.

44. After the Constitution was approved, the government formed a commission of state officials, representatives of black communities, and anthropological experts to elaborate a law regulating the collective property titles authored by transitory Article 55. The commission met for almost two years to hammer out thorny issues, including what "territory" implied (would it include subsoil resources, trees, the force of a river flowing through it?) and what type of entity would qualify to receive a title. The eventual law (Law 70 of 1993) envisioned that title would be granted to a "community council" (*consejo comuni-*

tario) responsible for enforcing locally agreed-upon rules about the division and use of land. It also allocated two seats in the lower house of Congress to representatives of black communities, granted them presence in the National Planning Council, called for elaboration of a special national development plan, created a state agency to manage "black" issues, and required the Education Ministry to create "ethno-education" programs to strengthen African cultural identity as well as research units to educate everyone on the history of blacks in the country and their contribution to the nation. Manuel Rodríguez, former minister, interview by the author, Bogotá, 1993. As of 2003, around 4.5 million hectares of land had been allocated to collective title, representing around 4 percent of the total national territory. Odile Hoffmann, "Espacios y región en el Pacífico sur: Hacia la construcción de una sociedad regional," in *Gente negra en Colombia: Dinámicas sociopolíticas en Cali y el Pacífico,* ed. Olivier Barbary and Fernando Urrea (Medellín: Cidse-Ird-Colciencias, 2004), 213.

45. Indigenous political organizing dates to the 1960s and 1970s, when groups such as the Consejo Regional Indígena del Cauca (CRIC; Regional Indigenous Commission of the Cauca) and AICO were formed, mostly in the southwestern provinces of Cauca and La Guajira, where Indians make up a significant minority of the population (though they constitute only around 2 percent of the total national population). In 1980, ONIC was created in the wake of the first nationwide congress of indigenous representatives. Some of these groups forged relations with political parties and mainstream movements, including the M-19 guerrillas, but for the most part indigenous activists steered clear of white and mestizo-dominated organizations and political institutions. Donna Lee Van Cott, *From Movements to Parties: The Evolution of Ethnic Politics in Latin America* (New York: Cambridge University Press, 2005).

46. Felipe Botero Jaramillo, "El senado que nunca fue: La circunscripción nacional después de tres elecciones," in *Elecciones y democracia en Colombia, 1997–1998,* ed. Andrés Davila and Ana María Bejarano (Bogotá: Ediciones Uniandes, 1999); Eduardo Pizarro Leongómez, "Colombia: Renovación o colapso del sistema de partidos?" in *Colombia ante los retos del siglo XXI: Desarollo, democracia y paz,* ed. Manuel Alcántara Sáez and Juan Manuel Ibeas Miguel (Salamanca: Ediciones Universidad de Salamanca, 2001); Eduardo Pizarro Leongómez, "Giants with Feet of Clay: Political Parties in Colombia," in *The Crisis of Political Representation in the Andean Region,* ed. Scott Mainwaring, Ana María Bejarano, and Eduardo Pizarro (Cambridge: Cambridge University Press, 2006); Matthew Shugart, Erika Moreno, and Luis E. Fajardo, "Deepening Democracy through Renovating Political Practices: The Struggle for Electoral Reform in Colombia," in *Peace, Democracy, and Human Rights in Colombia,* ed. Christopher Welna and Gustavo Gallon (Notre Dame, Ind.: Notre Dame University Press, 2006).

47. In addition, a third indigenous candidate came to occupy a general Senate seat. The candidate who came in third in the indigenous contest received more votes than 12 candidates winning seats from the ordinary district. Indigenous organizations protested to the electoral authorities, who subsequently took a seat away from the one who has received the lowest number of votes nationwide and gave it to the Indian candidate. This experience showed indigenous leaders that they could compete successfully in an open field, and in subsequent elections they presented candidates in the ordinary district as well as the reserved one. Senator Gerardo Jumí, interview by the author, Bogotá, June 24, 2004.

48. Van Cott, *From Movements to Parties,* 203–7.

49. Gerardo Jumí interview, 2004.

50. Van Cott, *From Movements to Parties.*

51. They include Manuel Mosquera Garcés, who served as minister of education in the 1950s; Diego Córdoba, senator in the 1970s; and Jacobo Pérez, secretary general of the Con-

stituent Assembly. Fernando Cepeda, personal communication with the author, October 4, 2005.

52. Elisabeth Cunin, "La política étnica entre alteridad y esterotipo: Reflexiones sobre las elecciones de marzo de 2002 en Colombia," *Análisis Político* 48 (January–April 2003): 81.

53. Carlos Agudelo, "Etnicidad negra y elecciones en Colombia," *Journal of Latin American Anthropology* 7, no. 2 (2002): 184–85 and n. 34.

54. In lower-house races, the five reserved seats (one for an Indian, two for blacks, and one for a representative of Colombians living abroad) are elected from a special national district. Only specified deputies can run in the district, but anyone can vote for them. The national candidates appear on every ballot nationwide, and voters may opt to support them or the politicians contesting provincial elections. To qualify to run, blacks require the endorsement of a "black community" organization registered with the Interior Ministry. The other 162 lower-house deputies run for seats allocated to the provinces according to population (with each province getting a minimum of two).

55. Carlos Agudelo, "Comportamiento electoral en poblaciones negras: Algunos elementos para el analisis," in "Impactos de la Ley 70 y dinámicas políticas locales de las poblaciones afrocolombianas: Estudios de caso," by Carlos Agudelo, Teodora Hurtado, and Nelly Rivas, Working Paper 50, Cidse-Ird, Universidad del Valle, Cali, July 2000, 122.

56. María Isabel Urrutia received only 421 votes in the Chocó, and Welington Ortiz received 31. Over half of Welington's votes came from Bogotá and one-third of María Isabel's from the Valle province, where she had spent her sports career.

57. Cunin, "La política étnica entre alteridad y esterotipo."

58. Welington Ortiz, interview by the author, Bogotá, June 23, 2004; María Isabel Urrutia, interview by the author, Bogotá, June 15, 2004.

59. Welington Ortiz interview, 2004.

60. Mala Htun, "From Racial Democracy to Affirmative Action: Changing State Policy on Race in Brazil," *Latin American Research Review* 39, no. 1 (February 2004): 60–89; Edward Telles, *Race in Another America: The Significance of Skin Color in Brazil* (Princeton, N.J.: Princeton University Press, 2003).

61. They make up between 60 and 70 percent of the population and are evenly split between Quechuas and Aymaras. A small minority (2 percent of citizens) belongs to other groups living mostly in the tropical lowlands.

62. Felipe Quispe's Movimiento Indígena Pachakutik (MIP; Pachakutik Indigenous Movement), not the MAS, is classified as an ethnic party. Quispe wants the Aymara to form their own country and separate from the rest of Bolivia. Whites, whom he disparagingly calls *q'aras,* are not welcome.

63. Anthony Downs, *An Economic Theory of Democracy* (New York: Harper, 1957).

64. Alicia Muñoz, interview by the author, La Paz, May 10, 2005.

65. Ibid.

66. Salvador Romero, National Electoral Court, interview by the author, La Paz, May 17, 2005.

67. Jim Schultz, "Bolivia's Election Stunner," blog post, The Democracy Center, San Francisco, December 19, 2005, www.democracyctr.org/blog/2005/12/bolivias-election-stunner.html (accessed September 17, 2007).

68. Van Cott, *From Movements to Parties.*

69. Victor Hugo Cardenas, interview by the author, La Paz, May 17, 2005.

70. Van Cott, *From Movements to Parties.*

71. Xavier Albó, *Pueblos indios en la política* (La Paz: Plural Editores, 2002), 82.

72. Van Cott, *From Movements to Parties.*

73. Albó, *Pueblos indios en la política,* 95.

74. René Antonio Mayorga, "Bolivia's Democracy at the Crossroads," in *The Third Wave of Democratization in Latin America,* ed. Scott Mainwaring and Frances Hagopian (New York: Cambridge University Press, 2006); René Antonio Mayorga, "Outsiders and Neo-Populism: The Road to Plebiscitary Democracy," in *The Crisis of Democratic Representation in the Andes* (Palo Alto, Calif.: Stanford University Press, 2006); Donna Lee Van Cott, "From Exclusion to Inclusion: Bolivia's 2002 Elections," *Journal of Latin American Studies* 35, no. 4 (2003): 751–75.

75. Van Cott, "From Exclusion to Inclusion."

76. America Vera-Zavala, "Evo Morales Has Plans for Bolivia," December 18, 2005, www.inthesetimes.com/article/2438 (accessed September 17, 2007).

77. Salvador Romero interview, 2005.

78. Felipe Quispe, interview by the author, La Paz, May 11, 2005.

79. Teresa Canaviri, interview by the author, La Paz, May 13, 2005.

80. Salvador Romero interview, 2005.

81. Notwithstanding this sentiment, the party voted in favor of the constitutional reform bill, including the reserved seats, as a way to "demonopolize" representation in the country. Alicia Muñoz interview, 2005.

82. Quoted in Jim Schultz, "Bolivia's Election Stunner."

83. "El MAS desecha la cuota para los indígenas y los sindicatos," *La Razón* (La Paz), February 23, 2006, www.la-razon.com/Versiones/20060223_005461/nota_249_252327.htm.

84. Note that women's presence is also compatible with authoritarian tendencies. Perhaps more than any other recent Latin American president, Alberto Fujimori brought women into his inner circle of confidants and appointed them to senior positions in his administration. Far from feminist activists or even democrats, these women served at the front lines in his authoritarian consolidation and centralization of power. (Of course, so did many men.)

85. This section draws from Mala Htun, "Democracy and Political Inclusion: The Andes in Comparative Perspective," in *Nadando contra la corriente.*

86. Renata Segura, *The Politics of Constitution Making in Colombia and Ecuador: Struggles for Recognition and Redistribution,* Ph.D. diss., New School for Social Research, New York, 2007.

87. Mayorga, "Outsiders and Neo-Populism." Also various interviews by the author in La Paz, May 2005.

Chapter 5. Argentina

1. Indeed, Argentina is viewed as a prototypical case of delegative democracy. See Guillermo O'Donnell, "Delegative Democracy," *Journal of Democracy* 5 (January 1994): 55–69.

2. See Carlos Nino, *Un país al margen de la ley* (Buenos Aires: Emecé, 1992); O'Donnell, "Delegative Democracy"; and Steven Levitsky and María Victoria Murillo, eds., *Argentine Democracy: The Politics of Institutional Weakness* (University Park: Pennsylvania State University Press, 2005).

3. Edward L. Gibson, *Class and Conservative Parties: Argentina in Comparative Perspective* (Baltimore: Johns Hopkins University Press, 1996); James W. McGuire, *Peronism without Peron: Unions, Parties, and Democracy in Argentina* (Palo Alto, Calif.: Stanford University Press, 1997).

4. Enrique Peruzzotti, "Towards a New Politics: Citizenship and Rights in Contemporary Argentina," *Citizenship Studies* 6 (March 2002): 77–93.

5. These included national organizations, such as Conscience, Citizen Power, the Center for Legal and Social Studies, and local groups created in response to specific abuses. See Peruzzotti, "Towards a New Politics."

6. Enrique Peruzzotti, "The Nature of the New Argentine Democracy: The Delegative Democracy Argument Revisited," *Journal of Latin American Studies* 33 (February 2001): 142.

7. Catalina Smulovitz and Enrique Peruzzotti, "Societal Accountability in Latin America," *Journal of Democracy* 11 (October 2000): 147–58.

8. The mafia boss, Alfredo Yabran, committed suicide in the face of imminent arrest.

9. Steven Levitsky, *Transforming Labor-Based Parties in Latin America: Argentine Peronism in Comparative Perspective* (New York: Cambridge University Press, 2003).

10. Guillermo O'Donnell, *Modernization and Bureaucratic Authoritarianism: Studies in South American Politics* (Berkeley: University of California–Berkeley Institute of International Studies, 1973).

11. Levitsky, *Transforming Labor-Based Parties in Latin America.*

12. Ruth Berins Collier and David Collier, *Shaping the Political Arena* (Princeton, N.J.: Princeton University Press, 1991).

13. Levitsky, *Transforming Labor-Based Parties in Latin America,* 130–39.

14. Javier Auyero, *Poor Peoples' Politics* (Durham, N.C.: Duke University Press, 2000); Levitsky, *Transforming Labor-Based Parties in Latin America,* 187–91.

15. Ernesto Calvo and María Victoria Murillo, "Who Delivers? Partisan Clients in the Argentine Electoral Market?" *American Journal of Political Science* 48 (October 2004): 742–57; Calvo and Murillo, "The New Iron Law of Argentine Politics? Partisanship, Clientelism and Governability in Contemporary Argentina," in *Argentine Democracy,* ed. Levitsky and Murillo.

16. On the links among Peronism's provincial electoral strength, legislative majorities, and governability, see Calvo and Murillo, "The New Iron Law of Argentine Politics?"

17. Indeed, Calvo and Murillo ("The New Iron Law of Argentine Politics?") go as far as to suggest a new "iron law" of Argentine politics: only Peronism can govern the country.

18. Steven Levitsky and María Victoria Murillo, "Introduction," in *Argentine Democracy,* ed. Levitsky and Murillo, 2–3.

19. Nino, *Un país al margen de la ley;* Levitsky and Murillo, "Introduction"; Pablo T. Spiller and Mariano Tommasi, "Institutions and Public Policy Making in Argentina," in *Argentine Democracy,* ed. Levitsky and Murillo.

20. Gretchen Helmke, *Courts under Constraints: Judges, Generals, and Presidents in Argentina* (New York: Cambridge University Press, 2004).

21. Delia Ferreira Rubio and Matteo Goretti, "When the President Governs Alone: The Decretazo in Argentina, 1989–93," in *Executive Decree Authority,* ed. John M. Carey and Mathew Soberg Shugart (New York: Cambridge University Press, 1998), 285–90.

22. Delia Ferreira Rubio and Matteo Goretti, "Executive-Legislative Relationship in Argentina: From Menem's *Decretazo* to a New Style?" paper presented at the conference Argentina 2000: Politics, Economy, Society and International Relations, Oxford University, May 15–17, 2000, 1–4.

23. Gretchen Helmke, "Enduring Uncertainty: Court-Executive Relations in Argentina," in *Argentine Democracy,* ed. Levitsky and Murillo.

24. Nino, *Un país al margen de la ley;* O'Donnell, "Delegative Democracy."

25. Spiller and Tommasi, "Institutions and Public Policy Making in Argentina."

26. On horizontal accountability in Latin America, see O'Donnell, "Delegative Democracy."

27. Enrique Peruzzotti, "Demanding Accountable Government: Citizens, Politicians, and the Perils of Representative Democracy in Argentina," and Juan Carlos Torre, "Citizens

versus Political Class: The Crisis of Partisan Representation," both in *Argentine Democracy,* ed. Levitsky and Murillo.

28. Torre, "Citizens versus Political Class."

29. Ibid.

30. Peruzzotti, "Demanding Accountable Government"; Torre, "Citizens versus Political Class."

31. Sebastián Etchemendy, "Old Actors in New Markets: Transforming the Populist/ Industrial Coalition in Argentina, 1989–2001," in *Argentine Democracy,* ed. Levitsky and Murillo.

32. Javier Auyero, "Protest and Politics in Contemporary Argentina," in *Argentine Democracy,* ed. Levitsky and Murillo.

33. "FMI: 'La Argentina deberá probar una medicina amarga,'" *Clarín* (Buenos Aires), April 18, 2002, www.clarin.com/diario/2002/04/18/e-00801.htm.

34. See Joseph Stiglitz, "Argentina, Shortchanged: Why the Nation that Followed the Rules Fell to Pieces," *Washington Post,* May 12, 2002, B1.

35. Data collected by Centro de Estudios Nueva Mayoría (see www.nuevamayoria .com).

36. Peruzzotti, "Demanding Accountable Government," 246.

37. Ibid., 247–48.

38. See, for example, Mariano Grondona, "¿Por qué estamos tan mal? Porque pensamos mal," *La Nación* (Buenos Aires), March 31, 2002, 23.

39. Between 1995 and 2000, Argentina was consistently located in the middle of the pack on Transparency International's annual Corruption Perception Index, more or less on a par with Brazil and Mexico; only a notch below the Czech Republic, Greece, and Italy; and far better than China and India.

40. See Kenneth Roberts, "Neoliberalism and the Transformation of Populism in Latin America," *World Politics* 48, no. 1 (1995): 82–116; Kurt Weyland, "Neopopulism and Neoliberalism in Latin America: Unexpected Affinities," *Studies in Comparative International Development* 31, no. 3 (1996): 3–31.

41. Political analyst Luis Tonelli, quoted in "Not So Super Powers," *Economist,* August 10, 2006, 42.

42. These included Misiones party boss Ramon Puerta and Vice President Daniel Scioli (although Scioli later found his way back into the president's good graces).

43. "Acuerdan limitar el uso de decretos presidenciales," *La Nación,* June 14, 2006, 1.

44. "Supreme Court President Blinks First," *Latin American Weekly Report,* July 1, 2003, 292.

45. The government claimed that Suez had violated regulations for nitrate levels in the water. See "Military Coup Anniversary Blighted by Scandal," *Latin American Brazil and Southern Cone Report,* March 2006, 15.

46. In March 2006, the government responded to rising domestic meat prices by suspending virtually all beef exports for 180 days.

47. "Kirchner Accused of Using Piqueteros," *Latin American Brazil and Southern Cone Report,* March 2005, 3.

48. "Economistas respaldan los acuerdos de precios, pero con matices," *Clarín* (Buenos Aires), January 11, 2006, www.clarin.com/diario/2006/01/11/um/m-01122529.htm.

49. Sebastián Etchemendy and Ruth Berins Collier, "Trade Union Resurgence and Neo-Corporatism in Argentina (2002–2006): Evidence, Causes, and Implications," paper presented at the Annual Meetings of the American Political Science Association, Philadelphia, August 31–September 3, 2006.

50. Etchemendy and Collier, "Trade Union Resurgence and Neo-Corporatism in Argentina," 20.

51. "Military Coup Anniversary Blighted by Scandal."

52. "Jubilaciones: Llevan a $ 470 la mínima y suben 11% el resto," *Clarín* (Buenos Aires), May 10, 2006, www.clarin.com/diario/2006/05/10/elpais/p-00301.htm.

53. Argentina's offer gained 76 percent acceptance among bondholders, which was considered a major success.

54. The 1986 Full Stop Law established a deadline after which new human rights cases could not be launched. The 1987 Due Obedience Law protected junior military officers from prosecution.

55. "Más de 500 represores en el banquillo," *Página/12* (Buenos Aires), January 2, 2006, www.pagina12.com/ar/diario/elpais/1-61197-2006-01-02. The Kirchner government also sought judicial annulment of Menem's 1990 pardon of top officials of the dictatorship, and in September 2006 a federal judge revoked some—though not all—of the pardons awarded to General Jorge Videla and two other officials of the dictatorship.

56. "Planes sociales: Más de la mitad son para afiliados a los partidos," *Clarín* (Buenos Aires), September 11, 2005, www.clarin.com/diario/2005/09/11/elpais/p-00315.htm.

57. "Los piqueteros electos," *Página/12* (Buenos Aires), October 30, 2005, www.pagina 12.com.ar/diario/elpais/1-58614-2005-10-30.html.

58. In several provinces, including Buenos Aires, Córdoba, La Rioja, Misiones, and San Juan, Peronist lists finished first *and* second in the election.

59. Peruzzotti, "Demanding Accountable Government," 248.

60. Omar Sanchez, "Argentina's Landmark 2003 Presidential Election: Renewal and Continuity," *Bulletin of Latin American Research* 24 (2005): 457.

61. Ibid., 459.

62. Peruzzotti, "Demanding Accountable Government."

63. "Un Congreso a la medida de Kirchner," *Clarín* (Buenos Aires), January 2, 2006, www.clarin.com/diario/2006/01/02/elpais/-00901.htm.

64. Helmke, "Enduring Uncertainty" and *Courts under Constraints.*

65. "Diputados aprobó la reforma en Magistratura," *Clarín* (Buenos Aires), February 22, 2006, www.clarin.com/diario/2006/02/22/um/m-01146507.htm; "Kirchner Strengthens Grip on Judiciary with Divisive Reform," *Latin American Brazil and Southern Cone Report,* February 2006, 1; "Opposition Unites against 'Bid to Control Judiciary,'" *Latin American Weekly Report,* January 3, 2006, 8.

66. "La SIP condenó el trato que se le da a la prensa en la Argentina," *Clarín* (Buenos Aires), March 22, 2006, www.clarin.com/diario/2006/03/22/sociedad/s-03501.htm; "Kirchner Strengthens Grip on Judiciary with Divisive Reform."

67. See "Como un lanzamiento, pero sin decirlo," *Página/12* (Buenos Aires), September 3, 2006, www.pagina12.com.ar/diario/elpais/1-72446-2006-09-03.

68. UCR leader Roberto Iglesias, quoted in "Entre intolerancias y exageraciones," *Clarín* (Buenos Aires), September 3, 2006, www.clarin.com/diario/2006/09/03/opinion/0-03301.htm.

69. ARI leader Elisa Carrió, interview by the author, Harvard University, April 28, 2006.

70. For example, Mariano Grondona, "Argentine Politics on the Eve of National Elections," presentation at the David Rockefeller Center for Latin American Studies, Harvard University, Cambridge, Mass., October 4, 2005.

71. See "Blumberg, más referente social que candidato," *Clarín* (Buenos Aires), September 3, 2006, www.clarin.com/diario/2006/09/03/elpais/p-00601.htm.

72. See O'Donnell, "Delegative Democracy." A useful comparison may be Alan García's

first presidency in Peru. Like Kirchner, García was a highly energetic and popular leader who concentrated power in the presidency. Unchecked even within his own party, García made a series of decisions—such as that regarding the 1987 bank nationalization—that destroyed his presidency.

73. Examples include "neo-Peronist" party bosses who defied Perón during the 1960s, the Renovation faction during the mid-1980s, and José Octavio Bordón in the mid-1990s.

74. Prior to 2003, the UCR had never won less than 17 percent of the vote in a presidential election, and only once—in 1995, when it finished third—had it finished worse than second.

75. "Political Representation Explodes into Small Fragments," *Latin American Weekly Report,* September 28, 2004, 3.

76. Calvo and Murillo, "The New Iron Law of Argentine Politics?"

77. Marcelo Escolar and Ernesto Calvo, "Ultimas imágenes antes del naufragio: Las elecciones del 2001 en Argentina," *Desarrollo Económico* 42 (April 2002): 25–44; Torre, "Citizens versus Political Class."

78. Collier and Collier, *Shaping the Political Arena;* Gibson, *Class and Conservative Parties;* McGuire *Peronism without Perón.*

79. Scott Morgenstern and Luigi Manzetti, "Legislative Oversight: Interests and Institutions in the United States and Argentina," in *Democratic Accountability in Latin America,* ed. Scott Mainwaring and Christopher Welna (New York: Oxford University Press, 2003).

80. Morgenstern and Manzetti, "Legislative Oversight."

81. Ernesto Stein, Mariano Tommasi, Koldo Echebarría, Eduardo Lora, and Mark Payne, *The Politics of Policies: Economic and Social Progress in Latin America, 2006 Report* (Cambridge: Inter-American Development Bank and David Rockefeller Center for Latin American Studies / Harvard University Press, 2006), 55.

82. Mark P. Jones, Sebastián M. Saiegh, Pablo T. Spiller, and Mariano Tommasi, "Amateur Legislators—Professional Politicians: The Consequences of Party-Centered Electoral Rules in a Federal System, *American Journal of Political Science* 46 (2002): 656–69.

83. Stein et al., *The Politics of Policies,* 55.

84. Ibid., 88. By contrast, Uruguay ranked first, Chile second, Brazil third, and Mexico sixth.

85. Helmke, *Courts under Constraints.*

86. Ibid.

87. Stein et al., *The Politics of Policies,* 86.

Chapter 6. Bolivia

1. A few books and journalistic interviews are now available that provide a glimpse into the life of Bolivia's president. See, for example, Darwin Pinto and Roberto Navio, *Un tal Evo: Biografía no autorizada* (Santa Cruz de la Sierra: Editorial El País, 2007). An interesting evaluation of Morales's first 18 months in office can be found in *Evo en el análisis: 26 lideres de opinión evalúan el proceso de cambio* (La Paz: Pulso Internacional, 2007).

2. For the best early analysis of the results of the December 2005 elections, see Carlos Toranzo Roca, *Bolivia: Una Revolución Democrática* (La Paz: Nueva Sociedad, 2006).

3. These were the central elements of the 1952 MNR Revolution. The best treatment of the revolution continues to be James M. Malloy, *Bolivia: The Uncompleted Revolution* (Pittsburgh: University of Pittsburgh Press, 1970).

4. Under the terms of 1994 Constitution, if the winner does not attain 50 percent plus one, Congress elects the president from the top two finishers. In earlier elections, the MAS had fared less well, but the trend was always upward. The electoral participation of the MAS-IPSP began in the 1999 municipal elections, in which the coalition won barely 3 percent of the vote. In the 2002 general elections, it placed second with 20.96 percent, and in the December 2004 municipal elections it won first place with 18 percent. Then, in the first-ever elections for prefects (governors), the MAS won three of nine departments, and in the July 2006 elections for representatives to the 2006 Constituent Assembly, it won 50.74 percent of the votes cast.

5. Through a strange agreement with the MNR, the MAS won control of the leadership of the Senate. This agreement lasted for the first year only; after August 2006, the opposition won back the leadership of that chamber.

6. Felipe Quispe broke with García Linera and has never been a supporter of Evo Morales. Since Morales's ascendance to power, Quispe has declared himself a member of the opposition, claiming that the MAS and Morales are not true representatives of indigenism.

7. The best work available on the collapse of the traditional party system is Jorge Lazarte Rojas, *Entre los espectros del pasado y las incertidumbres del futuro: Partido y democracia en Bolivia a principios del Siglo XXI* (La Paz: IDLIS and Plural, 2005).

8. For a discussion of these dynamics, see Eduardo A. Gamarra and James M. Malloy, "The Patrimonial Dynamics of Party Politics in Bolivia," in *Building Democratic Institutions,* ed. Scott Mainwaring and Timothy Scully (Stanford, Calif.: Stanford University Press, 1996), and James M. Malloy and Eduardo A. Gamarra, *Revolution and Reaction: Bolivia 1964–1985* (Piscataway, N.J.: Transaction Books, 1988). Despite the transition to democracy, neopatrimonial practices changed little. Until 2005, neopatrimonialism was rooted in the employment needs of Bolivia's urban middle classes, who comprised the leadership and the bureaucratic cadre of the leading political parties.

9. In the 1990s, the economic strategy included the capitalization of seven state enterprises, including hydrocarbons, airlines, railroads, electricity, and telecommunications. Capitalization was an innovative form of privatization under which 50 percent of shares and management were sold to foreign private investors. Much controversy surrounded this economic strategy, which was launched during the first administration of Gonzalo Sánchez de Lozada (1993–97). Foreign direct investment increased significantly, to the extent that by 1999 over US$1 billion had entered the national economy. At the same time, because the strategy was largely capital intensive, its impact on labor markets was small and its impact on employment was minimal. This was particularly significant in a country where over 70 percent of the economically active population was in the informal sector.

10. No greater controversy exists in Bolivia than that over the interpretations of what occurred in October 2003. Former president Sánchez de Lozada argues that it was a vast conspiracy—including Carlos Mesa, his own vice president, and Evo Morales—that toppled him (Sánchez de Lozada, interviews by the author, Washington, D.C., October 2003 and April 2007). A careful reading of the press during those 14 months provides ample evidence of the strong desire of myriad groups to end his presidency. These disparate efforts coincided in September and October 2003, mainly as a result of the government's violent rescue of foreign tourists who had been kidnapped by followers of Felipe Quispe in the Altiplano town of Warisata. The escalation of events included a massive and well-organized march toward La Paz that concentrated in the neighboring city of El Alto.

11. Following General Hugo Banzer's death from cancer in 2001, Quiroga became president of Bolivia for 12 months (August 2001–August 2002). He founded PODEMOS as an *agrupación ciudadana* (citizen's group) and essentially buried ADN, the party that had

given him a political life. Similarly, Doria Medina broke away from the MIR, which refused to give him the leadership of the party, to found Unidad Nacional (UN; National Unity). See Eduardo A. Gamarra, "The Future of Political Parties, Agrupaciones Ciudadanas and Comunidades Indígenas: An Analysis of the Impact of the 2004 Municipal Elections on Bolivia's Political System," report to USAID, La Paz, 2005.

12. Government of Bolivia, "Vivir bien: La nueva estrategia de desarrollo de Bolivia," PowerPoint presentation, Ministry of Hydrocarbons, delivered June 2007.

13. For a similar argument, see Fernando Molina's *Crítica de las ideas políticas de la nueva izquierda boliviana* (La Paz: Editorial Amauta, 2005) and *Evo Morales y el retorno de la izquierda nacionalista* (La Paz: Editorial Amauta, 2007).

14. Nonetheless, the growth rate for 2006 was below that registered during the 1970s or the 1990s and below the Latin American average growth rate of 5 percent. The recovery of the Bolivian economy began at least two years before the election of Evo Morales. In 2004, Bolivian exports surpassed US$2 billion for the first time since the late 1970s. In 2005, exports exceeded US$2.7 billion, and in 2006 exports surpassed US$4 billion. This export success has translated into US$2.7 billion in international reserves, an increase in the value of the Boliviano, and a positive commercial and fiscal balance. The point is that these favorable results have had little to no relation to the Morales government's economic strategy. They are largely due to the positive growth rate of the world economy and the export boom of raw materials worldwide.

15. For a similar analysis, see "Informe Milenio sobre la Economía en el año 2006," report 22, Fundación Milenio, La Paz, March 2007.

16. It is also correct, however, to note that representative democracy worked well mainly for urban middle-class sectors tied to the apparatuses of the traditional political parties and that rural Bolivians were largely ignored. This situation changed dramatically in the mid-1990s as a result of the Popular Participation Law.

17. Carlos Toranzo Roca, "Making Mestizos more Visible and Cholifying Social Discourse," *Hemisphere* (Summer 2007): 16–17. For a more comprehensive discussion of *mestizo* politics in Bolivia, consult Carlos Toranzo Roca, *Rostros de la democracia: Una mirada mestiza* (La Paz: ILDIS and Plural, 2006).

18. Ximena Costa, "15 meses de Evo," *Hemisphere* (Fall 2007): 8–9.

19. In mid-2007, the contradictory nature of simultaneous demands became clear to the Morales administration when *campesinos* of Apolo in the northern region of the La Paz department marched into the Madidi National Reserve demanding the land they had been promised by the government's agrarian reform program. They were met by *originarios,* indigenous people from the region who live in the park as partial recognition of their protection of the natural habitat. Many unresolved incidents like this one have occurred, revealing the weakness of the use of the term *indigenous.*

20. See "Torrico defiende los clanes del MAS Investigación: La oposición dice que indagará el presunto nepotismo y favoritismo del partido oficialista en el aparato estatal," *La Razón* (La Paz), April 10, 2007, www.la-razon.com/versiones/20070410_005872/nota_247 _412454.htm; "El MAS pide pruebas de militancia en el caso avales CASOS: Al menos cuatro de los investigados mencionaron que trabajaron para el masismo," *La Razón* (La Paz), April 5, 2007, www.la-razon.com/versiones/20070405_005867/nota_247_410892.htm; and "Tráfico de avales: MAS expulsa a 3 dirigentes y los somete a la justicia ordinaria," *Bolpress* (La Paz), March 20, 2007, www.bolpress.com/art.php?Cod=2007070601.

21. "La Suprema dice que si Evo no prueba, comete delitos: Molestia los magistrados aseguran que el Jefe de Estado es irresponsable y que miente," *La Razón* (La Paz), March 23, 2007, www.la-razon.com/versiones/20070323_005854/nota_247_405687.htm.

22. The focus group findings can be found in Eduardo A. Gamarra, "The Future of Political Parties, Agrupaciones Ciudadanas and Comunidades Indígenas: An Analysis of the Impact of the 2004 Municipal Elections on Bolivia's Political System," Report to USAID, La Paz, 2005.

23. "El aparato público, al servicio del plan masista: Además de la distribución de espacios entre el instrumento político y las organizaciones sociales, se realizan descuentos para el partido," *La Razón* (La Paz), April 2, 2007, www.la-razon.com/versiones/20070402 _005864/nota_244_409469.htm.

24. For an analysis of the implications of the nationalization decree, see Mauricio Medinacelli Monroy, *La Nacionalización del Nuevo Milenio: Cuando el precio fue un aliado* (La Paz: Fundemos and Hanns Seidel Stiftung, 2007). A more specific way to describe the nationalization decree is as part of a complex process of modification of contracts that yielded greater control for YPFB as well as up to 82 percent participation for the state and 12 percent for the private investor.

25. The Vinto Smelter was capitalized in the late 1990s by a British firm that then sold it to COMSUR, the company owned by former president Sánchez de Lozada. COMSUR sold the smelter to the Swiss-based Glencore for a hefty profit in 2002. The Morales government claims that the sale to Glencore was unethical and illegal; thus, it has been reticent to negotiate with the company. It has also claimed that it would withdraw from the World Bank's International Centre for the Settlement of Investment Disputes, where Glencore has claimed it will go for arbitration.

26. See Roberto Laserna, *La trampa del rentismo* (La Paz: Fundación Milenio, 2006), 26.

27. Malloy and Gamarra, *Revolution and Reaction.*

28. For an expansion of this definition, see Roberto Laserna, *Rentismo y conflicto social en Bolivia: Una investigación exploratoria* (Washington, D.C.: World Bank, 2005).

29. See "Se quiebra el diálogo y Apolo decide protestar, la comisión del Ejecutivo que fue a dialogar con los *campesinos* abandonó ayer Apolo: Los apoleños dieron un plazo de 24 horas para que el Jefe de Estado vaya a la zona a dialogar; Amenazaron con anexarse a Perú y marchar," *La Razón* (La Paz), June 1, 2007, www.la-razon.com/versiones/20070601 _005924/nota_250_434493.htm, and "Comunarios bloquean ruta La Paz–Apolo—Las comunidades de Correo y Yuyo controlan el tránsito: El Ejecutivo pide diálogo," *La Razón* (La Paz), June 2, 2007, www.la-razon.com/versiones/20070602_005925/nota_250_435031 .htm.

30. A huge march staged in January 2005 in the city of Santa Cruz de la Sierra forced then-president Carlos Mesa to call a referendum on autonomy and to allow for the election of prefects. Two and a half years later, a clear definition of autonomy is still lacking. Moreover, Santa Cruz leaders are ambiguous about their commitment to the Constituent Assembly, because it could roll back their notions of autonomy and the role of the recently elected prefects.

31. These interviews and focus groups were conducted for USAID in 2004 and have again been conducted since January 2007 as part of an ongoing book project. See Eduardo A. Gamarra, "The Future of Political Parties."

32. The final results showed that those voting "Yes" to departmental autonomy predictably won in the half-moon departments of Beni, Pando, Santa Cruz, and Tarija and that those voting "No" won in Chuquisaca, Cochabamba, La Paz, Oruro, and Potosí. The referendum question clearly notes that the binding results apply to each department and not nationally, as the MAS has argued. While the half-moon departments demand that the Constituent Assembly design an architecture that guarantees autonomy, the government

believes it won a national referendum and thus the Constituent Assembly can proceed to design an autonomy conceived by the middle-class indigenist intellectuals of the MAS.

33. See "Iyambae, el pueblo cruceño se hizo presente," *El Deber,* December 15, 2006, www.eldeber.com.bo/2006/2006-12-15/index.php; "Autonomía moviliza a un millón de personas," *El Deber* (Santa Cruz), December 16, 2006, www.eldeber.com.bo/2006/2006-12-16/index.php; and "Media Luna y MAS miden sus fuerzas en cabildos simultáneos," *Los Tiempos,* December 15, 2006, www.lostiempos.com/noticias/12-15-06/nacional.php.

34. "Ocho periodistas agredidos por bloqueadores en San Julián," *El Deber,* December 15, 2006, www.eldeber.com.bo/2006/2006-12-15/vernotaaldia.php?id=23.

35. European envoy messages to President Morales apparently swayed the government to order the coca growers and other groups to abandon their attempts to topple Reyes Villa.

36. The 25-five-year war on drugs in the Chapare yielded dozens of dead coca farmers and members of the unions that Evo Morales led. As has been documented by human rights organizations and the People's Ombudsman, Morales was also a recurrent victim of the human rights abuses that characterized this so-called war.

37. Although Morales was never formally charged in court, his expulsion from the National Congress was reversed by the Constitutional Tribunal. The irony is that, in 2007, Morales attempted to expel from the Tribunal the very members of that body who had allowed him to return to Congress in 2002.

38. For a useful early treatment of this phenomenon, consult Kevin Healy, "The Political Ascent of the Coca Growers," *Journal of Interamerican Studies and World Affairs* 33, no. 1 (1991): 87–121.

39. See "Los cocaleros ratifican a Evo en la dirigencia: Tendrá como misión fundamental despenalizar la hoja a nivel internacional; Pidieron la anulación de la Ley 1008 y el respeto al 'cato de coca' por familia," *La Razón* (La Paz), February 14, 2006, www.la-razon.com/versiones/20060214_005452/nota_256_248841.htm, and "Crisis política en Bolivia sin salida," *Los Tiempos,* January 12, 2007, www.lostiempos.com/noticias/1-12-07_ultimas_nac7.php.

40. A *cato* is about 1,600 square meters (about 0.16 hectares).

41. Coca chewing is legal in Bolivia, as is the use of the leaf for brewing tea, which is said to be effective in treating altitude sickness.

42. The reference to U.S. universities is curious because Morales and many of his followers refer to a study by Harvard University that they claim states that coca is the most nutritious leaf in existence. The only Harvard study conducted on the subject is one by J. A. Duke, D. Aulik, and T. Plowman, *Nutritional Value of Coca,* Harvard Botanical Museum Leaflets, 1975, 113–19.

43. In February 2006, when Evo Morales was reelected as head of the Federation of Coca Growers, the members of these groups demanded that the new Bolivian president authorize one *cato* per individual. Although the president did not give in to this request, in authorizing the increase from 12,000 to 20,000 hectares he has accomplished the same objective.

44. The Bolivian government claimed that the demand for industrialized products was not only internal. Morales argued that demand in northern Argentina was great and that products such as coca liquor, toothpaste, shampoo, and coca tea were also to be sold in China, Cuba, and Venezuela. Evo Morales, interview by the author, La Paz, November 7, 2004.

45. These assessments include the annual International Narcotics Control Strategy Report and the Office of National Drug Control Policy reports. A critical review of these re-

ports, which defend the Morales approach, can be found in Coletta A. Youngers and Eileen Rosin, *Drugs and Democracy in Latin America: The Impact of U.S. Policy* (Boulder, Colo.: Lynne Rienner, 2005).

46. Even President Morales has noted this link, at least in the case of the Apolo *campesinos* who continue to move into the Madidi park. Another indication of the explosion of this phenomenon can be measured by newspaper coverage. Between January and early June 2007, 87 articles (an average of 17.4 per month) about cultivation in parks appeared in the La Paz daily *La Razón* alone.

47. For example, buses, cars, trains, and trucks are frequently found with cocaine shipments hidden in compartments. These methods are used to move cocaine and its precursors throughout Bolivian territory.

48. On May 31, 2007, the Fuerza Especial de Lucha contra el Narcotráfico (FELCN) carried out an anti-drug raid dubbed "Cristal de Invierno" against one of the largest cocaine labs ever found in Bolivian territory. The FELCN claimed that the lab was capable of producing 100 kilograms of the drug per day. The significance of the lab was not only its production capacity but the fact that Bolivians, Colombians, and Peruvians were arrested at the site. In March 2007, Colombians who claimed to be demobilized members of the FARC were arrested in Santa Cruz.

49. See "Policía: Es difícil evitar ingreso de los extranjeros indeseables. Motivo: No hay medios y la frontera boliviana es inmensa," *El Deber* (Santa Cruz), April 25, 2007, www .eldeber.com.bo/2007/2007-04-15/index.php, and "Indagan la inmigración de narcos colombianos. Preocupación: El director nacional de la FELCN indicó que las acciones de Inteligencia se centrarán en Santa Cruz para determinar el grado de la presencia de mafias extranjeras ligadas al narcotráfico," *El Deber* (Santa Cruz), June 5, 2007, www.eldeber .com.bo/2007/2007-06-05/vernotaseguridad.php?id=1196.

50. According to a report in *La Razón,* 1,714 Bolivianos are serving prison time for trafficking drugs around the world. See "Mas de 1500 bolivianos cumplen sentencias por trafico de drogas en el exterior," *La Razón,* June 5, 2007, www.la-razon.com/irn.asp?ver =1846&C=244&id=519667.

51. Humberto Vacaflor, "La refundación de Bolivia," *La Razón* (La Paz), March 9, 2008, www.la-razon.com/versiones/20080309_006206/C_246.htm.

Chapter 7. Brazil

I thank Amaury de Souza, Jorge Domínguez, Kathryn Hochstetler, Peter Kingstone, Eduardo Leoni, Octavio Amorim Neto, Timothy Power, Michael Shifter, Paulo Sotero, and Kurt Weyland for helpful comments.

1. Rachel Meneguello, *PT: A formação de um partido* (São Paulo: Paz e Terra, 1989); Margaret Keck, *The Workers' Party and Democratization in Brazil* (New Haven, Conn.: Yale University Press, 1992).

2. William Nylen, "The Making of a Loyal Opposition: The Workers' Party (PT) and the Consolidation of Democracy in Brazil," in *Democratic Brazil: Actors, Institutions, and Processes,* ed. Peter Kingstone and Timothy J. Power (Pittsburgh: University of Pittsburgh Press, 2000), 126–43; David Samuels, "Sources of Mass Partisanship in Brazil," *Latin American Politics and Society* 48, no. 2 (2006): 1–27.

3. Scott Mainwaring, "Presidentialism, Multipartism, and Democracy: The Difficult Combination," *Comparative Political Studies* 26, no. 2 (1993): 198–228.

4. Bolívar Lamounier and Rubens Figueiredo, *A era FHC: Um balanço* (São Paulo: Cultura, 2002), 270.

5. Evaluations of the Cardoso administration include Lamounier and Figueiredo, *A era FHC*, and Fabio Giambiagi, José Guilherme Reis, and André Urani, eds., *Reformas no Brasil: Balanço e agenda* (Rio de Janeiro: Nova Fronteira, 2004). In English, see Mauricio A. Font and Anthony Peter Spanakos, eds., *Reforming Brazil* (Lanham, Md.: Lexington Books, 2004).

6. For Lula's 2002 platform, see Partido dos Trabalhadores, *Programa de governo 2002 coligação Lula presidente* (São Paulo: Comitê Lula Presidente, 2002).

7. Inês Magalhães, Luiz Barreto, and Vicente Trevas, eds., *Governo e cidadania: Balanço e reflexões sobre o modo petista de governar* (São Paulo: Editora Fundação Perseu Abramo, 1999); Nylen, "The Making of a Loyal Opposition."

8. David Samuels, "From Socialism to Social Democracy? The Evolution of the Workers' Party in Brazil," *Comparative Political Studies* 37, no. 9 (2004): 999–1024.

9. This was known as the *Carta ao povo Brasileiro* (Letter to the Brazilian people). It contrasted with a party resolution from just six months earlier known as the *Carta de Recife* (Letter from Recife), which had articulated more radical positions. Partido dos Trabalhadores, *Carta ao povo brasileiro* (São Paulo: Partido dos Trabalhadores, 2002), available at www.pt.org.br.

10. Lourdes Sola, "Financial Credibility, Legitimacy and Political Discretion: The Lula da Silva Government," in *Statecrafting Monetary Authority: Democracy and Financial Order in Brazil,* ed. Lourdes Sola and Laurence Whitehead (Oxford: Centre for Brazilian Studies, Oxford University, 2006), 237–68.

11. See, for example, Partido dos Trabalhadores, *Carta ao povo brasileiro,* which contains information from government ministries.

12. For details on participatory budgeting and the debates surrounding its political importance, see Brian Wampler, "Expanding Accountability through Participatory Institutions: Mayors, Citizens and Budgeting in Three Brazilian Municipalities," *Latin American Politics and Society* 46, no. 2 (2004): 73–99; William Nylen, *Participatory Democracy versus Elite Democracy: Lessons from Brazil* (New York: Palgrave Macmillan, 2003); and Gianpaolo Baiochhi, ed., *Radicals in Power: The Workers' Party and Experiments in Urban Democracy in Brazil* (London: Zed Books, 2003).

13. Kathryn Hochstetler, "Organized Civil Society in Lula's Brazil," paper presented at the Latin American Studies Association 2006 Conference, San Juan, Puerto Rico, March 15–18; Brasilio Sallum Jr. and Eduardo Kugelmas, "Sobre o modo Lula de governar," in *Brasil e Argentina hoje: Política e economia,* ed. Brasilio Sallum Jr. (São Paulo: EDUSC, 2004).

14. The reform Lula's government achieved was, however, watered down from the initial proposal. See Vinícius Carvalho Pinheiro, "Reforma da previdência: Uma perspectiva comparada," in *Reformas no Brasil,* ed. Giambiagi, Reis, and Urani.

15. Sallum Jr. and Kugelmas, "Sobre o modo Lula de governar"; Timothy Power, "The October 2006 Elections in Brazil," PowerPoint slide presentation obtained from the author, Chatham House, London, October 9, 2006; Hochstetler, "Organized Civil Society in Lula's Brazil."

16. Instituto de Estudos Socioeconômicos, "Reforma agrária no governo Lula: Residual e periférica," *Nota Técnica* 105 (March 2006): 2. This claim is somewhat ironic given that the Movimento dos Sem-Terra (MST; Landless Peasants' Movement), along with thousands of other civil-society organizations, receives substantial subsidies from the federal government. Hochstetler, "Organized Civil Society in Lula's Brazil."

17. See Francisco H. G. Ferreira, Phillippe G. Leite, and Julie A. Litchfield, "The Rise and Fall of Brazilian Inequality: 1981–2004," World Bank Policy Research Working Paper 3867 (Washington, D.C.: World Bank, March 2006); Cláudio Couto and Paulo Baia, "Lula's Administration: The Limits of Change," paper presented at the Latin American Studies Association 2006 Conference, San Juan, Puerto Rico, March 15–18; Ricardo Paes de Barros, Mirela de Carvalho, Samuel Franco, and Rosane Mendonça, "Uma análise das principais causas da queda recente na desigualdade de renda Brasileira," Discussão 1203 (Rio de Janeiro: Instituto de Pesquisa Econômica Aplicada, 2006).

18. Fundação Getúlio Vargas, "O segundo real," PowerPoint slide presentation, Centro de Pesquisas Sociais, Fundação Getúlio Vargas, Rio de Janeiro, 2006, www.fgv.br/cps/pesquisas/site_ret_port/RET_Apresentacao_port.pdf.

19. Ibid. See also Ferreira, Leite, and Litchfield, "The Rise and Fall of Brazilian Inequality."

20. Couto and Baia, "Lula's Administration."

21. Power, "The October 2006 Elections in Brazil."

22. Sérgio H. Hudson de Abranches, "Presidencialismo de coalizão: O dilema institucional Brasileiro," Dados 31, no. 1 (1988): 5–38.

23. Wendy Hunter, "Democracy and Social Policy in Brazil: Advancing Basic Needs, Preserving Privileged Interests," paper presented at the conference Democracy and Human Development: A Global Inquiry, Boston University, Boston, November 12, 2004.

24. Barry Ames, The Deadlock of Democracy in Brazil (Ann Arbor: University of Michigan Press, 2001); Argelina Figueiredo and Fernando Limongi, Executivo e legislativo na nova ordem constitutional (Rio de Janeiro: Editora FGV, 1999).

25. Octavio Amorim Neto, "As consequências políticas de Lula: Novos padrões de recrutamento ministerial, controle de agenda e produção legislativa," paper presented at the seminar Revisiting Governability in Brazil: Is Political Reform Necessary? Centre for Brazilian Studies, Oxford University, Oxford, May 26, 2006, 2.

26. Couto and Baia, "Lula's Administration," 7.

27. Ibid.

28. The expelled petistas went to other parties on Brazil's left. These included Senator Heloísa Helena, who challenged Lula in the 2006 presidential election as the candidate of the Partido Socialismo e Liberdade (Party of Socialism and Liberty).

29. Amorim Neto, "As consequências políticas de Lula," 11.

30. Ibid., 16.

31. Observers have pointed to several other weaknesses in Lula's administration: the president's hands-off personal management style, which may have facilitated the corruption within his administration; a lack of a broad set of goals to guide government action; and a lack of policy coordination across ministries. Sallum Jr. and Kugelmas, "Sobre o modo Lula de governar"; Couto and Baia, "Lula's Administration."

32. Sallum Jr. and Kugelmas, "Sobre o modo Lula de governar," 274. See also Lúcia Hippolito, Por dentro do governo Lula: Anotações num diário de bordo (São Paulo: Editora Futura, 2005), 53–77.

33. This contributed to low administrative capacity because many PT nominees had little experience in public administration. Sallum Jr. and Kugelmas, "Sobre o modo Lula de governar," 275.

34. Ames, Deadlock of Democracy.

35. As if things could not get any worse for the administration, the winning candidate resigned from the Chamber later that year after it was revealed that he had extorted money from the owner of a restaurant in the Congress building.

36. Couto and Baia, "Lula's Administration," 12.

37. An excellent summary of the scandals surrounding the Lula administration can be found in David Fleischer, "Pilgrim's Progress: How (and Why) Lula and the PT Lost Their Way Once in Power—The Political Corruption Scandals in 2003–2005," paper presented at the Latin American Studies Association 2006 Conference, San Juan, Puerto Rico, March 15–18.

38. "Roberto Jefferson: 'Não sou pior do que os caras do PT,'" *O Dia On-line*, April 15, 2006, http://odia.terra.com.br/brasil/htm/geral_31650.asp.

39. Transparency International 2006, *Transparency International Corruption Perceptions Index 2006*, www.transparency.org/policy_research/surveys_indices/cpi.

40. See José Antônio Giusti Tavares, Fernando Schüller, Ronaldo Moreira Brum, and Valério Rohden, *Totalitarismo tardio—O caso do PT* (Porto Alegre: Mercado Aberto, 2000).

41. They also allege that corruption was far more widespread than Jefferson and congressional inquiries have managed to expose—and thus that the scandals impeded even greater harm. Although it was perhaps not intended, this view has perversely allowed Roberto Jefferson to claim the mantle of martyr for democracy.

42. Marco Aurélio Garcia, *Revista Fórum* (São Paulo), April 15, 2006, www.revista forum.com.br/vs3/artigo_ler.aspx?artigo=a0a5fe9a-ec8f-4bdf-a676-324040ec038f& pagina=&Query=daslu&Assunto=&Edicao=&Autor= (accessed February 6, 2008); Tarso Genro, "O governo Lula está sob cerco politico," interview in *O Estado de São Paulo*, April 15, 2006, http://clipping.planejamento.gov.br/Noticias.asp?NOTCod=261468 (accessed February 6, 2008).

43. Eugênia Lopes, "MPF denuncia 40 pessoas por envolvimento no mensalão," *O Estado de Sao Paulo*, April 11, 2006; Rodrigo Rangel, "Entrevista do procurador-geral da república, Antonio Fernando de Souza, à revista Istoé," *Istoé Online*, April 23, 2006, www.estadao .com.br/arquivo/nacional/2006/not20060411p56842.htm.

44. "Entrevista com Luiz Gushiken," *O Globo* (Rio de Janeiro), July 18, 2005, http:// jg.globo.com/JGlobo/0,19125,VTJ0-2742-20050718-102960,00.html (accessed February 7, 2008).

45. Hunter, "Democracy and Social Policy in Brazil."

46. David Samuels, "Does Money Matter? Campaign Finance in Newly Democratic Countries: Theory and Evidence from Brazil," *Comparative Politics* 34 (2001): 23–42; Samuels, "From Socialism to Social Democracy?"

47. David Samuels, "Incentives to Cultivate a Party Vote in Candidate-Centric Electoral Systems: Evidence from Brazil," *Comparative Political Studies* 32, no. 4 (1999): 487–518; Samuels, "Sources of Mass Partisanship in Brazil."

48. David Samuels, "Incumbents and Challengers on a Level Playing Field: Assessing the Impact of Campaign Finance in Brazil," *Journal of Politics* 63, no. 2 (2001): 569–84; David Samuels, "Pork-Barreling Is Not Credit-Claiming or Advertising: Campaign Finance and the Sources of the Personal Vote in Brazil," *Journal of Politics* 64, no. 3 (2002): 845–63.

49. Samuels, "From Socialism to Social Democracy?"

50. Hunter, "Democracy and Social Policy in Brazil."

51. Samuels, "From Socialism to Social Democracy?"

52. Some have come to call this the "*caixa três*" to differentiate it from the decentralized *caixa dois*. Evidence that the PT had begun to centralize the distribution of campaign finance for its own candidates can be found even in the PT's official campaign finance balance sheets for 2002. That year, the PT became the first party to record substantial (and perfectly legal) intraparty financial transfers to candidates other than its presidential candidate. For Brazilian campaign finance data, please contact the author at dsamuels@umn.edu.

53. Those who made such accusations were ignored or silenced, and some left the party. For example, former *petista* Chico de Oliveira suggests that PT radicals knew long ago what was brewing and did nothing, thus tacitly approving of PT corruption. A critical reference is the interview of former PT treasurer Paulo de Tarso Venceslau, "Exclusivo: Ex-secretário denuncia corrupção no PT," *Jornal da Tarde* (São Paulo), May 26, 1997, www.ternuma.com.br/revela.htm (accessed February 8, 2008). Several other former *petistas* have gone on record with similar accusations.

54. Leonardo Avritzer, "O PT não acabou," *Agência Carta Maior,* June, 29, 2005, www.cartamaior.com.br/templates/colunaMostrar.cfm?coluna_id=2074; Peter Flynn, "Brazil and Lula, 2005: Crisis, Corruption and Change in Political Perspective," *Third World Quarterly* 26, no. 8 (2005): 1221–67; Amorim Neto, "As conseqüências políticas de Lula"; Couto and Baia, "Lula's Administration"; Hunter, "Democracy and Social Policy in Brazil"; Carlos Pereira, Timothy Power, and Lucio Rennó, "Under What Conditions Do Presidents Resort to Decree Power? Theory and Evidence from the Brazilian Case," *Journal of Politics* 67, no. 1 (2005): 198–200.

55. Ames, *Deadlock of Democracy.*

56. Pereira, Power and Rennó, "Under What Conditions Do Presidents Resort to Decree Power?"

57. Hunter, "Democracy and Social Policy in Brazil."

58. Brasilio Sallum Jr., "Metamorfoses do estado Brasileiro no final do século XX," *Revista Brasileira de Ciências Sociais* 18, no. 52 (2003): 35–54.

59. Scott Mainwaring, *Rethinking Party Systems in the Third Wave of Democratization: The Case of Brazil* (Palo Alto, Calif.: Stanford University Press, 1999); Ames, *Deadlock of Democracy;* Lamounier and Figueiredo, *A era FHC.*

60. Lamounier and Figueiredo, *A era FHC,* 289.

61. Argelina Figueiredo and Fernando Limongi, *Executivo e legislativo na nova ordem constitutional* (Rio de Janeiro: Editora FGV, 1999).

62. Cláudio Gonçalves Couto and Rogério Bastos Arantes, "Constituição, governo e democracia no Brasil," *Revista Brasileira de Ciências: Sociais* 21, no. 61 (June 2006): 41–62.

63. Ernesto Stein, Mariano Tomassi, Koldo Echebarría, Eduardo Lora, and Mark Payne, *The Politics of Policies: Economic and Social Progress in Latin America* (Washington, D.C.: Inter-American Development Bank, 2006), www.iadb.org/res/ipes/2006/index.cfm?language=English. See also Leslie Armijo, Philippe Faucher, and Magdalena Dembinska, "Compared to What? Assessing Brazil's Political Institutions," *Comparative Political Studies* 39, no. 6 (2006): 759–86.

64. Stein et al., "The Politics of Policies."

65. Kurt Weyland, "The Growing Sustainability of Brazil's Low-Quality Democracy," in *The Third Wave of Democratization in Latin America: Advances and Setbacks,* ed. Frances Hagopian and Scott P. Mainwaring (Cambridge: Cambridge University Press, 2005).

66. Amaury de Souza, "Political Reform in Brazil: Promises and Pitfalls" (Washington, D.C.: Center for Strategic and International Studies, 2004); Jairo Nicolau, "Cinco opções, uma escolha: O debate sobre a reforma do sistema eleitoral no Brasil," unpublished paper, 2007, http://jaironicolau.iuperj.br/artigos.html.

67. The case of Itamar Franco is certainly instructive. He was not directly elected to the presidency and was not affiliated with any party yet managed to sustain democratic governance in the aftermath of a jarring political scandal and in the face of economic crisis. He did so by constructing an extremely broad cabinet coalition.

68. If political reform that involves campaign finance occurs, it will be because cam-

paigns have become so expensive that politicians' uncertainty about their careers has increased.

69. Silvia Cervellini, "Corrupcão na política: Eleitor vítima ou cúmplice?" paper presented at the second Brazilian Research Congress, São Paulo, March 22–24, 2006; Samuels, "Sources of Mass Partisanship in Brazil."

70. Charles Davis, Roderic Ai Camp, and Kenneth Coleman, "The Influence of Party Systems on Citizens' Perceptions of Corruption and Electoral Response in Latin America," *Comparative Political Studies* 37, no. 6 (2004): 677–703.

71. Hochstetler, "Organized Civil Society in Lula's Brazil," 23.

Chapter 8. Chile

I thank Javier Corrales, Peter DeShazo, Jorge Domínguez, Steven Levitsky, Cynthia McClintock, David Myers, and Michael Shifter for useful comments and suggestions.

1. On the *estado de compromiso,* see Manuel Antonio Garretón, *The Chilean Political Process* (Boston: Unwin Hyman, 1989), 4, 48, 81.

2. Barrett has made a similar argument. However, his analysis focuses on the new compromise as it is reflected in the party system and its mediation of capital accumulation and distribution. See Patrick S. Barrett, "Chile's Transformed Party System and the Future of Democratic Stability," *Journal of Inter-American Studies and World Affairs* 42, no. 3 (2000): 1–32.

3. Many have referred to Chile's "unfinished" or "incomplete" transition. Most notably, Felipe Agüero's chapter in the second edition of this volume was entitled "Chile: Unfinished Transition and Increased Political Competition," in *Constructing Democratic Governance,* 2nd ed., ed. Jorge Domínguez and Michael Shifter (Baltimore: Johns Hopkins University Press, 2003): 292–320.

4. Shifter and Jawahar note the importance of differentiating leaders commonly grouped together as "leftists" in "The Divided States of the Americas," *Current History* 105, no. 688 (2006): 51–57.

5. International Monetary Fund, *World Economic Outlook Database,* April 2006, www.imf.org/external/ns/cs.aspx?id=29.

6. Inter-American Development Bank, *Chile Country Indicators,* www.iadb.org/countries/indicators.cfm?language=English&id_country=CH&pLanguage=ENGLISH&pCountry=CH&parid=8.

7. Alan Angell, "Democratic Governability in Chile," paper presented at the conference Democratic Governability in Latin America, Kellogg Institute, University of Notre Dame, South Bend, Ind., October 7–8, 2005, 9; Banco Central de Chile, *Fundamentals of the Chilean Economy* Santiago: Banco Central de Chile, June 2006), 42.

8. Pilar Vergara, "In Pursuit of 'Growth with Equity': The Limits of Chile's Free-Market Social Reforms," in *The Political Economy of Social Inequalities: Consequences for Health and Quality of Life,* ed. Vincent Navarro (Amityville, N.Y.: Baywood, 2002), 229–37.

9. See Silvia Borzutzky, "The State and the Market: Confrontation or Cooperation? Social Security and Health Policies, 1989–2004," in *After Pinochet: The Chilean Road to Democracy and the Market, 1990–2004,* ed. Silvia Borzutzky and Lois Hecht Oppenheim (Gainesville: University of Florida Press, 2006).

10. The Chicago Boys were a group of influential young economists who served in the Pinochet government, many of whom were trained at the University of Chicago under the tutelage of free market economist Milton Friedman.

11. Marcus Kurtz, "State Developmentalism without a Developmentalist State: The Public Foundations of the 'Free Market Miracle' in Chile," *Latin American Politics and Society* 43, no. 2 (2001): 1–25.

12. The best summary of the Pinochet era and post-transition economic reforms is Ricardo French Davis's *Economic Reforms in Chile: From Dictatorship to Democracy* (Ann Arbor: University of Michigan Press, 2002).

13. Andrew Schrank and Marcus J. Kurtz, "Credit Where Credit Is Due: Open Economy Industrial Policy and Export Diversification in Latin America and the Caribbean," *Politics and Society* 33, no. 4 (2005): 671–702.

14. Andrés Marinakis and Juan Jacobo Velasco, "Salario mínimo 2004: Indicadores para evaluar su reajuste," *Informe de la Oficina Internacional del Trabajo* (Santiago), June 2004, www.oitchile.cl/pdf/publicaciones/ele/elec002.pdf.

15. Ministerio de Hacienda, "Estadísticas de Finanzas Publicas," www.hacienda.cl/contenido.php?id=769.

16. On the evolution of economic policy making under Concertación governments, see Lois Hecht Oppenheim, "Chilean Economic Policy under the Concertación: Triumph of the Market," in *Traversing the Past: The Chilean Road to Democracy and the Market,* ed. Silvia Bortzutzky and Lois Hecht Oppenheim (Gainesville: University of Florida Press, 2006).

17. For an elaboration of this point, see Alan Angell, "Democratic Governability in Chile."

18. Small portions of this section are drawn directly from Peter Siavelis, "Accommodating Informal Institutions and Chilean Democracy," in *Informal Institutions and Democracy: Lessons from Latin America,* ed. Gretchen Helmke and Steve Levitsky (Baltimore: Johns Hopkins University Press, 2006).

19. Delia Boylen, "Taxation and Transition: The Politics of the 1990 Chilean Tax Reform," *Latin American Research Review* 31, no. 1 (1996): 23.

20. Constitution of the Republic of Chile, Article 64.

21. Eduardo Silva, "Capitalist Regime Loyalties and Redemocratization in Chile," *Journal of Interamerican Studies and World Affairs* 34, no. 4 (1992): 103.

22. Centro de Estudios Públicos, *Encuesta de Opinión Pública,* November–December 2000, DT 317/320, www.cepchile.cl/enc_main.html.

23. Ibid.

24. Arturo Valenzuela, *The Breakdown of Democratic Regimes: Chile* (Baltimore: Johns Hopkins University Press, 1978); Giovanni Sartori, *Parties and Party Systems: A Framework for Analysis* (Cambridge: Cambridge University Press, 1976).

25. Arturo Valenzuela, "Party Politics and the Crisis of Presidentialism in Chile," in *The Failure of Presidential Democracy,* ed. Juan Linz and Arturo Valenzuela (Baltimore: Johns Hopkins University Press, 1994), 165–244.

26. See J. Samuel Valenzuela and Timothy Scully, "Electoral Choices and the Party System in Chile: Continuities and Changes at the Recovery of Democracy," *Comparative Politics* 29, no. 4 (1997): 511–27; Peter Siavelis, "Continuity and Change in the Chilean Party System: On the Transformational Effects of Electoral Reform," *Comparative Political Studies* 30 (December 1997): 651–74. For a counterargument, see John Carey, "Parties, Coalitions, and the Chilean Congress in the 1990s," in *Legislative Politics in Latin America,* ed. Scott Morgenstern and Benito Nacif (New York: Cambridge University Press, 2002), 222–53.

27. Valenzuela, *The Breakdown of Democratic Regimes;* Sartori, *Parties and Party Systems.*

28. See "PDC asume dividido pérdida parlamentaria" and "Triunfo del PS-PPD en el Congreso," *El Mercurio* (Santiago), December 12, 2005, C22.

29. See Mark P. Jones, *Electoral Laws and the Survival of Presidential Democracy* (South Bend, Ind.: University of Notre Dame Press, 1995).

30. "Q & A: Chile's Election Run Off," *BBC Online,* January 11, 2006, http://news.bbc.co.uk/2/hi/americas/4603126.stm.

31. Ministerio del Interior, Sitio Historia Electoral (Ministry of the Interior, database of past elections), www.elecciones.gov.cl/SitioHistorico/index2005_p2v.htm.

32. "Las mujeres votaron más por Bachelet y Lavín que los hombres," *El Mercurio* (Santiago), December 12, 2005, C1; "No descarto ser presidenciable el 2009," *El Mercurio,* January 22, 2006, D7.

33. Jorge Domínguez, "Constructing Democratic Governance in Latin America: Taking Stock of the 1990's," in *Constructing Democratic Governance in Latin America,* 2nd ed., 375.

34. For a detailed account of the constitution-making process see, Robert Barros, *Constitutionalism and Dictatorship* (New York: Cambridge University Press, 2000). On authoritarian enclaves, see Garretón, *The Chilean Political Process.*

35. For a discussion of the role of each of these institutions and the military's role in appointing some of their members, see Peter Siavelis, *The President and Congress in Post-authoritarian Chile: Institutional Constraints to Democratic Consolidation* (University Park: Pennsylvania State University Press, 2000), 1–42.

36. Domínguez, "Constructing Democratic Governance," 375.

37. On Chile's constitutional history, see Fernando Campos Harriet, *Historia constitucional de Chile* (Santiago: Editorial Jurídica, 1969). For legal rather than politically focused treatments of the 1980 constitutions, see José Luis Cea Egaña, *Tratado de la Constitución de 1980* (Santiago: Editorial Jurídica, 1988), and Fernando Campos Harriet, *Historia constitucional de Chile* (Santiago: Editorial Jurídica, 1969). Carlos Andrade Geywitz analyzes the 1989 reforms in *Reforma de la Constitución política de la República de Chile* (Santiago: Editorial Jurídica, 1991).

38. Andrés Allamand, "Las paradojas de un legado," in *El modelo chileno: Democracia y desarrollo en los noventa,* ed. Paul Drake and Ivan Jacksic (Santiago: LOM, 1999), 169–90.

39. Off-the-record interview by the author with a high-level official in the Ministry of Justice, Santiago, June 23, 1995.

40. Valenzuela, *The Breakdown of Democratic Regimes,* 14.

41. For a full account of the Supreme Court reform, see William Prillaman, *The Judiciary and Democratic Decay in Latin America* (Westport, Conn.: Greenwood, 2000), 144–50.

42. Antonio Marangunic and Todd Foglesong, "Charting Justice Reform in Chile: A Comparison of the Old and New Systems of Criminal Procedure," report prepared for the Vera Institute of Justice, New York, December 2004.

43. For an analysis, see Agüero, "Chile: Unfinished Transition," and Peter Siavelis, *The President and Congress in Post-authoritarian Chile: Institutional Constraints to Democratic Consolidation* (University Park: Pennsylvania State University Press, 2000).

44. See J. Esteban Montes and Tomás Vial, "The Role of Constitution-Building Processes in Democratization: Chile Case Study" (Stockholm: IDEA, 2005).

45. For such an argument, see Patricio Navia, "Tapar el sol con un dedo," *La Tercera Online,* September 24, 2005, www.expansiva.cl/columnas/detalle.tpl?idcolumna=09262005112221.

46. Juan Linz and Alfred Stepan, *Problems of Democratic Transition and Consolidation* (Baltimore: Johns Hopkins University Press, 1996), 205–7.

47. On the evolution of the Chilean military under democracy, see Gregory Weeks, *The Military and Politics in Postauthoritarian Chile* (Tuscaloosa: University of Alabama Press,

2003). The real extent of the subordination of the armed forces has been a contentious issue. See the dialogue between Weeks and Paul Sigmund in *Revista de Ciencia Política* (Santiago) 23, no. 1 (2004): 227–31.

48. This is from a from a ranking of the 100 countries for which there is income inequality data listed in the *CIA World Factbook,* www.cia.gov/library/publications/the-world-factbook/.

49. Superintendencia de ISAPRES, "Aprendiendo sobre el Sistema Isapre," October 2004, www.supersalud.cl/568/propertyvalue-1527.html.

50. Century Foundation, "Chile's Experience with Social Security Privatization: A Model for the United States or a Danger Sign," *Issue Brief* 4 (New York: Century Foundation, June 11, 1998).

51. Ibid., 4.

52. Manuel Riesco, *Private Pensions in Chile, a Quarter Century On* (Santiago: Centro de Estudios Nacionales de Desarrollo Alternativo, December 2004, www.cep.cl/Cenda/Cen_Documentos/Pub_MR/Articulos/Varios/Pensiones_USA_1.html.

53. "Protests Paralyse Chile's Education System," *The Guardian,* June 7, 2006, www.guardian.co.uk/world/2006/jun/07/chile.schoolsworldwide.

54. "How Chile's Growth Skipped Its Schools," *Christian Science Monitor,* June 14, 2006, www.csmonitor.com/2006/0614/p06s01-woam.html.

55. "Protests Paralyse Chile's Education System."

56. The Chamber of Deputies' 120 members are elected from 60 two-member districts, and two senators are elected from each of 19 districts.

57. Peter Siavelis and Arturo Valenzuela, "Electoral Engineering and Democratic Stability: The Legacy of Authoritarian Rule in Chile," in *Institutional Design in New Democracies: Eastern Europe and Latin America,* ed. Arend Lijphart and Carlos Waisman (Boulder, Colo.: Westview, 1996), 77–100; Valenzuela and Scully, "Electoral Choices and the Party System in Chile"; Siavelis, "Continuity and Change in the Chilean Party System."

58. The party-integrative and -stabilizing tendencies of the electoral system are underscored by, among others, Eugenio Guzmán, "Reflexiones sobre el sistema binominal," *Estudios Públicos* 51 (Winter 1993): 303–25, and Rhoda Rabkin, "Redemocratization, Electoral Engineering, and Party Strategies in Chile, 1989–1995," *Comparative Political Studies* 29 (June 1996): 335–56.

59. *Informe Grupo de Trabajo sobre Reforma del Sistema Binomial* (Santiago: Comisión Boeninger, June 8, 2006), www.flacso.cl/flacso/biblos.php?code=1803.

Chapter 9. Colombia

1. Malcolm Deas, "Violent Exchanges: Reflections on Political Violence in Colombia," in *The Legitimization of Violence,* ed. David E. Apter (London: Macmillan, 1997), 350–90.

2. Sebastián Mazzuca and James Robinson, "Political Conflict and Power-Sharing in the Origins of Modern Colombia," Working Paper 12099 (Cambridge, Mass.: National Bureau of Economic Research, December 2005), 3, www.nber.org/papers/w12099.

3. Ibid.

4. Ibid., 4.

5. See Harvey Kline, *Colombia: Portrait of Unity and Diversity* (Boulder, Colo.: Westview, 1983), 40–41. Kline counts 13 coalitions in the period from 1854 to 1949. The best book on this type of government in Colombia is Jonathan Hartlyn's *The Politics of Coalition Rule in Colombia* (Cambridge: Cambridge University Press, 1988).

6. Secretaría de la Cámara de Representantes de Colombia, *Por qué y cómo se forjó el Frente Nacional* (Bogotá: Imprenta Nacional, July 20, 1959). The results of the plebiscite were as follows: "Yes," 95.27 percent (4,169,294 votes); "No," 4.73 percent (206,864 votes). Research Center on Direct Democracy, *Referendum Experience Database,* http://c2d.unige.ch/.

7. See Malcolm Deas, "La tradición civilista Colombiana," in *Fortalezas de Colombia,* ed. Fernando Cepeda Ulloa (Bogotá: Ariel, 2004).

8. Mario Latorre Rueda, *Hechos y crítica política* (Bogotá: Universidad Nacional de Colombia, 1986), 20.

9. Constitución Política de Colombia, 1886, Article 120.

10. See Malcolm Deas and Carlos Ossa, *El gobierno de Barco: Política, economía y desarrollo social* (Bogotá: FEDESARROLLO, 1994); Fernando Cepeda Ulloa, "Una Colombia nueva: La visión política de Barco," in *El gobierno de Barco,* ed. Deas and Ossa, 49–78; and Fernando Cepeda Ulloa, *El esquema gobierno-oposición* (Bogotá: Ministerio de Gobierno, Imprenta Nacional, 1987).

11. Alfonso López Michelsen was the first Liberal president since 1946 to be elected without a bipartisan agreement. He scored a resounding victory, with 57.92 percent of the vote, against 33.32 percent for the Conservative candidate, Álvaro Gómez Hurtado; 9.73 percent for the daughter of former dictator Gustavo Rojas Pinilla; and 2.71 percent for a leftist coalition called Unión Nacional de Oposición (UNO; National Opposition Union). UNO's candidate was Hernando Echeverría Mejía, the brother of Gilberto Echeverría Mejía. The latter Echeverría Mejía had served as cabinet minister and ambassador during the terms of López Michelsen and Julio César Turbay Ayala and then as minister of defense during the Samper government. He was kidnapped and murdered by the FARC during the first term of Álvaro Uribe. Figures from Registraduría Nacional del Estado Civil, *Elecciones presidenciales y vicepresidente de la República,* May 28, 2006.

12. *Revista Causa Común,* April–May 1977, 19; cited in Jonathan Hartlyn, *Política del régimen de coalición: La experiencia del Frente Nacional en Colombia* (Bogotá: Tercer Mundo 1993).

13. Thomas A. Marks, *Sustainability of Colombian Military/Strategic Support for "Democratic Security"* (Carlisle, Pa.: Strategic Studies Institute, U.S. Army War College, July 2005), www.strategicstudiesinstitute.army.mil/pdffiles/PUB610.pdf. Thomas Marks is one of the leading scholars on Colombia's military forces and their past and present strategies against illegal armed groups. By the same author, see also *Colombian Army Adaptation to FARC Insurgency* (Carlisle, Pa.: U.S. Army War College, January 2002), and "Un modelo de Contra Insurgencia: El apoyo Militar Colombiano a la Seguridad Democrática," in *Sostenibilidad política democrática en Colombia,* ed. Fernando Cepeda Ulloa (Bogotá: United States Embassy, 2005).

14. Michael Shifter, *Toward Greater Peace and Security in Colombia* (Washington, D.C.: Inter-American Dialogue, October 2000), 10.

15. Manuel José Cepeda Espinosa, *La constituyente por dentro: Mitos y realidades* (Bogotá: Imprenta Nacional, 1993).

16. Fernando Cepeda Ulloa, *La reglamentación de la elección popular de alcaldes* (Bogotá: Ministerio de Gobierno, 1987).

17. Manuel José Cepeda Espinosa, *La constituyente por dentro.*

18. Mala Htun, "La representación de los indígenas y los negros en la política colombiana," in *Fortalezas de Colombia II,* ed. Fernando Cepeda Ulloa (Bogotá: Editorial Alfaomega, 2006).

19. "Poder, justicia e indignidad: El juicio al Presidente de la República Ernesto Sam-

per Pizano," *Informe de la Comisión Ciudadana de Seguimiento* (Bogotá: Utópica Ediciones, 1996).

20. Ministerio del Interior, *Comisión para el Estudio de la Reforma de los Partidos Políticos: Memoria de trabajo* (Bogotá: Publicaciones Audiovisuales, 1996).

21. Alfredo Rangel, ed., *Gobernabilidad y seguridad* (forthcoming); see the chapter of this book by Fernando Cepeda Ulloa.

22. Madeleine K. Albright, "Colombia's Struggle and How We Can Help," *New York Times*, August 10, 1999, op-ed page.

23. Ibid.

24. Bill Clinton, "Remarks by the President in a Video Address to the People of Colombia," White House Press Release, August 29, 2000.

25. *El Tiempo*, July 13, 2006, 1–4. See statement by Juan Carlos Iragorri to the effect that Pastrana is the "continuation" of Uribe, in "Colombian Envoy's Title Is New, but Mission Is Same," *Washington Post*, July 5, 2006, A10.

26. Bill Clinton, *My Life* (New York: Knopf, 2004), 921.

27. Luis Alberto Moreno, "Aiding Colombia's War on Terrorism," *New York Times*, May 3, 2002, A23; Andrés Pastrana, "High Stakes in Colombia," *Washington Post*, April 15, 2002, A21.

28. Alfredo Rangel, ed., *Sostenibilidad de la seguridad democrática* (Bogotá: Editorial Kimpres, 2005).

29. Claudio Fuentes, ed., *Bajo la mirada del halcón: Estados Unidos–América Latina post 11/9/2001* (Buenos Aires: Biblos, 2004).

30. Thomas A. Marks gives an excellent description of the entire process in *Sustainability of Colombian Military/Strategic Support*, 67–111. Also see Marks, "Colombian Army Adaptation to FARC Insurgency." Interestingly, whereas Clinton saw Plan Colombia as a military strategy for defeating the guerrillas, Thomas Marks criticized it precisely because it was based on "the failed logic according to which Colombia's problem was principally drug-trafficking and that war was merely a result of it." According to all indications, something else in fact occurred. As Marks explains, "American urgings that Colombian armed action focus upon a narcotics center of gravity were rejected by the military leadership (apparently, often in conflict with Pastrana officials)." As a consequence, the U.S. role during this period, as far as Colombian military leadership was concerned, was appreciated but not directed at the real issue, counterinsurgency. Once President Pastrana's peace process had failed, he claimed he had dealt a "strategic defeat" to the FARC. He says he had caused the guerrillas' "political defeat." Marks, "Colombian Army Adaptation to FARC Insurgency," 72.

31. Álvaro Uribe, "La seguridad democrática es sostenible," in *Sostenibilidad de la Seguridad Democrática*, ed. Rangel.

32. Marks, *Sustainability of Colombian Military/Strategic Support*, 7.

33. Ibid.

34. The remainder of this section draws on Fernando Cepeda Ulloa, "Colombia: En busca del fortalecimiento de la gobernabilidad democrática," *Anuario*, Instituto Real Elcano (Madrid: Ariel, 2005).

35. Álvaro Uribe, "La seguridad democrática," in *Colombia: En busca del fortalecimiento*, ed. Ulloa, 14–15.

36. Ibid., 16.

37. Ibid., 18.

38. On this point, see Fernando Cepeda Ulloa, "Álvaro Uribe: Dissident," Inter-American Dialogue, Washington, D.C., 2003; María Jimena Dussán, *Cómo nos gobiernan*

(Bogotá: Planeta, 2004); and María Izquierdo, *Álvaro Uribe Vélez, el hombre, el presidente* (Bogotá: R&P Editores, 2004). This marked the first time several books have been published on the governing style of a Colombian president in his first two years in office, which underscores the controversy unleashed by Uribe's unconventional behavior.

39. Colombian Ministry of Foreign Affairs, *Política exterior de Colombia 2002–2006: Gobernabilidad democrática, responsabilidad compartida, y solidaridad* (Bogotá: Imprenta Nacional de Colombia, 2004), 9.

40. Ibid., 17.

41. Alexander Hamilton, *Federalist 72*, March 12, 1788.

42. Corte Constitucional, Sentencia C-1040, 2005, inter alia.

43. Constitución Política de Colombia, 1991, Article 372.

44. The minister of defense, Juan Manuel Santos, in a speech to commemorate the first 100 days of Uribe's second term, made it clear that achieving peace is the fundamental purpose of the democratic security policy.

45. This topic is examined in greater depth in Fernando Cepeda Ulloa, "Reforma política en Colombia," October 11, 2002; "El comienzo de la presidencia de Álvaro Uribe," September 5, 2002; and "El nuevo gobierno en Colombia," July 10, 2002, all published by the Instituto Real Elcano, Madrid, www.realinstitutoelcano.org/buscar.asp.

46. The commission was introduced by Decree 763 of 1995 (passed on May 9) and amended by Decree 842 of 1995 (passed on May 23). The chairs of the parties' governing committees, independent political groups, unions, academics, and the industrial sector took part.

47. Ministerio del Interior, *Comisión para el Estudio de la Reforma.*

48. The texts of the legislative proposals and of the list of amendments can be found in Ministerio del Interior, *Reforma política, un propósito de nación* (Bogotá: 1999). Pages 299 ff contain a report from the international consultant hired by the government to answer 17 questions on concrete features of the political reform.

49. The article, which would have given vast power to the president—nearly those of a constituent power—had not even been published or debated in the media.

50. Cámara de Representantes, *Gaceta del Congreso* IX, no. 98 (April 2000), 5.

51. Bill 261 of 2000, Cámara de Representantes, *Gaceta del Congreso* IX, no. 98 (April 2000).

52. The implementation of the Law of Guarantees is currently being evaluated by the National Democratic Institute. I participated in an evaluation session in which representatives of political forces and NGOs as well as academics expressed their opinions.

53. Political parties had until October 19, 2006, to amend their bylaws in line with the new regulations. The law requires that decisions on the actions of a party bloc in Congress, assemblies, or town councils be made through democratic procedures. It also sets forth disciplinary rules that parties must draft allowing for sanctions ranging from warnings to expulsion or loss of the right to vote.

54. See John M. Carey and Matthew Shugart, "Incentives to Cultivate a Personal Vote: A Rank Ordering of Electoral Formulas," *Electoral Studies* 14, no. 4 (December 1995): 417–39, and Gary W. Cox and Matthew S. Shugart, "In the Absence of Vote Pooling: Nomination and Allocation Errors in Colombia," *Electoral Studies* 14 no. 4 (December 1995): 441–60.

55. Matthew Shugart, Erika Moreno, and Luis E. Fajardo, "Deepening Democracy by Renovating Political Practices: The Struggle for Political Reform," in *Peace, Democracy, and Human Rights in Colombia,* ed. Christopher Welna and Gustavo Gallón (Notre Dame, Ind.: Notre Dame University Press, 2007), 2.

56. Ibid., 37.

57. Ibid., 34.

58. *Boletín de Prensa* 10, Annex 2, reported that the number of parties had been reduced to 11 (July 14, 2006).

59. The D'Hondt Method is a way to allocate seats in a party-list proportional representation system, one that slightly favors larger parties and coalitions.

60. Manuel José Cepeda Espinosa, "La defensa judicial de la onstitución," in *Fortalezas de Colombia,* ed. Fernando Cepeda Ulloa (Bogotá: Ariel, 2005), 155.

61. Ibid., 152.

62. Constitución Política de Colombia, 1991, Article 86.

63. Catalina Botero Marino and Juan Fernando Jaramillo, "El conflicto de las altas cortes colombianas en torno a la tutela contra sentencias," 22, www.dejusticia.org.

64. Cases on home financing have included Corte Constitucional de Colombia, Decisions C-383, 1999; C-700, 1999; and SU-846, 2000, inter alia. Those on displaced populations have included Corte Constitucional de Colombia, Decisions SU-1150, 2000, and T-025, 2004, inter alia.

65. Rulings on presidential reelection have included Corte Constitucional de Colombia, Decision C-1040, 2005, inter alia. Those on the peace process have included Corte Constitucional de Colombia, Decisions C-319, 2006; C-370, 2006; C-531, 2006; and C-575, 2006.

66. See Diego Eduardo López Medina, *El derecho de los jueces* (Bogotá: Editorial Legis, Bogotá, 2002).

67. The February 4, 2004, decision ("*auto*") handed down by the full bench of the Constitutional Court, and rulings SU-047 of 1999, C-426 of 2002, and SU-1185 of 2001 are examples of decisions by this court that have led to conflicts with the Supreme Court and the Council of State.

68. Jorge I. Domínguez, "Construcción de gobernabilidad democrática en América Latina: Una evaluación de la dérada de 1990," in *Construcción de gobernabilidad democrática en América Latina,* ed. Jorge I. Domínguez and Michael Shifter (Bogotá: Fondo de Cultura Económica, 2005), 387.

69. Ibid., 402.

70. Ibid., 404.

Chapter 10. Mexico

1. Luis Rubio, "Transición?" *Reforma* (Mexico City), March 25, 2007, www.reforma.com/editoriales/nacional/377/752156/default.shtm.

2. Mauricio Merino, *La transición votada: Crítica a la interpretación del cambio político en México* (Mexico City: Fondo de Cultura Económica, 2003).

3. I am indebted to Moisés Naim for the term "veto center," which he uses to describe political and economic actors that seek to protect their interests by blocking reforms.

4. Data culled from Alejandro Poiré, "Por una democracia de mejor calidad: La reforma política en México," in *México: Crónicas de un país posible,* ed. José Antonio Aguilar Rivera (Mexico City, Fondo de Cultura Económica, 2005), 158.

5. Salvador Camarena and Jorge Zepeda Patterson, *El presidente electo: Instructivo para sobrevivir a Calderón y su gobierno* (Mexico City: Planeta, 2006), 195.

6. Poiré, "Por una democracia de mejor calidad," 154.

7. Denise Dresser, "Punto final," *Reforma* (Mexico City), December 12, 2006, www.reforma.com/editoriales/nacional/358/714680/default.shtm.

8. Guillermo O'Donnell, "Delegative Democracy," *Journal of Democracy* 5, no. 1 (January 1994): 50–69.

9. Ibid. For an analysis of the necessary restraints on state power, see Andreas Schedler, Larry Diamond, and Marc F. Plattner, eds., *The Self-Restraining State: Power and Accountability in New Democracies* (Boulder, Colo.: Lynne Rienner, 1999). See also Poiré, "Por una democracia de mayor calidad," 157.

10. These include political party retreats at five-star luxury hotels, the trusts created to endow Supreme Court justices with pensions and discretionary bonuses, and the practice of "legislative tourism" in which representatives and senators routinely engage.

11. Alejandro Poiré, "Money in Elections and the Quality of Democratic Representation: Do Cash Subsidies Work?" Junior Fellow paper, Woodrow Wilson Center for International Scholars, Washington, D.C., September 2005, mimeo.

12. Poiré, "Money in Elections."

13. Lorenzo Córdova y Ciro Murayama, *Elecciones, dinero y corrupción: Pemexgate y Amigos de Fox* (Mexico City: Cal y Arena, 2006).

14. Jorge Herrea, "Para radio y TV, 70% de gasto en 2006: IFE," *El Universal* (Mexico City), April 23, 2007, www.eluniversal.com.mx/primera/28774.html.

15. See the essays on this issue in María Elena Cantú, *Medios y poder: El papel de la radio y la televisión en la democracia mexicana* (Mexico City: Grupo Editorial Norma, 2005).

16. Denise Dresser, "Extracción sin representación," *Reforma* (Mexico City), August 29, 2005, A19.

17. Juan Linz, "Democracy, Presidential or Parliamentary: Does It Make a Difference?" in *The Failure of Presidential Democracy*, ed. Juan Linz and Arturo Valenzuela (Baltimore: Johns Hopkins University Press, 1994).

18. As Jacqueline Pesachard states, "The PRI gambled on the strength of its electoral machinery to regain power six years later and the PRD calculated that the popular leadership that its former party leader and then mayor of Mexico City (Andrés Manuel López Obrador) would catapult it towards the presidency." As a result, neither party sought congressional collaboration with President Fox. See Jaqueline Peschard, "De la mutua incomprensión entre el Ejecutivo y el Legislativo en los tiempos de la alternancia," in *Qué país nos deja Fox: Los claroscuros del gobierno del cambio,* comp. Adolfo Sánchez Rebolledo (Mexico City: Grupo Editorial Norma, 1996), 69.

19. According to a poll published at the end of the Fox administration, 65 percent of Mexicans disapproved of how the president dealt with crime, 63 percent disapproved of how he handled unemployment, and 53 percent criticized his management of the economy. Nonetheless, 67 percent approved of his presidency because he "helped people and provided macroeconomic stability," and 69 percent had a favorable view of his personality. Carlos Ordóñez, "Desaprueban acciones pero no gestión de Fox," *El Universal* (Mexico City), November 30, 2006, A19.

20. Rebolledo, *Qué país nos deja Fox?*

21. See Denise Dresser, "Mexico: From PRI Predominance to Divided Democracy," in *Constructing Democratic Governance in Latin America,* 2nd ed., ed. Jorge Domínguez and Michael Shifter (Baltimore: Johns Hopkins University Press, 2003).

22. Peschard, "De la mutua incomprensión," 61.

23. Ernesto López Portillo, "La gestión de Vicente Fox en materia de seguridad pública y justicia penal," in *Qué país nos deja Fox?* comp. Rebolledo, 17.

24. The Atenco case proved to be one of the Fox administration's greatest failures in terms of respect for legality and the preeminence of the rule of law. In order to expand

Mexico City's cramped airport, the government decided to expropriate communal lands in the adjacent locality of San Andrés Atenco, but it encountered strong resistance from small farmers with a historic attachment to their land. The government demonstrated a notable incapacity to undertake negotiations that would have produced a satisfactory outcome for both sides. Disaffection ensued, and local farmers attempted to use legal avenues to block the expropriation, but to no avail. They then took to the streets, machetes in hand, forcing the government to cave in and abandon its plans and establishing a precedent of governmental incapacity to deal with social conflict.

25. Lorenzo Códova Vianello, "2000–2006: Claroscuros del Estado de Derecho," in *Qué país nos deja Fox?* comp. Rebolledo, 25–58.

26. Leonardo Curzio, "Las elecciones de la discordia," in *Elecciones inéditas 2006: La democracia a prueba* (Mexico City: Grupo Editorial Norma, 2006), 1–34.

27. Sidney Weintraub, "Governing a Demonstrably Divided Mexico," *Issues in International Political Economy* 81 (Washington, D.C.: Center for Strategic and International Studies, September 2006). Nonetheless, as Alejandro Poiré and Luis Estrada suggest, the "north-south divide" must not be overstated. Neither income, education, religion, nor rural status made a difference. The north-south divide is better understood as representing an increasing divide between left and right. See Alejandro Poiré and Luis Estrada, "Taught to Protest, Learning to Lose," *Journal of Democracy* 18, no. 1 (2007): 80.

28. A critical examination of Andrés Manuel López Obrador's political strategy in Mexico City is presented in Roger Bartra, "La izquierda ¿En peligro de extinción?" *Letras Libres* (Mexico City), August 2007, www.letraslibres.com/index.php?art=12319. A more sympathetic view can be found in Blanca Gómez, *Y quién es? Historia de un hombre enigmático* (Mexico City: Planeta, 2005).

29. The "desafuero" process is analyzed in Alejandra Lajous, *AMLO: Entre la atracción y el temor* (Mexico City: Océano, 2006), 225–33.

30. For analyses of the Calderón campaign, see Camarena and Patterson, *El presidente electo;* Sabina Berman, "Felipe Calderón y las tribulaciones de la fe," *Letras Libres* (Mexico City), June 2006, www.letraslibres.com/index.php?art=11292; and Carmen Aristegui, *Uno de dos. 2006: México en la encrucijada* (Mexico City: Grijalbo, 2006).

31. Camarena and Patterson, *El presidente electo,* 53.

32. Alejandro Moreno, "It's the Economy, Stupid! The Activation of Economic Voting in the 2006 Mexican Presidential Campaign," 2007, http://psweb.sbs.ohio-state.edu/intranet/cprw/moreno2.pdf.

33. Polls conducted after the election reveal that approximately 30 percent of citizens believe that electoral fraud occurred. See Pedro Salazar Ugarte, "La elección más larga," *Foreign Affairs en español* 7, no. 1 (2007): 109.

34. The IFE and the Federal Electoral Tribunal issued bans on 29 "denigratory" campaign ads, but campaign strategists and the Consejo Coordinador Empresarial (Business Coordinating Council) found ways to circumvent those constraints. In its postelectoral ruling the tribunal stated that these activities had indeed affected the quality of the race.

35. The IFE councilors did not make electoral trends public the night of the election. The reasons they gave for withholding that information were unconvincing, and their explanations as to why they had not computed the ballots with "inconsistencies" were presented in a clumsy fashion. Salazar, "La elección más larga," 115.

36. Salazar, "La elección más larga," 115.

37. For an account of López Obrador's campaign rhetoric, see "Las 10 frases más representativas del discurso de AMLO," *El Universal* (Mexico City), September 17, 2006, www.el-universal.com.mx/notas/375678.html.

38. For an account of López Obrador and the PRD's postelectoral saga, see Alejandra Lajous, *Confrontación de agravios: La post-elección de 2006* (Mexico City: Editorial Océano).

39. Poiré and Estrada, "Taught to Protest," 84.

40. José Woldenberg, "El peor enemigo del PRD," *El Norte* (Monterrey), December 7, 2006, www.elnorte.com/editoriales/nacional/697937/default.shtm.

41. A poll published after the PRD attempted to block Calderón's swearing-in ceremony revealed that 76 percent disapproved of the PRD's behavior, 61 percent said that the image of the PRD had become worse, and 68 percent opposed the party's calls for "civil resistance." See "Cae imagen del PRD," *Reforma* (Mexico City), December 2006.

42. According to a Parametría poll conducted in November 2006, 45 percent believed that Andrés Manuel López Obrador's reputation had worsened; 63 percent believed that he had little credibility; and 66 percent thought his alternative, "legitimate" presidency weakened his political standing.

43. Kathleen Bruhn and Kenneth Greene, "Optimismo moderado: Cómo podría desvanecerse el conflicto partidista mexicano," *Foreign Affairs en Español* 7, no. 1 (2007): 132–43.

44. Ibid., 141.

45. An example of this diaspora away from radicalism and in favor of a more centrist option occurred in the gubernatorial race in Tabasco just three months after the July 2 presidential race, in which the PRI candidate won in López Obrador's home state.

46. José Woldenberg, "La izquierda en su laberinto," *Reforma* (Mexico City), October 26, 2006.

47. Chappell H. Lawson, *Mexico under Calderón: The First Hundred Days and the Challenges Ahead,* special report, Pacific Council on International Policy, Los Angeles, April 2007.

48. For an analysis of how state governors have emerged as subnational authoritarian leaders who perpetuate provincial authoritarian regimes and explain subnational variations in democratic institutionalization, see Edward L. Gibson, "Boundary Control: Subnational Authoritarianism in Democratic Countries," *World Politics* 58, no. 1 (2005): 101–32.

49. According to Jeffrey Weldon, the three conditions that allowed the Mexican president to exercise "meta-constitutional" powers were (1) PRI electoral majorities, (2) the loyalty of those majorities to the president, and (3) the existence of a unified government. Those three conditions have been eroded since 1997, when the PRI lost its majority in Congress. See Jeffrey Weldon, "The Legal and Partisan Framework of the Legislative Delegation of the Budget in Mexico," in *Legislative Politics in Latin America,* ed. Scott Morgenstern, Scout Nacif, and Benito Nacif (Cambridge: Cambridge University Press, 2002), 121.

50. Sergio Sarmiento, "La violencia," *Reforma* (Mexico City), March 20, 2007, www.reforma.com/editoriales/nacional/668759/default.shtm.

51. Adam Thompson, "Interview with Agustín Carstens, Mexico's Finance Minister," *Financial Times* (London), February 14, 2007, www.ft.com/cms/s/0/81a102fe-bc51-11db-9cbc-0000779e2340.html.

52. Salazar, "La elección más larga," 111.

53. Poiré, "Por una democracia de mayor calidad," 168.

54. Ciro Murayama, "Las condiciones de la competencia: Dinero, medios y elecciones," in *Elecciones inéditas 2006,* 123–44.

55. Denise Dresser, "Paisaje después de la batalla: Reflexiones sobre la Ley de Radio y Televisión," *Perspectivas Progresistas,* a series of working papers produced at Fundación Friedrich Ebert, Mexico City, 2006, www.fesmex.org/Documentos%20y%20Programas/Paper%20Ley%20Medios%202006.pdf.

56. As Joel Migdal argues, accommodating capital by appealing to the long-term benefits of regime preservation is a necessary strategy in contexts of state weakness. See Migdal, *Strong Societies and Weak States: State-Society Relations and State Capabilities in the Third World* (Princeton, N.J.: Princeton University Press, 1988), 235.

Chapter 11. Peru

1. A *chullo* is a traditional Quechua wool cap. The Pachamama is Mother Earth, a pre-Columbian deity. A *pututu* is a large ceremonial conch producing a booming, stirring sound.

2. The *chakana*, or Inca cross, represents the connection between the Kay Pacha, or this world, and the Hanan Pacha, the higher world. Pachacuti united and expanded the Inca empire.

3. From 1980 to 1999, Peru suffered through the political violence unleashed by the Shining Path insurgency. This conflict resulted in some 70,000 dead and missing. See Truth and Reconciliation Commission, *Final Report,* Vol. 9 (Lima: 2003).

4. In 1990, in the midst of the worst economic crisis and at the height of the armed internal conflict that marked the end of Alan García's first term in office, Alberto Fujimori, a Peruvian of Japanese origin, became the first outsider to be elected president

5. In the runoff election of 2001, Toledo obtained 53 percent of the vote nationwide and 68 percent of the vote in the southern Andean departments, home to most of the country's indigenous population. See Pajuelo Teves, *Ramón: Participación política indígena en la sierra peruana; Una aproximación desde las dinámicas nacionales y locales* (Lima: Instituto de Estudios Peruanos / Konrad Adenauer Stiftung, 2006).

6. The populist Alianza Popular Revolucionaria Americana (American Popular Revolutionary Alliance) party was the most important political party in the country for most of the twentieth century and is again the only functioning party in the country.

7. The informal chief spy of the regime, Vladimiro Montesinos, was a former military officer, expelled in the 1970s, who became the "power behind the throne" and chief corruptor, especially during Fujimori's second term. On Montesinos, see Sally Bowen and Jane Holligan, *The Imperfect Spy: The Many Lives of Vladimiro Montesinos* (Lima: Peisa, 2003).

8. Impeachment was first brought up in 2002 by the pro-Fujimori media, which saw in Toledo's mistakes an opportunity for a restoration coup.

9. About the Fujimori government, see Charles D. Kenney, "¿Por qué el autogolpe? Fujimori y el Congreso, 1990–1992," in *Los enigmas del poder: Fujimori 1990–1996,* ed. Fernando Tuesta Soldevilla (Lima: Fundación Frederich Ebert, 1996), 75–104, and *Fujimori's Coup and the Breakdown of Democracy in Latin America* (Notre Dame, Ind.: University of Notre Dame Press, 2004). About his impudence—and its consequences—as his defining trait, see Juan Carlos Ubilluz, *Nuevos Súbditos: Cinismo y perversión en la sociedad contemporánea* (Lima: Instituto de Estudios Peruanos, 2006).

10. A month later, he reversed himself, saying that "fighting a dictatorship was easier than governing." Martín Tanaka, "El gobierno de Alejandro Toledo, o cómo funciona una democracia sin partidos," *Revista Política* (Universidad Autónoma de México) 42 (Fall 2004): 129–53.

11. An issue that dogged him throughout his term was his refusal to acknowledge his paternity of a daughter born out of wedlock, in spite of incontrovertible evidence. Overwhelmed by public pressure, he recognized her in October 2002.

12. Public anger forced Toledo to cut his salary to $12,000.

13. The interim government had been impeccably austere, while both Fujimori and Montesinos never lost a chance to show themselves as tireless workers. See Luis Jochamowitz,

Ciudadano Fujimori: La construcción de un politico (Lima: Peisa, 1993), and Luis Jocha-mowitz, *Vladimiro: Vida y tiempo de un corruptor* (Lima: Empresa Editorial del Comercio, 2002).

14. Toledo was a professor at the School of Business Administration and had taught at Harvard. A Bolivian influence had come to him through adviser Carlos Urrutia, who had spent time in Bolivia.

15. The Constitution of 1993 instituted a unicameral 120-member Congress. As of the writing of this chapter, parties receiving less than 4 percent of the national vote cannot be represented in Congress.

16. Notable victims include Lima mayor and Somos Perú leader Alberto Andrade, as well as Luis Castañeda, head of Solidaridad Nacional. About media and politics during the 2000 election campaign, see Carlos Iván Degregori, *La década de la antipolítica: Auge y huida de Alberto Fujimori y Vladimiro Montesinos,* Ideología y Política 13 (Lima: Instituto de Estudios Peruanos, 2000), Sec. 2, Chaps. 5–8.

17. See Sally Bowen. *El expediente Fujimori: El Perú y su presidente 1990–2000* (Lima: Monitor S.A., 2000); Sally Bowen and Jane Holligan, *El espía imperfecto: La telaraña sinies-tra de Vladimiro Montesinos* (Lima: Peisa, 2000); Yusuke Murakami, *Perú en la era del chino: La política no institucionalizada y el pueblo en busca de un salvador* (Lima: Instituto de Es-tudios Peruanos, 2007); Jane Markus-Delgado and Martín Tanaka, *Lecciones del final del Fujimorismo,* Colección Mínima 47 (Lima: Instituto de Estudios Peruanos, 2001); and Fer-nando Rospigliosi, *Montesinos y las fuerzas armadas: Cómo controló durante una década las instituciones militares,* Ideología y Política 14 (Lima: Instituto de Estudios Peruanos, 2000), among others.

18. A few days before the runoff date, after meeting with the prime minister and the head of the Elections Office, Stein said: "There are disquieting signs that the scenario of the first round may be repeated. . . . We don't know if there will be enough guarantees for a clean, transparent election." Clifford Krauss, "International Observers Say They Fear Fujimori May Steal Peru's Election Runoff," *New York Times,* May 15, 2000, http://query .nytimes.com/gst/fullpage.html?res=9C02E6DD103BF936A25756C0A9669C8B63.

19. The four corners of the Incan empire are known as *suyos.*

20. The level of discontent was greatest in the cities, because the rate of urban un-employment remained practically unchanged during Fujimori's decade in power (8.3% at the start versus 7.8% at the end). See Richard Webb and Graciela Fernández Baca, *Perú en números* (Lima: Cuánto S.A., 1992).

21. In Congressional elections, there is no provision for a second-round vote.

22. The PP was not the only victim. Montesinos managed to lure away fully 30 percent of the opposition legislators (19 of 62), achieving a comfortable, albeit spurious, majority in Congress. Luis Castañeda's Solidaridad Nacional lost all of its five congressmen. No party was immune to Montesinos' ministrations. See Carlos Iván Degregori and Carlos Meléndez, *El nacimiento de los otorongos: El congreso de la república durante los gobiernos de Alberto Fujimori* (1990–2000) (Lima: Instituto de Estudios Peruanos, 2007).

23. The situation was compounded by the Political Parties Act, which did not require internal elections, and by "preferential vote" provisions that promoted competition within slates and rewarded candidates with the deepest pockets.

24. A minister of women's issues was relieved after four days on the job when corrupt practices in previous public posts were discovered, for example.

25. Personal communication.

26. Journalists wrote a "who's who" of his associates. In addition to the inner circle of presidential advisers, there was an "operational circle," a "circle of ministers," a "circle of

relatives," and a "circle of friends." See Paola Ugaz, "¿Silenciando las protestas? El presidente Toledo encuentra una no muy efectiva solución en sus allegados," agenciaperu.com, May 5, 2002, www.agenciaperu.com/investigacion/2002/may/circulos.htm.

27. Alejandro Toledo et al., "Compromiso de Diálogo para un Acuerdo Nacional," Lima, March 5, 2002, www.acuerdonacional.gob.pe/compromiso.html.

28. Ignoring the National Accord's potential was yet another consequence of the debacle of the previous decade. By way of comparison, the Bolivian party system managed to survive an even weaker economy.

29. García had to wait until Ollanta Humala's emergence to win back the vote of the liberals and conservatives who had preferred Lourdes Flores. They voted for him as the lesser evil.

30. Unidad Nacional and the FIM lost everywhere. With the political party system in a state of collapse, the regions were swept by independent regional movements.

31. Ibid.

32. The first Defense Minister was PP leader and Second Vice President David Waisman. He knew next to nothing about defense and was replaced after several embarrassing blunders.

33. In January 2003, at the behest of the police, Costa was replaced by PP member Alberto Sanabria. His tenure was so disastrous that Rospigliosi was called back. In May 2004, a civil commotion in Puno forced Rospigliosi's resignation once again. He was replaced by Javier Reátegui, then by a retired policeman, and finally by another PP member. Conditions steadily declined at the ministry until practically the end of Toledo's term.

34. See Rocío Trinidad, *Entre la ilusión y la realidad: Las nuevas tecnologías en dos proyectos educativos del estado* (Lima: Instituto de Estudios Peruanos, 2005).

35. These evaluations included the Quality of Education Assessment Unit, created by Toledo within the Education Ministry (see Santiago Cueto, *Las evaluaciones nacionales e internacionales de rendimiento escolar en el Perú: Balance y perspectivas,* www.grade.org.pe) and the Organisation for Economic Co-operation and Development's Program for International Student Assessment, which assesses the scientific, reading, and mathematical literacy of 15-year-olds.

36. The Ayacucho strikers were commemorating 35 years of teacher-student demonstrations in defense of free education. To some extent, these events had heralded Shining Path's subsequent rise.

37. As regional governments elected in 2006 provide a conduit for grievances, García faces a somewhat less fragmented regional scenario. However, disputes between mining companies and community and regional stakeholders are on the rise.

38. *Etnocacerismo* is an ethnic supremacist, ultranationalistic movement that arose after the defeat of Shining Path guerrillas. Founded by the Humalas, an Ayacucho family, it has successfully recruited discharged soldiers. About *etnocacerismo,* see Carlos Basombrío and Fernando Rospigliosi, "La seguridad y sus instituciones en el Perú a inicios del siglo XXI," in *Reformas democráticas o neomilitarismo* (Lima: Instituto de Estudios Peruanos, 2006).

39. About the Ilave case, see Carlos Iván Degregori, *Ilave: Desafío de la gobernabilidad, la democracia participativa y la descentralización,* Cuadernos Descentralistas 13 (Lima: Grupo Propuesta Ciudadana, 2004).

40. Ibid., 55–57.

41. For a summary of decentralization efforts, see Javier Azpur, *La descentralización: Una reforma democratizadora que avanza sin norte ni conducción estratégica,* in *Perú hoy: Los mil días de Toledo,* ed. Javier Azpur et al. (Lima: DESCO, 2004); Consorcio de Investi-

gación Económica y Social (CIES), *Aportes para el Gobierno Peruano 2006–2011* (Lima: CIES, Universidad del Pacífico Centro de Investigación, 2006); and Grupo Propuesta Ciudadana, *Perú: Balance del proceso de descentralización,* Serie Ecuador Debate 61 (Lima: Grupo Propuesta Ciudadana, April 2004). About participation and conflict, see Carlos Iván Degregori, "Hasta las ultimas consecuencias: Gobierno local y conflicto en Ilave," *Revista Europea de Estudios Latinoamericanos y del Caribe,* April 2004, 89–99, and Ramón Pajuelo Teves, *Municipalidades de centros poblados y conflicto local / Las lecciones del caso Ilave* (Lima: Oxfam, 2005).

42. Spoiled ballots: 6.3%; blank ballots: 1.7%. Data from the Elections Office.

43. Owned by the Discovery Channel, the Travel Channel, and Check Six Productions.

44. There have been four shows to date, featuring Jordan (2002), New Zealand (2002), Peru (2005), and Jamaica (2005).

45. The script was drafted by Peruvians based on producer guidelines. Eyewitnesses report that tough negotiations with the producers were undermined during filming by an obsequious Toledo, who was eager to please his American guests, even against the advice of his public relations advisers.

46. The Truth Commission noted that no Peruvian university grants degrees in Spanish-Quechua translation, let alone degrees involving the Aymara language or any of the dialects spoken in the Amazon region.

47. Ramiro Escobar, "Un diálogo inolvidable," Ideele Radio, June 14, 2006.

48. As in Bolivia, sacking Toledo involved the risk to members of Congress that the public would demand that they be thrown out as well.

49. As recalled by Mirko Lauer in "La encrucijada de Julio," *La República,* July 20, 2007, 6.

50. Belaúnde was supported by Acción Popular and the Partido Popular Cristiano. García was elected on the APRA slate. All three parties were represented in the 2001–6 Congress.

51. As opposed to leading APRA members such as Agustín Mantilla, who was convicted of taking bribes from Vladimiro Montesinos.

52. Toledo's two other economy ministers were Javier Silva Ruete and Jaime Quijandría. Silva matched Kuczynski's experience with international financial organizations, and both were more flexible on privatization and public utility rates. These issues had been front and center in the Arequipa protests that toppled Kuczynski.

53. Not unlike Shining Path and the Túpac Amaru Revolutionary Movement in previous decades and under different conditions.

54. The FIM failed to achieve the 4 percent required for parliamentary representation and, for all practical purposes, ceased to exist—at least until the 2011 elections.

55. Data from the DESCO Weekly Summary (Lima), Year 29, no. 1392, July 12–18, 2006.

Chapter 12. Venezuela

I thank Cynthia Arnson, Javier Corrales, Jorge Domínguez, Jennifer McCoy, and Michael Shifter for their careful reading and helpful comments on a preliminary draft of this chapter.

1. Michael Shifter, "In Search of Hugo Chávez," *Foreign Affairs* (May–June 2006): 45–59.

2. Jim Rutenberg and Larry Rohter, "Bush and Chávez Spar at Distance over Latin Visit," *New York Times,* March 10, 2007, www.nytimes.com/2007/03/10/world/americas/10prexy.html.

3. *Punto Fijo* is the name of the residence in Caracas at which Venezuela's political and economic leaders negotiated a power-sharing pact that set the stage for a representative liberal democracy that lasted for 40 years.

4. Corporación Latinobarómetro, *Informe Latinobarómetro 2006* (Santiago: Corporación Latinobarómetro, 2006), 18.

5. This survey, released on June 27, 2006, measured pride across 10 specific domains: democracy, world political influence, economic system, social security, science, sports, arts, military might, history, and fair and equal treatment of groups.

6. There is an extensive literature on elite settlement and democratization. The best theoretical treatment is Michael G. Burton and John Higley, "Elite Settlements," *American Sociological Review* 52 (June 1987): 295–306. For a perceptive treatment of Venezuela's post-1958 democratic regime from this perspective, see Terry Lynn Karl, "Petroleum and Political Pacts: The Transition to Democracy in Venezuela," *Latin American Research Review* 22 (June 1987): 63–94.

7. I acknowledge Jennifer McCoy's work in developing the continuum on which this section is based. Her work is part of a collaborative project between the two us that explores how and why an unraveled liberal democracy evolves. When discussing transitions to and from democracy, some social scientists take a dichotomous approach. They draw a sharp line between democracy and autocracy on the basis of the existence of a competitive electoral process and the political and civil freedoms that accompany it. In this view, hybrid regimes do not exist; the polity is either democratic or not democratic, much as one is either pregnant or not pregnant. A dominant line in the literature, in fact, posits that the minimum condition for democracy will be competitive elections open to all but that a full liberal democracy will exhibit additional dimensions including rule of law, division of powers and horizontal accountability, absence of reserved domains, and some degree of "stateness." See Fareed Zakaria, *The Future of Freedom: Illiberal Democracy at Home and Abroad* (New York: W. W. Norton, 2004), and Wolfgang Merkel, "Embedded and Defective Democracies," *Democratization* 11, no. 5 (2004): 33–58.

8. Seen from this perspective, political regimes are subtypes of the political system. Almond's widely accepted definition of the political system views it as "that system of interactions to be found in all independent societies which performs the functions of integration and adaptation (both internally and vis-à-vis other societies) by means of the employment or threat of employment, of more or less legitimate physical compulsion. See Gabriel A. Almond, "The Political System," in *The Politics of the Developing Areas,* ed. Gabriel A. Almond and James S. Coleman (Princeton, N.J.: Princeton University Press, 1960), 3–64. See also Guillermo O'Donnell, Philippe C. Schmitter, and Laurence Whitehead, *Transitions from Authoritarian Rule: Comparative Perspectives* (Baltimore: Johns Hopkins University Press, 1986); Guillermo O'Donnell, "The Quality of Democracy: Why the Rule of Law Matters," *Journal of Democracy* 15, no. 4 (2004): 32–46; and Andreas Schedler, "The Logic of Electoral Authoritarianism," in *The Dynamics of Electoral Authoritarianism,* ed. Andreas Schedler (Boulder, Colo.: Lynne Rienner, 2006).

9. Aurel Croissant, "From Transition to Defective Democracy: Mapping Asian Democratization," *Democratization* 11, no. 5 (2004): 156–78; O'Donnell, "The Quality of Democracy"; Lucan Way, "The Authoritarian State and Hybrid Regimes," in *The Dynamics of Electoral Authoritarianism,* ed. Andreas Schedler (Boulder, Colo.: Lynne Rienner, 2006), 199–218.

10. Hagopian and Mainwaring refer to political regimes in the gray zone as semidemocracies. They discuss at length the transition from authoritarian political regimes to semidemocracies and democracies, which they view as a single process. See Francis

Hagopian and Scott P. Mainwaring, eds., *The Third Wave of Democratization in Latin America: Advances and Setbacks* (New York: Cambridge University Press, 2004), 25–32. See also Thomas Carothers, "The End of the Transition Paradigm," *Journal of Democracy* 13, no. 1 (January 2002): 5–21.

11. The most commonly discussed subtypes of full liberal democracy are *polyarchy*—the real-world variant of liberal democracy that is highly inclusive and open to extensive public contestation—and *feckless democracy*—a liberal democracy that performs poorly for reasons of corruption, patronage, clientelism, and so on. See Robert A. Dahl, *Polyarchy: Participation and Opposition* (New Haven, Conn.: Yale University Press, 1971), 8, and Thomas Carothers, "Debating the Transition Paradigm: A Reply to My Critics," *Journal of Democracy* 13, no. 3 (July 2002): 33–38.

12. Georg Sorensen, *Democracy and Democratization: Processes and Prospects in a Changing World* (Boulder, Colo.: Westview, 1998), 5–19; Larry Diamond and Leonardo Morlino, *Assessing the Quality of Democracy* (Baltimore: Johns Hopkins University Press, 2005), ix–xxxiv.

13. Guillermo O'Donnell, "Delegative Democracy," *Journal of Democracy* 5, no. 1 (January 1994): 55–69; Geoffrey Hawthorn, "Liberalisation and Democracy in Latin America," *Estudios Interdisciplinarios de America, Latina y el Caribe* 13, no. 1 (January–June 2002): 3–24.

14. Prominent examples include *illiberal democracy*—minimally acceptable elections, but governance that fails to fully respect the requirements of the rule of law being applied equally to all citizens, with the curtailment of some basic freedoms of organization and expression for selected groups (Zakaria, *The Future of Freedom*); *delegative democracy*—minimally acceptable elections but governance that overrides the division of powers and provides no horizontal accountability (O'Donnell, "Delegative Democracy"); and *tutelary democracy*—minimally acceptable elections but the elected lack full powers to govern, exercise veto powers, or reserve policy domains for unelected actors (Roda Rabkin, "The Alywin Government and Tutelatory Democracy: A Concept in Search of a Case," *Journal of Interamerican Studies and World Affairs* 34, no. 4 [Winter 1992–93]: 119–94).

15. Javier Corrales, "In Search of a Theory of Polarization: Lessons from Venezuela, 1999–2005," *Revista Europea de Estudios Latinoamericanos y del Caribe* 79 (October 2005): 105–18; Kenneth Roberts, "Social Polarization and the Populist Resurgence in Venezuela," in *Venezuelan Politics in the Chávez Era,* ed. Steve Ellner and Daniel Hellinger (Boulder, Colo.: Lynne Rienner, 2003), 3; Jennifer L. McCoy, "From Representative to Participatory Democracy: Regime transformation in Venezuela," in *The Unraveling of Representative Democracy in Venezuela,* ed. Jennifer L. McCoy and David J. Myers (Baltimore: Johns Hopkins University Press, 2004); Francisco Panizza, "Beyond Delegative Democracy: Old Politics and New Economics in Latin America," *Journal of Latin American Studies* 32, no. 3 (2000): 737–65.

16. Larry Diamond, "Elections without Democracy: Thinking about Hybrid Regimes," *Journal of Democracy* 13 (April 2002): 21–35.

17. Depending on the degree of uncertainty of electoral outcomes and what other dimensions are missing, we then find additional subtypes. *Competitive authoritarians* allow opposition contestation, and the opposition may even win in selected outcomes, but the regime is usually deficient in basic liberties or in horizontal accountability (Andreas Schedler, "Elections without Democracy: The Menu of Manipulation," *Journal of Democracy* 13, no. 2 [2002]: 36–50; Steven Levitsky and Lucan A. Way, "Elections without Democracy: The Rise of Competitive Authoritarianism," *Journal of Democracy* 13, no. 2 [2002]: 51–65. For a contrasting view, see Mark R. Thompson and Philipp Kuntz, "Stolen Elections: The Case of the Serbian October," *Journal of Democracy* 15, no. 4 [2004]: 159–72). *Exclusive democracy* or *liberal autocracy* excludes some groups from suffrage and thus does not fit

under electoral democracy (Merkel, "Embedded and Defective Democracies"; Zakaria, *The Future of Freedom*). *Hegemonic authoritarianism* (which can be sultanistic) does not allow for any meaningful contestation or for the chance that the opposition will win an electoral victory (Joy Langston, "Why Hegemonic Parties Rupture and Why Does It Matter?" paper presented at the Latin America Studies Association 2004 Conference, Las Vegas, Nevada, October 7–9; Andreas Schedler, "The Logic of Electoral Authoritarianism").

18. For an in-depth account of the fall of post-1958 democracy in Venezuela, see Jennifer L. McCoy and David J. Myers, *The Unraveling of Representative Democracy in Venezuela* (Baltimore: Johns Hopkins University Press, 2005).

19. David J. Myers and Robert E. O'Connor, "Support for Coups in Democratic Political Culture: A Venezuelan Exploration," *Comparative Politics* 30, no. 2 (January 1998): 193–212.

20. The best discussion of the origin of the Bolivarian movement is Alberto Garrido, *La historia secreta de la Revolución Bolivariana* (Caracas: Privately published, 2002).

21. Moises Naim, "The Launching of Radical Policy Changes, 1989–1991," in *Venezuela in the Wake of Radical Reform*, ed. Joseph S. Tulchin (Boulder, Colo.: Lynne Rienner, 1992), 4.

22. Ibid.

23. Ibid., 5.

24. Harold Trinkunas, *Crafting Civilian Control of the Military in Venezuela: A Comparative Perspective* (Chapel Hill: University of North Carolina Press, 2005), 4.

25. Rafael De la Cruz, "Decentralization: Key to Understanding a Changing Nation," in *The Unraveling of Representative Democracy in Venezuela*, ed. Jennifer L. McCoy and David J. Myers (Baltimore: Johns Hopkins University Press, 2004), 9.

26. The law governing the partida secreta gave the president wide discretion in using these funds. President Pérez was found guilty on a technicality. He had converted the funds of the partida secreta to U.S. dollars just prior to devaluating the bolívar. He then converted the dollars back to bolívares, which significantly increased the amount of funds available to him in the partida secreta. Pérez's chief of staff returned the partida secreta funds to the safe in the office of the president rather than depositing them into an account in the Ministry of the Interior, as required by law. Pérez maintained that this was an oversight that had occurred in the confusion that followed the Caracazo.

27. Caldera founded COPEI in 1936. He ran as the COPEI presidential candidate in the elections of 1947, 1952, 1958, 1963, 1968, and 1983. A younger generation of COPEI leaders took control of the party from him in 1985 and nominated Eduardo Fernández as the party's presidential standard-bearer for the 1988 election. Caldera failed in his bid to regain control of COPEI in early 1993 when the party he had founded chose Oswaldo Álvaraz Paz as its presidential candidate. Caldera then launched his ultimately successful bid for a second presidency. COPEI expelled Caldera from the party in March 1993.

28. Ruth De Kirvoy, *Collapse: The Venezuelan Banking Crisis of 94* (Washington, D.C.: Group of Thirty, 2000); Nelson Ortiz, "Profits without Power," in *The Unraveling of Representative Democracy in Venezuela*, ed. Jennifer L. McCoy and David J. Myers (Baltimore: Johns Hopkins University Press, 2004), 82–85.

29. *El soberano*—"the people"—is a term used by followers of Hugo Chávez to indicate that the people are sovereign. Groups and individuals opposed to the Bolivarian Revolution are excluded from *el soberano*.

30. Janet Kelly, "Reflexiones sobre la Constitución: La realineación de ideas acerca de la economia y los cambios en el sistema político de Venezuela," in *Venezuela en transición: eleccions y democracia 1998–2000*, ed. José Vicente Carrasquero, Thais Maingon, and Fredrich Welsh (Caracas: CDB, 2000), 244–67.

31. Voters in the "megaelections" not only chose the president but selected a broad range of legislative, regional, and local officials.

32. Abstention rates were higher in municipal and regional elections. See Table 12.1.

33. Trinkunas, *Crafting Civilian Control.*

34. Steve Ellner, "Organized Labor and the Challenge of Chavismo," in *Venezuelan Politics in the Chávez Era,* ed. Steve Ellner and Daniel Hellinger (Boulder, Colo.: Lynne Rienner, 2003), 9; Jonah Gindin, "Venezuela's Peasant Leaders Demand Justice and Protection," VenAnalisis.com, July 13, 2005, 9; John D. Powell, *Political Mobilization of the Venezuelan Peasant* (Cambridge, Mass.: Harvard University Press, 1971).

35. Eduardo Fernández of COPEI was the only major party leader appearing with Pedro Carmona when he announced that he had assumed the presidency.

36. A more comprehensive discussion appears in Daniel Levine, *Popular Voices in Latin American Catholicism* (Princeton, N.J.: Princeton University Press, 1992), 65–91.

37. "Exxon seeks arbitration in seizure payout dispute," *Miami Herald,* September 14, 2007, C2.

38. Damarys Canache, "Urban Poor and Political Order," in *The Unraveling of Representative Democracy in Venezuela,* ed. Jennifer L. McCoy and David J. Myers (Baltimore: Johns Hopkins University Press, 2004), 2.

39. Daniel Hellinger, "When No Means Yes to Revolution: Electoral Politics in Bolivarian Venezuela," *Latin American Perspectives* 32, no. 3 (2005): 8–32.

40. PODEMOS is an offshoot of the MAS that President Chávez enticed into the government in 2001. About the same time, the PPT became part of the governing coalition.

41. President Chávez initially decreased the number of central government ministries, but more recently the number has increased.

42. Organic Laws must be approved by a two-thirds majority of the Assembly. They have a status between regular legislation and provisions of the Constitution.

43. De la Cruz, "Decentralization," 9.

44. In 1993, Ramón Velázquez signed legislation that unified compensatory procedures and coordinated public sector investment. This legislation created the Fondo Intergubernamental para la Descentralización (Intergovernmental Fund for Decentralization).

45. Myers and O'Connor, "Support for Coups in Democratic Political Culture."

46. Data from the *Latinobarómetro* poll show that in 1995, when the level of disillusionment with Punto Fijo democracy was high, 60 percent of Venezuelans still preferred democracy over any other form of government. Seventy percent expressed this preference in 2006.

Chapter 13. Three Decades since the Start of the Democratic Transitions

This chapter is the successor to Jorge I. Domínguez and Jeanne Kinney Giraldo, "Conclusions: Parties, Institutions, and Market Reforms in Constructing Democracies," in *Constructing Democratic Governance in Latin America and the Caribbean in the 1990s,* ed. Jorge I. Domínguez and Abraham F. Lowenthal (Baltimore: Johns Hopkins University Press, 1996). I remain very grateful to Jeanne Kinney Giraldo for her superb work on that chapter. The current chapter is also a successor to Jorge I. Domínguez, "Constructing Democratic Governance in Latin America: Taking Stock of the 1990s," in *Constructing Democratic Governance in Latin America,* 2nd ed., ed. Jorge I. Domínguez and Michael Shifter (Baltimore: Johns Hopkins University Press, 2003). Ideas and passages from those earlier versions appear in this third edition. This chapter, like its predecessors, is not a freestanding chapter. Instead, it calls attention to, and to some degree summarizes, themes that emerge in the preceding chapters of this book and in the earlier editions. There are occasional textual references to the other chapters, but my debt to the authors in this book and its predecessors is much greater than these citations suggest. The views expressed here are mine alone, however. The Inter-American Dialogue and the authors are free to claim that this chapter's errors are all mine and all the insights are theirs. I am very grateful to Javier Corrales, Jeanne Kinney Giraldo, Nahomi Ichino, David Samuels, and Michael Shifter for comments on earlier drafts.

1. See Arturo Valenzuela, "Latin American Presidencies Interrupted," *Journal of Democracy* 15, no. 4 (2004): 5–19.

2. See Javier Auyero's analysis in "The Political Makings of the 2001 Lootings in Argentina," *Journal of Latin American Studies* 38 (2006): 241–65.

3. Domínguez and Giraldo, "Conclusions," 33–35.

4. I am grateful to Jeanne Kinney Giraldo for making this point forcefully.

5. Rut Diamint, "Military, Police, Politics, and Society: Does Latin America Have a Democratic Model?" in *The Construction of Democracy: Lessons from Practice and Research,* ed. Jorge I. Domínguez and Anthony Jones (Baltimore: Johns Hopkins University Press, 2007).

6. Anthony Downs, *An Economic Theory of Democracy* (New York: Harper and Row, 1957), 104–5.

7. Susan Stokes, *Mandates and Democracy: Neoliberalism by Surprise in Latin America* (Cambridge: Cambridge University Press, 2001), Chap. 2.

8. Ibid., Table I.2.

9. See David R. Dye, *Patchwork Democracy: Nicaraguan Politics Ten Years After the Fall* (Cambridge, Mass.: Hemisphere Initiatives, 2000), 12–18, 34.

10. For background, see Juan Rial, "Uruguay: From Restoration to the Crisis of Governability," in *Constructing Democratic Governance: Latin America and the Caribbean in 1990s,* ed. Jorge I. Domínguez and Abraham F. Lowenthal (Baltimore: Johns Hopkins University Press, 1996).

11. "Uruguay: The Next Chile," *Economist,* February 3, 2007, 39; "Latin America and the United States," ibid., March 3, 2007, 44.

12. Javier Corrales, "Market Reforms," in *Constructing Democratic Governance in Latin America,* 2nd ed., ed. Jorge I. Domínguez and Michael Shifter (Baltimore: Johns Hopkins University Press, 2003).

13. For a fine analysis of Venezuela's 1998 election, see Jana Morgan, "Partisanship during the Collapse of Venezuela's Party System," *Latin American Research Review* 42, no. 1 (2007): 78–98.

14. For related discussion, see Henry Dietz and David Myers, "From Thaw to Deluge: Party System Collapse in Venezuela and Peru," *Latin American Politics and Society* 49, no. 2 (2007): 59–86.

15. For an empirical summary of the Costa Rican case, see Fabrice Lehoucq, "Costa Rica: Paradise in Doubt," *Journal of Democracy* 16, no. 3 (2005): 140–54.

16. Michael Coppedge, *Strong Parties and Lame Ducks: Presidential Partyarchy and Factionalism in Venezuela* (Stanford, Calif.: Stanford University Press, 1994).

17. Kirk A. Hawkins and David R. Hansen, "Dependent Civil Society: The *Círculos Bolivarianos* in Venezuela," *Latin American Research Review,* 41, no. 4 (2006): 102–32.

18. See also "Venezuela: Rumbles in the Revolutionary Ranks," *Economist,* March 10, 2007, 33–34; "Defeat for Hugo Chávez: The Wind Goes Out of the Revolution," ibid., December 8, 2007, 30–32.

19. These respective programs are called Progresa, Oportunidades, Seguro Popular.

20. For an account of the effectiveness of parties, legislatures, and presidents engaged in the policy-making process, see Inter-American Development Bank, *The Politics of Policies: Economic and Social Progress in Latin America, 2006 Report* (Washington, D.C.: Inter-American Development Bank and Harvard University David Rockefeller Center for Latin American Studies, 2005), Chap. 3.

21. Ibid., 43.

22. World Economic Forum, *The Global Competitiveness Reports, 2003–2004* (New York: Oxford University Press).

23. Jeffrey Weldon, "The Legal and Partisan Framework of the Legislative Delegation of the Budget in Mexico," in *Legislative Politics in Latin America*, ed. Scott Morgenstern and Benito Nacif (Cambridge: Cambridge University Press, 2002).

24. See also Barry Ames, "Party Discipline in the Chamber," in *Legislative Politics in Latin America*, ed. Scott Morgenstern and Benito Nacif (Cambridge: Cambridge University Press, 2002).

25. "Brazil: Parliament or Pigsty?" *Economist*, February 10, 2007, 36.

26. See Timothy J. Power, *The Political Right in Postauthoritarian Brazil: Elites, Institutions, and Democratization* (University Park: Pennsylvania State University Press, 2000).

27. For the utility of competitive party politics in sustaining judicial independence in Argentina at the federal and subnational levels, see Rebecca Bill Chávez, "The Appointment and Removal Process for Judges in Argentina: The Role of Judicial Councils and Impeachment Juries in Promoting Judicial Independence," *Latin American Politics and Society* 49, no. 2 (2007): 33–58.

28. For evidence and analysis that support the proposition that party competition at the national level bolsters the independence of Mexico's Supreme Court, see Julio Ríos-Figueroa, "Fragmentation of Power and the Emergence of an Effective Judiciary in Mexico, 1994–2002," *Latin American Politics and Society* 49, no. 1 (2007): 31–57. For a similar argument that such competition at the subnational level also strengthens the independence of state legislatures and state courts in Mexico, see Carolina Beer, "Judicial Performance and the Rule of Law in Mexican States," *Latin American Politics and Society* 48, no. 3 (2006): 33–61; Jodi Finkel, "Judicial Reform as Insurance Policy: Mexico in the 1990s," *Latin American Politics and Society* 47, no. 1 (2005): 87–113; and Frederick Solt, "Electoral Competition, Legislative Pluralism, and Institutional Development: Evidence from Mexico's States," *Latin American Research Review* 39, no. 1 (February 2004): 155–67.

29. For background, see Gretchen Helmke, *Courts under Constraints: Judges, Generals, and Presidents in Argentina* (Cambridge: Cambridge University Press, 2004).

30. Domínguez, "Constructing Democratic Governance in Latin America," 381.

Index